THE GERMAN WARS

Books by D. J. Goodspeed

THE CONSPIRATORS
NAPOLEON'S EIGHTY DAYS
LUDENDORFF
THE TRAITOR GAME
THE GERMAN WARS

THE GERMAN WARS

1914 - 1945

D. J. Goodspeed

Illustrated with maps

HOUGHTON MIFFLIN COMPANY BOSTON

1977

The author is grateful for permission to quote from the
following sources: *The Origins of the World War,* Volume I, by
Sydney Bradshaw Fay, copyright 1928 by The Macmillan
Company; *The Schlieffen Plan: Critique of a Myth* by Gerhard
Ritter, reprinted by permission of Oswald Wolff Ltd.; *The
Origins of the War of 1914* by L. Albertini, translated and edited
by Isabella M. Massey (1953), Vol. II, reprinted by permission
of the Oxford University Press.

Library of Congress Cataloging in Publication Data

Goodspeed, Donald James, date
  The German wars.

  Includes index.
  1. European War, 1914–1918—Causes. 2. European
War, 1914–1918—Influence and results. 3. World War,
1939–1945—Causes. 4. European War, 1914–1918—
Campaigns. 5. World War, 1939–1945—Campaigns. I. Title.
D511.G593   940.4   77-4967
ISBN 0-395-25713-1

Printed in the United States of America

v 10 9 8 7 6 5 4 3 2 1

To Peter

PREFACE

IF A GENERAL SURVEY of the First and Second World Wars has any merit
at all, it must be in the attempt to provide a new set of broad outlines
for the subject. This is the perennial business of history — to reassess
the past in the light of what has come after, to reconcile what we knew
then with what we know now. There may be nothing of profit in the
exercise, for Bismarck's contention that we can learn from the experience of others is at the best a dubious one. But we have nothing else.

As we look back, a generation after the close of the Second World
War, many things seem different. Some of the old simplicities that
were accepted as axiomatic by contemporaries have either faded
away, as old soldiers are reputed to do, or have come to present a
much more complicated appearance. Victory crumbled in our hands
even as we seized it, and the second half of the twentieth century gives
indications of being not only very different from the first half, but
even more ominous.

Truth, it is said, is always the first casualty in war. But although this
may be excused on the plea of military necessity, there is surely no
justification for prolonging the habit of falsehood into the years of
peace. Any hope we may have of learning from our own or others'
experience is certainly betrayed if the experience itself is falsified.

Of course, historical truth is relative, for history is an inexact discipline, but this need not prevent us from forming sound general
judgments about the past. This book makes five such general judgments, which run like themes throughout the narrative.

The first is that, viewed from a distance, the two world wars of the
first half of the twentieth century can be seen to have been really one
war, possessing an organic unity, and this unity has to be perceived
before its component parts can properly be understood. In both wars
Britain, France, Russia, and the United States fought Germany and
various allies of Germany. The inconclusive result of the first conflict

led to a resumption of hostilities, and it was not until 1945 that a clear decision was obtained. Thus, Germany was central to both wars, although in two very different ways, and it is therefore appropriate to speak of the organic whole as the German Wars.

The second theme is that France, not Germany, was the power that desired and worked for a great European war in 1914. This conclusion is likely to be violently attacked, not least by those who regard historical analysis as merely another weapon in an ideological arsenal. Certainly too there will be ammunition for such an attack, for in any matter as complicated as the causes of the First World War it would be foolish to expect all the evidence to point one way. Yet conflicting evidence should not prevent us from reaching a reasonable and true conclusion, for not all evidence is of equal weight. There are six major obstacles to be overcome before anyone today can seriously reaffirm the verdict of Versailles, that the First World War was imposed on the Entente Cordiale powers by the aggression of Germany and her allies. In the first place, France was the only major nation whose aims could be achieved by no other means than a great war. Second, between 1894 and 1914 the Entente powers, France and Russia, and their unofficial ally, Britain, consistently spent far larger sums each year on armaments than did the Central Powers, Germany and Austria. Each year of that period Britain alone spent more on defense than did Germany. Third, and as a corollary to this, the armies of the Allies greatly outnumbered the armies of the Central Powers in 1914, and the Allies were also much stronger at sea. Fourth, the immediate cause of the war was the murder of the heir apparent to the Austrian throne as the result of a Serbian plot that had its roots in Russia's Balkan policy, a policy that was strongly supported by France. Fifth, in the final days of the crisis preceding the war the German government strove much harder to avoid a European conflict than did the governments of France or Russia. Finally, Russia, certainly with French foreknowledge, was the first power to order general mobilization, the decisive step to war, and Germany was the last.

A third theme that underlies the narrative is that the German Wars changed the world in ways that none of the combatant powers foresaw or desired and it therefore appears probable that warfare in an industrialized society is no longer an effective instrument of policy. This might seem to be an almost insulting statement of the obvious were it not that the statesmen of the world have clearly not accepted it as true.

The fourth thesis that must surely emerge from this tale of tragedy and terror is that the political leadership of all the powers in this century has been frighteningly inadequate, so inadequate, indeed, that, unless it soon improves, the extinction of all human life on the planet is a probable result. Perhaps the most urgent problem facing the world is how to improve the quality of the world's politicians.

Finally, it is a theme of this book that we live always in the shadow of the past, that our tomorrows are to a large extent determined by our yesterdays — and by our thoughts about our yesterdays. The German Wars were disasters of great magnitude, and the shadows they cast still darken all our futures. The only way to escape from those shadows is to dispel them with the light of truth.

The uncovenanted, unforeseen by-products of the German Wars were far more important than the intended consequences of victory. Pandora's box was opened in 1914 and the lid has not yet been replaced. Before the first war the major powers at least paid lip service to the same ethical principles, but by 1939 ideological differences had made Europe a spiritual madhouse. The Germany of the kaiser had become the Germany of Hitler; the Russia of Nicholas II had become the Soviet Union of Stalin. Since 1945 the breakdown of common values has progressed even further. Communism has ceased to seem to the world a monolith, and democracy in many instances has deteriorated until it is no more than a mindless quest for unrestricted personal liberty and ever higher consumption quotas.

The First World War was an unnecessary war. The differences between the belligerents, their conflicting ambitions, and their varying visions of the future were not so great or so fundamental as to demand a settlement by arms. And the war did infinitely more harm than good. It was a cul de sac down which the West should never have ventured. It killed the promise of a civilization, and it killed it frivolously, having nothing to offer in its place. Even those achievements that at the time appeared to be beneficial results of the conflict — the overthrow of tsardom, the weakening of empire, the establishment of a League of Nations — were stillborn. The tyranny of the Bolsheviks replaced the tyranny of the tsar, an exchange of whips for scorpions. The empires lingered on and defended themselves at Amritsar and in Algeria. The League failed. Quite possibly, had it not been for the First World War, Western civilization might have worked out its inner contradictions and progressed to a more just, generous, and creative society. As it was, in 1914 we stepped out into the night.

The Second World War was a direct consequence of the first, a continuation of it with only a brief and uneasy armistice separating the two episodes. Yet the Second World War was really a necessary war in a way that the first never was. Western civilization could not tolerate the presence of Nazism in its midst. Perhaps if the two totalitarian tyrannies of Nazism and communism had come into conflict with one another earlier, the West could have stood aside while they destroyed one another. Instead, of course, Hitler and Stalin became accomplices in the rape of Poland. In any case, a policy of neutrality would have entailed grave dangers for the West. The gingham dog and the calico cat might not have eaten each other up; Nazi Germany might have won a clear-cut victory and emerged too strong to be defeated.

So the West had to fight. The time and the occasion for fighting were badly chosen; Czechoslovakia in 1938 would have been a far better *casus belli* than Poland in 1939. Nevertheless, the war had to come. Since this is so, it follows that, unlike the first war, the Second World War did more good than harm, for what is necessary is never, in any absolute sense, bad. Nothing was gained, of course, by the war of 1939–1945, but something was saved. What was saved from the shipwreck of the West, however, was only a pitiful fraction of what had been on the ship.

Still, better that than nothing.

Whereas Germany was not primarily responsible for the outbreak of the First World War, it is undoubtedly true that the *immediate* responsibility for the Second World War falls on the Nazis and on the Germany that accepted the Nazis. Had the Germans been willing to abide by the verdict of 1918, to endure awhile and see injustice done, there need have been no second war. To ask this of a proud people who were by no means saints was to ask more than their nature could bear. The real guilt of the Germans would therefore seem to lie in the methods they were willing to accept to right injustice. And when the more remote causes of the Second World War are considered, those causes that created the Nazi party and shaped the Germany of the Third Reich, a wider responsibility becomes evident. One virtue in seeing the essential unity of the two world wars is that it tends to put causes into better perspective, to balance to some extent the France of Poincaré, the Russia of Izvolsky, and even the England of Grey against the Germany of Hitler. The balance is only approximate, for Hitler, who had temptations of power denied to Poincaré and Izvolsky, was far more evil in his acts and in his intentions than were the plotters of the first holocaust. Yet Hitler, no more than Poincaré or Izvolsky, saw the end of the road on which he set his feet.

But the malice, ambitions, and stupidities of men, or even of nations, were not solely and entirely responsible for the wars, although — since the wars came as a direct consequence of the actions of men — it is reasonable to place the primary responsibility here. Still, there is always one more question to be asked in history, one more curtain that separates us from the truth. What conditioned the actions of men? What made them malicious? What gave them their dreams? What placed the stupid in positions of power?

We may grant, then, that in a wider sense the conflicts of that half century were in part the result of what is rather foolishly called "blind historical forces": the world's unconscious attempt to adjust to industrialization, the partial substitution of nationalism and nationalistic values for religion and religious values, the attempt to perpetuate an ethic after abandoning its supporting metaphysic, the warring of the flesh against the spirit. These forces were all real and were actual contributory causes, but their action was so general and their exertion of pressure so fitful and uneven that it is difficult to assess their relative importance.

It is possible, however, to say that there is a sense in which the wars came about because of the inner contradictions in Western civilization. Christendom, which had once united the West, however inadequately, had been largely replaced by a philosophy of selfish materialism that was really no more than the law of the jungle. Much of the older and nobler concept indeed survived, but there was a perpetual conflict between this older essence of the West and the new industrial daemon who had enlisted in his service the plausible sophistries of 1789.

These contradictions need not have resulted in the wars, and so they were contributory rather than determinant causes. But just as it is often possible to look back after a suicide and see characteristics that indicated suicidal tendencies, so in the case of the West it is possible to look back after the wars and see characteristics that should have given forewarning.

Of course, such warning was given, but it went unheeded.

CONTENTS

MAPS

Book One

CHAPTER I

IN A SENSE, it all began the day the archduke came to Sarajevo. The immediate cause of the war of 1914 was the murder of Franz Ferdinand, the heir apparent to the throne of Austria-Hungary; and that murder was the result of a Serbian conspiracy aimed at the dissolution of the Dual Monarchy. If it had not been for the assassinations of Franz Ferdinand and his wife, Sophie, at Sarajevo on June 28, 1914, the war might not have come in August. Whether it would have broken out at a later date, on some other pretext, is by no means certain. In fact, if Franz Ferdinand had remained alive, he would have been a potent force for peace and a strong restraining influence on Austrian policy. In any case, the murders were undoubtedly the spark that lit the powder train.

Yet the Sarajevo murders by themselves were surely too small an event to bear full responsibility for the gigantic upheavals that shook the world. Men in general, and not merely historians, have an instinctive feeling that causes should in some way be commensurate with results, that human affairs are not dependent on the idle whims of the gods. Thus, the titanic results of the world wars, the millions of dead, the devastation of nations, and the overthrow of established orders of society appear to demand causes of like magnitude. It would offend both reason and instinct to believe that these tragedies were due to the act of a psychotic school boy. To understand what happened, it is necessary to go farther back and examine the circumstances by which Europe had become so tragically vulnerable to a single act of violence.

More than sixty years after the event, there is no longer any political purpose to be served by attempting to falsify the history of the time preceding the outbreak of the war. There are no longer neutrals to be influenced or living men with reputations to be defended. Since the generation of 1914 has all but passed away, it is no longer necessary to perpetuate falsehoods for fear of popular outrage, or to spare the sentiments of survivors. Sorrow, apprehension, and malice need no longer distort judgment or breathe their passions into the historical record. Poincaré, Izvolsky, Grey and Sazonov, Kaiser Wilhelm and Tsar Nicholas, Bethmann and Berchtold are as far beyond the reach of our censure as Alcibiades or Caligula.

Yet we are left to grapple with the results of their sins, errors, and miscalculations, and it may help us to do this — though it will help us but little and light our way only dimly — if we can understand what occurred, and, as far as it is possible, why. All history, of course, should be written with humility; the historian is setting himself a task that is ultimately beyond human capability. No art and no analysis will enable him to achieve Ranke's ideal of presenting the past "*wie es eigentlich gewesen.*" Nevertheless, if we know anything at all, it is about the past. The future is unknown and dark; the present does not exist except as a moving point in time. Only when we look backward is there any light of understanding, and when we look ahead it is only the reflected light from over our shoulder, from the past, that penetrates at all into the obscurity.

To blame the losers for the outbreak of the First World War, although this is still the prevailing theory in the Anglo-Saxon world, is too simple and too self-serving. On the other hand, attempts to explain the origins of the war by the operation of impersonal "historical" forces — economic imperialism, industrialism, militarism, nationalism, social Darwinism, and so on — are not really satisfying. The historical abstraction is always to some extent a falsification, useful as a tool but not to be mistaken for reality, although, of course, it is legitimate and necessary to ask to what extent the statesmen and diplomats were no more than the creatures of their time, reflecting attitudes and accepting assumptions that were not uniquely their own but the common property of the society to which they belonged.

All that happens has its origins and its roots in the past, and on the Day of Judgment it may indeed be given to man to understand history. In the meantime, practical considerations force us to limit our inquiries. In this case, the line between the relevant and the irrelevant in time can be drawn, with some justification, in 1871, at the conclusion of the Franco-Prussian War. There are, of course, serious objections to selecting this or any other date as a starting point for our investigations. If we settle on 1871 instead of, say, 1870, we exclude the Ems telegram and the machinations of Bismarck; but this exclusion is perhaps balanced by that of the hysteria of Paris, of the chauvinism of Gramont and the Empress Eugénie, and the little-remembered fact that it was France that declared war on Prussia in 1870 and not Prussia that declared war on France.

We must also, to a large extent, ignore the whole course of previous

Russian history: the cruelties of half-mad tsars and desperate peasants, the march and countermarch of armies across Russia's frontiers,
and the contention of opposing evils that resulted in the necessary
victory of tyranny over chaos. Nor will it be possible to consider the
theories that trace the origins of German national character (and attempt to explain its flaws) by pointing out that the civilization of imperial Rome stopped short at the Rhine or by seeing in Luther's Refor-
mation and the Wars of Religion sinister forces disruptive of European unity. The egalitarian nationalism of the French Revolution, the
militarism of Napoleon, and the disastrous opportunism of the
Second Empire must all be disregarded, though they contributed to
the shaping of Europe's destiny. Yet although we begin our story only
a hundred years ago, we should remember that these older ghosts are
there, unexorcised, and not without their haunting influence on the
events we shall be examining.

France had been the strongest single nation on the continent before
the Napoleonic Wars had bled her white and left her shaken and
exhausted. At one time or another, the French cavalry had stabled its
horses in all the major capitals of continental Europe, and during this
long period of French hegemony it had seemed that France was the
greatest threat to European peace and freedom. Britain had always
sought to offset French power, and time and time again it had been
British efforts, and especially the British navy, that had checked
French expansion.

If the French frequently found themselves frustrated by the Royal
Navy, they had more success in dominating their neighbors across the
Rhine. Richelieu and Mazarin, Louis XIV and Napoleon I, had all
worked successfully to keep the Germanies weak and disunited. However, the Germans had yearned for better things, and from the
fifteenth century on had intermittently dreamed of a national state.
There was often a strange, messianic quality to this dream, as in the
legend of Barbarossa, not dead but sleeping beneath the Kyffhäuser
mountain in Thuringia until his country should have need of him.*
The Germans awaited the predestined leader, the king, the *Feldherr*,
or the magician, sprung from the ranks of the people, who would
bring them into their own. When Bismarck emerged as the Prussian
chancellor, it seemed that this leader had at last appeared.

With the surrender of Napoleon III at Sedan, the tables were finally

---

*In Germany sleeping heroes and hollow hills are as common as cabbages. Siegfried,
Charlemagne, and Henry I are all reputed to have similar residences, at Geroldseck,
Paderborn, and Goslar respectively. But if these legends indicate, as has sometimes
been alleged, a romantic flaw in the German national character, what is indicated by
Francis Drake, slumbering between the round shot in Nombre Dios Bay, awaiting the
rumble of a distant drum?

turned. The defeat of France and the emergence of the new German Empire radically altered the European balance of power. Overnight, Germany became the inheritor of France's greatness, and Europe's center of gravity shifted across the Rhine to the middle of the continent.

The psychological results of this reversal were as serious as the actual shift of physical power. The German Empire, founded in the Hall of Mirrors at Versailles on February 26, 1871, was begun by a people imbued with exalted self-confidence and a confirmed belief in the efficacy of military solutions. This, like many aspects of German history, became far more readily apparent once the western democracies found themselves at war with Germany, a circumstance that made it far easier to forget that France, with equally good reason, also believed in war as the final court of appeal. The debacle of 1870 was followed not by any great upsurge of pacifist sentiment in France, but instead by army reforms, the introduction of universal compulsory military service, new fortifications, and new armaments. The French, humiliated and vengeful, could not reconcile themselves to the loss of past glories and were continually reminded of their shame by the "living wound" of the two lost provinces, Alsace and Lorraine, which Bismarck had annexed to the German Reich.* Influential elements in France continued to voice their hatred of Germany with what Bismarck regarded as a "feminine vindictiveness," and many Frenchmen took to heart at least half of Léon Gambetta's counsel in defeat: "Speak of it never; think of it always."

For his part, Bismarck hoped that France would eventually become reconciled to the annexation of Alsace-Lorraine, just as she had become reconciled to Waterloo; but on at least two occasions, in 1875 and 1887, the smoldering hatred between France and Germany burst into open flame. Not surprisingly, therefore, the aim of Bismarck's foreign policy was to keep France isolated. "Endeavour always to be one of three, so long as the world is ruled by the unstable balance of five great powers," he said, and in practice he tried to better his own maxim and remain on friendly terms with all the other European states.

It did not seem an impossible task, for in Bismarck's view Germany was now a "satiated power," which had no further cause to quarrel with her neighbors. This opinion was so obviously well founded that it was generally accepted both inside and outside Germany. During the

---

*Louis XIV had annexed these two German-speaking provinces in the seventeenth century. What the majority of the provinces' population desired, then or in 1871 or in 1918, there is no way of knowing for sure. It is interesting to note, however, that there was a strong separatist movement in Alsace-Lorraine between 1924 and 1929.

two decades after 1870, while Bismarck remained chancellor, he strove continuously and successfully to keep Europe at peace. Even later, when Germany began seriously to seek colonies and the status of a world power, the fundamental fact remained that it was never in Germany's interest radically to upset the status quo. There was no need to do so, for Germany was doing very nicely with things as they were. If only peace could be maintained, the time would soon come, as a German ambassador to Britain was later to say, "when everyone can have oysters and champagne for supper every night." Only the memories of 1870 and of Alsace-Lorraine seemed sufficient cause for a new war, but France by herself would never again be strong enough to pose a serious threat. The population of the new Germany already greatly outnumbered France's, and the German birthrate was rising while the French birthrate was declining; German industrialization had begun to forge well ahead of that of France. France by herself, then, was impotent in her hatred, but Bismarck had to prevent her from forming any alliance, for this would have exposed Germany to mortal peril. It was his "nightmare of coalitions" that drove Bismarck to enter into mutual defense treaties with other nations.

In his assessment of the international situation Bismarck recognized only five great powers: Britain, Germany, Russia, France, and Austria-Hungary. He never accepted at face value Italy's pretensions to greatness, and nothing in the history of the next fifty years calls this judgment into serious question. The United States lay outside Bismarck's sphere of interest, and the American tradition of noninvolvement in the affairs of Europe made it seem safe to disregard her. Britain presented few problems, for not only were British and German ambitions nowhere in conflict, but both nations had a common interest in safeguarding the peace. Moreover, Britain had a long tradition of hostility to France and was becoming increasingly suspicious of Russia's colonial aims. For a brief period, in fact, Bismarck toyed with the idea of making an alliance with Britain, but neither nation needed such an alliance or was willing to pay the price her partner would have demanded, so negotiations withered. Bismarck was not unduly concerned; so long as Germany remained a continental power with few colonies, no conflicts with Britain appeared likely to arise. Even in retrospect it seems a valid thesis. Certainly Bismarck would never have tolerated for a moment the building of a great German navy, and he realized, far better than the British, how dubious an asset colonial possessions actually were. "My map of Africa lies in Europe," he once said; and again, "Colonies for Germany are like the furs possessed by noble Polish families who have no shirts." True, he briefly recanted this doctrine, probably because he felt he could no longer resist the popular pressure to acquire colonies. In 1884, the Germans established themselves in German South-West Africa and went on to annex Togoland, the Cameroons, and German East Africa, but Bismarck never took these ventures very seriously.

For most of the period between 1870 and 1890, relations between the Russian and German governments were also good. Both nations had recognized their common interest as conservative monarchies ever since they fought together against Napoleon, and Prussia's considerate attitude toward Russia during the Crimean War and the Polish uprising of 1863 had strengthened the friendship, as had Russia's benevolent neutrality during the Franco-Prussian War. Furthermore, Kaiser Wilhelm I was the uncle of Tsar Alexander II, and the two men got along splendidly. Although, in moments of depression, Wilhelm I was wont to complain that it was "no easy task to be Emperor under such a Chancellor" as Bismarck, the old kaiser had considerable voice in policy, and retained a romantic loyalty to the ally of 1815.

In spite of all this, German friendship with Russia was not always easy to maintain. The German and Russian peoples tended to think of each other in elemental racist terms, nourishing an instinctive mutual hostility, as though "Teuton" and "Slav" were species as different as cat and dog. Western Europeans, not least the Germans, were reluctant to admit that Russia was really a part of Europe, and the Russian aristocracy, for its part, hated and feared the western political concepts of liberty and equality, which had been given currency by the French Revolution. Throughout western Europe the process of industrialization was transforming society, altering values, and changing the temper of the times. Living standards were rising, and the newly rich bourgeoisie was mingling with the old aristocracy to form a new amalgam. In Holy Russia, however, the middle class was still small and weak; the peasants, who had been liberated from serfdom only in 1861, were sullen and discontented; and the autocracy, even had it wished to continue with fundamental reforms, would have been unable to initiate changes sufficiently rapidly to satisfy the liberal intelligentsia, who were adopting, with their own violent variations, the revolutionary and utopian ideals of western Europe's Marxists.

These evidences of Russian political weakness did not altogether displease Bismarck, for an autocracy threatened by republican revolutionaries seemed unlikely to make an alliance with republican France, the seed bed of revolution. Still, the possibility of a Franco-Russian alliance was always the most terrifying of Bismarck's nightmares, because such an alliance would threaten Germany with a war on two fronts, and because Bismarck, an East Elbian Junker, had a deep ancestral dread of the Slavic masses hovering just beyond the last outposts of German civilization.

Friendship with Austria-Hungary presented Bismarck with fewer difficulties and tensions than did friendship with Russia. For one thing — and this was the most important consideration in Bismarck's mind — Austria was far weaker than Russia. Prussia had already beaten Austria in war, in 1866, and Germany could certainly do so again. Bismarck, constitutionally unable to distinguish between an ally and a subordinate, preferred friends who were dependent on him, and, as befitted one who had been born in the Old Mark of Brandenburg, he was more than slightly contemptuous of all South Germans, who had distressing tendencies toward Catholicism, the arts, and even liberalism. The farther south they lived, the worse they were, but they all lacked in some degree the ruthless Prussian drive and singlemindedness. "A Bavarian," he once said, "is a cross between a man and an Austrian."

Austria, in fact, had been in decline for at least half a century. In the revolutionary year of 1848, the Hungarian half of the empire had been prevented from gaining its independence only by the intervention of Russian troops. The France of Napoleon III had defeated Austrian armies in 1859 at Magenta and Solferino, and as a result Lombardy had been lost to the empire, and the Kingdom of Italy had been formed. In 1866, Bismarck had forced Austria out of Germany. Italy, not for the last time, had seen a chance of booty and had entered the war on Prussia's side. Things in Austria may have been in a bad way, but they were not so bad that Austrian armies could not still defeat Italian ones. Nevertheless, with Prussia's victory, Austria had lost Venetia. But Bismarck had treated Austria with great leniency after her defeat, and Austria, by remaining neutral in 1870, had missed her chance for revenge.

The root of the troubles of the Hapsburg Empire lay in the fact that it was an anachronism. In an age of nation-states, Austria was not a nation but a feudal conglomerate. Austria-Hungary was not even two nation-states joined together by allegiance to a common crown, although this had been the theory ever since the Ausgleich (Settlement) of 1867, which had established the Dual Monarchy. Austria-Hungary was a family affair, a dynastic state that was owned by the Hapsburg emperor, and it contained at least eleven nationalities. Vienna and Budapest each had a parliament, but there were joint Austro-Hungarian ministries of war, foreign affairs, and finance. The Hungarians, who owed their somewhat more than semiautonomous position to the Prussian victory of 1866, periodically blackmailed the emperor by threatening secession, and systematically exploited those of their subject peoples who were not of Magyar blood. The Magyars were a feudal aristocracy famous for cavalry regiments, racehorses, beautiful women, Gypsy music, and Tokay wine. Their reactionary policies were the most disruptive element in Franz Josef's domains, and their continual thrusting pressure left that poor emperor with no energy to spare for the pursuit of colonial ambitions and with no relish for adventurous foreign policies. Yet peaceful intentions are no guarantee of a quiet life, and Austria's weakness became a more serious threat to peace than even Austrian expansion would have been.

It would be a mistake, however, to exaggerate the internal difficulties of Austria-Hungary during the closing decades of the nineteenth century. Franz Josef, who had mellowed a good deal since he came to the throne in the midst of the troubles of 1848, ruled with a paternal authority, but there was little real separatism in his empire. The Czechs, it is true, wanted a constitution similar to that which the Hungarians had gained, but they envisioned its being promulgated under the emperor. Some few Germans desired an *Anschluss* with Germany. But Prime Minister Eduard von Taaffe, who held office between 1868 and 1870 and again between 1879 and 1893, was reasonably successful in his policy of keeping all the nationalities "in a balanced state of mild dissatisfaction."

Perhaps it was the atmosphere of the empire more than any policy that was responsible for Taaffe's success. Certainly in the capital, Vienna, life proceeded at a very different tempo from life in Berlin. The Austrians took things more easily and tended to make light of their troubles. Vienna was a lovely, graceful city. The spire of St. Stephen's Cathedral looked down on the best cafés in Europe. The Danube swept serenely by; the Vienna Woods were only half an hour's drive away. By and large, Viennese life seemed to move in Strauss's waltz time. The insouciant, good-natured inefficiency of the Viennese, which the Prussians so much deplored, might be a vice but it did take some of the sting out of political differences. As the parliamentary system of government disintegrated because of the multiplicity of parties, Emperor Franz Josef came more and more to rule by invoking Article 14 of the constitution, which allowed him, "under exceptional circumstances," to govern by emergency decree without consulting parliament. Viennese wits quipped that Austria was neither a democracy nor an autocracy but a state of emergency. The remarkable thing was that so few people really seemed to mind very much. As the Viennese themselves said, the situation was desperate but not serious.

In September of 1872, Emperor Franz Josef, Tsar Alexander II, and Kaiser Wilhelm I of Germany met in Berlin and agreed to coordinate their foreign policies. The formal treaty, which was signed on October 22, 1873, was not world-shaking. It looked back with a certain wistfulness to the Holy Alliance of 1815. The new Three Emperors' League emphasized monarchical solidarity and conservative sentiment. The three rulers agreed that in the event of aggression by another power they would consult together and consider the possibility of joint military action.

Bismarck was especially pleased by the Dreikaiserbund, for he foresaw that the most likely danger to his diplomatic system was the threat of Austro-Russian rivalry in the Balkans. He did not want his two friends to quarrel, thus forcing him to choose between them, because the rejected friend might make an alliance with France. "I am holding two powerful heraldic beasts by their collars," he said later, "and am keeping them apart for two reasons: first of all, lest they should tear each other to pieces; and secondly, lest they should come to an understanding at our expense." During all his period in office, Bismarck attempted to keep the lid firmly on the Balkan pot. "The whole Eastern question," he declared in a Reichstag speech in 1876, "is not worth the healthy bones of a Pomeranian musketeer."*

Yet it was not long before things began to go wrong, and in exactly the area where Bismarck had feared trouble. The Balkan Christians had been under Turkish rule for four centuries without having become reconciled to it — naturally enough, for it was both inefficient and oppressive. Early in the century the Greeks had won complete independence, and the Serbs partial independence, and now, as Turkish power declined, the other Balkan nationalities dreamed of freedom. Because of ties of race and religion, they had traditionally looked to Russia for sympathy and support.

Two principal motives underlay Russia's Balkan policy, reinforcing and complementing each other, often so entwined as to be indistinguishable. First of all, and for hundreds of years, Russia had longed to possess Constantinople and the Dardanelles. The economic and strategic advantages of such a conquest would have been immense: Russia would have gained an ice-free port and access to the Mediterranean, and the Russian Empire, crouched in a great semicircle around Europe, would have outflanked the continent at both extremities. Mysticism and religious mythology were interwoven with this predatory ambition. Moscow was destined to be the "third Rome," perpetuating both the imperial and religious splendors of the first two empires, the Roman and the Byzantine.

If the first motive was merely the desire for material aggrandize-

*Bismarck repeated this bon mot on several subsequent occasions, and in the course of repetition the musketeer became a grenadier.

ment at the expense of Turkey, the second had its origins in nothing more substantial than the romanticized folklore of Pan-Slavism. The Pan-Slav doctrine was simple, and as false as simple doctrines usually are: all peoples speaking a Slavic language were really one people and should reunite to affirm the unique spiritual values of the Slavic culture. Not surprisingly, the Russians, who were by far the largest group of Slavs, found much merit in Pan-Slavism, although the tsar and his government displayed a sensible coolness to the theory. Nevertheless, the Pan-Slavs were often able to influence Russian policy, for their vision had an attraction that was irresistible to many minds. Incidentally, such dreams die hard, since they are almost infinitely adaptable, and even today, after the great convulsions that are the subject of this book, the imprint of an imposed Pan-Slavism can be traced — and not too dimly — on the face of much of eastern Europe.

Thus, when the Christian peasants of Bosnia and Herzegovina rebelled against the Turks in 1875, the Pan-Slavs loudly demanded that Russia go to the aid of her "little brothers" in the Balkans. By midsummer, Russia was full of an evangelical bellicosity. All through this period the tsarist empire seemed to have a plentiful supply of rather sinister ambassadors; the Russian representative at Constantinople, General Nikolai Ignatiev, was a fanatical Pan-Slav who worked hard to bring war to the Balkans. Largely because of Ignatiev's incitement, the Bulgarians rose in revolt in September 1875 and again in May 1876. Both times they were bloodily suppressed.

The crusade was also preached in the little principality of Serbia, which now owed only a nominal allegiance to the Porte. The Serbian prince, Milan Obrenovich, twenty-two years old and timid, wanted no war and dismissed his regent, Jovan Ristich, who did. However, the domestic politics of Serbia had been somewhat unsettled since the Serbs had rebelled against the sultan, in 1804, under the leadership of a peasant known as Kara George. "Black George," a formidable guerrilla fighter, had gained himself a principality before he was assassinated in 1817 by one of his lieutenants, Milos Obrenovich. Milos had replaced Kara George as prince of Serbia, and had thereby inaugurated a murderous feud between the Karageorgevich and Obrenovich families, who remained rivals for the Serbian throne. Thus, in 1876 it was fairly simple for General Ignatiev to bring pressure to bear on young Prince Milan; he had only to intimate that the pretender, Peter Karageorgevich, was willing to follow a more belligerent policy. Prince Milan recalled Ristich to power in May, and on June 30 both Serbia and Montenegro declared war on Turkey.

Tsar Alexander II and his seventy-eight-year-old chancellor, Prince

Alexander Gorchakov, viewed these events without conspicuous enthusiasm. They had no desire to provide a new "Crimean coalition"
against Russia, and resolved that if they were to be forced into a war
against Turkey they should at least make sure that Austria-Hungary
would remain neutral. Bismarck, anxious as always to preserve peace
and the balance of power, had invited Gorchakov and Count Julius
Andrássy, the Austrian foreign minister, to Berlin in May 1876; and
on July 8, at Reichstadt in Bohemia, the two men had a further meeting, accompanied this time by their royal masters, Tsar Alexander II
and the Emperor Franz Josef. Alexander II still hoped to keep out of
the war, but he agreed that if Serbia was victorious she should be
given part of Bosnia and Herzegovina, and that the Sanjak of
Novibazar, the strip of land that separated Serbia from Montenegro,
should be divided between those two countries, giving them a common border. Austria could have the rest of Bosnia and Herzegovina,
and Russia, for her part, would be satisfied if she regained the territory she had lost in the Crimean War.

However, despite Russian aid, the Serbs were decisively defeated by
the Turks at Djunis on October 29, 1876. Alexander II thereupon
demanded that hostilities cease. The sultan, Abdul Hamid II, agreed,
and a conference of the powers met at Constantinople in December to
force reforms on the Turk. Abdul Hamid II did what many other sul-
tans had done — he promised to meet all the demands for reform and
then completely ignored his promises. When the Constantinople Conference failed, Alexander II, foreseeing a Russo-Turkish war, hastily
concluded a new agreement with Austria.

The tsar was now prepared to grant Austria an even higher price
for her benevolent neutrality than he had agreed to at Reichstadt. No
great Slav state was to be created in the Balkans, but Bulgaria,
Rumelia, and Albania would become independent; Thessaly, part of
Epirus, and the island of Crete would go to Greece; Constantinople
would become a free city; Russia would annex Bessarabia; and Austria would annex Bosnia and Herzegovina, except for the Sanjak of
Novibazar. Perhaps these terms were an indication of the tsar's restraint and moderation; more probably they reflected a consciousness
of Russian military weakness and fear of the old Crimean coalition. In
any event, the Russian people were determined to liberate the Balkan
Christians, and the wave of popular feeling could not be withstood.
Russia declared war on Turkey on April 24, 1877.

At first the war went badly for Russia, who had underestimated her
enemy. The Russian mobilization and deployment were inefficient
and slow, and the Turks fought much more tenaciously than had
been expected. The Bulgarian town of Plevna, defended by the Turks

on the windswept hills that encircled it, resisted two Russian attacks in July, and it was not until General Frants Todleben, the famous defender of Sebastopol, was brought out of retirement to command the investment that Plevna finally fell, on December 10. Another Russian army in the Caucasus had been experiencing similar difficulties, but the fortress of Kars was at last taken by storm on November 18. More and more Russian troops were called out, until by the end of the year the tsar's armies greatly outnumbered the sultan's. By the middle of January 1878, the Russians were at Adrianople and by the end of the month they were encamped outside Constantinople. Turkey asked for, and was granted, an armistice.

These events had caused considerable apprehension in Europe, in large part because Britain was determined that Turkey should not be destroyed. The British prime minister, Lord Beaconsfield, as Disraeli was now called, was more interested in the gaudy glories of empire than in the sufferings of Christians in far-off lands. No atrocity in Bulgaria or massacre in Armenia was capable of moving him as they had moved more generous spirits in Russia. As the Russian army had approached the Turkish capital, the British Mediterranean Fleet had passed through the Dardanelles. For a time it looked as though Russia and Britain might go to war.

This prospect thoroughly alarmed Bismarck, who called for a conference of the powers to settle the matter peacefully. Russia, elated by victory, had imposed terms on Turkey that bore little relationship to the prior agreements with Austria. By the Treaty of San Stefano, Russia created an independent Bulgaria larger than any other Balkan state; Bosnia and Herzegovina did not go to Austria but became autonomous; Russia still got Bessarabia; and Rumania and Montenegro became fully independent. This instance of Russian bad faith is significant, not because it advanced the powers toward a European war, but because it was a clear signal that Russia hoped to dominate all the Balkan area.

Austria, of course, was outraged, and promptly occupied Bosnia, Herzegovina, and the Sanjak of Novibazar. Britain backed Austria and tried hard to enlist French support. The Congress of Berlin, which opened on June 13, saw Bismarck acting as the "honest broker" of Europe, seeking nothing for Germany but the keeping of the peace.*

The congress forced Russia to abandon most of the gains she had

---

*Or almost nothing. He did, perhaps, and with some success, encourage the rivalries of other states so that each of them would need Germany's friendship. Lord Salisbury, the British foreign minister, who did not much like this policy, described it as "employing his neighbours to pull out each other's teeth."

made at San Stefano. The big Bulgaria, which was to have been estab-lished as a Russian satellite, was much reduced and a new state of Eastern Rumelia was created. On the motion of Disraeli, Austria-Hungary was to occupy and administer Bosnia and Herzegovina, al-though these provinces were still to be nominally under the sultan. *Nationalism* Austria was given permission to station garrisons in the Sanjak of Novibazar; Britain, for no very obvious reason except that she wanted it, was given the island of Cyprus; Serbia, Montenegro, and Rumania became fully independent; Russia gained Bessarabia and Ardahan, Kars and Batum, in Asiatic Turkey.

The Congress of Berlin ended on July 13, and Bismarck departed for the spa of Kissingen to try — unsuccessfully — to get his weight down. Turkey, naturally, was disgruntled because she had lost more than one third of her European territory. The smaller Bulgaria mourned because she was small and was forbidden to unite with East-ern Rumelia. Rumania, although she had fought the Turks at Russia's side, had been deprived by her ally of Bessarabia and given only the Dobruja in exchange. Italy sulked furiously because she had received no "compensation" in the Trentino for Austria's protectorate over Bosnia and Herzegovina. The Hungarians were perhaps the most unhappy of all, because they feared that the acquisition of Bosnia and Herzegovina would endanger the Magyar domination of the eastern half of the Dual Monarchy. They wanted no more Slavs in the empire.

In general, these grievances resembled the jealousy and dissatisfac-tion found in a selfish family after the reading of a will, but in the case of Russia the sentiment went deeper. Although Russian idealism and Russian arms had forced the Turk to relinquish his grip on Europe, Russia's just reward had been snatched away at Berlin. Or so it ap-peared to the Russians. The Pan-Slavs, of course, were especially en-raged. Most unfairly, the Russians blamed Bismarck more than An-drássy or Disraeli, and Alexander II spoke bitterly of the Congress of Berlin as a "European coalition against Russia under Bismarck."

This attitude enraged Bismarck, who felt that he had saved Russia from a probably disastrous war against Austria and England. His re-sponse was to seek a defensive alliance with Austria against Russia. He and Andrássy met at Gastein in Salzburg on August 27 and 28, and prepared a draft treaty. It provided that if either Austria or Germany was attacked by Russia, the other would enter the war with all her forces and that neither would conclude a separate peace. If either Aus-tria or Germany was attacked by a power other than Russia (that is, if France attacked Germany, or Italy attacked Austria), the other ally would maintain a benevolent neutrality. However, if the attacking power was aided by Russia, the other ally would intervene with her full fighting strength. The treaty was to last for five years but was to be renewed automatically. To meet the objections of Wilhelm I, a memorandum was appended to the treaty, declaring that no sufficient cause of quarrel then existed to justify war against Russia and that neither Germany nor Austria would attack or menace the Russian Empire.

The Austro-German alliance certainly did not cause the First World War, but in the end, by encouraging Russia to ally with France, it brought that war a step closer. At the time it did not seem so. Not only did there appear to be very formidable obstacles to any alliance between tsarist Russia and republican France, but the Austro-German alliance seemed positively to advance the cause of peace, because it would prevent any Russian attack on Austria and because Bismarck would be able to control and moderate the foreign policy of his Austrian ally. The Iron Chancellor's aim was still to hold the two heraldic beasts by their collars. The treaty of Dual Alliance was signed on October 7, 1879, in Vienna; it was to remain in force until both the high contracting parties were sucked down and disappeared in the maelstrom of defeat in 1918.

Tsar Alexander II was not overly disturbed by the Austro-German Treaty, and he was prepared to accept his uncle's assurances that there was no cause for a quarrel between the two nations. As a consequence, he was quite willing to renew the Dreikaiserbund in 1881. Bismarck was well satisfied with this, for now it seemed that German interests were doubly protected and that the three empires would continue to make common cause.

Meanwhile, the internal situation in Russia had taken a significant turn. The political assassinations of the 1860s had been isolated incidents, and the spontaneous movement of the Narodniki, or "going to the people," had failed by 1876. A new revolutionary party, Zemlya i Volya, "Land and Liberty," was formed, but it was little more than an emotional protest, without a reasoned tactical aim or a definite goal of social and political reform. Land and Liberty split in the summer of 1879, and at a conference held at the watering resort of Lipetsk in June the most extreme elements resolved to turn to terrorism. By ones and twos, the delegates made their way to the meeting place in the birch woods outside the town and there, under the trees, passed sentence of death on Tsar Alexander II. Two extremist leaders, Alexander Mikhailov and A. I. Zelyabov, formed a new secret party, the Narodnaya Volya, "People's Will," dedicated to murder.

Between the beginning of July 1879 and March 1881, six separate attempts were made to assassinate Alexander II. The revolutionaries hunted him like a wild beast, exploded dynamite beneath his private dining room in the Winter Palace, blew up the coaches of his imperial train, and finally killed him by the banks of the Catherine Canal on the icy Sunday morning of March 1, 1881. The bombs that blew off Alexander's legs also killed a little messenger boy and twenty other innocent bystanders, but the terrorists, with the customary egotism of their kind, had a lighthearted disregard for the lives of ordinary people.

The new tsar, Alexander III, although a colder and less amiable man than his father, was equally peace-loving and was willing to renew the Dreikaiserbund when it fell due in June 1881. The new treaty was somewhat more specific than the old, but the aim was the same: to ensure the cooperation of the three great empires of continental Europe in keeping the peace and preserving monarchical institutions. By the terms of the new Three Emperors' League, Austria, Russia, and Germany agreed that if any of them found herself at war with a fourth power, the other signatories would maintain a benevolent neutrality. Russia promised to respect the Austrian interests acquired by the Treaty of Berlin. No change would be allowed in the status quo of Turkey in Europe without mutual agreement, and all agreed to use their influence to prevent Turkey's opening the Dardanelles to another power for naval operations in the Black Sea. In a protocol to the treaty, Austria-Hungary was given permission to annex Bosnia and Herzegovina at her discretion and to occupy the Sanjak of Novibazar indefinitely. Germany got nothing from the Dreikaiserbund except the guarantee of a Europe that would develop conservatively and in peace.

In the meantime, France, acting on the permission she had received from England and Germany at the Congress of Berlin, had occupied Tunis and established a protectorate there. Some in France opposed this imperial expansion on the grounds that it would distract the nation from recovering Alsace-Lorraine; some favored it on the grounds that it would strengthen France by giving her new markets, raw materials, and black soldiers. As it turned out, those who advanced the first argument need not have worried; they underestimated the tenacity and ruthlessness of their compatriots who had their hearts set on revenge.

In Italy the public outcry at the French seizure of Tunis was hysterical, for the Italians had had colonial ambitions of their own in North Africa. Bismarck, as usual, put his finger on it. He said that Italy " had a large appetite but very poor teeth." Not a first-class power in her own right, Italy strove perpetually to be accepted as the equal of Britain, Germany, Russia, France, and Austria. This caused her to be treated with contempt, and she resented the contempt keenly.

Motivated by her jealous hostility toward France, Italy asked Bismarck if it would be possible for her to have an alliance with Germany, but was told that she would first have to resolve her differences with Austria — "the way to Berlin led through Vienna." Although Italy hated Austria, her traditional enemy, she took Bismarck's advice, and negotiations for a tripartite alliance were soon underway.

Bismarck was the readier to consider such an alliance because the two heraldic beasts were again straining at their collars. Austria was always complaining about Russia, and the new tsar, Alexander III, was being influenced toward a racist foreign policy by Pan-Slavs like General Ignatiev and the Procurator of the Holy Synod, Konstantin Pobedonostsev. When a well-known Pan-Slav fanatic, General Mikhail Skobelev, speaking to some Serb students in Paris on February 17, 1882, advocated a war to the death between Teutons and Slavs, it was taken as a sign of the times.

The treaty of Triple Alliance was signed in Vienna on May 20, 1882, by Germany, Austria, and Italy. At Austria's suspicious insistence, it was supplementary to, and did not supersede, the Austro-German Treaty of 1879. The signatories promised to enter into no alliance or engagement directed against any one of them. In the event of an unprovoked attack by France on Italy, Austria and Germany would support Italy with all their forces, and Italy, but not Austria, would go to Germany's aid if France made an unprovoked attack on her. If one or two of the signatories was attacked without direct provocation by two or more powers, all three would enter the war. If one of the allies found herself forced to make war on a great power not signatory to the treaty, the other two allies would maintain a benevolent neutrality. If the military clauses became operative, all three signatories bound themselves not to conclude a separate peace. The treaty, which, as its opening declaration stated, was "essentially conservative and defensive," was to be secret and was to last for five years.

To Bismarck, the Triple Alliance appeared to be another prop shoring up the peace of Europe. It was a strictly defensive treaty and it seemed to ensure that, even if the worst happened, if the Dreikaiserbund broke up and if Russia allied with France, the Triple Alliance would be too strong to be attacked. Three considerations were eventually to vitiate this calculation: Britain was to abandon her neutrality; Austria and Italy were never able to overcome their mutual hostility; and Italian politicians in the post-Risorgimento period were not men who felt themselves bound by their pledged word.

It was a great time for alliances and secret treaties. Austria-Hungary had already entered into a defensive alliance with Prince Milan of Serbia, who had virtually signed away his country's independence. On June 28, 1881, Milan had agreed not to enter into any treaty with a foreign power unless he had Austria's consent. In exchange, he had gained Austrian support for his dynasty against the Karageorgevich family and a promise of Austrian recognition and diplomatic help if he should proclaim himself a king. This alliance, which was prudently kept secret from the Serbian people, lasted until 1895.

Rumania, bitter about the Russian acquisition of Bessarabia, concluded a defensive alliance with Austria and Germany on October 30, 1883, and with Italy on May 15, 1888. Thus, the Triple Alliance became in effect a quadruple alliance. This Rumanian alliance, like the one with Italy, was to endure until it was betrayed in the First World War.

Meanwhile, in 1885, the Eastern Question again blew up into an eastern crisis that exposed the fundamental weakness of the Dreikaiserbund. A portion of the Bulgarian army mutinied in September and forced the union of Bulgaria and Eastern Rumelia. Russia had always desired such a union, but was unwilling to accept the independent Prince Alexander of Battenberg as the ruler of Bulgaria. The tsar's government wanted a Bulgaria that would in all things be subservient to Russia, and Alexander had other views of his princely duties.

King Milan of Serbia thought he saw an opportunity to seize territory at the expense of a neighbor, so he declared war on Bulgaria on November 13, 1885.* The Serbs were promptly defeated, but Bulgaria agreed to make peace after Austria threatened to enter the conflict on Serbia's side. In April 1886, Turkey, under pressure, agreed that the prince of Bulgaria could also be governor of Eastern Rumelia for a five-year period. Shortly afterward, a group of Bulgarian army officers, acting on Russian instructions, staged a coup d'état and deposed Prince Alexander. A counter-revolution brought him back, but Russia forced him to abdicate on September 7.

In spite of the Ruritanian atmosphere that surrounded these events, real blood was shed, and, of more serious consequence, Russia and Austria were further estranged. The union of Bulgaria and Eastern Rumelia, which now had been brought about, was contrary to the terms of the Treaty of Berlin; and it seemed to Austria that Russia had changed the status quo in the Balkans to her advantage, contrary to her pledge given in the Dreikaiserbund. Russia, for her part, had exactly the same complaint to make against Austria, but with somewhat less reason; although Austria had indeed given diplomatic support to Serbia, the entire crisis had been brought about by the Bulgarian annexation of Eastern Rumelia. Bismarck, seriously disturbed and anxious above all things to prevent a war between Russia and Austria,

*Milan had cashed in on Austria's guarantee and had proclaimed himself king in 1882.

exercised a moderating influence in Vienna. He was still resolute against sending Pomeranian grenadiers to the Balkans.

He was also keeping an especially wary eye on France at this time because that country was experiencing an outbreak of chauvinistic nationalism and was seething with talk of a war of revenge against Germany. Ever since the little Corsican led them to their hour of glory, the French have entertained a peculiar, almost housemaidish tenderness for generals. Between 1886 and 1889, the idol of great masses of the French people was General Georges Boulanger, a former commander of the army in Tunis who had returned to France to enter politics. Boulanger was a demagogue who was known on the Paris boulevards as "Général Revanche"; he rode about on his white horse, struck postures, and was the very picture of *le brav' général*; he made hundreds of warlike speeches, declaiming, "We remember that they are waiting for us in Alsace and Lorraine." When, in January of 1886, he became minister of war in Henri de Saulces de Freycinet's cabinet, he set about increasing and modernizing the army, and in the autumn of 1887 he went so far as to order a partial mobilization. Boulanger received tremendous popular support. Paul Déroulède's Ligue des Patriotes rallied around him; the Bonapartists lined up behind him, as did the supporters of the Comte de Paris; and Boulanger's own journal, *La France Militaire*, and a dozen other chauvinistic newspapers clamored for *la guerre sainte*, as though France had suddenly gone Moslem.

Maurice Rouvier, the premier, had the courage to exclude Boulanger from his cabinet in 1887, and the army expelled him for insubordination the following year, but the adulation of the mob only increased. He was elected to the Chamber of Deputies in 1888, and when he resigned in pique, dozens of constituencies all across France elected him their deputy. Boulanger was probably preparing a coup d'état in 1889, when the government issued a warrant for his arrest. When *le brav' général* was warned of this, his nerve failed him and he fled ignominiously from France. He was convicted of treason in absentia in October, and the excitement that had so inflamed the French died down. In September 1891, Boulanger, a showman to the end, committed suicide on the grave of his mistress in Brussels, but the Boulanger crisis had demonstrated how deep was the hatred of the French for Germany and how dear to many French hearts was the idea of a war of revenge.

Because of his resentment against Austria, Tsar Alexander III had refused to renew the Dreikaiserbund when it lapsed in June 1887. This was a misfortune for Europe, for while the league existed, it had been a sure and certain guarantee of peace. No other power, or combination of powers, would have been able to challenge the three great empires as long as they remained united, and it is tempting to speculate how Europe might have developed if the three emperors had had the wit to see where their true interests lay. In the end, their own falling-out brought all their empires down and opened the floodgates to new systems of government, new concepts of order, and new philosophies of life.

Tsar Alexander III, however, desired no quarrel with Germany. To replace the Dreikaiserbund, he had his foreign minister, N. K. Giers, draft a treaty of alliance with Germany alone. When the Russian ambassador, Count Peter Shuvalov, showed Bismarck the draft treaty, the German chancellor, who was always frank and open when he stood to gain by it, produced a copy of the Austro-German Treaty of 1879 and read it aloud, suppressing only the clause that dealt with automatic renewal. Bismarck and Shuvalov then agreed to a formula whereby Russia and Germany were bound to benevolent neutrality in a war between one of them and a third power, except in the case of an attack by Russia on Austria or by Germany on France. Once again, it seemed that peace was assured, for Germany had no intention of attacking France, France without an ally would never attack Germany, and Russia would not attack Austria if it meant bringing Germany in against her. Other articles of this "Reinsurance Treaty" recognized Russia's preponderant influence in Bulgaria and Eastern Rumelia, guaranteed the status quo in the Balkans, and reiterated that Turkey was not to be allowed to open the Dardanelles to any naval power in time of war. A protocol promised German support for "regular and legal government" in Bulgaria, and German opposition to any restoration of Prince Alexander of Battenberg. Germany promised neutrality and diplomatic support in case Russia found it necessary to seize the Dardanelles.

The Reinsurance Treaty, signed in Berlin on June 18, 1887, was to remain secret because the tsar feared that Russian public opinion would be unfavorable. The three emperors were still, in a sense, linked together because both Russia and Austria were bound to Germany. The three crowns, each of which had been linked to both of the others in the Dreikaiserbund, were now interlinked linearly, with the German crown in the center. While they remained joined, there could be no great European war, nor could the forces of revolution or of revolutionary nationalism destroy the fabric of Europe. Looking back now across a gap of nearly a century, one does not have to be a conservative or a monarchist to believe that, in comparison with what actually happened, it would have been infinitely better for the world had that linkage remained unbroken.

CHAPTER II

Bismarck has been severely criticized for signing the Reinsurance Treaty with Russia at the same time as Germany was bound to Austria and the Triple Alliance, but these criticisms, like much historical writing since 1914, have often been colored by the passions created by subsequent events. In fact, Bismarck's treaties, which were strictly defensive, were perfectly consistent with one another. Moreover, the Reinsurance Treaty explicitly excluded the cases of a Russian attack on Austria or of a German attack on France precisely in order that Germany's engagement to Russia would not conflict with her prior engagement to Austria. On the other hand, there is more substance to the criticism that, though there was no duplicity involved, Bismarck had complicated international relations by his network of treaties. The old kaiser, Wilhelm I, had once said to his chancellor: "I wouldn't want to be in your shoes. You strike me at times like a man on horseback who is juggling five balls in the air and never lets one of them fall." Yet even this comment smacks somewhat of exaggeration, and historians have perhaps been too ready to agree with Wilhelm I. What may have appeared infernally complicated to that rather simple old man was not, on analysis, really so very difficult to comprehend.

More to the point was the fact that by 1887 Bismarck was growing old and bad tempered. When he was angered by an anti-German outburst in the Russian press, he forced Russian bonds off the Berlin exchange, with the result that Russia turned to France for capital. Early in 1888, French financial houses floated a Russian loan for a half a million francs. Since the French had plenty of capital and the interest rate was good, the loan was oversubscribed. Further loans soon followed, and by the fateful year of 1894 there was the equivalent of more than $800 million of French money invested in Russia.

These were undoubtedly danger signals, but it is easily possible to make too much of them. The statesmen of the 1880s were not men who would involve their countries in war because of minor irritations. The overriding national interest of each of the three empires was still, on the whole, clearly perceived, even though there were already some indications of the emergence of a new and less rational mood. For instance, some high government officials in Russia, and almost all the Pan-Slavs, believed that Russia could not fulfill her "historic mission" to dominate the Balkans and capture the Dardanelles without a war against the Teutonic powers, and that in such a war France was Russia's "natural ally." Both Alexander II and his son, Alexander III, had been too wise to listen to the Pan-Slav voices, but the voices were getting stronger.

In Germany, too, some believed in the inevitable war between Teuton and Slav. One of these was Count Alfred von Waldersee, who became Chief of the Prussian General Staff in 1888. Waldersee used to go about advocating a preventive war against Russia; it was his opinion that "if Germany hopes to survive, she will have to begin dealing out death right and left." Few Germans took this nonsense seriously, and Waldersee's ravings would not have mattered at all had it not been that Germany now had Wilhelm II as her kaiser.

The old kaiser had died on March 9, 1888, in his ninety-first year. Lord Salisbury, the British foreign minister, had been filled with forebodings when he heard the news. "This is the crossing of the bar," Salisbury wrote. "I see the sea covered with white horses."

Wilhelm I had been succeeded by his son, Friedrich, a man of liberal views who was thought to be much influenced by his English wife, a daughter of Queen Victoria's. But by March 1888, the views of the new emperor did not in the least matter, for poor Fritz was dying of cancer of the throat and had only three months to live. He died on June 15, and his son, Wilhelm, became kaiser — the last kaiser, as it turned out, for Bismarck's German Empire was to have a remarkably short life span.

For some time, the relationship between Wilhelm II and Bismarck had been strained, for the young kaiser had none of his grandfather's wisdom and humility. One June morning in 1888, while at breakfast, Bismarck had been told that Fritz might die at any moment. *"Wehe meinen Enkeln!"* he said. "Alas for my grandchildren!" Later, Bismarck complained that Wilhelm II was "like a balloon. If you don't keep fast hold of the string you never know where he'll be off to." The new kaiser, for his part, had his own ideas. "I'll let the old man shuffle on for six months, then I'll rule myself," he said.

In any case, Wilhelm II was perhaps the only influential man in Germany inclined to listen seriously to Waldersee's babblings about preventive war. This terrified Bismarck, since the last thing he wanted was war with Russia. So for a time these two men, Bismarck and Waldersee, strove, as it were, for the soul of the young kaiser. Fortunately, Bismarck won. His clinching argument was that if Germany were to fight France, Russia might stay neutral, but that if Germany were to fight Russia, France would be sure to attack Germany from the rear. The kaiser, who was really no fool, saw the force of this reasoning, and, indeed, it was almost certainly true. Waldersee was no longer heeded, and Bismarck heaved a great sigh of relief. The kaiser now agreed that he would renew the Reinsurance Treaty when it fell due in June 1890.

Wilhelm II had said that he intended to get rid of Bismarck in six months, but in this, as in more important matters, he was overly optimistic. Bismarck remained chancellor for a year and a half after Wilhelm came to the throne. By the time the break came, there was almost nothing on which the two men agreed. The real issue was fundamental and irreconcilable; in the words of Humpty Dumpty in *Through the Looking Glass*, it was "which is to be master, that's all."

This contest of wills was a reflection — almost a portent — of a far deeper cleavage in German society. Bismarck represented an older generation and an older order of society; the kaiser represented the new, industrial Germany and the expansionist forces of the future. Bismarck was intent on the preservation of the past; he wished to command the clock to stand still. Had it not been impossible, such an achievement might have been to Europe's advantage.

The thirty-one-year-old kaiser, on the other hand, was also a creature of his time, and more truly representative of the Germany of the nineties than was the chancellor. "Wilhelmine Germany" is a convenient label to describe the kaiser's Reich, but it should be remembered that the kaiser was far more influenced by the Germany in which he lived than Germany was influenced by her kaiser. And by 1890, Germany was expanding its production, growing richer and more self-confident by the day, and taking on, as though by inexorable necessity, all the least lovely aspects of material success. Germany's steel production surpassed Britain's in 1895, and German firms were achieving worldwide fame in the newer and more sophisticated industries — I. G. Farben in chemicals, Krupp in armaments, Daimler and Diesel in internal combustion engines, Siemens in electrical equipment, and Zeiss in optics. The empire that had replaced the "little Spartan Prussia, the land of the king and the knight and the liege," was becoming enormously powerful and, as is always the case, was willingly paying the price for power.

Germany's rate of industrial growth was outpaced only by that of the United States. The American industrial takeoff was largely ig-

nored because in the last decade of the nineteenth century few Europeans could convince themselves that anything but the most primitive
barbarism existed beyond the old center of their own continent. For
the Germans, French, Austrians, and Italians, the outposts of civilization stood along the borders of Russia and the Balkans. For the
British, the "wogs" began at the Channel.

Bismarck knew little of the new forces at work in Germany. In the
Bismarckian constitution — designed by Bismarck for the maintenance of his own power — the kaiser was the font of all authority, because the chancellor and ministers were responsible to him, not to the
Reichstag, the representative body that Bismarck had established to
be the "fig leaf of absolutism." The Reichstag could not initiate legislation, could not appoint or dismiss the chancellor or ministers, and had
soon lost much of its control over military expenditures. Even the
chancellor had no authority over the army or the navy. Thus, it remained for the kaiser to coordinate foreign and military policy, if they
were to be coordinated. Nevertheless, Wilhelm Liebknecht, who
coined the phrase "fig leaf of absolutism," was not entirely fair in his
judgment. The Reichstag did have very considerable obstructive
power and could have done much more than it did had its members
so desired. Poor Fritz, before he died, had been nearer the truth; he
had called Bismarck's system "ingeniously contrived chaos." When
Wilhelm I was kaiser and Bismarck was his chancellor, the system had
functioned well enough. Under a kaiser like Wilhelm II, who was both
indolent and irresponsible, and chancellors who did not possess Bismarck's genius, sensitivity, and prestige, the German system of government can hardly be said to have worked at all.

Wilhelm II dismissed Bismarck on March 19, 1890. Ten days later
the old man left Berlin for his country estate at Friedrichsruh, taking
with him thirteen thousand bottles of wine from the cellars of the
Reichschancellery and three large packing cases, filled with official
documents to which he had no vestige of a legal title. The kaiser dispatched an exultant telegram to his old tutor, Georg Hinzpeter, saying, typically: "It has fallen to me to be officer of the watch on the ship
of state. The course remains the same, and now full speed ahead!"

But would the course remain the same? The English comic maga-
zine *Punch* expressed the British sense of unease by publishing its famous cartoon "Dropping the Pilot." Russians like Giers and Shuvalov
were dismayed to see Bismarck go, for they knew that Russia had lost
a friend, and they felt instinctively that Bismarck's stabilizing influence would be sorely missed in Europe.

The French, on the other hand, were delighted to see the old chancellor forced into retirement. He was the man they held responsible

for their defeat in 1870, and with his departure they felt relieved of a burden. Almost immediately a subtle but sinister change came over French foreign policy; it became more dynamic, more confident, and more aggressive. With Bismarck's fall, ears all over France pricked up, and those who had never ceased to hope for a reversal of the verdict of the Franco-Prussian War felt their pulses quicken. That same summer of 1890, the French government sent the French Chief of the General Staff, General Boisdeffre, to St. Petersburg. Boisdeffre held long talks with his Russian counterpart and was a deeply interested observer of the annual Russian maneuvers. Back in Paris, the French government began for the first time to harass and arrest Russian revolutionaries living there in exile. This was obviously done to make a good impression on the tsar, nor did it fail of its intended effect.

Bismarck was succeeded as chancellor by a Prussian general, Count Leo von Caprivi, a professional soldier of the best type — intelligent, simple, honest, sincere, and reasonable. When the kaiser was unsuccessful in getting Bismarck's son, Herbert, to stay on at the Foreign Office, he appointed a South German, Baron Adolf Hermann Marschall von Bieberstein, foreign minister. Neither Caprivi nor Marschall was at all experienced in foreign affairs, since Bismarck had been careful not to share his knowledge and his power. Caprivi said quite frankly that he was not the man to juggle five balls in the air at one time as Bismarck had done, and his honest nature was particularly susceptible to the argument of Friedrich von Holstein, his colleague at the Wilhelmstrasse, that the secret agreement with Russia was contrary to the spirit, if not the actual wording, of the alliance with Austria. Caprivi therefore recommended to the kaiser that Germany should now pursue "a peaceful, clear and loyal policy" and that the Reinsurance Treaty should not be renewed.* The kaiser, who was also reacting against everything Bismarckian, agreed.

In retrospect, it is quite obvious that the decision not to renew the alliance with Russia was a grievous mistake on Germany's part. It could, in fact, be taken as a classic example of the proposition that God punishes men and nations more severely for their blunders than for their sins. Caprivi certainly bore no malice toward Russia, and was as firmly dedicated to peace as Bismarck had been. Part of the truth may be that men who live for long in the shadow of some potential danger that never becomes actual learn to ignore and forget it — the peasants who dwell on the slopes of Mount Vesuvius, the inhabitants of the flourishing cities built along the San Andreas Fault, the statesmen of the world who have learned to live with the atom bomb.

*The implication was that Bismarck had been devious and disloyal to the Austrian ally.

Twenty years had passed since the Franco-Prussian War, and France had made no move. Bismarck had never forgotten or underestimated this danger; the kaiser, Caprivi, and Marschall had less understanding of basic international realities.

The plea that Bismarck had been secretive does not really excuse or justify this naïveté, for Bismarck's system was not all that complex, and the fundamentals of the international situation were not all that hard to understand. Germany had an alliance with Austria dating from 1879; she was a member of the Triple Alliance, along with Austria and Italy; she had a defensive alliance with Rumania, as had her partners in the Triplice; she had the Reinsurance Treaty with Russia. Bismarck's primary aim had been to maintain the peace of Europe in order to give the new German Empire a chance to settle and harden, and to preserve monarchical and conservative ideals and ways of life in the heart of the continent. Bismarck's successors, and the kaiser himself, adhered to the same aims, but were less astute. None of the four chancellors who followed Bismarck between 1890 and 1914 had so firm a grasp as he of the essentials of the European situation.

Stated simply, in terms of national interests, these fundamentals were as follows: Britain was a colonial power, far more interested in her empire and in trade than in European affairs; so long as none of her vital interests was affected, she could be counted on to remain in her "splendid isolation," to uphold the principle of the European balance of power, and to be hostile to any European aggressor, not because she was of superior moral stature but because British interests were furthered by peace and might be endangered by war. Austria-Hungary suffered from serious internal difficulties, and the Hungarian half of the empire could be expected to resist any expansionist policy. Russia and Germany had no conceivable cause for quarrel and no conflict of interest. Russia, however, had ambitions in the Balkans and coveted the Dardanelles and Constantinople, desires that might bring her into conflict with Austria because if the Balkans were given over to Pan-Slavism this would exert a powerful disruptive force on the heterogeneous Austrian Empire. Because Austria was Germany's most reliable ally, Germany had to support her and resist any attempt to dismember her empire. France nourished her hatred of Germany and had never become reconciled to the loss of her predominance on the continent and of Alsace-Lorraine. Italy was basically a second-rate power but an inordinately greedy and ambitious one. She could be counted on to play the part of the jackal. The only two constant political emotions held by Italian governments were hatred of the ally Austria and fear and dislike of the papacy, but Italy lacked both the strength and the courage to initiate a European war.

Imperialisms

Thus the European situation, viewed dynamically, showed Russia's eagerness, intermittent but long manifest, to expand southeastward and break out to the Mediterranean, and France's continuing desire to regain Alsace-Lorraine and exact revenge for 1870. Germany, Britain, and Austria, in contrast, desired to preserve the European status quo. France and Russia, then, were the potentially aggressive powers, with ambitions that could be satisfied only by war. But so long as these two thrusting forces remained separated, neither was, by itself, strong enough to upset the equilibrium of Europe.

These facts formed the basic framework of the European situation between 1871 and 1914. They were modified and complicated by later developments — by the Dual Entente between France and Russia, by the growth of a rabid Serbian nationalism fostered by Russia, by the Anglo-German naval rivalry, and by Italy's treason to the Triple Alliance. But though these additional factors made the European situation more dangerous, they were not the main source of danger. A British prime minister had once said that "interest never lies," meaning that to understand the international situation one should look not at the words of statesmen but at the necessities and ambitions of nations, which could always be relied on to act in accordance with what they believed their own interests demanded. The axiom, of course, is no infallible guide, for statesmen, like other men, are capable of miscalculating their true interests. Yet the axiom does present a serviceable way of looking at the world — an obvious way, indeed — so obvious that one can only wonder why it has not been used more often. One possible explanation, of course, may be that the real aim, conscious or unconscious, of many of the statesmen and historians who have written about the origins of the First World War has been to obscure the truth, not to reveal it.

The Russian foreign minister, Giers, was deeply disturbed when he was told that Germany would not renew the Reinsurance Treaty, and he attempted unsuccessfully in May and in August of 1890 to change the decision of the German Foreign Office. The Germans, among their other more serious faults, have never been very good at explaining their own point of view, and, naturally enough, the Russians were suspicious of the German refusal to continue a purely defensive treaty. The Russians, among their other more serious faults, have often been overly suspicious of the motives of their neighbors, and now they were unable to believe that Germany was merely trying to pursue "a peaceful, clear and loyal policy." Without the alliance with Germany, Russia appeared to be in a dangerously isolated position. Tension had recently been increasing between Russia and Britain as Russian influence had been extended toward Persia, Afghanistan, and the frontiers of India. Ever since the Congress of Berlin in 1878, Russia had resented Austria, and its ill will had been intensified by the Bulgarian crisis of 1885. Italy was too weak and too far away to be considered a possible ally, and the Russian autocracy had a deep aversion to the republicanism of France, to the French revolutionary tradition, and to the long-established sympathy felt by the French toward the national aspirations of the Poles. When the link between Russia and Germany was broken, it seemed that Russia had lost her only friend.

Nevertheless, few influential Russians viewed the matter as seriously as Giers. Tsar Alexander III was not worried. Russia might be a little lonely now in the concert of Europe, but she was certainly in no danger. Thus, when in March 1891, just a year after Bismarck's fall, the French ambassador to St. Petersburg asked the tsar what his attitude would be in the event of a war between France and Germany, he received a brusque reply. The question betrayed far too aggressive an attitude for Alexander III's liking, and in any case he rightly believed that Russia did not need a formal agreement with France. In the unlikely event of a war between Russia and Germany, there was no question in the tsar's mind of what France would do. And so, since Russia could count on French support, why should she strike any bargains? Alexander's own prejudices against democracy probably played a part as well, as did the fact that the Third French Republic seemed chiefly notable for its internal squabbles and sordid political scandals.

Rebuffed by Russia, the French turned next to Italy and proposed a treaty of alliance. Despite Italy's membership in the Triple Alliance, the Italians nibbled at the bait, as they always nibbled, but Britain advised Italy not to proceed with the negotiations, and the Italians complied. Britain at this time saw much that was commendable in the Triple Alliance, which could be counted on to keep both the French and the Russians in order. A clumsy French attempt to put financial pressure on Italy miscarried, and the Italians decided that they would, after all, remain loyal members of the Triplice.

The French were still too angry at the British for having occupied Egypt in 1881 to seek an alliance in that quarter, but an alliance of some sort France had to have, so renewed overtures were made to Russia. For their part, the Russians feared that Britain might be considering joining the Triple Alliance, though the British had persistently rejected all German suggestions that they do so. At about this time, however, Kaiser Wilhelm II visited England, where he was welcomed enthusiastically, and the Russians took this as a sign that Britain was about to join the Triplice. The truth was quite different;

Wilhelm II and his Uncle Edward, Prince of Wales, detested each other, and the kaiser's visit had been far from a success. Wilhelm made little secret of his belief that "fat old Wales" was a dissolute waster and a discredit to royalty, and Edward felt that his young nephew was too big for his boots. There was considerable truth in both points of view, and these personal antagonisms played their part, albeit a minor one, in poisoning international relations.

The Russians were scarcely aware of all this, and their fears of being faced with a potentially hostile coalition of Britain, Germany, Austria, and Italy made them the readier to listen to the French proposals. On July 23, 1891, a French naval squadron put in at the Russian naval base of Kronstadt. Tsar Alexander III turned up to welcome his guests and stood bareheaded while the naval band played the "Marseillaise," the French revolutionary anthem, which was officially banned everywhere in Russia. For the next two weeks the French sailors and their officers were feted in St. Petersburg; vodka and champagne flowed and there was much mutual enthusiasm. This Russian reception of the French was a forerunner of the far more sinister reception that was to be given to high French government officials twenty-three years later, in July 1914.

Still, it was not the Russians who seduced the French in 1891, but the French who seduced the Russians. In August, France and Russia signed a rather innocuous entente, which stated in general terms that no cause of quarrel existed between the two countries, that the two governments would act together on all matters that endangered the peace of Europe, and that if either was menaced by aggression the two governments would consult together on what measures were to be taken. At the moment, Tsar Alexander refused to commit himself further, and with this vague agreement the French had to be content. As events were to show, they did, in fact, have considerable reason for satisfaction.

The French now had their foot inside the door and they very skillfully proceeded to force it wide open. At the suggestion of France, military staff talks were begun between the two countries. It is interesting to compare this with what happened in the case of Britain a few years later. In both instances, military staff talks with France, which the French were quick to agree did not in any way bind the governments concerned, led to an actual commitment to French policy. The French were extraordinarily good at this kind of maneuver. The historian is almost tempted to conclude that between 1890 and 1914 France possessed the only really skillful diplomats in Europe, and it seems ironic that this was probably the one excellence that the French themselves, who have never been much noted for modesty in such matters, would have earnestly denied.

The French diplomatic achievement in winning an alliance with Russia is the more remarkable because there was considerable divergence of national interest. France, as always after 1870, felt that her main enemy was Germany, but Russia had no reason to fight Germany. To Russia, the main enemy was Britain, and France certainly had no desire to fight Britain. Indeed, the Franco-Russian treaty would have been in Russia's interest only if Britain actually had been allied with Germany. But the French eventually had their way, and a military agreement was drawn up by the two Chiefs of Staff and was ready for signature by August 1892.

The treaty of the Dual Entente was in two parts: a political statement purposely kept vague, general, and high-principled, so that it would be easily ratified by the French Chamber of Deputies; and a secret military supplement that had the advantage of not having to be revealed to the French legislature at all. There would seem to be good reason to distrust the motives of statesmen who invoke secrecy in order to conceal their doings, not from a possible enemy, but from their own people.

The secret military supplement to the treaty was anything but vague. It provided that if France was attacked by Germany, or by Italy supported by Germany, Russia would employ all her forces to attack Germany. If Russia was attacked by Germany, or by Austria supported by Germany, France would employ all her forces to attack Germany. If the Triple Alliance, or any member of the Triple Alliance, mobilized, then both France and Russia, immediately and without prior consultation, would mobilize all their forces and move them as close as possible to their frontiers. France agreed that for her attack on Germany she would utilize 1.3 million men, and Russia agreed that she would attack Germany with between seven hundred thousand and eight hundred thousand men. The two General Staffs were to work out the military details of their campaigns and coordinate them. If war came, there was to be no separate peace. The agreement was to last as long as the Triple Alliance endured and was to be secret.

Tsar Alexander III still had his doubts, and in August 1892 would do no more than agree in principle. This, of course, meant that the agreement had no legal force because it bore only the signatures of the two nations' Chiefs of Staff. However, the French bided their time agreeably and were rewarded sixteen months later, on January 4, 1894, when the tsar was finally persuaded to sign the military supplement to the Dual Entente. The French were later to bide their time much longer with the British in almost exactly similar circumstances, and once again their patience received its reward.

When the Dual Entente was signed, it was a strictly defensive pact aimed solely at Germany. Russia had no wish to support France in a war against Italy, and France had no need of such support; France had no wish to support Russia in a war against either England or Turkey. Because the Dual Entente was defensive, it was, on the face of it, no more a threat to peace than was the defensive Triple Alliance. The time was to come, as we shall see, when the terms of the Dual Entente were changed and it became an offensive treaty, and yet, even before this — in fact from the outset — the Dual Entente was a very different type of treaty from the Triple Alliance. For one thing, as has been noted, the Dual Entente provided that mobilization by any power of the Triple Alliance would result in immediate mobilization by both Russia and France. Thus, if Russia and Austria quarreled over the Balkans, and Austria mobilized against Russia, France would at once be forced to put her forces at the ready. But France had no frontier with Austria and would therefore have to mobilize against Germany and move her forces to the German frontier. Of course, this would inevitably lead to a German countermobilization and a European war. There is no doubt at all that both the French and the Russian general staffs knew exactly what they were doing and realized that this clause of their agreement would make any Balkan dispute between Russia and Austria the possible cause of a great European war. At the time of the signing of the Dual Entente, General Boisdeffre was at pains to point out to the tsar that mobilization was equivalent to a declaration of war. "To mobilize," he said, "is to oblige one's neighbor to do the same. Otherwise to allow a million men to mobilize on one's frontiers without at once doing the same thing oneself is to find oneself in the position of an individual with a pistol in his pocket who allows a neighbor to point a weapon at his head without reaching for his own." The tsar replied: "Yes, that is my understanding of the matter too." It is true that the clause pertaining to mobilization was modified in 1900 so that France would be required to mobilize only in response to German mobilization, but the original wording of the treaty was indicative of the mood of the soldiers who had drafted it.

More serious even than the scope of the Dual Entente was the difference between the aims of Germany and Austria on the one hand and of France and Russia on the other. Bismarck had signed the Austro-German Treaty, and the Triple Alliance after it, to ensure the peace of Europe, to restrain Russia from attacking Austria over the control of the Balkans, and to preclude France's waging a war of revenge to regain the lost provinces. Tsar Alexander III certainly, and the French government probably, intended the Dual Entente to be equally defensive. Yet undoubtedly many in France hoped from the outset that the Dual Entente would promote a war of revenge against

Germany, and some in Russia hoped that it would bring about the victory of Pan-Slavism. These influences, manifest behind the scenes and especially in military circles, were ominous forces tending toward a general European war. The two powers that had hoped, separately, to change the status quo were now united. This did not merely double the danger to peace, but rather increased it many times over; not only was France committed to support Russian interests and Russia committed to support French interests, but the Dual Entente was now strong enough to pursue policies that neither partner had previously been capable of pursuing alone.

Bismarck's "nightmare of coalitions" had become a reality with the signing of the Dual Entente. Many have claimed that the initial mistake was Bismarck's treaty with Austria in 1879, and the claim will undoubtedly continue to be advanced, though the arguments in support of it are weak at best. There are much better grounds for considering as a disastrous error Caprivi's refusal to renew the Reinsurance Treaty, a decision that severed the linear linkage that bound the three empires together. Yet it was the emergence of the Dual Entente, uniting the two European powers intent on changing the status quo, that marked the decisive turn toward war. The French were the initiators of this trend, but if the Russians were used as cat's-paws for the recovery of Alsace-Lorraine, they proved very willing to be so used. In the end, the alliance with France proved catastrophic for the Russian Empire and, indirectly, for all Europe and the world.

The propaganda occasioned by two world wars has created many myths, but few have been as persistent as that which has credited Germany before 1914 with being the soul and center of European militarism. Perversely, the Germans themselves contributed not a little to the legend. They were inordinately proud of their army, believing it to be the personification of the nation. The German Empire had been forged in war, and the glories of Sadowa and Sedan were always present in the national consciousness. If one looked only at the kaiser's vainglorious boastings, it would be easy to conclude that Germany was an armed camp and the possessor of the largest army in the world. The truth is different. In 1892, France, with a smaller population than Germany's, only about forty million to Germany's sixty-five million, and therefore with only about 65 percent of Germany's available manpower, was actually training 30,000 more recruits a year than Germany. The French army was considerably larger than the German army and it remained larger right up to the outbreak of war in 1914. The Russian army was already very large by 1894, and after the signing of the Dual Entente it became enormous, until by 1914 it numbered more than two and a quarter million men. Between 1894 and

1914, the Dual Entente powers always had a much larger military establishment at their disposal than had the powers of the Triple Alliance, and this disparity increased year by year throughout the period. In 1914 the strength of the German army was 761,000; the French army numbered 790,000; the Russian, 2,300,000; the Austrian, 500,000; the Italian, 400,000. This gave the Dual Entente a numerical superiority of nearly two-to-one over the Triple Alliance. When Italy's troops were subtracted from the Triple Alliance, the superiority of the Dual Entente approached three-to-one.

Caprivi managed to get a small army increase through the Reichstag in 1890, and two years later, in November 1892, after the entente cordiale between Russia and France had been announced, he asked for a further increase of 90,000 men, which would have raised Germany's regular army from 512,000 to 602,000. As a quid pro quo, to appease a Reichstag that was by no means eager to incur the additional expense of a larger army, Caprivi offered to reduce the term of service from three years to two and to arrange for the military budget to be voted every five years instead of every seven. This army increase was eventually passed, though not before Caprivi was forced to dissolve the Reichstag and fight an election on the issue.

Caprivi was too honest a man to survive for long as chancellor of the state that Bismarck had bequeathed to him. He soon began to have his troubles with the kaiser, and in this he was not alone; Wilhelm II was an erratic and unpredictable man. People in Germany and abroad were actually beginning to ask themselves out loud whether he was entirely sane. He loved to make speeches, and no one was quite sure what he might say next. It was commonly said that he approached all problems with an open mouth. He was also fond of dressing up in one or another of his more than two hundred uniforms. Once, when he went to the opening night of *The Flying Dutchman*, he turned up in his opera box wearing the full regalia of an admiral of the fleet; and when he visited the Holy Land, it was only with the utmost difficulty that he was persuaded not to don a crusader's costume.

So it is not surprising that Caprivi soon found the kaiser interfering, in the most irresponsible way, with matters of government. Caprivi also had his difficulties with the Junker landlords of East Prussia over agricultural policy, and Bismarck, in retirement at Friedrichsruh, did not help matters at all by publishing, in various newspapers, acidulous criticisms of Caprivi's conduct of foreign affairs. Those three packing cases of official documents that Bismarck had filched from the Reichschancellery were now being put to good use. At all events, Caprivi resigned in October 1894, to be replaced by Prince Chlodwig von Hohenlohe-Schillingsfürst, the seventy-five-year-old uncle of the kaiser. While Hohenlohe was chancellor, the kaiser came to exert more and more influence on both domestic and foreign policy.

Waldersee had been retired as Chief of the General Staff after the fall maneuvers of 1890. The new Chief of the General Staff, Count Alfred von Schlieffen, could not have been more different from Waldersee. Waldersee had been a political general, but Schlieffen was a soldier pure and simple, a military technician without political ambitions or interests. Under Schlieffen, the Prussian General Staff became, in Friedrich Engels' phrase, "a sword-bearing scholasticism," completely divorced from the political life of the nation. In its way Schlieffen's policy proved to be even more disastrous than Waldersee's intrigues had been.

For one thing, German strategy was planned by Schlieffen in a political vacuum, and military men came more and more to accept, tacitly, the inevitability of a two-front war. After Schlieffen became Chief of the General Staff, meaningful discussion between army headquarters on the Bendlerstrasse and the Foreign Office on the Wilhelmstrasse virtually ceased. If the diplomats had thought that a two-front war was likely, that Germany would be attacked by both France and Russia, Schlieffen would have tried to find a military solution to the problem. But he would never have dreamed of suggesting to the diplomats that they might have practiced their profession to lower the odds against Germany and make a two-front war less likely. Moreover, since Schlieffen had little use for the Austrians, there was almost no communication between the Austrian and Prussian staffs, and this was to have unhappy consequences in the opening months of the First World War.

Waldersee, whatever his faults, at least had had the good sense to oppose the plans that were now being advanced by a group of Germans, headed by the kaiser, to increase the size of the German navy. The first German naval increase in 1889 was a modest one, only some five ships, but it was the forerunner of more ambitious policies. Waldersee, and indeed most army officers, argued that Germany, as a continental power, could not afford both a large army and a large navy, but Schlieffen was far too subservient to the kaiser and far too much the pure military technician to take a stand on what he regarded as primarily a political issue. In fairness it should be added that, given the kaiser's personality, his love of the sea, and his jealousy of the Royal Navy, which staged such fine reviews for his British relatives, no opposition from Schlieffen would have been likely to prevent the building of a great German navy.

Although her central position in Europe made her liable to attack from two sides, Germany had certain military advantages. Her wonderful railway system, with four great trunk lines running east to west across the country, each capable of carrying two army corps from East Prussia to the Rhine in eighteen hours, meant that she could mobilize much more rapidly than her neighbors and that she could switch her troops east or west with greater facility. Then, too, Germany and Austria possessed the two large armament firms of Krupp and Skoda, which were technically in advance of armament firms in other countries. More important than any of this was the excellence of the German army, which was a very serious and professional organization. It was not by any means the largest army on the continent, but it was by all odds the best. Since 1864, the Prussian General Staff had been recruited on the basis of ability; it was highly trained and dedicated, but was open to the influence of new military ideas. German regimental training and discipline were also superior to those of other continental armies, though not, of course, equal to that of the long-service British Regular Army, in which enlisted men normally served for a minimum of seven years.

France, on the other hand, had certain grave military weaknesses — the more critical because they were not readily apparent at the time. So long as memories of 1870 remained fresh, French military doctrine was sensible and realistic. Yet it was not long before the reaction set in, marked by the attempt to explain away the French defeat and to compensate for the French inferiority complex that had been occasioned by that defeat. Was France in all material things weaker than Germany? Was her population smaller, her industry less fully developed? Never mind; the victory was not always to the strong. The French spirit would triumph over all these disadvantages.

So a dangerous, semimystical quality developed in French military thought, bound up with the idea of revenge and the recovery of the lost provinces. Perhaps the hero worship afforded to the memory of Napoleon also had its part in the new French thinking. The legends of dashing marshals and "old Mustaches," the eagles of the emperor, the glories of conquest and the roll call of splendid victories — Marengo, Austerlitz, Jena, Wagram, and Eylau — were all balm to the wounded French self-esteem and seemed an earnest of heroic days to come. Colonel Grandmaison, the head of the Operations Branch of the French General Staff in the 1890s, was the principal spokesman of the new school. He objected that the French war plan, which was basically a defensive one, surrendered the strategic initiative to the enemy, and he argued that the best guarantee against surprise would be the speed with which the enemy would be engaged, that the inherent power of the offensive would impose its own pattern on the battlefield, forcing the enemy to conform. By this reasoning, Grandmaison elevated one single principle of war, that of offensive action, to an entirely irrational position of dominance. He said at one time, "Imprudence is the best safeguard." But paradox is an insufficient basis for military doctrine.

The emphasis on the attack was, of course, reflected in French tactics, and it may even be said to have been reflected in French policy. The saying attributed to Napoleon, "The moral is to the material as three is to one," was much quoted, and the French talked a good deal about the bayonet — *l'arme blanche* — and a good deal about élan. In one sense, this new French doctrine was a direct result of the Dual Entente. When France had stood alone, without allies, a defensive strategy was the only one possible for her. With the Russian alliance, France appeared to have regained the initiative, and in the exuberance engendered by this belief the doctrine of the offensive à *l'outrance* came to be accepted — to France's most grievous loss in the years to come.

Russia, like France, had territorial ambitions in Europe in the 1890s, but there was no immediate hurry to realize them. Someday — probably quite soon — the Ottoman Empire would collapse of its own accord, and then would be time enough to move. In the meanwhile there were problems enough elsewhere. Russia was a nation of contradictions. Serious famines occurred in 1891, 1892, 1897, 1898, and 1901, and many hundreds of thousands of people died of starvation. Russian industrialization had hardly begun. Yet by 1897, largely because of the influx of French capital, the Russian government was able to begin the great project of the Trans-Siberian Railroad, which was to span some seven thousand miles of desolate countryside and was decisively to alter Russian foreign policy for the next decade.

In 1894 Tsar Alexander III died unexpectedly, at the age of forty-nine. He had been a reactionary ruler who had set his face firmly against political reform, but at least he had been a man who knew his own mind. His son was twenty-six when he ascended the throne as Nicholas II. In part because he had been educated by the same Pan-Slav, Pobedonostsev, who had been his father's tutor, and partly because he had lived all his life in the shadow of his father's overpowering personality, he was completely unprepared for his new responsibilities. In 1895 he married Princess Alexandra of Hesse-Darmstadt, a former Lutheran who had been converted to the Orthodox faith. The new tsarina, as is sometimes the case with converts, at once became more Russian than the Russians and more Orthodox than the Metropolitan. She professed a mystical belief in the union of the crown and the people, but her religiosity was never very far removed from superstition. Because her son, the tsarevitch, was a hemophiliac, she developed the weakness for quacks, faith healers, and pseudomystics that was later to give Rasputin his entrée into court circles, and was thus to play a part in the downfall of the autocracy.

Nicholas had not been groomed to be tsar, for there had seemed no likelihood that he would so soon replace his father. He had not even been told of the existence of the Dual Entente before he became Autocrat of All the Russias, and he had had far too childish a mind to interest himself to any extent in affairs of state. He was well meaning, religious, and devoted to his family, but he did not possess either intelligence or force of character. Another important aspect of Nicholas' personality was that he did not much like his cousin Kaiser Wilhelm II. Although their relationship appeared friendly, the tsar almost certainly entertained a secret resentment and hostility toward the kaiser, which boded no good for the future. Probably — in this at least — the tsar faithfully reflected Russia, as though in a small mirror, for Russians in general were resentful and suspicious of the West and most especially of the Germans.

In the nineties, indeed, Russia turned her back on Europe and looked toward the East. With the completion of the Trans-Siberian Railroad, Russia hoped to open up a vast new market in China and to capture much of the British trade in the Far East, which now moved through the Suez Canal. The Russian admiralty desired an ice-free port on the Yellow Sea or in Korea, and Russian entrepreneurs hoped for the economic dominance of Manchuria. Germany did her best to encourage this new orientation. Certainly Wilhelm II was always lecturing his cousin Nicky about Russia's historic mission to defend Europe from the Yellow Peril. Little profit is to be gained by questioning the sincerity of Wilhelm's actions, for some problems are beyond the reach of even the most psychoanalytic of historians. Perhaps the truth is that the kaiser really believed in the Yellow Peril and also realized how much stronger Germany's international position would be if Russia turned to the East. Probably, too, Russia, at one and the same time, wanted to be told that it was her historic mission to civilize the Orient, yet resented the sacrifice the West was eager to thrust on her. Nicholas was not very bright, but he was surely bright enough to see through his cousin's rather obvious attempts to embroil Russia in troubles on the far side of the world.

Once the gaze of Russian officialdom turned eastward across the steppes, the Turks felt they could safely resume one of their favorite national sports, the massacring of the Christian subjects of the Ottoman Empire. On this occasion, it was the Armenians who felt the Muslem fury. Between 1894 and 1896, many thousands of Armenians were killed — some thirty thousand of them in Constantinople alone in one month. Britain, for a change, wanted to intervene, but Russia was busy elsewhere, and Germany actually supported Turkey in the hope that, by doing so, she might aid in opening a gate through which German influence could be extended to the Near East. Ever since Disraeli's day, British advice had carried much weight at Constantinople, but now Germany saw a chance to elbow in as well. And so the Armenians went unavenged.

European affairs were now complicated by an event in the Far East that was ultimately to affect profoundly the European balance of power. In 1895 Japan suddenly attacked China and, in less than eight months, drove the Chinese armies out of Korea and Manchuria. Of all the European nations, only Britain was sufficiently well served by her diplomats to realize what this meant. For the first time, an Oriental nation had emerged as a world power, and even the British had no real conception of what this portended. At the moment, Japan seemed a very acceptable counterbalance to Russia in the Far East.

At the end of the Sino-Japanese War, Japan claimed large areas of Manchuria, Korea, and the naval base of Port Arthur. Russia was unwilling to permit this Japanese expansion and, having arranged for the support of France and Germany, persuaded these nations to join her in sending a note to Japan, demanding, on threat of war, that Japan abandon her gains on the mainland of China. Britain refused to associate herself with this threat, and through the words of the polite diplomatic rejection can be heard the faint, still-distant bugle notes of the Russo-Japanese War.

The Japanese gave way, but not without anger. In particular, they were bitter about the German interference. They could understand that Russia might have interests of her own in the Far East and they knew that France was Russia's ally, but Germany's stand appeared completely gratuitous. The Japanese also bridled at the note of rudeness that was creeping into German diplomacy. The German ambassador to Japan had been brusque; he had, in fact, flattered himself on his outspokenness. He reported back to the Wilhelmstrasse, "My remarks made an obvious impression." They did indeed. The Japanese were to repeat those remarks verbatim in their declaration of war on Germany in 1914.

As Russia turned her attention to the East during the second half of the 1890s, the likelihood of a conflict between Russia and Japan increased, but the political situation in Europe itself became easier. In 1897, Emperor Franz Josef and his foreign minister, Goluchowski, visited St. Petersburg and reached an agreement with Nicholas II and his foreign minister, Muraviev, for the preservation of the status quo in the Balkans. And for the next ten years, while Russia was busy in Siberia and Manchuria, the Balkans were "put on ice." Naturally, as soon as Russian eyes were distracted from the Balkans, the tension between Russia and Austria abated. As a result of this relaxation of tension and of Russian involvement in Asia, the German Foreign Office began to believe that it could adopt a bolder foreign policy.

The year 1895 was a difficult one for Britain. As one looks back, indeed, it seems a turning point in British affairs, marking the watershed between the years of peaceful and happy prosperity and the years of mounting trouble and danger. The real turning point, of course, was much earlier — probably around 1870 — but 1895 was the year when Britain's difficulties first began to be seriously noticed. Lord Salisbury, in addition to being prime minister, was acting as his own foreign secretary, and he had given the Colonial Office to the Liberal Unionist Joseph Chamberlain, who, more than any man in British public life, represented the spirit of British imperialism. Chamberlain was not, all things considered, a fortunate choice. Trouble was already shaping up in South Africa. After the Boer republics had defeated the British at Mjuba Hill in 1881, Gladstone had granted independence to the Transvaal under a nominal British suzerainty, but British entrepreneurs and adventurers had poured into the territory after gold was found in the Witswatersrand and diamonds were discovered near Kimberley. "Oom" Paul Kruger, the president of the Transvaal, had allowed the British in, had taxed them heavily, and had refused to give them any political rights. With the money Kruger obtained from the Uitlanders, he was now buying arms from Germany. He felt he would have need of them. And he was right, because Cecil Rhodes, the president of Cape Colony and, what was more important, president of the British South Africa Company, was dreaming imperial dreams — dreams of a Cape to Cairo railway and of a strip of British territory that would run north to south down all Africa. The Transvaal blocked the realization of these dreams. Rhodes was refreshingly candid about his views and quite sure that destiny was on his side. "History teaches," he said, "that expansion is everything, and that, the world's surface being limited, the great object of present humanity should be to take as much of the world as it possibly can."

By July 1895, the Boers, with German capital, had completed a railway that linked Delagoa Bay to Pretoria, thus providing an alternate route to the one that ran through Cape Colony. This may have been what made Rhodes decide that it was time to strike. Whatever the precipitating factor, he planned a coup d'état that would oust the Boer government at Pretoria and replace it with one headed by his brother, Frank, the leader of the Uitlanders in the Transvaal.

On December 29 a force of 470 armed men, led by Cecil Rhodes's friend and employee, Dr. L. S. Jameson, a medical doctor who found it more congenial and profitable to be a captain of condottieri than to practice his profession, invaded the Transvaal. The Jameson Raid was supposed to coincide with a rising by the Uitlanders in Pretoria, but on this occasion, the good Dr. Jameson found himself opposed not by ill-led and ill-armed blacks, but by white settlers who were thoroughly familiar with the country.* The uprising in Pretoria did not occur, but this hardly mattered because Jameson never reached the Boer capital. At the end of the first day out from Cape Colony, Jameson's raiders were met by deadly accurate rifle fire from invisible marksmen. Although Jameson's band had three field guns and eight machine guns, it had no opportunity to deploy its superior firepower. As British casualties mounted steadily, it soon became apparent that Jameson's party was surrounded. Before long, the raiders surrendered ignominiously.

Perhaps for the very reason that the Jameson Raid was such a complete fiasco, it provoked an almost universally hostile reaction in Europe. German public opinion was especially anti-British, and the German foreign minister, Marschall, wanted to break off diplomatic relations with Britain because he felt this would teach the British how much they needed German friendship. It was a remarkable theory, but rather typically German. Instead of breaking off diplomatic relations, Marschall, Holstein, and a few other officials at the Wilhelmstrasse, in conjunction with the kaiser, who at least had the good sense to be unenthusiastic about the project, composed a telegram to be sent to President Kruger. It was signed by the kaiser and dispatched on January 3, 1896. It read:

> I should like to express my sincere congratulations that you and your people have succeeded, without having had to invoke the help of friendly powers, in restoring peace with your own resources in the face of armed

*Two years previously, in October and November 1893, Dr. Jameson had conquered King Lobengula of the Matabele tribe south of the Zambesi River with the aid of Gatling guns, which had mowed down the natives in a most satisfactory manner. Hilaire Belloc, an English anti-imperialist who did not much approve of this type of warfare, was to comment:

> *Whatever happens,*
> *We have got*
> *The Gatling gun,*
> *And they have not.*

These exhilarating little campaigns and tiny colonial wars, though they contributed to the formation of the Boy Scout movement, taught the British many false lessons in tactics and organization for which the British army was to pay dearly when it fought a continental war.

bands which had broken into your country as disturbers of the peace, and have been able to preserve the independence of your country against attacks from outside.

To the British, the reference to "the help of friendly powers" seemed to imply a threat of war, and British opinion flared up in anger against Germany. Eighteen years later, in August 1914, the British ambassador in Berlin told the Belgian ambassador that the Kruger telegram had been the beginning of the Anglo-German misunderstanding that led to the war. This was certainly a gross exaggeration, but it was nevertheless true that the Kruger telegram did awaken British public opinion to the realization that the Germans viewed the British rather differently from the way in which the British viewed themselves. Such a realization is seldom a happy experience, and British journalists proved themselves to be as chauvinistic and bellicose as their counterparts on the continent. Their fulminations did much to exacerbate and inflame the crisis. Until now Britain had regarded France as the traditional enemy, and, after France, Russia. But a new alignment began to take form in people's minds, and Germany was being thought of as the enemy.

The German newspapers were equally irresponsible, and there was even some loose talk about the possibility of landing German marines at Delagoa Bay. However, since the Royal Navy controlled the seas, no obvious way of getting a German force to South Africa presented itself and the matter was dropped. The British government reacted strongly to the Kruger telegram, assembling and sending to sea a naval flying squadron of overwhelming strength. Dr. Jameson's silly little venture was really causing a great deal of trouble — more, indeed, than anyone at the time realized. Germany was forced to recognize her helplessness in the face of British sea power, and the knowledge was unpalatable. All those elements in Germany that were potentially anti-British were enormously strengthened and helped by Germany's sense of humiliation; and Holstein, Admiral Alfred von Tirpitz, and the kaiser himself were given splendid ammunition in their fight for a large German navy.

Strictly speaking, what the British did in the Transvaal was no business of the Germans, and though it is possible to sympathize with their moral indignation, it is also true that, since no German interest was at stake, the German government was unwise to take the action that it did. No more representative example of the faults of German diplomacy under Wilhelm II can be found than the Kruger telegram; it achieved nothing but the heightening of international tensions and the creation of ill will. The episode is also an interesting example of how colonial conflicts were contributing, though secondary, causes of the European war. Lenin and the Bolsheviks were almost entirely wrong when they blamed imperialism as the principal cause of the war, because conflicts of interest over markets, raw materials, and colonies were never of primary importance in the minds of European statesmen, most of whom would, in their hearts, have agreed with General Garnier des Garets that all the empires of Asia and Africa were not "worth an acre of the earth where I fought in 1870, and where the *Cuirassiers* of Reichshoffen and the Zouaves of Froeschwiller lie." Nevertheless, imperialism did much to set the mood of the period, a mood that was all too often chauvinistic, intolerant, and aggressive. As early as 1860, Richard Cobden had asked about Britain's Indian empire, "Is it not just possible that we may become corrupted at home by the reaction of arbitrary political maxims in the East upon our domestic politics, just as Greece and Rome were demoralized by their contact with Asia?" The question was even more pertinent by 1895 and was by then applicable to several European powers besides Britain. Of course, the real roots of the Anglo-German naval rivalry can be found in the belief that colonies were good things for great powers to own and that navies were needed to defend them.

In November 1897, on the excuse offered by the murder of two German missionaries, Germany seized the Chinese port of Kiaochow. Russia promptly took "compensation" by seizing the ports of Talienwan and Port Arthur, much to the indignation of the Japanese, who had been forced to disgorge Port Arthur so short a time before. Britain thereupon demanded that China grant her the port of Weihaiwei as a naval base, and France seized Kwangchowan. The British government came under sharp criticism in the House of Commons for thus forsaking its principle of upholding the territorial integrity of China, but it pleaded necessity, the force that proverbially knows no law. Another and more basic principle was soon to be likewise abandoned.

Britain, much disturbed by the increase of Russian influence in the Far East and the rivalry with France in Africa, renounced her policy of "splendid isolation" and sought an alliance with Germany. The prime mover in this attempt was Joseph Chamberlain, who believed it would be a fine thing to unite the naval power of Britain with the military power of Germany. The British prime minister, Lord Salisbury, was not so sure, but he went on a holiday and left the negotiations to the colonial secretary, who proposed the alliance to the German ambassador, Count von Hartzfeldt, on March 29, 1898. However, the German foreign minister, who was by now Bernhard von Bülow, was afraid that Britain intended to use Germany as a sword against Russia and believed, in any case, that Germany was in no immediate need of such alliance. Bülow feared, too, and with some justification, that the British Parliament might not ratify such a treaty. Chamberlain pressed his case, threatening that if Germany did not conclude an alliance with Britain "it would not be impossible for her to reach an understanding with Russia or France." Bülow thought this highly improbable, and though Chamberlain publicly suggested an Anglo-German alliance in a speech at Birmingham on May 13, the German chancellor was unwilling to estrange Russia by appearing to enter a coalition against her. Lord Salisbury, who had resumed the direction of foreign affairs at the end of April, quietly poured cold water on Chamberlain's scheme, and the negotiations died. Thus was lost the last real opportunity of a coalition of those powers whose paramount interest was the maintenance of peace. None of the negotiators, on either the British or the German side, had considered this aspect of the situation or realized that French and Russian ambitions might someday pose a danger to Europe. In 1898 a European war appeared most unlikely. Chamberlain and Salisbury, like Bülow and the kaiser, were preoccupied with the minor pieces on the diplomatic chessboard — prestige, colonies, and minor diplomatic successes — and overlooked entirely the distant threat of deadly checkmate, which would eventually bring their game to an end. It is unlikely that either Bismarck or Disraeli would have been so shortsighted.

As the nineteenth century waned, Britain found herself in various difficulties around the world. Lord Kitchener had conquered the Sudan in 1897 and had subsequently advanced up the White Nile, where he found a French expedition under Major Marchand already encamped at Fashoda. Neither the British nor the French would withdraw, and for six months Britain and France teetered on the verge of war. The crisis was resolved only when the French foreign minister, Théophile Delcassé, decided that France could not really afford the luxury of two enemies, and ordered Fashoda evacuated. Several factors contributed to Delcassé's decision: the Royal Navy could command the Mediterranean; the Dreyfus case was then at its height, with the French army and French politicians at each other's throats; and most decisive of all, in Delcassé's own words, "Alsace is more important than Africa." No colonial quarrel could long distract French attention from "the long blue line of the Vosges."

If Delcassé had held out a little longer, he might have obtained better terms, for in October 1899 the Transvaal and the Orange Free State declared war on Britain, invading Natal and investing Kimberley and Ladysmith. Britain was caught with only fourteen thousand troops in Cape Colony to oppose the Boers' fifty thousand excellent mounted rifles, and as a consequence the South African War was to be a prolonged affair. To its considerable surprise, the British government found itself facing a hostile world — a Russia grown aggressive in the East, a France embittered by Fashoda, a Germany estranged by the Jameson Raid and a difficult and humiliating war on the veldt. Even the United States could not be counted as a friend, as the Venezuela Boundary Dispute of 1895 had shown. The long Victorian peace was broken, though not yet irretrievably; the strong Victorian self-confidence was shaken, though not yet lost. But as the century drew to a close, Britain suddenly felt a little chilly in the sunlight.

Perhaps this brief premonition was experienced elsewhere as well. In August 1898 the tsar had surprised and annoyed most of the European powers by suggesting that they should hold a disarmament conference. The French were more than a little disconcerted by the suggestion of their Russian ally, and the newspaper *Le Temps*, which, as a rule, accurately reflected official French opinion, commented, "As long as the injustice of 1871 has not been righted . . . the true heirs of the Revolution cannot subscribe to the principles of Count Muraviev." The Germans pointed out that, though the Russians were suddenly talking about disarmament, Russia in the previous five years had spent much larger sums on armaments than had Germany, and had been building strategic railways and raising new divisions. The kaiser suggested that all his cousin Nicky really wanted was to avoid another increase in the Russian budget. There was, in fact, some truth in this. The Russian finance minister, Sergei Witte, had been horrified when he had seen the estimates for modernizing the Russian artillery, and it had been he who had suggested the disarmament conference to the tsar.

However, since no nation was willing to incur the stigma of being the one to sabotage so benevolent a suggestion, a conference was convened in the Hague in May 1899, each of the powers attending in the secret hope that one of the others would wreck the proceedings. They need not have worried, as it turned out, for all that came from three months of debate and discussion was the establishment of an international court of arbitration and some modest conventions outlining the rules of war.

In a sense, it was fitting that the nineteenth century should end with the failure of a peace conference. There had been no general European war since the fall of Napoleon in 1815, and the long, sunny decades of peace seemed to have forced the final flowering of Western civilization. Trade had increased; technological development had blossomed wonderfully; life was easier, healthier, and seemingly more secure; slavery and serfdom had been virtually abolished throughout the world; freedom seemed to be prevailing inexorably over old tyrannies; science and reason were held to be keys that would unlock all doors; faith in progress had merged with, or supplanted, faith in God. Yet at the very moment when European civilization had been universally accepted, when Asia and Africa had fallen under the European spell, as North and South America had done before them, the Europeans themselves began to falter, the achievements began to lose their charm, new doubts began to take the heart out of the secular optimism that had but recently seemed so self-evident and so justified. The gas-lit city of Western civilization was full of marvels and very fair to see, but it was neither the New Jerusalem nor the City of God, and men began to ask themselves — generally without knowing why — if they had labored in vain to build it.

Looking back on all of it now, it seems to the observer that there was a sort of fever about the last decade of the nineteenth century, a restlessness, an instability, and a materialism that had not previously been apparent. The nineties have been labeled "gay" or "naughty," depending on the describer's point of view, but certainly there was everywhere a new temper to the times. In Britain the high principles and moral purpose of the middle Victorian era began to disintegrate and to be replaced by a fin de siècle overripeness. The two Jubilee years of 1887 and 1897 were, perhaps, responsible for some of the manifestations of this new mood — military reviews at Aldershot, naval reviews at Spithead, fires blazing from the hilltops, patriotic crowds, and such pomp and circumstance that even Kipling, of all people, had his recessional doubts.

But the mood was by no means confined to Britain, nor was vociferous patriotism its only expression. The Third French Republic seemed to be doing its best to tear itself apart with quarrels between, on one side, republicans, anticlericals, and all the self-proclaimed inheritors of the Revolution, and, on the other, the army, the church, royalists, and conservatives. The Dreyfus case, which symbolized this division, was only the principal scandal of a scandalous decade. Across the continent, Russia was reaching out to conquer a vast new empire on the Pacific, and leaving behind, in the heart of European Russia, festering social and economic problems that were to prove mortal. In the south, the Italians suffered a humiliating military defeat at Adowa when they attempted to conquer an empire of their own in Abyssinia. The Italians, however, were unique in their failure, for by the close of the decade all Africa, except Abyssinia, had been partitioned among the nations of Europe, and great portions of China and Southeast Asia had suffered the same fate. In the United States, the period was marked by the Populist and Progressive movements and by an entirely unexpected and irrational outbreak of American imperialism, which betrayed the basic ideals on which the American nation had been founded.

In Germany, too, strange new ideas were in the wind. An unfamiliar word, *Weltanschauung*, or world view, was heard with greater frequency. Germany, it was said, should exert her influence on the world stage; it was her manifest duty not to confine so much Germanic virtue solely to the continent of Europe. In part, this ambition was imitative, the looking with jealous eyes on the vast colonial empires of France and Britain. Germans demanded "a place in the sun," by which they meant new colonies — as though the sun shone only in Africa and Asia — and they accepted easily enough the corollary that they should have a strong navy as an instrument of world power. For this, of course, they would have to acquire bases and coaling stations, new colonies in Africa, new concessions in China, and increased influence in the Middle East. A German Navy League was formed, as was a Pan-German League, and both of these nationalist organizations received strong middle-class support. How different it all was from the philosophy of Bismarck, who had said, "My map of Africa lies in Europe"!

CHAPTER III

AFTER THE FAILURE of the Hague Peace Conference, Delcassé visited St. Petersburg and persuaded the tsar to change the Dual Entente from a purely defensive pact for the maintenance of peace to a much broader alliance, which could be invoked to maintain "the equilibrium among the European forces." But Delcassé wished to use the Dual Entente as a means of ensuring Russian help against Germany for the repossession of Alsace-Lorraine. To achieve this, he offered Russia French support against Austria in any Balkan quarrel, and as additional bait he offered a protocol to the military convention that promised Russia French support in a war against England. If Britain attacked Russia, France would concentrate 150,000 men on the Channel and threaten a landing in the British Isles; if Britain attacked France, Russia promised to use 300,000 men to create a diversion against India, as soon as the Orenburg-Tashkent railway was completed. So as to eliminate any doubt about the binding nature of this protocol, France forthwith lent Russia the sum of 425 million gold francs for the construction of the Tashkent railway.

France had now obtained what some of her diplomats had all along desired, a military alliance with Russia that could be used as an instrument for a war of revenge against Germany. The hook had been baited to suit the Russian taste, with emphasis on Austria and England, Russia's principal opponents; but though Delcassé talked about the possibility of a British attack on Russia, he had his mind fixed intently on Alsace-Lorraine.

Events were playing nicely into the hands of the French diplomats who wished to weaken Germany. After Italy had been defeated by the Abyssinians at Adowa in 1896, she was inclined to blame Germany for not having given her stronger support. Bülow replied harshly that the Italians had mistaken the nature of the Triple Alliance, which was a conservative, defensive pact, not an association for grabbing other people's territory. Italy renewed the Triple Alliance when it fell due, but she signed a commercial treaty with France, which further weakened her ties to her alliance partners.

Toward the end of 1902 the Balkans again began to erupt into violence as Macedonian guerrilla forces, or *comitadji*, secretly supported by Bulgaria, revolted and seized the Kresna Pass in the Struma Valley. Bulgaria, which had hoped to annex an independent Macedonia, mobilized, and war with Turkey seemed imminent. However, neither Russia nor Austria desired a Balkan war, and their combined pressure forced Prince Ferdinand of Bulgaria to moderate his policy. At the Alpine resort town of Mürzsteg, in October 1903, Tsar Nicholas II and Emperor Franz Josef, both accompanied by their foreign ministers, signed an agreement to maintain the existing status of the Balkans and to force Turkey to make reforms in favor of her Christian subjects. The sultan, as was his custom, agreed to the demands of the Mürzsteg program but took no further action. Still, Mürzsteg seemed a happy omen, for Russia and Austria were now cooperating in the Balkans. As long as this cooperation continued, one of the two principal danger points in Europe was effectively defused.

By now Germany was taking a great deal of interest in Turkey. The former German foreign minister, Marschall, was ambassador there; General Kolmar von der Goltz headed a German military mission in Constantinople; a Turkish branch of the Deutsche Bank had been established; and Germany was making Turkey sizable loans in exchange for railway concessions. Neither Russia nor Britain much liked this new German interest in the Near East, and both were alarmed when the kaiser visited Damascus and declared in a public speech that he himself was a direct descendant of the Prophet Mohammed and the true defender of Islam. Germany, the kaiser said with uncomfortable accuracy, was the only major nation in Europe that had no Moslem subjects and no designs on any Moslem territory.

However, the increase of German influence in Turkey was only a minor irritation compared with the German decision to build a large navy that would be competitive with Britain's. For many years, Britain had maintained the "two-power standard," directed against France and Russia, whereby the Royal Navy was maintained at a strength 10 percent above the combined strength of the world's next two largest navies. Until the end of the last decade of the century, Britain had never considered Germany a possible naval rival, and as late as 1896, the Royal Navy greatly surpassed the German navy.

At the same time that Bülow replaced Marschall as German foreign minister in 1897, Admiral Tirpitz became naval minister. For the next few years, Bülow and Tirpitz cooperated wholeheartedly in increas-

ing German naval power. Almost immediately after assuming office,
Bülow managed to get the Reichstag to approve an addition to the
navy of seven battleships, two heavy cruisers, and seven light cruisers.
The Radicals and Socialists opposed the measure, but they were voices
crying in the wilderness. If Germany were ever to find her place in the
sun and become a world power, a strong navy seemed a necessity. The
kaiser, who was an enthusiastic amateur yachtsman, agreed completely with this line of reasoning. He argued that colonies were the
Achilles' heel of a Germany that had hitherto been out of England's
reach, and he declared, in 1897, "I will never rest until I have raised
my navy to the same level as my army." The following year he predicted, "Our future lies on the water." The British, holding dominion
over palm and pine, were not, for the time being, much disturbed by
these declarations of intent.

The new German world policy, based on sea power and colonies,
found considerable support within Germany. In 1897 two thirds of
German trade was inside Europe whereas two thirds of British trade
was outside Europe; but the Germans, naturally enough, saw no reason why the British should be exempt from competition, especially
since they had long enjoyed such exemption and had, as a result, become somewhat slipshod and careless. German industries were, on
the whole, more efficient than British industries, partly because Britain, having been the first nation to industrialize, was now saddled with
much obsolescent equipment; partly because of the natural advantages possessed by latecomers to the process of industrialization,
especially in the second phase, where more complex and sophisticated
industries, such as electrical machinery, chemicals, and machine tools,
replaced in importance the primary industries of iron, steel, and
coal-mining; and partly because the long period of Britain's virtual
monopoly of industrialization had given British firms a complacent
philosophy of business and inefficient organization. To the Germans
it seemed only natural and right that the long-held British supremacy
should be challenged, and there was general agreement that, for the
challenge to be effective, a strong German navy was a prerequisite.

What seemed to the Germans right and natural seemed to the
British outrageous — though it took a considerable time for their
sense of outrage to develop. The existing disparity in naval forces was
too great to cause the British much alarm, even when a second naval
bill was introduced into the Reichstag in December 1899, providing
that, within sixteen years, Germany would have thirty-four
battleships, fourteen heavy cruisers, thirty-eight light cruisers, and
eight torpedo boats. Bülow, in introducing this bill, said quite
explicitly that its purpose was to give Germany a navy so strong that it

could not be attacked by any other power, and he added that in the new century that was dawning Germany "would be either hammer or anvil."

Tirpitz, a man of great energy and excellent organizing ability, did much to marshal German public opinion behind the navy. The armament firm of Krupp, of course, enthusiastically supported the Navy League, for it made money with every keel laid down. The kaiser again ardently supported Tirpitz' plans. For many years he regularly attended the annual British naval maneuvers at Spithead, and was always jealous of the British battle squadrons on parade. It was not that the kaiser ever seriously considered fighting a naval war, but what he did picture to himself was a splendid naval review in which the German fleet outshone the British.

In the realm of grand strategy, however, Tirpitz was much less adept and was just as inclined as Schlieffen to take a narrow professional view. Tirpitz developed his so-called risk theory, which argued, in effect, that if Germany was prepared to enter a naval race with Britain, there would be a period when there would be a risk of naval war on terms disadvantageous to Germany. Once this "danger zone"* had been passed, however, the British fleet would not fight the German for fear that, even if it was victorious, the Royal Navy might suffer such serious damage as to risk losing the mastery of the seas to a third power. Besides, Tirpitz argued, Germany did not need naval equality with Britain because Britain's many overseas commitments forced her to keep her fleet dispersed around the world, whereas the German navy could remain concentrated. All Germany needed, Tirpitz used to plead, was a "respectable" navy.

The real question was whether Germany could afford the navy that Tirpitz, the kaiser, and Bülow wanted. Navies are very costly, consuming vast amounts of money and industrial resources, and no German soldier would have agreed that Germany was spending enough on her army. Because of lack of funds, Germany was training only slightly more than 50 percent of her available manpower, in comparison with a French conscription of over 80 percent. And the army was vital to Germany. Lying as she did in the heart of the continent, and surrounded by potentially hostile powers, Germany's survival depended on her army. The naval enthusiasts, of course, argued that without

---

*In fact, there was little reason to fear that the danger zone would be very dangerous, for the political climate in Britain would not have permitted a surprise attack on the German fleet. Admiral John "Jackie" Fisher, the British First Sea Lord, in his blunt, saltwater way, used to thump the table and express a desire to "Copenhagen 'em" — by which he meant that he wanted to sink the German navy at its bases without a declaration of war, as the British had done to the Danes in 1807. But no one took Fisher seriously on this point.

sea power Germany would be unable to fight a land war on two fronts because such a war might last for a long time and cause Germany to run short of raw materials. This argument was unconvincing at the time, and is even less convincing in retrospect. Nothing in the history of the First or Second World War really bears out the contention, for in each conflict Germany was able to survive for long periods of time without control of the seas, and her defeat in each instance was far more attributable to losses on the land than on the seas.

In any case, Tirpitz ignored the real crux of the problem, which was the British reaction. Tirpitz feared the unlikely possibility of a British surprise attack more than he did the probability that Britain would not allow the naval ratio to change to Germany's advantage. Britain, in fact, had no intention of allowing herself to be outstripped by Germany, and once she realized clearly the import of the German naval program, the naval race was on. It was wickedly expensive for both countries, but Germany was far less able to afford it because every mark spent on the navy was a mark denied to the army. And it was all in vain. By 1914 the Royal Navy was still so superior to the German High Seas Fleet that the latter service was forced to play a passive role throughout almost the entire war.

Moreover, Tirpitz was far too simple in his basic assumptions. He saw only his growing navy, and assumed that German foreign policy could adjust itself to the naval program. And he was most culpable in failing to consider the possibility that his challenge to British sea power might drive Britain out of her isolation and into alliance with the Dual Entente, thus upsetting the European balance of power. Such considerations were not, of course, Tirpitz' primary responsibility; they were the responsibility of the kaiser, the chancellor, and the foreign minister, and these were the men by whom Germany was most ill served.

At the time of Bülow's second naval bill, however, Britain had other preoccupations. The war in South Africa was going badly* and was eventually to require some 450,000 British troops before it could be won. During the South African War, the attitude of the German government was perfectly correct. The kaiser had refused to see President Kruger when he came to Europe to enlist support, and Germany consistently rejected Russian suggestions that the European powers should make a demonstration against Britain.† Still the German press

---

*Not surprisingly. The commission that subsequently investigated the British conduct of the war came to the conclusion that throughout the entire conflict there had never been an overall plan of campaign.

†The kaiser received less credit than he deserved for these evidences of friendship, perhaps because of his tendency to brag about them. Nor were the British noticeably grateful when the kaiser sent them a plan of campaign for subduing the Boers, drawn

was violently anti-British, and Admiral Tirpitz made good propaganda out of the Royal Navy's stopping and searching two German
steamships wrongly suspected of carrying contraband to the Boers.

Late in the autumn of 1900 Bülow became chancellor. He believed
quite firmly that Britain was a declining power and Germany a rising
one; and was also convinced that Russia and Britain could never settle
their differences, that the "lion and the bear" would never lie down
together. Indeed, Britain's apprehension about Russia's continual expansion toward the borders of India afforded some justification for
Bülow's view. In the unlikely event that Britain and France became
friends, Bülow thought that Russia would withdraw from the Dual
Entente. All Germany had to do, in his opinion, was to sit tight and
play the other powers off against each other. The kaiser would then
be the *arbiter mundi*, because other nations needed Germany more
than Germany needed them. By attempting to play Bismarck's game
without possessing Bismarck's ability, Bülow, in the next nine years,
missed opportunity after opportunity and made one miscalculation
after another.

When Queen Victoria died in January 1901, her son at last became
king as Edward VII. Edward had the reputation of being anti-
German — which may not have been true — but there is no doubt at
all that he disliked his nephew, the kaiser, or that he was, for not altogether reputable reasons, strongly pro-French. It might be unjust to
accuse Edward VII of setting the tone of the Edwardian age, either in
morals or in diplomacy, but he certainly exemplified his time in both
spheres.

If the diplomatic tide was now running against Germany, it was
running just as strongly in favor of France. In December 1901,
shrewd French diplomacy led to an agreement between France and
Italy by which France recognized Italian interests in Tripoli in exchange for Italian recognition of French interests in Morocco. This
was merely the forerunner of a much more momentous agreement.
On June 30, 1902, Italy signed a secret treaty with France, which assured that Italy would remain neutral if France was "the object of a
direct or indirect aggression on the part of one or more powers."
Prinetti, the Italian foreign minister, went further, and promised
France that Italy would remain neutral even "if France, in consequence of direct provocation, should find herself compelled in defense of her honor and her security to take the initiative in the declaration of war." This secret treaty with France was a flagrant violation

---

up by the Prussian General Staff. Wilhelm was probably right in believing that the
British could have done with such a plan, but he was certainly wrong if he thought he
would be thanked for it.

of the Triple Alliance, which Italy had formally renewed only two days previously.

Camille Barrère, the French ambassador to Rome, and Delcassé, the French foreign minister, both looked forward to the day when France could engage in a successful war of revenge against Germany, so they had reason to congratulate themselves on the secret agreement with Italy. From this time on France had little reason to worry that she would find Italy among her enemies. There was, indeed, some reason to hope that the military plans of Germany and Austria might be thrown into disarray by the unexpected defection of their Italian ally. The Italian treachery of 1902, by seriously weakening the Triple Alliance, made war that much more probable.

But the time for war was not yet. France had come a long way since 1890, when she had been isolated in Europe. Russia was now France's ally, and the Dual Entente had been broadened to anticipate almost any eventuality, whether offensive or defensive. Italy had defected secretly from her alliance with Germany and Austria, but more remained to be done. Rumania also had an alliance with the Central Powers, and Britain still retained her freedom of action. The French had waited thirty years for their *revanche*. They could afford to wait a little longer.

While Italy and France had been negotiating their treaty, Japan was engaged in diplomatic conversations with both Britain and Russia. For the Japanese the issue was a clear-cut one — peace or war — a treaty with Russia that would divide Manchuria and Korea into spheres of influence, or a treaty with Britain that would protect Japan's back when she went to war with Russia. Japan could have had either treaty, but the Russians were slow in coming to an agreement, and the talks with the British went well. As a result, the Anglo-Japanese Alliance was signed on January 30, 1902.

The British had been anxious for the alliance with Japan, and had made considerable concessions to get it. For several years past, splendid isolation had not looked so splendid anymore. Negotiations for an Anglo-German alliance had finally withered in 1901, in large part because Bülow had believed that he would later be able to extract a higher price from Britain. The South African War, which was now drawing to a close,* had revealed very serious weaknesses in the British army. In a sense, too, the Anglo-Japanese Alliance seemed to be a compromise between isolation and involvement, for Japan, of course, was not a European power. Almost certainly, no British statesman or diplomat foresaw the long-term consequences of the

---

*Peace was signed in May 1902, after thirty-two months of hostilities.

commitment to Japan, although the British knew that once the Japanese had their alliance war was likely to break out in the Far East. As early as August 1901, Baron Gonsuke Hayashi, the Japanese ambassador to Britain, in expressing his willingness to open negotiations for an alliance, had plainly said that Japan would defend her interests in Manchuria and Korea by war if she could be assured that no third power would go to Russia's aid. The British were not noticeably disconcerted by this statement.

The terms of the Anglo-Japanese treaty stipulated that if, in the defense of British interests in China or of Japanese interests in China or Korea, either of the contracting parties should become involved in a war, the other party would remain neutral and would do its best to prevent any other power from joining in the war. If, however, another power did enter the war, the *casus foederis* would arise for the other ally. There would be no separate peace; the treaty was to remain in effect for five years; and it was to be automatically renewed unless it was denounced prior to the date of expiry. Britain obviously got less from these terms than did Japan, and the phrasing of the treaty (". . . should become involved in war . . .") made the Anglo-Japanese Alliance more an offensive pact than a defensive one, for it became operative no matter who initiated hostilities.

Bülow was not displeased to learn of the Anglo-Japanese treaty, for he reasoned that it would be another obstacle in the way of any possible rapprochement between Britain and the Dual Entente. The French, on the other hand, were distressed by the agreement because they feared that, should war break out between Russia and Japan, they might be drawn in on Russia's side and Britain might be drawn in on the Japanese side. Even if France managed to remain neutral in such a war, as she might conceivably do since the terms of the Dual Entente did not cover the case of a Russian war against Japan, her neutrality would almost certainly cost her the alliance with Russia. And if the Dual Entente somehow survived, war between Britain and Russia would end all French hopes of luring Britain into the orbit of the Dual Entente. Thus, as early as June 1901, while the conversations between Britain and Japan were continuing, France approached Britain with the suggestion that the two nations come to some agreement about Morocco. The British did not take up this suggestion at the time, but the French diplomats were not discouraged and were soon to try again.

At the other end of the continent, the Balkans were living up to their reputation for savagery and bloodshed. A secret revolutionary organization in Macedonia, the Internal Macedonian Revolutionary Organization, was committing outrages against the Turks as far afield

as Constantinople; comitadji bands, half patriot, half bloodthirsty
bandit, were roaming the Macedonian hills; and the Turks in reprisal
were burning, massacring, and looting.

Although the violence in Macedonia was more widespread, it was
ultimately of far less significance than the concentrated violence that
broke out in the Serbian capital, Belgrade, on the night of June 10,
1903. Alexander Obrenovich, the last of his line, was on the Serbian
throne, and many Serbs felt that Alexander, like his father, King Milan, was too pro-Austrian. Since the time when Serbia had gained its
complete independence at the Congress of Berlin, the little country
had fallen victim to a virulent supernationalism. Serbia was poor as
dirt, exporting little besides plums, an inferior plum brandy known as
slivovitz, maize, and pigs, but Serbia was proud and overweeningly
ambitious. After four hundred years of servitude, independence, like
slivovitz taken on an empty stomach, went to Serbian heads. Because
there was scarcely any middle class, the Serbian army wielded a disproportionate influence in the state, and army officers, most of whom
were themselves the jumped-up sons of peasants, were intoxicated
with the possibilities of creating a great Serbian nation that would take
its place beside, or very nearly beside, the great powers. They
dreamed of the day when Belgrade would be the capital of a new
South Slav, Pan-Serb state, which would include the Serbs (as the
dominant class, of course) as well as the Bosnians, the Herzegovinians,
the Croats, the Montenegrins, the Albanians, the Macedonians, and
even some Bulgars. Just as Italy had been formed around the nucleus
of Piedmont by Mazzini, Garibaldi, and Cavour, and as Germany had
been formed around Prussia by Bismarck, so could Serbia, if she was
properly led, become the nucleus for the South Slavs. The dream
could hardly be realized without a major European war, for the Serbian aspirations entailed the dismemberment of both the Turkish and
the Austro-Hungarian empires, but this was a consideration that the
Pan-Serbs took in their stride. They were a brave, hardy folk with a
bloody past, not much given to humanitarian sentiments.

To the Serbian nationalists, Alexander Obrenovich seemed an obstacle to the fulfillment of their dream. His house had traditionally
looked to Vienna for support, whereas the Karageorgevich had
looked to St. Petersburg. The Pan-Slavs in Russia supported the Pan-
Serbs in Belgrade, but the Austrians were bound to oppose the creation of a Greater Serbia because such a state, besides wresting away
Bosnia and Herzegovina from the monarchy, would also exercise a
magnetic pull on the other Slavs living within the empire. King Alexander was personally unpopular, and his wife, Queen Draga, was detested. To the rabidly nationalist Serbian army officers and the pro-
Russian Radical party the solution seemed obvious.

On the night of June 10, just as the big bell of St. Sava's Cathedral on Prince Michael Street was striking the hour of midnight, an infantry regiment surrounded the Konak, or royal palace, in Belgrade. Some thirty army officers and a few Radical party politicians, who had primed themselves for the night's work by getting half drunk on slivovitz, blew down the great front door of the palace with a dynamite bomb and burst in. All the lights in the palace had gone out with the explosion, either because the electrical system had been damaged or because some loyal member of the royal household had thrown the switch. So, for the next two or three hours, the drunken officers and their politician friends wandered around inside the Konak, candles and drawn swords in their hands, searching for the king and queen. A few of the Royal Horse Guards who were on duty at the palace that night put up some resistance before they were shot down, and General Lazar Petrovich, the principal aide-de-camp to King Alexander, and young Captain Milkovich of the Royal Horse Guards were brutally murdered when they refused to disclose the whereabouts of the monarchs. The conspirators tore the clothes out of clothes closets, broke the mirrors and ikons on the walls, ripped down the tapestries and curtains, and poked about among the wine barrels in the cellars without finding their prey.

In fact, King Alexander and Queen Draga had taken refuge in a secret room that opened off the royal bedchamber. They would probably have been safe there had not Alexander, being the man he was, neglected to shut the secret door properly. One of the officers, running his hand along the wall, found the crack, forced the door open, and discovered the king and queen in their nightclothes, cowering in the little closet. They were dragged out to stand before their officers, all of whom had sworn an oath of fidelity to them. One officer raised his saber above the queen, called her a filthy whore, and slashed a large piece of flesh out of her thigh.

At that, the rest of the officers went mad. Alexander's body was later found to have suffered nineteen bullet wounds and five saber cuts, and that of his more unpopular queen, thirty-six bullet wounds and over forty saber cuts. All the fingers and one thumb were severed from King Alexander's hands, presumably as he tried to grasp his assassin's swords; Draga had also lost most of her fingers. Each of those present allegedly struck at least one blow, perhaps because they had previously sworn to do so in order that all would be equally implicated. The bodies were then thrown out the bedroom window to lie on the lawn by Prince Michael Street.

While the king and queen were being murdered in the Konak, other groups of army officers were breaking into private houses throughout Belgrade and shooting down the supporters of the House of Obrenovich. Queen Draga's two brothers, Nikodem and Nikola Lunjevitsa, were hauled before a firing squad; the Serbian premier and commander of the Serbian army, General Tsintsas-Markovich, was murdered in his home, as was the minister of war, General Pavlovich, who was cut down in the presence of his wife and daughter.

The next morning Belgrade rejoiced. The murderers sat about in cafés, drinking the brandy that admirers bought them and boasting to the newspaper correspondents of what they had done. The church bells rang out gladly, and at a Te Deum service held in St. Sava's Cathedral the Metropolitan of Belgrade, Monsignor Innocent, publicly thanked the army officers for their patriotic service. The murderers, sitting in full uniform with white gloves in the front pews of the cathedral, burst into spontaneous applause at this evidence of the church's understanding.

Peter Karageorgevich was brought back from Geneva to be proclaimed king, to attend a second Te Deum mass, and to review his loyal troops. Peter, who was now fifty-seven, had not lived in Serbia since 1885, when his father, Prince Alexander Karageorgevich, had been deposed. Peter had lived for a time in Austria, but in 1868 Prince Michael Obrenovich had been murdered in the royal park at Belgrade and a Hungarian court had been inconsiderate enough to sentence Prince Alexander Karageorgevich to eight years' penal servitude for complicity in the murder. Fortunately, this decision had been reversed by a higher court, and the Karageorgeviches, father and son, had left for the more congenial sanctuary of Russia. With King Peter Karageorgevich now back from exile and on the Serbian throne, Serbia's foreign policy became decidedly anti-Austrian and pro-Russian.

The Serbian army looked after its own, following the murders. A special medal was struck for the occasion, a little white-enameled Maltese cross with golden rays between the arms, which looked very handsome on the white Serbian tunics. The principal conspirators were promoted to higher ranks in the army, and naturally came to exert considerable influence on Serbian affairs. King Peter Karageorgevich may have been embarrassed by his retinue of assassins, but he was, after all, in their debt. Later, for reasons of policy, most of the conspirators retired from public life and made their careers in the army, which they controlled absolutely. Two of these men, Dragutin Dimitrievich, who as a twenty-seven-year-old captain had been a driving force behind the murderers, and Lieutenant Voja Tankosich, who had commanded the firing squad that had shot Queen Draga's two brothers on June 10, will be heard of again in this narrative.

The Radical party, which was pro-Russian, anti-Austrian, strongly nationalistic, and deeply implicated in the murders of Alexander and Draga, came to power soon after the return of a Karageorgevich to the Serbian throne. The party leader, Nicholas Pasich, who had had foreknowledge of the plot against the Obrenoviches in 1903, served as Serbia's prime minister and minister of foreign affairs between 1906 and 1918, and was to have foreknowledge of the murder of Archduke Franz Ferdinand.

Strangely enough, since the outbreak of the First World War, Serbian history has not been discussed by historians of the countries of the Entente, and most of Serbia's bloodstained past has been conveniently forgotten. Yet it is important to bear in mind the kind of government Serbia had before 1914 and the kind of men who were in charge of Serbian affairs. The murderers of King Alexander and Queen Draga were to murder again — many times, indeed — but the most important of their victims were to be the Austrian Archduke Franz Ferdinand and his wife, Sophie. When one remembers what happened in Belgrade on June 10, 1903, it is easier to understand the harshness of the Austrian ultimatum to Serbia eleven years later, the Austrian insistence that Serbia should be punished, and the kaiser's mistaken opinion that Russia would not support a nation that "had stained itself by assassination." Certainly the millions of dead of the First World War could scarcely have been sacrificed on a less worthy pretext than the protection of the Serbian government and the House of Karageorgevich.

It was not long before the murders of the Obrenoviches began to bear fruit in foreign affairs. In August 1904 Serbia and Bulgaria signed a secret treaty that bound them to take joint action against Austria if Austria should attempt to change the status quo in the Balkans to her advantage. Austria, of course, was well aware of the change in Serbian foreign policy that had taken place with the restoration of a Karageorgevich, but she was too preoccupied with her own internal affairs to do much about it.

However, these events in the Balkans, though of the gravest significance in the long run, had little immediate impact on the great powers because the outbreak of war in the Far East focused attention there. In 1900 the Chinese, goaded to desperation by the predatory European powers, had risen in revolt, and the "Boxers"* had vented their fury impartially against all the "white devils" in China. An international European force, under the command of none other than the former Prussian Chief of the General Staff, Waldersee, was dis-

*So called because they took as their symbol the clenched fist.

patched to put the Boxers down, which was done brutally and to the accompaniment of much indiscriminate looting. Russia seized this opportunity to occupy virtually all of Manchuria, much to the disgruntlement of Japan, who had her own designs on the area. Disreputable Russian entrepreneurs were pushing for economic concessions at Japan's expense in Korea and on the Yalu River, and they obtained support from corrupt circles at the tsarist court despite the despairing opposition of Witte, the brilliant Russian finance minister. At first Japan attempted to negotiate with Russia, but when these efforts failed Japan broke off diplomatic relations with Russia on January 6, 1904. A few days later Japanese forces, without any declaration of war, made a sudden surprise attack on the Russian fleet at Port Arthur.

The Trans-Siberian Railroad, linking Manchuria with Russia proper, was only a single-track line, and for a considerable stretch among the mountains by Lake Baikal there was no line at all. This was but one of Russia's disadvantages in the Russo-Japanese War: the Japanese initially deployed some 180,000 troops in Manchuria as compared with the Russians' 100,000; the Anglo-Japanese Alliance guarded Japan against the intervention of any other power on Russia's side; and both Britain and the United States gave the Japanese financial backing. But more serious than any of these handicaps was the fact that Russia was torn by internal dissension and was in no position to fight a war.

The Russian defenders of Port Arthur held out valiantly for 140 days before surrendering, and though the Japanese won the campaign in Manchuria, the Russians fought tenaciously and inflicted heavy casualties. The most serious Russian defeats occurred at sea. The squadron at Port Arthur was annihilated by Admiral Heihachiro Togo in August 1904, when it sallied forth in an attempt to reach Vladivostok. Thereupon, the Russian Baltic Fleet was fitted out and sailed forth to travel halfway round the world to engage the Japanese in the Pacific. While it moved through the North Sea one foggy night off the Dogger Banks, it ran into the British fishing trawlers out from Hull. The Russian admiral immediately leaped to the improbable conclusion that he was being attacked by Japanese torpedo boats, and opened fire. He sank two British fishing smacks, killing seven British fishermen and wounding eighteen. Undeterred, the Russians continued on their way, wintered at Madagascar, and were efficiently wiped out by the Japanese in the Tshushima Strait on May 27, 1905.

The British did not take kindly to the Dogger Banks incident, and it looked for a time as though they might join their Japanese allies in the war against Russia. The French, needless to say, were horrified at these developments, and urgently pressed the Russians to offer an apology and compensation. The tsar reluctantly took the French advice, and the crisis passed.

Meanwhile Kaiser Wilhelm II had suggested to Tsar Nicholas that this would be a splendid time for Russia and Germany to make a defensive pact against Britain. Once this had been done, France could be asked to join the alliance. What Wilhelm was really suggesting, of course, was a combination of the Triple Alliance and the Dual Entente. This would have been a fine idea, except that it ignored entirely the French hope that the Dual Entente could eventually be used to regain Alsace-Lorraine. Tsar Nicholas thought the kaiser's suggestions had merit, but because of his war with Japan he desperately needed French loans, and therefore insisted that France be approached before Russia and Germany signed any treaty. Wilhelm was realistic enough to know that such a course would lead nowhere, so the matter was dropped for the time being.

In the meantime the French had persisted with their efforts to reach an understanding with Britain. France wanted to acquire Morocco but knew she could not do so without British agreement. With the outbreak of the Russo-Japanese War, the French were all the more eager to come to an accord with Britain, and were prepared to make sizable concessions to that end. Both the British and the French were well aware that Russia's impending defeat would alter the European balance of power to Germany's advantage, and the British believed that an agreement with France, giving them a free hand in Egypt, would enable Britain to concentrate on the new threat being posed by the German navy. In British minds there was no question of any alliance; an agreement with France would be merely a settlement of colonial differences, which would increase Britain's freedom of action without involving her in any European commitments. Few calculations have proved more erroneous.

As the two governments felt their way toward a rapprochement, the French and British people were noticeably cool toward the idea. The French especially seemed unwilling to forget so easily their humiliation at Fashoda. However, the visit of King Edward VII to Paris in the spring of 1903 succeeded in charming many influential Frenchmen, and the tone of the French newspapers became much more cordial. The entente was signed in April 1904.

By the terms of the agreement, France gave up her offshore fishing rights in Newfoundland; she received the port of Gambia, the Los Islands off the Ivory Coast, and some territory near Lake Chad in Africa; and spheres of influence were delimited in Siam and the New Hebrides. The vital portion of the agreement, however, dealt with

Egypt and Morocco and was outlined in a document entitled "Declaration between the United Kingdom and France respecting Egypt and Morocco, together with the secret articles signed at the same time." Article I of this declaration began: "His Britannic Majesty's Government declare that they have no intention of altering the political status of Egypt." Article II began with a similar self-denying ordinance: "The government of the French Republic declare that they have no intention of altering the political status of Morocco." This sounded highminded and was meant to be reassuring. Unfortunately, the published treaty was flatly contradicted by the secret appendix, for the secret articles anticipated the day when France and Spain would partition Morocco between them and Britain would annex Egypt. France and Britain promised each other diplomatic support to that end.* The Entente Cordiale was signed by Lord Lansdowne, the British foreign secretary, and by Paul Cambon, the French ambassador to Britain, on behalf of their respective governments. It was a discreditable treaty, being both deceitful and grasping, but in the end Britain was to pay in blood for these faults out of all proportion to their gravity. Another subsequent agreement between France and Spain also publicly declared that these two nations would respect the independence of Morocco, but, again, a secret convention contradicted the public utterance and arranged for France and Spain to partition Morocco between them. Britain was fully informed of the Franco-Spanish agreement, and had, indeed, insisted on it, because she was willing to see Spain, but not France, in possession of the African mainland opposite Gibraltar.

French diplomats valued the Entente Cordiale the more highly because France's only ally, Russia, appeared to be disintegrating as a world power. In the process of losing the war against Japan, Russia fell victim to revolution. On Sunday, January 9, 1905, a great crowd of St. Petersburg workers, together with their families, marched peacefully toward the Winter Palace to lay a petition before the tsar. They were led by an Orthodox priest, Father Gapon, and carried ikons and religious banners. Their petition emphasized such revolutionary requests as an eight-hour day, no work on Sundays, and the abolition of child labor. The troops on guard at the Winter Palace opened fire, killing and wounding many hundreds of unarmed marchers, and western newspaper correspondents were much shocked later in the day to witness the Russian soldiers amusing them-

*Typical of subsequent British and French efforts to minimize the real nature of the Entente Cordiale and to gloss over the duplicity involved in the contradiction between the published text and the secret articles was Sir Edward Grey's comment, in his memoirs, that the agreement with France "was all made public except a clause or two of no importance."

selves by shooting down out of the trees the little street urchins who had climbed up there to watch what was happening.

Bloody Sunday was too much for the Russian people. Political assassinations, riots, mutinies in the army and navy, and a general strike forced the tsar to promise representative government. It was a promise he had no intention of keeping, as the Menshevik agitator Leon Trotsky warned at the time, but it served to split the opposition. Order was gradually restored, and with the signing of the Treaty of Portsmouth the Russo-Japanese War was brought to an end. Japan received Korea, Port Arthur, and the Southern Manchurian Railway. The Far East was divided into spheres of influence, with Japan exerting a controlling interest in Korea, Southern Manchuria, and Inner Mongolia, and Russia having as her sphere Northern Manchuria and Outer Mongolia.

But the drawing together of Britain and France in the Entente Cordiale was making Germany very uneasy on two grounds. First, and most important, she quite correctly foresaw that France would not long be content with merely a limited agreement but would press for a firm alliance with Britain. Second, Germany feared that France intended to annex Morocco, where Germany had considerable interests, without consulting her, even though the Treaty of Madrid, signed in 1880, granted most-favored-nation guarantees to all nations trading with Morocco. Germany was naturally unwilling either to allow France and Britain to squeeze out German commercial interests in Morocco by a separate agreement, or to accept the slight to her prestige that this arrangement would entail. As Holstein said at the time, "If we let our toes be stepped on in Morocco without saying a word, we will encourage others to do the same somewhere else." France had bought off Italy by promising her support in Tripoli, had bought off Spain by promising her part of northern Morocco, and had bought off Britain by promising her a free hand in Egypt, but Delcassé had not been able to bring himself to seek any agreement with Germany.

Bülow felt that things might not yet have gone too far to be remedied. The Dual Entente had been weakened by war and revolution in Russia, and perhaps something could still be done to break up the Entente Cordiale. The chance came early in 1905, when France sent a mission to Fez in Morocco to demand that the sultan impose certain "reforms." This was obviously a first step toward annexation, and Germany felt it had strong legal and moral grounds — as indeed it had — for landing at Tangier. Here, on March 31, the kaiser, who had been persuaded by Bülow, against his will, to undertake the venture, made a speech that touched off a serious international crisis.

The officials of the Wilhelmstrasse were not the only ones with the wit to see that France intended to annex Morocco; the sultan of Morocco realized very well what the French demands portended. He and his people welcomed the kaiser warmly as a possible friend in need. The kaiser rode through gaily decorated streets, lined with cheering Moroccans, to the German embassy, where he received the French agent in Morocco, Count Cherisey, and spoke to him bluntly about the independence of Morocco and German interests there. In his public address, the kaiser said:

> It is to the sultan in his capacity as an independent sovereign that I am paying my visit today. I hope that under his rule a free Morocco will remain open to the peaceful rivalry of all nations, without monopoly or annexations, on a basis of absolute equality. The reason for my visit to Tangiers is to make it known that I am resolved to do all in my power effectively to protect German interests in Morocco, since I regard the sultan as an absolutely independent ruler.

Germany made no territorial or new commercial claims for herself in Morocco, and no evidence has ever come to light to justify Britain's fear that the Germans really wanted a naval base there. What did occur to Bülow and Holstein was that they might be able to wrench France away from her newly found friendship with Britain. Delcassé had, as it were, been caught with his fingers in the till, and if Germany shouted loudly for the police both France and Britain would be in a very embarrassing position. Bülow calculated that Britain would not go to war over Morocco, and that when the French discovered that Britain would not support them they would become disillusioned with their British friends.

The sultan of Morocco, having listened to German advice, demanded a conference of the powers. Germany, of course, strongly supported this demand. Delcassé wished to brazen it out, but the French premier, Rouvier, the rest of the French cabinet, and the Chamber of Deputies failed to support his intransigent stand. Delcassé quite correctly argued that Germany did not intend to go to war over the issue and that the German threats were bluff. However, the French cabinet felt that Delcassé was leading France into a war for which she was unprepared. Russia was weak, and the Royal Navy, not being able to run on wheels, would be of little help if the German army invaded France. Delcassé found himself isolated in the cabinet and, accordingly, resigned on June 6. Although French policy had thus suffered a humiliating setback, there was an obvious sense of relief throughout France.

The fall of Delcassé did not cause Bülow to give up his demand for an international conference, and tension remained high. The kaiser now decided that he would solve matters by a diplomatic stroke of his own, and secretly arranged to meet his cousin Tsar Nicholas II. In the last week of July, the two royal yachts, the *Hohenzollern* and the *Polar Stellaris*, came together in the Bay of Björkö off Finland and the sovereigns met aboard ship on two successive days. Nicholas was in a mood to listen to Wilhelm. With some justification, the tsar blamed Britain for the outbreak of the Russo-Japanese War, and he was irritated by the attitude his ally France had displayed at the time of the Dogger Banks incident. After some conversation, in which they found themselves in amiable agreement,* the kaiser produced a paper from his pocket, saying that it just so happened that he had with him a copy of a draft treaty that had been prepared the previous winter. At this point the diplomatic conversations began to take on the overtones of a dialogue between a high-pressure door-to-door salesman and a gullible housewife who is beginning to become convinced that a set of illustrated encyclopedias is, after all, exactly what she needs.

The draft was of a mutual defense pact between Germany and Russia, restricted to Europe. France was to be informed of the treaty and invited to join. This would, in effect, have meant the fusing of the Dual Entente and the Triple Alliance into one alliance, which could only have been in opposition to Britain. As soon as he had read the draft treaty, the tsar impulsively signed it.

The kaiser was naturally exultant at the success of his salesmanship. The two cousins parted on the best of terms, and the tsar was much taken aback when, on arriving home, he found that his ministers, and especially his foreign minister, Count Vladimir Lamsdorf, were horrified by what he had done. The treaty signed at Björkö, they said, was a betrayal of France, and could not possibly be ratified. Accordingly, the tsar wrote the kaiser in October to tell him that France would have to be invited to join in the pact before, and not after, it was ratified. The kaiser, seeing his customer thus trying to evade the agreement, replied emotionally that "what is signed is signed and God is witness to it!" Nicholas, safe in St. Petersburg, and protected from the dominating personal influence of the kaiser, was able to stand firm. The treaty became a dead letter, and Wilhelm's reproaches served only to place a strain on the relationship between the two monarchs.

Meanwhile the Morocco crisis was continuing. On October 7, 1905, the Paris newspaper *Le Matin* increased the tension by publishing a report, presumably written by Delcassé, about the cabinet meeting of June 6, at which he had been forced out of office. According to this

---

*The tsar spoke of King Edward VII as "the greatest mischief maker and the most dangerous intriguer in the world," sentiments that could scarcely help appealing to Wilhelm.

account, the British government had promised Delcassé full support, even in the event of war, and had specifically mentioned such actions as the mobilization of the Royal Navy, the seizure of the Kiel Canal, and the landing of a 100,000-man expeditionary force in Schleswig-Holstein. It seems almost certain, however, that the report in *Le Matin* was inaccurate,* for the policy of mobilizing the fleet, capturing Kiel, and landing a British force in Schleswig was not at all the policy of the British government but rather the private policy of Admiral "Jackie" Fisher, the First Sea Lord, who advocated it tirelessly, in and out of season. *Le Matin*'s report did, however, clearly show the lines along which the French cabinet had divided. Delcassé, the *revanchist,* had sought the isolation and encirclement of Germany, but this policy had appeared too dangerous to his cabinet colleagues. "You have succeeded too well in the policy you have initiated in regard to Germany," Prime Minister Rouvier was quoted as saying. "You have detached Spain from her, you have got hold of England, *vous avez débauché l'Italie.*" This French government at least, in contrast to later French governments, recoiled from the prospect of a general European war, which would be the inevitable end of such a policy of encirclement. In 1906 French public opinion was in accord with Rouvier rather than with Delcassé. Time, increased armaments, the further entanglement of England, and continued propaganda combined in a few years to change this popular mood. In August 1914 the French were to be wildly enthusiastic for war.

By the Entente Cordiale of 1904 Britain had done no more than promise France diplomatic support over Morocco, but as the crisis evolved after the kaiser's visit to Tangier, the British government, encouraged, no doubt, by the attitude of a large section of the British press, which was vociferously anti-German and "more French than the French," prepared to go a step further. Lord Lansdowne had agreed to an exchange of notes† with the French government, authorizing conversations between the staffs of the British and French armed forces. With Delcassé's resignation and the cautious attitude adopted by the Rouvier government, the proposed exchange of notes did not take place, but official navy conversations and unofficial army conversations between the two staffs continued.

The Unionist government was replaced by a Liberal administration

*Lord Lansdowne, "with the greatest decisiveness and without equivocation," had already denied, on June 16, 1905, to the German ambassador, Count Metternich, that Britain had offered France any military alliance, and Sir Thomas Sanderson, the undersecretary of state for foreign affairs, specifically denied *Le Matin*'s report in October. He opened his conversation with the German ambassador by saying, "To begin with, we haven't got one hundred thousand men to land anywhere."

†A process that did not have to be revealed to the British or French legislatures.

under Sir Henry Campbell-Bannerman on December 11, 1905, and Sir Edward Grey replaced Lord Lansdowne at the Foreign Office. Paul Cambon now inquired of Grey whether, if the international conference on Morocco failed and Germany attacked France, Britain would join the war at France's side. Grey replied that the British government would be unable to pledge itself in advance on such a matter, but he repeated, as his personal opinion, the statement Lord Lansdowne had made previously to the German ambassador: if Germany attacked France, British public opinion would strongly favor intervention on France's side.

Cambon had to be content with this. He had better luck with his suggestion that all armed forces' staff talks be continued on an official basis. Grey agreed, and arranged that the military conversations, which had hitherto been conducted by a go-between, Colonel C. A. Repington, the military correspondent of the *Times*, should, in the future, take place directly and officially between General J. Grierson, the Director of Military Operations and Planning at the War Office, and the French military attaché, Major Huguet. At the same time, Grey was careful to point out that these staff conversations were not binding on either government but served only the purpose of ensuring that "all preparations were ready so that, if a crisis arose, no time would [be] lost for want of a formal engagement."

These staff conversations were to continue right up to the outbreak of war in 1914 and, as will be seen, were to constitute a moral commitment to France, which was, in everything except the purely legal sense, every bit as strong as a formal defensive alliance would have been. France was encouraged to expect quite specific British aid — naval action in the Channel and the North Sea, and the landing of a British expeditionary force in France to extend the French line of battle on the left. The repeated caveat that the staff talks did not bind the governments was thus almost meaningless; the truth was that the British found themselves morally bound to support France in a war, but without any of the rights of supervision over French policy likely to lead to war, which could have been obtained under an alliance.

Even more deadly was the fact that the British commitment to France, which was kept secret even from the majority of the British cabinet, left Germany with the reasonable expectation that she could count on British neutrality in a war that might break out over some issue that did not affect British interests. Sir Edward Grey and the British Foreign Office continually supported and strengthened this German illusion by their oft-repeated denials, which were only formally true, that Britain had no military alliance with France. In the face of these British assurances, Germany could scarcely have assumed that Britain would go to war at France's side should the French support Russian policies in the Balkans. What was Serbia to Britain that she should fight for her? By far the worst of all this was that France's secret knowledge of the virtual certainty of British support encouraged later French politicians to lay a trap for the unwary Germans, and to confront them suddenly with a war in which Britain was ranged against them and their ally Italy was forsworn.

If it had not been for the fatal British commitment to France, there might have been no war in 1914, for France would hardly have acted as she did without that commitment. And if there had been no war in 1914, there would have been no Chancellor Hitler and no war in 1939. Thus, it is not too much to say that the British Empire suffered well over a million and a half dead, the loss of almost all her colonial possessions, relegation to the position of a second-rate power, the transformation of her entire way of life, and the domination of much of Europe by a savage and criminal tyranny — all for reasons that were murky, obscure, secret, and most imperfectly comprehended even by those who directed British policy. Since the tragedy has been so great and so unrelieved, and the loss so grievous and enormous, it is small wonder that strenuous and persistent attempts have been made to becloud the truth and to conceal from the ordinary citizen the true significance of what occurred.

In a secret memorandum to the British cabinet, written on February 20, 1906, Sir Edward Grey's simple view of the world can be seen:

> If there is a war between France and Germany it will be very difficult for us to keep out of it. The *Entente*, and still more the constant and emphatic demonstrations of affection (official, naval, political, commercial, municipal and in the press) have created in France a belief that we should support her in war . . . If this expectation is disappointed, the French will never forgive us. There would also, I think, be a general feeling in every country that we have behaved meanly and left France in the lurch. The United States would despise us. Russia would not think it worthwhile to make a friendly arrangement with us about Asia. Japan would prepare to re-insure herself elsewhere, we should be left without a friend and without the power of making a friend, and Germany would take some pleasure, after what has passed, in exploiting the whole situation to our disadvantage . . .

The conference of the powers demanded by Bülow to discuss the Moroccan crisis met at Algeciras on January 16, 1906, and continued in session until April 7, 1907. Germany did not receive the support she had hoped for or to which the justice of her case entitled her. Spain did not support her because she had been promised northern

Morocco. Italy, Germany's ally in the Triple Alliance, did not support her because she had been promised a free hand in Tripoli. Russia, as a matter of course, supported her ally France. Britain was bound by the secret articles appended to the Convention of 1904 to give full diplomatic support to France in return for a free hand in Egypt. The United States, which neither knew nor cared much about the issues involved, was perhaps antagonized by the intransigent tone of German diplomacy. Austria, anxious to avoid war and almost completely uninterested in colonial questions, gave Germany only halfhearted support and appeared, on the whole, annoyed that so much fuss was being occasioned by so insignificant an issue.

The French and German governments had privately agreed, at German insistence, that the principle of the sovereignty and independence of the sultan of Morocco would be respected, as would that of the integrity of Morocco, and that all nations were to enjoy free trade with Morocco on a basis of complete equality. All that was left to discuss, therefore, was the nature of certain police and financial reforms in Morocco and the extent of France's particular influence in the country. France's special interests were recognized because of her possession of the adjacent colony of Algeria, which she had seized by force of arms in 1834. In the outcome, the Algeciras Conference agreed in principle with Germany that Morocco was the concern of all the powers and not merely of France, but the practical decisions of the conference gave France certain pre-eminent rights over the Moroccan police and the state bank. These concessions ultimately proved sufficient for the French to achieve what had all along been their aim, the conquest and annexation of the territory. As will be seen, France declared a "protectorate" over Morocco in 1912, and from then until 1934 fought a series of military campaigns against the Moroccans, who wished to retain the independence of their country. France, therefore, had firm control over Morocco for only six years, from 1934 until 1940, and shortly after the Second World War France lost even her "legal" title to the country.

Nevertheless, if we accept the standards of the time, France emerged victorious from the first Moroccan crisis, French colonial ambitions in the area were well on the way to being realized, and the German attempt to support the independence of Morocco had been thwarted. The French victory had unfortunate results for others than the Moroccans. During the crisis, there had been a substantial hardening of French opinion. Formerly, many in France believed that it was time to forget the past, to turn their eyes away from the lost provinces along the Vosges, and to come to terms with Germany. Those who held this view had deplored all the talk about *revanche* and the recovery of Alsace-Lorraine at the price of a great European war. The Socialist leader Jean Jaurès never tired of pointing out that so long as the wages of French workmen remained low and so long as France had problems of poverty, injustice, and social inequality to combat at home she should not waste her energies on adventurous foreign policies. After the first Moroccan crisis, these voices were largely silenced, and when — as in the case of Jaurès — they were not silenced, they were no longer much heeded. Furthermore, French public opinion was now converted to the enthusiastic support of the Entente Cordiale, for it was Britain that had given France the victory. More might be expected from so profitable an alliance — and more, much more, was, in due time, to be demanded. The Franco-British staff talks continued with a professional zest that, on the British side at least, recked little the cost.

In Germany, on the contrary, there was bitterness that the patently better German case had failed. The crisis had not broken up the Entente Cordiale, as Bülow and Holstein had hoped. Instead, France and Britain had drawn closer than before. Italy had, in the first test, already proved an unreliable ally. The consequence of all this was that Germany began to recognize her increasing isolation and to fear encirclement, and she turned more and more to her only loyal friend, Austria.

In June 1907, a second Hague Peace Conference was convened, and ran on until October. This conference was, if anything, even more ineffectual than the first. By now all the major European powers, without exception, were opposed to any limitation of armaments. The subject of disarmament was not, in fact, even placed on the agenda. Sir Eyre Crowe, the senior clerk at the British Foreign Office, wrote a memorandum that helped to define the British position. "German maritime supremacy," Crowe wrote, "must be acknowledged to be incompatible with the existence of the British Empire. But even if that Empire disappeared, the union of the greatest military and the greatest naval power in one state would compel the world to be rid of such an incubus." It should be noted that all Crowe's assumptions were very much open to question and that at least one was erroneous. In the first place, Germany was not the world's greatest military power; both France and Russia maintained larger military establishments and spent much more on their armies. Second, it was by no means axiomatic that the existing British Empire would be threatened by the growth of German naval power. Finally, the facile suggestion that the "world" would have to overthrow any preponderant power on the continent, presumably by war, was both unreasoned and reckless.

Still, there was no doubt that the British had been growing perturbed by the German naval rivalry. Perhaps the truth is that this naval rivalry was felt, dimly and instinctively, to have been symptomatic of Britain's relative decline. Here was something that could be seen and grasped by the mind, something, moreover, that could be responded to aggressively but without any fundamental change in society or in national outlook. If Germany was building warships, Britain would build more warships. This response was easier and less demanding than having to respond to other, less apparent challenges. An enormous effort of modernization — social, commercial, and industrial — might well have halted and reversed the trend toward decline, but to most of those who could have effectively supported such a modernization the cure seemed worse than the disease. Yet between 1870 and 1903, Britain had increased its pig-iron production from 6 million tons to 9 million tons. Germany, in the same period, had increased its pig-iron production from 1.4 million tons to 9.8 million tons, and the United States had increased production from 1.7 million tons to a huge 18 million tons. Growing competition for world markets and an increasing industrial challenge were leading Britain to retreat more and more into her empire, and into those areas where she did not have to face competition, such as finance and commerce.* Even more disconcerting than these economic facts were certain social comparisons. By 1913, in the whole of Britain, there were only 9000 university students, as compared with 60,000 in Germany. Worse still, from the British point of view, Germany by 1913 was producing 3000 graduate engineers a year, but England and Wales together were annually producing only 350 graduates in all branches of mathematics, science, and technology.

None of this was sharply present in the British consciousness; there was only a feeling of uneasiness and a disquieting awareness that life, which had seemed so splendid so short a time before, was now doubtful and less assured. The German naval program was a concrete manifestation of this vague and more encompassing challenge, and it was in reaction to it, more than for any other reason, that Britain now turned to make an agreement with her formidable colonial rival, the Russian Empire.

Shortly after the conclusion of the Entente Cordiale, in 1904, King Edward VII had suggested to Alexander Izvolsky, then Russian am-

---

*Empire was at sunset, too. In the great days of her unchallenged industrial supremacy, Britain had had a healthy contempt for colonies, regarding them as liabilities to be liquidated rather than as possessions to be cherished. It was only as competition became sharper on the world market that Britain retired into her empire as into an old-age home, finding there a quiet shelter where it was no longer necessary to bustle about for business, to keep improving the product and refining the process.

bassador in Copenhagen, that Britain and Russia might well come to an understanding similar to that arrived at by Britain and France. At the time the idea had seemed far-fetched, since Russian opinion very rightly held Britain largely responsible for the Japanese aggression in the Russo-Japanese War. British public opinion was also opposed to any such rapprochement because it very rightly held that the Russian autocracy was a bloodstained and reactionary regime. However, in neither country did the statesmen feel that they had to take much account of what the public thought.

The French, of course, saw great advantages accruing to themselves from an understanding between their two friends, and directed their diplomatic efforts, both in London and St. Petersburg, to bringing it about. The British, for their part, were beginning to believe that they had gone too far in the Anglo-Japanese Alliance. It had been no part of their intention to drive Russia to desperation and possibly force her into an alliance with Germany. Furthermore, ever since the German navy had begun to increase in size, the British had been perceptibly less willing to fight a naval war in the Pacific. This was, in a sense, a justification of Tirpitz' risk theory, although hardly in the way that Tirpitz had intended.

In May 1906 Izvolsky became Russian foreign minister. He was an ambitious, touchy man who counted himself a liberal in the contemporary Russian sense, an admirer of the English, and a man who believed that Russia's destiny lay in Europe rather than in the East. He was also vain and something of a dandy, going about in a perpetual odor of violet scent. Izvolsky intended to turn Russia back from the Far East and orient her policy toward the Balkans. This was, in any case, the only policy an ambitious foreign minister could follow, for after Russia's defeat in the Russo-Japanese War the road to the East was barred. So Izvolsky, determined to make a name for himself, dreamed the ancient Russian dream of acquiring Constantinople and the Dardanelles. He knew that any move in this direction would bring him into opposition with Austria, and therefore with Germany, and this made him the readier to come to terms with Britain.

Nevertheless, the negotiations between Russia and Britain lasted fifteen months before an agreement was finally signed in August 1907. On the British side, negotiations were conducted by Sir Arthur Nicolson, the ambassador to St. Petersburg, a diplomat who took the German menace very seriously and who favored meeting it by the formation of a triple entente of France, Russia, and Britain. Indeed, he was later inclined to take his wishes for reality, and to refer in his official dispatches to "the Triple Entente," as though such a grouping of treaty-bound powers actually existed, and for this he was gently rebuked by Sir Edward Grey.

The Anglo-Russian agreement was very far indeed from being an alliance. Like the Entente Cordiale, it was limited to colonial concerns and said no word about Europe. The two powers agreed to maintain the status quo in Persia but to divide that country into spheres of influence — a Russian sphere in the north, a British sphere in the south, and a central area left to the Persians themselves, who would have to struggle on there as best they could, without imperial patrons. Neither the shah nor the Persian people, needless to say, were consulted about this arrangement. It was also agreed that Afghanistan would be in the British sphere of influence and that Tibet would remain independent under the suzerainty of China.

Britain hoped by the agreement with Russia to be rid of a whole set of colonial worries and quarrels, but while it is true that India no longer seemed threatened, the Russians were continually breaking their word in regard to Persia, and British-Russian relations were often acrimonious. At the time of the Anglo-Russian conversations preceding the signing of the entente, Izvolsky had raised the question of opening the Straits of the Dardanelles to Russian warships.* Sir Edward Grey had declined to discuss any revision of the Black Sea clauses of the Treaty of London, but Izvolsky hoped that once the Anglo-Russian entente was in operation Grey might change his mind. In the meantime, he visited Vienna and talked to the new Austrian foreign minister, Alois Aehrenthal, about his ambitions regarding the straits.

Aehrenthal knew the Russians well; he had just returned from being ambassador in St. Petersburg. He had reason to know that Russia was at the moment exceedingly weak, having been defeated by Japan and torn by revolution. To Aehrenthal the time seemed propitious for Austria to pursue an active policy in the Balkans. With both Izvolsky and Aehrenthal turning their attention to the area, the Balkans were rapidly coming off the ice, but whereas Izvolsky was primarily interested in Constantinople and the Dardanelles, Aehrenthal was primarily interested in Bosnia and Herzegovina, the two provinces that had been administered by Austria ever since the Congress of Berlin. On the face of it, there did not seem to be any clash of interest here, or at least none that negotiation could not smooth away.

However, Bosnia and Herzegovina, which had a predominantly

---

*The Treaty of Paris in 1856 at the end of the Crimean War closed the straits to all warships and forbade Russia or Turkey to have naval vessels in the Black Sea. Russia had declared herself no longer bound by these clauses in 1870, and the Treaty of London of 1871 permitted both Russia and Turkey to maintain warships in the Black Sea, but also permitted the sultan to admit foreign navies through the straits if he deemed this necessary for the safeguarding of other articles of the Treaty of Paris. Thus, Russian ships could not get out, but warships of other powers could get in — a situation that Russia naturally regarded as highly disadvantageous.

Slavic population, were much coveted by the Pan-Serbs, who, ever since the installation of the Karageorgevich dynasty following the murders of 1903, had been bitterly anti-Austrian. Relations between Austria and Serbia were far from good. The natural antipathy of the House of Hapsburg to regicides was reinforced by a number of other factors. Since the new regime had been established in 1903, Serbia had been purchasing its military equipment from the French firm of Creusot rather than from the Skoda works in Bohemia; and some Hungarian Magyar landlords claimed that Serbian agricultural exports were underselling their own produce on the Austrian market. A tariff war, the so-called Pig War, ensued when the Austro-Serbian commercial treaty expired in 1906, but the Austrian economy suffered more than the Serbian, because Serbia found other outlets for her produce.

All this was certainly in Aehrenthal's mind as he sat back with hooded eyes and listened noncommittally to Izvolsky's exposition of his ambitions. The Austrian minister replied merely that he hoped Izvolsky would give him ample warning before Russia raised the question, with the powers, of opening the straits, as he would certainly give Russia ample warning if Austria should decide to annex Bosnia and Herzegovina. Izvolsky was disappointed and annoyed by Aehrenthal's attitude, so much so, in fact, that at a council of ministers, held in January 1908, he argued strongly that Russia should move aggressively into the Balkans, even at the risk of a war with Austria. The entente with Britain would, he felt, greatly strengthen Russia's hand.

P. A. Stolypin, the Russian prime minister, was a sensible, realistic man who was not prepared to listen to Izvolsky for a moment on this theme. He told the foreign minister quite plainly that it would be at least ten years before Russia had recuperated from the troubles she had recently been through and that only a strictly defensive policy was possible. The ministers of war, navy, and finance, as well as the Russian Chief of the General Staff, General Palitsyn, all agreed with Stolypin. Izvolsky, perforce, had to accept this, but he was nothing if not determined. If he could not achieve his ends in opposition to Austria, perhaps he could achieve them by striking a bargain with Austria. On July 2, 1908, Izvolsky sent an indiscreet note to Aehrenthal, suggesting conversations to settle the joint problems of the Austrian annexation of Bosnia, Herzegovina, and the Sanjak of Novibazar and the Russian control over Constantinople, its adjacent territory, and the Dardanelles. In the note Izvolsky expressed the opinion that inasmuch as these problems would require revision of the Treaty of Berlin, they could be settled only with the consent of the powers.

The annexation of Bosnia and Herzegovina by Austria would mean merely a formal change, for Austria had been administering the two provinces since 1878. At the Congress of Berlin, Britain had urged Austria to annex Bosnia and Herzegovina, and on several occasions since then the annexation could have been readily carried out with the consent of all the powers. Russia had specifically given her consent to the annexation under the terms of the Dreikaiserbund. In each case it had been the Hungarian opposition to having any more Slavs in the empire that had prevented Austria from annexing the territories.

Two days after Izvolsky's note to Aehrenthal, however, an event occurred in Turkey that was destined to accelerate the annexation of Bosnia and Herzegovina. There had been much discontent in Turkey with the capricious and autocratic rule of Sultan Abdul Hamid II. A group of young Turkish army officers, who through their profession had been exposed to European ideas, had founded a secret revolutionary society known as Vatan, or "Fatherland." By and large, these "Young Turks" were freethinkers rather than Moslems, and many of them were members of Masonic lodges in Istanbul and Salonika. They were all strongly nationalistic and believed in constitutional government, representation by population, modernization, industrialization, and mass education. There are, in fact, few better examples of how European technique and technology, as distinct from European culture, appealed to non-European peoples. The Young Turks admired European power and wished to transplant to Turkey what they considered the roots of that power. They should not be too much blamed for this, for the Europeans themselves knew no more than the Turks the things that were for their peace.

Mustapha Kemal, a cavalry officer, and Enver Bey, a staff major in the III Corps in Macedonia, were prominent leaders in Vatan. On July 8, Turkish troops under Enver Bey revolted in Macedonia, killed the loyalist general at Monastir, and subverted the forces the sultan dispatched to suppress them. The revolt spread rapidly throughout Turkey, and on July 23 the sultan gave way and proclaimed a constitution.

Both Russia and Austria viewed the Young Turk revolt with very mixed feelings. It had been assumed that the "sick man of Europe" would eventually die, at which time his estate would be divided. Now the Young Turks, by their enthusiasm, vitality, and eagerness for reform, threatened to revive the ailing Ottoman Empire. Aehrenthal was particularly concerned, fearing that the Young Turks might demand the return of Bosnia and Herzegovina, which were still nominally under the suzerainty of the sultan, and fearing also that the granting of a constitution in Turkey would stir up discontent in these provinces, which were ruled autocratically. Nor could a constitution be granted legally to Bosnia and Herzegovina until they were annexed to Austria.

During that August of 1908, Izvolsky was leisurely touring Europe, discreetly sounding out the diplomatic reactions to his plans for opening the Dardanelles. At Carlsbad he met the new Austrian ambassador to St. Petersburg, Count Leopold von Berchtold, who arranged a meeting between Izvolsky and Aehrenthal at his castle at Buchlau in Moravia.

The two foreign ministers met at Buchlau on September 16 and 17. Since there were no witnesses to their conversations, it is impossible to be certain which of the two subsequent versions of the Buchlau talks is correct, if, indeed, either is. Certainly, though, promises were exchanged. Apparently Izvolsky and Aehrenthal agreed not to oppose each other's demands, Aehrenthal agreeing to support Russia's claim for the opening of the straits and Izvolsky agreeing to support Austria's annexation of Bosnia and Herzegovina. They also agreed to recognize the proclamation of Bulgaria's independence, which would be another affront to Turkey. FN 2

The Buchlau Conference is an example of secret diplomacy at its worst. Aehrenthal, who was determined to assert his independence of German tutelage, had not informed the Wilhelmstrasse of what he intended because he knew that Germany, which had steadily been increasing its influence in Constantinople, would oppose the weakening of Turkey. Izvolsky, on the other hand, had not even informed his own prime minister, Stolypin, because the latter favored a cautious policy until Russia had recovered from 1904–1905 and because the annexation of Bosnia and Herzegovina by Austria would certainly be opposed by Pan-Slav circles in Russia.

When Izvolsky left Buchlau, he continued his European tour, going by way of Berchtesgaden and Paris to London. Arriving in Paris on October 4, Izvolsky learned from a letter of Aehrenthal's that the Emperor Franz Josef would formally announce on October 7 the annexation of Bosnia and Herzegovina and the simultaneous evacuation of Austrian garrisons from the Sanjak of Novibazar. The Serbian ambassador to Paris, Milenko Vesnich, called on Izvolsky on the afternoon of the 5th to protest against the annexation, but was told:

omit

You Serbs surely cannot be thinking of driving Austria-Hungary out of Bosnia and Herzegovina by force of arms. And we Russians, on the other hand, cannot wage war on Austria on account of these provinces . . . I have foreseen this step of Austria-Hungary's and it did not surprise me. For that reason I made our acceptance of it dependent upon her renunciation of her rights to the Sanjak of Novibazar; and then will follow the revision or alteration of the Treaty of Berlin, which we shall demand; upon this occasion, Serbia too, will be able to present her wishes as regards the rectification of her frontiers . . . I do not understand your state of agitation. In reality you lose nothing, but gain something — our support. I trust that the Serb people in Bosnia and Herzegovina will continue as hitherto their cultural activity for their own renaissance, and awake as they are, it will never be possible to denationalize them.

Izvolsky was soon shaken out of his calm, for the Austrian announcement of the annexation caused an immediate and very serious diplomatic crisis. Russia, Serbia, and Turkey were all outraged. Since Izvolsky had not informed Stolypin or the cabinet of his note of July 2 to Aehrenthal, or of what had taken place at Buchlau, the Russian government naturally assumed that the annexation was a unilateral Austrian move, which would have to be resisted. When Stolypin was informed of Izvolsky's part in the affair, he advised the tsar that it would be best to disown the foreign minister and announce that he had acted solely on his own initiative, without the consent of the government. Turkey initiated a boycott against Austrian goods, and Serbia began to mobilize her army.

London was annoyed that a treaty had been broken, the more so because Sir Eyre Crowe and Sir Arthur Nicolson at the Foreign Office were sure — mistakenly — that Germany was behind it all. In fact, the kaiser was furious at what Aehrenthal had done, partly because he had not been informed and partly because he feared that the Austrian move would greatly weaken German influence in Constantinople. The German chancellor, Bülow, insisted, however, that Austria would have to be supported for the sake of the Dual Alliance, and he had his way. Izvolsky was received with great consideration when he went to London, but he discovered to his chagrin that the Anglo-Russian entente of 1907 had not changed the British government's mind about opening the straits to Russian warships.

In this respect, at least, the Bosnian crisis of 1908–1909 has strongly ironic overtones. At times, indeed, it almost appears as though the entire business was no more than a game of blindman's buff in which all the players were blindfolded. For what it considered to be strategic reasons, the British Foreign Office in 1908 was adamantly opposed to the opening of the Dardanelles to Russian warships. If Grey had given his consent to this proposal of Izvolsky's, the worst of the crisis would certainly have been avoided. He withheld it, and the international situation never really recovered from the subsequent storm. Yet only seven years later, after the world had been at war for nearly a year, a British expeditionary force was to sacrifice more than 214,000 men in a vain attempt to open those same straits for its Russian ally.

Izvolsky was now faced with the unpleasant task of returning to St. Petersburg and explaining why he had agreed to the Austrian annexation of Bosnia and Herzegovina and why Russia had got nothing in exchange. Stolypin was sending him angry little notes, demanding to know what was going on, and the Pan-Slav press in Russia was calling for his resignation. He attempted to escape from this predicament by a lie.* He proclaimed loudly that Aehrenthal had deceived him, that the announcement of the annexation was a unilateral action on Austria's part and completely unexpected by him, and that all he and Aehrenthal had agreed to at Buchlau was that they would put their two proposals before a conference of the powers so that they could be implemented legally.

Emperor Franz Josef, for his part, could not understand what all the fuss was about. He wrote to the tsar and asked him, pointing out that Russia had agreed in 1877 that Austria could annex Bosnia and Herzegovina at any time and that this had been subsequently reaffirmed on at least three occasions.† It says something for Russian diplomacy that until he received Franz Josef's letter Nicholas II had never heard of the agreement by which Austria could annex the two provinces at her pleasure.

Izvolsky was, by now, demanding a conference of the powers to re-open the entire question. Britain supported his demand, and France felt bound to support her ally Russia despite the fact that the French government had no desire at this time to fight a war over obscure Serbian claims in Bosnia and had already assured Franz Josef that France would "contribute to the desired agreement inspired by the feelings of cordial sympathy with which the Austro-Hungarian Government has likewise shown itself animated towards us and which corresponds to the excellent relations existing between our two countries." In Britain, the anti-German bloc in the Foreign Office, headed by Nicolson and Crowe, was urging that the ententes between Russia and Britain and between France and Britain should be transformed into firm military alliances. Sir Edward Grey, who opposed such a policy, had all he could do to resist it.

*Aehrenthal's account of the Buchlau conversations (the only account that has so far come to light) indicates that he told Izvolsky that "the main lines of such a revision must in any case be settled by negotiations between the Cabinets in which, of course, there would be no more talk of Bosnia-Herzegovina," but that a ratifying conference should be held in Constantinople. In reply to Izvolsky's question as to when Austria would announce the annexation, Aehrenthal said that it would probably be early in October, before the meeting of the Austro-Hungarian delegations. Izvolsky asked that the announcement be postponed until the middle of October, when he would be back in St. Petersburg and would have had time to influence public opinion, but Aehrenthal replied that this was impossible, adding, however, the assurance that he would let Izvolsky know ahead of time the exact date of the annexation. Significantly, Izvolsky removed his version of the Buchlau conversations from the Russian archives. Both the British ambassador in Paris, Sir Francis Bertie, and Sir Arthur Nicolson told Grey that they thought Izvolsky was telling less than the truth.

† The Treaty of Budapest, January 15, 1877; the Berlin Protocol of July 13, 1878; protocol to the Dreikaiserbund, June 18, 1881; renewal of Dreikaiserbund, June 1884.

Austria refused to consider a conference of the powers unless it was agreed beforehand that the annexation would be approved, a policy, it may be noted, that was consistent with Aehrenthal's account of the Buchlau conversations. Turkey also rejected a conference because she feared that it would merely ratify the fait accompli. In February 1909, however, Austria obtained Turkey's recognition of the annexation in return for a payment of 2.5 million Turkish pounds and the withdrawal of Austrian garrisons from the Sanjak. Once Turkey had recognized the annexation, of course, any case Serbia might have had was gravely weakened. But the agitation in the Serbian press continued. The Serbian crown prince, George, and Nicholas Pasich, the leader of the Serbian Radical party, had already visited St. Petersburg to petition for Russian help, and the Serbian prime minister, Milovanovich, had toured the major European capitals to drum up support for Serbia. The Pan-Serbs in Belgrade founded a society known as Narodna Odbrana, or "National Defense," to undertake propaganda and agitation in Bosnia and Herzegovina, where the reaction of the Slavs to the annexation was not all that the Serbs could have wished. Many of the Slavs within the monarchy were pleased by Aehrenthal's action, which they regarded as a step toward the transformation of Austria-Hungary into a trialistic state, as, indeed, Aehrenthal intended.*

Narodna Odbrana was by no means only a cultural organization; the founding members included Radical party politicians and army officers who had been regicides in 1903. Dragutin Dimitrievich, rewarded for his part in the murder of Alexander and Draga by having been promoted to the rank of colonel, Major Voja Tankosich, and Vladmiro Gacinovich, the revolutionary son of a Herzegovinian Orthodox priest, were all prominent in the new society. As well as undertaking the "encouragement and promotion of national [that is, Serbian] feeling" in Bosnia and Herzegovina, Narodna Odbrana formed, armed, and trained secret revolutionary units, or comitadji, in the two provinces and established a clandestine factory for the manufacture of bombs.

As the Serbian disturbances increased, Austria began to arrest Serb agitators in Bosnia. Some Austrian officials went so far as to use forged documents in one of the treason trials held in Zagreb, and late in 1909 the famous Austrian historian Heinrich Friedjung, of Vienna

---

*In general, the Moslems and Roman Catholics in Bosnia and Herzegovina were supporters of the Hapsburg monarchy, and only some of the Orthodox subjects were Pan-Serbs. Even among the Orthodox, support for Serbia often came from the younger rather than from the older generation, and active support was, on the whole, limited to those who were rebels by temperament. In 1909 the total population of Bosnia and Herzegovina was some 1.8 million Serbs, Croats, Bulgars, and Hungarians; only some 800,000 were Orthodox Serbs.

University, was sued for libel because of an article he had written in *Die Neue Freie Presse*. It was disclosed during the trial that the article had been based on documents that were forgeries. The Friedjung trial raised much bitter feeling among the Serbs and Croats in the monarchy, and tended to discredit the Austrians.

Austria demanded that Serbia recognize the annexation, stop the agitation of her secret societies and the propaganda campaign conducted by her press, and renounce all claim to Bosnia and Herzegovina. There was, by now, a war party in Vienna, headed by the Chief of the General Staff, Count Franz Conrad von Hötzendorf, who ever since 1903 had held the opinion that Austria would sooner or later have to settle accounts with Serbia. Neither Emperor Franz Josef nor the heir apparent, Archduke Franz Ferdinand,* wanted a war with Serbia, even apart from the fact that it might lead to a war with Russia. Franz Ferdinand's policy was, in a sense, the direct opposite of that advocated by Conrad. He declared, quite bluntly: "I don't want anything from Serbia. Not a single pig. Not a single plum tree." His aim was to take the coat off the man's back by the sun rather than by the wind, for he hoped that by changing the Dual Monarchy into a tripartite monarchy the Slavs in the empire would be treated so well that Serbia would be drawn into the Austrian orbit.

On March 14, 1909, Germany made a diplomatic move in response to a Russian request, conveyed by the Russian ambassador at Berlin, Count von der Osten-Sacken. Izvolsky had been much alarmed by a threat from Aehrenthal to publish the memoranda of the Austro-Russian conversations held in the summer of 1908 and Izvolsky's two letters to Aehrenthal written after the meeting at Buchlau. These documents would certainly have compromised Izvolsky's position, for they would have shown the extent of his agreement with Aehrenthal concerning the annexation, his foreknowledge of it, and the fact that he had concealed vital information from both the tsar and the Russian government. Chancellor Bülow agreed to intercede with Aehrenthal not to publish, and offered his services as mediator. The German

---

*Franz Ferdinand was the nephew of Emperor Franz Josef and had become heir apparent when Franz Josef's son, Rudolf, shot his mistress, Marie Vetsera, and himself at the royal hunting lodge of Mayerling outside Vienna in the autumn of 1889. Franz Ferdinand's marriage in 1900 to the Czech Countess Sophie Chotek had estranged him from the emperor and was also probably responsible for the sympathy with which he viewed the Slav subjects of the empire. In 1904, Franz Ferdinand was already beginning to form the opinion that the monarchy could survive only if it converted from dualism to trialism, that is, if the Slavic peoples were given an equal share in government and equal rights with the Austrians and Hungarians. Naturally, since trialism could be introduced only at their expense, the Hungarian Magyars viewed these ideas with abhorrence, as did the Serbs, who, when they came to learn of them, feared that a policy of justice for the Slavs in the empire would spell the end of any possibility of a great South Slav Serbia.

Foreign Office suggested to St. Petersburg that all the powers sanction the annexation of Bosnia and Herzegovina, and specifically asked Russia to consent beforehand to this suggestion. When Izvolsky replied evasively, Germany sent a firm, but still friendly communication on the 21st. The German ambassador, Count Friedrich von Pourtalès, was instructed to make it clear that a definite answer was expected. Bülow telegraphed to Pourtalès:

> Please say to M. Izvolsky that we are prepared to propose to the Austro-Hungarian Government an appeal for the Powers' consent to the abrogation of Article 25 of the Treaty of Berlin concerning the Austro-Turkish agreement already brought to their knowledge. But before making such a proposal to Austria-Hungary, we must be certain that Russia will return an affirmative answer to the Austrian note and declare, unreservedly, her agreement to the abrogation of Article 25. Your Excellency will make clear to M. Izvolsky that we expect a definite answer: Yes or No; any evasive, involved or unclear answer would have to be regarded by us as refusal. We would then withdraw and let matters take their course; the responsibility for all further events would fall entirely on M. Izvolsky after we have made a last sincere effort to be of service to M. Izvolsky in clearing up the situation in a manner acceptable to him.

In this communication to St. Petersburg, Bülow was agreeing to comply with both the Russian request for mediation and Izvolsky's personal request that Germany persuade Aehrenthal to suppress the correspondence concerning their Buchlau agreement, but Bülow made Germany's mediation conditional on Russia's prior recognition of the annexation. If Izvolsky refused this condition, or again returned an evasive reply, Germany would wash her hands of the matter and let events take their course. That course would have been the publication by Aehrenthal of the correspondence with Izvolsky, which would have shown Izvolsky to have been a liar and would have undercut Russia's entire diplomatic position, as well as ruining Izvolsky personally. Also, in the highly unlikely event that Serbia would have continued to press her claims for compensation without Russian support, Austria might actually have invaded Serbia. This second possibility was far from likely, at least until all diplomatic efforts to reach a solution had failed, for Franz Josef, Franz Ferdinand, and Aehrenthal all wished to avoid a war with Serbia. Izvolsky was certainly more afraid of the probability that Aehrenthal would publish the Buchlau correspondence than of the possibility that Austria would attack Serbia, because he could, at any time, have prevented such an attack by withdrawing Russian support to the Serbs. It should be noted that Sir Edward Grey, too, had proposed mediation and had told Austria that if that failed he would draw back and let events take their course.

No one has accused Sir Edward Grey of presenting an ultimatum to Austria, but Izvolsky, after he had prudently accepted Bülow's offer, passionately declared that Germany had humiliated Russia and forced her compliance by a threat of war. Sir Arthur Nicolson gave currency in England to this false interpretation, and the Russian press spread the story within Russia.* The tsar, at least, knew better; he telegraphed the kaiser, thanking him for Germany's mediation, which had made a peaceful solution possible. The tsar, in fact, was inclined to dismiss Izvolsky, but was persuaded not to do so by the intercession of King Edward VII and Sir Arthur Nicolson, both of whom pleaded on Izvolsky's behalf. Thus was perpetuated the career of one of the most irresponsible and dangerous diplomats in Europe.

The Russian government accepted the German suggestion and on March 22 recognized the Austrian annexation of Bosnia and Herzegovina. England, France, and Italy followed the Russian and Turkish example, and the annexation was regularized. Once Russia withdrew her support from Serbia, the Serbs promptly backed down. On March 31 Serbia accepted a circular note agreed to by the powers, and drafted jointly by Britain and Austria, to the effect that no Serbian rights had been infringed by the annexation, that Serbia recognized that Bosnia and Herzegovina were now Austrian territory, that she would "renounce the attitude of protest and opposition" she had adopted, and that she would in the future live "on good neighborly terms" with Austria. It will be seen in what manner Serbia abided by these pledges.

The Bosnian crisis was by far the most serious and far-reaching of the crises that led up to the First World War. In itself a complicated affair, the Bosnian crisis has been made more difficult to understand by the deliberate obfuscation effected by both participants and historians. It may therefore be worthwhile to glance again at the salient points in the crisis. The whole affair began on Izvolsky's initiative, when he proposed that Russia and Austria make a deal: Russian support for the Austrian annexation of Bosnia and Herzegovina in exchange for Austrian support for the opening of the Dardanelles to Russian warships. The main difference in these two aims was that once Russia had consented to the annexation of Bosnia and Her-

---

*Bülow, indignant at the falsehoods being spread by Izvolsky, wanted to publish all the diplomatic documents in order to show "how well-intentioned, friendly, courteous and successful had been the mediation which Germany had undertaken at Russia's request and so put an end to the malicious insinuations spread abroad." Charikov, acting minister for foreign affairs in Izvolsky's absence, gave his consent; but this decision was promptly reversed as soon as Izvolsky returned. Kaiser Wilhelm II certainly did not help to dispel this legend of a German threat to Russia when he boasted in Vienna in 1910 that he had stood behind Austria "in shining armour."

zegovina none of the other powers had any serious reason to oppose the move, whereas Austrian consent to the opening of the straits was unlikely to alter Britain's fundamental objection. Aehrenthal saw this and Izvolsky did not. Aehrenthal certainly had no legal right to proceed with the annexation, and to do so with such abruptness, without obtaining the consent of the powers signatory to the Treaty of Berlin. This was an unwise and precipitate move, and it placed Austria's ally Germany in a false and embarrassing position. There is, however, on the evidence, every reason to believe that Izvolsky subsequently lied about the extent of his knowledge of Aehrenthal's intentions and about the extent of his commitment to Austrian policy. He believed, far too optimistically, that the Anglo-Russian entente of 1907 would dissolve British objections to the opening of the straits, and it was only after he realized that he would have to return empty-handed to St. Petersburg that he attempted to revoke the agreement he had made with Aehrenthal. Izvolsky's terror — it is not too strong a word — at Aehrenthal's threat to publish the Buchlau correspondence, his subsequent removal of the Buchlau documents from the archives, and his refusal to allow Bülow to publish the documents relating to the German offer of mediation all constitute strong evidence of Izvolsky's guilt. Aehrenthal was certainly wrong in the way he went about the annexation, but the annexation itself, after all, was merely the formal recognition of a state of affairs that had existed ever since 1878. Izvolsky's subsequent attempts at self-justification and his later vindictive intrigues against the Central Powers were criminally irresponsible, motivated as they were by no more edifying emotions than wounded vanity and hatred. In August 1914, at the outbreak of the great European war, Izvolsky was to declare exultantly to a group of newspapermen, "C'est ma guerre!" He credited himself with too much importance by this observation, but there was more than a kernel of truth in what he said.

Men like Sir Eyre Crowe and Sir Arthur Nicolson felt defeated and resentful at the outcome of the Bosnian crisis, for they persisted in the mistaken belief that it had all been instigated by Germany in order to facilitate her plans for a Berlin to Baghdad railway. They felt quite certain that Germany was an enemy and that war with Germany was probably inevitable — and a belief in the inevitability of war is frequently realized. What is more blameworthy is that Crowe and Nicolson do not appear to have viewed the prospect of a major war with serious alarm.

In Russia, the Pan-Slavs were even angrier than the British Foreign Office. Many of them believed Izvolsky's claim that Russia had been forced to retreat in the face of a German "ultimatum." Izvolsky remained on as foreign minister until September 1910, when the embassy in Paris fell vacant. Where better could he go if he wished vengeance? Before he left for France, he selected his own successor, Sergei Sazonov, a former subordinate who had been a protégé of Izvolsky's throughout his entire career. Sazonov had been better suited by temperament and ability for his previous appointment as ambassador to the Vatican; as foreign minister he proved weak and easy to influence.

Thus, when Izvolsky went to Paris the nerve center of Russian diplomacy moved with him, and Sazonov carried on Izvolsky's policies at Izvolsky's suggestion. From then on, Izvolsky worked wholeheartedly for war. He spent huge sums in bribing the venal French press, and many French newspapers began to receive regular subsidies of Russian money from Izvolsky's hands.* From his headquarters in Paris, Izvolsky worked hand in glove with those French politicians who were intent on *revanche* and the restoration of Alsace and Lorraine. From Paris Izvolsky also remained in contact with the Pan-Slav Russian ambassadors he himself posted to Belgrade and Sophia. N. H. Hartwig, who had been Russian minister at Teheran, was posted to Belgrade by Izvolsky in 1909, and in 1911 Izvolsky arranged for A. Neklidov, who had been counselor to the Russian embassy in Paris, to become ambassador to Bulgaria. The support of these ambassadors was henceforth given to any anti-Austrian activity in the Balkans, even when such a policy conflicted with that which the Russian government wished to pursue.

In spite of her promises to live on friendly terms with Austria, Serbia redoubled her Pan-Serb propaganda and her illegal activities in Bosnia, Herzegovina, and Macedonia. The distinctions that Entente apologists are fond of drawing between the Serbian government and the Serbian secret revolutionary societies break down on closer examination. For one thing, most of the funds that supported the secret societies came, in one way or another, from Serbian government sources, though some, at least, came from embezzlement. More important, high Serbian government officials, both civilian and military, were from the outset involved in the activities of Narodna Odbrana, Mlada Bosnia ("Young Bosnia"), and, later, the Black Hand. The Karageorgevich royal family, which had come to the throne with the murderous assistance of the Pan-Serbs, was also deeply involved in these intrigues and conspiracies. King Peter's elder son, Crown Prince George, had been almost pathologically bellicose at the time of the Bosnian crisis. He had inherited more than royal blood from the

*When Poincaré became French president, he and Izvolsky between them established a "slush fund" with $60,000 of Russian money to bribe French journalists during the Balkan Wars.

Karageorgeviches, and when he murdered his valet in a fit of rage in March 1909, it was deemed prudent to retire him in favor of his younger brother, Alexander. Russia looked on the illegal Serbian activity benignly, and there is reason to believe that the Russian ambassador at Belgrade, Hartwig, was fully in the confidence of Colonel Dragutin Dimitrievich, the head of the Black Hand. In addition, Russia had made specific promises to the Serbs at the same time as she counseled them to accept the circular note of the powers. The Serbian ambassador in St. Petersburg was advised by Alexander Guchkov, a prominent member of the Duma:

> When our armaments have been completed, we shall then settle accounts with Austria-Hungary. Do not begin a war now, because this would be suicidal; hide your purposes, and prepare; the day of your joy will come.

The tsar and Izvolsky gave similar advice, the tenor of which was: "Bide your time and wait until the Entente's rearmament program is completed; then you will see that the annexation of Bosnia and Herzegovina is not permanent." The Serbs, for their part, listened to such advice eagerly and followed it.

If the Serbs never really accepted the Austrian annexation of Bosnia and Herzegovina, the Turks were equally displeased with the outcome of the crisis and naturally blamed their government for recognizing the annexation. The Young Turks were challenged in the spring of 1909 by the Moslem Brotherhood, which had no use for westernization or reform. Bloodthirsty mobs, led by students from the Moslem seminaries, roamed the streets of Constantinople, and Abdul the Damned appeared to encourage them. However, a Turkish army under Enver Bey and Mustapha Kemal fought its way into Constantinople from Salonika, suppressed the brotherhood, and deposed the sultan, replacing him with his half brother, Mohammed V. Once back in power the Young Turks imprisoned their opponents, began murdering Armenians again, and, worst of all from the British point of view, restored the German influence in the army. Within a year or two the Young Turks had proved so arrogant that they had achieved the feat, by no means an easy one, of uniting the rest of the Balkans against them.

While these events were taking place on the international scene, an unfortunate interview, given by the kaiser in October 1908 to Colonel Berkeley of the *Daily Telegraph*, raised much criticism in Germany and annoyed the British. Wilhelm had been at his tactless worst, proclaiming that he was almost Britain's only friend in Germany, being patronizing about British military difficulties in South Africa, and declaring that the German navy, far from being a threat to Britain, would prove a definite asset to her someday in the Far East. As usual, he had meant no harm, and as usual, he would have done better to have remained silent. However, the only lasting result of the affair was that Bülow forfeited the kaiser's confidence by not defending him with sufficient enthusiasm in the Reichstag. Bülow, accordingly, resigned as chancellor in July 1909.

Even the kaiser's confidence was shaken by the reaction to his *Daily Telegraph* interview, or perhaps it would be closer to the truth to say that his self-doubt and timidity at last broke through the veneer of bluster and braggadocio. From then on, he ceased to play his former active role in diplomatic affairs. This was hardly an unmixed blessing, for though Wilhelm II was often erratic and excitable, his influence in times of crisis had generally been on the side of moderation and peace. He had opposed the policy of Bülow and Holstein at the time of the Kruger telegram and the first Moroccan crisis, as he had opposed Bülow's firm support of Aehrenthal during the Bosnian crisis. After the *Daily Telegraph* affair, the kaiser was more amenable to advice than he had been previously, but those who advised him were not as wise as he — which says little for German diplomacy.

Bülow was replaced as chancellor by Theobald von Bethmann-Hollweg, a career civil servant, an honest, melancholy, rather colorless man, by no means a mediocrity but not the man to guide Germany safely through the racing, troubled seas ahead. Here again, Germany may have been unfortunate, for though Bülow's policies, and especially his support of the naval program, had been disastrous, he had been acquiring a measure of wisdom just before his retirement. He knew that the Bosnian crisis had left Russia and Britain very resentful of Germany, and he had been having serious second thoughts about the naval race.

By now the British First Sea Lord, Admiral Fisher, had greatly strengthened the Home Fleet and had begun to build a new class of battleship, the dreadnought. Fisher had established the principle that Britain should build six dreadnoughts for every four that Germany laid down. In March 1909, relying on mistaken naval intelligence, the First Lord of the Admiralty, Reginald McKenna, had told the House of Commons that in 1911 Germany would have thirteen dreadnoughts to Britain's sixteen. It was not at all true; the intelligence estimate had been based on Germany's capacity, not on her naval budget. By 1912 Germany would have twelve dreadnoughts to Britain's eighteen, but McKenna's speech hit the British public like a thunderclap. Throughout the land the supporters of the British Navy League, the subscribers to the *Daily Mail*, and all those who believed in the inevitability of war sent up the cry:

We want eight
And we won't wait.

The agitation was successful. Britain laid down eight dreadnoughts, even though the Admiralty had asked for only six. David Lloyd George, then chancellor of the exchequer, had to find the money somewhere. He did it by a radical budget, which the House of Lords rejected and which provided a heaven-sent election issue. Herbert Asquith, the Liberals, and Sir Edward Grey were returned for a second term of office in the elections of January 1910.

In April, King Edward VII, whose health had long been impaired by his eating, drinking, smoking, and sexual habits, died after a brief illness. His wife, Queen Alexandra, charitable to the end, summoned his favorite mistress, Mrs. Keppel, to his bedside. George V succeeded to the throne, but British policy did not change.

One German suggestion for a limitation of naval armaments had been put forward in the spring of 1909 by the deputy foreign minister, Alfred von Kiderlen-Wächter, but as a precondition Germany wanted Britain either to join the Triple Alliance or to give a guarantee of neutrality in the event of a European war. Neither alternative was acceptable to Britain. Bethmann took up again in August the possibility of a naval détente with Britain, and the talks dragged on until May 1910. Although Germany refused to scrap her naval program, she did suggest that construction should be spread over a longer period of time. Britain rejected this offer, and in the end Germany broke off the talks.

The Germans undoubtedly had a right to a navy of their own, but their pursuit of this goal showed a singular lack of diplomatic sensitivity. Sincerely anxious to avoid a European war, which could not possibly be to their advantage, they nonetheless gravely underestimated the depth of the ill will they had aroused. There was implacable hatred in France, soon to find point and expression in the highest posts of the French government. Bound by her alliance to Austria, Germany could scarcely avoid the antagonism of the Pan-Slavs in Russia. These two enemies, powerful as they were, would have hesitated to let events be decided by arms if they had stood alone. It was German folly, rather than any wickedness, that drove Britain to join the hostile encirclement. And that very folly stands as proof that Germany wanted no major war, for if Germany had planned war and intended it, she would surely not have blundered on so blindly. In any longer view, of course, it was not only the Germans who were blind. France wanted Alsace and Lorraine, and she was to get them, but at a price of which she had never even dreamed. Russia wanted Constantinople and the straits, and did not get them, but paid a terrible price anyway. Britain wished to retain her empire and remain mistress of the seas; she did neither, but she, too, paid with the best blood of two generations.

The enemies of Germany and Austria were beginning to close in. Izvolsky's first important move in his campaign for vengeance came in October 1909, when he arranged a meeting between the tsar and King Victor Emmanuel of Italy. The meeting took place at the castle of Racconigi, near Turin, and the European press was quick to note that the tsar and Izvolsky took pains to avoid setting foot in Austria. At Racconigi, the Italian foreign minister, Tommaso Tittoni, and Izvolsky signed a highly secret agreement, the principal point of which was that both Russia and Italy would "uphold the application of the principle of nationality" in the Balkans in the event of any change in the status quo. This meant that Russia and Italy would seek to bar an Austrian advance in southeastern Europe. Other parts of the Treaty of Racconigi provided that Russia and Italy would cooperate in any agreement made with a third power about the Balkans, and Italy promised to support Russian ambitions for the straits in exchange for Russian support of Italian ambitions in Tripolitania and Cyrenaica.

The secret Russo-Italian Treaty of Racconigi, then, was the counterpart to the secret Franco-Italian treaty of 1902. Perhaps no better comment on Italian diplomacy can be made than that of the Italian foreign minister himself. When asked by Izvolsky at Racconigi why Italy did not leave the Triple Alliance, Tittoni replied, "We shall come out someday, and when we do it will be to go to war."

What Izvolsky already had in mind was the formation of a Balkan league to oppose both Austria and Turkey. This plan of Izvolsky's, which was aimed at nothing less than the destruction of Austria, was a giant step on the road to a European war. It is not surprising that Austria's ally Italy should have been so extremely anxious that the terms of the Racconigi agreement remain secret.

Perhaps, given the character of Tittoni and of Italian diplomacy at this time, it is not surprising, either, that Italy, having falsely assured Austria that she had no engagement, either written or verbal, with Russia, should then sign a pact with Austria that promised that neither Austria nor Italy would make any treaty with a third power without the participation of the other and that any offer made by Russia to one of the allies would be communicated to the other. This Italo-Austrian pact was to remain secret, except that Germany was to be informed. This remarkable example of Italian statescraft shows Italy, within a matter of less than two months, signing two completely contradictory treaties, the first of which was in violation of the Triple Alliance and the second of which was based upon an outright lie.

The German Foreign Office had been suspicious of the Racconigi meeting, but it was far from accepting the view of Conrad and the war party in Vienna that Italy was preparing to betray the Triplice. The tension in Europe had never really abated after the Bosnian crisis; it was soon to flare up again into a new crisis that once again threatened the possibility of war.

In March 1911, a French army officer, Colonel Charles Mangin,* had two Moroccan soldiers publicly executed for desertion, and thus provoked an uprising in Fez. It was a convenient revolt for the French, who moved troops into Morocco, sent out punitive expeditions, and occupied Rabat. The German government's view was that these actions were contrary to the Algeciras pact, which had pledged the independence of Morocco. German suspicions were increased by the fact that Delcassé was now back in the French cabinet.

At first Kiderlen-Wächter, now holding the full title of foreign minister, reacted gently to the news of the French expedition to Morocco, but his reaction was deceptive. He had resigned himself to the fact that France would eventually seize Morocco, but he intended that Germany should be granted compensation elsewhere in Africa. The French had agreed in principle that Germany should be compensated, without making a definite offer, when the kaiser authorized the sending of the gunboat *Panther* to Agadir "to protect German commercial interests in Morocco." The *Panther* dropped anchor in Agadir harbor on July 1, and the second Moroccan crisis was underway.

On July 15 Kiderlen-Wächter suggested that France cede the French Congo to Germany as compensation, but France refused and negotiations lapsed. France now asked both Britain and Russia if they would support her. Their response was unenthusiastic. Neither Britain nor Russia wanted to go to war so that France could grab Morocco. The tsar cautioned Georges Louis, the French ambassador at St. Petersburg: "Keep in view the avoidance of a conflict. You know our preparations are not complete." This was true, but it was also true that Russia was still resentful at the lack of French support during the Bosnian crisis.

In Britain, other considerations had to be taken into account. In the first place, the Entente Cordiale, which had given Britain a free hand in Egypt, had promised support for France in Morocco. Now for the second time that bill was being presented for payment. Moreover, Sir Arthur Nicolson, now undersecretary of state for foreign affairs, was convinced — wrongly — that Germany intended to seize Agadir and convert it into a naval base. The mere suggestion of a German naval base on the Atlantic coast of Morocco sent British blood pressure up.

For these reasons, Prime Minister Herbert Asquith and Grey allowed Lloyd George to make a belligerent speech at the Mansion House in London on July 21. Lloyd George said, in part:

*We shall meet Mangin again as a French general in the 1914–1918 war.

I believe it is essential in the highest interests, not merely of this country, but of the world . . . that Britain should at all hazards maintain her prestige among the Great Powers of the world . . . But if a situation were to be forced upon us in which peace could only be preserved by the surrender of the great and beneficient position Britain has won by centuries of heroism and achievement, by allowing Britain to be treated, where her interests were vitally affected, as if she were of no account in the Cabinet of nations, then I say emphatically that peace at that price would be a humiliation intolerable for a great country like ours to endure.

This was the strongest public statement any British politician had made in years. The Germans reacted furiously to the threat, and for a time it appeared as though war might result. Sir Edward Grey went so far as to warn McKenna that the British fleet might be attacked at any moment.

Nothing was further from the German government's intentions. Both the kaiser and Chancellor Bethmann-Hollweg were determined that no war should result over Morocco, and the more aggressive Kiderlen-Wächter was restrained. In the event, France and Germany reached an agreement, in November, whereby, in return for part of the French Congo, Germany recognized the French protectorate over Morocco.

The effect of the Agadir crisis on the international situation was indirect but important. France, of course, got Morocco — for a space of years and to her own ultimate sorrow. British government opinion had turned more favorable than ever toward France and Russia. After Agadir, British foreign policy was so firmly committed to the Entente that Britain had virtually no room left in which to maneuver. It was unfortunate that the French and Russian governments realized this more clearly than the majority of the British cabinet. Sir Edward Grey had found it expedient to say to the Russian ambassador, Alexander Benckendorff, in August, "In the event of a war between Germany and France, England would have to participate." At the end of August, General Auguste Dubail, the French Chief of the General Staff, confidently told the Russians that the French army was ready to mount an offensive against Germany "with the aid of the English army on its left wing." The British Parliament would have been dumbfounded to learn of this statement, even though the British General Staff had worked out all the logistical details for such an operation.

It was in France, however, that the Agadir crisis produced the most fateful effect. In the opinion of the French public, Joseph Caillaux, the premier, had been too submissive to Germany, and he was forced to resign in January 1912. His place was taken by a provincial lawyer and noted anticleric, Raymond Poincaré.

Poincaré had been born in Lorraine, and he never for an instant forgot it. He had once said publicly that his generation "had no reason for existence other than the hope of recovering the lost provinces." With Poincaré in power in France, a new element was introduced into European diplomacy. Poincaré's policy was to prepare for war, to increase armaments, and to strengthen the Entente. When, in his judgment, these three means appeared to be sufficiently advanced, he would not shrink from a general European war by which alone Alsace and Lorraine could be recovered.

IN THE AUTUMN of 1911, partly in reaction to Lloyd George's Mansion House speech and Germany's diplomatic defeat over Agadir, Admiral Tirpitz introduced into the Reichstag a new naval bill, known as the "Novelle." The Novelle provided for a third naval squadron of three new dreadnoughts and five other ships, all to be completed within six years. Bethmann-Hollweg was seriously disturbed both by the cost and by the effect of the Novelle on Anglo-German relations. Even the kaiser had his doubts, especially after Albert Ballin, the Jewish head of the Hamburg-America Steamship Line and Wilhelm's personal friend, had given him a solemn warning that if the naval rivalry continued it would inevitably result in war with England.

Ballin's attitude became known in Britain, and as a consequence Winston Churchill, Sir Edward Grey, and Lloyd George asked Sir Ernest Cassel to undertake an unofficial mission to Ballin in Berlin to propose that if Germany would undertake to cease expanding her navy Britain, in return, would offer her all possible assistance in the acquisition of colonies. Cassel, like Ballin, was a Jew and had many contacts in Germany. Nothing specific came of Cassel's mission, but in February 1912, Viscount Haldane, the secretary of state for war, went to Berlin, where he talked to the kaiser, Bethmann, and Tirpitz. The Germans agreed to cancel the Novelle but only on condition that Britain guarantee her benevolent neutrality in a European war. Again, Britain refused to give such a promise. Bethmann, who did not believe in the Novelle or in the continuance of the naval race, threatened to resign. In the face of this threat the kaiser agreed to postpone the Novelle, but Admiral Tirpitz thereupon threatened to resign, so the kaiser reverted to his former position. Bethmann gave in and remained on as chancellor.

Haldane's mission had failed but there was no deterioration of Anglo-German relations as a result. The German Foreign Office, in fact, continued the negotiations with Britain, and for a time it seemed as though progress were being made. In March 1912 Sir Edward Grey drafted a formula, which he handed to the German ambassador, Count Metternich: "England will make no unprovoked attack upon Germany and pursue no aggressive policy towards her. Aggression upon Germany is not the subject, and forms no part, of any treaty, understanding or combination to which England is a party, nor will she become a party to anything which has such an object."

This was a vague formula, made deliberately so by the insertion of the adjective "unprovoked," for when the time came who would define provocation? The Germans had asked for a guarantee of neutrality, and, at least on the face of it, this seemed to be nearly that, though such an interpretation is difficult to reconcile with Grey's words to the Russian ambassador a short time before: "In the event of a war between Germany and France, England would have to participate."

Whatever Grey's draft formula may actually have meant, the French were alarmed by the Anglo-German negotiations. In March 1912 Poincaré telegraphed Paul Cambon in London:

> The essential thing is that England should not undertake to remain neutral between France and Germany, even in the hypothesis of the attack seeming to come from our act. To take but one example: could the responsibility for an aggression legitimately be imputed to us if a concentration of German forces in the Aix-la-Chapelle region compelled us to cover our northern frontier by penetrating into Belgian territory?

Poincaré also informed the British government that the signing of any Anglo-German agreement pledging British neutrality would mean the end of the Entente with France. The French prime minister later boasted to Izvolsky that it had been this that had wrecked Haldane's mission and the subsequent Anglo-German conversations.

Nicolson and Crowe at the Foreign Office, and some British ambassadors, notably the Francophile Sir Francis Bertie in Paris and Sir George Buchanan, the British ambassador in St. Petersburg, also opposed the negotiations with Germany.

In reply to Grey's draft formula Germany made a counterproposal, objecting that the word "neutrality" had not been mentioned and suggesting that Britain make a guarantee of neutrality except in the case of aggression by Germany. Grey, who was probably glad of an excuse to terminate the conversations, rejected this German suggestion, and negotiations were dropped in April. If Sir Edward Grey had given the guarantee of neutrality that the Wilhelmstrasse had sought, the First World War would almost certainly not have happened, for

France and Russia would not have dared to take the stand they did unless they had been able to count on British support. The fact, too, that in the spring of 1912 Germany was anxious to obtain a guarantee of British neutrality except in the case of German aggression is proof positive that, at that time at least, Germany desired peace and had no aggressive intentions.*

France now suggested that Britain enter into an actual military alliance with her. Grey rejected this offer as well, on the significant grounds that British public opinion would not welcome such an alliance at this time. In Germany, both Bethmann and Kiderlen-Wächter were belatedly trying to make Tirpitz see reason about his naval program, but they got nowhere at all. With that narrow professionalism that made him such an unmitigated menace to Germany, Tirpitz now claimed that the "risk zone" had been safely passed and that Germany no longer needed to fear a naval war with Britain. He also claimed that two German battleships were the equal of three British, and, allowing for some exaggeration, there may have been some technical justification for this opinion. Germany was building excellent battleships, which were superior in ship design, fire power, gunnery control, and communications to their British counterparts.

Winston Churchill, now First Lord of the Admiralty, began withdrawing ships from the Mediterranean to strengthen the Home Fleet, and the French moved their North Sea Fleet from Brest to Toulon on the Mediterranean. Poincaré, eager to tighten British obligations to France, pressed the British government for a written naval convention. Churchill warned Grey of the dangers inherent in such a commitment:

> Freedom will be sensibly impaired if the French can say that they had denuded their Atlantic seaboard and concentrated in the Mediterranean on the faith of naval engagements made with us. Consider how tremendous would be the weapon which France would possess to compel our intervention if she could say, "On the advice of and by arrangement with your naval authorities, we left our northern coasts defenceless." Everyone must feel, who knows the facts, that we have the obligation of an alliance without its advantages, and above all without its precise definitions.

These were wise words, but Grey did not heed them and at last agreed to an exchange of letters between himself and Paul Cambon.

*The point would hardly seem worth making if it were not that one or two ideologically motivated German historians have recently revived the most extreme denunciations of Germany's prewar policy, repeating charges — such as that Germany timed the war for the summer of 1914 because that was the date of the completion of the Kiel Canal — that were originally leveled in Entente nations during the war but which in more thoughtful days were everywhere repudiated.

In this instance, Grey felt that the whole cabinet really had to be told what was going on, for though staff conversations could be kept secret, the reallocation of substantial numbers of naval vessels could not, so the ministers were informed for the first time of the staff talks with the French, which had been in progress since 1905. Grey later sought to minimize the cabinet reaction to this startling news, but Lloyd George probably gives a truer picture:

> There is no more conspicuous example of this kind of suppression of vital information than the way in which the military arrangements we entered into with the French were kept from the Cabinet for six years. They came to my knowledge, first of all, in 1911 during the Agadir crisis, but the Cabinet as a whole were not acquainted with them before the following year . . . When in 1912 (six years after they had been entered into) Sir Edward Grey communicated these negotiations and arrangements to the Cabinet, the majority of its members were aghast. Hostility barely represents the strength of the sentiment which the revelation aroused — it was more akin to consternation.*

A fascinating historical question is why Grey had, in fact, kept his cabinet colleagues in the dark for so long. It was certainly a question that occurred to the ministers. Is not the obvious answer in this case most likely to be the true one — that Grey knew the cabinet as a whole would not support his policy? Nicolson, Crowe, and of course the French would presumably have influenced Grey to adopt his course of deception. When the cabinet did learn of the staff talks, it demanded that the fact of the military conversations' being noncommittal should be put into writing. Thus Grey wrote to Cambon on November 22:

> From time to time in recent years the French and British naval and military experts have consulted together. It has always been understood that such consultation does not restrict the freedom of either Government to decide at any future time whether or not to assist the other by armed force. We have agreed that the consultation between experts is not, and ought not to be, regarded as an engagement that commits either Government to action in a contingency that has not arisen and may never arise. The disposition, for instance, of the French and British fleets respectively at the present moment is not based on an engagement to co-operate in war.
>
> You have, however, pointed out that if either Government had grave reason to expect an unprovoked attack by a third Power it might become essential to know whether it could, in that event, depend on the armed assistance of the other.

*When he wrote those words Lloyd George may have forgotten that the staff talks had actually begun in 1905, under the Conservative administration, not in 1906 as he implies.

I agree that, if either Government had grave reason to expect an unprovoked attack by a third Power, or something that threatened the general peace, it should immediately discuss with the other whether both governments should act together to prevent aggression and to preserve peace, and if so, what measures they would be prepared to take in common. If these measures involved action, the plans of the general staffs would at once be taken into consideration, and the Governments would then decide what effect should be given to them.

Even allowing for the customary understatement of diplomacy, this was rather bare faced. Years previously those involved in the Anglo-French staff talks had decided that a British expeditionary force of 100,000 men should land in France, concentrate in the north, and take up a position extending the French left. No alternative plan had been made. Grey's equating this plan with action "to prevent aggression and to preserve peace" may have pacified his cabinet colleagues but was certainly less than frank.

Grey's letter satisfied the British cabinet ministers, who wanted to keep their hands free from any entanglement with France, but this merely shows that they were less astute than Churchill had been. Poincaré knew better. He assured Izvolsky that the Anglo-French military agreement was of as definite and complete a character as the Franco-Russian agreement. "The only difference consists in the fact that the former bears the signatures of the two Chiefs of Staff and for that reason is, so to speak, not binding on the Government."

Italy had originally entered the Triple Alliance because of her colonial rivalry with France over North Africa. The Triplice had not satisfied Italian hopes for an African empire, being, as Bülow had said, a conservative, defensive pact and not an association for grabbing other people's territory. Now France had got Morocco, and Italy could bear it no longer. She determined to seize Tripolitania and Cyrenaica. After issuing a trumped-up protest over the treatment of Italian nationals in Tripoli, Italy hastily declared war on Turkey on September 29, 1911. The Italian military effort was hesitant and slow, and sporadic Arab resistance caused Italy to send heavy reinforcements to her expeditionary force, which eventually reached a figure of well over 100,000 men. Nevertheless the Italian army suffered a sharp little defeat at Sciara-Sciat in October, and only more reinforcements from Italy persuaded the Italian soldiers to retain their positions. The Italian military reputation, never high, sank even lower in the estimation of Europe — a view no later event has substantially contradicted.

Britain was mildly annoyed at this evidence of Italian aggression, but France was cordial and Russia warmly supported the Italians.

Austria and Germany, of course, were displeased that their alliance partner should go chasing after mirages in the Tripolitanian desert. In Austria, Conrad von Hötzendorf, who accurately guessed what had occurred at Racconigi, urged that Austria take this opportunity to attack Italy. The old emperor, Archduke Franz Ferdinand, and Aehrenthal were all adamantly opposed to any such step, and when Conrad persisted in his advocacy he was relieved of his post in November.

While Italy was thus busily stirring up mischief, Aehrenthal died of cancer, to be succeeded in February by Count Leopold von Berchtold, an elegant, superficial aristocrat who loved racehorses and women but who had little success with either. Berchtold dressed impeccably, had charming manners, and was profoundly ignorant. His elevation to the post of Austrian foreign minister further lowered the already low caliber of European statescraft. As it happened, Count Berchtold was to be put to the test more directly than most European statesmen and diplomats in the testing time of 1914. He came out very badly indeed, and historians have, on the whole, and very rightly, dealt harshly with him.

Yet it should be noted that Berchtold was all too typical of his time. Who were his peers? Grey in England, melancholy after the tragic death of his wife, well meaning, with his preference for trout-fishing over diplomacy, capable of infinite self-deception. Bethmann in Germany, even more well meaning, equally melancholy, holding on to office not because he wished it but because he feared what would happen if he resigned. Sazonov in Russia, temperamental, deeply religious but with that strain of fatalism and superstition that has so often marred Orthodox faith, a reed swayed by the winds created by Izvolsky, the military archdukes, and the Montenegrin archduchesses. Was ever a generation so badly served? Only in France, of all the great powers, were there men who knew their own minds and were their own masters. In Austria, England, Germany, and Russia the statesmen who held the levers of power in their well-manicured hands were hesitant, uncertain, hopeful, middling honest,* and, according to their knowledge and lights, humane. In France, Poincaré, the advocate, the single-minded man, the freethinker for whom all was clear-cut and dried, played out his hand without doubts, or pity, or any fear that he might be wrong. Berchtold, as it happened, was a fool, but he had a multitude of companions. And perhaps at the end the clever

---

*This judgment is in general true of foreign ministers, but it shou'd not be taken to have too wide an application — as the recurrent scandalous corruption in France, the Marconi case in England, the mishandling of government funds to support East Prussian landlords in Germany, and the embezzlement attendant on the Russian rearmament program all bear witness.

ones, who were more responsible than he for bringing Europe down, were the greater fools. Had Europe produced, anywhere in her five great powers, one statesman of the caliber of Disraeli, or Goluchowski, or Bismarck, or Andrássy, surely the disaster would never have been allowed to happen.

Of less significance, but still in those far-distant times of some importance, was the quality of the reigning monarchs. It is true that they reflected rather than originated policy and national sentiment, and so had, in a sense, abdicated before their time. Even when in theory they were absolute, as in the case of Tsar Nicholas II, the Autocrat of All the Russias, they were the creatures of forces they were insufficiently strong to resist. King George V of England, of course, had no chance at all. After the death of Victoria no one paid much attention to what the British monarch thought, unless it happened to be convenient to do so. Wilhelm II of Germany, who was so sedulously hated in his generation, was a timid, basically decent man, though given to erratic and emotional judgments and to bluster and bombast that concealed nervousness and uncertainty. In happier circumstances and with wiser counselors, he might not have done badly at a difficult job. Emperor Franz Josef, old, hide-bound, two generations out of date, and bowed down by the weight of personal sorrows such as few men have had to bear, also had his heart in the right place but exercised no real control over events. Another kaiser or another tsar might have been able to prevent the situation from developing so fatally, and if Franz Josef had died three years before he did and Franz Ferdinand had become emperor, Europe might have been spared. In this connection, however, it should be noted that hereditary monarchies are not predicated on the intelligence or virtue of the monarch, for that would be an impossible precondition, but, just like democracies and republics, rely on the intelligence and virtue of responsible officials. And it was exactly here, in the years between 1890 and 1914, that there was a fatal failure everywhere in Europe.

Turkey was not doing badly in her war with Italy — a not unusual circumstance, for Italy since her creation in 1861 had shown herself incompetent on every battlefield. However, the Italian aggression in Tripoli had set other forces in motion. The Balkan states, alerted by Izvolsky two years before, saw Turkey's involvement in the Italo-Turkish War as an opportunity they should not miss. Izvolsky in Paris was enthusiastically of the same opinion, and Hartwig in Belgrade and Neklidov in Sophia were eager instruments of his will. Seeing the dangers gathering in the Balkans, the Turkish government, without the approval of its parliament, concluded peace with Italy by decree on October 19, 1912.

Balkan comitadji, especially the Serbian and Bulgarian groups, had long been active in Turkish Macedonia. The ancient hatreds, the sanction of patriotic emotion, the comradeship and adventure of irregular warfare in the hills, and the sense of personal power that is the root of all sadism lured these guerrilla bands to their raids, bombing outrages, massacres, and looting. There was little personal risk involved. The attack on an isolated police barracks, the blowing up of a bridge, the murder of the unarmed inhabitants of a village, the burning of a mosque, all provided glory and usually only the illusion of danger. The men and boys — and most of the comitadji were boys — who did these things did them from personal preference. Patriotism provided the excuse and the justification, just as it was later to do in the case of the German *Freikorps* and Nazi SA and SS. Turkish rule was certainly bad; the comitadji alternative was far worse. Nor was it only the Turks the comitadji attacked. Far more often, because they provided safer targets, it was rival Christian nationalities who were slaughtered. And in the Macedonian hills, where murder was accepted as valor and cruelty as manliness, was bred a type of man who could be used for the political purposes of those who from the beginning had directed these campaigns.

Izvolsky in Paris regarded the Balkan comitadji with a mild and benevolent eye. He was encouraged by the intense wave of French nationalism that had followed the Agadir crisis, and by the fact that the French General Staff had advised Poincaré that a great European war might well occur in 1912. Izvolsky's first thought, suggested to him by Charikov, the Russian ambassador at Constantinople, had been to create a barrier against Austria in the Balkans by an alliance of Serbia, Bulgaria, and Turkey — an impossible ambition and one that clearly reveals Izvolsky's ignorance of Balkan realities. Serbia and Bulgaria had conflicting claims on Turkish Macedonia, and German influence at Constantinople would never have permitted such a combination. But hatred is a natural tactician, and Izvolsky discovered a way around his difficulty. A Serbian-Bulgarian alliance, together with the cooperation of Greece, might achieve his ends just as well, and a change of government in Bulgaria in 1911 and the outbreak of the Italo-Turkish War had made the new alignment possible.

Russian aims in the Balkans were not, of course, the same as the aims of the Balkan states themselves. Russia desired an anti-Austrian bloc in the Balkan peninsula that would help her achieve the control of Constantinople and the straits. The Balkan nations, on the other hand, wanted the dismemberment of Turkey in Europe to their own territorial aggrandizement, and Serbia wanted also the dismemberment of the Austro-Hungarian Empire so that she could seize the territories she considered to be South Slav. The Serbian ambition could be achieved only by a war that would wrest Bosnia and Herzegovina from the Dual Monarchy. Sazonov, the Russian foreign minister, did not want a general war — at least not until Russia had completed her rearmament program in 1917. Russia was recovering rapidly from her defeat in the Russo-Japanese War and — apparently, at least — from the revolution of 1905. Larger intakes of conscripts were coming into the Russian army every year; the artillery was being modernized; and, most important of all, Russian strategic railways were being pushed forward toward the German frontier with the aid of French money. Stolypin, the prime minister, was in no hurry. He believed, very sensibly, in a long period of recuperation for Russia and in the formation of a class of wealthy Russian peasants who would provide a stabilizing basis for Russian society. Stolypin, unlike Izvolsky, took the long view. He was prepared to endure a lengthy period of peaceful rebuilding. But in September of 1911 Stolypin was murdered in the Kiev Opera House by a terrorist who was also a secret police agent, and with Stolypin's death the last strong, conservative, restraining influence on Russian policy was gone. The field was now left clear for Izvolsky and his foolish and emotional theories.

To the Balkan states the Italo-Turkish War appeared to be a chance that might not come again. Turkish difficulties were Balkan opportunities, but this tide of fortune had to be taken at the flood. Russia was of the same view, although as always she was more interested in acquiring Constantinople and the Dardanelles for herself than in seeing the Balkan Slavs expand their territory. Nevertheless, perhaps the Balkan states could be used as Russia's cat's-paw. Conversations between Serbia and Bulgaria for a military alliance were arranged by the Russian ambassadors Hartwig and Neklidov and began in Belgrade in September 1911. Ivan Geshov, who served as Bulgarian prime minister and foreign minister, met his Serbian counterpart, Milovanovich, in a railway compartment, and in the course of a three-hour train journey outlined a military alliance for the joint seizure of Turkish territory in Europe. It was to be another five months before these two mutually suspicious and hostile nations came to an agreement, but the efforts of Hartwig and Neklidov were finally successful. A secret military agreement between Serbia and Bulgaria was signed on March 7, 1912, and a week later the Serbo-Bulgarian Treaty was signed. The political treaty provided for a mutual guarantee of each other's territory and independence, for military assistance if either nation were attacked or if any other state attempted to occupy territory under Turkish rule, or if either nation felt that there was a threat that this might happen.

This was strong enough, but what was far worse was the secret military annex, which stated that if disorders in Turkey endangered the national interest of Serbia or Bulgaria and the status quo, Serbia and Bulgaria would discuss joint military action. The decision as to whether there would be a war was reserved to Russia, and the tsar was to mediate any disputes over the acquisition of territory. Three zones of Turkish territory were outlined, one to go to Serbia, one to go to Bulgaria, and a third, about which the two nations could not agree, would be apportioned by the tsar. In May a military convention was signed that set out the number of troops Serbia and Bulgaria would deploy against Turkey or Austria. The tsar and Sazonov were shown the Serbo-Bulgarian Treaty in May, and approved it, though Sazonov piously urged that there should be no war in the Balkans.

Sazonov, in fact, was worried about the possible outcome of the Serbo-Bulgarian Treaty, as well he might have been. He had approved it, but the policy had been not his but Izvolsky's, and the more he thought about it, the less he liked it. Hartwig, however, argued from Belgrade that without the secret military annex the treaty would be useless and Russian interests would soon suffer because of the differences between Serbia and Bulgaria. On May 28, 1912, the Serbian foreign minister warned the French ambassador in Sophia that when the Archduke Franz Ferdinand came to the throne he would substitute a tripartite state for the Dual Monarchy, and this new government would threaten to absorb Serbia. Therefore, the Serbian foreign minister argued, the Balkan League should act while Franz Josef was still alive, and the Dual Entente should support Serbia in this action. With this forecast of things to come was combined a thinly veiled threat that if France and Russia did not support her, Serbia would inevitably drift into the Austrian orbit.

The treaty between Serbia and Bulgaria was only the first of the interlocking treaties that came to constitute the Balkan League. On May 24 Greece and Bulgaria promised each other military assistance against Turkey. There was no provision in this treaty for the sharing of territory since both Greece and Bulgaria wanted Salonika, and any attempt to divide that particular bearskin before the bear was dead might well have resulted in the hunters' falling out among themselves. The offensive military convention between the two nations was not signed until October 13, only four days before they went to war. But in July Bulgaria and Montenegro began talks and, though no formal treaty was signed, agreement was reached. Thus, by autumn, all was organized and in readiness for war in the Balkans.

When Izvolsky revealed the existence of the Serbo-Bulgarian Treaty to Poincaré in April, the French prime minister was much disturbed, even though he was not then informed of the secret military provisions of the pact. He went to St. Petersburg in August specifically to discover what Russia was up to in the Balkans. Sazonov then showed him the full text of the treaty. Poincaré realized at once that it was an imminent danger to peace, being designed for a war not only against Turkey, but also against Austria. *"Mais c'est là une convention de guerre!"* he said to Sazonov, who admitted that it was, indeed, a pact for war, but added — because he may have believed it, being that sort of man — that the Balkan states could not implement the treaty without Russia's consent.

However, in August of 1912, Poincaré seemed noticeably less disturbed by the prospect of war than he had been in April. The substance of his conversations with Sazonov was that if the Balkan states began a war and were attacked by Austria, and if Russia then attacked Austria, France would not intervene. If Germany went to Austria's support in such a situation, France would recognize that the *casus foederis* had arisen, and would immediately attack Germany with all her forces. Poincaré added, gratuitously, that Britain would join with France in the attack on Germany.

Poincaré was thus prepared to accept the risk of a general European war, which could break out if Russia took action in the Balkans: and since Russia could defeat Austria by herself, Poincaré's statement to Sazonov was scarcely calculated to restrain Russia or the Balkan League. Indeed, it was almost certainly designed to have the opposite effect and to encourage Russia and, consequently, the Balkan League to begin the process of disrupting the Ottoman and Hapsburg empires. This pledge of Poincaré's to Sazonov marked the complete conversion of the originally defensive Dual Entente into an offensive pact.

On his return to Paris, Poincaré asked Alexandre Millerand, the French minister of war, for the General Staff's appreciation of the situation that would develop in the event that a major European war broke out in the Balkans. Millerand's reply was that, because Italy would not support Austria and because the Balkan states would formidably augment the anti-Austrian forces, such a war would probably have a favorable outcome for the Entente, and the map of Europe could then be redrawn in France's favor. This General Staff assessment had a decisive effect on Poincaré's future policies. From now on, it was not a question merely of building up French armaments, preparing for war, and tightening the solidarity of the Entente. Henceforth, there was the pervasive belief that a general war, especially if it originated in the Balkans, would regain for France the lost provinces. Poincaré circulated the General Staff's appreciation to the principal

French embassies on September 13. The opinion of the French General Staff had not been formed overnight in reply to Poincaré's request. As is common with all such strategic appreciations, it had been constantly discussed by military men, and its conclusions had been in the wind for months before they were formally embodied in the General Staff paper. Almost certainly, Poincaré had heard of them long before he went to St. Petersburg in August. What Millerand's paper did was to make the opinion official. The General Staff's view, of course, also explains why Poincaré was prepared to give French support to the immoderate ambitions of Serbia at the expense of Austria-Hungary. For Poincaré, war was no longer a specter to be dreaded but a chance to be seized by the bold.

It is perhaps not too much to claim that this evaluation by the French General Staff, which was so optimistic about French prospects in a major conflict, was a deciding factor in bringing about the First World War in 1914. From that time on, certainly, Poincaré directed his efforts not to avoiding war, but to ensuring that when it came it would come under circumstances favorable to France. Two considerations especially recommended themselves to him. First, it would be better if the war broke out over a Balkan question, both because this would elicit wholehearted Russian participation and because Italy, a rival of Austria in the Balkan area, would remain neutral under the terms of the secret agreement she had signed with France in 1902. Second, it must be made to appear that the Central Powers were the aggressors, for otherwise there would be strong objection in Britain to becoming involved in a world war over a matter that was purely Balkan. These considerations were to some extent conflicting, but French diplomacy was able to resolve the conflict with a consummate skill worthy of a better cause.

At the end of September, the Balkan states, knowing that the Italo-Turkish War was drawing to a close, and anxious lest they miss their best opportunity of attacking Turkey, mobilized their armies. With this evidence of imminent war, Sazonov lost his nerve, and even Izvolsky began to have serious second thoughts about the wisdom of the course he had been pursuing. The Russians now began to worry that if Turkey defeated the Balkan states Russian prestige might suffer. Worse still, if the Balkan states defeated Turkey, they rather than Russia might possess Constantinople and the Dardanelles. It was late in the day to be entertaining such doubts, but Sazonov even went so far as to try to persuade Serbia not to honor her agreement with Bulgaria. This greatly enraged the French ambassador in Sophia, Hector Panafieu, who had read Millerand's assessment of the military situation. Panafieu protested that it was Russia that had brought about the alliance between Serbia and Bulgaria, and he recalled that at the time of the Bosnian crisis Russia had promised the Serbs that "the day of their joy would come." At all events, Sazonov now worked hard to head off the war that Izvolsky and the Russian ambassadors had striven so diligently to bring about. Perhaps Sazonov had his doubts about the French belief that this would be an excellent time to start a general war, or perhaps he remembered Stolypin's opinion that a war policy for Russia would be "madness." He attempted to insist that the agreement between Bulgaria and Greece should include no aggressive intention against Turkey, but the Bulgars, hardy folk that they were, would have none of this. Bulgaria replied that if Greece was discouraged she would swing over to Austria.

Poincaré and Sazonov at last agreed on a common policy. France and Russia would condemn any move by the Balkan League to break the peace; administrative reforms would be demanded from the sultan; and neither Russia nor France would recognize any changes in the status quo that might be brought about by war. The sincerity of this démarche is more than somewhat open to question, at least in part. Again, perhaps, the best way of judging such a problem is to look at what actually happened. In this case, war came and French and Russian interests were safeguarded. Indeed, this three-point program gave Russia the best of both worlds. If the Balkan League lost its war against Turkey, as most experts believed would be the case, Russia and France would see to it that the Balkan states were not penalized. If the Balkan League won, none of its members could claim Constantinople or the straits. London, Berlin, Rome, and Vienna all concurred in the Sazonov-Poincaré initiative, and on October 7 Russia and Austria, acting for all the powers, sent a joint note to the members of the Balkan League, sternly telling them that they must not go to war.

Not surprisingly, when one considers all that had gone before, this note had absolutely no effect. The very next day, October 8, Montenegro declared war on Turkey. Nine days later, on the 17th, Serbia, Bulgaria, and Greece followed Montenegro's example. Since the Montenegrin army was run by Russian officers, there was some natural doubt in Europe as to whether Russia could have been completely unaware of what was going to happen. Paul Cambon, one of the few French diplomats who was really dedicated to peace, questioned whether Sazonov was actually in control of Russian policy. The truth, of course, was that he was not.

To the surprise of most of the soldiers and politicians of Europe, the Balkan League was immediately successful in its war against Turkey. Within a month the Bulgars were just outside Constantinople.

Most of European Turkey was quickly overrun. The Greeks captured Salonika on November 9, and a Bulgarian division joined them there the next day. The Serbs defeated a Turkish army at Kumanovo in Macedonia, occupied the Sanjak of Novibazar jointly with the Montenegrins, and sharply defeated another Turkish army near Monastir. They then pushed forward to the Adriatic and, together with the Montenegrins, laid siege to Scutari.

In Austria there was understandable alarm at the Balkan League's success and especially at the Serbian and Montenegrin occupation of the Sanjak. Conrad was desperately urging that Austria intervene and separate Serbia and Montenegro. This time the old soldier was almost certainly right, and positive action by Austria, even at this late date, might have saved the empire. But Conrad had been too belligerent too often, and had destroyed his credibility. Count Berchtold was weak and passive where he should have been strong and decisive, just as he was later to be reckless and unheeding when he should have been cautious. Austria made no move to intervene, but Conrad was recalled as Chief of the General Staff in December.

On December 3 Bulgaria, Serbia, and Montenegro agreed to an armistice with Turkey. Greece, which still wanted to occupy some Aegean islands and to reduce Janina, remained at war. Negotiations for peace began in London in January 1913. Serbia demanded an outlet to the Adriatic, a proposal that Austria was quite unwilling to accept. In Russia, the army, led by the Grand Duke Nicholas and by Vladimir Sukhomlinov, now the minister of war, favored supporting Serbia even at the risk of a general war, but the tsar, Sazonov, and the prime minister, Vladimir Kokovtsov, all insisted that Russia was not yet ready. The Russian army was increased by 25 percent, but Russia told Serbia plainly that she would not go to war to gain Serbia a port on the Adriatic.

Poincaré was far from pleased with the pacific Russian attitude, and took the opportunity of reiterating that "if Russia goes to war, France will also go to war." Izvolsky reported back to St. Petersburg on December 18 that the French General Staff, the French ministers, the public, and the press were astonished and displeased that Russia was not taking a harder line. "It is no longer the idea that France might see war forced on her for foreign interests that I shall have to combat," Izvolsky wrote, "but rather the fear that we are too passive in a question touching the position and prestige of the whole Entente." Poincaré became president of the Republic on January 17, 1913, and Charles Jonnart became minister of foreign affairs, but nothing changed; Poincaré continued to exercise a decisive influence on foreign policy. After talking to Poincaré and Jonnart in January, Izvolsky reported to St. Petersburg that France would fully support Russia in the Balkans, and added only that "the French Government urgently begs us not to undertake any unilateral action without a pre liminary exchange of views with our French ally, for it is only on this condition that the Government can successfully prepare public opinion for the necessity of taking part in the war." The reason war did not come in 1912 or 1913 was not that France did not want it, but because Austria, Germany, and Russia were all intent on preserving peace.

Not long after Poincaré became president, he had the wise and peace-loving ambassador at St. Petersburg, Georges Louis, retired and replaced with none other than Théophile Delcassé. All Europe rightly took this to be a sign of increased belligerence on the part of France. Poincaré now threw his support behind the agitation to have the term of military service increased from two years to three, a measure that would increase the French regular army by one third. The three-year service bill was passed by the Chamber of Deputies on July 19, 1913, giving France a peacetime army of 790,000 men. A German army increase in July 1913 brought the German army up to a strength of 761,000.

The London Conference, meeting to settle the Balkan dispute, made slow headway. It is interesting to note that the Russian ambassador in London, Count Benckendorff, wrote to Sazonov on February 20, 1913, that France was the most belligerent power at the conference:

> France wanted one of these outright diplomatic triumphs that may end in cannonades. All the Powers were really working for peace. But of them all the one that would accept war with the greatest philosophy is France. France has recovered. Rightly or wrongly she has complete confidence in her army, and the old ferment of rancor is reappearing, and it may be that she regards conditions as more favorable today than they might be later.

This judgment of Benckendorff's was in every aspect sage and astute, not least in his reservation about the French confidence in their army. Moreover, it was still true, as it had been ever since 1871, that France, of all the European powers, was the only one whose vital interests seemed attainable by no other means than war. The return of Alsace-Lorraine and the restoration of France as the dominant power on the continent could be achieved only by the defeat of Germany in war. Russia, it is true, also wanted a revision of the status quo because she coveted Constantinople and the Dardanelles. Yet there was a major difference between French and Russian aspirations. France felt an urgency about the recovery of the lost provinces that was almost entirely absent from Russia's desire for Constantinople. Russia had desired Constantinople and the Dardanelles for centuries; she had already fought eight wars against Turkey without gaining her ends. Most Russians, therefore, did not view the problem as one that had to be solved within any strict time limit. In France, on the other hand, the loss of Alsace-Lorraine was an open wound that had been inflicted within the lifetime of most senior French statesmen. There was also the unspoken fear that, as the years went by, the French people might forget, might grow reconciled to the loss, might come to prefer peace even to a successful war of revenge, and also, of course, the fear that the German-speaking population of Alsace and Lorraine might, in time, give their full allegiance to Germany.

General Sir Henry Wilson was, perhaps more than any other British soldier, an ardent advocate of a military alliance with France. He told Sir Arthur Nicolson, who shared his views, that he had talked in February 1913 to some of the leading military men in France. The French soldiers, Wilson reported, believed that it would be better if war came soon, because if it broke out over the Balkans, France could be sure of Russian support, whereas if it came from some difficulty between Germany and France alone, Russia might not respond with the desired enthusiasm, the treaty of the Dual Entente notwithstanding.

The London Conference appeared to be making headway, but the Young Turks could not reconcile themselves to the loss of Turkish territory, and they staged a revolution that overthrew the Turkish government. Hostilities reopened in February 1913. This was a mistake on the part of the Young Turks, for their armies were soundly and promptly beaten for the second time. After the Bulgars occupied Constantinople, a new armistice was granted in April.

The First Balkan War ended with the Peace of London, which was signed on May 30, 1913. It spelled the end of Turkey in Europe, for the Ottoman Empire was left with only an insignificant enclave west of Constantinople. However, the division of the spoils was almost immediately the occasion for a new Balkan conflict. Serbia had been prevented by the London Conference from obtaining all the territory she had been promised in the Serbo-Bulgarian Treaty, and therefore demanded that Bulgaria give her more of Macedonia than the treaty allotted. While negotiations between Serbia and Bulgaria were still going on, Ferdinand of Bulgaria, who in 1908 had proclaimed himself tsar, suddenly attacked the Serbian army, on the night of June 29/30, without consulting his cabinet. Rumania and Greece promptly joined Serbia against Bulgaria, and Turkey intervened to recapture Adrianople. Bulgaria was quickly defeated in the Second Balkan War and was forced to sue for peace early in July. By the Treaty of Bucharest, which ended the conflict, Bulgaria lost most of the territory she had gained from Turkey and also had to relinquish the Southern Dobruja to Rumania. An independent Albania was created, and Serbia and Montenegro divided the Sanjak of Novibazar between them, giving them a common frontier, a development that was much to the strategic disadvantage of Austria.

In the Balkan Wars, Serbia was the chief gainer. She had nearly doubled her population and territory, and had brought her dream of a great South Slav state much closer to realization. The Serbs, who had never lacked confidence, were beside themselves with enthusiasm and patriotic ambition. Turkey had been defeated. Now it was to be the turn of Austria-Hungary. Belgrade filled up with unemployed comitadji, who sat about in the cafés, drinking and telling each other of their acts of heroism in the Balkan Wars.

Between March and October 1909, in angry reaction to the Austrian annexation of Bosnia and Herzegovina, Colonel Dragutin Dimitrievich and Ljuba Jovanovich, a lawyer and Freemason, had organized a new secret society, the Ujedinjenje ili Smrt, "Union or Death," more commonly known as the Black Hand. Many high government officials belonged to this society. The program of the Black Hand had two parts, one clandestine and the other public. It published its own newspaper, *Piedmont*, with Jovanovich as its first editor, but its secret work was the more important. Each member of the Black Hand swore an oath to be obedient to death and to take to his grave all the secrets of the society. The regicides of 1903, of course, were prominent in the new organization. The Black Hand's first president was Colonel Ilija Radivojevich, the head of the Serbian police and one of the murderers of King Alexander and Queen Draga, but the real leader was always Dimitrievich, who, in 1913, held the key post of head of the Serbian army's intelligence department. The clandestine portion of the Black Hand's work involved assassination. Politicians in Belgrade who were not considered sufficiently "patriotic" were intimidated or blackmailed; murder and outrages against Austrian officials and Serbian "traitors" were carried out in Bosnia and Herzegovina; and similar acts were undertaken against both Turks and Bulgars in Macedonia.

On June 3, 1910, on the Appel Quay in Sarajevo, Bogdan Zerajich, who had originally intended to murder Emperor Franz Josef, fired five shots at General Varesanin, the governor of Bosnia-Herzegovina, and then committed suicide with his sixth round. Zerajich had been armed and trained in Belgrade by Major Bozin Simich, a member of the Black Hand. Two years later Oskar Tartaglia of the Black Hand sent Lukan Jukich to assassinate Baron Cuvaj, the Ban of Croatia, in Zagreb. By 1911 Dimitrievich had already organized one unsuccessful attempt against the life of Archduke Franz Ferdinand, and he organized similar plots against Tsar Ferdinand of Bulgaria, King Constantine of Greece, Prince George Karageorgevich,* and Prime Minister Pasich.† Dimitrievich had been highly critical of the Serbian government ever since it had accepted the circular note of the powers in 1909 and promised to maintain good-neighborly relations with Austria. This suspicion and hostility was highlighted at the time of the Balkan Wars because the Black Hand felt that Pasich and the Radical party were too soft on Bulgaria. Pasich found an ally in Prince Alexander, now the heir apparent, because the younger of King Peter's sons had hoped to control the Black Hand himself. Dimitrievich had easily resisted this, but in the course of doing so made an enemy who would eventually have him murdered. A full account of the intrigues, murders, and conspiracies that were rife in Serbian official circles between 1903 and 1914 might make dramatic reading but would be less than edifying. Perhaps enough has been related to demonstrate that Serbia was an undesirable neighbor and that there was much justice in the Austrian view that Serb officialdom was no better than "a nest of assassins."

Meanwhile, in St. Petersburg, the well-meaning but ineffectual Sazonov strove for peace, while Hartwig in Belgrade and Neklidov in Sophia fanned the flames of Balkan nationalism, encouraged at every turn by Izvolsky in Paris. At the time of the Balkan Wars, the Pan-Slavs demonstrated noisily in the streets of St. Petersburg, demanding the annexation of Constantinople. Sazonov desired peace, but he was a nervous man and not at all strong enough to ignore Pan-Slav influences. It was partly in reaction to the Pan-Slav agitation that Sazonov objected so sharply to the appointment of the German general Otto Liman von Sanders to a high post in the Turkish army late in 1913. Liman von Sanders, who had headed the German military mission in

*Nothing came of the Black Hand plot to murder Prince George by poison, but Dimitrievich and Prince Alexander cooperated to bring about George's abdication after the heir apparent had killed his valet by kicking him in the stomach in March 1909. Prince Alexander Karageorgevich, who had been privy to the attempt to murder his brother, took no chances of having a rival near the throne. As soon as King Peter died, Alexander had his brother thrown into solitary confinement and kept him there for twenty years. Prince George was released only in 1941.

†Most of the Black Hand's murder plots against prominent personages failed, largely because of the poor caliber of assassins who were available as instruments. The Sarajevo conspirators were typical of the type of individual Dimitrievich employed — school boys in their teens, high school dropouts, pathologically rebellious youngsters who had quarreled with their parents and who had police records as juvenile delinquents. Imanuel Geiss, in his book *July 1914*, refers to them as "young south Slav intelligentsia" but does not reveal by what weird criteria he so designated them.

Constantinople, was given a corps command in the capital with the power to promote senior Turkish officers. Sazonov, fearing that if Germany controlled the Turkish army Constantinople might be lost to Russia forever, was very nearly prepared to go to war over this issue. The French, of course, supported Sazonov, but the British, who bore in mind that a British admiral had exactly the same type of command in the Turkish navy as Liman von Sanders had been given in the army, were unwilling to make a strong protest. This crisis was really resolved by the conciliatory attitude of Germany. Liman von Sanders was given an alternative appointment and a promotion that made him too senior to command a corps. Sazonov, perforce, had to express himself as satisfied, and the period of tension passed.

The real significance of the Liman von Sanders affair is that it is another indication that Germany was not seeking an excuse to go to war but was, on the contrary, striving hard to preserve peace in Europe. Once again, it was the two powers, France and Russia, whose aims could be achieved only by changes in the status quo, that threatened war, and this time on an essentially trivial pretext. If a more substantial occasion could have been discovered, war would probably have come at that time instead of seven months later.

During 1913 and 1914, wherever one looked in Europe, there was a French ambassador or minister whispering assiduously in the ear of some statesman. Things were no different in Rumania, which had come out of the Balkan Wars with some increase of territory and with her appetite whetted for more. Besides, Rumania was dissatisfied with the support Austria had given to Bulgaria. Now the French ambassador in Bucharest, Jean Blondel, was attempting to persuade the Rumanians that Austria-Hungary was breaking up and that they should leave the sinking ship while there was still time. Blondel told the Rumanian government that at the sharing of the spoils after a major war, the Entente would reward Rumania with the gift of Transylvania if Rumania forswore her alliance with Austria and Germany. The Rumanian government was in a mood to listen to Blondel's temptings, and when the tsar and tsarina of Russia, accompanied by Sazonov, visited King Carol of Rumania on June 16, 1914, at Constantza, Ioan Bratianu, the Rumanian prime minister, falsely assured Sazonov "that Rumania was under no obligation to take part in any war where her own interests were not at stake." Sazonov reported to the tsar that, in his opinion, "Rumania would try to join the stronger side and the one that could promise her the greater gains." This was a well-founded opinion. Of Germany's three allies in central Europe, two had now decided not to honor their pledge to her. This consideration did nothing to impose caution and restraint on France and Russia.

While these events were taking place, however, relations between Britain and Germany began to improve noticeably. Agreement was reached on the vexing question of the Portuguese colonies, and also on the financing of the Baghdad Railway. And although no compromise had been arrived at on the question of naval building, even this rivalry seemed less acute, since Britain was maintaining and even improving her relative position of about sixteen to ten in capital ships. In June 1914, for the first time in many years, a British naval squadron paid a visit to Germany, putting in at Kiel. The British stayed for a week; they and their German hosts drank together in the beer gardens of the town and dined in each other's wardrooms. Kiel was gaily decorated with the flags of both nations, and when a British aviator was killed flying a German aircraft, both navies had representatives at the graveside. The British squadron was still at Kiel on Sunday, June 28, when word suddenly came that Archduke Franz Ferdinand had been assassinated in the little Bosnian town of Sarajevo. On receiving a wireless message from the Admiralty, the British ships at once sailed home.

On that day, Archduke Franz Ferdinand and his wife, Sophie, had heard mass at nine o'clock in the morning at the Hotel Bosnia, where they were staying in the spa of Ilidze. The archduke had been attending the maneuvers of the XV and XVI Austrian corps, and as a conclusion to his visit to Bosnia he and his wife were to go by train from Ilidze to Sarajevo, inspect a new barracks, attend a municipal welcome at the Sarajevo town hall, open a museum, attend an official luncheon at the Konak, take a sightseeing tour, inspect a carpet factory, and return to Ilidze. They were met at the Sarajevo station at a quarter to ten by General Oskar Potiorek, the governor of Bosnia, and, after a quick inspection of the barracks, set out in a motorcade for the municipal reception at the town hall. The archduke and his wife traveled in the third car, an open touring model, with General Potiorek and Lieutenant Colonel Count Franz Harrach.

The streets of Sarajevo were bedecked with the black and yellow Austrian flags, and pictures of the archduke were much in evidence. In fact, the Bosnians received the royal couple with every evidence of affection and enthusiasm, for they knew that the heir apparent was well disposed toward the Slav subjects of the empire. The previous afternoon, Saturday, Franz Ferdinand and Sophie had slipped into Sarajevo for an unofficial visit and had walked in the streets and shopped in the bazaar, warmly greeted everywhere.

But on Sunday morning, June 28, four separate groups of assassins were distributed along the Appel Quay on the route of the royal motorcade. Colonel Dragutin Dimitrievich had armed his young thugs from Serbian army arsenals and had had them trained for their task by Voja Tankosich, a major on the Serbian army's active list and Dimitrievich's former accomplice in the Obrenovich murders. Then the assassins had been sent to Sarajevo to murder the archduke. The choice of Franz Ferdinand as the victim of the assassination plot had been by no means haphazard. He was marked for death precisely because he favored giving equal rights to the Slav subjects of the empire and because he and his Czech wife were regarded with hope and affection by the monarchy's Slavs. If Franz Ferdinand had been able to transform the Dual Monarchy into a tripartite monarchy, the towering ambitions of Dimitrievich and the Black Hand for a Great Serbia would have been checkmated.

The first assassination attempt was made by the Cumeria Bridge when a nineteen-year-old Bosnian Serb by the name of Nedeljko Cabrinovich hurled a bomb at the archduke's car. The archduke's chauffeur, seeing a black object hurtling through the air, accelerated, and the bomb landed on the folded canvas hood of the car, bounced onto the street, and exploded underneath the car behind. Twenty bystanders were wounded, some critically, and two officers in the car behind the archduke's were struck by bomb fragments. Cabrinovich jumped over the low wall that separated the Appel Quay from the Miljacka River, dropped twenty-six feet to the ground, and was promptly taken prisoner. He had been thoughtfully provided by the Black Hand with a capsule of poison so that he could commit suicide as a precaution against his revealing the origins of the plot. Cabrinovich loyally swallowed the capsule, but the potassium cyanide he had been given in Belgrade, though it made him very ill and impaired his health for the rest of his life, did not kill him.

The archduke ordered the cavalcade to proceed to the town hall, where the official reception lasted about half an hour. Franz Ferdinand then decided that before he went on to open the museum he would go to the hospital to visit Lieutenant Colonel Erich von Merrizzi, the more seriously wounded of the officers who had been hit. Sophie was to have gone directly to the Konak from the town hall, but she now declared that she would not leave her husband. Accordingly, the archduke and his wife again set out in the open touring car at a quarter to eleven. As a safety precaution, it had been decided that their route would be changed and that, instead of proceeding down Franz Josefstrasse, the motorcade would go to the museum by the Appel Quay.

The archduke was still in the third car, but this time Harrach rode on the running board to protect the archduke with his body. When the first car reached the intersection of the Appel Quay and Franz Josefstrasse, the driver, who had not been informed of the change of route, turned into Franz Josefstrasse. The second car followed and so did the one in which Franz Ferdinand and Sophie were riding. When General Potiorek shouted out to the driver that he was taking the wrong route, the chauffeur stopped and began to back into the Appel Quay.*

Just at that moment, Gavrilo Princip, nineteen years of age, consumptive, and a fanatical Pan-Serb, stepped out of the crowd and shot down Franz Ferdinand and Sophie at pointblank range with his Browning pistol.† Count Harrach, on the other side of the car, was a helpless spectator. Sophie fell sideways toward her husband and blood welled up from Franz Ferdinand's mouth. Harrach later recounted:

> As I was drawing out my handkerchief to wipe away the blood from the Archduke's lips, Her Highness cried out: "For God's sake! What has happened to you?" Then she sank down from her seat with her face between the Archduke's knees. I had no idea that she had been hit and thought that she had fainted from the shock. His Royal Highness said: "Sopherl, Sopherl, don't die, live for the sake of our children." Thereupon I seized the Archduke by the coat collar to prevent his head from sinking forward and asked him: "Is Your Highness in great pain?" To which he answered clearly: "It is nothing." His face was slightly distorted, and he repeated six or seven times, every time losing more consciousness and with a fading voice: "It is nothing." Then came a brief pause, followed by a convulsive rattle in his throat, caused by loss of blood. This ceased on arrival at the governor's residence. The two unconscious bodies were carried into the governor's residence where death was soon established.

Inside the Konak, the bodies were covered with white sheets while arrangements were made to transport them back to Vienna. At about noon on that Sunday morning, as the news of the murders spread through Sarajevo, each of the churches in town began to toll a single bell. Soon the whole of Sarajevo was filled with the mournful and ominous tolling of bells.

---

*Potiorek was later, and very justly, criticized for the inefficiency of the measures taken to protect the archduke, especially after the first bomb attempt. Now that most of the relevant facts about the assassination have been made public by Serbian admissions, it is no longer necessary to refute the suggestion that Potiorek (who, after all, sat in the same car as the archduke when Cabrinovich threw his bomb) connived at the assassination. This story, repeated in the Entente nations long after it had been conclusively proven groundless, is an example of "patriotic history" at its worst.

†Princip was at once seized by the police, who had to protect the assassin from the enraged crowd, which tried to lynch him. This action of the crowd is only one of many indications that the pro-Serbian agitators in Bosnia did not enjoy the overwhelming support of the Bosnians themselves.

CHAPTER V

DURING THE WAR and immediately after it, propagandists for the Entente, including more than a few historians, portrayed the Sarajevo murders as the private act of a small group of oppressed subjects of Austria-Hungary. The Serbian government was absolved of all complicity and guilt, and Austria was said to have used the assassination as the "pretext" for a war to impose her will on a gallant and innocent little state that desired no more than the preservation of her independence and freedom. The most outrageous parallels were even drawn between Serbia and Belgium (which really was such a gallant and abused nation), presumably on the theory of innocence by association.

In the 1920s, new evidence came to light, which made such a view of Serbia quite untenable, but the monstrous consequences of the assassination imposed strict limits to intellectual honesty. The case for a revision of the verdict, which had found Austria and Germany guilty of premeditated, aggressive war, was naturally weakened by the abhorrence felt by decent men toward the Nazis after they came to power in 1933, and with the outbreak of war in 1939 Germany was discredited retroactively. What had been blamed on the kaiser seemed to be proved by the actions of Hitler. The result was that a great silence fell on the subject of Serbian history from 1903 to 1914.

Yet the truth was that Serbia had followed a virulently anti-Austrian policy after the assassination of King Alexander and Queen Draga on June 10, 1903. It was never proved that King Peter Karageorgevich had foreknowledge of those murders (although the probability that he did must remain strong), but certainly he was willing to accept his crown from the bloodstained hands of particularly brutal killers.

Murder, of course, had long been the familiar that stood beside the Serbian throne. King Peter's father had been convicted of complicity in the murder of Prince Michael Obrenovich in 1868; King Peter's elder son, Prince George, was forced to abdicate for murdering his valet in 1909; and King Peter's younger son, Prince Alexander, was involved in a plot to murder his brother, Prince George, and was the instigator of the judicial murder of Colonel Dimitrievich on trumped-up charges in 1917. All three Karageorgeviches had been strong supporters of the Black Hand, and it appears probable that Alexander at one time may have been made a member of the organization.

The Black Hand was a powerful force in Serbian political life and had been largely responsible for the Serbian policies that had led to the Balkan League and the Balkan Wars. Apart from its open propaganda activities, the Black Hand was a murder organization pure and simple. What distinguished it from similar organizations that, from time to time, flourished in the barbarous conditions of southeastern Europe was the remarkable fact that most of the senior members of the Black Hand held responsible positions in the Serbian army, police, or bureaucracy. Most of them, too, in the expressive Mafia phrase, had "made their bones." The younger members, who had not yet had the chance so to prove their manhood, looked forward eagerly to the day when they could do so. Many of them were given the opportunity as comitadji and in the Balkan Wars. Those who, like Princip, had been unable to serve in comitadji units because of poor health or other reasons were the readier to attempt assassinations. Gavrilo Princip, the murderer of Franz Ferdinand and Sophie, was himself a member of the Black Hand, as were Danilo Ilich and Trifko Grabez, Princip's fellow conspirators. Princip and his fellows had been given their pistols and grenades by Major Voja Tankosich, who had instructed the assassins how to use their weapons. Tankosich had also arranged for Princip and his companions to travel from Belgrade to Sarajevo using one of the "tunnels," or secret routes into Bosnia, developed by Narodna Odbrana and also used by the Black Hand. Serbian customs officials and border guards, themselves members of the Black Hand, assisted the assassins in crossing the frontier.

All this would have been damning enough, but, in fact, the Serbian government's responsibility went much deeper. In 1924, Ljuba Jovanovich, who had been minister of education in Pasich's cabinet, blithely revealed that the Serbian government had known about the intended assassination some four weeks before it took place. Jovanovich wrote, in a commemorative pamphlet called *Krv Slovenstva* ("Blood of the Slavs"):

I do not remember whether it was the end of May or the beginning of June, when one day M. Pasich said to us (he conferred on these matters more particularly with Stojan Provich, who was then Minister of the Interior, but he said this much to the rest of us) that there were people who were preparing to go to Sarajevo to kill Francis Ferdinand, who was to go there to be solemnly received on *Vidov Dan*.

As they afterwards told me, the plot was hatched by a group of secretly organized persons and in patriotic Bosnian-Herzegovinian circles in Belgrade. M. Pasich and the rest of us said, and Stojan agreed, that he should issue instructions to the frontier authorities on the Drina to deny a crossing to the youths who had already set out from Belgrade for this purpose. But the frontier authorities themselves belonged to the organization, and did not carry out Stojan's instructions, but reported to him (and he afterwards reported to us) that the order had reached them too late, for the young men had already got across.

Thus the endeavors of the Government to prevent the execution of the plot failed, as did also the endeavor made *on his own initiative** by our Minister in Vienna, M. Joca Jovanovich, in an interview with the Minister Bilinski, to dissuade the Archduke from the fatal journey which he contemplated. And so the attempt at Sarajevo was to be carried out, in more terrible measure than had been anticipated and with results which no one could then have pictured even in his wildest dreams.

Confirmation of Jovanovich's story is provided by a document containing the report of Jakov Milovich, the guide who conducted Princip and Grabez into Bosnia. Milovich worked not only for the Black Hand but also for Narodna Odbrana and he sent his report through Narodna Odbrana channels to Belgrade, where it came to the notice of Provich, the minister of the interior, and Prime Minister Pasich toward the end of the first week in June.† The authenticity of the document is corroborated by the fact that it was summarized in Pasich's own handwriting. Pasich later vehemently denied Jovanovich's account in *Krv Slovenstva*, but only after Miss Edith Durham in England and Professor Sidney Fay of Harvard had drawn attention to its implications.

The Serbian minister in Vienna, Joca Jovanovich, a former captain of comitadji and himself probably a member of the Black Hand,‡ did attempt in a vague and roundabout way to warn the Austrian government about the assassination. He approached Leon Bilinski, the Austro-Hungarian joint finance minister, on June 21 and advised

---

*Italics added.

†Imanuel Geiss, in his disingenuous account of the Sarajevo crime, implies that Pasich knew only in a vague and general way, by rumors, of what was going to happen at Sarajevo on June 28. In fact, Pasich knew the actual names of the assassins, who could easily have been arrested in Bosnia if Pasich had passed this information to Vienna. Men who are not prime ministers, and who are thus privy to murder, risk being charged as accessories before the fact and are held in law to be equally guilty with the murderers themselves.

‡The Black Hand had selected Jovanovich to be foreign minister of the government that, it hoped, would replace Pasich's.

against the archduke's going to Sarajevo — on the grounds that he might be shot by one of his own soldiers. Not surprisingly, this piece of insolence was ignored.

One of the chief conspirators and organizers of the Sarajevo assassination, Milan Ciganovich, who had introduced Princip to Major Tankosich and had participated in the planning of the assassination, was an employee of the Serbian state railways. His name was mentioned by Cabrinovich to the Austrian authorities on the day after the murder, and Austria included in her ultimatum to Serbia a demand for Ciganovich's immediate arrest. The Serbian government replied that they could not find him. The truth was different and more complex. Ciganovich, besides having been one of the chief plotters of the Sarajevo assassination, was also a double agent, spying on the Black Hand for Prime Minister Pasich and the Old Radicals. Immediately after the assassination, therefore, Pasich had Ciganovich smuggled out of Belgrade and into Montenegro. In March 1915, seven months after the war broke out, Ciganovich returned to Serbia and received all his back pay from the state railways from June 1914. He was an important witness against Colonel Dimitrievich in the Salonika trial of 1917, and after Dimitrievich's execution, Pasich arranged for him to be given a false passport and sent to the United States. Ciganovich returned from the United States in 1919 and was promptly given a grant of land by the Serbian government.

The situation in Serbia in June 1914 was complicated by internal quarrels. Prince Alexander Karageorgevich and Colonel Dimitrievich had cooperated for a considerable time, but during the past few years they had become estranged. It was because of Dimitrievich's instructions that the plot to poison Prince George had failed, and shortly afterward Prince Alexander lured a group of regicides away from Dimitrievich and founded his own rival society, the Bela Ruka, or "White Hand." When the Black Hand criticized Pasich and the Old Radicals for their conduct of the Balkan Wars, Prince Alexander sided with Pasich in order further to undermine Dimitrievich's power. In June of 1914, matters came to a head over the question of whether the army or the civil authorities should be in control in the newly gained Macedonian territories. The army, as a whole, supported the Black Hand's stand, and King Peter was induced to dismiss Pasich and the Old Radicals. When the government drafted an order-in-council to retire Dimitrievich, Tankosich, and other Black Hand members, King Peter refused to ratify it, and Pasich was forced to resign on June 2. Prince Alexander intervened on Pasich's behalf, however, and Dimitrievich's companions in the Black Hand refused his suggestion that they stage a coup d'état. Pasich remained in office until June 24, when he dissolved the legislature and called an election for August 1. King Peter promptly abdicated and appointed Prince Alexander regent.

Not only Serbs were implicated in the Sarajevo assassination. Colonel Dimitrievich, both in his capacity as head of Serbian military intelligence and in his unofficial capacity as head of the Black Hand, worked in close daily association with Colonel Victor Artamonov, the Russian military attaché in Belgrade. Artamonov supplied Dimitrievich with certain secret funds, ostensibly in return for military intelligence reports collected by Dimitrievich's agents in Bosnia and Herzegovina. Colonel Bozin Simich, a member of the Black Hand, declared in 1925 that before Dimitrievich decided to murder the archduke he wished to make sure Russia would support Serbia in a war if Austria attacked her as a result of the assassination. Dimitrievich, therefore, informed Colonel Artamonov of the details of the Sarajevo assassination and requested the pledge of Russian support. According to Simich: "A few days later Artamonov gave his reply which ran: 'Just go ahead! If you are attacked, you will not stand alone.'" With whom Artamonov made contact to obtain this guarantee has not been definitely established, but it seems probable that General Sukhomlinov, the Russian minister of war, was the guilty party.*

Not all this was known at the time, of course, but the past history of Serbia and her former relations with Austria provided good and sufficient grounds for suspecting much of it. France and Russia, however, accepted the Serbian government's protestations of innocence without question, and though the British appear to have had some mental reservations, they made no awkward inquiries that might have embarrassed their allies. In excuse for this fatal naïveté, it has been pointed out that Britain was poorly served by her diplomatic representatives in Belgrade that summer. The British ambassador-designate had not yet arrived in Serbia, and the British chargé d'affaires was relatively new to the Balkans and, unfortunately, was ill. But this explanation accounts only for the British Foreign Office's particular ignorance of the Sarajevo assassination; it can scarcely be accepted as a reason for the general ignorance of Serbian conditions or of the type of man foremost in Serbian affairs.

*Colonel Simich's evidence about the foreknowledge and complicity of Colonel Artamonov is confirmed by Dimitrievich's nephew, Milan Zivanovich, and by Mustapha Golubich, a member of the Black Hand. Golubich claimed that, in addition to Artamonov, Hartwig, the Russian ambassador, Prime Minister Pasich, and Prince Alexander Karageorgevich all knew of the assassination ahead of time. We have seen that this statement is certainly true insofar as Pasich was concerned. The Italian historian Luigi Albertini interviewed Artamonov in Belgrade in 1937. Artamonov, of course, denied the allegations, but Albertini found his protestations unconvincing and reported that Artamonov's replies to questions were given with "embarrassed hesitation."

If the British Foreign Office was poorly served in Belgrade, the Quai d'Orsay was, in contrast, served too well for the liking of someone in France. The French ambassador in Belgrade, Léon Descos, knew very well where the responsibility for the assassination lay, and he had the courage to say so. He wrote to Prime Minister René Viviani, on July 1, that Serbia, for the first time in six years, found herself in the wrong. "The *Politka* [a Serbian newspaper] insists that the outrage can only be the deed of isolated elements," Descos wrote. "The *Pravda* imagines a plot set afoot at the vengeance of another Archduke on Franz Ferdinand. But the actual circumstances of the crime betray the existence of a national organization of which it is easy to suppose the aims." This outspoken honesty was not viewed kindly either in Serbia or France, and Descos was removed from his post on July 25.

Europe as a whole was shocked by the assassination but did not for a moment expect that it would lead to a major war. The French press remained preoccupied with the scandalous murder trial of Madame Caillaux, the wife of the former premier, who had shot Gaston Calmette, the editor of *Le Figaro*, for printing the love letters that Caillaux had written to her when she was his mistress. The British were far more concerned about the possibility of Ulster's resisting Home Rule by civil war than with what went on in the Balkans, and what attention the British public spared from Ulster was devoted to cricket. In Germany, the kaiserin was presented with a gold and diamond ornament from the German colonies, and there was a good deal of comment about the unexpected defeat of the Conservative candidate in a by-election in Labiau-Wehlau. General Helmuth von Moltke took the waters at Carlsbad, accompanied by his wife and daughters, and General Conrad von Hötzendorf vacationed in the Tyrol. The kaiser toured the Norwegian fjords in his royal yacht, the *Hohenzollern*, and Emperor Franz Josef rested at Ischl. The common people, too, were enjoying the last summer of peace: university students climbed mountains and tramped across the countryside; families went to the seashore; young lads, who would be dead before the year was out, indulged in their last flirtations.

Count Berchtold, the Austrian foreign minister, remained at his desk in the Ballplatz. On June 29, the day after the assassination, he told Conrad that the time had come to settle accounts with Serbia once and for all. Conrad, of course, agreed enthusiastically. The occasion certainly seemed propitious. The people of the Dual Monarchy were united in anger and grief over the assassination, although the Viennese court and the Hungarian Magyars felt that with Franz Ferdinand's death an enemy of their interests had been removed. The Hungarian premier, Count Kalman Tisza, opposed any strong action

against Serbia because he feared that parts of Serbia might be annexed to the empire, and the Magyars were determined to have no
more Slavs in the monarchy. However, Berchtold got around Tisza's
objection by promising him that Austria would not annex any Serbian
territory* and by telling him, "If we should compromise with Serbia
[the Germans] would accuse us of weakness, which would sensibly affect our position in the Triple Alliance and the future policy of Germany."

Austria's first move was to sound out official German opinion, and
in every way the result was satisfactory. The German government
agreed that Serbia would have to be punished and, indeed, favored
immediate offensive action. Germany and Austria found themselves
at one in their understanding of the situation. Both agreed that the
Balkan Wars and subsequent Serbian policy had endangered the very
existence of the Austro-Hungarian Empire, and that Austria, for the
sake of its own safety, could not afford to let matters drift. Germany
was unwilling to see its only reliable ally go down. In addition, the
kaiser had been a personal friend of the murdered archduke's. Only a
short time before the assassination, Wilhelm had visited Franz Ferdinand and Sophie at Konopischt, had walked with them in the famous rose gardens there, and had talked hopefully with them about
the future of their countries. And both the kaiser and the Austrian
emperor had reason to remember — what the statesmen of the Entente were so willing to forget — that the regime in Serbia had been
established by murder in 1903. At a conference in Potsdam on July 5
the kaiser expressed the opinion that Russia "would not enter the lists
for Serbia which had stained itself by assassination." He felt, too, that
at the moment France was in no position to fight a war, but he added
that the possibility of a Franco-German war would have to be borne in
mind.

Thus assured of German support, Count Berchtold began to draw
up an ultimatum to present to Serbia. He was in no hurry about it, in
spite of German advice that if he was going to strike at Serbia he
should do so quickly, while Europe was still shocked by the murders at
Sarajevo. Count Berchtold was constitutionally unable to hurry, and
he had the kind of vanity that made him reject advice. The ultimatum
to Serbia was not ready until July 19, and even then Berchtold did not
deliver it immediately. He first wanted to undertake certain preliminary military measures that would result in smoother mobilization.
On July 15 President Poincaré and Prime Minister Viviani of France

*Berchtold later came to the view, however, that portions of Serbia should be given
to Bulgaria, Greece, and Albania.

had set out on the cruiser *France* for St. Petersburg. Izvolsky had gone ahead of them to await their arrival. Berchtold, in his silly way, believed that it would be better to delay the sending of the ultimatum to Serbia until Poincaré and Viviani had left St. Petersburg, so that the Entente partners could not immediately confer on common action. What Berchtold thought Poincaré, Izvolsky, and Sazonov would be doing in St. Petersburg between July 20 and 23, if not coordinating Entente policy, is unclear.

While Berchtold was engaged in this sort of statesmanlike calculation, the other chancelleries of Europe waited anxiously to see what would happen. Crises had been recurring phenomena in the previous few years, and all of them had been successfully resolved, so no one was yet prepared to believe that the long-dreaded war would really come that summer — or almost no one.

The Wilhelmstrasse certainly did not think it likely. What Germany foresaw was a short, brisk war between Austria and Serbia, which, because of the disparity of forces, would probably involve very little fighting. Honor would be satisfied, Austria's position would be strengthened, and German prestige would be increased. The war between Austria and Serbia, moreover, was seen as a purely defensive measure, and one that would be dangerous, perhaps fatal, for Austria to neglect. There was surely much truth in this view. Neither Austria nor Germany would gain in territory by such a war; it would merely be a brief campaign to prevent the disruption of the status quo.

Sir Edward Grey was not entirely unsympathetic to Austria's position and had little use for the Serbs. His main concern was to keep the peace, and he felt that this could be done if Austria did not claim any Serbian territory and if Russia did not become too excited. And so, though warnings of Austria's intentions multiplied in London, Sir Edward Grey continued to be optimistic and noncommittal. On July 22 he suggested that Russia and Austria enter into direct conversations so that the Russians could emphasize the strength of pro-Serb feelings in Russia and attempt to have Austrian demands on Serbia "kept within reasonable limits."

When President Poincaré heard of this suggestion he at once opposed it, saying that "conversations *à deux* between Austria and Russia would be very dangerous at the present moment." Professor Fay rightly asks the pertinent question: " 'Very dangerous' to what?" And replies, "Certainly not to the peace of Europe." Poincaré wanted none of his allies talking separately to the enemy; the Triple Entente should stand as a firm unit against the Triple Alliance — or at least against that portion of the Triple Alliance that had not already been suborned.

The French reaction to Sarajevo is to be traced not in Paris, but in St. Petersburg. Poincaré and Viviani arrived early on the afternoon of July 20, and remained in the Russian capital until the late evening of the 23rd. Those four days they spent in the company of Izvolsky, Sazonov, the tsar, and Maurice Paléologue, the French ambassador.

Since Europe was in the grip of the gravest crisis of the century, there can be no doubt that the statesmen of the Dual Entente had weighty matters to discuss. It is all the more remarkable, then, that no record whatsoever of their conversations has survived. Not the Russian or the French archives, not the private papers of Poincaré or Paléologue, retain any trace of what was decided there during those four vital days. Viviani went one better; he left no private papers at all. Paléologue, usually verbose and fluent, had nothing of importance to report to the Quai d'Orsay on the subject of Russian reaction to the Sarajevo outrage.* Bruno de Margerie, the director of political affairs and Chef de Cabinet, was excluded from the talks and later claimed that he never saw a report of them. Paléologue is silent on the subject in his memoirs, though he describes the general atmosphere of the visit. Sazonov says only that the visit was "passed under the shadow of impending calamity."

Such reticence in diplomacy almost invariably has but one meaning: the participants in the conference are determined to hide their decisions not only from contemporaries but from posterity. In this case, unfortunately, they were successful; historians can deduce what was said only by examining what subsequently occurred. Yet even that type of deduction can be extremely revealing. As Thoreau points out, some circumstantial evidence can be very strong, "as, for instance, when you find a trout in the milk."

Jules Cambon, the brother of Paul Cambon and French ambassador in Berlin, had already warned Poincaré that Germany was likely to support Austria in her demands on Serbia and had no "intention of playing the role of mediator." The Berlin and Viennese stock exchanges were dropping dramatically as rumors of impending war spread through financial circles. On July 16 the Russian ambassador in Vienna, N. Shebeko, had reported that Austria was counting on Russia not to intervene on Serbia's behalf, and suggested to his government that Russia should make her position clear before any Austrian ultimatum was dispatched. On the 17th, Sazonov spoke to Sir George Buchanan, British ambassador at St. Petersburg, of the possibility of Russia's having to take some military measures preliminary to mobilization. Thus, the fiction cannot be maintained that Poincaré,

*Only two brief and inconsequential telegrams on the subject were dispatched by Paléologue, on June 30 and July 6.

Viviani, Izvolsky, and Sazonov were unaware of the gravity of the crisis or that they had other, more urgent matters to discuss.

Long before Poincaré's visit, those in France who favored a pacific policy were alarmed. In May, Georges Louis, the former ambassador in St. Petersburg,* had suggested to Joseph Caillaux that Poincaré should be refused permission to make the trip, and Jean Jaurès demanded that the Chamber of Deputies should withhold Poincaré's visa.

These fears were not without justification. Poincaré had more than once been disappointed by Russia's unwillingness to fight a major European war and, as Izvolsky had reported, had said as much to the Russian ambassador. He had determined now that another opportunity would not go by unused. General Millerand's opinion that, if war came, the map of Europe could be redrawn to France's advantage was one that Poincaré, the man from Lorraine, was not likely to forget. The present situation must have seemed, in all respects, ideal to him. The crisis involved Austrian relations with Serbia; if only Sazonov and the tsar could be brought up to scratch, the conditions considered so satisfactory by the French General Staff would be fulfilled, And since the *casus foederis* would arise out of a Russian initiative, there would be no peacemongering to fear from French Foreign Office officials, the Chamber of Deputies, or the French public. St. Petersburg, not Paris, could be made the focal point.

Poincaré began his task before he set foot on Russian soil. In the launch that took him off the *France*, he at once engaged the tsar in earnest conversation, and, according to Paléologue, it soon was only Poincaré who was doing the talking; Nicholas sat and merely nodded his agreement.

The days of July 20 to 23 in St. Petersburg were passed in an atmosphere of military bands, banquets, champagne toasts, and patriotic speeches. Behind Poincaré, Sazonov, and the tsar lurked the figure of Izvolsky, who knew well what game was afoot and did his best to forward it at every turn. Behind them, too, towered the huge figure of the Grand Duke Nicholas, the leader of the Pan-Slav war party in Russia and commander-in-chief of the army, who seldom

---

*After the war, Georges Louis published a two-volume collection of memoirs in which he reported that Stéphen Pichon, the French foreign minister between 1906 and 1911, the prominent French deputy Paul Deschanel, Paul and Jules Cambon, the French ambassadors to London and Berlin, and Adolph Messing, the French minister of war in 1914, all held that Poincaré was responsible for the outbreak of war in 1914. In 1915, Deschanel told Louis: "The majority of men who were ministers in July [1914] say openly that Poincaré is the cause of the war." The French Socialists, of course, also held this opinion and labeled the president "*Poincaré la guerre.*" It is an oversimplified view, but it contains much truth.

missed an opportunity to try to "stiffen" Sazonov and his own weak and amiable nephew the tsar.

On the night of July 22, the Grand Duke Nicholas gave a banquet in the French president's honor. Paléologue arrived early and found the two Montenegrin archduchesses in the banquet hall. These two women, the wives of the Grand Duke Peter and the Grand Duke Nicholas, were the daughters of the king of Montenegro and, quite naturally, had a somewhat Balkan outlook on matters of war and peace. Both of them began to chatter excitedly to the French ambassador. Anastasia, wife of the Grand Duke Nicholas, said:

> Do you realize that we are passing through historic days, blessed days! Tomorrow, at the review, the bands will play nothing but the "Marche Lorraine" and "Sambre et Meuse." Today I had a telegram from my father in the proper style [i.e., in code]. He tells me we shall have war before the month is out. What a hero my father is! He is worthy of the *Iliad*. Here, look at this little box — it never leaves me. It has Lorraine soil in it, yes, Lorraine soil which I collected beyond the frontier when I was in France two years ago with my husband. And now look there at the table of honor! It is decorated entirely with thistles; I would not have any other flowers put on it. Now then! They are Lorraine thistles, don't you see! I picked a few stalks in the lost provinces; I brought them here and had the seeds sown in my garden. Metiza, talk some more to the ambassador. Tell him all this day means to us, while I go and receive the tsar.

At the banquet table Paléologue sat next to the bubbling wife of the Russian commander-in-chief, and her conversation continued in the same vein:

> War is going to break out. Nothing will be left of Austria. You will recover Alsace-Lorraine. Our armies will meet in Berlin. Germany will be annihilated.

Then suddenly — "But I must control myself. The Tsar has his eye on me."

During Poincaré's visit two events that had some significance were recorded: Poincaré had a few words with the Austrian ambassador, Count Friedrich Szápáry, who reported to Vienna that the president's attitude was "threatening" and in marked contrast to the correct and reserved attitude of Sazonov; Szápáry concluded that Poincaré "would have anything but a calming effect here." The other event showed that Szápáry was right, for on the night of the 22nd, after the Grand Duke Nicholas' banquet, Sazonov sent off a telegram to the Russian embassy in Vienna, warning Austria of the dangerous consequences of any Austrian demands that were unacceptable to the dignity of Serbia. This was going further than Sazonov had cared to go before Poincaré's arrival; on the 18th he had told Baron Schilling, the director of the chancellery of the Russian Foreign Office, that there was no need to resort to threats.

On June 30 Alfred Zimmermann, the German undersecretary for foreign affairs, had advised the Serbian government to initiate its own judicial investigation of the Sarajevo murders. This might have done something to avert Austrian wrath, and Zimmermann warned Serbia that to neglect such a step might have serious consequences. Also, Austria asked, unofficially, whether Serbia was going to investigate the murder, but received the answer that "nothing has been done so far and the matter is no concern of the Serbian government." This Serbian attitude, however infuriating it may have been to Austria, was perfectly natural. In the first place, the Serbian government had no need of an investigation — it knew all about the assassination. Second, a public inquiry into the facts would have been disastrous, for the truth would inevitably have come out.

On July 10 the Russian ambassador at Belgrade, Hartwig, grossly overweight, in poor health, and suffering from asthma, dropped dead of a heart attack. Unfortunately, he did so while he was visiting the Austrian embassy, and the Serbs immediately proclaimed that he had been murdered. To a Serb, it must have seemed a perfectly natural conclusion.

The German Foreign Office had still not seen the contents of the Austrian ultimatum to Serbia when, on July 21, it advised the German ambassadors that Austria was to receive full support and that the quarrel between Austria and Serbia should be localized because outside intervention might well result in a major war. The ultimatum was delivered by the Austrian ambassador, Baron Vladimir Giesl, at a few minutes before six on the evening of July 23. Prime Minister Pasich was at Nish, electioneering, and, although the Austrian embassy had informed the Serbian government that morning that an "important communication" would be delivered in the afternoon, Pasich did not return to the capital.*

The Austrian ultimatum, which required a reply not later than 6:00 P.M. on July 25, contained ten demands on the Serbian government:

1. The suppression of any publication inciting hatred of Austria-Hungary.
2. The dissolution of Narodna Odbrana and all other propaganda

---

*This was typical of Pasich in moments of acute crisis. He had had foreknowledge of the murders of King Alexander and Queen Draga in June 1903, but instead of taking a stand beside his friends, the murderers, he slipped quietly out of Belgrade and did not return until the deed had been accomplished.

societies, and the taking of necessary measures to prevent the dissolved societies from continuing their activities under another name and form.

3. The elimination from Serbian schools of hate propaganda against Austria-Hungary.

4. The removal from the Serbian army and bureaucracy of officers and officials guilty of propaganda against Austria-Hungary.

5. The acceptance of the collaboration in Serbia of Austrian officials in the suppression of the subversive movement.

6. The arrest of the accessories to the murder plot of June 28, and the participation of Austrian officials in the investigation of the assassination.

7. The arrest of Major Voja Tankosich and Milan Ciganovich.

8. The suppression of the illegal traffic of arms and explosives from Serbia into Austria, and the punishment of the frontier officials who had helped the murderers to cross into Austria.

9. An explanation of "the unjustifiable utterances of high Serbian officials both in Serbia and abroad" who had, in interviews since June 28, expressed hostility to Austria-Hungary.

10. The notification of the Austrian government, without delay, of the measures taken.

Once the Austrian ultimatum had been studied by the diplomats of Europe, international tension immediately deepened. Berchtold had deliberately framed his demands in such a way as to make their acceptance either very difficult or impossible. Sir Edward Grey described the ultimatum as the most formidable document he had ever seen addressed by one state to another that was independent. In Russia, Sazonov read the ultimatum and decided that he would ask the tsar to order a partial mobilization against Austria but not against Germany. Unfortunately, the Russian General Staff had no plans prepared for such an eventuality but was prepared only for a general mobilization against both Austria and Germany. In spite of the fact that a partial mobilization against Austria would have chaotic military consequences for Russia if she had subsequently to mobilize against Germany, the Russian Chief of the General Staff, General Janushkevich, made no objection to Sazonov's proposal. Sazonov was encouraged to request partial mobilization by the assurances of Paléologue that France would fulfill all the obligations of her alliance and would go to war by Russia's side.

As soon as the council of ministers had decided to ask the tsar to declare partial mobilization, Sazonov at once informed Paléologue, but the French ambassador, very strangely, did not pass this vital information on to Paris. On July 25 Sazonov told Sir George Buchanan that "Russia cannot allow Austria to crush Serbia and become the predominant power in the Balkans, and, secure of the support of France, she will run all the risks of war." Germany made representations to Britain, Russia, and France, urging "the localization of the conflict" between Austria and Serbia should Serbia reject the ultimatum. Also on July 25, Berchtold assured the Russian chargé d'affaires, Kudashev, that even if Austria were forced to go to war with Serbia she would not annex any Serbian territory.

On that day, too, the tsar gave his consent in principle to partial mobilization against Austria, "but not before Austrian troops had crossed the Serbian frontier." By now Serbia had appealed to Russia for support, agreeing to accept those terms of the Austrian ultimatum that were in keeping with Serbia's independent status and, as well, those that the tsar might advise Serbia to accept. Thus, Serbia was prepared to adopt the one course of action Berchtold most feared — total acceptance of the Austrian demands — but only on condition that Russia advised her to do so. Until noon on the 25th the Serbian government was prepared to accept all the Austrian demands. This attitude changed, however, on receipt of word from Sazonov that Serbia should accept only those demands consistent with her dignity as an independent state. Sazonov also advised Serbia not to resist an Austrian invasion, but to withdraw without fighting and appeal to the powers. This advice was enough for the Serbian government, which now drafted its reply to the Austrian ultimatum in the light of the knowledge of Russian support.

As soon as the Serbian government had decided not to accept the Austrian ultimatum unconditionally, it ordered general mobilization. This order went out at three o'clock on the afternoon of July 25. Serbia was thus the first nation to mobilize in 1914. Prime Minister Pasich delivered the reply personally to the Austrian embassy and then he and the other cabinet ministers caught the six o'clock train for Nish. Government offices, military units, the archives, and the treasury also evacuated Belgrade that day. Giesl and the Austrian embassy staff left Belgrade at once, severing diplomatic relations with Serbia.

The statement has often been made that the Serbian government accepted the overwhelming majority of the Austrian demands and declined only those incompatible with its national honor. Even on the supposition that a state ruled by the Karageorgeviches possessed a "national honor," it requires only a comparison of the Austrian ultimatum and the Serbian reply to see how far wide of the mark is the idea that Serbia was meeting Austria's demands in a reasonable and conciliatory way.

The Serbian reply first expressed "pain and surprise" at the idea that Serbian citizens were accused of being implicated in the murders of the archduke and his wife, then dealt with each of the Austrian demands as follows:

1. Promised to amend the Serbian constitution to enable action to be taken against any publication that expressed hatred of Austria-Hungary, but claimed that no such action could be taken until the constitution was amended.
2. Promised to dissolve Narodna Odbrana and other propaganda societies, but ignored the Austrian demand that these societies should not be allowed to continue their activities under another name and form.
3. Promised to eliminate anti-Austrian propaganda from Serbian schools, but only when Austria furnished proof of such propaganda.
4. Promised to remove from the army all officers found guilty by a [Serbian] judicial inquiry of acts directed against Austria-Hungary.
5. Promised to accept the collaboration of Austrian representatives in the suppression of subversive movements, but only when such collaboration agreed with "the principle of international law, with criminal procedure and with good-neighborly relations."
6. Flatly rejected the Austrian demand that Austrian officials cooperate in the investigation of the murders of June 28.
7. Announced that Major Tankosich had been arrested but claimed that Milan Ciganovich could not be found.
8. Promised to reinforce and extend the measures already in force for the prevention of the smuggling of arms and explosives into Austria, and promised to punish frontier officials found guilty of assisting the murderers to enter Austria.
9. Promised to explain the anti-Austrian remarks of Serbian officials if the Austrian government furnished proof that the remarks had actually been made.
10. Promised to inform the Austrian government of the measures taken to carry out the above promises.

The Serbian reply to the Austrian ultimatum was undoubtedly cleverly conceived. Alexander Musulin, of the Austrian Foreign Office, who had drafted the ultimatum for Berchtold, regarded the Serbian note as "the most brilliant specimen of diplomatic skill that I have seen." The kaiser annotated his copy with the lines: "A brilliant achievement at forty-eight hours' notice. More than anyone could have expected. A great moral victory for Vienna but it removes any reason for war . . ." The observation was superficial. In any case, the kaiser, when he wrote these words, was already — and with good reason — getting cold feet.

In fact, Serbia declined to comply unreservedly with eight of the ten points of the Austrian ultimatum, and the Serbian acceptance of Point

10, "To notify the Imperial and Royal Government without delay of the execution of the measures comprised under the preceding heads," was meaningless unless the previous nine points were agreed to. In effect, Serbia in her reply to the Austrian ultimatum accepted without reservation only one point, number 8, which promised to prevent the illicit traffic of arms and explosives into Austria from Serbia and to punish the customs officials who had helped Princip and his accomplices cross into Bosnia.

The most important divergence between the Serbian reply and the Austrian demand concerned Point 6: "To take judicial proceedings against the accessories to the plot of the 28th of June who are in Serbian territory; organs delegated by the Imperial and Royal Government will take part in the relevant investigations." The Pasich government returned an outright rejection of this demand. What else could it do? If an impartial investigation were held in Serbia into the activities of the Black Hand, what would the results have been for the Karageorgevich dynasty or the Serbian government? Talk about the sovereign rights of Serbia, national honor, and dignity is mere cant. The fact was that Pasich did not dare to have Austrian officials investigate in Serbia the murder of Franz Ferdinand and Sophie because they would have discovered the truth.

On July 25 Austria ordered partial mobilization against Serbia, and the next day the British Foreign Office suggested that the crisis might be mediated by Britain, France, Germany, and Italy. France did not reply to this suggestion for forty-eight hours, and Sazonov replied that he would prefer to continue the direct conversations with Austria that had already begun. Berlin rejected the idea of a four-power European conference because she would certainly be outvoted by Britain, France, and Italy. Anyway, Bethmann was still insisting that the Austro-Serbian dispute should be settled without the intervention of other nations. Austria should not, in his view, be brought before "a court of arbitration." Bethmann felt secure in his stand because he knew that Sir Edward Grey, like himself and unlike France, drew a sharp distinction between the Austro-Serbian and the Austro-Russian quarrels, and Grey had no interest in upholding Serbia. Grey went so far as to say to Count Albert von Mensdorff, the Austrian ambassador, "If [Austria] could make war on Serbia and at the same time satisfy Russia, well and good; but, if not, the consequences would be incalculable."

The Germans were also much encouraged by the fact that on the morning of July 26 Prince Henry of Prussia had breakfasted with King George V, and the king had explicitly told him, "We shall try all we can to keep out of this and shall remain neutral." Sir Francis

Bertie, the British ambassador to Paris, though strongly pro-French, also had his doubts about this particular quarrel. He wrote to Sir Edward Grey on the 27th, suggesting that France "should be encouraged to put pressure on the Russian Government not to assume the absurd and obsolete attitude of Russia's being the protectress of all Slav states, whatever their conduct, for this will lead to war." Bertie, however, overestimated the French government's desire for peace, and Grey obstinately refused to intercede with either Russia or France for a more moderate Russian attitude.

The British fleet, which had been concentrated at Portland for annual maneuvers, had been due to disperse on Monday the 27th, but orders went out from the Admiralty to keep it mobilized. The next day, the 28th, Austria declared war on Serbia. Russia forthwith broke off the conversations she had been holding with Austria. Austria was thus the first nation to declare war in 1914, but Austrian military preparations, like Viennese diplomacy, moved in waltz time. The declaration of war was not followed by any blitzkrieg offensive. A desultory bombardment was opened up across the Sava, but no Austrian troops were yet ready to cross the Serbian frontier.

On this same day Kaiser Wilhelm saw for the first time the text of the Serbian reply to the Austrian ultimatum. He at once wrote to Gottlieb von Jagow, the foreign minister, at ten o'clock that morning:

> On reading through the Serbian reply which I received this morning I am persuaded that on the whole the wishes of the Dual Monarchy are met. The few reservations made by Serbia on single points can in my opinion be cleared up by negotiation . . . Nevertheless this scrap of paper with what it contains can be regarded as only of limited value so long as it is not translated into *deeds* . . . In order that these fine promises may become truth and fact, the exercise of *gentle violence* will be necessary. This will best be done by Austria's occupying Belgrade as *security* for the enforcement and execution of the promises and remaining there until the demands are *actually* carried out.

On July 24 Sir Edward Grey had proposed an almost identical *Halt in Belgrade*. Bethmann had already forwarded the kaiser's proposal to Vienna. When no reply had been received by shortly after ten o'clock on the evening of the 29th, Bethmann dispatched two urgent telegrams to Vienna, reiterating that the Serbian reply to the Austrian ultimatum was regarded as "a suitable basis for negotiations on the condition of an occupation of Serbian territory as a guarantee." In a further telegram, sent half an hour after midnight on the 30th, he urged Vienna to continue direct negotiations with St. Petersburg. Indeed, though Germany had certainly favored a localized war between

Austria and Serbia, as soon as the German Foreign Office realized that the war would probably not be localized, it insistently, almost frantically, tried to hold Austria back and save the peace. Between July 28 and 31 Bethmann did far more than Grey to avoid a major war; Poincaré, Sazonov, and Berchtold did nothing.

Bethmann sent for the British ambassador, Sir W. E. Goschen, late on the evening of the 29th and made a surprising bid for British neutrality. If Britain remained neutral, Germany would make no territorial gains from France in Europe and promised to respect the neutrality of Holland. If Belgium did not take sides against Germany, no territory would be taken from Belgium, but — significantly — Bethmann did not promise to respect Belgian neutrality. Finally, if England remained neutral, Germany would be prepared to discuss a general neutrality agreement with her in the future. Sir Edward Grey described this offer as "infamous"; it was certainly clumsy and revealing. It revealed not only German intentions to invade Belgium but also the way in which the German Foreign Office had been deluded by Sir Edward Grey's attitude into believing that Britain might remain neutral. This German misconception was one of the chief reasons why the Wilhelmstrasse lost control of events. A clear statement by Grey either of Britain's neutrality or of her belligerency on the side of the Entente would have prevented the war, in the first instance by restraining France and Russia, and in the second by causing Germany, much earlier, to restrain Austria.

Now, however, there occurred the event that was to make all further diplomatic endeavor useless. When the news of the Austrian declaration of war on Serbia reached St. Petersburg, the Russian General Staff at once began to exert pressure to have the tsar declare general mobilization. No one in a senior government position anywhere in Europe should have been under any delusion that once Russia ordered general mobilization peace could be saved. The Russians, the French, the Germans, and the Austrians all surely knew that a Russian general mobilization would, in every respect, be equivalent to a declaration of war. This had been stated plainly at the signing of the Dual Entente in 1894,* and nothing had happened to change this fact since then. Germany, of course, being in the center of Europe and liable to attack from two sides, and being, in addition, seriously outnumbered by her potential opponents, was especially sensitive to mobilization. Her only hope in a war was to take advantage of her superior technical skill and of her more rapid mobilization to strike at France before the huge army of the tsar was ready to crush her. Germany could not,

*See page 31.

therefore, as a matter of life and death, allow Russia the extra time that an uncontested mobilization would give her.

Sir Edward Grey seems to have been unaware of these elementary facts of the international situation. At all events, he said in his memoirs:

> I felt impatient at the suggestion that it was for me to influence or restrain Russia . . . If I were to address a direct request to [Sazonov] that Russia should not mobilize, I knew his reply. Germany was much more ready for war than Russia; it was a tremendous risk for Russia to delay her mobilization, which was anyhow a slow and cumbrous affair. If Russia took that risk in deference to our request, would Britain support her, if war did ultimately come and she found herself at a disadvantage owing to following our advice? To such a request the only answer could be that we would give no promise. If we give a promise at all it must be to France, and my promise to Russia must be only consequential on that. The Cabinet was not prepared yet to give a promise even to France. This consideration was always present to my mind in all communications to St. Petersburg during those critical days.
>
> But besides this I did most honestly feel that neither Russian nor French mobilization was an unreasonable or unnecessary precaution. In Germany, in the centre of Europe, was the greatest army the world had ever seen, in a greater state of preparedness than any other, and what spirit was behind?

It is very difficult, in reading the foregoing passage, to escape the conviction that Grey was being essentially dishonest. That the foreign minister of Great Britain should actually believe that Russian general mobilization was simply a necessary defensive measure, and not the pistol pointed at a neighbor's head that General Boisdeffre had called it in 1894, is all but incredible. It is equally difficult to believe that Grey really thought that Germany possessed "the greatest army the world had ever seen, in a greater state of preparedness than any other," when the real truth was that the regular armies of the Dual Entente greatly outnumbered those of Germany and Austria and that the Entente had for many years been spending much larger sums on armaments. For Germany to allow both Russia and France to mobilize without taking defensive action of her own would have been patently suicidal. One can feel a certain sympathy with Kaiser Wilhelm's anger in the note he appended to Prince Karl Max von Lichnowsky's dispatch from London, which related Grey's warning on July 29 that Britain would probably fight on the side of France:

> England shows her hand at the moment when she thinks we are in a corner and, in a manner of speaking, done for. The lowdown shopkeeping knaves have been trying to take us in with banquets and speeches. The grossest deception is the King's message to me by Henry: "We shall remain neutral and

try to keep out of this as long as possible." Grey makes the King out a liar and these words to Lichnowsky are utterances of the bad conscience he has for deceiving us. What is more, it is a threat combined with bluff, meant to detach us from Austria, stop our mobilizing and make us take the blame for the war. He knows quite well that if he says a serious, sharp deterrent word at Paris or St. Petersburg and admonishes them to remain neutral, both will at once keep quiet. But he takes good care not to say the word and threatens us instead! Contemptible scoundrel! England *alone* bears the responsibility for peace or war, not we now!

One can feel sympathy toward the kaiser without necessarily agreeing with him. Much of his indictment of Grey's policy was valid. Had Grey said "a serious, sharp deterrent word at Paris or St. Petersburg," the war would not have come. It would not have come because France would not have allowed it to come. But the alternatives were not all that simple at the end of July. If the Entente had backed down at Britain's behest, could it have held together? Grey thought not, and was prepared to fight a European war rather than see the Entente dissolve. Still, this had not been the position earlier, before Russia had taken so firm a stand in defense of Serbia. Had Grey exercised a moderating influence at any time before July 23, the peace could have been saved without endangering the Entente.

Paléologue had advised Sazonov to be circumspect about military measures undertaken on the German frontier because of the necessity of convincing England that Germany was the aggressor, but on July 28, after hearing of the Austrian declaration of war against Serbia, the French ambassador again repeated France's "complete readiness . . . to fulfill her obligations as an ally." On the 29th Sazonov telegraphed to the Russian ambassadors in London, Paris, Vienna, and Rome that "all we can do is to accelerate our armaments and count on the inevitability of war." What Sazonov meant by the euphemism "accelerate our armaments" was general mobilization.

A debate had been going on in St. Petersburg as to whether Russia should order the partial mobilization of thirteen army corps against Austria or general mobilization (which meant war) against both Austria and Germany. The Russian quartermaster general, Yury Danilov, who had been out of the city, returned to St. Petersburg on July 27 and was able to convince the Chief of the General Staff, Janushkevich, that the order for the partial mobilization of the military districts of Odessa, Kiev, Moscow, and Kazan against Austria would be disastrous from a strategic point of view; no plan existed for such a partial mobilization and it would gravely hinder any later general mobilization. On Janushkevich's urging, Sazonov, on the evening of July 28, ordered two orders prepared, one for partial mobilization and one for general mobilization, and on the morning of the next day the tsar signed both, but did not then decide which, if either, to send out.

On the evening of the 29th the tsar, very reluctantly, authorized general mobilization. This was done in spite of the fact that Bethmann, shortly after noon that day, had sent a telegram to Pourtalès. It read: "Kindly impress on M. Sazonov very seriously that further progress of Russian mobilization measures would compel us to mobilize and then a European war could scarcely be avoided." The minister of the interior, N. A. Maklakov, who had countersigned the mobilization order, spoke first of his fear that war would bring revolution to Russia. He crossed himself before countersigning the order; then added with characteristic Russian fatalism: "We cannot escape our destiny." At nine-thirty on the evening of the 29th, while the telegrams ordering general mobilization were actually being dispatched, an urgent message came from the tsar, countermanding the order and substituting the one for partial mobilization. Nicholas had been influenced to take this action by a telegram from his cousin the kaiser, urging that negotiations be continued and concluding: "Of course military measures on the part of Russia which would be looked upon by Austria as threatening would precipitate a calamity we both wish to avoid . . ." This "Willy-Nicky" correspondence continued, but was without result.

The tsar was desperately anxious to save the peace, but Sukhomlinov, the minister of war; the Grand Duke Nicholas, the commander-in-chief; Janushkevich, the Chief of the General Staff; Danilov, the quartermaster general; and even Sazonov urged on the tsar the immediate necessity for ordering general mobilization. Sazonov did not hesitate to say — perhaps not to Nicholas himself — that if Serbia were allowed to become the vassal of Austria, he feared for the life of the tsar; that there would be a revolution in the country. On the afternoon of July 30, at about four o'clock, the tsar finally, and most reluctantly, again gave his consent to general mobilization. The order went out at five o'clock, and by that evening the red mobilization posters were being pasted up on walls all across the empire.

War was now inevitable and imminent. Russia's action in proclaiming general mobilization meant that the direction of events had passed from the diplomats to the soldiers.

Paléologue, in St. Petersburg, was informed of all the Russian decisions concerning mobilization almost as soon as they were made. His right to be so informed was written into the military agreement of the Dual Entente, and for Russia to have ignored it would have given France just cause not to recognize the *casus foederis*. Indeed, under Article II of the military agreement as amended in 1913, France had to give its consent to Russian mobilization. However, Paléologue did not report the true state of affairs to the Quai d'Orsay. When the tsar first consented to general mobilization, Paléologue reported to Paris only that Russia was calling up thirteen corps on the Austrian frontier (that is, partial mobilization). The only possible reason for this deception of his own Foreign Office can have been that Paléologue was afraid that those in France who wished to preserve peace would demand that the Russian general mobilization be postponed until the consultations called for by the military agreement had taken place. The deception continued when Paléologue deliberately kept from the Quai d'Orsay the news that Russia was preparing to order general mobilization on the 30th. Even at a quarter past nine on the night of July 30, five and a quarter hours after the tsar had ordered general mobilization, Paléologue did not relay this information to Paris, but reported instead that "the Russian Government has decided to proceed secretly to the first measures of general mobilization." Paléologue was ensuring that nothing should be done at the last moment to interfere with the coming of the war he so badly wanted. He did not, in fact, inform Paris of the Russian general mobilization ordered at four o'clock on the afternoon of the 30th until 10:43 A.M. on the 31st — nearly nineteen hours later. His telegram reached Paris at eight-thirty on the evening of the 31st.

On the morning of July 30 Viviani instructed Paléologue to repeat France's resolve to stand by her ally but to advise the Russian government that Russia "should not immediately proceed to any measure which might offer to Germany a pretext for a total or a partial mobilization of her forces." This telegram may have been framed more with an eye on London than St. Petersburg, for France was desperately anxious to pull Britain into war on her side, and the French feared that this could be done only if Germany was made to appear the aggressor. None of it mattered, however, for Russian general mobilization was announced that afternoon. Viviani's telegram arrived too late to be taken into consideration, and when Paléologue did speak to Sazonov about it, he suppressed the important portion and did no more than repeat, as he had been repeating every day since Poincaré had left St. Petersburg, that Russia could be sure of French support.

Can Paléologue be presumed to have acted thus on his own initiative, deliberately lying to his own Foreign Office and concealing information on matters of the most vital importance to France? The supposition is incredible on every count. Nothing in Paléologue's character indicated that he would have dared to plunge Europe into war on his own authority. Less than a week before, Poincaré had been in St. Petersburg for four days and had had ample time to discuss the measures to be taken. Indeed, before he left, Poincaré had instructed Paléologue, "Sazonov must be firm and we must support him." These are the instructions that have survived, and they are accurate enough, but there were certainly more detailed orders given. That, of course, is why no record of Poincaré's conversations during his visit have survived. It was indeed a secret to be kept: the planning of the greatest war the world had ever seen. When the deceptions practiced by Paléologue became known after the war, and when it was discovered that the French *Yellow Book* of diplomatic documents was riddled with forgeries, Paléologue was bitterly attacked, but Poincaré never spoke a word against him. Why should he? It was not the French ambassador who was responsible for the deception practiced on the French Foreign Office, but the French president.

The French government ordered its covering forces into position along the frontier on the afternoon of July 30, but ruled that, except in certain special cases, they should not approach closer than ten kilometers to the border. This ruling was not to avoid the possibility of border clashes but to create a good impression in Britain. The telegram to Paul Cambon, informing him of the "ten kilometre withdrawal" and asking him to convey the news to Sir Edward Grey, ended: "In so doing we have no other reason than to prove to British public opinion and the British Government that France, like Russia, will not fire the first shot." France was taking good care on this occasion not to repeat her mistake of 1870, when she had forfeited considerable international sympathy by being the first to declare war.

By July 30, Chancellor Bethmann-Hollweg was making frantic attempts to moderate Austria's attitude. Now at last, and too late, Germany realized that her hope of a localized war between Austria and Serbia was impossible and that Britain would fight on the side of France. Germany had never intended to let it come to a European war and had believed, probably rightly, that if Britain remained neutral the Dual Entente would have to back down without fighting. Once this policy was seen to be mistaken, Bethmann sent telegram after telegram to Vienna to stop the machine, but it was already out of control.

General Helmuth von Moltke, the German Chief of the General Staff, reacted differently. In common with soldiers everywhere, Moltke knew that the Russian proclamation of general mobilization meant certain war. Therefore, as soon as he heard that general mobilization had been proclaimed in Russia his whole purpose was to fight the war on advantageous terms. He was extremely agitated by what he regarded as the slowness of government reaction both in Vienna and Berlin. Early on the morning of the 31st he telegraphed Conrad:

Stand firm against Russian mobilization. Austria-Hungary must be preserved, mobilize at once against Russia. Germany will mobilize. Compel Italy to do her duty as an ally by compensations.

At the same time as Moltke was telegraphing this message to Conrad, both Kaiser Wilhelm and Bethmann were making desperate appeals to Emperor Franz Josef and Berchtold to come to terms with Russia. Berchtold compared Moltke's telegram and Bethmann's and commented, "How odd: Who runs the government — Moltke or Bethmann?" But while it is true that Moltke had no business to overstep his authority and interfere in diplomatic matters, his view of the situation on July 31 was the correct one. Nothing could save the peace now that Russia was mobilizing.

Austria's reply to the appeals of the kaiser and Bethmann was to proclaim general mobilization at twelve-thirty on the afternoon of July 31. This was done some twenty hours after Russia proclaimed mobilization, but the French government, then and later, deliberately lied about this vital point, claiming that the Austrian general mobilization preceded the Russian. The French *Yellow Book* made this claim, and falsified and forged documents to prove it.* Poincaré and French historians were to repeat the lie after the war.

At three-thirty on the afternoon of the 31st, Germany sent a note to St. Petersburg demanding that every Russian war measure against Austria and Germany be suspended within twelve hours; if this was not done, Germany would mobilize. At the same time, a German note to Paris asked if France would remain neutral in a Russo-German war and demanded an answer within eighteen hours. The German government, of course, had no illusion that the French answer would be anything but a rejection, but the German ambassador in Paris was instructed, in case of French acceptance, to demand the handing over of the fortresses of Toul and Verdun as pledges of neutrality. This was not an attempt to force France into war, but reflected the well-founded German fear that, if the German army ever became deeply involved on the eastern front, France would be unable to resist the temptation of attacking Germany in the west. To the German note, France replied that she would act as her own interests dictated.

*Only the French and the Russians actually forged documents in their diplomatic books relating to the outbreak of the war. The German, Austrian, and British books omitted documents to strengthen their respective cases but did not find it necessary to forge them. In this instance, the French *Yellow Book* manipulated and distorted telegrams Nos. 102, 115, 118, 125, and 127; and this falsification was followed in the British *Blue Book* and the Russian *Orange Book*. For a complete analysis of this forgery, see L. Albertini, *The Origins of the War of 1914*, vol. III, chap. III. It is, of course, significant that the French and Russian governments alone found it necessary to resort to this type of falsification.

On the night of July 31, the French government definitely decided to go to war and so informed Izvolsky. France was thus the first nation officially to state that she intended to participate in a major European war. The formality mattered little. The real decision had been taken long ago by Poincaré.

Nothing could now prevent the catastrophe, but Austria, at German urging, made a last-minute attempt to reopen direct conversations with Russia. These negotiations were actually begun on July 31, but the next day Russia broke them off. At noon on August 1 France ordered general mobilization, and Germany followed suit five hours later. As Germany had repeatedly warned during the crisis, her mobilization meant war. Germany declared war on Russia at the same time as she ordered general mobilization, that is, at five o'clock on August 1. The German declaration of war on France was delayed until 6:15 P.M. on August 3.

The sequence of mobilization is in itself revealing. Serbia was the first nation to mobilize on the early afternoon of July 25; Austria ordered a partial mobilization of eight corps against Serbia on the evening of July 25; Russia ordered partial mobilization on July 29 but, before this could become effective, replaced it with the order for general mobilization at four o'clock on the afternoon of July 30; Austria ordered general mobilization at about noon on July 31; France ordered general mobilization at noon on August 1; and Germany, the last continental power to mobilize, ordered general mobilization at five o'clock on the afternoon of August 1.

The Italian attitude to the July crisis was not decided by Italy's adherence to the Triple Alliance, but neither was it decided by the pledge that Italy had given to France in the secret treaty of 1902. As early as July 29 the Italian foreign minister, Antonio San Giuliano, had made his position clear to the Austrian ambassador, Merey von Kapos-Mere. San Giuliano claimed that since the Triple Alliance was a purely defensive treaty, and since Austria had provoked the war by her action against Serbia and had done so without previous consultation with Italy, there was no obligation on Italy's part to go to war. This did not mean that Italy would necessarily remain neutral. It was more likely that Italy would still fight beside Germany and Austria, provided that Italian interests in the Balkans were safeguarded and provided that Austria would not seek to increase her influence in southeast Europe at Italian expense. San Giuliano repeated this policy the following day to Hans von Flotow, the German ambassador to Rome.

On July 31 Flotow officially informed the Italian government that Germany had proclaimed a state of *drohende Kriegsgefahr*, "imminent danger of war," which would most probably be followed by German general mobilization and a declaration of war. The German ambassador ended by saying, "Germany expects that Italy will fulfill her obligations arising under the alliance." San Giuliano replied that "in accordance with the spirit and letter of the treaty of the Triple Alliance, [Italy] does not hold herself bound to take part in this war, which is not of a defensive character."

Thus, after all, Italy did not come to the rendezvous. Her conduct, while hardly exemplary, is understandable — far more understandable than Austria's stupid obstinacy in refusing to give her the "compensation" and the assurances that would have brought her into the war on the side of the Central Powers. And it can be argued that the Italian government had a good case for remaining neutral. Italy had not been consulted about the diplomatic moves that had led to war, though she had certainly been entitled to such consideration. The criticism that can justly be leveled at Italian diplomacy in July 1914 is not that she betrayed the Triple Alliance then, but that she deliberately put herself on the auction block for sale to the highest bidder, and that this had been her intention for years, regardless of her treaty obligations. The Italian betrayal had taken place in 1902.

A legend has developed that it was the German invasion of Belgium that brought Britain into the war at the side of France and Russia, but a closer consideration of events does not support this view. The overwhelming majority of the British Liberal cabinet was in favor of Britain's remaining neutral unless attacked, but Asquith, Grey, and Churchill favored the full support of France. On the morning of August 1 Sir Edward Grey sent Sir William Tyrrell, his private secretary, to the German ambassador to ask whether, if France remained neutral in a war between Russia and Germany, Germany would guarantee not to attack France. Grey later telephoned Lichnowsky and repeated this query. The German ambassador assured Grey that Germany would accept such terms. When the matter was discussed in Berlin later that day, General Moltke objected that the German plan of mobilization called for deployment against both Russia and France, and that mobilization plans involving millions of men could not be improvised overnight. The kaiser replied, with justifiable annoyance, "Your uncle would have given me a different answer." Germany then promptly accepted the British offer;* Bethmann telegraphed his acceptance to Lichnowsky and the kaiser telegraphed his to King George. However, Grey by now had had second thoughts. He pretended that his offer to

---

*This fact has been consistently suppressed by historians who claim that Moltke's arguments carried the day. The truth is exactly the contrary. Moltke's objections were promptly and unceremoniously overridden.

Lichnowsky had all been a misunderstanding; and the offer was withdrawn. It had been an impossible idea in the first place, but Grey's attempt to evade the responsibility for it was less than creditable.*

Germany had already given strong indications that in the event of war it was her intention to attack France through Belgium. On August 1 Grey asked both France and Germany if they were prepared to respect the neutrality of Belgium. The French government promptly replied that it would, unless Belgian neutrality was violated by some other power. This decision had, in fact, been reached in November 1912, when General Joseph Joffre, the French commander-in-chief, learning of British political objections to a French invasion of Belgium, had modified his own plan, which had previously called for such an invasion. The German ambassador, Lichnowsky, asked Grey whether, if Germany respected Belgian neutrality, Britain would remain neutral. Grey's reply was that he could not give such a promise. Lichnowsky then asked whether it would not be possible for Britain to remain neutral if Germany also promised to respect the integrity of France and her colonies. Grey likewise refused this offer, saying that Britain must "keep her hands free."

Paul Cambon, the French ambassador in London, was far from satisfied with this attitude of Grey's and he now proceeded to remind the British that by the naval agreement of 1912 France had left her coasts undefended, relying on the protection of the Royal Navy. Churchill's prediction of 1912 was thus borne out in every particular.

The British cabinet still had a majority that favored neutrality, and for a time it looked very much as though Asquith and Grey would be forced to resign, which would break up the government. However, the Conservative party now came to the rescue of the Liberals who wanted Britain in the war. The Liberal imperialists in Asquith's cabinet, blinded by their imperialism, their economic and strategic calculations, and their class interest, may have had little idea of where their country's true interests lay; but the tragic fact is that the only alternative to Asquith's government, the Conservatives, was blinder still, and for basically the same reasons.

On August 2 Asquith received a letter from Andrew Bonar Law, the leader of the opposition, which read:

> Lord Lansdowne and I feel it our duty to inform you that, in our opinion, as well as that of the colleagues whom we have been able to consult, any hesitation now in supporting France and Russia would be fatal to the honour and future security of the United Kingdom, and we offer H.M. Gov-

---

*For a full discussion of this incident, the reader is referred to L. Albertini, *The Origins of the War of 1914*, vol. III, pp. 380–86.

ernment the assurances of the united support of the Opposition in all measures required by England's intervention in the war.

This meant, of course, that Asquith was saved, for he could now, if
necessary, form a coalition government with the support of the Conservatives. So strengthened, Grey and Asquith, at two o'clock that afternoon, were able to obtain cabinet authorization to promise France
that the Royal Navy would intervene to prevent the German fleet
from attacking the French coast. This authorization was given five
hours before the delivery of the German ultimatum to Belgium. John
Burns, the trade-union member of the cabinet, promptly resigned in
protest, and that evening Lord Morley, the old Gladstonian Liberal,
quietly told Asquith that he, too, would resign.

Before Lord Morley left, he presented to the cabinet a strong plea
for British neutrality, which included a strangely prophetic utterance:

> Have you ever thought what will happen if Russia wins? If Germany is
> beaten and Austria beaten it is not England and France who will emerge
> pre-eminent in Europe. It will be Russia. Will that be good for Western
> civilization? I at least don't think so.

The cabinet listened intently. Well they might have done, for they
were hearing the voice of Cassandra. The war that was begun in 1914
did not find its true end until 1945, but when it was really over, Lord
Morley's prediction had come true in every particular.

Paul Cambon, naturally enough, reacted differently from Burns
and Lord Morley to the British cabinet's decision:

> I heaved a sigh of relief, as you can well believe. I felt that the battle was
> won. Everything was settled. In truth a great country does not wage war by
> halves. Once it decided to fight the war at sea it would necessarily be led into
> fighting it on land as well.

On the night of August 2 the German ambassador in Brussels presented his government's ultimatum to Belgium. With German
thoroughness, it had been drafted previously and sent to Brussels well
ahead of time. Germany demanded free passage for her troops, the
surrender of the Belgian army, and the handing over of the Belgian
fortresses. To justify these terms, Germany claimed, falsely, that
France was about to invade Belgium, but promised the restoration of
Belgian sovereignty at the end of the war and an indemnity that
would cover the costs of a German occupation.

Grey had already informed Paul Cambon that Britain would not
regard the invasion of Luxembourg as sufficient cause for going to

war; but Belgium was another matter. Belgium had a seacoast. By the Treaty of London, signed on May 11, 1876, the European powers, severally and individually, had guaranteed the neutrality of Belgium, but the treaty had also gone on specifically to state that

> by a collective guarantee it is understood that, while in honour all the Powers who are parties to it severally engage to maintain, for their own part, a strict respect for the territory for which neutrality is guaranteed . . . yet a single Power is not bound to take up the cudgels for all the other Powers with whom she gave a collective guarantee.

This meant, very plainly, that, while Britain was herself obliged to respect Belgian neutrality, she had no obligation to defend that neutrality if it was violated by another power also signatory to the treaty.

Sir Edward Grey and the British cabinet were well aware of this. Prime Minister Asquith wrote to King George on the subject: "The Cabinet consider that the matter, if it arises, will be one of policy rather than of legal obligation." It was a nice legal point, but one that was not made clear to the British public.

Belgium, alone of the nations who went to war in the summer of 1914, had clean hands and a clear conscience. King Albert was a king out of legend, and of all those who talked of honor that disastrous summer he alone knew the true meaning of the word. There could be no doubt of what Belgium's decision meant for her — the Germans were desperately in earnest and were earnest in their desperation. The horrors that were to come upon Belgium were foreseen — the women and children killed or mangled, the cities destroyed, the long, long list of dead, the possible extinction of the nation. The decision taken by King Albert and his cabinet in the Royal Palace at Brussels on the night of August 2 shines like a pure light in the darkness of a barbarous and pagan century. Unanimously and with almost no discussion, the king and his government decided to reject the German ultimatum:

> Belgium has always been faithful to her international obligations; she has accomplished her duties in a spirit of loyal impartiality . . . Were the Belgian Government to accept the propositions conveyed to it, it would be sacrificing the nation's honour and betraying its engagements to Europe . . .

In his first draft of the ultimatum to Belgium, Moltke had attempted to bribe the Belgian government by an offer of French territory, but the German Foreign Office, belatedly showing some political acumen, had deleted this shameful suggestion. What remained was shameful enough, and Moltke knew it. Perhaps it was this, more than any other thing, that broke his spirit in the war, for men who are not dead to conscience find it hard to go against their better natures.

King Albert had no such difficulties. In all that desperate crisis, he lost his composure only once, for a few seconds. He had received a personal letter from the kaiser, urging acceptance of the terms of the German ultimatum and reminding him that he was himself a German prince. When he read this letter, King Albert indulged in a brief outburst of profanity — a very rare thing for him, for he was a religious man.

Germany began her invasion of Belgium on the morning of August 3. Asquith and Grey thereupon drafted an ultimatum to Germany, demanding that she respect Belgian neutrality; an answer was required by midnight on August 4. The ultimatum was dispatched at two o'clock on the afternoon of the 4th, and when no answer had been received by midnight Britain announced that a state of war existed between herself and Germany.

On the same day, after Paris had witnessed the moving funeral of Jean Jaurès in the morning,* the French Chamber listened to Viviani read an inaccurate and disingenuous message from Poincaré on the causes of the war. No mention was made of the Russian general mobilization, which had been the point of no return; and Poincaré lied about Russia's readiness to accept Grey's proposal for a *Halt in Belgrade*. Viviani then spoke on his own behalf, saying, among other things, that "Italy, with the clarity of insight possessed by the Latin intellect, has notified us that she proposes to preserve neutrality."

The French and Russian ministers in Bucharest had been working long and hard to prevail on Rumania not to honor her treaty with Germany and Austria. King Carol felt morally bound by the alliance, but Bratianu, the prime minister and minister of war, had no such old-fashioned ideas. He was, it is true, afraid of the German army, but on the other hand he was very much tempted by Sazonov's promise, made on July 31, to give Rumania Transylvania. The French ambassador at Bucharest, Blondel, was wiser than his Russian colleague, Poklevski, who was urging Rumania to enter the war on the Entente's

---

*Jean Jaurès, the French Socialist leader, had been a defender of Dreyfus, a foe of French imperialism in Morocco, and a vocal opponent of Poincaré's July visit to St. Petersburg. The right-wing *Paris Midi* had declaimed, on July 17:

> If on the eve of war a general were to detail half a dozen men and a corporal to put Citizen Jaurès up against a wall and pump the lead he needs into his brain at pointblank range — do you think the general would be doing anything but his elemental duty?

The work was done, not by half a dozen men and a corporal, but by a young French "patriot," Raoul Villain, who shot Jaurès through the open window of the café where he was dining on the night of July 31. Villain was tried for murder, and, like Mme. Caillaux, acquitted.

side. Blondel merely pressed for Rumania to declare her neutrality —
as a first step. This step the Rumanian cabinet took on August 3.

Two days later Montenegro declared war on Austria, much to the
distress of King Nicholas, who, when the time came, was far less anxious to fight than were his two daughters in Russia. Nicholas had become increasingly disturbed as he had learned more about the
Sarajevo assassinations — not unreasonably, for, as time was to prove,
he himself had some personal reason to fear Dimitrievich's Serbian
assassins. Montenegro's decision to go to the aid of Serbia did not save
her independence; after the war she was swallowed up in the South
Slav state of Yugoslavia.

Bulgaria, still smarting from her defeat in the Second Balkan War,
rejected the advances made by Serbia and Russia; she declared her
neutrality. Greece did the same. But on the other side of the world
Japan declared war on Germany on August 23. Britain had not originally desired Japan's participation, which was not at all called for
under the Anglo-Japanese treaty of 1902, but the Japanese, seeing an
opportunity to seize Germany's possessions in China, were not to be
denied.

Belatedly, and only after some pointed queries from Berlin, Austria
got around to declaring war on Russia at 6:00 P.M. on August 6.

To understand the rapidity with which Europe slid into the abyss, it
is necessary to bear in mind the German strategic position. As General
Boisdeffre had pointed out to the tsar in 1894, "Mobilization meant
war" for every nation. But this was especially true of Germany, both
because she was so greatly outnumbered by her opponents and because of the German war plan, which had been largely shaped by the
realization of Germany's numerical inferiority. Open to attack from
both the east and the west, from Russia and France, Germany would
be facing armies about twice the size of the combined German and
Austrian forces. If Germany divided her army more or less equally,
placing half in the east to face Russia and half in the west to face
France, the preponderance of strength against her might be impossible to withstand.

The plan that was finally adopted was worked out by Schlieffen,
who was Chief of the General Staff between 1891 and 1905. Schlieffen decided that the only possible course for Germany when faced
with a war on two fronts was first to concentrate to defeat one enemy
decisively, then to turn and deal with the other. Germany, in fact,
would have to fight two separate, consecutive wars, using almost the
whole of her concentrated strength for each. This course of action
was possible only because Germany could mobilize much more
rapidly than Russia. What Schlieffen was proposing to do was to

exploit this gap in time, between the completion of the German and Russian mobilizations, for a sudden attack on France. Three considerations made France the target for the first attack: she could mobilize far more rapidly than Russia and was therefore initially the more dangerous adversary; the Russian concentration might take place too far to the east for Germany to reach, so that any spoiling attack might fail; and, finally, the Russians might in any case retire "into the interior of [their] enormous empire," thus depriving Germany of the decisive victory she had to have.

The gap in time between the completion of the German and Russian mobilizations was no more than six weeks. In that six weeks, therefore, France had to be knocked out of the war, freeing Germany to turn east again and deal with the forces that would by then be pouring over her eastern frontiers. The margin of time was desperately small, and Schlieffen's plan was incredibly bold; everything was staked on Germany's being able utterly to defeat the French army, which was larger than the German army, within forty-two days.

But how to defeat France in six weeks? The French frontier with Germany was only some 150 miles long, and nearly half of it was covered by the Vosges mountains, with only the Belfort Gap providing any ready means of entry. Worse still, France had extended her natural defenses by a chain of fortifications that ran by way of Belfort, Epinal, Toul, and Verdun to the borders of Luxembourg and Belgium. Just past Verdun lay the Ardennes district, hilly and wooded and bound to slow any advance. Schlieffen was convinced, in any case, that frontal attacks could never achieve more than limited success, because the enemy, even if defeated, could usually fall back and fight again. From the German point of view, this kind of war was of no use at all, for with every hour that final victory was delayed in the west the Russian masses would be growing larger in the east. From his study of military history,* Schlieffen concluded that a decisive battle of annihilation was possible only if the enemy could be outflanked and enveloped. He regarded Hannibal's victory over the Romans at Cannae as the classic example of this type of operation.

There were, of course, only two flanks to the French defensive line. If the Germans moved by their left, they would have to pass through the Jura mountains of Switzerland, and their advance would be fatally delayed; they would, moreover, debouch far from any vital point in France. However, intensive studies made during staff rides convinced Schlieffen that, by moving very wide to the right, through Luxembourg, Belgium, and the Maastricht Appendix of Holland, it would be

*For a time, Schlieffen had served as director of the German army's Historical Section.

possible to by-pass the French defenses. The invasion of Dutch territory seemed necessary to Schlieffen because any German advance north of the Ardennes would run into the defile of the deep-cut Meuse valley, which was blocked by the formidable Belgian fortress of Liège. By marching north of Liège, through the Maastricht Appendix, the Germans could by-pass the flank of the Liège forts. Thus Schlieffen, at the same time as he was exploiting a gap in time, was also exploiting a gap in space. This double exploitation of the enemy's weaknesses was the key to the plan and a measure of the brilliance of Schlieffen's strategic concepts.

Schlieffen and the General Staff did not worry unduly about the morality of this plan of campaign. They believed that France intended to violate Belgian territory no matter what Germany did, and Schlieffen was shrewdly convinced that a German concentration in the Aix-la-Chapelle area could certainly lure the French army into crossing the Belgian frontier and taking up the natural defensive position in the Meuse valley south of Namur. By so manipulating the French, Germany would escape the odium of being the first to violate Belgian neutrality. We have seen that, until 1912, the French were indeed planning to invade Belgium, and that it was the political consideration of England's attitude that caused them to abandon the plan. Germany would have been much wiser to allow similar political considerations to modify her military plans. Such a modification would not have prevented Britain from going to war at France's side, but it would have meant Britain's entering the war divided, and the British government would subsequently have been under great pressure to accept a compromise peace. Schlieffen also hoped that both Belgium and Holland would do no more than protest a German invasion and would not oppose it by force of arms. None of these considerations, of course, can absolve Schlieffen from deliberately planning the invasion of three inoffensive neutral nations, two of which were expressly guaranteed by Germany against just such a violation.

Schlieffen devised his plan from the narrowest of military viewpoints, caring only for the quick victory in the west that Germany had to have. The invasion of Belgium would almost certainly be the signal for bringing Britain into the war against Germany, but Schlieffen, the pure military technician, was quite prepared to accept this. He asked himself only how large the British Expeditionary Force would be and where it would be employed. He was staking everything on a short and decisive campaign in France, and therefore did not feel it necessary to consider what influence the Royal Navy might exert in a long war or whether Britain might, in time, raise large new armies. Schlieffen had read and admired Bismarck's witty comment that if British forces invaded Germany he would have them arrested, and in

his plan he wrote that the British Expeditionary Force could easily be
shut up in Antwerp along with the remnants of the Belgian army.
They would, he said, be "securely billeted in the fortress much better
than on their island . . ." Indeed, if the bulk of the British Regular
Army could be trapped in Antwerp, that would be far better from the
German point of view than having it free to make seaborne descents
upon the German coast.

Schlieffen planned to leave only ten divisions in East Prussia to
guard against a Russian advance. All the rest of the German army
would be employed in the west against France, and the bulk of it
would go to the swinging right wing, which would pivot on Metz, pass
through Belgium and northern France, cross the Seine just above
Rouen, sweep around Paris to the west and south, and hammer the
French army back against the Swiss frontier. This hammerhead of a
right wing was to be "as strong as possible," Schlieffen emphasized,
and he allotted seventy-nine divisions to it — in theory, at least, for in
fact the German army in 1905 had only about eighty-one equivalent
divisions all told.* The German left wing, holding the line from Metz
to the Swiss frontier, was to be given only nine divisions, some Land-
wehr forces, and the garrisons of Metz and Strasbourg. Since Schlieffen rightly anticipated that at the outset of the war the French would
launch heavy attacks against Alsace-Lorraine, he planned for his left
wing to swing back, again pivoting on Metz, to lure the French away
from the decisive northern sector.

Schlieffen stipulated that ninety-four equivalent divisions would be
needed for the west, but in fact the German army never had so large a
disposable force at its command. Worse still, Schlieffen calculated that
he would have to detach six or seven army corps to invest the "gigantic
fortress" of Paris, and, consequently, the decisive battle south of Paris
would find the German army seriously short of soldiers. This would
have been true if only the French had to be faced, but the addition of
the Belgians and the British to the French order of battle and the later
subtraction of the five Italian corps and two cavalry divisions that were
to have fought at Germany's side in France† were to make the German troop shortage desperate.

*In the final 1905 version of his plan, Schlieffen pointed out with some indignation
that France, with a population of only 39 million, could provide 995 battalions for her
field army, while Germany, with a population of 56 million, provided only 971
battalions.
†In spite of many indications to the contrary, Moltke always believed that Italy would
honor her commitments under the Triple Alliance and "come to the rendezvous." But
at the time of the Italo-Turkish War in 1911 the Italian General Staff informed Moltke
that, because a strong force had to be retained in North Africa, the five army corps and
two cavalry divisions Italy had promised to send to the Rhine would not be forthcom-
ing. Moltke continued to count on Italy's holding French forces on the Franco-Italian
frontier. The French, of course, knew better.

This is one of the strangest aspects of the Schlieffen Plan and a further proof that Germany was not plotting aggressive war. The entire Schlieffen Plan was an enormous gamble in any case, and the odds against the gamble's succeeding were greatly lengthened by the fact that Germany never had sufficient troops to field the minimum force that Schlieffen considered necessary. Thus the plan, though brilliant, was riddled with imperfections and inadequacies.

General Helmuth von Moltke, the nephew of the great field marshal, had succeeded Schlieffen as Chief of the General Staff in December 1905. Moltke had not wanted the job, and he told the kaiser that he was "too reflective, too scrupulous, and, if you like, too conscientious for such a post." Wilhelm insisted, however, because he had been attracted by Moltke's famous name. Moltke was far from happy with the Schlieffen Plan; it was, he considered, far too much of a gamble. He was right, but his attempts to make it less of a gamble injured rather than improved its chances of success. Worried about the weakness of the German left wing from Metz to the Swiss frontier, and fearful lest a French offensive should cut in behind him and sever his lines of communication, Moltke allotted most of the new divisions that became available between 1905 and 1914 to the left wing rather than to the right. By doing so, Moltke gained a fancied security but ran, in reality, a far greater risk, for the whole point of Schlieffen's concept had been the weight of the swinging hammerhead of the right wing. The concentration of force on the right and the roundabout approach were to ensure that the German army would fight its decisive battle with a local superiority of force. The calculation was by no means certain, however, for the French might be able to switch their forces to the threatened sector in time to thwart the Germans. For this reason, the weakness of the German left was as much an integral part of the plan as was the strength of the right. The more deeply the French became committed to Alsace, the less hope they would have of extricating themselves in time and concentrating to meet the German swoop from the north. Moltke, by altering the relative strengths of his wings, proved that he had misunderstood the essence of Schlieffen's thought.

The second important change initiated by Moltke was the cancellation of the invasion of Dutch territory. He wrote:

> A hostile Holland at our back could have disastrous consequences for the advance of the German army to the west. Particularly if England should use the violation of Belgian neutrality as a pretext for entering the war against us . . .
>
> Furthermore it will be very important to have in Holland a country whose neutrality allows us to have imports and supplies. She must be the windpipe that enables us to breathe.

These comments are highly significant because they show that Moltke had already lost confidence in that speedy victory in the west that Germany had to have. "Imports and supplies" are vital considerations in any protracted war, but are of insignificant importance in a six-week campaign.

As the alternative to marching across the Maastricht Appendix, Moltke ruled that the potential bottleneck in the Meuse valley at Liège would have to be cleared at the very outset. He wrote:

> However awkward it may be, the advance through Belgium must therefore take place without the violation of Dutch territory. This will hardly be possible unless Liège is in our hands. I think it possible to take it by a *coup de main* . . . Everything depends on meticulous preparation and surprise. The enterprise is only possible if the attack is made at once, before the areas between the forts are fortified. It must therefore be undertaken by standing troops immediately war is declared. The capture of a modern fortress by a *coup de main* would be something unprecedented in military history. But it can succeed and must be attempted, for the possession of Liège is the *sine qua non* of our advance.

Holland was therefore spared from German invasion in 1914, but the necessity for the immediate capture of Liège at the outbreak of war meant that Belgium had to be invaded while the German mobilization was still going on. The time available for last-minute diplomacy was thus further shortened. Too much should perhaps not be made of this, however, for even in the original Schlieffen Plan little time was allowed for diplomatic measures. This was not an evidence of German "militarism," but a reflection of the bitterly harsh strategic realities with which Germany was faced.

The French plan of campaign, Plan XVII, which was completed in February 1914 under the direction of General Joffre, could not have fitted in better with German intentions if it had been devised by the Prussian General Staff. Plan XVII exuded that spirit of the offensive that had permeated French military thinking for the previous two decades. "Whatever the circumstances," the plan's preamble read, "it is the Commander-in-Chief's intentions to advance with all forces united to the attack of the German armies." French forces were to be assembled in five great armies: the First Army under General Auguste Dubail around Epinal, the Second under General Edouard de Castelnau around Toul, the Third under General Ruffey around Verdun, the Fifth under General Charles Lanrezac around Reims, and the Fourth Army under General Fernand de Langle de Cary in strategic reserve in the area behind Verdun.

It was intended that the British Expeditionary Force of about 160,000 men should concentrate on the extreme French left around

Le Cateau, but this was not included as an integral part of Plan XVII. (There is, indeed, some evidence that the French General Staff believed that the French army alone and unaided could defeat the Germans. Some years before 1914, when General Sir Henry Wilson had asked General Ferdinand Foch how many men Britain should send to the continent, Foch had replied: "Only one. And we'll take good care that he gets killed.")

Joffre had anticipated that Germany would invade Belgium, but he did not believe that the Germans would move in force west of the Meuse. A German advance through Belgium, in fact, was welcomed by the French for military as well as for political reasons, since Joffre calculated that if the enemy strengthened his right wing, either his left or his center must be weak. He therefore proposed, "whatever the circumstance," to attack first the German left in the country between the wooded district of the Vosges and the Moselle River below Toul, and to launch a second offensive against the German center north of a line from Verdun to Metz. The French intelligence staff actually succeeded in underestimating by twelve corps the German strength in the west. At the outbreak of the war, the French planned to use only their regular army, because they did not believe their reserve formations sufficiently trained. In this, they may well have been right, but they made the mistake of assuming the enemy followed a similar plan, and were therefore most unpleasantly surprised. Indeed, it was only the gross French military errors and miscalculations in August 1914 that to some extent compensated Germany for her shortage of troops and allowed the Schlieffen Plan to be as successful as it was.

Russia would have liked to concentrate first against Austria, and to leave the clash with Germany until the full Russian strength had been mobilized. Unfortunately, the military annex to the Dual Entente was quite specific and made such a strategy impossible. The French had insisted that a Russian attack against Germany be launched as soon as possible after the outbreak of war so as to relieve the pressure on their own forces in the west. The Russians agreed, with some misgivings, and the Russian plan, as a consequence, called for the advance of two Russian armies into East Prussia during the third week after mobilization. One Russian army would move north of the Masurian Lakes to turn the left flank of the defending German forces and cut it off from the fortress of Königsberg. A few days later, a second Russian army would march north from Warsaw, well to the west of the Masurian Lakes, to operate against the rear of the German defenders and cut them off from the Vistula.

The other four of Russia's initial six armies were to mount an offensive against the Austrians in Galicia. The main Russian offensive was to be launched toward Lemberg from the east with two strong armies, while a secondary offensive would drive down on the Austrian rear by way of Krasnik, Zamosc, and Komarov.)

The Austrians also had offensive plans — too many, in fact, because they had one plan for dealing with Serbia and another for attacking Russia. Conrad divided the Austrian army into three groups: Echelon A, of twenty-eight divisions, for use against Russia; Minimum Balkan, of eight divisions, for use against Serbia; Echelon B, of twelve divisions, in strategic reserve. Since Berchtold and Conrad were both anxious to get on with the business of crushing Serbia, Echelon B had begun to move toward the Serbian frontier the week before the war became general. On July 31, when it was apparent that Russia would attack, Conrad ordered Echelon B back to the Galician front. This was more than the Austrian railway system could cope with, and it was necessary for Echelon B to complete the move to the Sava, detrain, and then entrain again to be transported to Galicia. At the outbreak of general war, then, the Austrian forces were already in considerable disarray before they had met any foe in the field.

It has often been claimed that Europe was ripe for war between 1904 and 1914. "There was a strange temper in the air," Winston Churchill later recalled, and Theodor Wolff, the editor of the *Berliner Tageblatt*, said that "the light had grown more livid." On the other hand, these were hindsights, the recollections of men who had passed across the chasm of the war and whose judgments must therefore be treated with caution. It is more probable that the strange temper in the air and the livid light are the conjurings of retrospection. Indeed, it may actually be that the absence of such premonitions was a major contributing cause to the disaster. Of all the more general explanations, perhaps the least dissatisfying is that European statescraft prior to 1914 was governed by obsolete concepts that had not been adjusted to an industrialized age or to the implications of industrialized warfare. Ignorance rather than unusual wickedness may be said to have been responsible for the catastrophe. Even this, however, begs the ultimate question, for wickedness and the perverse heart of man, of course, lay at the bottom of it. But the wickedness that was responsible for 1914 was no more heinous than that of previous ages; men were merely sillier and more feckless because they failed to realize how enormously technology had raised the stakes in the game of war.

After all this has been said, however, it still remains true that, at one level, the First World War was brought about because of the shortcomings of a handful of individuals who were significant because they held in their hands the direction of policy. There is no doubt, either, that had those individuals acted differently the war could have been avoided. Thus, the assertion that it was all an accident, the stumbling of foolish men into an abyss, is much nearer the truth than either the simplistic view that the losers were to blame or the general explanation that indicts all European civilization. The statesmen of 1914 were certainly on the whole a poor and pitiable crowd, and there must always be a sense of wonderment that so great a tragedy was staged by such small actors. But it was.

Finally, to understand how the war came about, it is necessary to look at the interests of the powers. When this viewpoint is adopted, certain landmarks are clear. It was in the interests of Germany, Austria, and Britain to keep the peace. It was, under certain circumstances and certain presuppositions, in the interests of France and Russia to go to war. Desire and longing are the whips of God, and when the two revisionist powers, each with its separate offensive ambitions, united in the Dual Entente, peace was at once in jeopardy.

Germany also had her dreams, and it would be incorrect to underestimate their influence on events. Germany aspired to be a world power among the other world powers, to have colonies, a navy, and a right to be consulted in world affairs. These were, of course, foolish and vain ambitions, and led to foolish words and imaginings. But there is absolutely no evidence that any German government between 1871 and 1914 sought to realize those ambitions by war. There was no need to do so. Germany was the strongest industrial power in the world after the United States and Britain, and though the gap between the United States and Germany was widening, the gap between Britain and Germany was rapidly narrowing. Both the British and the Germans were aware of this.

Any impartial examination of the three great crises of the twentieth century that preceded the climax of 1914 must present a very different picture of the relative morality of the European states than that commonly presented by the historians of the Entente powers. In the first Moroccan crisis, a secret, imperialist agreement between France and Britain was the basis for French designs against an independent nation. France wanted to annex Morocco; Britain had promised, in secret, to help her do so in return for French assistance in the British annexation of Egypt. Germany opposed this change in the status quo — for a complex of reasons, not all of them creditable and none of them idealistic. Yet it is surely better to be on the right side for the wrong reasons than to be on the wrong side for reasons that are also wrong.

In the Bosnian crisis of 1908–1909, Austria played a more dubious and ambiguous role, for, strictly speaking, she had no right to annex Bosnia and Herzegovina without the consent of the powers signatory to the Treaty of Berlin.* Yet she had not promised not to annex the provinces. She had been repeatedly urged by other nations to do so; and before she took that action she had obtained the consent of the Russian foreign minister, who, presumably, represented the only power at all likely to object to the annexation. In any case, it was all done without Germany's knowledge.

The second Moroccan crisis, in 1911, was consequent on the first and had the same origin. France wanted to annex Morocco, and Britain had promised to help her do so. The flagrant imperial drive of France was at the root of this quarrel as it had been at the root of the quarrel in 1905.

Historians are still steaming cheerfully ahead in the artificial darkness created by the smokescreens that were thrown up by France and Britain at the time of these crises. The secret agreements to annex Egypt and Morocco are clauses "of no importance." Germany threatened Russia with war in 1909, when in fact all she did was threaten to let events take their course and allow Aehrenthal to publish the documents that would prove Izvolsky a liar. The German army was the greatest on the continent, when in fact it was outnumbered by the French army and enormously outnumbered by the Russian. Anyone whose life has been vitally affected by this sort of misrepresentation must feel a natural indignation on learning the truth. And which of us alive today has not been vitally affected?

But indignation is a profitless emotion. So it is perhaps better to go on with the analysis of how the old world died and say no more for now about the cost.

In truth, too, hubris was not the monopoly of any European nation by 1914. All of them, like Ephraim, were joined to their idols, and Germany not least. It was the German hubris, more than any other fault, that led to Germany's destruction and dismemberment. The statesmen and soldiers in all nations profoundly misunderstood the true nature of twentieth-century war. Their imaginations utterly failed to grasp the military implications of the mass armies and the weapon systems that would be employed. They believed that a major European war would be short, that it would be decisive, that it was, indeed, still a suitable instrument of policy. All these beliefs were fallacious.

In the fateful summer of 1914 the German calculation was, first of

*Incidentally, Austria in 1908 acted just as Russia had acted in 1870, when she unilaterally denounced the Black Sea clauses of the Treaty of Paris, but *tu quoque* is a poor argument.

all, that Austria had to deal harshly with Serbia if the Dual Monarchy was to survive, a proposition with which it is difficult to quarrel. Enough has been said about the conduct and nature of Serbia to indicate the strong probability that Austria, if she was not passively to acquiesce in her own dissolution, had little choice but to deal sternly with the Serbian menace. This, of course, must to some extent remain an open question, since it is a hypothesis contrary to fact. Austria *might* have survived without attacking Serbia, but it did not seem likely at the time, nor does it seem likely in retrospect. Second, Germany shared Austria's indignation against Serbia and could not bring herself to believe that even Russia would go to war in support of a nation that pursued its policies by such means. (Russian statesmen, ambassadors, and military attachés, as well as the Pan-Slav war party in Russia itself, had encouraged the Serbian aggressiveness toward Austria, including the final aggression of the murder of the heir apparent to the Austrian throne.) Much of this encouragement may have been given in contradiction to Russia's official foreign policy, but neither Sazonov nor the tsar took steps to prevent it. So Germany was wrong in her belief that Russia would admit the justice of the Austrian grievance against Serbia. (Third, Germany miscalculated what Britain would do. The German Foreign Office had been repeatedly assured by Sir Edward Grey that Britain was not bound by any alliance to France or Russia; Anglo-German relations had notably improved in the previous eighteen months; Britain had no interest of her own in the Balkans; and Sir Edward Grey had shown himself not insensible to the justice of the Austrian complaints against Serbia. Finally, Germany calculated — and was surely correct in doing so — that if Britain remained neutral there would be no war because France and Russia would not dare to attack Germany and Austria without British help.)

The chain of German logic broke down most seriously on its third link, and it is exactly here that Britain must bear some share of responsibility for the outbreak of war. The fatal inconsistency and contradiction in British policy that had begun with the secret Anglo-French staff talks in 1905 later confused and darkened the international scene. If the real aims of the powers in July 1914 are examined, it will be found that Britain sincerely wanted peace, complete peace if possible. But if such peace was not possible and a small Austro-Serbian war could not be avoided, Britain hoped that Austria could be persuaded to halt her advance after the occupation of Belgrade and that Russia would accept this, on the guarantee that Austria would not annex any Serbian territory. However, certain senior cabinet ministers in the British government were also determined that if a major war broke out Britain would not stand aside and allow Germany and

Austria to defeat France and Russia. They do not seem seriously to have contemplated the far more likely eventuality that if Britain stood aside there would be no war because France and Russia would not provoke one. This line of conduct would, of course, have meant a "diplomatic defeat" for the Dual Entente, but this argument is circular, since it would have meant a diplomatic defeat for the Entente only because of the Entente's firm stand in defense of Serbia; and that firm stand in defense of Serbia was adopted, in very large measure, because the French were sure of British support.

Thus, it would be fair to say that British policy was thoroughly confused in 1914. It was based on the inherent contradictions of believing that Britain retained her freedom of action and, at the same time, admitting a binding moral obligation to go to the support of France in however dubious a cause. Furthermore, it was not a policy that the British cabinet as a whole understood or agreed with. It was fortunate for Grey's reputation that Germany made the mistake of invading Belgium. Britain did not go to war in defense of Belgium. The decision to go to war was taken before the German invasion of Belgium, and on quite other grounds. What Belgium provided was a rallying cry, an ideal piece of propaganda, that united the British people as nothing else could have done. Had Germany not invaded Belgium, Britain would still have gone to war, but she would have entered the conflict disunited and uncertain.

Germany and Austria both wanted war in July 1914, but not a major European war. They wanted a small, localized, punitive war of Austria against Serbia. They calculated, for the reasons mentioned, that they could achieve this. Once it began to appear that this calculation was incorrect, Germany tried desperately to put on the brakes and restrain Austria. Count Berchtold, however, was not to be restrained, and with reckless stupidity held to his collision course. Had Britain, at any time prior to July 28, when Austria declared war on Serbia, frankly informed Germany that she would go to war beside France or frankly informed France that she would not go to war in defense of Serbian assassins, war could have been avoided.

If a case is to be made for German guilt for the outbreak of the First World War, it must rest on Germany's readiness to support Austria in a war against Serbia and on Germany's encouragement to Austria to fight such a war. All the rest of the arguments that have been put forward in such profusion since 1914 are a mere muddying of the waters, intended to conceal and confuse the truth. The building of a large German navy was undoubtedly an error, but it was not a moral fault. Not even Britain went so far as to claim that she was the only nation with a moral right to a fleet.

Austrian guilt is far more direct than German, and it lies not in Aus-

tria's desire to fight a punitive war against Serbia, but in Count Berchtold's readiness to persevere in his course even when it became apparent that this would result in a major European war. This obstinacy was
both criminal and unintelligent — if, in the last analysis, these adjec-
tives are not nearly synonymous in international affairs.

The Russian aims in July 1914 are more difficult to assess because
of the opposing influences on Russian policy. The tsar sincerely
wanted peace, but he was neither clever enough nor strong enough to
assert his will. The triumph of the war party in Russia was achieved by
persuading both the tsar and Sazonov to act against their better
judgment. What Russia hoped to gain by war was the control of the
Balkans, Constantinople, and the Dardanelles. To these aims can be
added the personal desire of Izvolsky for revenge against Austria and
the Pan-Slav desire to eliminate the Austro-German bloc in central
Europe, which stood in the way of Russia's drive to the southeast.
What Russia hoped to prevent by the war was the loss of Russian prestige in the Balkans and the weakening, and possible disruption, of the
Dual Entente. It should be noted that here again there is an element
of circularity in the argument, for Russian prestige had been staked
on Russia's forward policy in the Balkans, and that forward policy had
been possible only because of the strength gained by the alliance with
France. Russia's true interests, of course, had nothing in common
with such grandiose aims, as Stolypin had realized very clearly. For a
nation such as Russia to concern herself with international prestige
and the acquisition of vast new territories when her internal social and
economic problems meant that she was perpetually on the brink of
revolution was a stupidity of incredible magnitude. In 1914, all the
major powers believed that they were stronger than they were, and
acted in the light of this belief, but the Russian miscalculation was by
all odds the one most wide of the mark.

We come at last to the aims of France.* Ever since Poincaré had
come to power, French policy had aimed at achieving a state of affairs
that would make possible the regaining of Alsace-Lorraine and the
humbling of Germany. These results had, indeed, been desired by
French governments ever since 1871, but they had never been the
principal objectives of government policy. Rather, they had been
hopes that had appeared impossible of fulfillment, dreams to be indulged in, not goals to be attained. What Poincaré brought to the

*Perhaps here it should be pointed out — what is surely, in any case, evident — that
when the historian speaks of "France," or "Russia," or "Britain," he is employing a sort
of shorthand. He does not mean the totality of those nations but is, rather, speaking
only of the French or the Russian or the British government, and even, in many cases,
only of that sector of the government actually responsible for the policy under discussion.

conduct of affairs was a single-mindedness and a ruthlessness that had previously been absent. As is sometimes the case with men devoid of religious faith, Poincaré had found a substitute for religion — the holy cause, the sacred soil, the lands made infinitely beautiful and infinitely desirable by being lost. Such secular mysticism is the most terrible of emotions.   *Premère*

(France — that is to say, Poincaré and those of like mind — wanted war. Not a small, limited war in the Balkans, but a great European war by which alone Alsace-Lorraine could be restored to France.) In the pursuit of this aim there was, of course, very real delusion. The French military appreciation of 1912, which had decided Poincaré that the hour had struck, was — even though it was proved to be justified by subsequent events — an erroneous, overly optimistic, and ill-considered opinion. France at last regained Alsace-Lorraine, but at a cost in her young dead that was greater than the combined populations of those two provinces. Other costs (some of them still being paid) to France, her allies, Europe, and the world it will be part of the subsequent business of this book to reveal.

The case for French responsibility for the war is, in part, a circumstantial one, in which it differs not at all from the vast majority of cases tried before criminal courts in every nation every day. Circumstantial evidence is perfectly good evidence, which is just as well, since otherwise justice would rarely be done. There is no doubt that France, from the summer of 1912 until the outbreak of war, consistently encouraged Russia to take a hard line in the Balkans. "If Russia goes to war, France will go to war" was the insistent refrain during all that period. There is no doubt that France had prepared for war — by the three-year service law, by huge expenditures on armaments, by military loans to Russia, by the weaning away of Italy and Rumania from the Central Powers, and by the entangling of Britain in what was virtually a military alliance. There is no doubt that France made no move to disband the Balkan League and no effective move to halt the Balkan Wars. The thoughtful and peaceable French ambassador in St. Petersburg, Georges Louis, was replaced first by Delcassé and then by Paléologue, with the results we have seen. When the French ambassador in Belgrade told his government the truth about the Sarajevo assassination, he was unceremoniously removed from his post. There is no doubt that Paléologue deliberately kept the Quai d'Orsay in ignorance of the fateful Russian general mobilization that was the immediate cause of the major European war. There is no doubt that the French *Yellow Book* and the Russian *Orange Book* were the only two such books that contained forgeries and manipulated documents, or that the French *Yellow Book* was by far the most untruthful of such government publications. All these indictments are amply proven by hard, direct evidence, which there is no gainsaying.

By the nature of things, there is no such direct evidence of what was contrived by Poincaré, Paléologue, Izvolsky, and Sazonov in St. Petersburg between July 20 and 23. It is surely significant that no record whatsoever of those conversations was made or, if made, was allowed to survive. After those conversations, Russia certainly adopted a stronger line toward Austria, and advised Serbia, in effect, to reject the Austrian ultimatum. After those conversations, Russia ordered general mobilization, the first major power to do so, and took this action, moreover, in the full knowledge that it made a European war inevitable. The Russian general mobilization was apparently not discussed beforehand with Russia's ally France, *as the terms of the Dual Entente specified must be done*, and word of that mobilization was not passed to Paris by the French ambassador until nearly nineteen hours had been allowed to elapse; nor was France informed of the Russian general mobilization by the Russian ambassador in Paris, Izvolsky. Yet, by the terms of the Dual Entente, any such mobilization made without consultation would have given France the right to refuse to recognize the *casus foederis* and to declare her neutrality. Is it plausible that the Russians would have taken the chance that France might react in this way? Is it plausible that so momentous a step as general mobilization should have been taken without prior consultation? Is it plausible that the French ambassador would have dared to conceal the Russian general mobilization from his own government on his own authority? Is it plausible that the subsequent forgeries in the French *Yellow Book* and the Russian *Orange Book* about the priority of the Russian general mobilization, and the lies told by Poincaré and Viviani on this subject to the joint meeting of the French legislature on August 1, had any purpose other than to conceal French guilt? If there was consultation between the Russian and French heads of state and foreign ministers on the subject of Russian general mobilization and on French reaction to such a move, it must have taken place during the visit of Poincaré and Viviani to St. Petersburg between July 20 and 23; that is, before the delivery of the Austrian ultimatum to Serbia and long before the Austrian declaration of war on Serbia.

Such a hypothesis, and such a hypothesis alone, explains the unresolved questions raised by the sequence of events, by Paléologue's conduct, and by the subsequent French lies and forgeries. The evidence is circumstantial but it is very strong, and neither Poincaré nor Paléologue, when they were later accused of having plotted and brought about the war, ever issued any convincing refutation.

Book Two

CHAPTER I

NINETEEN FOURTEEN was a very bad year — a far worse year than the most pessimistic imaginings had forecast. In Berlin, Paris, London, and St. Petersburg, crowds packed the streets during the last days of the crisis, singing patriotic songs, demonstrating in front of enemy embassies, committing pointless acts of violence. Those who had desired the conflict and those who had dreaded it alike found their tensions released with the declarations of war. Some wept to see the lamps going out all across Europe, but these were a small minority. In all the belligerent powers, the young especially were filled with a sense of exaltation because they had come to the end of an era and were crossing the threshold of a new world. Rupert Brooke spoke for his generation of Europeans when he wrote:

> Now, God be thanked Who has matched us with
> His hour . . .

Yet before long, it became obvious that all the belligerents had seriously misjudged the nature of modern war. Arguing that no nation's economy could stand the strain of a prolonged conflict, Europe's statesmen, soldiers, and peoples had all been agreed that a decision could be reached in a single great campaign fought across the summer countryside, conducted in the classical manner with cavalry screens and wide-wheeling masses of maneuver. Berlin would be taken before Christmas, the French thought; the Germans, for their part, believed that Paris would be entered between harvest time and frost. What happened, of course, was very different, and infinitely worse.

The German army invaded Belgium in the early morning of August 4, striking toward Liège with the six regular brigades and two cavalry divisions that Moltke had set aside for the *coup de main*. The

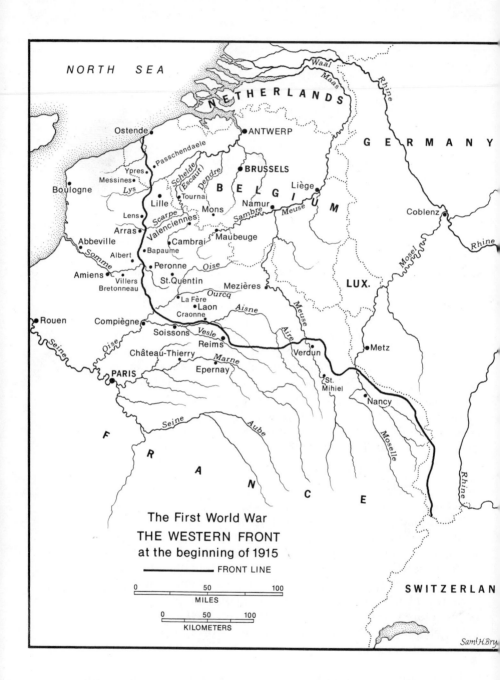

NORTH SEA

NETHERLANDS

GERMANY

Waal

Maas

Rhine

Ostende

ANTWERP

Passchendaele

BRUSSELS

Ypres

Schelde
(Escaut)

Dendre

Liège

Messines

Lys

BELGIUM

Boulogne

Lille

Tournai

Mons

Namur

Coblenz

Lens

Scarpe

Valenciennes

Sambre

Meuse

Arras

Rhine

Abbeville

Cambrai

Maubeuge

Mosel

Albert

Bapaume

Somme

Peronne

Oise

LUX.

Amiens

Villers
Bretonneau

St.Quentin

Mezières

Ourcq

La Fère

Laon

Aisne

Craonne

Meuse

Rouen

Compiègne

Soissons

Vesle

Aire

Metz

Seine

Oise

Reims

Verdun

Château-Thierry

Marne

Epernay

St.
Mihiel

Mosel

PARIS

Nancy

Seine

Aube

F

R

A

N

Moselle

C

E

Rhine

The First World War
THE WESTERN FRONT
at the beginning of 1915

━━━━━━━━ FRONT LINE

0   50   100
MILES

0   50   100
KILOMETERS

SWITZERLAND

Sam!H.Bry

Belgian garrison defended the fortress gallantly and inflicted heavy casualties on the attackers.

No European nation had fought a major war for many years, and the Germans had not fought at all since 1871, but this was by no means an adequate excuse for the tactics of 1914. Lessons that had been commonplaces by the end of the American Civil War and that had been repeated and emphasized in the Russo-Japanese War were everywhere ignored. The killing power of entrenched riflemen, the vulnerability of cavalry, the value of skirmishers, the advantage to be derived from attacking at first light — all these were tactical truths that had been known and forgotten. Was this, perhaps, merely another manifestation of the pervading European hubris that had caused the war, and another illustration of the truth that armies are mirrors of the societies from which they spring?

On August 7 a German staff officer, Major General Erich Ludendorff, forced his way into the center of Liège and took the surrender of the citadel. The fame he was to win for this exploit was to change his career and the history of the world, but since none of the forts had fallen, his act had only symbolic significance. The German government announced, wrongly, that Liège had been taken by assault, and on the 9th Chancellor Bethmann-Hollweg tried again to stop the fighting in Belgium. His conscience had always been uneasy about the invasion. He had admitted in the Reichstag on the 4th that it was contrary to international law, but he had declared, "The wrong — I speak openly — that we are committing we will make good as soon as our military aims have been attained." The Belgian government curtly rejected Bethmann's appeal and the fighting in Belgium continued.

On the night of August 9, German heavy siege artillery began to move toward Liège. By the evening of the 12th the siege guns were in position ready to open fire. But even before this, the German infantry had been able to capture two of the forts, Barchon and d'Evegnée, by storm. Once the big howitzers opened fire, it was merely a matter of time. By the 14th the right bank of the Meuse was cleared, and two days later the resistance of Liège was at an end.

The right wing of the German invasion forces, the First Army under General Alexander von Kluck and the Second Army under General Karl von Bülow, began to cross the Belgian frontier on August 14. Since German mobilization had not been completed until the 13th, the defense of Liège had delayed the Germans only a few hours, if at all. Nevertheless, the courage of the Belgian defense evoked the admiration of the world and increased the odium that Germany had brought upon herself by her lawless act of invasion.

Indeed, the German army in Belgium was already beginning to

display the almost hysterical ruthlessness that was to become one of its most deplorable hallmarks. Villages were razed to the ground, hostages were executed, Louvain, with its great libraries, was burned, priests whose only offense had been tending the wounded were shot out of hand, and an English nurse, Edith Cavell, was later killed by a firing squad for helping English prisoners to escape.

So far, the Schlieffen Plan was working almost exactly to its timetable, thanks to extraordinarily efficient staff work, but no indication was yet given to the Allies of the extent of the wheel through Belgium. The French air force brought back few useful reports, and what reports the airmen did make were generally disregarded. This was not altogether because of the reluctance of military men to accept a new and unconventional arm, though such sentiment was certainly present. The airmen were untrained in aerial reconnaissance, and made many gross errors both in map reading and in the identification of troops on the ground.

The German First and Second armies, each comprising six corps, would have the farthest to go, so they moved first. To their left, the Third Army under General Max Klemens von Hausen, the Fourth Army under Duke Albrecht of Württemberg, and the Fifth Army under Crown Prince Wilhelm advanced more slowly. The wheeling movement to the southwest would not begin until Kluck's First Army reached Brussels. In the first fifteen days of marching, Kluck's First Army covered some 180 miles. There had been virtually no fighting, even for the cavalry advance guards. The great mass of the German invasion marched across lands that were empty of any enemy.

On August 15, advance units of the German Third Army reached the Meuse at Dinant, but their first attempts to force a crossing were beaten back. The German hope of cutting off the Belgian field army on the Gette and preventing it from seeking refuge in Antwerp was also foiled, for the Belgians had no intention of standing on that river line and being destroyed. One Belgian division was caught on the Gette and suffered sixteen hundred casualties before it could break away, but by August 20 the Belgian forces, except for the 4th Division at Namur, were safely in Antwerp.

On that day, too, the Germans entered Brussels and forced a crossing of the Meuse at Dinant. Namur fell on August 25, and the road through Belgium was open. To the west of Lanrezac's Fifth Army there was nothing to stop the invader. If the right-hand man of the German right-hand corps had actually been "brushing the Channel with his sleeve," as Schlieffen had advised, he could have walked unopposed into the heart of France.

By now, the British Expeditionary Force of four divisions and a cavalry division had disembarked at Le Havre without interference and had concentrated south of Maubeuge. On the 21st it began to advance toward Mons to take up its position on the left of General Lanrezac's Fifth Army of ten divisions. As the British soldiers swung along the dusty roads of France, they sang a popular music-hall song, "Tipperary," which they effectively immortalized. At General Joffre's insistence, the combined Anglo-French force on the extreme left was moving into a trap where it was to be attacked from the north and east by the thirty-four divisions of the advancing German First, Second, and Third armies. Joffre, however, ignored all of Lanrezac's warnings about the width of the German sweep. Such ideas did not conform to Plan XVII.

As a curtain raiser, Joffre had ordered the French VII Corps of the First Army to invade Alsace on August 7. Joffre, like Poincaré, was a sound anticleric who found other outlets for what would normally be religious sentiment. This invasion of Alsace was mystical, not military. Launched at the far end of France near the Swiss frontier, it served no possible strategic purpose. The French troops presented arms as they moved across the long-watched, long-desired Vosges frontier, saluting the redemption of their Promised Land and, as is the way with soldiers, at the same time paying a compliment to themselves as well.

The next morning the German Seventh Army fell back according to plan, and the French occupied Mulhouse without fighting. On the 9th, however, the Germans counterattacked, and the French, who had spent more time rejoicing than in preparing defensive positions, were smartly swept out of Alsace again. There had been no point to this futile French expedition, and there was no point to the heavier assault that Joffre launched on September 11. Again the French got to Mulhouse, and again they were driven out.

The first major offensive called for in Plan XVII began on August 14 in Lorraine. On the right, General Dubail's First Army was to drive forward in the direction of Strasbourg, its right flank protected by the newly formed Army of Alsace under General Paul Pau. On the First Army's left, General Castelnau's Second Army was to capture Morhange. Thus, almost a third of the entire French army was to be committed to an offensive that, even if successful, would bring the French no great strategic prize. Indeed, if Schlieffen rather than Moltke had been German commander-in-chief, this silly French offensive into Lorraine would, in all likelihood, have spelled the defeat of France.

For four days the German Sixth and Seventh armies fell back before the French advance, inflicting heavy casualties with their rear guards and their artillery. They struck back on August 20, a strategic mistake on their part; they would have done much better had they adhered to the original Schlieffen Plan and continued their retirement. However, Crown Prince Rupprecht of Bavaria, commanding both the German Sixth and Seventh armies, saw the possibility of a considerable tactical victory and was loath to let the opportunity pass. Permission was given with an ominous readiness. Schlieffen had visualized Supreme Headquarters' holding all seven German armies in a tight rein, but Moltke, far back in his headquarters at Coblenz, exercised a far looser control. More important, Moltke's readiness to allow Rupprecht to counterattack suggested a lack of strategic sensibility. Had the three advancing French armies been lured on, they might well have become too deeply committed to send reinforcements to the threatened Allied left.

The French First Army attacked at first light on the 20th but was first stopped and then driven back in some confusion. The Second Army on the left also came under sharp attack, and here the situation was more serious. General Foch's XX Corps fought splendidly on the left, and its stand saved the day from complete disaster, but the center and right corps broke in panic and fled from the battlefield. Castelnau's army fell back rapidly to the fortified positions on the Grand Couronné, the heights above Nancy. Since the First Army's left flank was thus exposed, Dubail also had to continue his retirement back to his original starting line on the Meurthe River.

General Joffre was not greatly discouraged by the sharp defeat of the First and Second armies in Lorraine. The enemy had appeared in greater strength on the right than had been anticipated, but he could not be strong everywhere. If Lanrezac was even halfway correct in his alarmist expectations of what was about to happen on the left, the German front must of necessity be weak in the center. Or so Joffre and the staff at Grand Quartier Général at Vitry-le-François believed. Accordingly, the second great French offensive was launched on August 22 by General Ruffey's Third Army on the right and General Langle de Cary's Fourth Army on the left. A newly formed Army of Lorraine, under General Michel-Joseph Maunoury, was to act as right-flank guard against a possible German counterattack from Metz.

GQG was convinced that no more than eighteen German divisions could be in the Ardennes, an estimate based not on hard intelligence but on intuition. The conduct of the battle was thus determined by vain imaginings. It was far too soon for the French faith in the offensive to be shaken — among the French generals, that is. Their troops were already beginning to learn better. Joffre's headquarters instructed the Third and Fourth armies, "The enemy will be attacked wherever encountered." Hamlet, Prince of Denmark, had similarly claimed that nothing was either good or bad "but thinking makes it so." But Hamlet was pretending to be mad.

The German Fourth and Fifth armies had a total strength of some twenty-five divisions, rather than eighteen. On the afternoon of August 21 the Germans moved into the Ardennes forest several hours before the French got underway, and set about preparing ambushes for the impetuous Gallic attackers. August 22 was marked by a series of murderous clashes along the enclosed forest roads as the French, without adequate reconnaissance, pushed boldly into the traps that had been set for them. At Virton, Ochamps, Rossignol, and Neufchâteau the French advanced into killing grounds, where they were slaughtered by fire from unseen foes.

The Germans were lucky enough to have the best of both worlds that August. Where they launched their main offensive, the country was relatively open and they were opposed by quite inadequate forces; where they stood on the tactical defensive, the French obliged them by attacking blindly in close country. Thus, the Germans retained the initiative in both types of fighting and the French conformed to their will.

At Longwy, a French corps in the center of the Third Army broke to the rear, leaving its two adjoining corps dangerously isolated, each with an open flank. Much the same thing happened in the Fourth Army at Tintigny. These were isolated occurrences, and most of the French fought with a fanatical heroism; but it is undeniable that the French army, in these initial clashes of the war, was proving an instrument of uneven quality. The romanticism that had overemphasized élan at the expense of the more prosaic details of the profession of arms was now failing in the test of war. On the 26th, with Plan XVII everywhere in ruins, with his forces tragically depleted, and with his left flank so endangered that even he could no longer ignore the threat from the north, General Joffre ordered a suspension of the offensive in the Ardennes.

General Lanrezac, guarding the extreme left of the French line of battle, knew that between him and the Channel were only a few scratch units and some cavalry. He did not know where the British Expeditionary Force was, nor did he believe devoutly in its existence. He was too intelligent a man to have much faith in the abilities of Joffre or of GQG. And all his instincts told him that the German advance was going to reach far to the west, enveloping his open left flank.

When the British finally came up into position around Mons on August 22, Lanrezac's nerves were badly on edge and so were those of his staff. The British commander, Sir John French, now learned that

Lanrezac had been attacked on the 21st and had lost the crossings of the Sambre. This was grave news, and Sir John received little reassurance from the atmosphere at Lanrezac's headquarters. He spoke no French himself — which was just as well, considering some of the things that were being said — but he knew panic when he saw it. Nevertheless, he agreed to deploy his two corps along the Mons-Condé canal to protect the left flank of Lanrezac's Fifth Army.

August 23 was a Sunday, and in Mons and the outlying villages the Belgians went to mass as usual. This deceptive tranquillity did not last for long. The Germans advanced in the middle of the morning, attacking as though they had never heard of Schlieffen or the finding of an open flank. Kluck outnumbered the British by three to two, but he chose to fight a head-on encounter battle. There may not have been visible angels at Mons, but what was there, lining the left bank of the canal, was the best-trained infantry in the world, with a standard of musketry no continental army could equal. The German attacks withered away in the face of the deadly rifle fire, and though the British also suffered casualties, mostly from the enemy's well-sited field guns, the position was held nicely. It had, for all the world, been as though the British had been fighting in Wellington's time again, with the enemy coming on in the same old way and being beaten in the same old way. Certainly the British commander-in-chief was well pleased, for he had no idea as yet of the real weight of the forces that were closing with him.

What Sir John French could not take into account was that Lanrezac would retreat from his positions that night without troubling to inform the British on his left until a short time before the retirement. When the British learned at midnight that the French were pulling out in an hour or two, they had no choice but to do the same. Nor did Sir John French desire to stay any longer. He was utterly disgusted with Lanrezac's behavior, and felt that he had been badly let down by his ally. His reaction, indeed, was somewhat extreme, for he announced his intention of retiring all the way back to St. Nazaire, on the south coast of Brittany, where he would at least be in touch with a service on which he could rely, the Royal Navy. Lord Kitchener, the British minister of war, and the British cabinet were naturally disturbed when they heard of this drastic decision, and Kitchener was authorized to travel to France by destroyer to set the British commander-in-chief right. Kitchener interviewed Sir John French in Paris on September 1 and instructed him without ceremony to keep the British Expeditionary Force in the battle line in conformity with "the movements of the French Army."

In the meantime, the BEF had been falling back from Mons by

forced marches. On August 26 General Sir Horace Smith-Dorrien's II Corps stood and fought at Le Cateau, where the battle went better for the British than their dispositions entitled them to expect. The Germans allowed Smith-Dorrien to break off the action in full daylight, and failed to enact the forfeit that this maneuver should have entailed. The French Fifth Army likewise fought a delaying action at Guise on the 29th that caused Bülow's Second Army to halt for thirty-six hours and wait for the First and Third armies to come up. In the meanwhile, the Allied retreat continued all along the front westward from Verdun.

This was all to the good from the German point of view, but on the French right Castelnau's Second Army held fast to the Grand Couronné above Nancy and was even able to send troops west toward Paris. General Maurice Sarrail, who had replaced Ruffey as commander of the Third Army,* held on at Verdun. Under the Schlieffen Plan, these two armies should still have been advancing deeper into the net and should have had no formations to spare. Moltke had thus failed to grasp the subtlety of Schlieffen's strategic thought concerning the German left. He was now to prove that he had also misunderstood the situation on the German right.

On August 31 Kluck's First Army wheeled inward in the hope of finding the French flank and driving it east from Paris. This was a definite departure from the Schlieffen Plan, which had called for the German First Army to pass forty miles west of the French capital and to wheel inward only when well to the south of Paris. Now Kluck, with Moltke's too-ready concurrence, was shortening his march and making his wheel to the north of the city. Moltke, misled by the reports of success from the German Fourth and Fifth armies, had decided to drive forward in the center, while the First Army, which was to have been the hammerhead of the German assault, was relegated to the role of flank guard. With these decisions, the entire concept of the giant outflanking maneuver was prematurely abandoned for a frontal advance. What was far worse was that with every mile that Kluck marched east the risk increased that he, who had been intended to be the outflanker, would himself be outflanked by the French forces that were concentrating around Paris.

Joffre, who, to his great credit, maintained his usual imperturbable calm in the face of disaster, now formed a new Sixth Army under General Maunoury. By September 1 this army became part of General Joseph Gallieni's Army of Paris. The previous day the French government, in a state of near panic, had abandoned Paris and fled to

*Joffre also replaced Lanrezac with General Louis Franchet d'Esperey on September 3, and within a few days dismissed some twenty-five corps and divisional commanders.

Bordeaux. This was an unedifying spectacle and, as it turned out, quite unnecessary.

In fact, the advancing German armies were now in a state of some confusion, and Moltke was rapidly losing control of the situation. The fatal flaw in Schlieffen's master plan had always been that Germany did not have the minimum number of troops with which to implement it. This difficulty had been only partly overcome by the German use of reserve formations at the outset of the campaign, and Moltke had made a number of detachments that further weakened the strength of the field army and especially of the vitally important right wing. Two corps had been sent to invest Antwerp, and on August 26 two more corps had been sent to the Eighth Army in East Prussia. Now the Germans did not have enough troops in the west to perform the tasks set them. In addition, the long marches were straining the German supply system to the point of dislocation. On September 3 Allied aerial reconnaissance revealed Kluck's change of direction. The German First Army was marching diagonally across the face of the Paris defenses and exposing its flank to a counterattack from the fortress. Gallieni, the commandant of Paris, was probably the first to see the opportunity, and his pressure on Joffre may have helped the French commander-in-chief to make up his mind. At all events, at ten o'clock on the evening of September 4 Joffre issued orders for a general counterattack to be launched on the 6th* in the hope that the German First Army and part of the German Second Army would be crushed by converging attacks.

The plan looked admirable on the map, and if it had been implemented by other commanders it might have succeeded. As it was, the counterattack seemed to proceed in slow motion. Most of September 5 was taken up with getting the Allied armies to their starting lines. During the 6th, three corps of the German First Army recrossed the Marne to take up a position facing west to guard against the threat from Paris. The move, though necessary, was an indication of how badly the German plan had gone awry. Between the First Army and Second Army a gap was now created that was covered only by some cavalry and Jäger battalions.

On the 7th, both the British army† and the French Fifth Army advanced northward. They moved with exasperating slowness and caution, though there was almost nothing in front of them. By last light

*This had not been exactly Gallieni's idea. He had favored allowing the German advance to continue for a time so that the enemy would march deeper into the sack. Such a calculated risk, which promised to maximize the Allied strategic advantage, was foreign to Joffre's temperament.

†The BEF now consisted of three corps.

the British had pressed ahead only to within four or five miles of the Marne; Franchet d'Esperey's Fifth Army had not advanced quite so far. For a brief time there had been a chance to cut off and destroy the German First Army, but between September 7 and 9 this chance disappeared. The BEF had advanced only about eight miles a day and the French Fifth Army rather less. The Germans would lose the war on the Marne, but they were to be spared a tactical defeat. In this they were unfortunate, for a quick victory by either side in 1914 would probably have been preferable to the long-drawn-out agony that was actually in store.

By now, Moltke had almost no control over his armies. He sat in his headquarters, a broken man who realized all too clearly that his own inadequacies might well have lost Germany the war. The Schlieffen Plan had been abandoned for a will-o'-the-wisp; the German left was at a standstill and the right in a most hazardous position. Moltke dispatched his chief of intelligence, Lieutenant Colonel Hentsch, to visit the various army headquarters by staff car with authority to order a retirement if he considered it necessary. At Fifth, Fourth, and Third Army headquarters, Hentsch found everything satisfactory, but at Second Army he found Bülow very apprehensive. It was therefore agreed that if the British and French crossed the Marne in force, the Second Army should retire to the north.

The British got portions of I and II corps across the Marne by seven-thirty on the morning of the 9th, but they halted at eleven o'clock and did not attempt to resume their advance until late afternoon. The advance of the French Fifth Army was equally dilatory. Nevertheless, the German position remained critical. When Hentsch reached Kluck's headquarters, he ordered the First Army to retire. By last light* on the 9th, the First and Second armies and the western half of the Third Army were all falling back toward the Vesle and the Aisne. The remainder of the German Third Army had no choice but to conform to this retirement, and on September 11 Moltke ordered the Fourth and Fifth armies to retire as well. When the Battle of the Marne ended, at about noon on September 9, the British were only six or seven miles north of the Marne and no French unit had even crossed the river.

The Marne was far from being a tactical victory for the Allies. Yet the Marne was *the* great battle of the war, the decisive turning point. The Germans were never again to be so near to victory as they had been in those August and September days, not even in March and April of 1918. The great German plan had failed and now Germany

*The German Second Army began its retirement at noon and the First Army an hour or so later.

was faced with exactly that two-front war of attrition that her military leaders had always recognized she could not win.

By September 12 the German First and Second armies were safely back across the Aisne, having been pursued hardly at all. Rather than attempt to defend the river line, they took up positions on the commanding high ground some two miles north of the Aisne. The German front was firmly established by September 13 and was to remain so for the next four years. When Allied attacks on the 13th and 14th failed to make any impression, both sides began to entrench.

Westward from the Aisne, however, the countryside was empty of armies, presenting the last open flank in the west. Moltke was relieved as Chief of the General Staff on September 14, and his successor, General Erich von Falkenhayn, at once began to edge the German armies to the right in an attempt to revive the Schlieffen Plan and get around the Allied flank. This phase of operations has become known as the "Race to the Sea," and the sea was where it ended, but both armies were more concerned with the open wing of the opposing line than with their ultimate destination. The battle lines were extended almost due north by a series of short outflanking maneuvers, all of which failed. Significantly, both sides could find the necessary troops for their progressive extension of the front by thinning out the positions they already held, since far fewer soldiers were needed for defense than for attack. Early in October the British army was transferred from the Aisne to Flanders so that it would be closer to its seaborne communications.

The Germans had been too busy elsewhere to spare the troops needed for the reduction of Antwerp, but at the end of September the fortress came under attack. The British cabinet dispatched the infantry of the Royal Naval Division and the First Lord of the Admiralty, Winston Churchill, to assist in Antwerp's defense. Churchill thought that this was great fun and suggested that he stay on to command the British force, but Prime Minister Asquith quaintly replied that the navy needed him more. Once the Germans brought up their siege artillery, the end could not be long delayed, and on the night of October 6 the defenders of Antwerp began to withdraw westward along the coast. Most of them made good their escape, but one British brigade was forced to retreat over the Dutch border, where it was interned.

The British government was now doing its best to reinforce and enlarge the British Expeditionary Force, chiefly in response to demands from the force itself, where it was commonly believed that, with only a little more effort, the war could still be won by Christmas. Kitchener resisted these demands as well as he could, being all along convinced that the war would be a long one. No one had yet any inkling of the

terrible things that were to take place in Picardy and Flanders, though
the French might have guessed, in the light of what had happened to
them during the Battle of the Frontiers. In any case, the war was already out of control. It was no longer an instrument of policy but an
end in itself. Men's horizons had already narrowed so that they could
see ahead of them only the mirage of victory, and that shimmering
vision seemed enough. They no longer calculated profit and loss;
their only aim was to win the war. And they were confident that when
they had done so all else would be added unto them.

Falkenhayn fully realized the desperate strategic situation Germany
faced after the breakdown of the Schlieffen Plan and therefore re-
sorted to a desperate expedient: he tried once more to break out on
the right, even though he had none of the advantages of planning and
preparation that had preceded the first attempt. It is difficult to see
how Falkenhayn could have hoped to accomplish with two armies in
October what the Schlieffen Plan failed to achieve with three armies
in August.

General Foch, who had been placed in command of all French
forces in the north, also determined to attack, hoping to break the
enemy before he could organize his defense. The British held the
twenty-five-mile stretch of front between Béthune and Ypres; the
French on the left held the area north of Ypres to the Yser Canal; and
the Belgians held the remainder of the line along the Yser Canal and
Yser River to the sea. The First Battle of Ypres opened on October 19,
with both the British and the Germans advancing to the attack. On the
20th a newly formed German Fourth Army, under Duke Albrecht of
Württemberg, and the Sixth Army, under Crown Prince Rupprecht
of Bavaria, attacked between La Bassée and the sea. Four of the five
German corps were made up, for the most part, of volunteers too
young to have been called up but whose proffered services had
nonetheless been accepted by the Fatherland. Probably about one
hundred thousand of these young volunteers were killed or wounded
between the middle of October and the middle of November. The
German army could very ill afford the loss, for a high percentage of
these casualties were potential officer cadets. Falkenhayn later
claimed that he had no time to bring up experienced formations, but
the excuse is far from convincing. It might be nearer the truth to
suggest that there was a certain ruthless bloody-mindedness in Falkenhayn's character, a quality he displayed again and even more
strongly at Verdun. In Germany, the autumn fighting around Ypres
was given the bitter name of *der Kindermord von Ypern*, "the Massacre
of the Innocents at Ypres."

Between October 19 and 21, the French and British met the Germans in a series of encounter battles. The fighting was close and bloody, but the German attacks were halted. On the extreme left the Belgians blocked the culverts in the Dixmuide-Nieuport railway embankment and opened the sluices to let in the sea. Soon the area was flooded and that portion of the front became static. On October 22, new attacks struck the British, but again the defense, sorely tried, held, and as at Mons, inflicted heavy casualties with the accuracy of its rifle fire. French formations were hurried up to the hard-pressed British, and the line was not broken.

Falkenhayn was not yet prepared to admit that a breakthrough was impossible. A new assault was launched on October 31 with seven fresh divisions. The young German volunteers, many of them only seventeen years of age, stormed forward, singing their patriotic songs, until their bodies were piled up by the deadly blast of British rifle fire. This fighting was of a deadliness and intensity that had not been experienced by a British army since Waterloo. Messines Ridge had to be abandoned, but General Sir Douglas Haig, commanding the British I Corps, and General Pierre Dubois, commanding the French IX Corps, cooperated splendidly and fought a cool, tenacious defensive battle.

Falkenhayn made one more attempt before he admitted defeat. On November 11, a fresh German corps advanced down both sides of the Menin Road toward Ypres. The Prussian Guard drove through the thin British line north of the road and nearly reached the artillery lines before they wavered and were driven back by a hastily organized counterattack. The German failure on November 11 marked the end of the First Battle of Ypres. Sporadic fighting continued for another eleven days, but the danger was never again acute. On the 17th the situation on the eastern front was so serious that Falkenhayn was forced to begin moving divisions from the west to help the Austrians.

At First Ypres, British casualties had amounted to over 50,000 men; the French losses were at least as severe. The Germans paid a much higher price for their attacks than the combined total of French and British casualties in defense. Rather more than a quarter of a million men were killed or wounded contesting the control of those few flat and flooded fields around Ypres. When the battle died down, the front solidified to form the Ypres Salient, of evil memory. Before the war was over, the British Empire was to lose half a million men in this insignificant patch of ground. The fighting had been of an astonishing severity. The 160,000-man British Expeditionary Force, the elite of the British Regular Army, had, by the end of the year, lost 86,237 men, well over 50 percent — and this percentage was, of course, much higher in the infantry battalions.

Joffre, knowing that some German formations had been transported to the eastern front, launched two offensives in December. The first, which lasted between the 14th and the 24th, was marked by bitter but inconclusive fighting around Arras, and the second, which began on December 20 and lasted until March 17, 1915, was mounted in Champagne and was as abortive as the one in Flanders.

As winter set in, the whole stretch of front from Nieuport to the Swiss frontier congealed and hardened so that maneuver was no longer possible. Trenches, which had at first been mere scratches in the ground, were deepened, revetted, drained, and connected together to form a complete system with communication saps and dugouts. Barbed wire was strung in ever-increasing depth in front of the trench lines, strongpoints were built for machine guns, and gun pits were dug for artillery. In the winter of 1914–1915 the trench lines were not as strong as they later became — but they were strong enough. On Christmas Day on the British front there was an unofficial truce between the opposing armies, a brief interval of sanity in the madness that had gripped Europe. Germans and British met in no man's land, exchanged small and pitiful gifts of cigarettes or sausages, even organized a football match. Headquarters on both sides were outraged when they heard about it, and issued stern orders against any repetition.

While the Schlieffen Plan as implemented by Moltke had been breaking down in the west, the assumptions that Schlieffen had made about the Russian front were being wonderfully justified. Because of the barrier of the Masurian Lakes and the inadequate Russian roads, the Grand Duke Nicholas could not concentrate the whole of his force of half a million men either in the east or the south and move them united into German territory. For this reason, the Russian plan called for a double thrust into East Prussia. The Russians would strike two coordinated blows, catching the defenders between hammer and anvil. The trouble with the Russian plan was the gap between theory and practice, the difference between forecasting movements on the map and actually moving Russian armies on the ground. A further serious disadvantage was that, at French insistence, the twin Russian attacks had to be launched as soon as possible. General Pavel Rennenkampf's Russian First Army, some 246,000 men, concentrated at Vilna and then crossed into East Prussia on August 17, moving north of the Masurian Lakes. General Jilinksy, the commander of the Russian northwest front, deliberately held back the advance of General Alexander Samsonov's Second Army, which was to march from Warsaw, because he hoped to draw the German defenders eastward to meet Rennenkampf. The Russian Second Army, of 284,000 men, began its advance on August 19, striking up well to the west of the Masurian Lakes to come between the Germans facing Rennenkampf and the Vistula.

The Russian plan looked very formidable, the more so since the German Eighth Army, under Lieutenant General Max von Prittwitz, had only about 210,000 men to meet two Russian armies, each of which outnumbered it. If the Russian offensives could be properly coordinated, the Eighth Army would be crushed between them. This would leave open the road to Berlin, and no victory in the west could compensate for the loss of the capital and all northern and eastern Germany.

The German plan, of course, was to deal with each of the two advancing Russian armies in turn. No other plan was feasible, for the abandonment of East Prussia without fighting would have been politically impossible, and there was, in any case, no reason to believe that the line of the Vistula could be held against the combined strength of the Russian First and Second armies. In the task of dealing separately with Samsonov and Rennenkampf, the better road and rail communications in East Prussia and the superior quality of German formations seemed to promise some hope of success. Nevertheless, it was undoubtedly a very bold gamble, and for very high stakes.

A minor German victory against Rennenkampf at Stallupönen on August 17 was followed by a German defeat at Gumbinnen on the 20th. This convinced Prittwitz that he would have to abandon East Prussia and retreat behind the line of the Vistula. He informed Supreme Headquarters of this decision, adding that he doubted if he could hold even the Vistula line. The principal staff officers at Supreme Headquarters, therefore, promptly insisted that Moltke replace Prittwitz with a less timid commander. No one had a commander in mind, but it was soon agreed that General Ludendorff, who had just won the Pour le Mérite at Liège and who was one of the best staff officers in Germany, would do excellently as the Eighth Army's chief of staff.* Once this had been decided, Supreme Headquarters looked around for a figurehead and decided on the sixty-six-year-old General Paul von Hindenburg, who had retired three years before. Hindenburg and Ludendorff were immediately dispatched to East Prussia to try to save a desperate situation.

They arrived at Eighth Army headquarters at Marienbad on August 23, and from that moment East Prussia was saved. Hindenburg

---

*In the German system, a commander and his chief of staff functioned as a team, jointly responsible for all decisions. Thus, when a commander fell into disgrace, his chief of staff almost automatically shared his fate. Prittwitz's chief of staff, Count von Waldersee, was dismissed at the same time as Prittwitz.

and Ludendorff proved to be a very formidable combination indeed, for Ludendorff was highly intelligent, aggressive, and meticulous, and Hindenburg had nerves of steel and could always be counted on to steady and calm his more easily agitated chief of staff. These two men eventually went on to control the entire German war effort, but they were never quite as successful elsewhere as they were on the eastern front. Their success on this front was primarily due to their having inherited Prittwitz's chief of operations, Lieutenant Colonel Max Hoffmann, a staff officer who possessed what was probably the best military brain of the war.

The essence of the German plan was to concentrate the entire Eighth Army against Samsonov in the south. The Russian Second Army, anxious to reach the Vistula before the Germans could retire behind it, had hurried on too fast. By now it was strung out over a great extent of countryside, with nearly sixty miles between its extreme left and its extreme right. The Russian rate of advance — sixteen or seventeen miles each day in blazing August weather — had tired the troops and had played havoc with their system of supply. From loyalty to their French allies, the Russians had begun their move before mobilization was complete, and as a result there were not nearly enough horses, wagons, or field batteries available. By August 23 many units were going hungry, not having received even their minimum ration of black bread, cabbage soup, and tea.

The corps of the Eighth Army were moved down to concentrate against the Russian Second Army, and only a light cavalry screen was left in front of Rennenkampf. Ludendorff planned for one German corps to form a firm base with a refused flank to lure on the Russian center and then to drive the Russian wings into a gigantic sack by a double envelopment.*

The Russian right was struck on August 26 by the two marching German corps coming down from the north. At Lautern and Lake Bössau, the Russian right-hand corps was sharply defeated, and streamed away from the battlefield to take no further part in the fighting. By nightfall on the 26th the trap had more than half closed.

The decisive day of the battle was the 27th, when the Russian left wing was attacked at Usdau and driven away from the battlefield. The Russian center of three corps was now all but surrounded in the forests and swamps around Tannenberg, and the next day the Germans sealed the trap. On August 29 and 30 the Russians attempted in vain to break out of the tightening cordon around them. Samsonov and his staff tried to escape on foot, but when they found the Ger-

---

*The Germans' task was simplified by the fact that Russian headquarters issued orders in clear.

mans ahead of them, Samsonov moved a little distance away from his staff and shot himself.

By last light on August 30 it was all over. The Germans rounded up 125,000 prisoners, 95,000 of them unwounded. The number of Russian dead was never accurately computed, but certainly it was very high. Some 500 Russian guns fell into the Germans' hands.

In the long run, perhaps the most important result of the battle was that overnight the unknown Hindenburg became the idol of the German people. His calm old face, his huge square head — "like a woodcut" — and his inner strength and repose gave confidence to the frightened. The German authorities, needing good news to counterbalance the terrible failure in the west, deliberately encouraged this hero worship and Hindenburg himself did nothing to check the popular adulation. The legend of Hindenburg as the victor of Tannenberg was, like most legends, to serve its believers ill in the future.

Rennenkampf's First Army still remained to be dealt with. All through the Battle of Tannenberg it had made no offensive move, and on September 2 Rennenkampf ordered his troops to dig in on a line from the Baltic to the northern end of the Masurian Lakes. Ludendorff planned to grip the Russian First Army by a frontal attack with four corps while two more corps and two cavalry divisions wheeled wide to the south to strike the Russians' left rear, roll up their line, and pin them against the Baltic coast. It was to be a repetition of Tannenberg, except that on this occasion a double envelopment would be unnecessary since the sea would take the place of one of the closing pincers. To guard the enveloping German right wing against a flank attack, Ludendorff detached three divisions under General Rüdiger von der Goltz to act as right-flank guard.

The German advance began on September 5 and the assault on the Russian line was launched on the 8th. The frontal attack failed everywhere, with losses, as the Russians, in good deep trenches, easily held their own. To the south, however, the enveloping maneuver made excellent progress and the Germans broke out and fell on the Russian rear at first light on the 9th.

As soon as he heard that his left flank had been turned, Rennenkampf reacted with panic, a response that was more effective than Samsonov's fatalistic courage had been. A general retreat was ordered, to be covered by the suicidal counterattack of two divisions. This counterattack, delivered with great gallantry on September 10, prevented another German victory like Tannenberg, but the Russians still suffered severely. When the fighting ended on the 13th, what was left of the Russian First Army was back across the Niemen River.

Between August 15 and September 13 Samsonov and Rennenkampf between them had lost 310,000 men — considerably more than the total strength of the German Eighth Army. Worse still, this loss had been inflicted on the best-trained portion of the Russian regular army. Many Russians were now convinced that the war was lost and that no amount of courage could compensate for superior German organization, leadership, and training.

While the Russians were being defeated by the Germans, they were themselves inflicting a defeat of equal magnitude on the Austrians. Conrad, the Austrian Chief of Staff — in reality the commander-in-chief, for the nominal commander-in-chief, Archduke Frederick, was only a figurehead — determined to take the offensive against Russia as soon as possible. Conrad had only three armies immediately available: the Third, commanded by General Brudermann around Lemberg; the Fourth, under General Moritz von Auffenberg, farther to the left covering the fortress of Przemysl; and the First, under General Viktor von Dankl, in the triangle formed by the junction of the Vistula and the San. These three armies were deployed on a front of some 175 miles. Conrad intended to attack northward into the Polish salient with his First and Fourth armies, while the Third Army, later to be joined by the Second, which was to concentrate around Stanislau, would act as right-flank guard. If the Russians should attack from the east, the First and Fourth armies would execute a great right wheel and take them in the flank and rear.

The army group commander on the Russian front was General Nikolai Ivanov, who initially had four armies under his command, one more than Conrad. East of Lublin, facing south, was the Russian Fourth Army, commanded by General Evert, and on the Fourth Army's left, also facing south, was General Plevke's Fifth Army. Separated from this pair of armies by some sixty miles was a second pair, facing west toward Lemberg and Stanislau, the Third Army commanded by General Nikolai Ruzski to the north and the Eighth Army commanded by General Alexei Brusilov farther south. It was Ivanov's intention to hold the Austrians' eastward advance with his Third and Eighth armies, while his Fourth and Fifth armies came down on the enemy's rear.

Neither Conrad nor Ivanov had the least idea what the other was doing. In both cases their assumptions about the enemy were based on intuition and wishful thinking; in both cases the assumptions were wrong. Conrad began his northern advance in the general direction of Lublin on the 20th. Half of the Third Army moved north to support Auffenberg and Dankl and half moved northeast. Conrad was nothing if not bold.

The Austrian First Army defeated the Russian Fourth Army around Krasnik between August 23 and 25, and by the 28th Plevke's Fifth Army was almost surrounded. However, the Austrian Third

Army was sharply defeated at Zlochev by the combined forces of the Russian Eighth and Third armies, and now the Russians were reinforced with an extra army, the Ninth.

Greatly outnumbered, Conrad ordered a general retreat on the morning of September 11, intending to halt sixty miles to the rear and hold the line of the San. The river was reached on the 16th, but Conrad judged that he could not hold this line, and ordered the retreat to continue to the Dunajec, 140 miles west of Lemberg. He did, however, detach a corps to help hold the fortress of Przemysl.

Between August 23 and September 11, the Austrian armies had lost more than a third of their strength — 250,000 casualties and more than 100,000 prisoners. Austrian morale had been as badly damaged by the Battle of Lemberg as Russian morale had been by Tannenberg and the Masurian Lakes. Worse still was the high percentage of German-speaking officers who had been killed, for their place in the future had to be taken by inadequately trained men from the empire's subject nationalities. Although both sides had fought well, superior numbers had given Ivanov the victory. This boded ill for Austria because Russia could raise new armies much more readily than could the Dual Monarchy.

To meet the Russian threat, the Germans formed a new Ninth Army in Upper Silesia, leaving East Prussia weakly defended, and on September 28 this army began to advance toward the Vistula. Ludendorff was attacking with eighteen German and Austrian divisions against sixty Russian divisions deployed in four armies, but even so the German thrust nearly captured Warsaw. As it was, the odds were too great, and the Germans were forced to retreat on October 27. The Russian pursuit soon petered out, and Ludendorff promptly shipped the entire Ninth Army through Germany by rail to concentrate in the vicinity of Thorn, where it would be poised above the exposed right wing of the Russian armies in the center of the eastern front.

The next offensive opened on November 11, with the Ninth Army driving southeast toward Lodz through the thinly held joint between Rennenkampf's First Army and Scheidemann's Second Army. By the 19th Rennenkampf had been driven off and Scheidemann was all but encircled at Lodz. Plevke's Fifth Army, however, was pushing north by long forced marches, while Scheidemann continued to defend himself desperately. Three and a half divisions from Rennenkampf's First Army also began, though very slowly, to move south to Scheidemann's assistance.

The Germans encircling Lodz were now encircled in their turn. General Scheffer, with 60,000 German troops, was surrounded by vastly superior Russian forces, and the Grand Duke Nicholas gave orders for sixty trains to be shunted into sidings for the shipment of

German prisoners. But Scheffer had no thought of surrendering. All through November 21 and 22, his soldiers hurled back assault after assault, but when the belated order for them to retire was received after dark on the 22nd they were far more completely surrounded than Samsonov had been at Tannenberg. However, a dawn attack on the 24th against one portion of the Russian line was successful; the Germans broke through and after a day of breathless cut and thrust and hard marching Scheffer's 60,000 men rejoined the rest of the Ninth Army. Not only had they escaped through half a million encircling Russians but they also took with them the 10,000 Russian prisoners and sixty-four guns they had previously captured. In the fighting around Lodz the Germans captured some 135,000 prisoners and inflicted very heavy, but unrecorded, casualties on the Russians. Their own losses were not light — some 100,000 casualties, of whom about 36,000 had been killed. The Austrian First Army had lost another 30,000 men.

Even such legendary feats of arms as Scheffer's could not conceal the fact that both the German advance to the Vistula and the Battle of Lodz had failed. And what matters in war is not brilliance but success. Thus, in the east as in the west, the 1914 campaigns ended in apparent stalemate.

In the lesser theaters of war the Allies had been somewhat more successful. Marshal Potiorek, who had been so ineffective in Sarajevo in June, was equally incompetent when he invaded Serbia in August. The Serbs drove back the Austrians, who incurred heavy losses, and by the end of the year there were no more Austrian troops on Serbian soil and Potiorek had been dismissed. The British, sensitive about the Suez Canal, had reinforced Egypt, and a small British force was landed in Persia near Basra to protect the oil supplies there. The British defeated a weak Turkish column and advanced as far as Al Qurna, where the Tigris and Euphrates rivers join. A brigade group of West African Rifles captured German Togoland in August; German New Guinea fell to the Australians, and Samoa to the New Zealanders; but an invasion of German South-West Africa was postponed because of a Boer rebellion in South Africa. British, French, and Belgian columns invaded the Cameroons but they soon bogged down in the jungle and made no further advance for eight months. In German East Africa the British force that landed in November found itself opposed by a German soldier of genius, Lieutenant Colonel Paul von Lettow-Vorbeck, who drove the invaders back to their ships in some confusion.

The greatest Allied success — though it did not seem such at the time — was at sea. When war had broken out in August the British Grand Fleet, based on Scapa Flow in the Orkneys and on Rosyth on the east coast of Scotland, had a decisive superiority over the German High Seas Fleet based on Kiel and the Jade. The Austrian fleet was bottled up at Pola in the Adriatic, and the Russian Baltic Fleet was similarly bottled up at Kronstadt.

On July 20, when war seemed imminent, the British Admiralty seized two Turkish battleships that had been built in British yards and were ready for delivery to Constantinople. This naturally enraged the Turks, the more so since the cost of the ships had been met by public subscription. On August 3 Turkey signed a secret treaty of alliance with Germany. In the Mediterranean the German battle cruiser *Goeben* and the cruiser *Breslau* managed to evade the British fleet and escape to Constantinople, where their presence put great pressure on the Turkish government. To ensure Turkey's entry into the war, the two ships, now nominally part of the sultan's navy, steamed into the Black Sea and bombarded Odessa and some other Russian ports on October 28. Russia declared war on Turkey on November 4, and Britain and France followed suit the next day.

The first consequence of Turkey's entry into the war was that Enver Bey, the Turkish minister of war, decided to launch an attack into Russia through the Caucasus. The invading Turkish army of ninety-five thousand men endured the most appalling conditions of weather, was ill-supplied, and met fierce resistance. Finally, in January of 1915, the Turks were decisively defeated at Sarikamis and forced to retreat. Only eighteen thousand ragged, frostbitten, and starving soldiers returned to Turkey.

In the North Sea the British drew first blood when Vice Admiral Sir David Beatty's 1st Battle Cruiser Squadron thrust boldly into the Heligoland Bight on August 28 and sank the German light cruisers *Köln, Mainz,* and *Ariadne* as well as a destroyer. During September, however, U-boats sank four British cruisers with heavy loss of life. These sinkings impelled the Grand Fleet to withdraw temporarily to an anchorage in the north of Ireland while the defenses at Scapa Flow were improved, which was in itself a sorry comment on the Royal Navy's lack of preparation for Armageddon. The British battleship *Audacious* was sunk by a mine off the north coast of Ireland on the 27th.

Elsewhere on the oceans of the world German raiders were being hunted down. Admiral Maximilian von Spee, with his China squadron, consisting of the *Scharnhorst*, the *Gneisenau*, and the cruisers *Nürnberg* and *Leipzig*, got to South American waters and there at Coronel, off the coast of Chile, on November 1 attacked the badly outgunned squadron of Admiral Sir Christopher Cradock. Cradock fought gallantly, but the outcome was never in doubt. The British light cruiser *Glasgow* managed to escape, but the *Good*

Hope and the cruiser *Monmouth* went down with all hands.

Spee was not at large for long. When he attempted to shell Port Stanley in the Falkland Islands, he discovered to his horror that a fresh British naval force was lurking in the harbor. Admiral Sir Doveton Sturdee, with the two battle cruisers *Invincible* and *Inflexible*, outgunned Spee as heavily as Spee had outgunned Cradock. In the ensuing engagement, the *Scharnhorst, Gneisenau, Nürnberg,* and *Leipzig* were sunk, and although the light cruiser *Dresden* got away, she was caught and sunk off the Juan Fernández Islands in the Pacific on March 15, 1915. On his way to Cape Horn, Spee had dropped off the light cruiser *Emden* in the Indian Ocean, and there the German ship had a successful but brief career as a raider before she was pounded to death by the fire of the Australian cruiser *Sydney*, off the Cocos Islands on November 9. The German battle cruiser squadron shelled the English east-coast towns of Scarborough, Hartlepool, and Whitby on December 16, but failed to catch any British warships. On Christmas Day the French dreadnought *Jean Bart* was sunk by a U-boat in the Straits of Otranto.

At first glance it might seem that these naval actions had resulted in little more than pointless bloodshed, but the strategic results were in fact considerable. The blockade of Germany was working well, and the German merchant fleet was either sunk, captured, or lying idle in neutral harbors. The first five months of the war thus showed how completely fallacious was Tirpitz' naval policy.

Winter brought a halt to large-scale operations on the western front; the first phase of the war at sea had been decided in Britain's favor; and there was a lull on the eastern front. At the end of 1914 it was obvious that all the long-matured war plans of the powers had failed. Neither Berlin nor Paris, after all, had been taken before the snowflakes flew. Seldom has there been such a wholesale wreckage of plans, such a thorough dissolution of expectations, such a blighting of hopes. Yet it is only in a narrow military sense that the first five months of the war can be called indecisive. By the end of 1914 the shape of future events had, in fact, been decided for decades to come. The peoples of Europe had welcomed the coming of the war that bright summer. God had matched them with His hour. The bugles that had called the soldiers to the crest of the Vosges, to Masuria, to Liège, or to the sleepy little country town of Ypres had seemed to promise chivalry, exaltation, and high adventure. None of the promises had been fulfilled; none of the expectations realized. The war was going to be a long one. Defeat for either side was a distinct possibility, and the blood that had already been poured out seemed to cry from the ground for vengeance.

CHAPTER II

Each year of the First World War had its own special character, different from all the rest. Nineteen fourteen had been the year of the breakdown of the great plans and — in the west — the end of the war of movement. Nineteen fifteen was given its special character by the partial recognition that trench warfare had brought deadlock in France and Flanders. It was the year the Easterners — those who wanted to fight the war someplace else than the western front — had their chance and muffed it.

Both the Allies and the Central Powers had their Easterners and their Westerners. In Britain and France the eyes of the Easterners turned to Italy and the Balkans, to Salonika, even to Mesopotamia and Palestine. In Germany the Easterners were those who wanted to knock Russia out of the war first. In both cases the Easterners were, in general, more intelligent than the Westerners (Lloyd George and Churchill as opposed to French, Haig, and Robertson; Ludendorff and Hoffmann as opposed to Falkenhayn and Gerhard Tappen); but the difference was that the Allied Easterners were wrong and the German Easterners were right. It was typical of this war that the ones who were wrong were given a chance to prove it, and that the ones who were right never had such an opportunity.

Falkenhayn, having failed to break through at First Ypres and realizing that his Austrian ally would need considerable help to stay in the war, decided to stand on the defensive in the west and turn his attention to the east. This was the first time, but by no means the last, that German strategy would waver between east and west. The problem now was basically the same as the one Schlieffen had faced — so long ago, it seemed. Since Germany could not afford to divide her forces equally on her fronts, which front should be given priority? In essence the problem was so simple that the toss of a coin could have decided it — east or west, heads or tails. Nor would the German

strategists have done ill to settle the matter in this way; it would surely
have been preferable to what they actually did, which was to keep
changing their minds and striking blows first on one front and then
on the other.

In retrospect it would appear that Schlieffen had been wrong and
that the eastern front should have been given priority from the outset.
This was the strategy that the great Moltke had favored, and perhaps
this very fact had made Schlieffen look for an alternative rather than
merely follow tamely in the steps of his famous predecessor. For
priority to be given to the eastern front two questions had to be answered affirmatively. Could the Russian armies be caught and killed?
And could the western front be held against French and British attacks while Germany diverted large forces to the east?

Schlieffen had feared that the Russians might "withdraw into the
interior of their enormous Empire" rather than stand and give battle,
but in fact the Russians never had any such intention. On the contrary, they were committed by the terms of the Dual Entente to an
immediate offensive against East Prussia, and of their own free will
they undertook a simultaneous and much larger offensive against the
Austrian front in Galicia. Given the nature of the Dual Entente and
the long-standing Russian bitterness against Austria, this had been entirely predictable. Russia was the weaker member of the Dual Entente
and it is almost always a good idea to attack weakness rather than
strength. In the east there was space for maneuver, which would have
greatly favored the better-trained Germans. Since the Russian government was an autocracy, it could have made a separate peace more
easily than the French and British governments could. Victory or
peace in the east would have made considerable supplies of foodstuffs
available to Germany and would in large measure have countered the
effects of the British blockade.

A defensive in the west would have made the invasion of Belgium
unnecessary, and if Belgium had not been invaded, Britain would
have entered the war a divided nation. The stopping power of the defensive would probably have made it safe for Germany to employ
nearly two thirds of her army in the east while leaving only about
one third in the west. Germany's western front would have been
strained and hard pressed, but it would probably not have broken,
and France would have been bled white more effectively than she was
at Verdun.

All the arguments in favor of Germany's giving priority to the eastern front applied in 1915 just as they had in 1914. Perhaps even more
so, for the superiority of the defensive had been conclusively demonstrated in the first five months of the war, the British forces on the

continent were still small, the French army had suffered huge casualties, and the Russians still gave no sign of any voluntary retirement.

Falkenhayn, probably alone among all the generals on either side, did not believe in the possibility of decisive victory. That hope had died in him with the failure of First Ypres and now he sought only an acceptable peace. He believed that if France and Britain became convinced they could not win the war, he would have no trouble in reaching a peace with Russia. The proposition should have been reversed: if Russia makes peace, the French and British will be far more readily convinced that they cannot win the war. But basically Falkenhayn was a Westerner, who not only considered the western front the decisive one, but who also believed that the only way peace could be achieved was by striking the French so hard a blow that they would recognize the futility of continuing the struggle.

The trouble with Falkenhayn's strategy was that he did not have the strength to implement it. Warfare is necessarily a thing of makeshifts and expedients, where the ideal must continually be subordinated to the possible.* Falkenhayn could not assemble sufficient forces to deal with the French while the Russians remained a threat in the east, and Conrad was already beginning to worry about his ability to hold the Carpathians. Furthermore, in March the Royal Navy made a half-hearted attempt to force the Dardanelles, and if this enterprise were renewed with vigor, Turkey would be in grave danger. To assist Turkey it would first be necessary to knock Serbia out of the war. Reluctantly, therefore, Falkenhayn came to the conclusion that things would have to be tidied up in the east before he could turn west.

But Falkenhayn had no notion of knocking Russia out of the war. All he hoped to achieve was a "crippling" of Russia, a driving back of the tsar's armies, so that Germany could gain the time for another great effort in the west. Yet to achieve this it proved necessary, in the course of 1915, to raise the strength of the German army in the east to a total of sixty-five divisions. If another twenty or thirty divisions had been sent to the Russian front, it is probable that Russia could have been forced to make peace that year. Falkenhayn's strategy was essentially one of half measures, oversubtle and faint-hearted; it had the most profound effects on the outcome of the war and the future of the world.

Of course, what the Russians should have done in 1915 was make peace, but honor and the Dual Entente forbade. And the Russian high command, as opposed to the Russian army, still believed in the possibility of victory. Early in January 1915 the Grand Duke Nicholas

*The British minister of war, Lord Kitchener, at about this time was realizing the same thing — "We have to wage war as we can," he said, "not as we would like to."

was preparing for an offensive that he hoped would break through the Carpathians and into the plains of Hungary. The intelligence staff at *Ober-Ost* had little difficulty in piecing together the strategic plan of the Grand Duke Nicholas. Ludendorff and Hoffmann promptly decided to forestall him by striking first, in midwinter. *Ober-Ost* now controlled three armies: the Eighth, in East Prussia; the Ninth, near Warsaw; and the Tenth, southeast of Tilsit. The Russian Tenth Army under General Sievers was poised for the invasion of East Prussia but was somewhat weak on both flanks. The German plan was to attack these flanks and catch the Russian Tenth Army in a double envelopment. As a distraction, the German Ninth Army attacked at Bolimov on January 31, using, for the first time, eighteen thousand shells containing poison gas. Surprise was achieved, but the gas proved a disappointment because its effects were much reduced by the freezing cold.

A diversionary German-Austrian offensive in the Carpathians made little headway in January, but the German offensive in the north achieved complete surprise when it opened on February 7, in terrible winter weather. The Russian Tenth Army did its best to break away from the terrible twin claws closing in on it. Two of its corps managed to flounder back to comparative safety at Grodno, but the third corps and many thousands of stragglers were cut off and forced to surrender in the forest of Avgustov. This "Winter Battle of Masuria" was another epic German victory, with some 110,000 Russians taken prisoner and perhaps another 100,000 killed, but it made surprisingly little difference to the eastern front. The Germans had advanced seventy miles in two weeks, but they were still as far away as ever from defeating Russia.

Two plans for operations against Russia were presented to Falkenhayn in the summer of 1915. One, drawn up by Conrad, called for a penetration of the Russian front between Gorlice and Tarnow in the western Carpathians, and one, prepared by Ludendorff and Hoffmann, called for an enveloping offensive from the northwest to the southeast that would sweep around behind Warsaw. Conrad hoped to drive the Russians back; Ludendorff and Hoffmann, on the other hand, aimed at the destruction of the Russian armies and the elimination of Russia from the war. Falkenhayn chose Conrad's plan, for he considered *Ober-Ost*'s proposal too large and ambitious. Even when he was concentrating on the eastern front Falkenhayn was continually looking over his shoulder to the west. He was always anxious to hedge his bets, to be perfectly secure everywhere, so he refused to take calculated risks. Schlieffen, for all his faults, had better understood the nature of war, which, like fortune, favors the bold, if not always the brave.

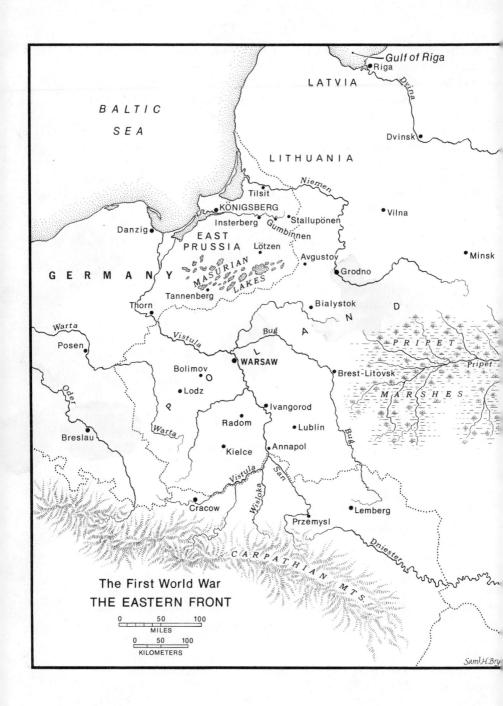

The First World War
THE EASTERN FRONT

The offensive was launched on May 2 along the thirty-mile stretch of front between Gorlice and Tarnow, and it was immediately success-ful. On most of the front the Russians simply abandoned their trenches and fled. The Grand Duke Nicholas fell back from the Car-pathians in disarray, having lost 140,000 in prisoners alone. By the middle of May General August von Mackensen reached the San. This was far enough for Falkenhayn, whose eyes were again turning back to the west, and only Conrad's pleadings persuaded him to continue the offensive. When Lemberg fell on June 22, the Eleventh Army wheeled north between the Vistula and the Bug toward Brest-Litovsk.

Hoffmann now argued desperately that Mackensen's offensive would never be decisive. What was needed was a way of catching and killing the Russian armies. Hoffmann's plan was that the German Tenth Army should attack from the west while the Niemen Army at-tacked from the north, encircling and capturing Kovno. With Kovno in German hands, the road to Vilna and the Russian rear would be open. The Niemen Army would then wheel south between Kovno and Grodno, marching between Brest-Litovsk and the Pripet Marshes. If successful, this enormous envelopment would virtually destroy the Russian army, and the nightmare war on two fronts would be as good as over.

Hoffmann convinced Ludendorff, but Falkenhayn was far too cau-tious and unimaginative to be attracted by so bold a concept. Yet the reinforcements that would have been required from the western front could easily have been spared; it would merely have meant that Fal-kenhayn would have had to give up his intention of striking France at Verdun. The kaiser, when appealed to, supported his Chief of the General Staff. The next German attack would be launched across the Narev, not the Niemen. It is very probable that this decision lost Ger-many the war, for if Hoffmann's plan had succeeded, Russia would have been forced to make a separate peace in 1915 instead of two years later.

The frontal attack southeast across the Narev opened on July 13. Warsaw fell on August 5, and the Grand Duke Nicholas withdrew from the line of the Vistula. Brest-Litovsk fell, and still the Russian retreat went on. By the end of September the front ran almost due north and south from Dvinsk to the Rumanian border. The Russians had by then suffered a million casualties and lost three quarters of a million men as prisoners. The Grand Duke Nicholas was relieved of his command, to be replaced by the tsar as commander-in-chief with General Mikhail Alexeiev as his Chief of the Imperial General Staff. The tsar was in no sense of the word a soldier, and Alexeiev, although a competent staff officer, was not a commander. The work of the Stavka could only deteriorate with the change of command.

Falkenhayn was well pleased with the result of the campaign, and, superficially, it had been a great success. Nineteen fifteen was the worst year for Russia in the entire war, and it was Russian losses in that year that eventually led to such a deterioration of morale that revolution swept the tsarist regime away. But although imperial Russia had been dealt a mortal wound in 1915, she was a long time in dying. Russia was battered, bleeding, all but out on her feet, but still sufficiently strong to require great German forces in the east. What was to haunt Germany everywhere throughout the war had been repeated here again — great tactical success, which fell just short of strategic victory. Hoffmann and Ludendorff did not share Falkenhayn's elation, and they had the better reasons for their attitude.

The British reaction to the events of 1914 had been not unlike the German. Although Britain was not faced with a war on two fronts, British counsels, just like German, were divided between those who sought a decision on the western front and those who looked for it elsewhere. Germany was limited to one alternative, Russia; but Britain had a variety of strategic choices open to her — or so it seemed — because of the mobility conferred by her sea power. As early as January 2, 1915, Kitchener wrote to Sir John French:

> I suppose we must now recognize that the French Army cannot make a sufficient break through the German lines of defense to cause a complete change of the situation and bring about the retreat of the German forces from northern Belgium. If that is so, then the German lines in France may be looked upon as a fortress that cannot be carried by assault, and also cannot be completely invested — with the result that the lines can only be held by an investing force, while operations proceed elsewhere.

This was masterly for the date on which it was written, and typical of the flashes of insight Kitchener occasionally had.* Traditionally, Britain had been a naval rather than a land power, and she had fought her wars economically, with small expeditionary forces in remote theaters. She had supported her allies by naval blockade and money rather than with large armies. Some members of the British cabinet hoped that she might do so still, for they failed to realize the implications of the fatal commitment to France. Paul Cambon, the French ambassador, had known better: "A great Power does not wage war by halves." Because France and Russia would have been defeated had not Britain assumed more and more of the burden of the war, the

---

*Kitchener had also predicted that the war might last three or four years, when everyone else expected to be in Berlin before Christmas. Lloyd George later was to compare Kitchener's mind to a lighthouse that every once in a while sent forth a penetrating beam of light and then relapsed into total darkness.

traditional British policy was no longer possible. Eventually the new policy that was forced on Britain was to result in her destruction as a great power.

Britain's primary mistake, like tsarist Russia's, had been the alignment with France, but this error had been compounded by the almost complete British subservience to French strategy. France had grievously overestimated both her own and Russia's strength. And the strength that the Dual Entente had possessed had been gravely weakened by military stupidity in the first few months of the war. There were three pressures that forced the British government to forsake its traditional policy and raise huge new armies of the continental type.

The most important of these pressures was the fact that the war could be won only by the defeat of the German army. Naval blockade by itself would be insufficient to ensure victory. The only alternative to defeating the German army in battle was to make peace, and that seemed a political impossibility. For a democracy like Britain, which had gone to war for insufficient and obscure reasons, it had been necessary to inflame popular opinion against the enemy and to present the war in sharply contrasting moral terms. The enemy was all black; the Allied cause, pure virtue. The angels that had allegedly halted the German advance at Mons had been doing nothing more than could reasonably have been expected of them. This attitude, so sedulously cultivated by propaganda, certainly had its short-term practical uses, but it severely restricted the British government's freedom of maneuver.

The second pressure was the fear that France might make a separate peace. Joffre actually threatened this in July 1915, to ensure British participation in his next offensive. If Britain did not seem to be "pulling her weight," the French might easily become discouraged, and any attractive German offer, such as a restoration of Alsace-Lorraine in exchange for the German retention of Belgium, might be accepted by the French government. The parallel between Britain and Germany is instructive; France and Austria could each blackmail its ally by threatening suicide.

The third pressure on the British government, though probably the weakest, was that exerted by the British high command, which opposed any weakening of the British armies in France in favor of "side shows." The fact that the high command was right was irrelevant. Had it been wrong the result would have been much the same, for the myth-making that is an indispensable part of modern mass warfare tied the government's hands. The replacement of a commander-in-chief who had been built up in the popular mind as a hero might bring about the downfall of the government. Lloyd George never felt strong enough to dismiss Haig, just as the kaiser never felt strong enough to dismiss Hindenburg.

None of this was as plain at the beginning of 1915 as it later became. Alternatives to the western front were being earnestly canvassed at the beginning of the year. Admiral Fisher was still advocating his mad scheme of landing an army in Schleswig. Lloyd George wanted to attack the Central Powers through Salonika or Dalmatia, "in conjunction with the Serbians, the Rumanians and the Greeks." He was quite undeterred in his advocacy of this plan by the fact that both Rumania and Greece were neutral. Lloyd George also advocated an attack on the Turkish army through Syria. The chancellor of the exchequer had a good deal to say about "bringing Germany down by the process of knocking the props from under her," though it was not Austria and Turkey who were propping up Germany, but vice versa.

These schemes and others like them were laudable in intent, being designed to avoid the killing match that would be inevitable if a decision were sought on the western front. Perhaps the time to have faced such unpleasant realities was July 1914 rather than January 1915, but there was no point in thinking of that now. Unfortunately, there was no real point either in the suggested strategies. The German army had to be beaten, and this could be done only in France. Furthermore, if the western front were starved of reinforcements and supplies so that these could be used in the Balkans or Asia Minor, there was the very real danger that the Germans might break through. An advance of forty or fifty miles in France might end the war, whereas Salonika or Syria was far from any vital point. Finally, what would be the good of any of these distractions? The defensive would still be superior to the offensive in any theater, and Germany could reinforce by rail more quickly than the Allies could build up by sea. The bitter truth was that the pattern of the war had been fixed on the outbreak of the war, and if the politicians found that it was not a pattern they liked or had anticipated, they really had no one but themselves to blame.

One scheme, however, appeared promising — the Gallipoli peninsula should be seized, the Royal Navy should enter the Sea of Marmara, and, with the aid of a Russian army, subdue Turkey. The virtue of this suggestion over all the others lay in its aim, which was not the opening of another front against Turkey but the opening of a sea route to Russia. When the "invisible portcullis" had fallen across the Dardanelles in August 1914, Russia had at a stroke been deprived of her trade outlet through the Bosphorus and the straits — and in peacetime 90 percent of her grain exports, 50 percent of all her exports, and about the same amount of her imports had been shipped by this route. With the closing of Russia's land frontiers by the war and with the German blockade of the Baltic, Russian exports declined by 98 percent and her imports by 95 percent. The Central Powers had their hands firmly on Russia's windpipe, and the giant was slowly but surely being strangled.

Apart from its strategic advantages, the idea of capturing the Dardanelles appealed to the British for other reasons. The navy would find more spectacular employment than sitting at Scapa Flow waiting for the High Seas Fleet to emerge; success here could mean that Italy, Greece, Rumania, and even Bulgaria might be induced to enter the war on the Allied side; the business of killing Germans could be undertaken by the Russians rather than by Kitchener's New Armies; Britain could again be triumphant by using her old weapons of sea power and money.

This was all true and it was all possible — or should have been possible. But what actually happened was more complex and more heartbreaking. Comparisons with Greek tragedy, of course, are maddeningly frequent, but it is really difficult to escape comparing the Gallipoli campaign to Greek tragedy: the audience can see the truth plainly, but the actors are blind; the chorus warns, but the warnings go unheeded; the key to it all is a fatal flaw in character.

To begin with there was the grim irony that a Dardanelles expedition should have been necessary at all. If in 1908 Sir Edward Grey and the pundits of the Foreign Office had been prepared to grant Izvolsky the control of the straits, Russia would not now have been choking to death. But, then, if Grey had agreed to the Russian control of the Dardanelles in 1908, there would have been no Bosnian crisis and probably no war. That, however, was no more than the opening chorus, although it might have conveyed a hint or two to the initiated as to how the main action of the tragedy was likely to unfold. The British government, which had drifted unthinkingly and carelessly into war, was now to be unthinking and careless again; it was to appoint commanders who typified itself; the end was in the beginning. Other bungled operations in this war were to cost the British army far more in direct casualties — though the butcher's bill at Gallipoli was to be 214,000 men — but no other operation was so negatively decisive. Britain here had a chance to win the war on the cheap, to maintain her position as a great power, to retrieve at one stroke all the errors and follies of the past.

Or did she? Was the failure, on the other hand, inevitable, grounded in some obscure dialectic of character, and did all the actors merely play out their roles in the only way they could?

On January 3 Winston Churchill, the First Lord of the Admiralty, telegraphed Vice Admiral Sir Sackville Carden, commander of the British naval squadron in the eastern Mediterranean, asking him whether he considered the forcing of the Dardanelles by ships alone a practical operation. Carden replied, as was expected of him, that he thought it was. Accordingly, a plan was drawn up for a new battle-ship, *Queen Elizabeth*, and eleven other ships, four of them French, to sail into the Hellespont and reduce the Turkish forts by gunfire. Naval suggestions that a land expedition should cooperate received short shrift; the troops, Kitchener said, were needed in France.

Carden began a leisurely bombardment of the Turkish forts on February 19. A week after the attack started, British marines and sailors landed without opposition and blew up the guns on some of the forts at the entrance to the Dardanelles. Cape Helles and the Asia-tic side were bare of Turkish troops, and the British strolled about freely in the open on ground that soon had to be taken at a high cost in blood. On March 18 the fleet sailed in to attack the forts at the Nar-rows, which one by one were battered into silence. Early in the after-noon, however, the French ship *Bouvet* struck a mine and sank within two minutes, with 640 of her crew. Within a few hours three old British ships were also sunk by mines. Vice Admiral John de Robeck, who had replaced Carden, refused to continue the action. At this time, as was later revealed, the Turks were beaten and a further British effort would have won the day, but the admiral turned his ships around and sailed for Tenedos, where he waited for the army to come to help him.

General Sir Ian Hamilton, a sixty-two-year-old soldier and poet who had been a protégé of Kitchener's during the South African War, had already been appointed to command a military expedition to Gal-lipoli. The War Office had given him no plan of operations, no defi-nite instructions, and no information about the enemy, and the maps with which he was supplied were out of date and inaccurate.* Hamil-ton's force consisted of the 29th Division, the last of the British regu-lar divisions, the Australian and New Zealand Army Corps (ANZAC) of two divisions under General Sir William Birdwood, the Royal Naval Division, and a French division. The force had been assembled in haste, and when the transports arrived at the base at Lemnos, it was discovered that they had not been tactically loaded (guns were sepa-rated from their limbers and ammunition; unit equipment was di-vided among several ships; important items were buried deep in the

*All this was in keeping with the British tradition for combined operations. General Sir John Moore had exactly the same complaints about the outfitting of his expedition to the Iberian peninsula in 1808.

holds under tons of superfluous material).* Hamilton decided there was nothing for it but to turn all the transports around, go to Alexandria, and repack.

By April 25, when the landings at last began, the Turks, under their German commander, Liman von Sanders, had made preparations to receive visitors. In fact the Turkish defending force now consisted of six divisions, as opposed to the five divisions Hamilton had for his assault. The British plan called for landings in two main areas: around Cape Helles on the toe of the peninsula and on the western beaches north of Gaba Tepe. General Hamilton decided to remain aboard the *Queen Elizabeth*, where he could exercise absolutely no control over the battle.†

The landings began in the dark, shortly after four o'clock in the morning. The Australians and New Zealanders got ashore without too much trouble at Anzac Cove, but everyone promptly got lost, units became mixed up, and no advance could be begun until hours after daylight. By then the Turks under Mustapha Kemal had rallied and counterattacked. At the end of the long day the Dominion troops were holding a precarious beachhead some two miles long by three quarters of a mile deep. The story at Cape Helles was far worse. Two of the landings went smoothly, but once the troops were ashore, no one knew what they were supposed to do next, so they lay about, cooked breakfast, and made tea while their comrades were being slaughtered a short distance away. On the southern tip of the peninsula, the British who attempted to disembark from the landing ship *River Clyde* were mowed down by Turkish fire. The British and Anzacs held on to their narrow toeholds on the beaches at Anzac Cove and Cape Helles, resisting every attempt to drive them back into the sea. But if the British were not to be driven from the peninsula, neither could they advance. The British government, afraid to admit defeat, and unable to think of a solution, left the Gallipoli front to fester.

Hamilton's force grew from five divisions to eight, but the Turks were reinforced too, and more easily. The War Committee of the cabinet was now renamed — fantastically — the Dardanelles Committee, and a new landing was decided upon. Two divisions of green

---

*Students of comparative military history may be interested in the reflection that almost exactly similar complaints about poor tactical loading of transports were made at the time of the Anglo-French invasion at Suez in 1956.

†Not from any lack of personal courage. Sir Ian Hamilton had the well-deserved reputation of being one of the most gallant officers in the British army, and he was to prove himself utterly fearless time and again at Gallipoli. What he lacked was not courage but rather the determination to impose his will on his subordinate commanders and events. He was, perhaps, too much a gentleman to be a good commander.

troops were brought out from England and thrown ashore at Sulva Bay, a few miles north of Anzac Cove. Hamilton had asked that this corps be commanded by a commander from France, but the War Office gave him instead the senior lieutenant general, the Honorable Sir Frederick Stopford, sixty-one years of age and a very pleasant gentleman who had been Lieutenant of the Tower of London. Stopford had never commanded troops in war, and it cannot really be said that he did so at Gallipoli.

Simultaneously with the landings at Sulva, an attack was to be launched at Anzac Beach, and the peninsula was to be cut at the Narrows. The operation began on August 6, but once again there was no firm hand in control, and initial success petered out. Hamilton stayed at Imbros; Stopford stayed aboard the sloop *Jonquil;* and the infantry commander ashore had a nervous breakdown. At the end of the operation the British were left with three beachheads instead of two, none of them connected, and with the tactical situation as hopeless as ever.

Prime Minister Eleutherios Venizelos of Greece, who was anxious to bring his country into the war on the Entente side, now asked for 150,000 Allied troops. The French at once agreed and began assembling a force under General Maurice Sarrail* for Salonika. In response to French pressure, the British moved the 10th Division from Sulva to join Sarrail. While all this was going on, Venizelos' policy was repudiated by the Greeks, who did not want to get involved in so unpleasant a war, and Venizelos was forced to resign, but the French and the British went ahead with their plans in any case. The first Allied troops invaded neutral Greece on October 5, an act not notably different from the German invasion of Belgium in 1914.

Hamilton was relieved of his command in the middle of October, and his successor, Lieutenant General Sir Charles Monro, arrived at Gallipoli on the 23rd, visited all three beachheads, and promptly recommended evacuation. At first the British cabinet would not accept such a solution, although it was not so much the predicted casualties that worried them as the belief that an admission of defeat at Gallipoli would cause the British to lose face in the East. Such staunch defenders of the empire as Lord Curzon and Lord Selborne were especially worried about the reaction among Britain's Moslem subjects.

Only more bitterness was in store for the Allies as 1915 drew to a close. Falkenhayn decided to crush Serbia because the best route for

---

*The French government was anxious to get Sarrail out of France because they feared his political influence. Sarrail, a left-wing anticleric and Mason, had been relieved of his command by Joffre in July, and his political friends were demanding his re-employment.

the relief of Turkey was across her territory. On October 7, German and Austrian armies advanced into Serbia, and on the 11th the Bulgarians attacked in Macedonia. General Sarrail, a very indifferent soldier, attempted to come to Serbia's aid by moving up the Vardar valley from Salonika, but the Bulgarians threw him back unceremoniously.

Within three weeks Serbia was effectively knocked out of the war. The tattered remnants of the Serbian army crossed the Albanian mountains, in terrible winter weather, to find refuge on the Adriatic coast. The Germans and Austrians were content to let them escape, but the Bulgarians, remembering many wrongs, pursued as fiercely as wolves. Of the 450,000-man Serbian army, fewer than 125,000 survived to be transported by the Allies to Corfu.

The British, who had never believed in the Salonika expedition, now wanted to withdraw, but the French refused. Reluctantly, the British agreed to maintain forces in Salonika for the sake of Allied harmony. The Salonika front was reinforced until at last there were more than half a million French and British troops bottled up in the port and the desolate hinterland. The Germans contemptuously, but with reason, referred to this theater as "our largest internment camp."

The British cabinet, dissatisfied with Kitchener's conduct of the war, greatly reduced his authority but left him in the government because he was idolized by the British public.* The cabinet did, however, agree to evacuate Gallipoli. The troops were withdrawn from Sulva and Anzac without trouble; not a man was lost; and by December 20 the last rear guard had safely embarked. On January 8 and 9 a similarly successful evacuation was conducted at Cape Helles.

The British government, desperately seeking some ray of sunshine, looked about the world and saw only disaster. The Russian armies had lost Warsaw and Kovno and Brest-Litovsk, and the Russian government was muttering angrily about the paucity of aid from its allies. Bulgaria had joined the Central Powers; Serbia had been overrun; Greece was hostile because of the invasion of Salonika. The operations in France and Belgium had turned out to be a bloody shambles. After Basra had fallen the previous December, the expedition to Mesopotamia had almost been forgotten, but in the meantime its ambitious commander, General Sir John Nixon, had inched his way forward to Kut-el-Amara, a hundred miles from Baghdad. The British cabinet, suddenly noting this, decided that it was the "one bright spot on the military horizon" and, for no better reason than that, informed the viceroy of India that "Nixon may march on Baghdad."

*As Lady Asquith remarked, he made "a wonderful poster."

Meanwhile, Italy had completed her transfer of allegiance and joined the Entente, declaring war on Austria on May 23, although — cautious even in treachery — she refrained for the time being from declaring war on Germany. Italy had had reasonable grounds for declaring her neutrality in 1914, but her entry into the war was quite frankly purchased by the Allies with promises of Austrian territory. In spite of the lavish Allied promises, a majority of the Italian Chamber of Deputies had wanted to keep Italy out of the war, but they had been intimidated by organized mobs who attacked the parliament buildings and staged mass demonstrations in Rome. Italy's prime minister, Antonio Salandra, spoke of his government's "*sacro egoismo*" and was at least half right.

In 1915 Italy was able to raise some forty-two indifferent divisions, poorly equipped and badly officered. With this force she launched four consecutive attacks against the Isonzo lines in the northeast. These abortive assaults, made uphill against smaller Austrian forces, were grandiosely named the First, Second, Third, and Fourth Battles of the Isonzo. None of them made any headway, and in this they were similar to the Fifth, Sixth, Seventh, Eighth, Ninth, Tenth, and Eleventh Battles of the Isonzo, which marked Italy's later contribution to the war. The unfortunate Italian infantry, driven into battle, in 1915, at the behest of megalomaniac politicians and journalists, suffered a quarter of a million casualties.

On March 12, Britain, by another secret treaty, promised Russia that after the war she could have Constantinople, Galicia, and the control of the Balkans. The French foreign minister, who now once again was Théophile Delcassé, signed a similar agreement with Russia on April 12. The British promised the French that they could have Syria, and encouraged people like T. E. Lawrence to promise the Arabs that they could create a great Arab state, which would include Syria, after the war. In truth, it was not only Palestine that was the much-promised land, although both Jews and Arabs were in fact given conflicting and contradictory assurances about that territory. Anything that might help to win the war seemed justified by 1915.

Although the western front in 1915 was for Germany a secondary theater, it could never be so for France. General Joffre had no such choice before him as Falkenhayn had. Joffre *had* to attack in 1915, for the strategic position of France was, to say the least, serious. France had suffered nearly three quarters of a million casualties in 1914, and had lost almost all of northern France, where much of her industry had been situated. Naturally, the chief preoccupation of French strategy was to regain this occupied territory. Allied resources still seemed sufficient to achieve this objective, for though the German army in the west was to reach a total of ninety-four divisions in 1915, it was still outnumbered by a ratio of more than three to two. France fielded 107 divisions in the year, and the British army on the continent grew from ten divisions to thirty-seven, including two Canadian divisions. These, plus the six divisions of the Belgian army, gave an Allied total of 150 divisions.

When the ebb and flow of battle had congealed into trench lines with the coming of winter, it was found that the German front from Verdun to Ypres bulged out to the west in a great salient whose apex was to the west of St. Quentin. Joffre's plan for 1915, like Plan XVII for 1914, was a simple one: attacks at either end of the salient would narrow the base and exaggerate the configuration of the bulge; then a third offensive from the direction of Verdun would cut in behind the Germans and cut their lines of communication through Belgium and Luxembourg. The plan looked reasonable on the map, and the French persisted in it throughout the entire war. It was never successful, and it never had any chance of succeeding, for the base of the salient was too wide, some 150 miles, and the salient itself too blunt for the entrapment of any considerable body of troops.

Such arguments, however, are entirely academic, for the Allies were never able to achieve a breakthrough. This was only partly because of the inherent tactical superiority of the defensive, though this factor was enormously important. Trenches, barbed wire entanglements, and defensive fire from both machine guns and artillery made frontal attacks very expensive, and because the trench system was continuous between Switzerland and the sea, only frontal attacks were possible. The French and British generals realized this, but not as soon as they should have, and came up with a simple answer — more artillery. As it happened, this was not the right answer. Sufficient defenders could usually survive even the heaviest bombardment, and artillery fire churned up the ground so badly that the attacking infantry was slowed to a crawl. Worse still from the attackers' point of view was the fact that strategic mobility had not been impaired, as had tactical mobility, by the weapons system in use. The defender could always reinforce by rail around the circumference of a breakthrough more rapidly than the attacker could advance in a straight line across country.*

In 1915 Joffre believed that the old methods would work, that

*Another point worth noting is that, through almost the entire war, the Germans, who intended to remain on the defensive, sited and constructed their trench systems with far more care and elaboration than the Allies, who intended at the first possible moment to abandon their trenches and advance. This often meant that the Germans lived in relative comfort, and the British and French endured severe and avoidable hardships.

trench lines could be broken by artillery preparation and massed infantry assaults. In any case the attempt had to be made, because if the
French army merely sat still in front of the German lines waiting for
something to turn up, Germany would be free to turn against Russia.
If that happened it might not even be necessary for the Germans to
destroy the Russian armies, for Russia would be unlikely to persevere
in a war in which she alone was bearing the burden of sacrifice. The
Triple Entente, which had seemed so formidable a combination before it was put to the test of war, was now demonstrating its basic
weakness. It was like three rifles piled together — if one rifle was removed, the other two would fall down. To prevent this sort of collapse, each of the Allies at one time or another was forced to undertake operations that it knew were strategically unsound and that could
end only in severe losses.

Joffre's first Battle of Champagne, which had opened on December
20, 1914, continued in March of 1915 with attacks between Arras and
Ypres. The French lost 90,000 men in unproductive assaults that
never endangered the German line at any point. Not to be outdone,
the British launched an attack of their own against Neuve Chapelle.
What possible strategic reason there was for this offensive is difficult
to fathom. It seems to have been undertaken chiefly because Sir John
French was irritated by Joffre's criticisms that the British "were not
pulling their weight." On March 10, Haig's First Army attacked after
a short preliminary bombardment. By the time the offensive bogged
down, British losses totaled 11,652 men, a high price to pay for some
400 acres of useless ground. An attack by two French armies against
the St. Mihiel Salient south of Verdun was persisted in for two weeks
in April, but resulted in nothing but more casualties.

The next move was made by the Germans. Although Falkenhayn
intended to stand on the defensive in the west in 1915, he permitted a
limited German offensive against the Ypres Salient in April to distract
attention from German troop withdrawals for the east. He also hoped
to pinch out the salient and to test a new weapon, chlorine gas.

In April 1915 the salient was being held by six divisions: two French
divisions on the left, the Canadian division in the center, and three
British divisions on the right. At four o'clock on the afternoon of
April 22 the Germans released a cloud of chlorine gas against the
French divisions on the left, and the French troops broke and fled,
leaving a gaping hole in the Allied line. Canadian reinforcements
were hurriedly sent to seal off this gap, and succeeded in doing so although they were desperately thin on the ground. The Germans were
unable to exploit their success because they were surprised by it and
did not have reserves available. Falkenhayn's policy of half measures

thus proved as unproductive in the west as it was to do in the east. Desperate fighting continued sporadically until the middle of May, but the most significant result of Second Ypres turned out to be the pig-headed British decision to hang on to the reduced salient. That little patch of Flanders proved to be a killing ground for British armies for the rest of the war.

Joffre was still far from discouraged by previous failures. With a persistence that would have been admirable had it not been completely divorced from reality, he attacked again on May 9 in Artois. The French Tenth Army under General Victor d'Urbal assaulted Vimy Ridge, but after seven days of very hard fighting the French had still not reached the crest and had lost more than one hundred thousand men. A small British diversionary attack against Aubers Ridge also failed, with heavy losses, but Joffre and Foch both pressed Sir John French to continue his attacks. Accordingly, Haig's First Army launched a fresh offensive north of the La Bassée Canal near Festubert on May 15. A series of gallant but suicidal attacks by Canadian and British troops advanced the line some 600 yards and cost sixteen thousand casualties. The ominous significance of Festubert lay in what it revealed of Haig's mentality, for he was to repeat the same sort of futility on a far larger scale in the future.

Nothing much happened in the west during the summer. Joffre, who took the German success at Gorlice-Tarnow as a proof that trench lines could be broken, prepared for a renewal of his offensives. His plan was still to attack both in Artois and Champagne at the sides of the great salient, and he was insistent that the British cooperate by an offensive between Lens and La Bassée. Neither Haig, whose army was to conduct this operation, nor Sir John French liked the chosen battlefield, which was covered with sprawling mining villages and slag heaps. The French high command appealed to the British government, and Lord Kitchener, worried about the possibility of Russia or France making a separate peace, ordered the British commander-in-chief to cooperate fully with Joffre's offensive. Haig was told that "[we must] act with all our energy, and do our utmost to help the French, even though, by doing so, we suffer very heavy losses indeed." Joffre, in his magisterial way, overruled British objections about the slag heaps and mining villages by simply declaring, "Your attack will find particularly favorable ground between Loos and La Bassée."

For various reasons the French offensives had to be delayed, so the Germans learned what was afoot. They were not seriously alarmed, but Falkenhayn did send four divisions back from the eastern front. The offensive in Champagne opened first, on September 25. Pétain's Second Army and Langle de Cary's Fourth Army attacked six German divisions, and though suffering heavy losses, gained some ground, but the Germans had prepared a second line, where they made their real stand. This was the first occasion when a second line of defense had been thoroughly prepared, with its wire and trenches beyond the reach of the attacker's field artillery. From this seed of an idea was later to grow the concept of all-round defense in depth. Even this first modification of the old idea of "one line and a strong one" was sufficient to baffle the attackers. By the 28th, Joffre had to break off the engagement.

Meanwhile the French Tenth Army and the British First Army attacked in Artois with similar results. The British assault at Loos was badly mismanaged by Sir John French, who kept his reserves too far back and was late in committing them. The British, despite what their propagandists had said about the barbarism of the weapon, now employed poison gas, although to little effect. On the 26th, Joffre halted the French attacks, telegraphing to Foch:

> Stop the attacks of the Tenth Army, taking care to avoid giving to the British the impression that we are leaving them to attack alone, or to the Germans that we are relaxing our efforts.

In this remarkable example of inter-Allied loyalty, it is to be noted that, though Joffre intended to deceive both the British and the Germans, he gave priority to the deception of the British.

Both of Joffre's offensives had thus failed ignominiously, and even though fighting later flared up around Hill 70 and in Champagne, nothing more of note occurred after the end of September. These futile attacks in the autumn of 1915 cost the British more than 48,000 casualties and the French more than 191,000. German losses were high, but very considerably less. One result of the failures of 1915 was that Sir John French was persuaded, not without difficulty, to tender his resignation on December 4. His successor was his former subordinate (who had, incidentally, conspired to get rid of him), Sir Douglas Haig.

For 1915 as a whole, French losses on the western front totaled an awful 1,624,000 men. British casualties were 296,500, and German casualties 873,200, less than half the Allied total. For this enormous price in dead and wounded the Allies, as Churchill said, had "of 19,500 square miles of German-occupied France and Belgium . . . recovered about eight square miles." The year petered out as it had begun, in discouragement, pain, and loss.

CHAPTER III

NINETEEN SIXTEEN was the most bloodstained year in history. On the western front it was a year devoted to mutual attrition, the trading of blood for blood, in the hope that the enemy would somehow get the worst of the bargain. The Allied generals still clung to the belief that one more concerted, all-out offensive would break the German army and win the war. There was no rational basis for this hope, unless it was the faulty intelligence appreciations that forecast a shortage of German reserves in 1916. At a conference held at Joffre's headquarters in December 1915, the British, French, Russians, and Italians had agreed to take the offensive the following summer. Because Kitchener's New Armies had to be trained and equipped and because Britain had to build up her stock of guns and ammunition, the date for the great offensives was set as sometime in August. Thus the decision at Chantilly was that 1916 would see a repetition of 1915 — the same frontal attacks against the German trench lines, but with more men and, above all, more artillery.

The area selected for the Anglo-French offensive was the Somme front in Picardy, chosen not because any great strategic prize was to be won there but simply because the British and French sectors happened to join in this spot. Neither Joffre nor Haig was disturbed by the fact that the Germans could safely retire for miles in this sector without losing any important railhead or vital industrial complex. Nor were they disturbed by the exceptional strength of the German defenses along the Somme. It was a plan devoid of imagination, without subtlety, and divorced from common sense. No provision was made for attaining surprise; there was no concept of exerting leverage; the great projected attack would have no center of gravity. It was to be a broad-headed battering ram applied to the strongest section of the wall. Such a plan might have been drawn up by a sergeant major who had spent most of his life aligning troops on the parade ground.

Meanwhile, Joffre continued his policy of *grignotage*, "nibbling away," oblivious of the fact that it inevitably cost France more men than Germany, and that France, with her smaller population and lower birthrate, could less afford the loss. This was the ultimate bankruptcy of generalship, since the only reason for having generals is to apply some principle of intelligence to the exercise of force. By 1916 the Allied commanders had abdicated this responsibility. They had become the mere pourers-out of blood, content if their container was deeper than the enemy's.

Falkenhayn recognized this characteristic of his opponents and decided to take advantage of it. But Falkenhayn was never satisfied with the obvious, even when the obvious was obviously true. He had an involved, tortuous way of thinking. When, for example, he had decided in 1914 that the western front was the decisive theater, his reasoning had led him to attack in the east, but without any intention of seeking a decision there. Now that that attack had been successful — but less than decisive — he turned back to the west, and again his convoluted reasoning led him to a remarkable conclusion.

In December 1915, Falkenhayn wrote a memorandum to the kaiser in which he argued that Britain was Germany's principal enemy. Unfortunately, Britain was primarily a naval power and was, moreover, an island that the German army could not reach. The British portion of the western front was not suitable for offensive operations, and therefore it was not possible to strike a crippling blow directly at Britain. Unrestricted U-boat warfare should undoubtedly be begun at once, but as far as land operations were concerned, Britain could best be injured by a blow at France. The logic was typical of Falkenhayn, and so was the recommendation to reopen unrestricted U-boat warfare, which had been abandoned the previous September in deference to American outrage over the loss of American lives when the *Lusitania* was sunk off Queenstown. (Falkenhayn's suggestion was, in fact, adopted and the U-boats were unleashed, but the unrestricted campaign did not last long. When the Folkestone-Dieppe packet the *Sussex* was sunk on March 24, President Wilson threatened to sever diplomatic relations with Germany. The kaiser, wiser than his military advisers, insisted on limiting U-boat activity. It would have been better for Germany if he had similarly overruled Falkenhayn's military plan for 1916.)

The Chief of the General Staff's memorandum went on to describe the plan for striking at France:

France has arrived almost at the end of her military effort . . . If her people can be made to understand clearly that militarily they have nothing more to hope for, they will reach their breaking-point and England's best weapon will be knocked out of her hand.

Was ever a commander more enamored of paradox? If you seek a decision in the west, strike in the east; if you wish to injure Britain, strike at France. But there was more of this logic to come. The attack against the French would not aim at seizing any vital point, at disrupting French communications, or at encircling French armies. The aim of this offensive would be the same as that commonly chosen for a defensive action: the inflicting of losses on the enemy. He would attack, Falkenhayn said, some point "for the retention of which the French will be compelled to throw in every man they have." By a series of limited advances, he would lure the French reserves into a killing ground where they would be pulverized by artillery fire. France would be bled white, but if the battle ever showed signs of becoming too costly for Germany, it could be broken off at any time. He recommended that the historic French fortress of Verdun on the heights of the Meuse be chosen as the point of attack since it would meet admirably his requirements for a killing ground. It was the strongest fortress in the world; it was something of a menace to German communications; but, more important, for reasons of prestige the French would defend it regardless of cost.

Perhaps never in the history of warfare has so remarkable an assessment been provided by a commander-in-chief. Everything was stood on its head; everything was seen reversed, as in a mirror. Defeat the British by attacking the French; use the methods of the offensive to attain the aims of the defensive; establish killing grounds by capturing them. Surely the only just comment is that Falkenhayn was too clever by half. If he had wanted to wear down the French, to bleed them white — and, incidentally, the British too — all he had to do was wait until August, when Joffre and Haig would have done his work for him.

Falkenhayn gave his murderous plan the code name "*Gericht*" (a place of execution), but he did not inform either Crown Prince Wilhelm, who commanded the German Fifth Army, which would conduct the attack, or the Fifth Army's chief of staff, Lieutenant General Schmidt von Knobelsdorf, of the true aim of Operation Gericht, preferring to let them believe that he really intended to capture Verdun. The intellectual arrogance is breathtaking, and it was the cause of a fundamental miscalculation, for as the battle of Verdun rose to an unprecedented crescendo, the city became a symbol for the Germans no less than for the French. To the German people the capture of Verdun came to be regarded as an earnest of victory —

to the utter negation of sound strategy and military common sense.

Since the initial German attack was to be launched on a narrow front, with only nine divisions, it did not take long to prepare. Nevertheless, the French did learn what was in store for them, of course, for in the First World War it was really impossible to conceal the administrative build-up for a great set-piece attack. But GQG proved deaf to warnings. Although Verdun certainly had been the strongest fortress in the world, it was so no longer. The fate of Liège and Namur and the French doctrine of *l'offensive à l'outrance* had seemed good reasons for stripping most of the guns from the Verdun forts in 1915 and sending them to support Joffre's offensive in Champagne. Moreover, since the front thereabouts had been quiet for some time, the field fortifications had been allowed to fall into disrepair, and morale among the defenders was not high.

The reasons for this last were complex. A philosophy of live and let live had grown up while the front was quiet, and some of the French senior officers had been woefully lacking in energy. But by far the most important reason for low morale was that the French army seldom bothered about the comfort or well-being of its troops. Leave was, in practice, very hard come by; the soldiers' food was generally abominable; and *pinard*, the cheap red wine on issue to the army, was far too plentiful. On top of all this, the poilu could see quite clearly that the war was not going well. Everywhere he looked he saw evidences of "*systeme D*," the muddling through that is always so depressing and enraging to soldiers; and he often knew from personal experiences how futile and costly the French attacks of 1914 and 1915 had been. All in all, therefore, the Verdun front was what one of the French corps commanders so aptly called it — "*un terrain à catastrophe*."

The German offensive opened with a tremendous bombardment on February 21, and by the 24th the commander of Army Group Center, Langle de Cary, decided to withdraw from the Plain of the Woëvre, which would have meant the abandonment of all the right bank of the Meuse. On the 25th, Fort Douamont was captured, which was a sickening blow to French morale. At the front it led to panic and retreat. French guns and deserters began to pour back through Verdun.

But help was already on the way. General Castelnau, Joffre's deputy, had visited Verdun on the 24th and had ordered the Second Army, under General Henri Philippe Pétain, to move to the defense of both banks of the Meuse. Castelnau's decision to defend Verdun was indeed exactly what Falkenhayn wanted and what he had predicted would happen. It is a decision that has since been much criticized. Certainly the military value of Verdun did not justify the horrible cost of its defense, but military values are not the only values in war. In theory it should have been easy for the French to abandon Verdun and the Plain of the Woëvre, to draw back a little way, thus dissipating the shock of the German attack. But panics are not halted by withdrawals, and if they are not checked soon, they have a habit of spreading beyond control. Castelnau's decision to stand and fight saved Verdun; it may well have saved France.

When the order came for General Pétain to report to Chantilly for instructions, he could not be found. Fortunately, one of his aides could guess where he was. Captain Serrigny drove hurriedly to Paris and there at the Hotel Terminus at the Gare du Nord he discovered the sixty-year-old Pétain spending the night with a lady friend. Serrigny, not without difficulty, managed to get Pétain out of bed and to deliver his message, but the Second Army commander refused to abandon his companion until morning, when he and Captain Serrigny set out for GQG together.*

Pétain assumed command at Verdun at midnight on February 25/26 and at once put fresh heart into the defense. Three corps arrived as reinforcements and Pétain ordered a halt to the suicidal counterattacks. His most immediate concern was for his communications, which were limited to one secondary road from Bar-le-Duc, forty miles to the south, and a poor, narrow-gauge railway along the Meuse. Traffic on the Bar-le-Duc road was organized by an engineering officer of genius, Major Richard, and in the next ten months, along that one winding secondary road, was to pass two thirds of the French army. Most of the poilus trudged up wearily on foot, well knowing that they were to endure indescribable things on the heights above the town. Nearly two hundred thousand of those who made the journey up never came back again. Not surprisingly, when Maurice Barrès called the road *la Voie Sacrée*, "the Sacred Way," the name stuck.†

By February 28 the German advance had come to a halt, and now French enfilade fire from the west bank of the Meuse forced Falkenhayn to extend his frontage of attack. The new assault on the left bank began on March 6. A series of desperate attacks on the dominating feature, a bare rounded hill known as *le Mort Homme*,‡ brought the

---

*This was in the best French military tradition. On September 26, 1810, Marshal Ney roused Marshal Masséna in similar circumstances at the inn at Moragoa in Portugal, demanding permission to attack the British on Busaco Ridge. Serrigny was more fortunate than Ney, however, for Masséna would not even open the bedroom door to talk to his fellow marshal. English admirals at moments of crisis traditionally play bowls.

†In December some embittered poilu tacked up a sign giving the road another title: "*Chemin de l'abattoir.*"

‡The name did not come from the current fighting; the hill had been called "The Dead Man" for many years before the war.

Germans to the crest, but they were unable to advance down the southern slope. The whole of the hill was not in German hands until the end of May. With its capture, the German offensive on the west bank came to a halt and the attacks switched once again to the area east of the Meuse.

At the beginning of the battle the German air force had dominated the skies, but the French soon rallied, and French fighter aces like Charles Nangesser, Jean Navarre, and Georges Guynemer wrested aerial superiority from the Germans until the arrival of the German fighter ace, Oswald Boelcke, shifted the balance once more in Germany's favor. In May the French air force was reinforced by the arrival at Verdun of the newly formed Lafayette Escadrille, a squadron of American volunteers under two French officers. The Americans greatly distinguished themselves, and the Lafayette Escadrille continued to fly with the French service until February 1918. With Boelcke's departure in June, the French regained mastery of the air and did not lose it again throughout the remainder of the battle.

By the end of May, in an area of less than thirty square miles, more than a quarter of a million men, French and German, had been killed or wounded. The French losses were higher than the German, although not appreciably so — some 125,000 men to 117,000. Already the Battle of Verdun had become the most prolonged and intense engagement of the war, and it still had seven months to run. For the fighting men on both sides, conditions were indescribably bad. Some soldiers went insane from the incessant shellfire; some committed suicide rather than continue to endure. The woods and coppices that had covered the hills were blasted away by high explosives and the whole area became bare mud, polluted with the festering dead.

In some ways the Germans were a little better off than the French, for they were better organized. French medical services, never good, were quite unable to cope with the flood of casualties from the Verdun fighting. Most French wounded had to wait more than twenty-four hours before receiving any treatment, and at the dressing stations the medical teams instituted the practice of *triage*, whereby the casualties were segregated into three categories: those who were "untransportable" and were therefore left to die; those who might recover but could not serve again in the army and were treated if there was time (there often was not); and those whom the surgeons could repair for further use. Of all the western powers, France had by far the highest proportion of casualties who died from wounds — some 420,000 as compared to 895,000 killed in action. French sanitation was also inferior to the German, with the result that many preventable deaths occurred from gas gangrene and tetanus.

Fort Vaux on the right bank fell to a German attack on June 7 after its commander, Major Raynal, had put up a courageous defense. General Robert Nivelle's attempts to relieve the beleaguered garrison had been hastily organized and had all broken down with heavy loss of life. Pétain, a compassionate commander who almost alone among senior Allied generals displayed a real desire to minimize casualties, did not much like Nivelle's eagerness to counterattack, but Joffre and GQG were far from happy with Pétain's commendable caution. From their remote headquarters in Chantilly the staff and the commander-in-chief yearned for some great stroke that would hurl the Germans back. Joffre was unable to dismiss Pétain as he had so many other generals, because the French nation now recognized Pétain, and rightly, as the "savior of Verdun." Joffre's own star, in any case, was already in decline. The solution found was typical of GQG: Joffre removed General Langle de Cary from command of Army Group Center and promoted Pétain to that post. Henceforth the command at Verdun would be exercised by Robert Nivelle, who could be trusted to attack in and out of season.

Nivelle was a self-confident little fire-eater of fifty-eight, who, when he marched into Pétain's former headquarters at Souilly on May 1, was heard to declare, "We have the formula!" It was a claim without foundation. There were, indeed, to be formulae discovered for the breaking of the trench deadlock on the western front, but not in 1916, and not by Nivelle. With the new commander of the Second Army, as his chief of staff, came Major d'Alenson, a tall, somber man who looked like a walking cadaver. D'Alenson was dying of consumption but he was determined to save France before he died. No one could possibly have been a worse influence on the optimistic Nivelle, who, instead of accepting d'Alenson into his retinue, should have paid a slave to keep whispering in his ear that he was mortal. With Nivelle, too, came Charles Mangin, the same soldier whose public execution of Moroccans had touched off the convenient rebellion in Fez in 1911. As a general, he was as careless of the lives of French troops as he had ever been of the lives of his Africans when he was a colonel. Fearless himself, he nevertheless thoroughly earned his nickname of "the Butcher." The French soldiers at Verdun were sorry to see Pétain go, and they had good reason.

By now it seemed to the combatants on both sides that this incredible battle might go on forever, under its own impetus, until everyone in both armies was dead. A young French second lieutenant, Raymond Jubert, who was later killed in action, had a thought about all this: "They will not be able to make us do it again another day; that would be to misconstrue the price of our effort." He was right — and for more generations than his own.

Papa Joffre was now holding back reinforcements from Verdun, hoarding them for the Somme, at the same time as he was urging Sir Douglas Haig to advance the date of the great attack. French divisions were going into the charnel house on the hills above the Meuse for the second or third time — and, an omen of things to come, the French army was beginning to crack under the strain. Some regiments took to bleating like sheep while they were being marched up to the line, and officers frequently had to pretend not to hear what their men were saying. Early in June an entire battalion of the 291st Regiment surrendered to the Germans, and later in the same day the regiment next to it, the 347th, fled from the battlefield, not stopping until it reached Verdun. Nivelle ordered officers and men accused of cowardice to be shot without trial. In Paris the left-wing newspaper *Bonnet Rouge* was proclaiming that the war was lost and that peace should be made at once.

The Germans certainly did not have this sort of trouble, but Verdun was also laying its deadly hand on them. Ever since April Crown Prince Wilhelm had been convinced that the offensive had failed and that Germany should cut her losses, but neither Falkenhayn nor the crown prince's own chief of staff, Knobelsdorf, agreed with him. A German attack at the end of June took Fort Souville, but this was the high-water mark of the advance. Nivelle's order of the day declaimed, *"Ils ne passeront pas!"* They did not pass, although it was Haig's offensive on the Somme rather than Mangin's counterattacks that prevented it. The crown prince ordered his army to assume a defensive posture and the intensity of the fighting at Verdun abated.

At the end of August, when Rumania declared war on Germany, the kaiser finally agreed that Falkenhayn would have to go. Hindenburg and Ludendorff were called to take over Falkenhayn's post, and Ludendorff at once ruled that there should be no resumption of the offensive at Verdun. The French, however, were not prepared to let well enough alone. On October 24 Mangin began to counterattack, recapturing the ruins of Forts Douaumont and Vaux. A further French counterattack on December 15 pushed the Germans back to the original front line of the previous February, but French losses were very high and once again there were ominous signs of a decline in French morale. When President Poincaré visited Verdun that month, stones were thrown at him and he was greeted with abuse.

The Battle of Verdun, judged only in military terms, had thus ended in a draw, though the French could claim a moral victory. French losses came close to 400,000, of which more than 162,000 were dead. German losses were nearly 350,000, of which more than 100,000 were dead, and though Germany could afford the losses better than France, the missed strategic opportunities of 1916 were gone beyond recall. By remaining on the defensive in the west and by trading ground for Allied lives on the Somme, Germany might well have been able to spare enough extra forces to have knocked Russia out of the war in 1916 rather than in 1917. Joffre's Somme offensive, even if it had been conducted with forty French divisions, would have failed. Under such circumstances Germany might conceivably have won the war, or if this had proved beyond her strength, she would have been in a position to obtain a reasonable peace. As it was, by the end of 1916 Hindenburg and Ludendorff could see little prospect of either the one or the other.

But to impartial observers in the spring of 1916 it seemed as though the Central Powers were winning the war. The Allied force at Salonika was still bottled up by the Bulgarians. General Sir Charles Townshend, who had failed to reach Baghdad and had been besieged at Kut since the previous December, was about to surrender his nine thousand troops to the Turks. The fighting on the western front had been at the best indecisive. Looking at all this, certain Irish rebels came to the conclusion that "England's difficulty was Ireland's opportunity." On Easter Monday, April 24, 1916, a nationalist uprising occurred in Dublin. The British quickly assembled five thousand troops, some field guns, and the gunboat *Helga* to suppress the rebellion, and on Saturday afternoon, April 29, the last of the insurgents surrendered in Parnell Street. The severity of the treatment meted out to the rebels permanently alienated the Irish, who had formerly, on the whole, been pro-British and prowar.

In the late spring of 1916, while French and German infantry were struggling desperately for *le Mort Homme*, the new commander of the German High Seas Fleet, Vice Admiral Reinhard Scheer, was planning to lure a portion of the British Grand Fleet out of its bases so that he could fight a naval battle with the odds in his favor. Scheer planned to send his battle cruiser squadron, under Vice Admiral Franz von Hipper, up the Norwegian coast in the hope that part of the British fleet — possibly Beatty's force from Rosyth — would hurry to the scene and be caught by the main High Seas Fleet, which would follow Hipper at an interval of some fifty miles.

The High Seas Fleet was therefore commanded by wireless to assemble in the outer Jade roadstead by seven o'clock on the evening of May 30. The British Admiralty intercepted this message and at once ordered the Grand Fleet to put to sea. Thus, as Admiral John Jellicoe, with twenty-four dreadnoughts and three battle cruisers, and Beatty, with four superdreadnoughts and six battle cruisers, sailed out to their rendezvous in the North Sea, a countertrap was laid for Scheer. The British forces were well on their way before either Hipper or Scheer left the Jade.

At dawn on the 31st Hipper's battle cruiser squadron of five battle cruisers, two cruisers, and three destroyer flotillas slipped out of harbor and steamed northward. Scheer followed behind with the High Seas Fleet of sixteen dreadnoughts and eight old battleships.

At a little after two o'clock on the afternoon of the 31st Beatty's and Hipper's ships sighted each other. Beatty, who was flying his flag on the *Lion*, turned south to get between the German battle cruisers and their base, but because of a communications failure the four super-dreadnoughts of Rear Admiral Sir Hugh Evan-Thomas' 5th Battle Squadron continued on their previous course for another twenty minutes. Beatty was left steaming into battle with a divided force, the heavier part of which was now some ten miles distant from his battle cruisers.

Beatty sighted Hipper's ships at 3:15 and at once decided to engage. Hipper, with more justification, also made up his mind to fight. When Beatty changed course again at 3:30 P.M., another confusion of orders resulted in Evans-Thomas and the superdreadnoughts again drawing farther away from the British battle cruisers. None of the opposing commanders was aware that his enemy's main fleets were in the vicinity. Hipper and Scheer believed that they had to deal only with Beatty, and Jellicoe and Beatty had been informed by the Admiralty that the High Seas Fleet was still at anchor in the Jade.

The opening salvos of the Battle of Jutland were fired by Hipper at 3:40 P.M., catching Beatty's battle cruisers while they were changing course in succession and without the support of the 15-inch guns of the superdreadnoughts. The day was bright and sunny but with a slight haze, and the sea was calm. The German gunnery at once proved itself uncomfortably accurate, and the five German ships were more than a match for the six British. The *Indefatigable* and the *Queen Mary* were sunk, and *Lion*, *Tiger*, and *Princess Royal* were all badly damaged.

By now, however, the first salvos from Evan-Thomas' superdreadnoughts were beginning to splash near Hipper's ships. Hipper turned away to the southeast to lead the British force toward the guns of the High Seas Fleet. Beatty followed, and at 4:33 P.M. the British 2nd Light Cruiser Squadron, commanded by Commodore William E. Goodenough, reported sighting Scheer's fleet. Courageously, Beatty continued on his course for another seven minutes, until he saw the High Seas Fleet himself, then turned north to lead Scheer to Jellicoe. As the British scouting force steamed away northward at its best speed, Beatty was disconcerted to find that, though he should have had a four-knot advantage in speed over the German battleships, he was doing no more than maintaining his distance. Evan-Thomas and the superdreadnoughts now covered Beatty's retirement.

Thus ended the first of the series of actions that was to constitute the Battle of Jutland. Beatty had lost a third of his force, his own ship was on fire, and worst of all, the German ships had been only lightly damaged.

Jellicoe's Grand Fleet in six columns, with its battle cruisers under Rear Admiral Sir Horace Hood some five miles to the east, was now converging on Beatty. Jellicoe had had no information from Beatty, but he had received a signal from Goodenough that had told him that the High Seas Fleet was near at hand, though he had no idea of its speed or course. The Royal Navy was now paying for its long reluctance to train staff officers, and indeed the British staff work at the Battle of Jutland was deplorable by any standard — as deplorable as its inferiority in shells, armor, equipment, and gunnery.

When at last, at 6:14 P.M., Jellicoe got the information he needed about Scheer's speed and course, he gave his order for deployment from column into line. Jellicoe deployed to port; that is, away from the enemy. He had what seemed to be excellent reasons for this decision, though it was later to be bitterly criticized. The deployment to port took the Grand Fleet away from any submarine ambush and gave Jellicoe the best possible visibility for his gunnery. Beatty now took up position behind the battleships of the Grand Fleet. Hood's 3rd Battle Cruiser Squadron, which had been out of position because it had made an error in reckoning, went into line ahead of Beatty.

The main fleet action at Jutland opened at 6:30 P.M. In the fire fight that followed, Hipper's flagship, *Lützow*, was put out of action, and Hood's flagship, *Invincible*, was sunk. But now Scheer suddenly found himself in a desperate position. Instead of having to deal merely with Beatty's force, he found the whole Grand Fleet looming up in front of him. He was outnumbered by twenty-eight to sixteen, and while his ships were sharply outlined against the scarlet sunset, the British ships were all but invisible in the battle smoke and the gathering darkness in the east.

Therefore at 6:35 P.M. Scheer gave the order for the High Seas Fleet to turn about. This was accomplished by means of a maneuver unknown to the Royal Navy, the *Gefechtskehrtwendung*, by which each ship turned completely about in succession from the rear. Scheer sailed away at sixteen knots, and contact between the two fleets was lost.

Once again Jellicoe displayed caution in refusing to follow Scheer. Instead, the Grand Fleet swept around to the southeast so as to come between Scheer and his base. At 6:55 P.M., however, the German admiral executed another right-about turn, probably in the hope of crashing through the rear of Jellicoe's line and getting safely back to the Jade.

For the second time Scheer found himself in serious danger, since he appeared out of the mist opposite the center of the British line, which could "cross his T" once more. The German admiral once again turned right about, ordering his battle cruisers and destroyers to make a suicidal diversionary attack on the British van. Jellicoe turned away 45 degrees, to avoid the destroyers' torpedoes, and Scheer made good his escape to the south. The German battle cruisers were hit repeatedly, but they were so well constructed that they were neither sunk nor put out of action.

Jellicoe was still between Scheer and the Jade, but he refused to fight a night action, fearing that the training of the Royal Navy was not up to it. Scheer had three possible routes by which he could get home, and he chose the shortest, by the Horn Reefs, even though this meant that he had to crash through the light forces at the rear of the Grand Fleet. Between eleven-thirty on the night of May 31 and two o'clock on the morning of June 1, the last action at Jutland was fought as Scheer's fleet steamed desperately for home. In this confused night encounter the Germans again had the better of it, sinking the cruiser *Black Prince* and five British destroyers for the loss of the old battleship *Pommern*. In this prolonged but intermittent engagement only one British ship thought it worthwhile to make a report to Jellicoe, but every German ship in action at once sent particulars by wireless to Scheer.

Not until 5:40 A.M. on June 1 did Jellicoe realize that Scheer had made good his escape. He then turned for home. In the battle the Germans had sunk three battle cruisers, three cruisers, and eight destroyers for a loss of one battleship, one battle cruiser, four light cruisers, and five destroyers. The comparative tonnages sunk tell the story better: 111,980 tons of British shipping had gone to the bottom, as compared with 62,233 tons of German. British casualties were 6945; German casualties, 2921.

Both Britain and Germany claimed Jutland as a victory, but obviously the Germans had better reason for doing so. Neither side had attained its objective of destroying the opposing fleet, but the Germans had — though not significantly — changed the ratio of strength to their advantage. The myth of British naval invincibility inherited from Nelson, and in itself responsible for much of the slackness, complacency, and conservatism in the Royal Navy, was dead, never to be revived. Admiral Jellicoe, who was later so harshly blamed for excessive caution, had in fact displayed a realistic tactical sense and a sober assessment of relative capabilities, but it is undeniable that these were not illuminated with the spirit of Nelson. Perhaps, in view of the technical disparities of the fleets, it was just as well.

Jutland changed nothing. Like the land battles of the war, it was in decisive — and for that reason was another proof that the building of the High Seas Fleet had been a fundamental error of German policy. The British blockade continued and was to have its effect, albeit slowly.

Four days after the close of the Battle of Jutland, the cruiser *Hampshire*, on its way to Russia with Lord Kitchener aboard, struck a mine and went down. When the British people heard of Kitchener's death, they experienced a sense of desolation and loss, as at the passing of some great champion.

The year 1916 marked the peak of the French effort at Verdun and of the Russian effort in Galicia, and as both France and Russia had passed their peak, the main burden of the war on the Allied side came to be assumed by Britain. In spite of the disasters of 1914 and 1915, the British were supremely confident. With the introduction of conscription, a seemingly limitless supply of manpower was available, and with the reorganization of munitions under Lloyd George, the British armies were getting huge quantities of new matériel. The new commander-in-chief, Sir Douglas Haig, and the new Chief of the Imperial General Staff, Sir William Robertson, both intended to fight the war until a decisive victory was won in the west.

This was also the intention of the British government. The German Zeppelin raids on England in February created a good deal of unnecessary panic, and it was the panic rather than the few casualties the Zeppelins caused that intensified the hatred of the Germans. The press, with the same generous irresponsibility it had displayed before the war, inflamed the popular mood and was much aided in this by a government bureau of propaganda. Asquith and his colleagues knew that if they did not follow the popular line, the British would find another government that would. The Asquith coalition managed to remain in office throughout most of 1916 by surrendering to the concept of total victory, but it can hardly be said to have governed the country or directed the war.

When, in a conference on May 26, Haig mentioned the possibility of postponing his offensive on the Somme until the middle of August, General Joffre blew up, excitedly declaring that "the French Army would cease to exist if [the British] did nothing until then." Haig and his staff, in Haig's words, "looked on at this outburst of excitement" and then — having tried their ploy and scored one up by keeping their heads while all about them were losing theirs — they agreed to attack on July 1. Because of the losses at Verdun, Joffre reduced the French portion of the Somme offensive from forty divisions to eight and the French frontage of attack from twenty-five miles to eight.

The German defenses on the Somme were the strongest on the entire western front,* and there were also other handicaps at the Somme sufficiently serious to make any general less optimistic than Haig reconsider his plan. The local water supply was quite inadequate, and worse still, the axis of the Allied advance led steadily uphill because the Germans, in falling back to this position, had naturally decided to keep the high ground. The heights on the Somme are not impressive — though they look higher if viewed from ground level over the parapet of a trench — but they are commanding. The Germans could look down into the Allied lines and observe all that was going on there; the British, gazing uphill, could make out nothing.

None of this deterred Haig or even seemed to worry him unduly. He began his preparations months ahead of time, methodically, carefully, and with a complete disregard for secrecy. Everyone, not only at the front but also in England, knew what was coming. "The Big Push" was common gossip, as was Haig's belief that it would break through the German lines, roll them up, and finish the war. If the enemy still had any doubts about the coming offensive, these were removed when Arthur Henderson, the British minister of labor, made an incautious speech to munitions workers in which he gave away the approximate date of Haig's attack.

However, Henderson's indiscretion probably made little difference. The Germans could see with their own eyes what was going on. Day after day the munitions and storage dumps grew, new airfields were built, new railway lines were laid out, guns were moved in, and three quarters of a million men — in twenty-nine British and eight French divisions — assembled for the Big Push. Under his own control, in GHQ reserve, Haig assembled five cavalry divisions whose task it would be to ride through the rupture in the German front and exploit the victory in the open country well to the enemy's rear.

The Germans watched these preparations — incredulously at first, then with a sort of amazed belief. They took what countermeasures seemed necessary, but on the day the battle broke they had only eight and two-thirds divisions deployed along the frontage of attack, two thirds of them in reserve. Haig moved his headquarters nearer to the front, to the gracious gray stone Château de Valvion at Beauquesne. But the Château de Valvion was still twelve miles behind the front and

---

*Later the British soldiers were to be amazed at what they saw of the German trench system in the hills above the Somme: three lines of trenches, each fortified by two belts of thick barbed wire thirty yards wide; deep, spacious dugouts, often forty feet below the surface, carpeted, ventilated, furnished with bunks, tables, and armchairs and lit by electricity; plentiful stocks of cigars, brandy, canned meats, and bottled beer; and out side, on the spurs of the hillsides, concrete and sandbagged strongpoints that could bring down deadly enfilade fire across the front.

psychologically a million miles away from the awful realities of the battle zone. Neither Haig nor his staff officers went to the front to see for themselves the defenses that the infantry would be expected to pierce. As the date set for the attack drew nearer, Haig became more and more optimistic. So, strangely enough, did his subordinates, many of whom had earlier had their doubts. As time went by, these doubts had been stilled, and corps and divisional commanders began to be enthusiastic over prospects of success. Haig heard nothing from those around him to make him uneasy. A few days before July 1 he confided in his diary: "I feel that every step in my plan has been taken with the Divine help!"*

Soon now the British New Armies were to be blooded in battle, and the men in those armies, all volunteers, were wonderful material. No other British force in history had ever had so much talent and dedication in its ranks. Haig's plan for the battle had the virtue of simplicity. How could it have been otherwise, considering the maker of the plan? Before the infantry assault, there would be an artillery bombardment of seven days' duration; then the infantry would advance along an eighteen-mile front, aligned and equipped for consolidation. The British fire plan was as rigid and inflexible as that for the infantry assault: there was to be a creeping barrage, but it could be neither halted nor reversed, and the fire was distributed with a neat impartiality across the entire frontage of attack, with no special concentrations on strongpoints. Nevertheless, the preliminary bombardment seemed impressive. General Sir Henry Rawlinson, commander of Fourth Army, assured his subordinates that the infantry would merely walk over and occupy the pulverized German trenches. Reports from front-line battalions that the German wire was uncut in many places were generally disregarded, and on more than one occasion units were rebuked for their apprehensions. That staff officers, far to the rear, who had not taken the trouble to view the ground, should thus cast aspersions on the courage of front-line soldiers was evidence of an arrogance stunning in its proportions.

At seven-thirty on the morning of July 1 the hammering guns suddenly fell silent. All along the British front, officers blew their whistles and waved their men over the top. A hundred thousand volunteers clambered out of their trenches and stepped out into no man's land, where wild mustard, blue cornflowers, and red poppies grew. The

*Perhaps Calvinism sometimes has its practical drawbacks. Haig had long felt a sense of destiny, and no doubt this served him well when courage and determination were required. At the Somme, however, his belief in Divine guidance reminds one of the prayer of another Scottish Calvinist: "Lord grant that I may be right; for Ye ken I never change."

day was bright and warm. The sun had been up for three hours, for the British staff was taking no chances of these wartime soldiers losing their way or their alignment by an attack at first light. Since each advancing infantryman was burdened with a minimum of sixty-six pounds of ammunition, rations, entrenching tools, barbed wire, and other equipment, the long, straight lines proceeded toward the German trenches at a slow walk, the men standing upright.

General Rawlinson notwithstanding, the German defenders had not been killed nor had their defenses been destroyed. In their deep dugouts the enemy machine gunners had waited out the long barrage. When it lifted, they ran up to the surface, carrying their guns. Before the attackers had got far into no man's land, they began to be cut down by German machine-gun fire. The attackers fell in their thousands; long rows of khaki-clad dead lay where they had been mowed down like corn. But still the third and fourth waves advanced with great heroism to meet the same fate in their turn. Common sense occasionally triumphed over discipline, and some British soldiers threw down the equipment they were carrying and tried to advance by short rushes, using shell holes and what natural cover there was. These tactics often took them into the German front line, but the attackers who penetrated this far were too few and were killed or captured in the enemy trenches. More frequently the British reached the German wire only to find it uncut, and the remnants of battalions raged helplessly before this obstacle until death stilled them. For long stretches, the German wire was covered with khaki figures like bloody bundles of rags hung on a fence to dry.

South of the Somme, the French Sixth Army advanced about half a mile beyond its objectives, while north of the Somme it had secured all its objectives by midday. The British on the right, next to the French, also gained a little ground, but elsewhere the day was a bloody defeat for the British. In some sectors the Germans did not even bother to call up their reserve battalions, but held the line easily with only one third of their strength. When darkness fell, the task of rescuing the wounded began. There were more than 37,000 of them, for that first day of July had cost the British army 57,470 casualties, nearly 20,000 of them killed — by far the heaviest loss in its history.

Back at GHQ Haig, though disappointed that no breakthrough had been achieved, was not discouraged. Instead of calling off the battle, he persisted with his offensive, limiting it to the right flank, where some progress had been made. In August both sides brought up reinforcements; divisions were by now being committed for the second and sometimes for the third time. In Britain, Lloyd George, Winston Churchill, and some other cabinet ministers began to be appalled by the terrible casualties; but Haig continued his frontal, battering-ram attacks. Strict censorship and witlessly optimistic reports from staff officers who had never been to the front concealed the full and horrible truth from the British public.

The battle raged all through August, when the Canadian Corps was committed. By now the whole area had taken on a desolate, lunar aspect. Villages were mere rubble heaps, indistinguishable from the shell-torn ground around them. The stench of death was everywhere, and smoke and gas polluted the air. In the miserable holes the British called dugouts, the candles burned with only a feeble glimmer in the poisoned air. The battlefield looked like nothing so much as a sinister rubbish heap, littered with bits of bloodstained equipment, rotting bodies, broken rifles, unexploded bombs, and all the pathetic debris of the fighting.

In the skies the Allies had a clear superiority until October. The French Nieuports and Spads were better aircraft than the German Fokker monoplanes, and it was not until nearly the end of the Battle of the Somme, when the Germans introduced their new Halberstadt and Albatross fighters, that the Allies lost their command of the air. None of this, however, was of much help to the infantryman on the ground. The casualties mounted on both sides, and as hospitals in Britain filled up with disillusioned and embittered wounded, the truth could no longer be entirely hidden.

The angry mutterings at the losses on the Somme may have helped Haig to reach the decision he did in September. Against the advice of his technical experts and over the protests of Lloyd George and Churchill, Haig now threw thirty-two of the new and highly secret "tanks" into the battle. These first tanks were slow and cumbersome, but they were a possible answer to the machine gun's domination of the battlefield, and had they been employed in sufficient numbers and as a tactical surprise, they might have broken the trench deadlock and won the war. Lloyd George's later comment seems just: "And so the great secret was sold for the battered ruins of a little hamlet."

In October the rains came and soon the whole battlefield was thigh-deep in yellow, slippery mud. Wounded men drowned or suffocated in shell holes or mud-filled trenches, and the walking wounded took four or five hours to cover the two miles to the nearest dressing station. Although there were strict orders against fraternization, British and German stretcher bearers often met in no man's land and worked side by side, sometimes dressing each other's wounded. By now the front-line soldiers on both sides had little hatred left for the enemy they fought so fiercely; the dimly understood causes of the war and the finely phrased war aims of the statesmen had an unreal quality at the front, like dreams that had drifted in from another world.

British GHQ had no intention of calling off the battle yet. Haig's staff and his apologists had long been claiming that the British commander-in-chief had never intended a breakthrough; his aim, they said, had all along been attrition, the wearing down of the enemy. Lord Cavan, the commander of the British XIV Corps, recognized the futility of the battle and was one of the very few senior officers with enough moral courage to protest to higher authority. Perhaps even in wartime there were advantages to being an earl. Cavan not only said that further attacks were senseless, but added the pointed reproach: "No one who has not visited the front can know the state of exhaustion to which the men are reduced."

The Germans by now were probably suffering equally with the British, although for many weeks Haig's policy of attrition had resulted in more British than enemy casualties. Certainly it is safe to say that on both sides about three million soldiers took part in the battle and that about a million of them were casualties. The official figures, admittedly inaccurate, are bad enough: British casualties, 419,654; French, 204,253; German, 465,525. This was an excessive price to pay for a maximum gain of eight miles on a twelve-mile front.

Haig was finally forced to call off the Battle of the Somme toward the end of November. By then an infantryman marching back to a rest billet from the front was often so coated with half-frozen mud that his clothing, boots, and puttees would weigh 120 pounds. Incredible as it may seem, it does not appear that Haig was dissatisfied with the results of the Battle of the Somme. True, there had been no breakthrough, and the five cavalry divisions had had to go back into quarters instead of riding madly about the enemy's rear, but a lot of Germans had certainly been killed. Haig and Joffre met again at Chantilly and talked it over. They agreed that the offensive should be renewed again in the spring, in the same place, in the same way, but, of course, with fresh drafts of soldiers to fill the depleted ranks.

Fortunately, the French government and the German high command had more sense. Joffre was relieved of his command, promoted to marshal of France, and given a fine office but no further work to do. The German high command was also dissatisfied with the Somme battle. Ludendorff gave orders for the whole Somme area to be evacuated as soon as a new trench system, the Siegfried Stellung, known to the Allies as the Hindenburg Line, was prepared twenty miles to the rear. This move would shorten the German front by thirty-two miles and release fourteen divisions for employment elsewhere.

Because of Verdun and the Somme, the eastern front in 1916 had been kept short of reinforcements by Falkenhayn; and Conrad, eager to strike a blow at the perfidious Italians, weakened his front in Galicia in order to send troops to Italy. When Conrad attacked in the Tyrol, the Austrians made good progress. As Conrad's armies threatened Verona, the king of Italy appealed to the tsar for help, and as always the Russians responded generously. General Alexei Brusilov's offensive was initially intended to be no more than a demonstration in force by four armies along a 200-mile front, but when the Russians moved forward on June 3 they discovered to their surprise that the Austrian defenses everywhere collapsed. Entire battalions sometimes surrendered, and a number of Bohemian units fraternized with the attackers. By the 9th the Stavka was pouring reinforcements into the gap Brusilov had made. By the end of the month 350,000 Austrian prisoners had been taken and the Russian lines had advanced sixty miles.

German formations, however, had stood firm amid the Austrian collapse. Ludendorff sent Conrad five divisions, Falkenhayn was persuaded to part with four divisions from the west, and the situation was stabilized before the end of August, when Hindenburg and Ludendorff were summoned to Supreme Headquarters. The new commanders found themselves faced with a far worse situation than Falkenhayn had inherited from Moltke after the Marne. In spite of their disastrous losses, the Entente powers were still fiercely on the offensive — the British and French attacking on the Somme, the Italians attacking again on the Isonzo, the Rumanians invading Transylvania with 750,000 men, and the Russians preparing to attack again in Galicia. The superior industrial production of the Allies was also beginning to make itself felt, as was the Royal Navy's blockade. The 1916 harvest in Germany was poor, partly because of a shortage of labor, and morale in the Fatherland was not high.

Ludendorff scraped together what troops he could spare to form a new army in Transylvania to deal with the Rumanians. On September 29 at Hermannstadt, on October 8 at Kronstadt, and on November 11 at the Szurduk Pass, Falkenhayn and Mackensen inflicted sharp defeats on the Rumanian army, driving its demoralized remnants north into Moldavia.

Ludendorff now found himself in virtual control of the entire German war effort, and under his direction General Wilhelm Gröner was placed in charge of an *Allgemeines Kriegsamt*, which controlled foodstuffs, raw materials, labor, and munitions. A compulsory labor law was passed, and large numbers of prisoners of war and Polish and Belgian "help-workers" were coerced into the factories. Before the end of the year Germany was, to all intents and purposes, a dictatorship ruled by the First Quartermaster General. Ludendorff's administrative changes soon began to improve Germany's output of aircraft, ammunition, guns, and military equipment.

The German admiralty, now headed by Admiral Edouard von Capelle, was pressing for the resumption of unrestricted U-boat warfare, and Admiral Tirpitz was claiming that his fleet of 148 U-boats could make Britain sue for peace within six months. Chancellor Bethmann-Hollweg, who distrusted Tirpitz's optimism and who had a truer appreciation of the effect of the United States' entry into the war on the Allied side, resisted the navy's arguments and was able for the time being to obtain Ludendorff's rather doubtful support. Interventionist forces in the United States included some very influential men, whose motives varied from genuine idealism to a desire to protect their investments, but unless Germany provoked the United States by sinking American ships on the high seas, there seemed little danger that the American people could be persuaded to participate in the conflict that was destroying Europe.

On the other hand, Bethmann had reason to believe that a separate peace with Russia might be possible in the autumn of 1916. Boris Stürmer, the Russian prime minister, favored it, and unofficial talks were actually begun in Stockholm. They broke down because Ludendorff agreed to the establishment of an independent kingdom of Poland, foolishly believing the promise of Hans Hartwig von Beseler, the German governor general of Poland, that by the spring of 1917 Poland could provide Germany with five divisions and with a million men on the introduction of conscription. The proclamation of Polish independence in November killed all possibility of a separate peace with Russia, and, of course, Ludendorff did not get his Polish troops.

The opportunity lost here because of military shortsightedness may have been truly tragic for Europe. A separate peace at the end of 1916 between Germany and Russia might have induced the Allies to follow suit, and the war might well have been ended on the basis of a return to the status quo. Perhaps, though, it was already too late. With Ludendorff at the center of affairs in Germany, it would have been difficult for Bethmann to accept moderate peace terms. Even such reasonable Germans as Matthias Erzberger and Gustav Stresemann of the Center party had by now come around to the view that Germany was entitled to some compensation for her wartime sacrifices, and the German industrialists were looking greedily at Belgium. Among the Entente powers similar influences stood in the way of a moderate peace: the inflamed popular mood, deliberately whipped up by the governments and aggravated by the casualty lists, and the hope of obtaining benefits from the war — Alsace-Lorraine, colonies, the destruction of the German fleet, or the control of the Middle East. Here, as in the battles, the war seemed to have acquired its own self-perpetuating force.

In Austria the mood was different. On November 21 the Austrian emperor, Franz Josef, died in his eighty-seventh year. His great-nephew, Archduke Charles, ascended the throne, and Charles's wife, Empress Zita, well known for her pro-Allied sympathies, lost no opportunity for persuading her husband that nothing but peace could save his throne.

Colonel Edward House, President Wilson's personal representative, had been pressing the advantages of American mediation on Viscount Grey of Fallodon* since May, but without success. President Wilson's proposal was that France should be given Alsace-Lorraine, Germany should pay for the restoration of war-ravaged territories, Russia should get Constantinople, Italy should get the Italian-speaking portions of Austria, and an independent Poland should be created. In return, Germany would be given compensation in the form of colonies outside Europe. President Wilson further said that if Germany did not agree to these terms, the United States would "probably" enter the war on the Allied side. The Allies rejected Wilson's proposal as inadequate. France wanted the left bank of the Rhine as well as Alsace-Lorraine; Russia had no desire to see an independent Poland; Britain did not intend to compensate Germany with colonies; and Italy had been promised far more by the Treaty of London than the American President was prepared to offer her. That spring, by the Sykes-Picot Agreement, Britain, France, and Russia had arranged for the partition of Turkey among themselves.

Lloyd George publicly rejected the possibility of American mediation, saying in an interview with an American newspaper owner:

The fight must be to the finish — to a knock-out . . . Britain asked no intervention when she was unprepared to fight. She will tolerate none now that she is prepared, until the Prussian military despotism is broken beyond repair.

Grey was much upset by this blunt talk, declaring that the door that "should be kept open for Wilson's mediation . . . is now closed forever as far as we are concerned," but Lloyd George, knowing that he had gained greatly in popular support by his stand, was impenitent. Nevertheless, Lord Lansdowne, minister without portfolio in Asquith's cabinet, circulated a memorandum to his colleagues on November 13, suggesting that if there could be no guarantee of a de-

*Grey had been elevated to the House of Lords in July 1916.

cisive victory, the British government should consider a negotiated peace. Lansdowne's suggestion was sound, if belated, common sense, and it required an uncommon amount of moral courage to make it in 1916. However, Lloyd George had his way. And on December 7, as the climax to weeks of intrigue, Asquith resigned and Lloyd George became prime minister.

Chancellor Bethmann-Hollweg, like Lord Lansdowne, thought that the end of 1916 might be a good time to make peace. On December 12 Germany dispatched rather vague proposals for a negotiated peace, warning at the same time that she would continue to defend herself if the proposals were rejected. On the 18th President Wilson sent a circular note to the belligerents, asking on what terms they would make peace. In reply Germany suggested direct negotiations between the Central Powers and the Entente but did not outline what terms would be acceptable, probably because any terms that might be acceptable to Germany would almost certainly be considered outrageous by both the Allies and Wilson.

The Allies turned down out of hand Bethmann-Hollweg's offer of direct negotiations, declaring that it was not sincere. Since President Wilson could not safely be treated in such a cavalier manner, the Allies suppressed their natural irritation and replied to the American note on January 16, saying in effect that they were prepared to make peace if Belgium and Serbia were restored and compensated, if the Allies were paid compensation by Germany for the financial outlay of the war, if Alsace and Lorraine were given to France, if the Austrian Empire was broken up into national states, and if Turkey was forced out of Europe. Not surprisingly, the Central Powers, who had so far had the better of the fighting, were unwilling to accept defeat without having been defeated. And the war went on.

CHAPTER IV

NINETEEN SEVENTEEN was the most important year of the war — more important even than 1918, the year of victory, for the victory in 1918 was delusive, but the changes wrought in 1917 are with us still. In 1917 a small clique of revolutionaries seized control of Russia, an event that may yet prove as momentous as Constantine's conversion to Christianity. Balancing this, the United States intervened in Europe, and the New World permanently upset the balance of the Old. Thus, 1917 marked the destruction of European world power just as the Battle of Chaeronea in 338 B.C. marked the end of the Greek city-states, and the European nations, just like the Greek cities, had no one but themselves to blame. Henceforth if Europe were to find greatness, it would have to be in realms other than those of power.

At the beginning of 1917 the Allies still outnumbered the Germans on the western front by 175 divisions to 122, and the new French commander-in-chief, General Robert Nivelle, believed that he could break through the German lines between Reims and Soissons and win the war. The British were to cooperate with the French in a large diversionary offensive around Arras a few days before Nivelle struck his blow. Most French generals, including Pétain and Foch, had serious reservations about Nivelle's plan, and these doubts soon came to be shared by the French government. But Lloyd George, who deeply distrusted Haig, was impressed with Nivelle.

In Germany the pressure to resume unrestricted U-boat warfare had mounted steadily. The proponents of the submarine argued that Germany could not hope to defeat the Allied armies on land, that the Allies would reject a compromise peace, and that therefore the only alternative to defeat was to starve Britain by cutting her seaborne communications. It was recognized that unrestricted U-boat warfare would probably bring the United States into the war, but Ludendorff reasoned that the United States was in any case giving full material help to Britain and France, that it would be at least a year before an American army was ready to take the field, and that the U-boats would have knocked Britain out of the war long before then. Furthermore, the naval staff assured him that even if the United States raised a large army, the German submarines could prevent its being transported across the Atlantic.

This reasoning was fallacious on almost every count. The belief that Germany could not win the war on land was wrong because in the spring revolution broke out in Russia and by midsummer the eastern front had virtually closed down. The naval staff was wrong in believing that the U-boats could make Britain sue for peace or prevent American forces from landing in France. Bethmann-Hollweg, who felt much of this instinctively, did his best to prevent the declaration of unrestricted U-boat warfare, but Ludendorff was too strong for him. The kaiser was persuaded to unleash the U-boats on February 1, 1917. Bethmann commented bitterly, "With Falkenhayn we lose the war militarily; with Ludendorff we lose it politically."

The decision to resume unrestricted U-boat warfare was the greatest German error of the war after the invasion of Belgium. It is of interest that the basis of both errors was the same: a mistaken belief that the war might be won before adverse factors came into play. In both decisions there was a strong element of recklessness, almost of desperate recklessness. Behind the optimism lurked a deep strategic pessimism. Both Schlieffen and Ludendorff took counsel of their fears — fear of being crushed by the Russian "steamroller" and fear that Germany could not endure a prolonged war of attrition. In neither case was the situation as grave as the German strategists believed. It is easy, but superficial, to accuse Schlieffen and Ludendorff of overconfidence. In truth, their errors had a deeper and directly contrary cause.

Ludendorff decided to stand on the defensive in the west in 1917. This would give the U-boats time to do their work, and there was, in any case, little choice because the Allies outnumbered the Germans — 3.9 million men to the Germans' 2.5 million — on the western front. To counterbalance this numerical inferiority the German army now adopted an entirely new system of defensive tactics, which had originally been worked out by Colonel Fritz von Lossberg, the chief of staff to the First Army during the Somme fighting. Lossberg abandoned linear defense for a new concept of defense in depth. The defensive zone was deepened so that the attacker's artillery fire would be more dispersed, and the ratio of defenders to defended area was reduced to minimize casualties. Forces for immediate counterattack were stationed out of range of the enemy's field guns, and beyond these again were divisions designated for deliberate counterattack. The new emphasis on counterattack gave the defensive a measure of the flexibility that had previously been the prerogative of the offensive. The withdrawal to the Hindenburg Line was successfully completed in the last fortnight of March.

While the German army was adjusting to the new defensive doctrine, revolution broke out in Petrograd on March 12. The revolution was a spontaneous thing, not at all the work of the professional revolutionaries, who were as much surprised by it as anyone else. The tsar and his government made the Russian Revolution, and their single biggest contribution to that end had been going to war in 1914. Since then, the terrible casualties, the loss of battles and territory, and, perhaps most of all, the seemingly endless prolongation of the strain had killed hope.

Bread riots broke out in Petrograd, and a strike and lockout at the Putalov Metal Works put thirty thousand industrial workers on the streets. Angry crowds began to demonstrate against the tsar and the war. On March 13 some infantry battalions, and even some Cossacks, displayed a reluctance to fire on the crowds. When the mob sacked the headquarters of the Okrana, the tsarist secret police, and stormed the prison of Peter-Paul, it was obvious that the autocracy had lost the capital.

An emergency committee of the Duma was convened and a provisional government established. The tsar abdicated on the 15th, and the Grand Duke Michael, who had been named his successor, announced that he would accept the crown only at the hands of a duly elected constituent assembly and then abdicated in his turn. For the first time in centuries Russia found herself without a tsar. The provisional government possessed no real legality, and from the beginning its authority was duplicated, if not challenged, by the Petrograd soviet, a committee of elected representatives from the factories. After some soul-searching, the provisional government decided to continue the war, and initially the soviet agreed.

German military intelligence had been attempting without success to foment a revolution in Russia ever since 1914. In the spring of 1916 the leader of the Bolshevik party, Vladimir Ilich Ulyanov, better known as Lenin, had begun receiving German subsidies. Now, when revolution actually broke out, the German high command underestimated its effects and even feared that a new government might continue the war more efficiently than the tsar had been able to do. Since Lenin was publicly committed to a policy of immediate peace with Germany, however, Ludendorff agreed to have the Bolshevik leader and forty of his followers transported across Germany to Russia.

Arriving at the Finland Station in Petrograd on the evening of April 16, Lenin at once began to denounce the provisional government and the war. The Bolsheviks had no great popular following and most of them, as orthodox Marxists, did not believe that Russia was ready for socialism — the bourgeois stage of the revolution would have to come first. However, Lenin, almost alone until Trotsky joined him in May, had a shrewder understanding of tactical possibilities. The existence of the Dual Power, the government's error in continuing the war, the people's longing for peace, land, and bread, as well as the existence of an organized, if inadequately armed and trained, Red Guard gave Lenin reason to believe that he might be able to seize power. In May, when the provisional government assured the Allies that Russia would continue fighting, riots erupted in Petrograd.

A cabinet shuffle brought in the right-wing Socialist Alexander Kerensky to be minister of war. On June 3 the Menshevik and Social Revolutionary majority in the All-Russia Congress of Soviets supported Kerensky's plans for a new offensive on the Galician front. The idea was madness, for the Russian armies were in no condition to attack and the Germans had guessed where the main blow was to fall. Although Haig was even then preparing for his great stroke in Flanders, Ludendorff sent four German divisions from the western front to stiffen the German counterattack force, the last German troops to be switched from the west to the east. Once again Russia was drawing enemy spears to her bosom and aiding her allies at tragic cost to herself. When the offensive opened on June 29, it made slight initial gains before being brought to a halt. General Max Hoffmann, now the de facto commander-in-chief on the eastern front, launched a counteroffensive on July 18 and the Russians were soon in headlong retreat, their armies melting away as the soldiers "voted for peace with their legs" and deserted by the thousands. Thereafter, though Germany did not yet dare to withdraw substantial numbers of troops from the eastern front, the fighting in Russia was no longer at all demanding.

As Russia was breaking up in revolution, Germany gained a new enemy in the United States. Unrestricted U-boat warfare had provided the American interventionists with the issue they needed to swing public opinion over to their side. The downfall of tsardom also made it seem that the Allies were at last the pure representatives of democracy, ranged against the forces of militarism. President Wilson had broken off diplomatic relations with Germany on February 2, but had hoped to maintain American neutrality. Wiser than most of his generation, he feared what involvement might do to the American national character and to American traditions. The President was still "too proud to fight," but events were too strong for him. American ships were sunk by German submarines; American lives were lost.

British and French propagandists were far more astute than their German counterparts, and Britain controlled the transatlantic cables by which European news came to North America. Many wealthy Americans had a high stake in an Allied victory, since an Allied defeat would have meant the loss of their investments. A German victory would have removed the buffer between the United States and Europe that the Royal Navy had always provided.

To crown it all, the British secret service intercepted and decoded a telegram from the German undersecretary of state, Alfred Zimmermann, to the German ambassador in Mexico. The ambassador was authorized to inform the Mexican government, in case the United States declared war on Germany, that Germany would support Mexican claims to Texas, New Mexico, and Arizona in exchange for Mexico's entry into the war on Germany's side. Zimmermann also made the inept suggestion that the Mexican government should be asked to involve Japan in these ventures. The British waited until the revelation of this message would have maximum effect before informing the Americans, but when the text of the Zimmermann telegram was published in the United States it brought a furious reaction. The United States declared war on Germany on April 6.

At first the U-boats were dramatically successful against British shipping. One ship in four that sailed from British ports was sunk. In February, 105 British merchant ships went to the bottom; in March, 127; in April, 169. Britain was dependent on her maritime trade for most of her food, half of her iron ore, and most of her other materials except coal. She had also given hostages to fortune in the shape of large expeditionary forces in Palestine, Mesopotamia, and Salonika. With the resumption of the underwater war, much neutral shipping decided to stay in port rather than run the terrible risks involved in taking cargoes to Britain. The First Sea Lord, now Admiral Jellicoe, could see nothing ahead but starvation and defeat. Others were less pessimistic. Several junior naval officers had long been advocating the establishment of a convoy system, but their Lordships of the Admiralty would have none of it. The speed of the convoy, their Lordships said, would be reduced to the speed of the slowest vessel; the amount of shipping assembled together would present far too large a target; the merchant captains would not be able to "keep station"; the ports of arrival would not be able to handle such a concentration of cargo; it had never been done before. By including the figures from the coastal trade, the Admiralty reported that twenty-five hundred ships sailed each week from British ports* and that it would be impossible to find

*This was probably stupidity rather than intentional dishonesty, but Lloyd George was easily able to get the correct figure, 140, from the ministry of shipping.

escorts for so much shipping. Fortunately, Lloyd George talked to others besides their Lordships, and on April 26 he flatly overruled the Admiralty's objections and ordered convoys instituted.

The first convoy sailed on May 10, and by mid-August the system was in full operation. Allied shipping losses dropped sharply in May and June and continued to drop steadily for the rest of the year. In December 1917 only 117 British, Allied, and neutral vessels were sunk, and by then American and British shipyards were more than making good the losses.

But although the U-boat menace was defeated at the eleventh hour, there was still time for the Allies to lose the war. If Ludendorff underestimated the effects of American intervention, the French and British high commands were equally blind. They still believed that they could defeat the German army before the Americans arrived to share the glory.*

Nivelle hoped that the French army would gain this signal success — under his command, of course. Haig thought this silly. It was obvious to him that only the British army could win the war, and he intended to do it in Flanders as soon as Nivelle's offensive had failed. However, at Nivelle's request, the British army launched its diversionary attack in Arras on April 9. Haig planned for Sir Edmund Allenby's Third Army to attack on a ten-mile front between Bullecourt and Arras, break clean through the Hindenburg Line, and capture Cambrai. The left flank of this thrust would be covered by a subsidiary offensive by General Henry Horne's First Army against Vimy Ridge, and the right flank by an offensive against Bullecourt by General Sir Hubert Gough's Fifth Army. The cavalry was once again assembled to exploit the breakthrough.

If the high command had learned nothing from past failures, the same was not true of lower echelons, where the assault was prepared with unusual care and attention to detail. There was still no imagination or flair in the British tactics, but at least the old-style battle was fought more methodically. At 5:30 A.M. on Easter Monday, April 9, in a dawn dimmed by driving sleet and snow, the British and Canadians advanced behind their barrage. The Canadians, all four divisions abreast, stormed to the top of Vimy Ridge. North of the Scarpe River the British advanced more than three miles. The first day had gone well, but as so often happened in this war, the defense stiffened afterward and progress became slow and costly.

*The Serbian government-in-exile did not share this optimism. To Crown Prince Alexander and Prime Minister Pasich it looked as though the Allies were losing the war, and they prepared to make a separate peace. As a first step in this direction, they arrested Dragutin Dimitrievich on a trumped-up charge and had him and other Black Hand leaders shot by a firing squad in June. The secret of Sarajevo had to be kept at all costs.

Haig now paused to regroup, but resumed the offensive on April 23. Fighting and casualties were heavy and little ground was gained, yet Haig persisted in his attack. Even when Nivelle's offensive had definitely broken down, Haig continued to press his assaults, with mounting losses, until nearly the end of May. British casualties were close to 160,000. German losses were also heavy, about 140,000. This Third Battle of Arras, in spite of some brilliant minor victories, such as the capture of Vimy Ridge, had not achieved a breakthrough. The Germans had not been drawn away from the French front in Champagne, and British casualties had been heavier than German. Therefore, having failed in all its aims, Haig's offensive must be counted a complete failure.

By the middle of April Nivelle had assembled five armies for his attack around Reims. The Germans, of course, had learned what was coming. As early as February 15 they had acquired a number of top-secret French documents, including Nivelle's "Instructions as to the object and conditions of a general offensive." There was some reason to believe that these documents had been deliberately betrayed into German hands by a traitorous member of the Chamber of Deputies. A new German army, the First, under General Karl von Bülow, was moved into the line; and by the time Nivelle was ready to attack with his forty-six divisions, the Germans had forty-two divisions opposite him — a ratio that was far more than enough to check any offensive in this war. On April 4 the Germans took a French divisional order from the body of a dead warrant officer. Nivelle learned of this, but decided to go ahead with the attack. His subordinate generals had been becoming more and more doubtful of his scheme, with the notable exception of General Mangin, commanding the Sixth Army, who had boasted that on the night of the opening of the offensive he would drink his apéritif in Laon, ten miles and more behind the German front. Nivelle solemnly promised the French government that if the offensive was not at once an unqualified success, it would be broken off.

The delays and the long period of waiting had been hard on the French soldiers. Leave had been stopped in March; their food was poor; and as they huddled in their trenches or in crowded, leaky billets behind the front they remembered how every other offensive had failed with bloody losses. Moreover, a steady stream of antiwar pamphlets was reaching the front from Paris. Louis Malvy, the French minister of the interior, with a misguided liberalism that came close to treason, steadily refused to take action against pacifist agitators in the capital. The news of the Russian Revolution did not make the French troops more enthusiastic for the war; it occurred to some of them that what Russian soldiers had done, French soldiers could also do. This theme was pushed vigorously in pacifist propaganda. Two Russian brigades, which had been sent to France as a gesture of Entente solidarity and because Russia still had more men than she could equip, began to form their own soviets — not a good example to the disaffected French.

The weather did not improve with the coming of April. Rain fell from gray skies, and as the frost left the ground, mud was everywhere. At GQG in the Compiègne Palace only the commander-in-chief and his chief of staff, the dying Colonel d'Alenson, displayed much confidence. On the evening before the offensive Nivelle issued an order of the day to the armies who were to attack: *"L'heure est venue! Confiance! Courage! Vive la France!"*

Sharp at six o'clock on the morning of April 16 the barrage lifted and the soldiers of the Fifth and Sixth armies advanced. The enemy's defenses were held in depth and the preliminary bombardment had not destroyed his machine guns. Across most of the forty-mile frontage of attack, gains were small and casualties heavy. As usual, the French medical services broke down. With an optimism that nothing in the past could justify, the French had anticipated light casualties and had made preparations to evacuate only fifteen thousand wounded, instead of the ninety-six thousand that eventually had to be moved. As a result, the forward dressing stations could not cope with the flow, and the field hospitals were crowded beyond their capacity. The wounded men on the hospital trains that pulled into the Gare du Nord in Paris were not backward in telling the shocked crowds what they thought of the offensive and of the war. "Our friends are being murdered!" they screamed from the trains. "To hell with Nivelle!"

Although the offensive had failed on the first day, Nivelle decided to go on. On the 17th the Sixth Army drove up the heights of the Chemin des Dames, but nowhere else along the long front were there notable gains. The secondary attack to the east of Reims was put in as planned but made little headway. The story was the same on the 18th, and on the 19th, and on the 20th. General Mangin was still not appreciably nearer to drinking his apéritif in Laon.

In Paris the extent of the setback was certainly not minimized. Rumors exaggerated the French losses, and panic-stricken deputies were already repeating the words of the wounded, who were calling Mangin a murderer. During Haig's offensive on the Somme, England had come to realize only slowly what was actually occurring, for England lay across the Channel from the battlefield, and strict censorship and false reports had kept the British people long in ignorance. Reims, however, was only seventy miles from Paris, and Paris, like France, was by now desperately tired of the war.

On April 26 the minister of war, Paul Painlevé, attempted to gain the cabinet's consent to the replacement of Nivelle, but his colleagues did not dare to take so drastic a step. Mangin, however, was dismissed, and on the 29th Pétain was appointed Chief of the General Staff. The French attacks continued, and some two and a half miles of the first portion of the Hindenburg Line along the Chemin des Dames was taken. On May 10 the French government finally demanded Nivelle's resignation. He refused, and persisted in his refusal for five days before he finally left to be replaced by Pétain.

In the reserve area of the Fifth Army around Ville-en-Tardenois on May 19 an infantry battalion in the IX Corps was ordered to the front. Instead of obeying, the men fled from the camp and hid in nearby woods. On the same day mutiny broke out in the depot of the 69th Division. The soldiers, singing "The Internationale," broke into officers' quarters and appointed "delegates" to bargain with the commander. On the 20th a more serious mutiny broke out in the 128th Regiment at Proilly when drunken soldiers refused to march forward. When a battalion of the 68th Regiment mutinied on the 21st, a number of soldiers were selected at random and shot.

The rot was by now too widespread to be stopped even by such draconian measures. At Mainz, mutineers from the 18th Regiment set up machine guns in the streets and 300 men had to be arrested. North of Soissons four battalions of the 158th Division refused to go to the front on May 26, and that same night at Fère-en-Tardenois mutineers attempted to seize a railway train to go to Paris. The propaganda pamphlets that were being passed from hand to hand in the army urged the mutineers to rendezvous in the capital, where "the Commune awaits you." By now reports of the mutinies in the Fifth, Sixth, and Tenth armies were pouring into GQG daily. On the 29th, mutiny broke out in ten more regiments.

In Paris agitators were openly meeting the leave trains that pulled into the Gare du Nord and the Gare de l'Est; leaflets were handed out, urging the soldiers to desert; and in dingy little shops near the stations, secondhand clothing merchants were doing a brisk business, fitting out deserters with civilian clothes. Before long there were an estimated twenty-seven thousand deserters in Paris alone. Revolutionary newspapers like *Le Bonnet Rouge, La Tranchée Republicaine,* and *Ce Qu'il Feut Dire* were denouncing the war, the high command, and the government, and were calling for peace. A negotiated peace in 1916, when the Allies could have bargained from a position of strength, was a very different thing from the kind of peace that the agitators were recommending in May of 1917, with Russia out of the war and the French army slipping into chaos. Patriots might with good conscience have recommended that peace negotiations be opened at the end of 1916; only defeatists and traitors could advocate a peace of surrender five months later. Unfortunately, France had more than her share of defeatists and traitors.

The mutinies in the army continued to spread. The 36th and 120th regiments seized motor transport, hoisted red flags, and started to drive to Paris. What was really alarming was that some junior officers had joined this group of mutineers. The drive to Paris was halted by a loyal cavalry regiment, but by now the situation was becoming desperate. Pétain wrote a thoughtful memorandum to the government, blaming the army's leave policy, the mistakes of Nivelle, drunkenness, pacifist propaganda, and communist agitation for the mutinies. He proposed a more generous leave policy, a defensive strategy, a curtailment of the wine supply in the Zone of the Armies, and stern measures against traitors, traitorous publications, and agitators.

By now the whole of the French army between Reims and Soissons was seething with revolt, and the only consolation Pétain could find was that the troops in the front line were prepared to hold the trenches, although not to attack. There was little actual desertion at the front, and when a German raid captured 180 prisoners near Vauxaillon, none of them revealed the true state of affairs behind the French lines. The Germans had had some indications of the breakdown of French morale, however. Three German prisoners who had escaped from the camp near Fismes made their way back to their own lines, bringing with them stories of mass breakdown of discipline, drunkenness, and demoralization in the French rear areas. These reports were passed back through the crown prince's headquarters to Supreme Headquarters, but were discounted. Perhaps the rumors seemed too good to be true. Perhaps Ludendorff had set his mind too firmly on a purely defensive policy in the west while the U-boats starved out Britain and the Russian army disintegrated.

Early in June Pétain sent his chief of staff, General Debeney, to Haig's headquarters at Bavincourt to explain, guardedly, why he could not cooperate in the Flanders offensive. With a most peculiar concept of his duties as British commander-in-chief, Haig decided to regard the information on the French mutinies as a "military secret," which he was not at liberty to divulge to his own government. He wrote to Robertson:

> For the last two years most of us soldiers have realized that Great Britain must take the necessary steps to win the war by herself, because our French allies had already shown that they lacked both the moral qualities and the means of gaining victory

In fact, the French army was disintegrating just as the Russian had done, and just as rapidly. A great riot staged by drunken poilus in Soissons on June 2 affected more than half a dozen regiments. Pétain established special courts-martial to deal with the ringleaders among the mutineers, and on Monday, June 4, the French cabinet was told for the first time how very grave the situation was. Poincaré was bluntly informed by Painlevé that between the German lines and Paris there were only two wholly dependable divisions, both cavalry formations. If the Germans attacked now, they could finish the war in a week.

By June 9 mutiny had spread to fifty-four French divisions, and even in formations where there was no actual mutiny more than half the soldiers returning from leave reported back drunk. However, Pétain's corrective measures were now beginning to make themselves felt. The courts-martial were having the worst offenders shot or were sentencing them to long periods of penal servitude; in many instances mutineers were shot without the formality of a trial. Often, in cases where it was not possible to ascertain who the real ringleaders were, the men with the longest records of military offenses were selected for execution. In some instances, mutineers were turned loose in no man's land, to be destroyed by their own artillery. The actual number of executions is a matter of speculation. Certainly the official French figures of 412 death sentences, of which 356 were commuted, is much too low. The French army subsequently admitted that 170 acts of mutiny had occurred, of which the worst outbreaks had involved seventy-nine infantry regiments, eight artillery regiments, twenty-one chasseur battalions, a dragoon regiment, and a Senegalese battalion. Nevertheless, the full story of the French mutinies has never been told, nor is it likely that it ever will be. While the war was still going on, of course, there were excellent reasons for this reticence, but the policy of suppressing the facts and of stifling all discussion after the war is less easy to justify. Shame and pride are bad counselors, and the causes of the catastrophe in French morale that occurred in 1917 were never brought out into full daylight, where they could have been analyzed and perhaps cured. That no real cure was effected, the debacle of 1940 conclusively proved.

Pétain, however, achieved wonders, and it was primarily thanks to him that France did not follow the same path as Russia. Harshness toward mutineers, though the most important ingredient in his solution, provided only part of the answer. Pétain liberalized the army's leave policy, improved the food, medical service, and rest camp facilities, and personally visited ninety divisions to talk to the men himself. He promised them that there would be no more suicidal attacks, that lives would be economized, that conditions would be improved, and that mutiny would be dealt with ruthlessly. He was as good as his word on all counts, and the recovery of the French army began by about June 20. It was a slow recovery and was never a complete one. French formations participated in the great battles of 1918, both defensive and offensive, but the old élan was gone. Too many French soldiers had become convinced that victory was not worth the price being demanded of them. This conviction, which became widespread in 1917, was transmitted undiminished to the next generation.

In a sense, the French mutinies were merely a part of a larger picture. There had been a partial collapse of Austrian morale in the summer of 1916 in the face of Brusilov's offensive, and some units, especially Bohemian ones, had deserted en masse. No mutiny had occurred in the Austrian army, however, and there had been no threat of revolution. The Russian army had not broken until revolution had occurred in Petrograd in March. Even then the Russian front had held, and in July the Russian army was capable of one final offensive effort. The truth was that by 1917, after two and a half years of war, all the belligerent nations were being subjected to great strains, and those nations that were weakest broke first under the strain. Italy, as we shall see, was likewise to break before the year was out.

By the end of May, with the French armies refusing to fight, Haig knew that the brunt of the work for the remainder of the year would fall upon the British. This remarkable man does not seem to have been perturbed by the prospect. He had long wanted to launch a great offensive in Flanders. Now he was to have his chance. There was much to be said for an advance on the Allied left near the coast: the U-boat bases at Ostend and Zeebruge might be cleared and the German right flank turned; after the Germans were pushed back off the ridge near Ypres, amphibious landings might be possible in the enemy rear.

Unfortunately, the area that was strategically attractive was tactically forbidding. The Germans held the high ground, and the salient was under constant, observed fire. The land around Ypres was impervious clay soil, reclaimed from the sea, artificially drained and protected by a system of dikes and ditches. Artillery bombardment would destroy the drainage system, and Haig was warned that "the weather broke early each August with the regularity of the Indian monsoon." Before the offensive was launched, every one of Haig's army commanders was to express strong reservations about his plan. General Foch, for once not optimistic, said that the idea of making "a duck's march through the inundations to Ostend and Zeebruge [was] futile, fantastic, and dangerous." Prime Minister Lloyd George and some cabinet ministers were most apprehensive about the outcome of Haig's offensive, fearing another blood bath like the Somme.

Haig, however, claimed that "success seems reasonably certain" and argued that even if "a full measure of success is not gained . . . our purpose of wearing down [the enemy] will be given effect to" and that to break out of the salient would "reduce the heavy wastage which must occur there next winter as in the past, if our troops hold the same positions." What could have made Haig believe that "success seems reasonably certain" must remain forever a mystery. Nothing in past experience justified such an opinion. The ground was appalling; the French army was in mutiny and could not cooperate;* and both his own army commanders and the leading French generals lacked faith in his plan. The "wearing down" of the enemy could scarcely help wearing down the British armies even more. Finally, the argument that a breakout from the salient had to be attempted in order to reduce "wastage" during the coming winter implicitly rejected the simple expedient of withdrawing from the death trap to a shorter and stronger line along the base.

The brilliant tactical success at Messines in the second week of June gave Haig a fine talking point with his opponents in the war cabinet. He assured them that the Germans were demoralized, that he could capture the Flemish coast and win the war, and he made the same promise that Nivelle had made to the French government: if a significant initial success was not achieved, he would break off the offensive rather than pile up needless casualties. The British government, unsure of the support of the House of Commons, had little room for maneuver. Russia was in revolution, and the Russian government, in May and again in July, had called for a peace of reconciliation "without annexations or indemnities." The German Reichstag had passed a similar resolution, and peace talk was very much in the air in both France and Italy. An Austrian initiative for peace was made through the brother-in-law of Emperor Charles, Prince Sixte of Bourbon, but this broke down because Italy held out for all the territory she had been promised by the Treaty of London. Socialism was gaining strength everywhere. Some 200,000 British workers had gone on strike in April and May, and the Independent Labour party and the British Socialist party were advocating a revolution in Britain similar to the one in Russia. Viscount Esher summarized the British dilemma well in a letter to the king's private secretary in August:

If we fail to beat the enemy and have to accept a compromise peace, then we shall be lucky if we escape a revolution in which the Monarchy, the Church and all our "Victorian" institutions will founder . . . The institutions

*Although in June Haig promised the war cabinet that the French would cooperate fully, this was a deliberate deception; General Debeney had told him plainly on the 2nd that no French help was possible for some time at least.

under which a war such as this was possible, whether monarchial, parliamentary or diplomatic, will go under. I have met no one who, speaking his inmost mind, differs from this conclusion.

The British war cabinet, in fear and trembling between the alternatives of another Somme and the possibility of revolution, decided to let Haig proceed with an offensive in which few ministers had any faith.*

The series of operations known as the Third Battle of Ypres began on July 31 with an attack by Gough's Fifth Army against Pilckem Ridge. It did not advance even halfway to its first objectives, and in four days cost 31,850 casualties. Just as Haig had been warned, the weather now broke and heavy rain caused a suspension of operations until August 16, when renewed attacks broke down. For ten days, between August 15 and 25, the Canadian Corps fought a bitter diversionary battle at Hill 70 near Lens, but though the Canadians took Hill 70, the German high command was not deceived and no German reserves were moved from Flanders. On the 20th Pétain launched a meticulously prepared small attack at Verdun, which was successful, but this had no effect on the main operation in Flanders. When Gough recommended that the offensive be abandoned, Haig turned over the principal role to Major General Herbert Plumer's Second Army. By the end of August British losses had amounted to more than sixty-seven thousand men. The plans for amphibious landings were now abandoned.

On September 2, in London, Haig persuaded a reluctant war cabinet to let the offensive proceed. He claimed that Pétain was urging him to attack so as to give the French more time to recover, and Haig's apologists have since repeated this claim. In fact, the only comment of Pétain's that is recorded is a letter to Haig, dated June 30, in which the French commander-in-chief wrote: "*L'offensive des Flandres doit être assurée d'un succès absolu, imperieusement exigé par les facteurs moraux du moment.*" What Pétain was telling Haig, of course, was that if he was determined on his offensive, he should make absolutely certain of success because Allied morale could not stand another failure like Nivelle's in Champagne.

Plumer's tactics, unlike Gough's, envisaged no breakthrough. He intended to take Passchendaele Ridge in three bites, each carefully prepared. A spell of good weather intervened and Plumer's common sense had its reward. The three battles of Menin Road Ridge, Polygon Wood, and Broodseinde were all successful. The October rains now

*Only Smuts and Carson in the war cabinet professed any belief in Haig's being able to do what he planned.

set in in earnest, and both Plumer and Gough told Haig that it would be better to discontinue the offensive. Against all reason the British commander-in-chief decided to continue the attacks. He was no longer talking of capturing Ostend and Zeebruge, of clearing the Flanders coast, rolling up the German right flank, and winning the war. His eyes were now fixed hypnotically on half a dozen map squares of mud.

Haig had promised that if substantial initial success was not achieved, he would halt the operation, but there was a simple way around this. He now claimed that substantial success had in fact been achieved. This technique of the deliberate falsehood had worked for him at the Somme. Military secrecy made the real facts hard to come by, the British public was anxious to believe the best, and certain newspapers and politicians took the attitude that any criticism of the generals was unpatriotic. At the end of October, after three months of bloody fighting and enormous numbers of casualties, objectives that were to have been captured on the first day still remained in enemy hands.

The troops who marched up through the broken arch of the Menin Gate, across the footbridge over the Yser Canal, and made their way to the line came on a dreary plain that stretched as far as the eye could see. It was a nightmare landscape, featureless, evil-smelling, a gray waste of scum-coated water and mud. The road to the front, made of planks laid on fascines, crossed a vast swamp. It was dangerous to slip off the road or off the greasy duckboards farther up, for it was all too easy to sink down and suffocate in the stinking mud. Horses, mules, and men were often lost this way, and many of the walking wounded never reached the regimental aid post. The thousands of shell holes were filled with water, and in some the water was reddened with blood and in some there floated horribly bloated corpses.

The German defenses in the salient had been organized by Colonel Lossberg, for Ludendorff moved Lossberg to threatened sectors of the front just as a medical expert might be called in for consultation. Lossberg made the most of his resources. Men were thinned out of the front line, and in their place concrete pillboxes dotted the battlefield in checkerboard patterns, each pillbox invulnerable to all but a direct hit from a heavy gun. In all that waste of desolation the machine gunners in these pillboxes were the only men who fought in relative comfort and safety. No elaborate preparations were made for counterattack because the German high command had a more just appreciation than did the British of the value of that water-logged ground. If the attackers were prepared to pay for it, they were welcome to keep it.

The Australians and New Zealanders made little progress in the first attempt to take Passchendaele Ridge on October 22. The Canadian Corps moved in to attack on the 26th and fought its way up foot by foot through the German strongpoints to capture the ridge and Passchendaele village by November 10. The Canadians suffered nearly sixteen thousand casualties. At last even Haig was persuaded to call off the battle.

The Third Battle of Ypres had gone on for 109 days; it had deepened the Ypres Salient at the point of farthest advance by four and a half miles. All but nine of the sixty British divisions on the western front had been committed at one time or another. As with the Somme, and for the same discreditable reasons, there is still doubt about the true casualty figures. Probably Haig's armies lost more than 300,000 men in the Flanders offensive. The Germans in the same period of time lost 270,710 on the entire western front, including the much longer portion facing the French and Belgian armies.

The casualties at Passchendaele, then, were rather less than at the Somme, but when one deals with casualties of the magnitude of hundreds of thousands the imagination in any case boggles. What these casualties, and the Somme casualties, really cost is in the truest sense imponderable — the problems that were never solved, the sons that were never born, the poetry that was never written, and all the valor that was heedlessly poured out into the ground. No excuse whatsoever existed for the latter half of the battle and it may well be doubted whether even the first half was wise or necessary. True enough, the same comment could be made about the whole war, but the war, although a far greater fault, was not the fault of the generals. This reflection necessarily gives rise to another. Was Passchendaele the fault of Haig and his staff, of — in Lloyd George's words — "this secluded little community [that] reeked of that sycophantic optimism which is the curse of autocratic power"? Or were Haig, Kiggell and Charteris, Joffre, Nivelle and Falkenhayn, the Grand Duke Nicholas and all the rest no more than reflections of the society that had promoted them, given them command of these mighty armies, and sent them into aimless battle unprepared by training or aptitude to fight intelligently?

As 1917 drew to a close, Haig was left with an army grievously weakened both in numbers and morale. Riots occurred at the British base depot at Etaples and, although there was never any question of mutiny among combat formations, the average British soldier had lost much of his confidence in the high command.

Ludendorff had been so little worried by Haig's attacks in front of Passchendaele that in October he sent a new German army, the Fourteenth, under General Otto von Below, to the Italian front to aid the Austrians. The Italians had fought the Tenth and Eleventh Battles of the Isonzo in April, and in August and September, and had achieved some local success. As autumn drew in, however, the Italian commander-in-chief, General Luigi Cadorna, decided that he would have to go over to the defensive. His armies had suffered heavy losses, he was short of trained officers, guns, and ammunition, and the morale of his troops was uncertain.

Austrian morale was also poor, and Austrian Supreme Headquarters informed Ludendorff that its armies could not endure another winter of war or a twelfth Italian attack on the Isonzo. When Ludendorff's chief of operations, Lieutenant Colonel Wetzel, urged an attack at some Italian "soft spot," two German officers made a reconnaissance of the Italian front and reported that an attack might well succeed.

Pack artillery and special mountaineering equipment were hastily scraped together, and the six German divisions of Below's army assembled secretly in a small bridgehead on the west bank of the Isonzo River near Tolmino. Nine Austrian divisions also moved up without the Italians realizing what was happening.

In the early morning of October 24, after a five-hour bombardment, the Germans and Austrians advanced in a cold misty rain that partly blinded the defenders, the Italian Second Army, commanded by General Luigi Capello. A clean breakthrough on a four-divisional front was achieved at Caporetto in the center, and Below hastened to reinforce success. At 9:00 P.M. on the 24th, General Cadorna decided on a limited retirement, intending to stand on the line of the Tagliamento River, but he delayed in ordering the forty-mile retreat until the afternoon of the 27th, and by then it was too late. Many Italian soldiers had already decided that they had had enough of the war and were fleeing rearward, blocking the roads and making the forward movement of reinforcements impossible. The Second, Third, and Fourth Italian armies were all flowing backward now, and the Second Army had virtually dissolved. It was unkindly described by an Entente observer as being composed of 180,000 prisoners and 400,000 stragglers. By October 31 the Third Army, not much molested, got most of its troops back across the Tagliamento. Some disorganized remnants of the Italian Second Army also scrambled to safety beyond the river.

When a German and an Austrian division forced a passage of the Tagliamento on the night of November 2, Cadorna ordered a retreat to the Piave, another thirty miles to the southwest. The troops were not unwilling; they fell back with alacrity, jostling to get out of the way of their pursuers. The Third and Fourth armies were across the Piave by the 9th, and there the retreat halted. Cadorna was replaced as commander-in-chief by General Armando Díaz.

At Caporetto the Italian army lost 275,000 prisoners and 2500 guns; some 100,000 Italians deserted and went home. Below had originally intended to halt at the Tagliamento, but the Italian route had been so complete that he allowed his forces to accompany the Austrians to the Piave. Thereupon Ludendorff ordered them back to the western front.

The British and French governments, greatly alarmed by the news of Caporetto, were not noticeably cheered to hear that the Italian prime minister, Vittorio Orlando, was talking bravely of carrying on the war from Sicily. Six French and five British divisions were dispatched to Italy (despite protests from Haig) and took over a portion of the Italian front on November 25. Thereafter talk of further retreats died down. One side effect of Caporetto was that Lloyd George was finally able to get agreement for the creation of the Supreme War Council, composed of the American and Allied heads of government and their military advisers. This council was to meet at Versailles and coordinate the overall strategy of the war and the allocation of reserves.

The fighting around Arras, the Nivelle offensive, the French mutinies, Passchendaele, and Caporetto had made 1917 a bitter year for the Allies, and the promise of American aid in the future was, of course, dependent on Britain and France holding on until that aid could be effective. There was serious reason to doubt that this could be done, for on November 7,* Lenin and the Bolsheviks seized power in Petrograd by a coup d'état, took over the Winter Palace where some cabinet ministers of Kerensky's government were meeting,† dissolved the pre-parliament at the Mariinsky Palace, and entered into peace negotiations with Germany.

On December 2 the Russian armistice delegation arrived at *Ober-Ost* at Brest-Litovsk, and Hoffmann at once began sending German divisions to the west. Trotsky, the head of the Russian delegation, firmly believed that the Russian Revolution would soon spread across the world, bringing about the downfall of the capitalist and imperialist system and ushering in the communist millennium. So he was in no particular hurry at Brest-Litovsk, preferring to talk about world revolution rather than about peace. Hoffmann finally had enough of this and bluntly outlined the German terms, telling the Russian delegation to accept them or face a resumption of the war. The terms were very

*October 25 by the old Russian calendar.
†Kerensky had become prime minister in July.

severe. Trotsky refused them, but declared that this did not mean that Russia was still at war with Germany; he was demobilizing the Russian army, he announced, and the war was therefore over. There would be "neither peace nor war."

Hoffmann, who was perhaps not familiar with the intricacies of socialist theory, signed a separate peace with the Ukraine and ordered a general advance of his armies all along the eastern front. The forward movement began on February 18, 1918, against virtually no opposition, and although the Bolsheviks were indignant that an imperialist power should thus persecute the revolution, they surrendered abjectly five days later. The Peace of Brest-Litovsk, signed on March 3, gave Finland and the Ukraine their independence, deprived Russia of Courland, Lithuania, Poland, Batum, and Kars, allowed the German army to occupy Estonia and Latvia, provided for the demobilization of the Russian army and for an immediate end to Bolshevik propaganda. A separate peace with Rumania was signed on May 7.

One more military operation in the west remains to be recorded for 1917. At the end of the Passchendaele offensive Haig looked about him for something "to restore British prestige and strike a theatrical blow against Germany before the winter." Colonel J. F. C. Fuller of the Tank Corps suggested a raid near St. Quentin, where good tank country was to be found. This was not ambitious enough for GHQ, which transformed the raid into an offensive. General Sir Julian Byng's Third Army was allotted the task and given a total of nineteen infantry divisions and more than 300 tanks. The plan was to break through the Hindenburg Line, cross the St. Quentin Canal, and capture the German second position covering Cambrai. The Cavalry Corps of five divisions was placed in reserve to exploit the breakthrough. Pétain placed three French infantry and two cavalry divisions at Haig's disposal for the exploitation phase. In the event, the British commander-in-chief did not use this force, for he wanted the credit to be the British army's alone.

The British attack went in at 6:20 on the morning of November 25. In four hours the main Hindenburg position was overrun and the advance had penetrated between three and four miles along a six-mile front — a greater gain than had been achieved by fifty-one British divisions in four months of bloody fighting at Third Ypres. In England, at the suggestion of the War Office, church bells were rung to celebrate the victory and there was much inspired rejoicing. This was to prove premature, for the British offensive had already lost its momentum. The German front re-formed like a scab around the penetration, and on November 30, after a heavy bombardment, the

Germans counterattacked. When the battle was over on December 2, the Germans had regained slightly more ground than they had lost to the original British thrust.

The end of 1917 thus witnessed the nadir of the Allied cause. Russia was out of the war and the United States not yet effectively in it. The French army was convalescing after its mutinies, and the British army, now woefully understrength because Lloyd George was refusing Haig the reinforcements he demanded, was recuperating after Passchendaele. Each week more German divisions were being shipped to the west from the eastern front. It was not surprising that the thoughts of the British cabinet turned to peace. Lord Lansdowne had again raised the possibility, publicly this time, in a letter to the *Daily Telegraph* on November 29. The South African General Jan Smuts, a member of the British war cabinet, talked in Geneva with Count Albert von Mensdorff, a former Austrian ambassador to Britain, and found the Austrian not unwilling to listen, if, as Smuts hinted, Austria was given Russian Poland. In a public speech on war aims, Prime Minister Lloyd George was remarkably conciliatory, rejecting any enforced change of government in Germany and asking only for the restoration of Belgium and Serbia and of the territories of France, Italy, and Rumania occupied by the Central Powers. In exchange, he said, "I will not attempt to deal with the question of Russian territories now in German occupation." In other words, if Germany gave up her conquests in the west, she could compensate herself at Russian expense. "I went as near peace as I could," the British prime minister said later.

But the time for peace had long passed. The French government had fallen on November 13 and Poincaré had reluctantly appointed his old enemy Georges Clemenceau as the new prime minister. Clemenceau outlined his intentions to the Chamber of Deputies later in the month: "You ask what is my policy. It is to wage war. Home policy? It is to wage war. Foreign policy? I wage war. All the time, in every area, I wage war." Clemenceau at once began a purge of traitorous and pacifist elements in France. Caillaux was among those brought to trial for treason. When the Bolshevik government suggested a negotiated peace, the idea was rejected out of hand. Nor was the German government now in any mood for negotiation. What Bethmann-Hollweg would have granted with a light heart, Ludendorff would never agree to. He had already decided to stake everything on a decisive victory in the west before the Americans could intervene in strength. The self-generating momentum of the war had not yet run down.

CHAPTER V

NINETEEN EIGHTEEN was the year when the breaking point was reached. Bulgaria, Turkey, Austria-Hungary, and Germany finally crumbled under the weight of Allied attacks. Once the United States had entered the conflict, this result was probably inevitable, but it was hastened because General Ludendorff gambled desperately to stave off defeat, lost his gamble, and in doing so broke Germany's defensive capability. However, Ludendorff's last throw was also the result of American intervention, for it was the threat of massive American forces on the western front that dictated the timing and nature of the Ludendorff offensives.

On January 8, 1918, in a message to Congress, President Wilson outlined his Fourteen Points as a basis for peace. They included "open covenants, openly arrived at," freedom of navigation on the seas in peace and war, the removal of economic barriers between nations, the reduction of armaments, the adjustment of colonial claims with the interests of the colonies being taken into account, the evacuation of conquered territory in Russia and Belgium, the restoration of Alsace-Lorraine, and the recognition of the principle of national self-determination in Europe.

Lloyd George, who perhaps had had some advance notice of what the American President intended to say, tried to take the wind out of his sails by getting in first with a statement of British war aims. It was late in the day to be asking what had been the purpose of the long day's labor, but if Wilson insisted on raising such an awkward question, he could not be allowed to have the floor to himself. In an address to a trade-union conference in London on January 5, the British prime minister mentioned some twelve of Wilson's Fourteen Points and added a demand for reparations. The German, French, and British governments were all displeased at Wilson's initiative and embarrassed by the political idealism it portrayed. Ludendorff had his heart set on carving out a Greater Germany that would completely dominate the continent. The French dreamed similar dreams at Germany's expense; when Clemenceau heard of Wilson's Fourteen Points, he growled: "The good God had only ten." The British did not much like the sound of "freedom of navigation on the seas in peace and war" or of an adjustment of colonial claims in which the interests of colonial subjects would be considered.

Meanwhile there was still the war, and it had not yet been won. Although Ludendorff was obviously preparing a great blow in the west, Haig was not preparing to defend himself but was pressing to be given more men and resources so that he could resume his attack beyond Passchendaele. However, Lloyd George had no intention of providing the British commander-in-chief with more drafts to be squandered in more Passchendaeles. In any case, Britain's manpower resources were rapidly dwindling; the British army could have been brought up to strength in the winter of 1918, but it could not be kept up to strength for any prolonged period of fighting.

Ludendorff had called his first staff conference on the 1918 spring offensive, code-named "Michael," on November 11, 1917, at Mons. Once again Germany was working within strict time limits. The British and French armies would have to be crushed in the interval between the drying of the ground in the spring and the time in midsummer when American formations could be expected to begin arriving in force. For a brief period before the Americans began to arrive, the Germans, for the first time in the war, would actually have a slight numerical superiority over the western Allies — 194 German divisions to 173 Allied divisions, six of them American. The German superiority would really be less than this, for each American division was roughly twice the size of its British or French counterpart.

Ludendorff decided to strike the British army between Arras and St. Quentin. This was the old Somme battleground and contained no vitally important strategic objectives, but the British, for that reason, were holding the area weakly. Moreover, Ludendorff did not intend to stake everything on a single blow. Operation Michael would be merely the first of a series of attacks designed to "shake the hostile edifice by closely connected partial blows so that the whole structure would collapse." This concept was a natural corollary to Ludendorff's very proper emphasis on tactical success, but it did have the effect of blurring the aim of the German offensive. Hoffmann, with shrewder strategical insight, would have preferred a single mighty effort, and then, if that failed, a retirement to the frontiers of Germany and a defensive policy aimed at securing a reasonable peace. What

Hoffmann feared was that each of Ludendorff's attacks, even if successful, would consume more of Germany's limited reserves, whereas the British and French had only to stave off utter defeat until American reinforcements would guarantee them final victory.

The German army had not launched a full-scale offensive in the west since 1914; Verdun had aimed at no more than attrition. Thus the army in the west was not well trained in offensive tactics, and the formations brought back from the east were used to fighting a quite different kind of war. Ludendorff decided to revise completely the German tactics for the offensive just as he had done in 1916 for the defensive. These two fundamental changes of doctrine, implemented not in the leisurely atmosphere of peacetime when experiment and criticism would minimize error, but in the haste and distraction of war, were perhaps the greatest German military achievement of the years 1914 to 1918.

In the fall of 1917 Ludendorff assembled a group of carefully selected young officers with combat experience and put them to work devising new offensive tactics for the conditions of static warfare. The new tactics employed the same weapons that had been in use for the past two years but employed them in a radically different way. The previous emphasis on weight gave way to a new emphasis on flexibility. There would be no elaborate preliminary bombardment but only a short, whirlwind barrage of the kind that Lieutenant Colonel Bruchmüller, the German artillery expert, had employed so effectively on the eastern front. The fighting line would not consist of wave after wave of carefully aligned attackers advancing almost shoulder to shoulder; instead, it would be kept thin but would be fed constantly from behind. As had been done for the defensive, manpower was to be replaced as much as possible by machine-power. A new tactical formation, the infantry group, would be the basic unit and would consist of only a few riflemen and a light machine gun. This would confer a greater degree of articulation on the attacking formations; instead of a closed fist smashing the opposition, innumerable tentacles would reach out to explore the enemy's soft spots. Specially trained storm troopers would move forward in front of the main infantry assault, leaning hard against the rolling barrage, probing for weak spots, bypassing centers of resistance, and exploiting success. There would be no effort made to maintain a uniform rate of advance or to align formations; the battlefield was considered in terms of depth as an area to be controlled, just as had previously been done in the defense, and the security of flanks would no longer be a consideration. The new German offensive tactics thus abandoned the concept of the battering ram, pounding heavily and head-on against a fortified line, and substituted in its place the principle of pervasiveness, by which the attackers, like a flood of water, would penetrate the defense, flow around and isolate obstacles and centers of resistance, and move by a thousand different routes into the enemy's territory.

All this was, in many ways, the obverse of Lossberg's defensive doctrine, with an emphasis on fluidity, initiative, and replenishment from the rear. Once the idea of defense in depth had been accepted, it was only logical that the attack would have to be modified to meet it — another illustration of Clausewitz's maxim that "the defensive is the stronger form of war," for it was the defense that dictated the nature of the attack rather than vice versa. Geometrical tactics, with the emphasis on lines and points, were to be replaced by concepts of area; it was almost as though a new dimension had been added to the battlefield. The correct employment of reserves was obviously the key to success in this type of battle, and here, as it turned out, the new doctrine was better understood by the fighting formations than by Supreme Headquarters.

Operation Michael called for an assault by three armies between Arras and La Fère. The northern portion of the attack, undertaken by Below's Seventeenth and Georg von der Marwitz' Second armies, was to be controlled by an army group headquarters commanded by Crown Prince Rupprecht; the most southerly army, Oskar von Hutier's Eighteenth, came under Crown Prince Wilhelm. The frontage of attack was some forty-three miles but the main thrust was to be north of the Somme, where the Seventeenth Army would strike for Bapaume and Arras and the Second Army would take Péronne and Doullens. Hutier's Eighteenth Army on the Somme would act as flank guard. The British were to be separated from the French and driven to the sea.

Although the British had attempted to adopt the German defensive tactics, the idea of holding a line still dominated British tactical thought. The area to be defended was divided into three so-called zones: a lightly held forward zone to cushion the initial impact of the attack, a battle zone two or three miles farther back, and a rear zone, which, in fact, was never constructed because the necessary labor was not available. The net result of these changes was that the defensive would now rely on two lines rather than on "one line and a strong one." The importance of counterattack to the defense was not emphasized, and about one third of the British defenders were placed in the forward zone — too few to hold it but too many for the battle zone to be properly manned.

General Byng's Third Army held eighteen miles of the front north of the Somme, and General Gough's Fifth Army held the southern sector, forty-two miles long. Neither of these armies was up to strength. Gough's Fifth Army had recently taken over fourteen miles of front from the French, and these trenches were, as usual, in very poor condition. Thanks to Haig's jealous obstruction, there was no general Allied reserve, but Pétain had agreed that if the need arose, he would send the British six divisions at short notice.

Sharp at 4:40 A.M. on March 21 the German preliminary bombardment crashed out. The foggy morning favored the attackers, but Byng's Third Army, strongly posted north of the Somme, fought well and gave ground slowly. In the center, Marwitz' Second Army did better and got well into the battle zone. South of the Somme, Gough's thinly spread Fifth Army crumbled before the assault.

The following day the German attacks continued. The field gray battle groups worked their way forward with disconcerting ease, spreading like a stain into the British areas until they dominated them. By nightfall only patches of Byng's battle zone were still being held, and the Fifth Army, in increasing confusion, had everywhere fallen back to the unfortified rear zone or beyond. Headquarters lost touch with units, vital railway bridges fell intact into the enemy's hands, and 500 British guns were captured. For the first time since 1914 a real breakthrough had been achieved on the western front, of sufficient width to make any sealing-off of the gap problematical. Fortunately, the situation was not completely dark, for the German Seventeenth Army was making no progress, and though the Second Army was still advancing, it was doing so slowly.

Pétain promptly honored his pledge to Haig and in fact was better than his word, sending nine divisions instead of six. It was a generous move, but as the British retreat continued on the 24th, Pétain, meeting Haig late at night at British GHQ, gloomily informed the British commander-in-chief that he did not believe the main German attack had yet been delivered and that French reserves would have to be moved southwest to cover Paris. When Haig demanded to know if this meant that Pétain would abandon the British right flank and allow the enemy to drive a wedge between the British and the French, Pétain nodded his head. Perhaps the successful defense of Verdun had taken its toll of Pétain as well as of the French army. Certainly this decision to leave the British army to its fate was a tacit admission by Pétain that he believed the war was lost.

Field Marshal Haig was not the most brilliant of men, but he was certainly no defeatist. He at once telephoned London, saying that unless General Foch or some other determined general were given supreme command, there would be disaster. At noon on March 26 Lord Milner, who was soon to be the new secretary of state for war, and the

Chief of the General Staff, Sir Henry Wilson, conferred with President Poincaré, Prime Minister Clemenceau, Foch, Pétain, and Haig at Doullens. Haig noted in his diary that Pétain "had a terrible look. He had the appearance of a commander who was in a funk." Pétain, for his part, had whispered to Clemenceau, when Haig had entered the room, "There goes a general who will soon have to surrender in the open field, and I after him."

Little General Foch, on the other hand, was as full of fight as ever, declaring: "We must fight in front of Amiens. We must stop where we are now." At Haig's suggestion, Foch was appointed "coordinator" of the Allied armies on the western front. This was still a long way from appointing an Allied commander-in-chief, and Haig, who had formerly opposed any subordination of his own position, now had changed his mind only because he was desperate. The British cabinet was displeased at even the moderate powers given to Foch, and on April 3 Lloyd George told the French premier that the idea of a French commander-in-chief was unacceptable.

Meanwhile the German advance continued. Albert fell on the 25th and Montdidier on the 27th. But the flexibility that had made possible the success of the German infantry groups in the field was not reflected in Ludendorff's handling of his armies. The German high command persisted too long in its attacks on Byng's Third Army on the heights around Arras instead of reinforcing the success of the Eighteenth Army south of the Somme. The British front hardened, and Foch sent twenty-one French divisions to his ally's assistance. On April 5, after the failure of a final German attempt to capture Amiens, Ludendorff called a halt to Michael.

On the whole, he was satisfied. In two weeks the Germans had advanced to a depth of forty miles along a forty-mile front. Allied casualties had amounted to 240,000 men, two thirds of them British. But strategic success had again eluded the German high command. The capture of Amiens, a focal point of railway and road networks, might well have forced the British and French armies apart and have ended the war. This had not been achieved. Even more significant was the fact that German casualties had been at least as high as the French and British. Of the 199 German divisions by then on the western front, 88 had been employed in Michael. And all the while the clock was ticking away remorselessly, bringing nearer the time when fresh American divisions would spell the end of all German hopes of victory. Another sinister portent was the action of German troops who had overrun the British rear areas; they often stopped attacking to loot the well-stocked supply depots. The German soldiers, who had been told that as a result of the U-boat campaign the British were starving, were much disillusioned to find that the enemy was in fact better fed and clothed than themselves.

Ludendorff's slowness in reinforcing his left, the prompt arrival of French reinforcements, and Haig's dogged defense had all contributed to the successful Allied resistance. A more important factor than any of these, however, was the insufficient German numerical superiority. In March of 1918, as throughout the entire war, the Germans simply did not have enough resources for the tasks they set themselves.

Ludendorff's next blow was to fall again on the British, this time in Flanders, on both sides of the Lys River. This offensive, which had initially been given the code name "George," would be mounted with only thirty-five divisions as opposed to the eighty-eight divisions that had been available for "Michael." For this reason the code name was changed to "Georgette." Such gentle irony was all very well, but Hoffmann's reservations about a series of offensives were already being grimly confirmed.

Ludendorff, however, again caught Haig on the wrong foot, because in spite of evidence to the contrary the British commander-in-chief had persisted in his belief that the next German blow would be against Vimy Ridge. At 4:05 A.M. on April 9 a Bruckmüller bombardment fell upon the British lines between the La Bassée Canal and Armentières. The infantry assault, launched by formations of General Friedrich Sixt von Armin's Fourth Army and Quart's Sixth Army, went in at 8:45 A.M. Immediately the overstrained Portuguese 2nd Division, north of Neuve Chapelle, broke. Before noon the entire British front was endangered by a German penetration of more than three miles, but by nightfall the German advance had been temporarily halted. On the next day, four fresh divisions of the German Fourth Army struck three depleted British divisions north of Armentières. Armentières was abandoned, and farther south the Germans forced a crossing of the Lys. The British commander-in-chief begged Foch for reinforcements, but all he obtained was a promise that the French Tenth Army of four divisions and three cavalry divisions would be in position behind Amiens by April 12. Haig had supported Foch's appointment as coordinator* because he hoped that Foch would be more generous with French reinforcements than Pétain had been, but now both Haig and Pétain complained that Foch was hoarding his reserves.

On the 11th, when the Germans thrust to within five miles of Hazebrouck, Foch refused to take over any of the British line and told Haig that his army "must hold on where it stood." Perforce, Haig took

*Foch was made commander-in-chief of all Allied armies on April 24.

this advice, declaiming, in his order of the day, "With our backs to the wall and believing in the justice of our cause, each one must fight on to the end." This exhortation was not needed, for the British troops were as usual persevering in the defense. Nevertheless, British observers south of Béthune, watching night after night in the clear April weather, saw with mounting apprehension a wedge of burning villages like a great fiery V moving farther and farther westward to the coast.

In the event, some British reinforcements were scraped together and Foch relented to the extent of contributing two divisions and three cavalry divisions. Renewed German attacks on the 13th and 14th made little headway, and when Haig asked Foch on the night of the 14th to relieve the tired British troops, the generalissimo refused, declaring, with sure insight, "*La bataille d'Hazebrouck est finie.*" Foch was correct, though Ludendorff did not recognize the fact until April 29, when he broke off the offensive.

Ludendorff's second great offensive had again failed to bring about a strategic decision. Ten British divisions had had to be broken up for reinforcements, but the Channel ports were still firmly in British hands. Since March 21 the Germans had lost 350,000 men to an Allied loss of 331,000. And time was still running out as more and more Americans landed in France.*

The third German offensive, code-named "Blücher," was intended as a diversion to draw reserves away from the vital Flanders area. Surely it was ominous that it took the Germans nearly a month to prepare, an interval they could ill afford. However, on May 27 the Germans attacked a thirty-nine-mile stretch of front along the Chemin des Dames. American intelligence had predicted this offensive, but neither Foch nor Pétain was inclined to believe that these amateur staff officers knew their business. As a consequence, the German blow struck a front that had been much weakened by the draining away of reserves.

At 3:40 A.M., while it was still deep night, seventeen German divisions stormed the Chemin des Dames ridge. Three battle-worn British divisions that had come to this "quiet" sector for rest were swept aside, as was the French division on the right. The Germans passed through and by noon had crossed the Aisne on bridges that had been left intact. Before darkness fell the Germans had advanced up to twelve miles and stood on the banks of the Vesle.

Originally Ludendorff had intended to halt on the Vesle, but his success tempted him to continue. Soissons fell the next day, and by evening on the 29th both that town and Fismes had been left far be-

---

*By the end of July there were twenty-seven United States divisions in France.

hind. In the center, the German Seventh Army had reached the Marne.

The United States 1st Division had been thrown into the battle on the 28th, capturing Cantigny near Montdidier in fine style. Two more American divisions, the 2nd and 3rd, entered the line at Château Thierry and Belleau Wood on June 1 and 6. General John Pershing, who had long insisted that the United States Army would have to fight united, had agreed to Pétain's urgent request for help to hold the Marne crossings. The U.S. 3rd Division broke repeated German attempts to cross to the south bank of the Marne, and the U.S. 2nd Division held like a wall west of Château Thierry. In this, the first operation in which American troops had been engaged, their splendid behavior was as discouraging to the Germans as it was uplifting for the British and French.

Now, too, for the first time in the war, some German divisions had shown no inclination to attack. Troops had frequently halted to search for food, and a staff officer reported that at Fismes "drunken soldiers were lying all over the road." The Germans and the Allies had each lost about 128,000 men in this third offensive, but the Germans had no means of replacing their casualties. By now a quarter of a million American soldiers were arriving in France every month. These fresh troops were sorely needed, for the British front-line infantry strength, which had stood at 754,000 men on July 1, 1917, was down to 543,000 men on June 1, 1918.

Ludendorff decided to launch a fourth offensive, to threaten Paris and attract Allied reserves from Flanders, where he still intended to strike his final blow. Hutier's Eighteenth Army was to advance south from Montdidier astride the Matz River. Since the time and place of this attack was revealed by a German prisoner,* the French Third Army under General Emile Fayolle was prepared to receive it when it came on the early morning of June 9. On the 11th the French counterattacked with five divisions — really with seven equivalent divisions, for the U.S. 1st and 2nd divisions, which participated, were both double the size of French formations. This counterattack halted the Germans in their tracks, and on the evening of the 12th Ludendorff called off the offensive. The Germans had advanced a maximum of nine miles, but Foch's reserves were still largely uncommitted. By now, too, the slender German numerical superiority had vanished; the arrival of American formations had shifted the balance back to the Allies.

---

*The increasing frequency with which Allied intelligence was now getting accurate information from German prisoners and deserters was a sure sign that German morale was at long last weakening. Until 1918 German prisoners had rarely cooperated with their captors.

Ludendorff still believed that he could win by defeating the British in Flanders, but he planned yet another diversionary offensive on both sides of Reims before the decisive switch to the Ypres sector. However, the French, warned as to both the time and the place of the attack, strengthened the Reims front with an additional thirteen divisions, four of them British.

In the middle of June, when the front was relatively quiet, an epidemic of "Spanish" influenza broke out almost simultaneously across the world. Within a year it was to kill more people than the war had done. Nothing so pandemic or so deadly had been seen before in history; not even the Black Death claimed so many victims over such a wide area. In the last seven months of 1918 and the first three months of 1919 more than twenty million people died of the disease. In the United States, where the percentage of deaths was much lower than in most other nations, 548,000 perished — more than four times the 126,000 American soldiers who died from all causes during the war. Civilian populations were hit harder than the armies, where the standard of physical fitness was high and the average age much younger.

In the last two weeks of June army after army reported to German Supreme Headquarters that the epidemic had so weakened their divisions that they could not resist an Allied attack, let alone mount one of their own. The British, French, and Americans also fell victim to the influenza, and Ludendorff hoped without reason that the Allies would be weakened more than the Germans. Quite predictably, the converse occurred, for the German army, thanks to the British blockade, had long suffered from dietary deficiencies. The epidemic raged through the latter half of June and July, died down, then broke out again with increased virulence in October.

Another illness, more insidious and more deadly even than Spanish influenza, was also beginning to attack Germany. Bolshevik propaganda, which had weakened France in the spring of 1917, was now being spread in the Reich. Some units brought back from the eastern front were considered to be so infected with Bolshevik ideas that they were not deemed suitable for employment in the west. Ludendorff found it necessary to promulgate a harsh order, on June 23, promising death and the confiscation of property to all deserters and making it clear that there would never be an amnesty. Nevertheless, increasing numbers of German soldiers slipped across the border into Holland. On June 24 the German foreign minister, Richard von Kühlmann, who believed in a negotiated peace, declared in the Reichstag that Germany could no longer hope to win the war by purely military means. Ludendorff, branding this as defeatism, demanded his resignation. The kaiser, by now accustomed to bowing to the will of Hindenburg and Ludendorff, reluctantly consented and appointed Admiral Paul von Hintze, the former military plenipotentiary at Petrograd, to be foreign minister.

Ludendorff's double offensive was at last ready for launching on July 15. The odds were now definitely against the Germans. Three and a half German armies, comprising fifty-two divisions, faced a French force of fifty-seven divisions, including nine American divisions. The French, having learned from prisoners that the German bombardment was to open at 12:10 A.M., began their defensive artillery fire half an hour earlier, slaughtering the enemy forming up for the assault and throwing his troops into confusion.

East of Reims the German offensive was a disastrous failure, and at noon on the 16th Ludendorff ordered his First and Third armies to switch to the defensive. However, General Max von Boehn's German Seventh Army crossed the Marne west of Reims without excessive casualties. The United States 3rd Division stopped the right wing of this assault, but southwest of Reims two Italian divisions crumbled at the first approach of German infantry and had to be relieved by two British divisions. As the German bridgehead was successfully expanded in the center to a depth of three miles, Paris appeared to be in danger for the first time since 1914.

Foch and Pétain had prepared a counterstroke against the western side of the German salient, and Foch's steady nerves had enabled him to watch the German advance with equanimity. Pétain ordered the counterattack postponed because he hoped that after the commitment of more German reserves the eventual counterattack would be more decisive. Foch was still too impetuous for such a strategy; he possessed neither Pétain's patience nor his pessimism. Often in the past Pétain would have been the better guide, but not by midsummer of 1918. Foch countermanded Pétain's order, and on the early morning of the 18th General Mangin's Tenth Army struck the western flank of the salient. General Jean Degoutte's Eighth Army joined the assault later in the morning. The French troops and tanks, concealed in the woods around Villers Cotterets, achieved complete surprise, driving forward more than four miles and threatening to cut off the six German divisions south of the Marne. But on the 19th, as so often before, the Allied attacks met increased opposition and made little headway. That night the German forces safely recrossed the river. The Germans continued to withdraw, abandoning Soissons on August 2 and falling back to entrenched positions behind the Vesle and the Aisne.

This was the end of the Ludendorff offensives. The great gamble had failed. Since March 21 the German army had suffered more than a million casualties, and the German general reserve now consisted of only sixty-six seriously depleted and battle-worn divisions. From Villers Cotterets on, the road led steadily downhill for the German armies; the initiative now rested with Foch, who was promoted to marshal of France on August 6.

Before the events of July, the best the Allies had been able to hope for was that they would somehow survive the German onslaught, hanging on by their teeth, until the Americans arrived. Then — perhaps in 1919, perhaps even later — they would attack and win the war. Lord Northcliffe, whose genius consisted essentially in being a sort of lowest common denominator of British public opinion, was even more pessimistic. As late as September he told one of his subordinates, "None of us will live to see the end of the war." Marshal Foch had a different vision, and now his unquenchable optimism finally found its justification. He later recorded his reflections on the military situation in these words:

> What am I risking, after all? I asked myself. You can prepare for the worst and another year of fighting, but there is no crime in hoping for the best — decisive victory within a few months.

In the first days of August there was a fresh scent in the air on the Allied side of the line — elusive, hard to define, but wonderfully, sweetly fragrant — the scent of victory. For the first time in long, bitter years the soldiers themselves — and not just the generals — sensed that the tide had turned. An army is extraordinarily sensitive to such impressions. Logic has nothing to do with it, nor calculation. Most probably it is transmitted from a hundred different sources — the bearing of prisoners, the quality of resistance, the relative casualties, the gain in ground, rumors from other formations, the attitude of senior officers — but it is in any case a critical indicator of reality. The Germans, on their side, sensed it too. Some, perhaps the majority, fought dourly on, but many now began to fight halfheartedly and to retreat or surrender before either of these expedients was really necessary.

Now that the Marne Salient had been reduced, it was the turn of the Amiens Salient, which had been formed in March. General Debeney's French First Army would cooperate with General Rawlinson's British Fourth Army in the offensive. By now even Haig had learned a trick or two, and this attack was prepared with the greatest secrecy. Tanks were used as they had been at Cambrai, and there was to be no preliminary bombardment. As the troops assembled, spirits were high.

For the first time since the Somme, British soldiers were singing on the march. Their songs now were less sentimental than they had been in the far-off days when the war was new, but no one minded that. One popular marching song, to the tune of "Take It to the Lord in Prayer," went:

> When this bloody war is over,
> Oh how happy I will be —
> No more pork and beans for breakfast,
> No more bully beef for tea,
> When I get my civvy clothes on,
> No more soldiering for me.

There were other verses, less printable, but the words mattered less than the fact that the men were singing again.

At 4:20 A.M. on the misty morning of August 8 the attack went in. Canadian, Australian, British, and French divisions hit Marwitz' weak Second Army. At the first blow, the Canadians and Australians shattered the enemy's front, overrunning gun lines and killing or taking prisoner the gunners. A divisional headquarters was captured, and a corps staff was shot up by armored cars. On this day an incredible thing happened. The cavalry at last went through. True, they did not accomplish much, for a horseman even in open country still presented a better target than a man on foot. But for the first time in four years of war the gap for the horsemen was there. The Canadian Corps advanced eight miles, the Australians seven, the French five, and the British two. British tanks losses were high, but there were fewer than nine thousand infantry casualties. German casualties were more than twenty-seven thousand, and the Allies captured some fifteen thousand prisoners and 400 guns. Ludendorff later wrote that August 8 was "the black day of the German army in the history of this war."

The next day, when the attack was resumed, surprise of course was not possible. Seven German divisions had arrived during the hours of darkness, and poor staff work at British Fourth Army headquarters resulted in a five-hour delay. The attack, when it finally went in, encountered stiff opposition, and the Germans managed to stabilize the position.

But for how long now could positions be stabilized? Several German divisions had been broken at Amiens, and though most of the prisoners the Allies captured still refused to admit that Germany had lost the war, the old spirit was lacking. On August 10, as Ludendorff was reporting to the kaiser on the military situation, Wilhelm interrupted him to say: "We must draw only one conclusion. We are at the limit of our capabilities. The war must be ended." A few days later the German government put out peace feelers through the queen of the Netherlands and the king of Spain.

The Allied command showed another unwonted sign of intelligence in refusing to press the offensive at Amiens after opposition had hardened. Foch now began a series of attacks, each limited in aim but designed to make the enemy react and thus weaken himself for the next blow, which would be struck somewhere else. This policy of "tapping" bore some superficial resemblance to Ludendorff's strategy in his spring offensives. The differences were that Foch's blows were lighter than Ludendorff's had been, more frequent, and better coordinated. Most important, Foch, unlike Ludendorff, possessed sufficient resources for such a strategy, and could keep Ludendorff hopping from one foot to another, like a tennis player desperately chasing well-placed sallies all over his side of the court.

On August 20, Mangin's Tenth Army struck between Soissons and Compiègne, driving forward five miles. The French Third Army and the British Third Army attacked on the 21st north of Albert. The British Fourth Army astride the Somme then joined the offensive. The Canadian Corps, with a Scottish division under command, thrust forward five miles on the Scarpe, and reached the Canal du Nord. The Germans now withdrew along a fifty-five-mile stretch of front, and Ludendorff ordered a withdrawal into the main Hindenburg Line. All the territory that the Germans had captured in their 1918 offensives had now been relinquished.

General Pershing was given the task of eliminating the St. Mihiel Salient near Verdun. The U.S. First Army, supported by the French 2nd Colonial Corps, began its attack on September 12; and by the next night the salient, from which the Germans were in any case withdrawing, had been eliminated. The fighting had not been severe and most of the German heavy artillery had moved out before the Americans had attacked, so it may be that Foch's effusive congratulations and the sending of French staff officers to study American methods were part of the generalissimo's technique for dealing with a recalcitrant ally. The U.S. First Army now moved to the Meuse-Argonne sector for a fresh assault in the direction of Mézières.

Foch's master plan envisaged a huge encirclement, with a Franco-British force driving in on the northwest and a Franco-American force on the south. He had a total of 220 divisions to put in against Ludendorff's 197, and only some 50 of the German formations were at all battleworthy. To aid in the encirclement, attacks were to be pressed all along the front — as Foch put it: "*Tout le monde à la bataille.*" As it happened, there was no encirclement, for the Germans gave ground in the center and held on the flanks.

The southern offensive opened on September 26, with the U.S. First Army and the French Fourth Army on its left lunging for Mézières and Sedan. Five of the nine American divisions in the assault had not been in action before and four of them had to rely on French artillery. The French fought their way forward only some ten miles in a fortnight of exceptionally bitter fighting, and the Americans, after a rapid advance along the Meuse, became seriously entangled in the Argonne forest. Errors of command and inadequate staff work, rather than any greenness of the troops, accounted for the American difficulties. Clemenceau was bitterly disappointed with the results of the Argonne fighting. "Those Americans will lose us our chance of a great victory before winter," he declared. "They are all tangled up with themselves." He tried to have Pershing relieved of his command, but Foch supported the American commander and nothing came of this suggestion. On October 12 a new U.S. Second Army was formed under Lieutenant General Robert L. Bullard, and the First Army was taken over by Lieutenant General Hunter Liggett. Pershing became the commander of an American army group. The costly American frontal attacks were resumed, but it was not until the end of October that the Argonne forest was cleared.

The day after the French and Americans opened their offensive in the south, the British First and Third armies struck in the center along the line of the Sensée Canal. The Canadian Corps swept across the Canal du Nord, and the British Fourth Army crossed the Canal de St. Quentin and pierced the Hindenburg Line. Once again Ludendorff withdrew along a wide sector of front.

On September 28, ten British, twelve Belgian, and six French divisions attacked in the north between Messines and Dixmuide, but after rapid initial progress against indifferent German opposition, the difficulties of advancing across the water-logged Flanders plain slowed the forward movement to a crawl. Both the German flanks, around Ypres in the north and in the Argonne in the south, were holding firm, and the three French armies in the center were advancing with more caution than enthusiasm. It was clear, though, that the German army, everywhere in retreat, was a beaten force.

If the German position in the west was bad, that of Germany's allies was worse. Ludendorff had stripped most of the German troops from the Eleventh Army in Salonika, and when six Serbian and two French divisions under General Franchet d'Esperey attacked on September 15, the Bulgarians abandoned their trenches and fled without fighting. In the next week the Bulgarian army dissolved itself. Tsar Ferdinand abdicated, and Bulgaria signed an armistice on September 12.

In Palestine a British army under General Edmund Allenby decisively defeated the Turks at the Battle of Megiddo in September and pursued the fleeing remnants headlong to Damascus. Another British army, under General William Marshall, advanced up the Tigris to the oil fields of Mosul, and Turkey was granted an armistice on October 30.

In Italy an Austrian offensive had failed in June, and on October 23, British troops under Lord Cavan and French troops under General Jean Graziani led a counterthrust. The British and French got across the flooded Piave River, but an Italian attack on the Monte Grappa broke down with heavy losses. By October 29 Cavan's troops had reached the Monticano River, and by November 2, the Tagliamento. On that day the newly formed Republic of Hungary recalled all Hungarian units from the front. By now the Austrian army was disintegrating, with entire divisions surrendering. As the Austro-Hungarian armies dissolved, the Italians advanced and "captured" some 300,000 prisoners. Perhaps Italy, with her military record, can not be altogether blamed for hailing this as the brilliant "victory of Vittorio Veneto" and a mighty feat of arms.

The German high command had realized at the end of September that the game was lost. On the 28th the leaders of the Reichstag were told that Germany would have to sue for peace, and the kaiser ruled that President Wilson should be asked for an armistice not later than October 1.

Chancellor Georg von Hertling was replaced by Prince Max of Baden, who formed a cabinet responsible to the Reichstag and not to the kaiser. Prince Max begged for "ten, eight or even four days, before I have to appeal to the enemy," but Ludendorff, as panic-stricken now as he had been grimly optimistic in the spring, merely repeated over and over again, "I want to save my army." Prince Max therefore sent a note to President Wilson on October 4, stating that Germany was willing to accept the Fourteen Points and the President's subsequent pronouncements as a basis for peace negotiations.

The American people, less moderate than the American President, favored harsh terms for Germany. "Peace without victory" is a most undemocratic ideal, quite foreign to the nature of popular government, and once the United States had entered the war, the majority of Americans became fiercely bellicose. Clubs advocating unconditional surrender sprang up all across the country, dedicated to victory and revenge. American newspapers were sharply critical of the President, and it seems probable that the main reason for the sharp Democratic setback in the congressional elections of November was dislike of Wilson's negotiations with Germany. President Wilson replied to the German note on October 8, asking whether Germany would really accept the Fourteen Points as a basis for peace. Prince Max replied on the 12th that Germany did indeed accept the Fourteen Points and asked if the Allies did the same. This was a shrewd point, for as Wilson well knew the Allies were almost foaming with rage at these one-sided negotiations, fearing, with some reason, that the American President might attempt at the last minute to cheat them of the fruits of victory.

On the same day as Prince Max dispatched his second note, a German U-boat sank the *Leinster* in the Irish Sea with the loss of 450 passengers, some of whom were Americans. This outraged President Wilson and gave him the excuse he needed to stiffen his terms. Indeed, the decision not to discontinue unrestricted U-boat warfare while peace negotiations were underway was an incredibly stupid one, another sign of the insensitivity to world opinion that has so often marked, and vitiated, German policy. Wilson replied on the 16th, demanding that an armistice be worked out by the Allied and American military authorities, that armistice terms "provide absolutely satisfactory safeguards and guarantees of the maintenance of the present military supremacy of the armies of the United States and her Allies in the field," that U-boat warfare be at once halted, and that the German government prove that it was truly democratic.

Prince Max accepted these new terms on October 20, despite Ludendorff's opposition to them. On the 23rd Wilson replied, agreeing to discuss the possibilities of an armistice but reasserting his demand for military supremacy and adding that if the United States had to negotiate with "the military masters and the monarchial autocrats of Germany" it would demand "not peace negotiations, but surrender." The German answer, on October 20, promised far-reaching constitutional changes and invited the Allies' armistice proposals.

The Allies, and the United States as an "Associated Power," were by no means unanimous as to what should be demanded of a defeated Germany. The world, of course, would have to be "made safe for democracy," and it would have to be a world "fit for heroes to live in"; Prussian militarism would have to be eliminated, as would autocracy. President Wilson had his own ideas, which included a League of Nations and an end to all the shabby European oppression of small nationalities and to the deceitful European diplomacy. But Wilson was the only head of a major power who wanted an idealistic peace — except Lenin, who (always allowing for a certain amount of class bias) talked in terms that were not notably different from Wilson's.

The British and the French certainly did not see eye to eye about peace with Germany. At this late date — more than four years after it all began — the British government was not quite sure why it had gone to war. Belgium, certainly. Belgium would have to be restored to its former independent status. And the German navy would have to be swept off the seas — preferably into British ports, where it would contribute substantially to Britannia's rule of the waves. The German colonies would presumably be nice to have, though some of Turkey's former possessions were really more attractive. Apart from these points, the British were not too sure what they should demand.

They brought Haig back to London on October 19 to ask his opinion. Haig pointed out that if the German armies continued to retire, they would shorten their front from 250 miles to 155 miles, which would give them an uncomfortable number of reserve divisions for 1919. He was therefore of the opinion that Germany should be offered a "soft" peace. Lloyd George, Milner, and Bonar Law all saw the force of this, and only the Chief of the Imperial General Staff, Sir Henry Wilson, disagreed. His reason for differing was a strange one — to anyone but an Ulsterman. He hoped that if the war went on into 1919, conscription would have to be imposed on Ireland and there might be an opportunity of getting some of those Irish Catholic rebels killed off. The British government, however, ignored this curious opinion, as well it might have done, and members of the British cabinet found themselves agreed in their opposition both to the tough demands of Clemenceau and to the Wilsonian idealism.

The French wanted, quite simply, the permanent weakening of Germany, Alsace-Lorraine, of course, and the left bank of the Rhine incorporated into France. They did not really care what happened to the German fleet but they were very anxious that the principle should be established that Germany should somehow pay for the war. On only one point were the British and French in substantial agreement — the danger of Bolshevism. Even Foch was willing to allow the Germans to retain some sort of army to put down German communists and to act as a buffer against the Russians. The American commander-in-chief, General Pershing, favored the French terms because he felt that the task his armies had been sent to Europe to accomplish had not yet been fully completed.

By now the German Empire was in the process of dissolution. When the sailors of the High Seas Fleet at Kiel were ordered to put to sea for a "death or glory" encounter with the Royal Navy, they mutinied, elected soviets, and raised the red flag. Dock workers in Lübeck and Hamburg joined the sailors' revolt, and by November 5 those cities were in the hands of self-constituted soviets. The kaiser went to Supreme Headquarters at Spa "to be with the army," but by now it was too late to save anything of the former Germany. By November 8 the communist revolution had spread to the Ruhr and Bavaria. King

Louis III of Bavaria abdicated and Soviet republics were proclaimed in Munich, Cologne, Frankfurt, Stuttgart, and Leipzig.

On November 5 Prince Max received President Wilson's last note, stating that Germany could send an armistice delegation behind the Allied lines and that the terms of the Armistice would then be revealed. The four-man Armistice delegation, headed by Matthias Erzberger, the Center party leader, met with Marshal Foch and Admiral Weymss in Foch's private railway coach on a siding in the Compiègne Forest on November 8.

In Berlin Prince Max resigned as imperial chancellor on the 9th, turning over the government to a reluctant Majority Socialist party, headed by the former saddler and *Gasthaus* owner Friedrich Ebert. On this day too, the Socialist deputy Philipp Scheidemann, on his own considerable initiative, proclaimed the republic from a window of the Reichstag. At Spa, Hindenburg, who should have done it himself, delegated to Wilhelm Gröner, Ludendorff's successor as First Quartermaster General, the task of informing the kaiser that he would have to abdicate. Early the next morning the kaiser crossed the frontier into Holland, where he was granted political asylum.

At five o'clock in the morning of November 11 Erzberger signed the Armistice. Under its terms, Germany agreed to hand over huge amounts of arms and munitions, numerous warships, railway engines, and rolling stock. France, Belgium, Luxembourg, and Alsace-Lorraine were to be evacuated by the German army within two weeks, and the left bank of the Rhine and a number of enclaves on the right bank were to be evacuated within a month. Germany would also have to get out of East Africa and all conquered Russian territory when it suited the Allies. The treaties of Brest-Litovsk and Bucharest were annulled, and the Allies were to be allowed free access to all parts of Germany and to requisition supplies for their armies. The blockade of Germany was to be continued. In exchange for these considerable concessions, the Allies were to permit a cessation of hostilities at eleven o'clock on the morning of November 11.

Thus, at eleven o'clock on the morning of the eleventh day of the eleventh month of the year the guns fell silent on the western front. Some saw symbolism in the timing of the Armistice: Europe had been saved at the eleventh hour. Far more to the point was an incident that occurred on the British front that morning. At a minute or two before eleven a solitary German machine gunner manned his gun and fired off an entire belt of ammunition at the British lines. Then he stood upright in the open field, took off his coal-scuttle helmet, bowed, turned, and walked away. To those who witnessed this performance it seemed the salute of a duelist who promises a return engagement.

Book Three

CHAPTER I

THE SOLDIERS on the western front generally accepted the news of the Armistice with a sort of numb disbelief in their good fortune at having survived the war, but in London, Paris, and New York the rejoicing was hysterical. It was as if a spell had been broken. For more than four years the people of Europe had lived with sacrifice, sorrow, and heroism, keeping pace with these stern companions by an extraordinary effort of will. When the guns fell silent, the reaction set in, and the spirit of rejoicing was soon replaced by weariness and disillusionment. Even the most unthinking realized that there must have been something radically wrong with a system that had perpetrated the horrors of the war. The hopes that the nineteenth century had so confidently held — of inevitable progress, of ever-increasing prosperity, and, indeed, of the ultimate perfectability of man — all these had withered. After so bloody a conflict, the doctrine of original sin seemed more in keeping with reality than the doctrine of progress. Since then the world has largely regained its confidence, but it has never recaptured its lost optimism.

Perhaps it is just as well, for the optimism had been false and had contributed not a little to the terrible outcome. Peace brought not renewed hope, but disenchantment and fear of the future. These emotions were strong among the victors and even stronger among the defeated. As compensation for vanished certitudes, men and women turned to the pursuit of pleasure, to irrational philosophies, and to various kinds of magic. In some ways it was more difficult for the victors to understand what had happened to their world than for the defeated, for the defeated could blame their misfortunes on their defeat. Everyone, of course, continued to blame the enemy. The manner in which the war had been fought and the emotions that had been aroused precluded any true peace. For four years the world had been a jungle; it was a jungle still. The Peace Conference of 1919, held in

Versailles, marked not the end of the war but rather its continuation by other means.

Bolshevik revolutions sprang up in Bavaria, the Ruhr, Hungary, and the Baltic states; Russia was given up to civil war, which was exacerbated by Allied intervention; and starvation threatened the population of Europe. In Britain, where there was a general election in December, the Coalition Unionists announced their intention of hanging the kaiser. Sir Eric Geddes, the First Lord of the Admiralty, declared that Germany would have to pay for the war. "We will get out of her all you can squeeze out of a lemon and a bit more," he declaimed. "I will squeeze her until you can hear the pips squeak."

In France, for a brief time after victory, the "old tiger," Clemenceau, was extraordinarily popular. On the other hand, the congressional elections in the United States in November had resulted in a sharp defeat for President Wilson and the Democrats. In spite of this, Wilson made no effort to consult his political opponents about the business of peace-making, and only one Republican was a member of the American mission to Paris. Yet if Wilson's popularity was slipping badly at home, he was still regarded with adulation in Europe. This reinforced his belief that the peoples of Europe, tired of their own corrupt governments, would willingly accept his arbitration of their affairs. Wilson was convinced that the Americans "will be the only disinterested men at the peace conference" and that "the men with whom we are about to deal do not represent their own people." There was, in fact, more than a little truth in this point of view, but it did nothing to endear the American President to other heads of government.

Partly because victory had come sooner than had been anticipated and partly because killing the bear had seemed to take precedence over dividing up his skin, almost nothing had been done to prepare for peace. No preliminary agreements had been reached among the Allies, who were to make peace as they had waged war — separately and in competition with one another. The victors sent their delegates to Paris not to meet with the representatives of the defeated nations, but to decide among themselves what terms would be imposed upon the vanquished.

They were a strange group of men who had been chosen for the task of remaking the world. President Wilson was a self-righteous professor turned politician, with a mind that had been compared to the soil of New England — "essentially barren but highly cultivated." Little Lloyd George, "the wizard from Wales," was a shifty demagogue, nicknamed, with reason, "the Goat." He saw practical issues with great clarity and was not devoid of idealism, but readily suppressed his principles for his political ambitions. Clemenceau, seventy-seven years of age and embittered by many vicissitudes, burned with fierce hatred of Germany. Orlando of Italy was smooth and slippery but had little influence.

Both Wilson and his secretary of state, Robert Lansing, professed themselves horrified to learn of the secret treaties the Allies had signed before the United States entered the war. Now the American delegation claimed that because the United States had not been a party to, or indeed even been informed of, these secret pacts, it had no obligation to honor them. This reasonable point of view was highly irritating to statesmen who hoped to profit from the war.

At Wilson's insistence, the first business of the Peace Conference was the establishment of the League of Nations. In fact, Wilson saw to it that the peace terms and the League were inextricably bound together; he did this to ensure that the United States would have to accept the League. It proved a colossal miscalculation, but he is not perhaps to be blamed for failing to foresee that his countrymen would refuse to sign the peace treaty rather than participate in an international organization.

The first session of the conference opened on January 18, 1919. The defeated nations were excluded, and so was the Soviet Union, which in any case regarded the League as "a bourgeois swindle." The Russian Bolsheviks established their own organization, the Third International, or Comintern, which was designed to subvert the workers of the world from their national loyalties.

The Covenant of the League expressed the desire of its members to reduce armaments, and specified that all member nations were to inform the League of their military expenditures. War was renounced in favor of arbitration; aggressors would be jointly resisted, first by economic sanctions and eventually, if necessary, by force. No provision was made, however, to compel members to participate in either economic or military sanctions. All nations were to register treaties with the League secretariat, which would publish them.

With the Covenant out of the way, the delegates at last got down to the business of making peace. The Italians insisted on all that Italy had been promised by the Treaty of London and claimed Fiume as well. Unfortunately, Wilson had already violated his own principle of self-determination by agreeing that Italy should be given the South Tyrol and the Brenner frontier, together with 200,000 new German-speaking subjects, who had — to put it mildly — no desire to become Italians. On the question of Fiume, however, Wilson refused to compromise, and on the strength of a three-day visit to Italy told Orlando, "I know the Italian people better than you do." In this at least he was wrong, for when the Italian delegation walked out of the conference Italy rallied behind Orlando and repudiated Wilson.

While Orlando was gone, Lloyd George and Clemenceau took the opportunity to partition Germany's African colonies, leaving none for Italy. Lloyd George also persuaded Wilson and Clemenceau to consent to a Greek army landing in Smyrna, a Turkish territory that had been promised to Italy. Orlando, seeing the sort of thing that was going on in his absence, hastily returned to Paris. Japan was given a mandate over the German colonies in the North Pacific islands, but the Japanese request that the principle of racial equality be recognized in the Covenant of the League was rejected. Japan was given the former German railway and mining rights in Shantung, on the understanding that they would eventually be restored to China.

The main business of the Peace Conference, of course, was to make peace with Germany, and it was exactly here that the peacemakers failed. The task was admittedly one of enormous difficulty. Passions still ran high and the Allies were not agreed among themselves. Clemenceau spoke for France in his demand for a harsh and vindictive peace, one that would forever remove the German threat to French security. Lloyd George, in spite of what he had said during the "khaki election," favored a peace of conciliation. With the internment of the German navy at Scapa Flow on November 21, 1918, the evacuation of Belgium, and the division of Germany's colonies, British aims had largely been achieved. No British territory had been devastated by the war and British financial experts were already saying that a restored German economy would be necessary for world trade. Britain did not want to keep military forces in Europe, nor did the British relish the prospect of France's becoming the dominant power on the continent, as would inevitably happen if Germany were too gravely weakened. Moreover, a healthy Germany seemed an essential bulwark against the spread of Bolshevism.

Clemenceau, on the other hand, wanted to take the entire left bank of the Rhine and to establish there, as a French satellite, an autonomous Rhineland republic. He wanted to have Allied garrisons stationed indefinitely on bridgeheads at the major Rhine crossings and he pressed strongly for the dismemberment of Germany. He also demanded that, in the Saar, France should be given "the French frontier of 1814, and by way of reparation, the right of occupation without annexation of that part of the Saar coal basin not included in this frontier." But the population of the Saar was German, and Wilson was not prepared to sanction this violation of the principle of self-determination. He was not impressed by the argument that Napoleon had claimed this territory for a short time in 1814. "That was a hundred years ago," he told Clemenceau. "A hundred years is a very long time." Clemenceau snarled, "Yes — a very long time in the history of the United States."

Clemenceau feared, not unreasonably, that in any future war with Germany, France would be in a weaker position than in 1914. France had been a victor in the war but she had certainly not beaten Germany by herself. The Russians, the British, the British Dominions, and finally the United States had all come to her aid. Would they ever do so again? Russia seemed to be lost for good; indeed, Clemenceau feared that the Soviet Union might form an alliance with Germany. And Germany by herself was still potentially stronger than France.

The British and Americans rejected the idea of dismembering Germany. Lloyd George proposed a compromise whereby Germany would keep the Rhineland and the Allied occupation would be limited to fifteen years. In exchange, France would be given a military alliance with Britain and the United States to guarantee her against any future German aggression. Reluctantly but realistically, Clemenceau accepted this proposal. The French Chamber and Senate ratified the treaty, as did the British Parliament. But in the United States the Senate Committee on Foreign Relations did not even present the treaty to the Senate for a vote, and the guarantee to France was aborted. British ratification had been conditional on American ratification, and with the American rejection the British were glad enough to withdraw. So in the end France got nothing — neither the Rhine republic nor the Anglo-American guarantee.

All this time, at French insistence, the blockade of Germany had continued. Both Wilson and Herbert Hoover opposed this policy, the latter vehemently, but the French got their way. As a result, all through the winter of 1918–1919 the suffering in Germany was severe, and many thousands of Germans, especially children and the aged, died. Yet under the terms of the Armistice the victors were to "provision Germany as shall be found necessary." At the War Office, Churchill, who saw the iniquity of the blockade, did his best to get it lifted, but other politicians were more responsive to the mood in the country. In fact, the blockade was not lifted until the British government took its courage in both hands and did so unilaterally on July 12, 1919, eight months after the Armistice. By this time the bitterness in Germany had greatly increased because it was felt that the continued starvation of a nation that had surrendered was both illegal and immoral.

The German delegation, headed by Foreign Minister Count Ulrich von Brockdorff-Rantzau, was presented with the peace treaty on May 7. Brockdorff-Rantzau rejected out of hand the Allied demand that

Germany confess to having caused the war. "Such a confession in my mouth would be a lie," the foreign minister stated. He was right, but the Allies were scarcely in a mood to admit it. The Treaty of Versailles was in many respects a remarkably harsh document. Alsace-Lorraine, of course, went back to France without any plebiscite. France received the Saar as a temporary mandate for fifteen years, at which time a plebiscite was to determine its future. Germany lost a little territory to Belgium and Denmark. The rump state of Austria was forbidden to unite with Germany. An independent Poland was created and received a considerable portion of former German territory, including a corridor through East Prussia. Danzig became a free city under the League of Nations but with a Polish administration. The city of Memel went to the new state of Lithuania. All Germany's colonies were taken from her on the grounds that she was unfit to govern subject peoples.

The German army was limited to one hundred thousand men, and enlisted men were to serve for a minimum of twelve years and officers for twenty-five, so that there would be no accumulation of reserves. The General Staff was abolished and Germany was forbidden to own military aircraft, tanks, or submarines or to manufacture poison gas. The German navy was limited to six battleships of under ten thousand tons apiece, six light cruisers, and twelve destroyers. The entire left bank of the Rhine and a strip fifty kilometers wide on the right bank were to be permanently demilitarized, and Allied garrisons were to remain there for fifteen years.

Article 231 of the treaty, the "war guilt clause," stated:

> The Allied and Associated governments affirm and Germany accepts the responsibility of Germany and her allies for causing all the loss and damage to which the Allied and Associated governments and their nationals have been subjected as a consequence of the war imposed upon them by the aggression of Germany and her allies.

This was the clause that had stuck in Brockdorff-Rantzau's throat. Almost all Germans agreed with him that it was an intolerable affront and an injustice. Perhaps the statesmen who framed the treaty — or at least some of them — believed that Article 231 was a true statement of responsibility. If so, Poincaré, Izvolsky, Sazonov, and Pasich could have enlightened them.

Provision was also made in the Treaty of Versailles for the trial of German war criminals. By this the Allies did not mean primarily German officers or men who had been guilty of atrocities but rather the kaiser and leading German politicians and generals, who were to

be accused of having caused the war. In the outcome, little was done
to enforce this clause. The Dutch government refused to extradite the
kaiser so that he could stand trial, and when calmer counsels prevailed
the Allies were probably as well pleased. Such a trial would inevitably
have led to damaging revelations.

The economic provisions of the Treaty of Versailles were fantastic.
Clemenceau suggested that Germany pay $200 billion. He demanded
that Germany should return the French indemnity of 1871, at 5 percent interest, and added in for good measure the capital value of the
lives of the Frenchmen who had been killed in the war. President Wilson's speech of February 11, 1918, had promised that there would be
no "punitive damages," although Germany was to pay for all damage
to civilian property in the occupied areas. At Versailles the French
demanded that Germany be made to pay the entire cost of the war.
Wilson, disagreeing, said:

> I feel that we are bound in honor to decline to agree to the inclusion of war
> costs in the reparation demand. The time to think of this was before the
> conditions of peace were communicated to the enemy originally. We should
> dissent publicly if necessary, not on the ground of the intrinsic injustice of it
> but on the ground that it is clearly inconsistent with what we deliberately led
> the enemy to expect and cannot now honorably alter simply because we
> have the power.

This was reasonable and fair, but unfortunately the final decision
was at variance with these sentiments. The French got their way. The
treaty provided that Germany make an initial payment of twenty billion gold marks by May 1, 1921, but this was merely a first installment;
the total figure would be fixed later. Reparations were to be a first
charge against the German national revenue until the unspecified obligation was finally paid off.

The Allied and Associated Powers had adopted President Wilson's
Fourteen Points and his subsequent declarations on war aims as the
basis for peace with Germany. The Germans were later to claim, with
some justification, that they had been tricked and betrayed; that after
they had signed the Armistice in good faith and carried out its provisions, the Allies abandoned the Fourteen Points and violated many
of them by the peace treaty. The treaty, in its territorial provisions,
may have been at least a partial victory for the principle of self-
determination, but it was drafted in haste, in anger, and in considerable ignorance. The Germans from the beginning regarded it as an
abomination, and not merely because they were the losers by it.
Within a very few years a substantial body of opinion in the United
States, Britain, and even France came to share this opinion and to feel

that a policy of *vae victis*, "woe to the conquered," had been immoral and unwise. Much of the history of the 1930s — the disillusioned isolationism of Americans, the readiness of the British to appease Germany, the moral rot in France — is understandable only in the light of this policy.

Perhaps the task of peace-making in 1919 really was beyond human ingenuity, as the war itself had been beyond human control. What is at any rate certain is that the peacemakers failed. Marshal Foch realized this very clearly. "This is not peace," he declared; "it's an armistice for twenty years." Foch's solution, of course, would have been a peace that destroyed Germany as a great power. This would have been feasible if Foch could have obtained agreement to it. Almost certainly it would have been a better solution than the one the peacemakers reached, which was to injure Germany and humiliate her, but to leave her with the potential soon again to become the strongest nation in Europe. Machiavelli had long ago urged in his advice to the prince that one should never inflict insufficient injuries. A man should either be killed or ruined beyond all hope of recovery or he should be treated generously; any other course would lead inevitably to retaliation. Machiavelli was wiser in his generation than the Allied and Associated Powers at Versailles.

A third possibility may have existed, though this should not be too readily assumed. Perhaps in 1919 it was too late for a generous peace of reconciliation — a Versailles without reparations, war guilt, war criminals, Danzig, Memel, or the Polish Corridor. Yet even so it would almost certainly have been better to attempt this solution than the one that was adopted. A peace "without annexations or indemnities," a "peace without victory" is how an unnecessary war should have ended. The Bolsheviks and the President of the United States, when they were able to feel some detachment from the war, both realized this clearly enough. Perhaps it was too much to expect that the British or French could share either the detachment or its resulting insight.

Brockdorff-Rantzau resigned rather than ratify the Treaty of Versailles, and when the terms were published in Germany there was great outcry against the *Diktat*. At Scapa Flow the officers and sailors of the interned High Seas Fleet scuttled their ships, and for weeks it seemed that the war might be renewed. However, the German General Staff confessed that this was impossible. The German government made a last desperate counterproposal, agreeing to sign the treaty if the war guilt clause and the provision for the trial of war criminals were removed. The Allies were in no mood to bargain; if Germany did not agree to sign the treaty by 7:00 P.M. on June 25, the Allied armies would invade Germany. The German government resigned on June 20 and a new government ratified the treaty on the 23rd. The treaty was formally signed on June 28, five years to the day after Gavrilo Princip had murdered the Archduke Franz Ferdinand and his wife in Sarajevo. So that the Germans could taste the full bitterness of defeat, the signing took place in the Hall of Mirrors at Versailles, where the German Empire had been proclaimed in 1871.

Peace treaties were later signed with Austria, Bulgaria, and Hungary, and all of these nations lost extensive territories. Peace with Turkey was not made until July 24, 1923, because Mustapha Kemal had successfully driven the Italians out of southern Anatolia and halted a French army in Cilicia. The Allies were weary of war by 1923, so they granted Turkey more generous terms than any of the other defeated nations. Turkey lost only Syria, Palestine, Arabia, and Mesopotamia.

When President Wilson returned to the United States shortly after the Treaty of Versailles was signed, he found much opposition to American participation in the League of Nations. All through the summer of 1919 the Americans debated the pros and cons of membership in the League. Isolationism had deep roots in the American public consciousness, and until after the Second World War the United States did in fact have a free choice between involvement and noninvolvement in European affairs. The Atlantic and Pacific oceans were wide barriers that eliminated any threat of invasion, and hostile air power did not have the capability of striking at North America. Because of their strategic invulnerability the Americans could decide for themselves what their course of action should be. Moreover, the United States was economically almost self-sufficient, and the western hemisphere contained virtually all the raw materials she required. The tradition of avoiding "foreign entanglements" was as old as the nation itself. The American declaration of war in 1917 was already being sharply criticized on these historic grounds, and many Americans were asking themselves whether the United States had not been lured into a conflict that had been none of her concern.

In September Wilson set out on a speaking tour to drum up support for his policy. He prophesied that if the United States rejected the League there would be another world war within a generation, but he refused to make any substantial concessions. Had he been willing to consider amendments to the treaty and the Covenant, he would almost certainly have obtained the two-thirds majority necessary for ratification, but he remained unbending. During his tour he fell ill, and in October a stroke left him paralyzed. When the vote was taken in the Senate on March 19, 1920, forty-nine senators voted for ratification and thirty-five voted against. Because this was seven votes short of the required majority, the United States did not join the League of Nations. The United States, an Associated Power to the bitter end, signed a separate peace with Germany on August 5, 1921.

This American retreat into hemispheric isolation seriously handicapped the work of the League of Nations. With the United States out of the League, and with the Soviet Union and Germany excluded, the control of the organization fell by default to Britain and France. These governments did not have the same aims in international affairs. Britain looked forward to the day when a reconciled Germany could be brought back into the concert of Europe; France looked forward to an indefinite period of French hegemony on the continent. The American people repudiated Versailles formally; the British, with an increasingly guilty conscience, repudiated it in their hearts and sought for ways to appease their former enemies.

The Weimar Republic, as the new German state was called, had been created to meet Wilson's demand that Germany convert herself into a democracy. But the Weimar Republic was from birth an unwanted child and from birth it faced a whole range of potentially deadly problems. When the Spartacists, led by Karl Liebknecht and Rosa Luxemburg, had attempted to bring on a communist revolution in January 1919, they had been suppressed with the aid of the *Freikorps*, volunteer paramilitary forces organized by ex-officers. Liebknecht and Luxemburg were murdered by the *Freikorps* while the Spartacists were being put down in Berlin, and in the spring the Communists were broken elsewhere in Germany. By now *Freikorps* had sprung up all over Germany, from the Polish marches to the Austrian border, until there were soon an estimated 400,000 Germans enlisted in some 200 illegal paramilitary organizations. Wartime ex-officers, anxious to retain the social status they had acquired during the war, front-line veterans who enjoyed soldiering, young idealists who sought to serve the Fatherland, students who saw no purpose in continuing their education, and adventurers on the make — all enlisted in the *Freikorps*. When a Polish army invaded Silesia before the plebiscite that was to determine the province's fate, the French openly supported the Poles but the *Freikorps* more than held their own.

The Weimar Republic needed the *Freikorps* in 1919 and early 1920 for protection against both its internal and external foes because the new 100,000-man Reichswehr, allowed under the Treaty of Versailles, was still in the process of being formed. However, the members of the *Freikorps* themselves constituted a danger to the state. German nationalists were already claiming that the republican politicians were the "November criminals" who had stabbed the undefeated German army in the back. Legends to account for the loss of the war were already taking root in the German mind. The story that the German army had not been defeated in the field was made the more plausible by the claim that Germany had been betrayed after its acceptance of Wilson's Fourteen Points. The first claim was false, for though the German lines had still been intact at the time of the Armistice, the German army had taken such a beating that it could not long have continued the war. But the second claim was true; the Allies had refused to abide by the pre-Armistice contract and the Fourteen Points. The German army had been defeated, which should have made betrayal unnecessary, but the making of peace had been as badly bungled as the waging of the war.

By the middle of 1920, after the failure of a *Freikorps* attempt to overthrow the government by a coup, the situation in Germany was under control and the *Freikorps* were officially disbanded. In fact, however, many of these bands of free-booters remained in being, until a little later they merged with various Nazi organizations. Some of the *Freikorpskämpfer* who enjoyed violence for its own sake and did not much care under whose banner they fought turned communist and brawled in the streets with their former comrades. After Hitler came to power in 1933 most of these revolutionaries joined the winning side and enlisted in Röhm's SA, becoming "beef-steak Nazis" — brown on the outside and red on the inside.

Representatives of the Allies met in Paris in February 1921 to settle the question of German reparations. Their demands, known as the Paris Resolutions, called on Germany to pay $52 billion over forty-two years and imposed an annual levy of 12 percent on Germany's export trade. When the German government protested that it could not possibly pay such a huge amount, Marshal Foch promptly occupied Duisberg, Düsseldorf, and Ruhrort with French troops.

The Weimar Republic, already unfairly blamed by the radical right for the loss of the war, was further discredited by this French move. On August 26, 1921, Matthias Erzberger, the Catholic Center party leader who had signed the Armistice, was shot down by nationalist gunmen while walking in the Black Forest. Germany was a spiritually sick country; defeat and humiliation lent credence to extremist doctrines and gained a hearing for any demagogue who claimed to know the cure for the nation's ills. The symptoms of this disease were certainly repulsive, and were to become far more repulsive as time went on, but they did not indicate any special wickedness in the German people. Russia in defeat had thrown up the Bolsheviks, a party as violent, ruthless, doctrinaire, and inhuman as the radical right in defeated Germany. Would not the same terrible extremism have sprung up in France or Britain if those nations had lost the war? The thought is so unpleasant that one instinctively shrinks from it, yet there are numerous indications that it would have been so.

In April 1922 a European economic conference was held in Genoa. Representatives from the Soviet Union, Britain, France, Italy, and Germany, as well as from some smaller nations, met to see if they could improve their trade relations. However, the Soviet delegate, G. Chicherin, seizing the opportunity for propaganda, presented the Allies with a huge bill for damages inflicted on Russia during the intervention and civil war; the French countered by demanding repayment of the loans made to tsarist Russia in the days of the Dual Entente.

On Easter Sunday, April 16, Walter Rathenau, the German foreign minister, and Chicherin slipped away to meet for lunch in the little resort town of Rapallo. There they signed a treaty that provided for the resumption of diplomatic relations between their two countries, renounced all mutual reparation claims, and agreed to facilitate Russo-German trade. A secret agreement had already been made between the Soviet Union and the Weimar Republic by which German soldiers would be able to undergo tank and aviation training in the Soviet Union, and Germany would be provided with forbidden war materials manufactured in Russia. In exchange, Germany would give the Soviet Union technical assistance in establishing new industries.

What had happened at Rapallo was that the two outcast nations of Europe had very sensibly agreed to draw closer together. The move was so obviously to their mutual advantage that the Allies should not have been surprised. Rathenau had served his country well but this did not save him from the rage of the extreme nationalists. When much of Upper Silesia was awarded to Poland by plebiscite, the radical right in Germany denounced Rathenau as a traitorous Jewish internationalist. On June 24 he was murdered in his car on a highway near Berlin.

In July 1922 Germany declared that she could not meet her reparations payment and asked for a two-year moratorium. With the mark standing at 500 to the dollar, inflation was ruining the middle class. In Britain, Balfour, with cabinet approval, made the very reasonable proposal that Britain would renounce all reparations and cancel all war debts if other nations did the same. Although Britain owed large sums to the United States, she was owed rather more by her debtors, but the revival of international trade now appeared more important to the British economy than the acquisition of gold, which was promptly shipped to Fort Knox, or of reparations in kind, which undercut her home industries.

However, Poincaré, who had just become premier of France, intended that Germany should pay to the uttermost pfennig. He proposed to extract what he called "productive guarantees" if Germany could not pay — by which he meant the Ruhr mines, the Rhine forests, the German dye industry, and the entire German customs service. Poincaré blandly put forward these thoughts as a counter-proposal to Balfour's.

The United States also rejected Balfour's plan. The Americans, as the world's chief creditors, were outraged that such a solution should even have been suggested. As Calvin Coolidge was later to say, "They hired the money, didn't they?"

As 1922 ended, Germany was sinking deeper and deeper into economic depression. France discovered "an almost microscopic shortage in German deliveries of timber" — in fact, some 140,000 telegraph poles. The German government admitted the shortage and requested three months in which to make it good, but to the French this seemed a typical German evasion. Poincaré referred the matter to the reparations commission and urged that Germany be declared in default. Neither the British nor the Americans approved of the French attitude, but the reparations commission voted Germany in default, with the British delegate dissenting. On January 20, 1923, French troops marched into the Ruhr.

The separation of the highly industrialized Ruhr from Germany could lead only to economic chaos in the Reich, which was exactly what Poincaré hoped to bring about. World public opinion was outraged, but the French premier showed himself as single-minded now as in July of 1914. The German chancellor, Wilhelm Cuno, decided to resist the French demands by nonviolent methods. A policy of passive resistance was proclaimed, a general strike was called in the Ruhr, and all reparations payments to France were stopped.

The French were in no mood to tolerate this. They confiscated German property, deported some 147,000 German workers, hauled German municipal officials before military courts, and moved in black troops from North Africa to intimidate the inhabitants of the Ruhr. Riots and demonstrations were answered by fire from the French soldiers, and the toll of dead and wounded mounted steadily.

Inflation swept over Germany until in August one American dollar was worth five million German marks. The savings of the German middle class were wiped out while wealthy industrialists grew wealthier by paying off their debts with worthless currency and landowners bought up more land. The very class that would have proved the backbone of a democratic republic in Germany was ruined, and the natural enemies of the republic increased their power. The rage and humiliation caused by the French occupation of the Ruhr was a godsend to the extremists of the radical right.

On August 13 Cuno resigned because of the failure of his policy in the Ruhr. The new government, headed by Gustav Stresemann, abandoned passive resistance, ordered the Ruhr workers back to work, resumed reparations payments, and established a new currency. By now France had extracted $106 million worth of goods from the Ruhr, and it seemed as though Poincaré had been victorious all along the line.

So he would have been, if he had known when to stop, but he now began to stir up separatism in the Ruhr, the Rhineland, and the Palatinate. In these areas there were almost no real separatists, but French officials gladly gave their backing to criminals and psychopaths. Censorship of the press and a travel ban isolated the area from the rest of Germany. On September 30 French-sponsored separatist bands attacked the municipal offices in Düsseldorf. After heavy fighting had gone on for some time, the French at last intervened to disarm the police. On October 21 a "Rhineland Republic" was proclaimed and Poincaré recognized it at once. In November the Palatinate was declared an independent state.

The British and Americans viewed all this with much displeasure and disgust, but when the British government protested, Poincaré merely replied that it was, after all, a quarrel among Germans in which France had no desire to take part. In January 1924, British patience at last gave out, and Britain threatened to take France before the World Court in the Hague. With this threat Poincaré backed down. In other ways, too, his policy had failed. He had estranged his former American and British allies, he had evoked a good deal of sympathy for Germany, and the French franc had dropped by 25 percent in the past year. As soon as the separatists were deprived of French support, their movement collapsed. In February angry Germans killed most of the separatist leaders.*

These troubles were symptomatic of the first half of the new decade. The war was not really over. Only the methods of waging it had been changed and the system of alliances somewhat altered. Now Europe was divided into victor nations, defeated nations, and, in a twilight that was neither victory nor defeat, the new successor-states, which had been formed by the breakup of the Austro-Hungarian Empire and the diminution of Russia and Germany. In 1924 the League of Nations greatly reduced Hungarian reparations, but this

*History does not repeat itself, but that is not to say that men do not try to make it do so. Although the French encouragement of the Rhineland separatists failed dismally in 1923, this did not prevent them from trying to play the same card again in Canada in 1967. It would be a mistake, however, to believe that the French learned nothing with the passage of time. In 1923 Poincaré attempted to use separatism against France's former enemies and conquerors; in 1967 De Gaulle had progressed to using separatism against France's former friends and liberators.

did not reconcile the Magyars to their new and lesser status. Three million of them were living unhappily as citizens of Czechoslovakia, Rumania, and Yugoslavia, and irredentist feeling ran high. As a result, the other successor-states of the Dual Monarchy were fearful of Hungary and were determined to allow her no chance of revising the status quo.

Yugoslavia, the land of the South Slavs, was a realization of the Pan-Serb dream. In spite of the invasion of their country and the terrible losses of the war, most Serbs felt that it had all been well worthwhile. On the Appel Quay in Sarajevo, opposite the spot where Princip had murdered the archduke and his wife, the Serbs erected a commemorative plaque, not to the murdered couple but to their murderer, who had died of consumption in an Austrian prison during the war. Yet it was not long before the Croats and Slovenes, who had been liberated from what some of them had considered the yoke of Austria, began to look back longingly to their former state. King Alexander Karageorgevich was inclined to deal highhandedly with his new Catholic subjects, and civil liberties were frequently in abeyance. Before long a Croatian independence movement was turning the weapon of terrorism against the Serbs.

In August 1920 Czechoslovakia and Yugoslavia signed a military convention at Belgrade, providing that they would come to each other's aid if either was attacked by Hungary. Later that month Rumania and Czechoslovakia signed a treaty with the same stipulation; and in June of 1921 Yugoslavia and Rumania formed a similar alliance, though this one was against both Hungary and Bulgaria. France concluded military treaties with Czechoslovakia in January 1924, with Rumania in June 1926, and with Yugoslavia in November 1927. This network of bilateral treaties became known as the Little Entente. French military loans now poured into the Little Entente, just as they had formerly poured into tsarist Russia.

In her search for security and for a substitute for the lost friendship of Russia, France also turned to Poland. During the Russian civil war, the Polish marshal Josef Pilsudski, taking advantage of his ancient enemy's vulnerability, had led Polish troops into the Ukraine and occupied Kiev. In retaliation a Bolshevik army under General Mikhail Tukhachevsky invaded Poland in August 1920 and advanced on Warsaw. France sent aid to Poland, the Polish peasants did not rise to support the communist invaders as the Bolsheviks had confidently expected, and the French general Maxime Weygand defeated Tukhachevsky's army outside Warsaw, forcing it to withdraw. The Poles pursued, and in March 1921 the Bolsheviks reluctantly signed the Treaty of Riga, which moved the Polish border far to the east. Poland thus took sovereignty over some six million Russians, an act of greed that was to prove dangerously unwise. In February 1921 France and Poland signed a mutual defense pact, following this up the next year with a commercial treaty.

For the time being it appeared that France was in an unassailable position. On paper, at least, military alliances with the Little Entente, Poland, and Belgium provided a very considerable augment to the strength of the French army, by itself the largest on the continent. Yet this apparent strength concealed real weakness. The potential disparity between France and Germany remained, and was without cure. French hostility to the Soviet Union had replaced the former French alliance with tsarist Russia. This hostility sprang from the feeling that the Bolsheviks had betrayed the Dual Entente and from the Soviet Union's refusal to honor the debts that the tsarist regime had contracted with France. Ideological differences also played their part; the revolutionary propaganda that the Third Communist International conducted within France and her colonies was resented by patriotic Frenchmen.

France and Britain had also drifted apart as soon as the war was over, partly because of differences over the role of the League of Nations, the treatment of Germany, war debts, reparations, and disarmament. Perhaps a deeper reason was the British reaction against the war, the feeling that French diplomacy had been too clever and that Britain had been duped into a life-and-death struggle for French interests. This opinion was by no means universally held in Britain, and to have expressed it openly would have been to admit to a shameful gullibility, injurious to national pride. The violent deaths of a million of one's fellow countrymen could not be lightly dismissed as a mere error in judgment. No British statesman went as far as Salisbury had in commenting on the Crimean War or said bluntly that Britain "had backed the wrong horse," but there was at least the strong suspicion that this was so.

French weakness, then, lay in the loss of her great wartime allies; the little successor-states who ranged themselves at France's side were in truth liabilities rather than assets. Over and above all this, and far more serious, was the psychic damage the war had done to the French people. Victory brought merely the admission of exhaustion and the end of courage.

Though disillusionment and the forces of disintegration worked strongly on France, they were present in Italy in far more acute form. The war had been an unrelieved disaster for the Italian people. Many Italian formations had fought bravely, but no amount of heroism could counteract the effects of poor leadership and inefficient administration. Italy had lost 600,000 dead and had as her reward the humiliation of Caporetto, her own sense of shame, and the scarcely concealed contempt of her allies. Although the peace treaties had given Italy generous additions of territory, most Italians felt cheated of all that was their due. Nationalists raised the cry that Italy had won the war at Vittoria Veneto but had been swindled at the conference table. Those who could believe the first half of this proposition would have no difficulty in swallowing the second half.

During the war the Italian government, like most of the belligerent governments, had made extravagant promises to its people about the utopian world that would come into being with victory, but in Italy the contrast between promises and reality was more than usually stark. Italian servicemen returned home to poverty, unemployment, corruption, and inefficiency. The Italian left, which had opposed the war, now encouraged strikes and riots. There was bloodshed in the streets, and in the countryside manor houses began to be burned down.

A new Italian party, the *Fasci di combattimento*, was founded in Milan on March 23, 1919, by Benito Mussolini, a Socialist turncoat who had been bribed by French money to advocate Italy's intervention in the war. Mussolini, an astute opportunist, saw that two revolutionary forces were at work in Italy: the discontent of the poor and the disappointment of the nationalists. He believed that if only these forces could be combined they might together be strong enough to overthrow the government. The nationalists and the proletariat had little in common but their discontent, but that was enough. Socialism and the army, the two chief influences in Mussolini's own life, became the basis of fascism. Yet the Fascist party program did not call for an international socialist revolution. Some of the social and economic platform of the Communist party was taken over, but communism was labeled the enemy. Mussolini's socialism was to be national, and patriotism was appealed to as much as radicalism. Italy would acquire new territory and more colonies, the military virtues would be cherished, and Italy would take her rightful place as a great power, reviving the ancient glories of Imperial Rome.

It was all nonsense, of course, and insincere nonsense at that, but it had a tremendous appeal. Mussolini believed only in power. The flamboyance of the fascist movement concealed an emptiness as black as night, just as Mussolini's warlike rantings concealed military impotence.

The Fascists sent gangs of thugs, or *squadristi*, into the streets, armed with pistols, cudgels, and bottles of castor oil, to terrorize their opponents. The Socialist mayors and councils of Milan, Cremona,

Verona, and Florence were driven out of office, and in August 1922 the Fascists broke a general strike called by the Confederation of Labor, a Communist-dominated organization. In September Mussolini made a sudden switch and declared himself a monarchist, which gained him the support of the army and the right-wing Nationalists. A group of senior army officers now began to push Mussolini forward toward a coup d'état. On October 27, Fascist meetings were held all over Italy, and that evening tens of thousands of black-shirted Fascists marched to the railway stations, climbed aboard the trains without buying tickets, and demanded to be taken to Rome. At the last moment the king gave way and called on Mussolini to form a government. The first Fascist government was a coalition that included Nationalists, Liberals, members of the People's party, and even three Democrats, but Mussolini himself took the offices of prime minister, minister of foreign affairs, and home secretary.

When, in June 1924, five Fascist thugs murdered one of Mussolini's most outspoken opponents, the Socialist Giacomo Matteotti, the revulsion of feeling in Italy almost swept Il Duce from power. For the next four or five months the Italian strongman lived in perpetual fear of a popular rising. However, when his enemies took no action, Mussolini pulled himself together, dismissed the non-Fascist members of his cabinet, outlawed other political parties, banned trade unions, and introduced censorship. By the end of 1926 Italy was a police state, with Mussolini ruling as dictator.

Under Mussolini, Italian foreign policy came more and more to side with the revisionist powers, which were dissatisfied with the Versailles settlement. Relations with Yugoslavia deteriorated as Italy began to exert economic and political pressure in the Balkans, supported the Internal Macedonian Revolutionary Organization, and granted large loans to Bulgaria. France and Italy became naval rivals in the Mediterranean, and Mussolini began to press territorial claims on Corsica, Nice, and Savoy.

In Germany, after the abortive Kapp Putsch of 1920, many of the *Freikorps* leaders made their way to Munich, in Bavaria, where the writ of the Weimar government could scarcely be said to run. Adolf Hitler was only one of many nationalist agitators in Munich in the first years after the war. By birth an Austrian, Hitler had served in a Bavarian infantry regiment, rising to the rank of corporal.* After the war Hit-

*It was symptomatic of the Europe of the interwar years that the corporals should come into their own. Mussolini and Hitler had both held this rank; and in the armies of the First World War it would have been difficult for them to have risen higher. Stalin was the son of a peasant. These new rulers were all revolutionaries, believing in fundamental change. They saw the world in crude, primary colors. This is perhaps the clue to the oft-noted similarity between the radical right and the radical left, a similarity so strong and many-sided that it dwarfed whatever differences might have existed. Hitler

ler was for a time employed by the Reichswehr as a propagandist and spy. It was in the latter capacity that he came across a tiny political party calling itself the National Socialist German Workers' party. He joined it and soon became its leader. The comparison with Mussolini is obvious and fascinating — both former corporals in the army, both considering themselves socialist revolutionaries, both professing as well an extreme nationalism.

The differences, however, were as great as the similarities. Whereas Mussolini was a cynical opportunist, Hitler was fanatically sincere in his illogical and terrible beliefs. Hitler believed in at least the negative side of socialist doctrine; he never had any use for the aristocracy, the middle classes, the rich, the religious, or those who had been born to positions of power, and he quite honestly considered himself a revolutionary all his life. He was, but his revolution was nihilistic rather than socialistic. Hitler believed in the destruction of the Versailles settlement, the resurrection of Germany, the gathering in of all Germans into a *Gross Deutschland* greater than the empire Bismarck had created, the elimination of Jews and Jewish influence, and the seizure of *Lebensraum* in the east. He added in the mystique of the German blood and the German soil, proclaiming that the Germans belonged to a *Herrenvolk*, a "master race," whose destiny it was to rule the world. Nothing in the Nazi "philosophy" was intellectually respectable; nothing in it was in keeping with the great traditions of Western civilization. Hitler himself was an ignorant man, uncouth and with a manifest lack of breeding, but these characteristics were all assets to a demagogue.

Around Hitler gathered a grotesque and sinister group of men: Captain Hermann Göring, who had been an air ace and the second-in-command of Baron Manfred von Richthofen's flying circus and was now a drug addict; Captain Ernst Röhm, a homosexual tough who believed in the socialist side of Nazism; Rudolf Hess, who acted as Hitler's private secretary; Emil Maurice, an ex-convict who acted as his bodyguard; Alfred Rosenberg, a German from the Baltic states who passed as the "philosopher" of the party; and Heinrich Himmler, a man who had failed at everything he had put his hand to, from chicken-farming to schoolteaching.

By now Poincaré's occupation of the Ruhr was causing terrible hardship in Germany, a circumstance that could not but help the Nazi party. The time seemed auspicious for Hitler to make his bid for power. On November 9, 1923, Ludendorff, who had also been in-

---

and Mussolini were nationalists who did not understand the subtleties of nationalism; Stalin was a communist who did not understand the subtleties of communism. By the 1930s the control of much of the world had fallen into new hands, and these hands, though strong and able, could not by their nature be delicate.

volved in the Kapp Putsch, joined him and the Nazi storm troopers in a march from the Bürgerbräu Keller in Munich to the center of the city. The attempted coup was easily foiled by the Bavarian state police, and both Ludendorff and Hitler were arrested. At their trial, Hitler and eight other Nazis were found guilty and sentenced to terms of fortress detention, though Ludendorff was acquitted. During his spell in prison, Hitler passed the time dictating *Mein Kampf*, but it appeared as though the fiasco of the Beer Hall Putsch had forever ruined his political career.

In 1924, with the new German chancellor, Stresemann, committed to a policy of "fulfillment" of the Treaty of Versailles, the British government asked the United States to cooperate in a new inquiry into reparations. A committee, headed by an American general, Charles Dawes, submitted its report in April. The British, Belgians, Italians, and Americans all agreed that the German budget should be balanced, the German economy stabilized, and Germany's reparations reduced. Premier Poincaré of France set out a list of so-called additions to the Dawes Committee's report, but fortunately Poincaré's government fell on May 11, and a conference in London in July and August agreed substantially to implement Dawes's proposals. An international loan was floated for Germany, most of it raised in the United States, and Germany's internal economic situation would henceforth govern the amount of reparations payments. When the Dawes Plan went into effect in September 1924, French troops began to leave the Ruhr.

Stresemann, as a patriotic German, had aims in international affairs that were in many particulars the same as those of Hitler and the Nazi party. He desired the downward revision of reparations payments, the incorporation of the Germans who were excluded from the Reich by Versailles, and territorial revisions in the east that would restore Danzig, the Polish Corridor, and the lost portions of Upper Silesia to Germany. To achieve these ends he was willing to come to an agreement with the western democracies. In October 1925, Austen Chamberlain, Aristide Briand, Stresemann, Eduard Beneš of Czechoslovakia, Dino Grandi of Italy, and representatives from Belgium and Poland met in Locarno in Switzerland. The deliberations took time, but finally, in December, the protocol, the seven treaties, and the note, which together made up the Locarno Pact, were signed.

The protocol promised the peaceful solution of differences and cooperation with the League in disarmament. The Rhineland agreement, between Britain, France, Italy, Belgium, and Germany, guaranteed the western frontiers of Germany and the continued demilitarization of the Rhineland. Under the terms, France, Belgium, and Germany promised not to attack or invade one another, unless they were acting under the sanction of the League of Nations. The agreement was to take effect as soon as Germany became a member of the League. Four arbitration treaties were signed between Germany on the one hand and France, Belgium, Poland, and Czechoslovakia on the other. France signed defensive alliances with Czechoslovakia and Poland. The note appended to the Locarno Pact clarified Germany's obligations to cooperate in military sanctions under Article 16 of the League Covenant.

Chamberlain returned to Britain to announce that Locarno marked the real dividing line between the years of war and the years of peace. It did indeed seem that this opinion was well founded and that the troubled postwar period of readjustment was at an end. Only the Soviet Union viewed Locarno with suspicion, as foreshadowing a new coalition against communism. Allied forces evacuated Cologne and Coblenz in February 1926, and, after rather more delay and obstruction than had been anticipated, Germany was admitted to the League of Nations on September 8 and was given a permanent seat on the League Council.

The Locarno era of conciliation, which lasted until the onset of the Great Depression at the end of 1929, proved to have been a false spring, but there was nothing inevitable about this outcome. Europe might well have found her peace at the time — and a better peace than she has since been able to achieve. Of course, since politics are the work of men, there were naturally flaws and imperfections in the "Locarno spirit." After Locarno, men put too much faith in the efficacy of treaties. Pacifism was almost universally popular, and the prevalence of this mood was regarded as being in itself a guarantee against war. Much was heard of during these years about the "weight of public opinion" and the deterrent effect this would have upon would-be aggressors. These ideas were immensely popular and immensely wrong-headed.

Economic policies in the 1920s were also a reaction to the war, as were many trends in domestic politics. In Britain in 1926 a general strike was broken by the government, trade union membership declined, and an uneasy industrial peace settled on the United Kingdom. Communist propaganda was blamed for the unrest in India and other parts of the empire, although in truth it was the war that was responsible. Between 1914 and 1918, Britain's subject peoples had realized for the first time that Britain, which had formerly seemed the still center of the world, was really only one of several great powers. The unedifying spectacle of the European nations waging war had also convinced Asians and Africans that European supremacy had no moral base.

France's internal difficulties were greater than those of Britain, for

France had been injured more seriously by the war. Nearly half of her young men of military age in 1914 had been killed or wounded, and even after the restoration of Alsace-Lorraine the French population was smaller than it had been before the war. In 1920 the French Socialist party joined the Third International and became the French Communist party, while the less radical minority, led by Léon Blum, tried to rebuild the cause of moderate socialism. Numerous reactionary groups on the extreme right advocated a French brand of fascism. Action Française, led by Charles Maurras, had the most popular success, until it was condemned by the Vatican in 1926. The French center, which was split into some thirty parties, ruled the nation with a series of uneasy coalition governments.

With Locarno, the worst of Germany's economic problems appeared to be over. American loans poured in and were spent enthusiastically. Industrial production climbed and foreign investors hastened to participate in the boom. The threat to the democracy of Weimar, whether from the radical right or the radical left, diminished appreciably with the coming of prosperity. Early in 1929 a committee under the chairmanship of an American, Owen D. Young, fixed the total sum of reparations Germany was to pay, making yet another substantial reduction from previous figures. Germany accepted the Young plan, in spite of nationalist protests, and in September 1929 the Allied armies of occupation began to withdraw from the Rhineland, five years ahead of schedule. In the elections of May 1928 the Nazi party elected only twelve deputies to the Reichstag, and party membership totaled no more than 178,000. The symbol of German moderation and unity, and of the reconciliation of the old order and the new, seemed to be Field Marshal von Hindenburg, who had been elected president of the republic in April 1925.

Russia, isolated from the rest of Europe behind the barrier of the new successor-states, went its own way after the end of Allied intervention and the civil war. The Russian people, who had already suffered so much, now found that they had been delivered into the hands of a ruthless faction that was prepared, in the name of its ideology, to impose still greater hardship upon them. The Bolsheviks had not fulfilled their promises of "peace, land, and bread"; instead, the Russians had to endure war and famines in which millions died. The Soviet Union became a one-party dictatorship, ruled by terror and the secret police.

When Lenin died in January 1924, a struggle for power ensued between Stalin and Trotsky. Stalin's position as party secretary, as well as his complete lack of scruples, gave him the victory. Once Stalin was in undisputed control of the state he embarked upon the first of his

Five-Year Plans to collectivize farms, increase industrial production, stamp out religion, and suppress national minorities. Russia, still an empire composed of many subject peoples, was now governed by a tyrant as bloodstained and as far removed from humanity as Ivan the Terrible. Stalin, too, was part of the bill for the First World War.

Across the world the other potential superstate presented a diametrically different picture. The United States was the embodiment of capitalism, democracy, and, in the 1920s, unparalleled prosperity. American production had greatly expanded during the war. For the first time the United States had been a creditor nation rather than a debtor, and gold from war debts piled up in Fort Knox. Installment buying, mass production, planned obsolescence, and ruthless advertising all perpetuated the postwar boom. The crash came on Black Thursday, October 24, 1929, when blind panic gripped American investors. By the middle of November the market had lost 50 percent of its value as of six weeks previously; commodity prices plummeted; steel, coal, and automotive production fell sharply; and unemployment soared.

The Wall Street crash, however, was no more than the detonator that set off the Great Depression. The explosive mass itself had long been accumulating. And once again the First World War was the major cause. War debt payments had concentrated much of the world's gold supply in the United States. Overproduction, caused by the war, depressed world prices. Many formerly prosperous nations were impoverished, and reparations damaged the economy of the recipient more than that of the donor. Many of the small states in Europe adopted a shortsighted economic nationalism.

But there was worse to come. Just as the war had led to the depression, so now the depression was to lead to a new and even more terrible war.

CHAPTER II

THE GREAT DEPRESSION spread like an epidemic, its severity and duration varying from country to country but with considerable cross-infection and reinfection. As American imports were cut back by two-thirds from 1929 to 1932, European nations reduced their imports from the United States. Thus the value of American exports dropped from $5.2 billion in 1929 to $1.6 billion in 1932. The year 1932 marked the nadir of the depression in the United States, with steel production down to only 12 percent of capacity, bread lines and soup kitchens common sights in every city, and a great mass of transient unemployed roaming the continent in the vain search for work. The effect of the depression on international affairs was to confirm and deepen the American urge to isolationism. Like a sick dog preoccupied with his own troubles, the United States turned its back on the rest of the world.

The depression reached Britain in 1930, but its effects were uneven. The fall in world commodity prices reduced the cost of British imports, but the price of British exports of manufactured goods did not fall to anything like the same extent. Secondary industry flourished, though the older industries of cotton-manufacturing, shipbuilding, and coal-mining stagnated. During the depression the British trade balance actually improved by 20 percent. And since wages remained stable and prices fell, those who were employed in Britain actually experienced a significant rise in living standards, which some economists estimate at as much as 40 percent. So the troubled thirties were a time of relative prosperity and comfort for most of the British people.

This perhaps explains some of the British reluctance to face the hard facts of the international situation. In the 1920s the British had yearned for a return to the prewar world. By the middle of the 1930s this desire seemed to have been fulfilled. The world, of course, was not quite the same as it had been before 1914. It was no longer so definitely divided into officers and enlisted men, and the empire had degenerated into a commonwealth. But things were not half bad. Rupert Brooke's church clock still stood at ten to three, and there was honey still for tea. Though the Conservative governments that ruled Britain in the 1930s were blind to international realities, they accurately reflected public opinion. The British did not want to be disturbed. Aggression was to be condemned, but so was military action to halt aggression.

The British desire for a quiet life was certainly a factor considered by Japan before the invasion of Manchuria in the autumn of 1931. After a brief, undeclared war in 1929 between the Soviet Union and China along the line of the Chinese Eastern Railway, the Japanese calculated that the Soviet Union would be slow in coming to the defense of China. The United States, the only other power with interests in the Far East, was far too preoccupied with the depression to take any strong action on the other side of the Pacific.

Japan, as an exporter of luxury goods, had been disastrously affected by the depression. Within one year Japanese foreign trade declined by more than 30 percent and agricultural prices fell sharply. To the influential military and nationalist circles in Japan the answer to industrial unemployment and hardship in the home islands appeared to be a "forward policy" in Asia. In Manchuria, Japan could find new markets, raw materials, and an outlet for surplus population. Japanese interests in Manchuria seemed to be threatened by the extension of Nationalist Chinese influence there, which could not be tolerated. A brief flare-up of fighting in 1928 had seen Japanese troops temporarily reoccupy Shantung province, and the Chinese were building a new railroad that would compete with the Japanese-controlled South Manchuria Railway. As economic conditions in Japan worsened, the arguments of the imperialists gained more and more popular support. Nor were the arguments only verbal. When the premier, Yuko Hamaguchi, attempted to institute a measure of naval disarmament in 1930, he was murdered by a secret nationalist society.

The pretext for the invasion of Manchuria was provided on the night of September 18/19, 1931, by a bomb explosion on the South Manchuria Railway north of Mukden. There seems little doubt that the Japanese army staged the explosion. At all events, the following day Japanese forces began a full-scale invasion of southeast Manchuria without any declaration of war. When China appealed to the League of Nations, she received cold comfort. The League Council called on both sides to cease fighting and accept arbitration. Within five months the Japanese army was in effective control of Manchuria, and in March 1932 Japan established Manchuria as the puppet kingdom of Manchukuo under the former boy-emperor of the Manchu dynasty.

In the 1920s pacifist idealists had loudly claimed that world opinion would deter would-be aggressors. Now the Japanese occupied Manchuria and Jehol province without paying the least heed to world opinion, and the members of the League of Nations excused their inaction by claiming that pacifist public opinion made it impossible for them to honor their obligations under the League's Covenant. When a League of Nations commission returned a report adverse to Japan, Japan withdrew from the League. In December 1934 Japan denounced her naval agreements with Britain and the United States, and the Japanese army advanced west and south into Chahar and Hopeh. Two other results flowed from the Japanese conquest of Manchuria. In 1933 the United States at last recognized the Soviet Union, and in Japan itself the success of the Manchurian adventure greatly strengthened the hand of the nationalists and militarists. In 1936 militarist secret societies began to murder moderate Japanese politicians, and in June 1937 Prince Fumimaro Konoye became the head of a nationalist government dedicated to expansion on the Asian mainland.

Meanwhile the Great Depression was breeding violence in Europe as well. In France the depression came late and was never as severe as in more highly industrialized nations. Not until the end of 1931 did the French economy begin to feel the pinch, and even then unemployment was relatively mild. Nevertheless even this was enough to shake the political stability of the Third Republic. When Premier Édouard Herriot's government was overthrown in December 1932, it was followed by a succession of nearly impotent Socialist and Radical-Socialist administrations. The moderate, ineffective politicians of the French center came under increasing attack from the radical right and the radical left. Right-wing political leagues dramatically increased their membership. Action Française, Jeunesses Patriotes, Solidarité Française, Le Francisme, and Colonel de La Rocque's Croix de Feu sent their gangs into the streets, rioting, beating up political opponents, and disrupting the life of the capital. Paris newspapers of all shades of political opinion added their intemperate voices to the uproar.

In January 1934, when the Stavisky scandal climaxed a whole series of sordid financial scandals involving French politicians, the fascists began rioting in earnest. The government of Camille Chautemps weakly resigned, to be replaced by a new ministry under Édouard

Daladier. The violence continued and on February 5 the Croix de Feu, Action Française, and Solidarité Française raised formidable mobs. The next day the communists joined the fascists in the attempt to overthrow the government of France. Some forty thousand rioters battled with the police; public buildings were set afire; French deputies slunk away from the Chamber and went into hiding; and before the insurrection failed, seventeen persons were killed and more than two thousand wounded. Daladier resigned, to be replaced by the seventy-one-year-old Gaston Doumergue. The street violence spluttered on for another week, then died down. France was left fearful and shaken, and no subsequent French government dared to take a strong line on any contentious issue for fear of the possibility of civil war.

The Soviet Union very largely escaped the effects of the Great Depression, for it was not dependent on world trade. This isolation behind a "cordon sanitaire" might have proved a blessing for the Russian people were it not that they were being afflicted with far worse ills than those caused by the fluctuations of the capitalist economy. The West was scourged with the whips of supply and demand; the Soviet Union was scourged with the scorpions of Stalin's Five-Year Plans and purges. In January 1930 Stalin decided to collectivize the enormous majority of privately owned peasant farms in Russia. Two and a half years later, livestock holdings were down by more than two-thirds because the peasants had slaughtered their farm animals rather than turn them over to the commissars, agricultural production had dropped dangerously, and millions of peasants had been killed or deported for resisting collectivization. In 1930 and 1931 hundreds of thousands of Russians starved to death, and in the Ukraine especially the suffering was worse and more widespread than any that Europe had seen in a thousand years.

Stalin's first Five-Year Plan also called for the doubling of Russia's industrial capacity between 1928 and 1933. This Georgian peasant, with nothing but the dim light of an outdated Marxism to guide him, proposed to accomplish in the Soviet Union within five years what it had taken the nations of the West some three generations to achieve. In the West the unplanned industrial revolution had brought its full share of horrors, but these were nothing in comparison with the horrors brought on the Russian people by the forced and planned industrialization now begun by the Communist party. Real wages in Russia dropped by more than 40 percent, and when the state was the employer, no nonsense of trade unionism, collective bargaining, or the strike was tolerated. Instead, harsh labor regulations were enforced by the secret police, with death or deportation to slave camps in

Siberia commonly invoked as disciplinary measures. Factory mana-
gers were given control over the workers' ration cards and housing.
By these methods Russian industry did indeed make great advances,
especially in the production of such basic commodities as coal, steel,
chemicals, gasoline, and electricity. Consumer goods were hardly
produced at all, and housing was badly neglected. The long-suffering
Russian people, who had thrown off one tyranny only to be subjected
to a far more brutal one, were incessantly assured that they lived in a
socialist paradise and that conditions in the unregenerate West were
infinitely worse.

Of all the European nations Germany was most affected by the depression. Short-term American loans were hastily recalled in the first
few months after the Wall Street crash, and this undermined the entire German economy. With the withdrawal of credit and the drying
up of trade, Germany soon found herself unable to meet her reparations payments or the interest charges on her loans. Attempts by the
government to curtail expenditures and increase taxes brought hardship to the population without assisting the economy. Bankruptcies
became common and unemployment increased. The Weimar Republic had not done too badly so long as American money had bolstered
the economy. The republic's greatest handicap was that it was the
creature of Versailles. Democracy had come to Germany in the bag-
gage train of the Allied armies of occupation and appeared to be
merely another imposition of the victors on the vanquished. Nevertheless, with Field Marshal von Hindenburg as head of state, with the
relaxations in tensions that followed Locarno, and with the prosperity
that marked the second half of the 1920s, there seemed every reason
to believe that Weimar might endure. In 1929 the German National
Socialist Workers' party was little more than a collection of extremists.
Lack of political success led to lack of money, so Hitler turned more
and more for financial backing to the big industrialists. This in turn
caused internal difficulties within the party, for many old Nazis from
the days of Munich — men like Otto and Gregor Strasser and Ernst
Röhm — were socialist revolutionaries who hated the party's new
orientation.

By the election of September 1930, the depression had created a
portentous change in German political life. The Nazis won 107 seats
in the Reichstag and became the second largest party. The reasons for
this sudden increase in Nazi support were complex, but the most important were economic. The sense of despair evoked by the depression led many Germans to turn to a desperate remedy. In addition,
the Nazis campaigned in and out of season; Hitler was given a certain
respectability when the Nationalist party leader, Alfred Hugenberg,

entered into the National Front with him; Nazi propaganda, directed
by Dr. Joseph Goebbels, was very clever; and the Nazi street-fighting
organizations, the SA and the SS, were swelled by the unemployed.

Seeking some solution to their difficulties, the German and Austrian governments announced, in March 1931, a plan for economic
union, with the proviso that other nations might later join under the
same terms. France at once objected and was seconded in her protest
by Czechoslovakia. When the matter came before the Permanent
Court of International Justice in the Hague, eight states voted against
the union and seven states, including Britain and the United States,
voted in favor of permitting it. The plan was abandoned, and the
internal situation in Germany grew worse. This was to be the last time
before the Second World War that France was able to block German
recovery. In this case the French initiative had been particularly
shortsighted, for it contributed to the mounting frustration in Germany, which was to culminate in the establishment of a government
that cared nothing for courts or international justice or French objections.

After winning the presidential election in April 1932, Hindenburg
agreed to Chancellor Heinrich Brüning's demand that the SA and SS
be outlawed. However, Brüning was soon succeeded by Franz von
Papen, a vain and inconsequential man whom few had ever taken seriously. Papen promptly lifted the ban on the storm troopers, dissolved the Reichstag, and called new elections.

By now Germany's industrial production was only half of what it
had been in 1929, and commodity prices had dropped by 25 percent.
More than six million Germans were unemployed. The Nazi party
had profited greatly from the nation's distress — naturally so, for
where the carcass is there will the vultures be gathered. In January
1931 the party membership had climbed to 400,000. One year later,
in January 1932, it stood at 900,000.

With the lifting of the ban on the storm troopers, Nazi violence in
the streets at once burst forth again. In the elections that were held in
July the Nazis polled 13.4 million votes and won 230 seats out of the
total of 608 in the Reichstag. This was a frightening increase in Nazi
strength but was still far short of a working majority — something the
Nazis never achieved by democratic methods. Papen was forced to resign in September and another election was called for November 6. In
that election the Nazis lost two million votes and forty-four seats,
being reduced to 196 deputies. General Kurt von Schleicher, a political soldier, became chancellor, only to be dismissed within two
months.

Berlin was full of intrigue in January of 1933. Hindenburg declared that he would never make "that Bohemian corporal" chancellor of Germany. He was, however, induced to change his mind, partly because the Nazis and the Nationalists could between them command a majority in the Reichstag and partly because his son, Oskar, had struck a bargain with Hitler on January 22.* Papen became vice chancellor, representing the nationalist, conservative interests that believed that they could "control" Hitler. This calculation was largely based on the power of the president, but Hindenburg at eighty-five was a shaky reed on which to lean.

The Nazis immediately banned all Communist meetings, suppressed Communist newspapers, and began to arrest Communist leaders. On February 20, Hermann Göring, Hitler's right-hand man and now president and minister of police of Prussia, ordered his policemen to shoot Communists on sight. Many Communists were murdered in the streets, and when, on the night of February 27, the Reichstag caught fire and a half-witted Dutch Communist, Marinus van der Lubbe, was conveniently discovered in the burning building, the Nazis declared that they had uncovered a Communist plot to seize power. Some 4000 Communists were arrested and thrown into hastily organized concentration camps. At the height of the red scare, Hitler called new elections for March 5.

The Nazis polled only seventeen million votes, or 43.6 percent of the total cast. With only 288 Reichstag seats, the Nazis were still a minority party, dependent on Nationalist support. This embarrassing situation was somewhat eased when Hitler managed to prevent the eighty-one Communist deputies from taking their seats. On March 23 the new Reichstag voted, by 441 to 94, to pass the so-called Enabling Act, which gave Hitler full dictatorial powers for a period of four years. Only the Social Democrats voted against the bill.

Since 1945 it has often been claimed that the German people did not know what manner of man Hitler was or where he was leading them. The second part of the claim is certainly true, but the first proposition requires qualification. The Nazi appeal lay not so much in the half-baked and simple-minded ideology of Alfred Rosenberg or in the vicious anti-Semitism of Julius Streicher as in the aura of self-confidence and decision that the Nazi leadership exuded. The Nazi promises appealed to all classes and conditions of men — workers and bosses, farmers and city dwellers, old and young, rich and poor. But what was promised was of secondary importance. The Germans wanted some positive action and they recognized instinctively that

*Oskar von Hindenburg was subsequently promoted from colonel to major general in the Reichswehr and was given a large, tax-free grant of land to be added to the family estate in East Prussia.

Hitler was the man to give it to them. In many particulars, too, Hitler spoke for the overwhelming majority of the German people. When he condemned the "slave treaty" of Versailles, when he demanded an end to Germany's humiliation, when he promised to revise the verdict of defeat, he echoed the sentiments of almost all Germans. Yet other politicians, on the right and in the center and even on the left, had said the same. The difference was that Hitler was able to convince people that he would act. Because of this conviction much was forgiven or ignored. Though before they came to power the Nazis were careful to conceal the full extent of their wickedness, it must have been apparent to the discerning that they were wicked, that Hitler was "a flame kindled from foul gases." The full extent of Nazi sadism, the corruption of the party, the nihilism of the Nazi philosophy, and the blood lust of the Führer and his entourage could not, of course, have been fully guessed in March of 1933, but none of these things had been entirely hidden or should have come as a complete surprise. Hitler was not, as the Marxists so neatly claimed, the final rank flowering of capitalism, its last despairing attempt to ward off the inevitable victory of communism. Rather he was the result of all the history that had gone before and especially of the First World War. Defeat, injustice, humiliation, and economic chaos were the swamps where the Nazis bred.

With the passage of the Enabling Act, democracy was dead in Germany, legality was replaced by the will of the Führer, and morality was whatever the party desired. Other political parties were soon outlawed; censorship was imposed on press and radio; the secret state police, or Gestapo, began arresting all possible opponents of the regime. Before the year was out some 100,000 Germans were in concentration camps; the trade union movement was absorbed into the Nazi Labor Front under Dr. Robert Ley; the student body of each school and university could not be more than 5 percent Jewish; and the concordats that had been signed with the Catholic and Lutheran churches were being consistently broken. Anti-Semitism first took the form of plundering the Jews — "frying the fat out of them," in Streicher's phrase — and then it became merely an excuse for sadistic impulses. The physically or mentally unfit were murdered, and German boys and girls were enrolled in Baldur von Schirach's Hitler Jugend and Hitler Mädchen for their systematic corruption.

In October 1933 Germany withdrew first from the Disarmament Conference and then from the League of Nations. However, Hitler was careful to point out that his withdrawal from the Disarmament Conference did not mean that Germany was becoming warlike. He would return to the conference, he said, if Germany was allowed to have an army of 300,000 men, if German civil aviation was freed from supervision, and if the Saar was immediately returned to Germany. The figure of 300,000 for the army was nicely calculated: this was the maximum number, according to the German General Staff, that could be trained in the next three years. France indignantly rejected Hitler's offer, but both Britain and Italy were ready to negotiate. None of these demands was in fact unreasonable, except on the old premise that Germany had been guilty of causing the world war.

At a great party rally in Nuremberg in September 1933, Hitler, as he was to do many times in the future, spoke words of peace, promising to disarm if other nations would do the same. Germany was still militarily weak and would remain so for a number of years, so Hitler sought to dispell the suspicions his regime was awakening in other nations. The civilized world had been horrified and disgusted by the Nazi treatment of the Jews; France, Poland, and Czechoslovakia were seriously alarmed by the Nazi assumption of power; and even the Soviet Union, long friendly to Germany, was now hostile. Hitler's apparent moderation made a good impression in Britain, however, where a considerable body of opinion held that many of the German claims were just, that the Treaty of Versailles had been too harsh, and the French, too vindictive.

Some few men with sounder instincts — or perhaps only with more bellicose dispositions — hated Hitler from the outset and warned of what his coming portended, but they could scarcely have made a logical case for their beliefs at the time. Although the Nazis' domestic policies were often abominable, they were certainly no worse than the policies that had been pursued in Russia by Lenin and Stalin. Intervention had been tried in Russia and had failed. French intervention in the Ruhr had failed in 1923. Now, with the world in the depths of a terrible economic depression and with pacifist sentiment overwhelmingly strong, intervention in Germany was unthinkable. Nor did it seem necessary. Hitler, after all, was a statesman like any other, who could be trusted to follow national interest in a rational way. There is, of course, considerable retrospective irony in this. Poor old Kaiser Wilhelm had been falsely accused of having plotted aggressive war against the world. By 1933 few thinking men any longer believed that accusation was true. They were therefore the readier to discount a similar charge against another ruler of Germany, and those who had for a time believed that Wilhelm was a wolf were the more easily deceived by Hitler's sheepskin.

With the coming to power of the Nazis, Poland began to have doubts about the value of her alliance with France, and sought further assurance by signing a nonaggression pact with Germany on January

26, 1934. The members of the Little Entente proclaimed their loyalty to France and to each other, but each of them assessed for itself the implications of the Nazi rise to power. Czechoslovakia, with three million Sudetan Germans within her borders, was the most disturbed, and with good reason. On the other hand, Rumania now hoped that the new Germany might be an ally against the Soviet Union. Yugoslavia, too, thought that a Nazi Germany might not be too serious a threat, for the Yugoslavs considered Italy their chief enemy.

Stalin was well aware of Hitler's often-stated intention of restoring the terms of the Treaty of Brest-Litovsk at Russia's expense. The Nazis' doctrine that the living space they required could be obtained in the east was not a comforting one for the Communist dictator, nor was he reassured by the anti-communism that Hitler so frequently expressed. The Soviet Union was also apprehensive about Japanese intentions in Manchuria. Placed thus between two fires, Stalin discovered belatedly that there was virtue in the principle of collective security and that the League of Nations was not, after all, merely a "bourgeois swindle." In September 1934 the Soviet Union joined the League, sponsored by France, Britain, and Italy.

By the summer of 1934 Hitler, after eighteen months in power, had very considerable achievements to his credit. Unemployment had been greatly reduced as rearmament stimulated industry and a network of new superhighways was begun. Mass rallies and torchlight processions, military bands, propaganda films, and a controlled press combined to assure the Germans that they were living in a new age and that the Fatherland was once more on the road to greatness.

The nonaggression pact with Poland, however, was regarded sourly by many Nazis, and there were mutterings in the party ranks when Hitler proclaimed, as he did more than once, that he had no intention of absorbing Austria into the Reich. More ominous was the split that was appearing between the right and left wings of the party. Ernst Röhm's brown-shirted SA had taken seriously the Führer's promises of class warfare against the rich. They believed in the socialist content of national socialism, and now that the party was in power they expected their reward. Time hung heavy on the hands of these lower-middle-class thugs when there were no more political opponents to beat up. The obvious solution seemed to be to incorporate the SA into the Reichswehr, but the mere suggestion horrified the German generals. General Walther von Brauchitsch certainly spoke for the officer corps when he declared, "Rearmament is too serious a business to permit the participation of peculators, drunkards and homosexuals." As a result, Hitler found himself saddled with two and a half million disgruntled storm troopers who were anxious that the Nazi revolution continue until society had been completely overturned and they themselves were on top. Röhm and his associates, the Strasser brothers, were talking about the "second revolution," which would bring in the social changes they had always desired.

Accordingly, Hitler made a deal with the army, in May 1934, whereby he would reduce the SA, disarm it, and guarantee that the Reichswehr would be the sole bearer of arms in Germany. In return the army agreed that when Hindenburg died (an event that could not in the nature of things be far off), Hitler should be the old gentleman's successor, combining the functions of president and chancellor in his own person.

The internal situation in Germany was growing intolerably tense, with Hitler's wealthy backers calling for a turn to the right in Nazi policy and Röhm and the SA demanding that the party march forward to socialism. Early in June Hitler gave the SA a month's leave and forbade the members to wear their uniforms during that period or to participate in any public gathering. This was a device to gain time but it only increased the pressure from the right. The generals now warned the Führer that if the tense situation was not ended they would ask Hindenburg to declare martial law and turn the country over to the army. Ever since the abdication of the kaiser, the ultimate question in German politics had always been "Which way would the big gray cat jump?" So far the Reichswehr had not jumped at all, but it now seemed to be gathering itself together for a spring. And by now, of course, the army was the only possible alternative to the Nazi party as the government of Germany.

Thus, in the last two weeks of June 1934 Hitler found himself in a very dangerous position indeed. He solved his problem by murder. On the early morning of June 30 Himmler's SS surprised and shot Röhm and most of the SA leaders in Bavaria, while Göring conducted a simultaneous purge in Berlin. June 30 was a Saturday, and the killing went on all through the weekend. Hitler later boasted in the Reichstag that this prompt action had saved Germany from a left-wing revolution. The Nazis admitted to having killed seventy-seven persons in this "Night of Long Knives," but in actual fact more than a thousand were murdered. The German people, who were tired of the coarseness and brutality of the SA, accepted Hitler's explanation and applauded him. Why not? Their elected representatives, by passing the Enabling Act, had already placed him above the law.

On August 2, 1934, Hindenburg died, and Hitler, though he did not take the title, assumed the powers of the president of the republic. Hitler was now head of state and commander-in-chief of the armed forces, whose officers and men were required to swear an oath of personal allegiance to him. When a plebiscite was held later in August to ask the Germans whether they approved of Hitler's assuming these new powers, it was reported that 90 percent of the voters did approve. Perhaps the plebiscite was fraudulent; there is, unfortunately, little reason to think so.

Dr. Engelbert Dollfuss, the Austrian chancellor, was determined to defend his country's independence, and he moved against both the radical left and the radical right, disarming the illegal paramilitary Schutzbund of the Social Democrats and outlawing the Austrian Nazi party. But as animals are excited by the smell of a slaughterhouse, the Austrian Nazis were stimulated by the reek of the blood that had been spilled in Germany on the Night of Long Knives. On July 25, 1934, Austrian Nazis seized the chancellery in Vienna, murdered Dollfuss, and announced that the pro-Nazi ambassador to Rome, Anton Rintelen, was to be the new chancellor. The old but tough Austrian president, Dr. Wilhelm Miklas, refused to be intimidated, and ordered the Nazis put down. Loyal Austrian army and police forthwith surrounded the chancellery and moved against the Nazis in the countryside. Mussolini, who was by no means prepared to see a rearmed Germany on the Brenner Pass, at once moved four divisions to the Alpine frontier and warned that Italy would not tolerate an *Anschluss*. The Austrian Minister of Justice, Dr. Kurt von Schuschnigg, assumed the chancellorship, and when the army stormed the chancellery, he had thirteen of the Nazi leaders hanged out of hand. Hitler backed down promptly, disclaiming any prior knowledge of the rising and expressing deep shock at Dollfuss' murder.

The failure of the Putsch in Vienna made Hitler cautious for a time. For the rest of the year, on every public occasion, he was careful to speak of peace and goodwill among men. Meanwhile, of course, German rearmament continued, although it was actually a slower process than was long believed. By October the Reichswehr had expanded to 300,000, submarines were being assembled at Kiel, and the secret German air force began to take shape under Göring.

By the end of 1934, with Nazism secure in Germany, Hitler could begin to look outward at the world. It was a purely European world that he saw, for he had little interest in colonies or sea power, as the kaiser had had. His aim was to establish German hegemony on the continent. It was not, in fact, a particularly revolutionary program. Except for the policy of expansion in the east — and it is admittedly a very large exception — a good case could be made for Hitler's other objectives in foreign policy. But to claim that many of Hitler's objectives in foreign policy were reasonable is not for a moment the same as condoning Hitler's foreign policy. Good ends are invariably corrupted by bad means, and Hitler himself was a bad means, a murderer, a liar, a terrible petit bourgeois barbarian without formal education or culture or honor or morality.

In January 1935 the plebiscite in the Saar, promised by the Treaty of Versailles, was held under international supervision. Some Nazi intimidation occurred but not on a scale that could account for the result. More than 90 percent of the population of the Saar voted to return to the Reich, even though it was now the Third Reich of Adolf Hitler.

On March 10 Hitler announced that Germany now had an air force, contrary to the provisions of Versailles, and six days later he announced that Germany was introducing conscription and already had an army of half a million men. In April Prime Minister Ramsay MacDonald of Britain, Premier Pierre Flandin of France, and Mussolini met in Stresa, where they condemned Germany's illegal rearmament, reiterated their support of the League of Nations, and promised to "act in close and cordial collaboration" for the maintenance of the peace of Europe. Mussolini had stressed that this declaration applied only to Europe, for he was already planning the invasion of Ethiopia. The British and French, aware of Mussolini's intentions, were so anxious to maintain the "Stresa Front" against Germany that they tacitly accepted the Italian dictator's position.

On May 21 Hitler made a speech in which he protested his loyalty to the Locarno Pact and proclaimed that Germany had no wish to interfere in the internal affairs of Austria or to bring about an *Anschluss*. Finally, he proposed a treaty with Britain whereby German naval strength would be restricted to one third of the British. This was sheer insolence, since under the terms of the Treaty of Versailles Germany was allowed to have only an insignificant number of warships of not more than 10,000 tons' displacement each. The *Scharnhorst* and the *Gneisenau*, then being built, were each 26,000 tons, however, and the British Admiralty thought it might be wise to close with Hitler's offer rather than face another naval race similar to that of 1894–1914. Accordingly, the British signed a bilateral naval agreement with Germany behind the backs of the French.

By the agreement Germany was allowed a navy one-third as large as Britain's, but in submarines Germany was allowed to have 60 percent of the British strength, or if the Germans considered it necessary, 100 percent. What the Admiralty or the British government hoped to achieve by this arrangement is difficult to fathom. Since Hitler was already breaking the terms of the Treaty of Versailles, what grounds were there for believing that he would abide by the terms of the naval agreement unless it suited him? At the cost of strained relations with

France, Britain gratuitously allowed Hitler to legalize his disregard of Versailles. More than this, the fact that the British government would sign such an agreement was a sure indication to the German dictator of the type of man in Britain with whom he would have to deal. He was later to speak of them contemptuously as "little worms," and surely the epithet was not too harsh.

The western democracies were thus in some disarray when the Ethiopian crisis blew up in the autumn of 1935. The pretext was a clash between Ethiopian and Italian native troops at the little watering place of Walwal on the borders of Italian Somaliland, but it soon became apparent that Mussolini intended to add Ethiopia to his African possessions. Between September 1934 and October 1935 Mussolini prepared quite openly for his war. Pierre Laval, the French foreign minister, had already promised France's benevolent neutrality, and British public opinion was divided, with mass circulation newspapers like the *Daily Mail* and the *Daily Express* upholding the fascist side. The League of Nations was impotent, having been unable to deal with Japanese aggression in Manchuria or even to halt a vicious war between Bolivia and Paraguay. The United States was not, of course, a member of the League, and, in any case, American public opinion on international affairs was both selfish and uninstructed. No wonder that it seemed to the dictators that the world was full of rich prizes for anyone bold enough to seize them.

In the spring of 1935 Anthony Eden, then minister without portfolio for the League, was sent to Rome to buy Mussolini off. If Il Duce would abandon his military plans, Britain would see that he received the fertile lowlands of Ethiopia. Britain would compensate the Ethiopian emperor, Haile Selassie, with a portion of British Somaliland, including a corridor to the sea. By this means it was hoped to maintain the Stresa Front against Germany and spare the League of Nations the embarrassment of putting collective security to the test. Mussolini, by now enamored of the prospect of his war, turned Eden down out of hand, and that rising young diplomat came away from Rome embittered against fascism. In a speech to the League Assembly in September, Sir Samuel Hoare, the British foreign minister, seemed to place Britain firmly on the side of collective security and resistance to aggression. He spoke well and with some emphasis on morality, but it was all a sham; Hoare and Laval had in fact already agreed that they would under no circumstances oppose Mussolini by force, that they would not institute a naval blockade or close the Suez Canal. Both Britain and France banned the export of arms to Ethiopia but undertook no similar action against Italy.

Three Italian army corps invaded Ethiopia on October 3, 1935.

The British Chiefs of Staff Committee had advised the government that Mussolini would need at least two campaigning seasons to subdue the country, and predicted great difficulties for the Italian invaders. In this they were mistaken, though not nearly as mistaken as were their Lordships of the Admiralty, who had unblushingly informed the cabinet that the British Mediterranean Fleet, even if reinforced by the entire Home Fleet, would be unable to control the Mediterranean. These military opinions probably reinforced the British government's already pronounced disinclination to interfere with the Italian aggression.

Nevertheless something was owed to respectability. On October 7 the League Council branded Italy an aggressor and demanded sanctions. The sanctions that were imposed included an arms embargo on Italy, the lifting of the embargo on Ethiopia, the freezing of all financial transactions with Italy, and an embargo on Italian imports and exports, although Italy was still permitted to import oil, scrap iron, and certain other supplies essential for war. These sanctions, intentionally made ineffective against Mussolini's war effort, succeeded only in rallying Italian public opinion behind the dictator.

In December 1935 Hoare and Laval, meeting in Paris, revived Eden's plan of the previous spring for buying off Mussolini. The British cabinet approved its foreign minister's action, and Italy might have agreed to accept the Hoare-Laval plan — the war was not going well — had not someone, possibly Laval himself, leaked the agreement to the French press. A quite unexpected storm of opposition burst forth in England. The British government, long used to doing what it liked in foreign affairs, was taken aback by the violence of the objections. Stanley Baldwin, who had replaced MacDonald as prime minister in June, blamed Hoare. The latter was hurriedly recalled from a skiing holiday in Switzerland, told that he was a sick man, and forced to resign "for reasons of health." Mussolini now rejected the repudiated plan, and the smaller nations of Europe, reflecting on the disparity between Hoare's ringing words to the League Assembly in September and the shabby reality of the deal with Laval, began to look about for some more certain help in time of trouble than collective security.

Mussolini began to badger his generals, replaced the commander-in-chief, and raised the number of troops in Ethiopia to 400,000. The man who years before had achieved the miracle of making Italian trains run on time now achieved the even greater miracle of forcing an Italian army to move expeditiously. By the spring of 1936 Ethiopia had been overrun. Emperor Haile Selassie fled from his capital, Addis Ababa, on May 1, and made his way to Geneva, where he wandered, a pathetic and embarrassing figure, about the halls of the League of Nations until it was decided that he represented no one but himself. On May 6 the conquering Italians marched into Addis Ababa, and in Rome Mussolini grandiloquently proclaimed the inauguration of the Second Roman Empire. In June 1936 Neville Chamberlain, the British chancellor of the exchequer, publicly declared that, now that the Ethiopian war was over, the continuance of sanctions against Italy would be "the very midsummer of madness," and on June 18 the British government dropped sanctions.

Large portions of the British public were less ready than Chamberlain to forget and forgive, and from this time on a strong current of opposition to the policies of appeasement flowed against the government, dividing the country. France and Britain were estranged by the Hoare-Laval revelations, and Hitler, if he needed it, had been given another demonstration of the kind of statesmanship then being practiced in the western democracies. The most important result of the Ethiopian war, however, was that it had driven Italy out of the Stresa Front and forced her into closer relations with Germany. This was to be disastrous for Italy, who could never hope to maintain her freedom of action in such a partnership.

At the beginning of 1936, French and British intelligence sources persistently reported that Hitler was about to reoccupy the Rhineland. The German high command was very apprehensive about this plan of the Führer's because the German army, inferior in size, equipment, and training, was quite unprepared to stand up to the French. Hitler, however, knew better. He assured his anxious generals that France and Britain would make no move, but he did go so far as to promise them that if the French opposed him by force the German troops could at once retreat.

On the morning of Saturday, March 7, a small German force marched into the Rhineland and sent three battalions across the Rhine to the left bank. As the German troops were marching into the forbidden territory, the German foreign minister, Konstantin von Neurath, informed the French and British ambassadors in Berlin of what was happening, and denounced the Locarno Pact, which Hitler had publicly guaranteed the previous May. He then proposed a new twenty-five-year nonaggression pact between Germany, France, and Belgium, to be guaranteed by Britain and Italy; similar nonaggression pacts between Germany, Poland, and Czechoslovakia; and the demilitarization of both sides of the Franco-German frontier. The last proposal, of course, amounted to a suggestion that the French scrap the Maginot Line — which, as it turned out, might not have been such a bad bargain for France after all.

In Britain, Lloyd George suggested that it would be a good thing if everyone kept his head. Lord Snowden, who had been chancellor of the exchequer under MacDonald, was in favor of accepting Hitler's new peace offer and of taking him at his word when he had declared in the Reichstag that he had no territorial demands to make in Europe and that Germany would never break the peace. Prime Minister Baldwin, with tears in his eyes, assured Premier Flandin of his sympathy but confessed that he was helpless because the British people simply would not entertain the possibility of another war. The best summary of all was that of Lord Lothian, who would later be ambassador to the United States. He said, of the occupation of the Rhineland, "After all, [the Germans] are only moving into their own back garden."

By the end of the week following the occupation, it was apparent to everyone that Hitler had got away with it.

The British and Belgians were very glad that he had, for they certainly had no wish to support France with military measures. On March 19 the League Council condemned the German action, a gesture that impressed no one. Only Maxim Litvinov, the Soviet foreign minister, suggested that sanctions be imposed on Germany, and this proposal met with no support in the League Assembly.

The German occupation of the Rhineland is frequently said to have been the last occasion on which the western democracies could have stopped Hitler without a war. On the face of it, the opinion has much to recommend it, but closer analysis raises certain doubts. If France had moved armed forces into the Rhineland, the Germans would, as we now know, have retired without fighting. What would have happened then? Could France have remained indefinitely in occupation of the Rhineland, facing the sharpened hostility of a rearming Germany and the disapproval of Britain? In 1923, only four years after the end of the First World War, a far stronger France failed to maintain its occupation of the Ruhr against a far weaker Germany. Nor is it likely that Hitler would have lost popular support no matter how the march into the Rhineland had turned out; the German people were too enthusiastic about the project for that. If the move had failed, the government would have gained sympathy; once it succeeded, the Nazis were hailed as saviors. In the plebiscite he held after the event, Hitler got a solid vote of confidence from 98.8 percent of the German voters. Furthermore, the Führer had been proved right and his more timid generals had been proved wrong — a circumstance that both Hitler and the generals were to remember.

The truth surely is that Hitler's reoccupation of the Rhineland exposed the false basis of French policy, revealing the weakness that had always lain beneath the show of strength. How could France expect that, seventeen years after the war, a German nation one-third larger than the French would continue to accede to the demilitarization of a vital part of its territory? The Germans were indeed only moving into their own back garden. The real turning point in European affairs was therefore not the British and French acquiescence in the occupation of the Rhineland. That turning point had been reached three years earlier, when Hitler and the Nazis had fastened their hold on Germany. The French error had been to hang on for seventeen years to an indefensible position and to pretend to wield a control over Europe that could not be maintained. If the true situation had been recognized earlier and if the Treaty of Versailles had been modified as justice and reality indicated, the Nazis would have lost most of their appeal and would, in all probability, have remained an insignificant and crackpot party followed by none but cranks.

With the occupation of the Rhineland, the whole of the French façade cracked wide open. France's partners in the Little Entente, Czechoslovakia, Rumania, and Yugoslavia, quickly took note of the new situation. If France, with a hundred divisions and the strongest air force in Europe, found herself unable to oppose three German battalions on the left bank of the Rhine, what prospect was there of her coming to the aid of distant allies in the east of Europe? Poland was confirmed in her belief that friendship with Germany was her best policy, and the Soviet Union, which until now had greatly overrated French strength, began to have doubts. Moreover, with the Wehrmacht on the Rhine, how could France, even if she found the courage, support Poland, Czechoslovakia, Rumania, or Yugoslavia? The Germans immediately began to build their own fortifications in the west, and once the Siegfried Line was completed, of what use would be the hundred French divisions? They might be able to defend the frontiers of France, but they could be no help at all to Poland or the Little Entente. While the French army was breaking its teeth on the Siegfried Line, the great bulk of the new German army would be free to turn east.

This sudden reversal of fortune posed fundamental questions to both France and Britain. Within a period of two years the illusory protection of Versailles and Locarno had dissolved like mist in a morning breeze. How could the damage be repaired, the losses cut, the peace maintained? The policy that was in fact followed proved to be in almost every respect the worst possible one. The reoccupation of the Rhineland, which caused the stripping away of French illusions, was a traumatic experience for the French nation. From now on it was Britain that took the lead while the French followed. The French, afraid to walk alone, could do nothing else. The British policy, soon to be given the name of "appeasement," was to rebuild a Europe in which

Germany could take its rightful place as a great power. In many ways this was an enlightened and moral policy, for it sought to undo the injustices that had sprung from the First World War. What was wrong with it was that it was too late. Had Locarno come sooner, had war debts and reparations been abandoned, had the Weimar Republic been granted as rights what Hitler was determined to take by force, then appeasement would have been noble and generous. As it was, with the Nazis in firm control of Germany, appeasement was futile since it could no longer achieve its aim, the reconciliation of Germany. Nor was it only futile; it also had the appearance of being cowardly, of giving way before blackmail and the threat of force. In this case the appearance coincided to a considerable extent, though not exactly, with the reality. The British and French governments from 1936 to the outbreak of the Second World War were indeed overly anxious to maintain the peace and went beyond the bounds of honor and self-interest in this vain endeavor. This was not so much because they feared defeat in war as because they had a very understandable horror of war itself. The French believed that the Maginot Line, even though it petered out at Malmédy, afforded them a sure protection against German attack. The British, with more reason, counted on their insular position and their sea power.

Neither Britain nor France was willing to draw the true lessons from the Rhineland occupation, and the British in particular grossly deceived themselves as to the nature of Nazism. Yet in fact all was not lost in 1936. It was probably already too late to save Europe, but the western democracies could still have saved themselves had they acted vigorously.

The first prerequisite of any Franco-British policy after the spring of 1936 was a strong military position. German rearmament had as yet hardly begun and Britain and France were still much, much stronger than Nazi Germany. This, by itself, was part of the trouble, for it led to an underestimation of the danger. No real effort was made in either Britain or France to overhaul defenses, to modernize them, and to increase their industrial base. Britain did begin a very modest rearmament program that was limited and hampered at every turn by the pacifist idealists of the left. Thus, when rearmament was eliminating German unemployment, the British and French economies were working at far less than capacity, and Germany soon became militarily stronger than the democracies. Perhaps even more important than the purely physical side of rearmament was the disparity of spirit between Germany and the west. British and French leadership was timid, cautious, and uninspiring, and in France national morale was very low. Germany, on the other hand, was filled with a wild enthusiasm. If there is any truth in Napoleon's dictum that the moral is to the physical as three is to one, Nazi Germany was already stronger than Britain and France.

Yet after 1936 Britain and France could have made themselves secure against German aggression, though they could not by themselves have prevented Hitler from carrying out the rest of his program at the expense of Austria, Czechoslovakia, and Poland. After the reoccupation of the Rhineland, these states could not be defended by the west for any length of time, even at the cost of another great European war. None of them could be reached from Allied territory, which in the end would have proved a decisive handicap to their defense.

But a way of saving Europe remained open in 1936, and even later. This was for the western democracies to make a military alliance with the Soviet Union. The Russians professed to desire this, and since it was manifestly in their own national interest, there is no good reason to doubt their sincerity. The Soviet Union, France, and Britain would in combination have been strong enough to contain Nazi Germany, prevent her aggressions against both Czechoslovakia and Poland, and defeat her in war if she were foolish enough to initiate one. The British government turned its face resolutely from any such alliance until it was too late, and the Franco-Soviet Pact of Mutual Assistance had, at the request of France, been so watered down as to be of no value. The reasons for the British attitude were fear and distrust of Bolshevism, underestimation of the military power of the Soviet Union, and the persistent belief that it would be possible to come to terms with Hitler. Some British politicians may even, as the Russians allege, have entertained the hope that Germany would leave the west in peace and turn east.

An alliance with the Soviet Union would undoubtedly have had its dangers, although it would have been far less dangerous than the policy actually followed. If an alliance between the Soviet Union and the western democracies had resulted in war with Germany, communism would very probably have gained a hold on much of eastern Europe. The crux of the matter, however, is that an alliance with the Soviet Union might well have prevented war, for even Hitler might have hesitated long before challenging so strong a combination. Blindly, and with a quite unjustified smugness, British statesmen continued to reject this hopeful policy, thus bringing down upon their heads a war that they were required to fight under the most adverse conditions. Nor did British policy save eastern Europe from communism.

On July 11, 1936, Hitler signed a pact with Austria, promising that he would not attempt to influence Austria's internal affairs and that he would refrain from giving any encouragement to the Austrian Nazi party. Five days later, on the 16th, Hitler ordered the German General Staff to prepare for the invasion of Austria, and the Austrian Nazis were ordered to increase their agitation for union with Germany.

Hardly had the palpitations caused by Hitler's march into the Rhineland died down than civil war broke out in Spain. The situation in Spain resembled that in France but in more acute form: the left and the right had become so bitterly hostile that they could no longer meet on any common ground. Violence was endemic; peasants seized land; the cities were periodically swept with riots; churches and monasteries were burned and priests, monks, and nuns murdered. The Spanish temperament, which seems to include so much fanaticism, fierceness, and unwillingness to compromise, made any reasonable solution impossible to achieve. In the general elections of February 1936, the right received slightly more of the popular vote than the left, but because of the distribution of electoral districts the left coalition emerged with a small majority in the Cortes. Left-wing political prisoners were released and the prisons were refilled with right-wing supporters. Between February and July 1936, the political violence got completely out of hand. Revolutionary clubs sprang up across the country, and the center and right coalesced against the left.

The murder of a rightist deputy, Calvos Soleto, touched off the civil war. On July 17, Spanish garrisons in Morocco declared against the government, as did the troops in a dozen cities in Spain itself. General Francisco Franco, the governor general of the Canary Islands, flew to Morocco and subsequently landed with an army in the south of Spain. The Popular Front government in Madrid panicked, forming and re-forming itself three times on July 17 and 18. Some of the Spanish navy and air force declared for the government but the great majority of the army joined the revolt. In the capital and some other cities, government officials opened the arsenals and armed the mob.

By the end of 1936, Franco's forces controlled about three fifths of Spain, but the republic continued to defend itself ferociously, and retained possession of Madrid, Barcelona, Valencia, and some other large cities. The war was marked by bravery and cruelty on both sides; prisoners were rarely taken, as the example of indiscriminate killing set by the anarchists spread. By September the members of the left coalition were feuding bitterly with each other, the Trotskyites and Stalinists, the anarchists and syndicalists, being almost as intent on defeating the doctrinal opponents in their own camp as in saving the republic.

Long before the civil war had broken out both the Soviet Union and Italy had been interfering in Spain's domestic politics. Léon Blum's Popular Front government in France also sympathized with its counterpart across the Pyrenees. Because of difficulties of transportation, Soviet aid to the Spanish government was limited to food, munitions, pilot instructors, technical experts, and a few selected officers. Italian intervention was more direct and massive because now that the Ethiopian war was over, Italy had troops to spare. By the spring of 1937 four Italian divisions were in Spain and nearly 150 Italian naval vessels operated in Spanish waters. Hitler also intervened in Spain, but for reasons of his own, which had little to do with ideology. As the Nazis saw it, the longer the Spanish civil war continued, the better, for it would serve to widen and make impassable the breach between Italy and the western democracies.* The campaigns in Spain were also an excellent opportunity to test new military equipment and tactical doctrines under combat conditions. Hitler's aid to Franco, therefore, was calculated to be less than decisive and was restricted to aircraft, artillery, technicians, a few small tank units, and the Luftwaffe's Condor Legion.

The sympathy of the French Popular Front for the Spanish left was tempered by a lively fear of the civil war's spreading to France, a possibility that seemed by no means improbable. As a result, the French government, in August, proposed to the British and Italians that everyone should adopt a policy of nonintervention in Spain. By the end of the month Britain, France, Italy, Germany, the Soviet Union, and Portugal had all promised to adhere to a nonintervention agreement and all of them, except the British, were breaking the terms of the agreement before the signatures of their representatives were dry on the paper. In October the Soviet Union repudiated nonintervention; Germany and Italy recognized General Franco's government and granted it belligerent rights in November.

By the beginning of 1937, eastern Spain from Madrid to the sea still flew the red flag; Catalonia, which was separatist, halfheartedly embraced the republican cause; and the Basques and the Asturians on the Bay of Biscay formed a little republican enclave surrounded by nationalists. The rest of Spain was Franco's. When an Italian warship and the German cruiser *Deutschland* were bombed by government planes in May 1937, German warships retaliated by shelling the town of Almeria. That spring near Madrid the Italians upheld tradition by suffering a sharp defeat, but elsewhere the republic was in desperate

*The calculation was correct. The Rome-Berlin Axis pact was signed in October 1936; in November 1936 Germany and Japan signed the Anti-Comintern Pact, which Italy joined in 1937.

straits. Bilbao fell to the Nationalists in June, and by October the northern coast was cleared of republican troops. In February 1938 the Nationalists began advancing down the Ebro to the sea, and by the summer the government forces were split in two. A check on the Ebro line prolonged the war into 1939, but Barcelona fell in February of that year and Madrid was entered in March.

Aside from Spain, the rest of Europe dwelled in uneasy calm in 1937. Hitler had promised that the year would bring no surprises, and because it suited him he kept this promise. Work proceeded apace on the Siegfried Line, and newly inducted recruits sweated on parade grounds and training areas all across Germany. Stanley Baldwin retired as British prime minister to be replaced by Neville Chamberlain, who was even more committed to a policy of appeasement than Baldwin had been. Eden remained foreign minister, but under Chamberlain he had far less latitude than Baldwin had given him.

In the Far East 1937 was marked by renewed Japanese aggression against China. The invasion of Manchuria had helped the Japanese economy, which by 1935 had regained its pre-1929 level. Even moderate opinion in Japan was impressed, and the militarists found increased credence for their claim that only conquests on the Asian mainland could give Japan the standard of living it required. In July 1937 Japanese forces attacked Peking, and in August heavy fighting broke out at Shanghai. After three months the Japanese captured Shanghai and began to push up the valley of the Yangtze toward the interior of China. The Chinese capital of Nanking fell in December, but Generalissimo Chiang Kai-shek moved to Shantung and carried on the war as best he could.

Although the Sino-Japanese War did not merge with the Second World War until the Japanese attacked Pearl Harbor in December 1941, it had an important influence on the European situation. After the signing of the Anti-Comintern Pact, western statesmen and diplomats tended to lump Germany, Italy, and Japan together as the "Axis powers" and to credit them with a far more coordinated policy than they in fact pursued. This served to increase western timidity; the British Chiefs of Staff were especially apprehensive that they might have to counter Japanese moves in the Far East while honoring a commitment to France in northwest Europe and meeting a threat from Italy in the Mediterranean. Fear is a paralyzing emotion, and it did much to vitiate British policy in the years immediately preceding the war.

The United States, too, was distracted by the Japanese aggression against China. The American government and people were bitterly hostile to Japan, for reasons that are not altogether clear. Certainly neither strategic nor economic considerations alone can account rationally for the American attitude toward the Far East, and the United States was already in the process of liquidating, rather shamefacedly, its aberrant empire in the Philippines. Yet the sentiment was there, whatever its origins, and it deeply affected American policy, turning it away from Europe and to some extent alienating it from Britain and France. However, no American government could possibly have taken military measures in support of China or even have begun preparations that would make such measures feasible. In the 1930s the Americans, deploring the fact that they lived in a wicked world, were quick to condemn the British and French failure to stand up to Hitler and Mussolini, but they had absolutely no intention of becoming involved themselves.

The Soviet Union, like the United States but with better cause, was also distracted and alarmed by the Japanese attack on China. Clashes between Japanese troops and Soviet border guards in Mongolia became frequent, and in June 1939 the Japanese launched another undeclared war in the Khalkhin-Gol region. In August a Soviet army under General G. K. Zhukov counterattacked the Japanese forces that had invaded the Mongolian People's Republic and inflicted a severe defeat upon them. Yet, though the Russians were successful in the Khalkhin-Gol, the Japanese menace meant that they could not concentrate exclusively on European problems. Large military forces had to be maintained in Asia, and Stalin, as well as the British, was apprehensive about the possibility of having to meet attacks from more than one direction. Hitler and Mussolini profited from Japanese actions, but there was no common Axis policy and no coordination, except the instinctive coordination of wolves attacking a flock of sheep.

Early in 1938 Eden resigned as foreign minister and was replaced by Lord Halifax, who clothed in fine words his inflexible determination to continue to retreat. The thronging ghosts of the Somme and Passchendaele haunted the corridors of Whitehall, and British statesmen made the unnecessary resolve that history should not repeat itself. Had Chamberlain, Halifax, Hoare, and the other appeasers of the 1930s held the reins of power in 1914, Europe might have been spared a great calamity, but the world had moved on since those days. Hitler bore no resemblance to the kaiser, nor the Third Reich to the Second, and yesterday's solution was of no help in dealing with the problems of today.

In January 1938 Hitler carried out a purge of the high command of the Wehrmacht. The minister of defense, Werner von Blomberg, had married his secretary, unaware that she had formerly been a registered prostitute, and this gave Hitler the excuse he was seeking to dismiss him. The commander-in-chief, General Werner von Fritsch, had no such private vulnerability, so the Nazis falsely accused him of homosexuality and retired him in disgrace. The occasion was also taken to get rid of some sixteen other general officers who were anti-Nazi. Hitler himself assumed the Supreme Command of the Wehrmacht, with General Wilhelm Keitel as Chief of Staff and General Walther von Brauchitsch as head of the army command. Until this time senior army officers had retained the illusion that the army could still be the ultimate arbiter of Germany's destiny, that, if it came to a showdown, the army would prove stronger than the party. It had not been true since Hindenburg's death but it took the purge of the high command to bring home to the generals the fallacy of their belief.

In the five years since Hitler had become chancellor, the army had been forced to make concession after concession. The rearmament program and the twelvefold expansion of the army preoccupied the officer corps at the same time as it diluted its formerly homogeneous quality by bringing in thousands of new officers from the lower middle class. These new officers, who had none of the conservative, monarchist, and Christian traditions of the old officers corps, were out-and-out Nazis or Nazi sympathizers, and a split developed between the junior and senior ranks. This split was the more disastrous for the high command because Hitler and the party could play on it by promoting those officers who favored Nazi policies.

On November 5, 1937, at a conference in the chancellery, Hitler had outlined three possible eventualities that would result in Germany's going to war: a civil war in France, which would be the occasion for a German invasion of Czechoslovakia; a war between France and Italy (Hitler thought that this might occur in 1938), in which case Germany would deal with both Czechoslovakia and Austria; and finally the arrival of the year 1943, when Germany would move in any case, since after that time her relative position could only deteriorate. But Hitler was not an architect; he was an artist, producing improvisations rather than blueprints. When he found that the French and British governments were quite prepared — at some time — to see Germany annex Austria, Danzig, and the Sudetenland, provided only that "any alterations should come through the course of peaceful evolution and that methods should be avoided which might cause far-reaching disturbances," he recognized the acquiescence of the democracies and tended to regard their qualifications as mere face-saving quibbles. Why then wait until 1943 or until civil war broke out in France or until France and Italy went to war?

On February 12, 1938, the Austrian chancellor, Schuschnigg, met with the Führer at his mountaintop eyrie at Berchtesgaden. In all probability, what occurred had not been planned. It is likely that Hitler merely felt like bullying someone that day and became more violent as he saw how Schuschnigg was being intimidated. At all events, Hitler demanded that the Austrian Nazi Artur von Seyss-Inquart be made minister of the interior, with the police under his control; that Austria follow the German lead in economic and foreign policy; that Nazis be made ministers of war and finance; that the Austrian army and the Wehrmacht exchange officers; that all restrictions on Nazi propaganda be lifted; and that all imprisoned Nazis be liberated, including the murderers of Dollfuss. Schuschnigg was given three days to meet these terms, on pain of a military invasion.

Schuschnigg, overwhelmed by Hitler's ranting and abandoned to his fate by Britain, France, and Italy, agreed to meet the Führer's demands. But when he returned to Vienna, the Austrian chancellor, realizing that the independence of his country was at stake, announced that he intended to hold a plebiscite to ascertain whether Austrian opinion favored an *Anschluss* with Germany. Hitler was furious that Schuschnigg seemed to be trying to cheat him at the last moment. On the 11th Germany closed the border with Austria, and German troops began to concentrate near the frontier. When Schuschnigg appealed desperately to Mussolini, he was told that Italy could do nothing to help him. In France there was no government, for Camille Chautemps had resigned as premier and Léon Blum had not yet taken office. Chamberlain's government in Britain, of course, had never intended to do more than protest if Hitler invaded Austria.

Schuschnigg gave way and revoked the plebiscite, and when told that this was no longer sufficient, he resigned and was replaced by Seyss-Inquart, whose first act as chancellor was to ask for German troops. They were already on their way. On March 12 the German army rode into Austria, not without a good many mechanical breakdowns en route. At Linz, Hitler announced that Austria was incorporated into the Reich. That same day at the Vienna railway stations the Gestapo, with lists in their hands, were screening out those refugees who were destined for concentration camps. In the first few weeks after the Anschluss some forty thousand Austrians, many of them Jews, were sent to Buchenwald and Dachau. Thus the Nazi culture came to Austria.

When the Soviet Union proposed, on March 18, that Britain and France join her in a conference to implement collective security, the offer was rejected. France was still staggering from one political crisis to another and was, moreover, distracted by a wave of strikes that was sweeping the country. Chamberlain still persisted in his policy of throwing things out of the sleigh in the hope that the pursuing wolves would be delayed.

The Anschluss was an episode not at all like the occupation of the Rhineland. In 1936 the German army had moved only into German territory, and though the action had broken two treaties, it was undoubtedly wildly popular with the population of the occupied area. In annexing Austria, on the other hand, Hitler was committing a definite act of aggression, was seizing territory that had never historically been a part of the Reich, and was doing so, almost certainly, against the wishes of a majority of the Austrian population. Not only was the Anschluss Hitler's first external aggression; it was also an act that drastically altered the strategic situation in Europe. Germany gained seven million new subjects, and the Austrian army was merged with the German. Germany now gripped Czechoslovakia on three sides, and the entire communications system of eastern Europe, which by road and rail as well as by river followed the Danube valley, was in Nazi hands. Hungary, Yugoslavia, and Italy had a new neighbor that would in time overawe and physically occupy each of them.

On March 14 Premier Blum promised Czechoslovakia that France would honor her pledge under the mutual defense treaty, and when, on April 10, Blum was replaced by Daladier, the new French government repeated the assurance. It is doubtful if anyone took such words seriously. Chamberlain had already firmly decided that he would not give any guarantee to the Czechs or to the French in connection with their obligations to Czechoslovakia, and France was unlikely to act without British support.

The German generals, who knew more about war than their Führer, were alarmed by the strength of the Czech defenses, by the fact that only five regular and eight reserve divisions would be available for the defense of the Siegfried Line (which was not yet completed), by the hundred divisions that France could mobilize, and by the thirty-four excellent divisions that the Czechs could deploy. The Skoda munitions works in Bohemia were among the best in the world, and the frontiers of Czechoslovakia, naturally strong, had been fortified more thoroughly than the Maginot Line. Over and above all this, the German soldiers knew that the Soviet Union was pledged to come to Czechoslovakia's support provided only that France moved first.

Hitler, who was politically far shrewder than his generals, did not share their fears. On his instructions, the Sudeten Czechs, led by Konrad Henlein, began to riot and demonstrate. The German press also began to beat the drum, printing stories of alleged "atrocities" against the German minority in Czechoslovakia.

In July Chamberlain succeeded in forcing the Czech government to accept a British mission, headed by Lord Runciman, to arbitrate the quarrel between the Sudeten Germans and the Czechs. Runciman arrived in Czechoslovakia early in August, visited extensively with the Sudeten aristocracy, and quickly decided that the only possible solution was for the Czechs to give the Sudeten Germans everything they demanded. The Czech response was to pass a "nationalities statute" that removed any reasonable grounds for grievance that the Sudetenlanders might have had, but Henlein's only reply was to put forward fourteen new demands. To increase the problems of the beleaguered Czechs, Poland and Hungary now began to press claims on Czech territory.

General Ludwig Beck, the Chief of the German General Staff, warned Hitler that the Siegfried Line could be held against the French for only three weeks, and when his warning was ignored he resigned. Hitler appointed General Franz Halder to the post but kept Beck's resignation secret. Nevertheless, by the beginning of September a number of senior German generals, including both Beck and Halder as well as General Brauchitsch, the commander-in-chief, had formulated a plot to overthrow Hitler and establish a military government rather than allow the Nazi dictator to lead Germany into a hopeless war. Whether this plot would have succeeded, it certainly existed. Had its implementation been attempted, even if it had proven abortive, it would almost certainly have weakened the Nazi regime so gravely that the European war would have been brief and decisive. Everything favored the defense of Czechoslovakia in 1938 — everything except the will of those pledged to defend her and of those who stood to gain immeasurably from her defense.

On September 2 Russia again assured France that she was prepared to honor her obligations to the Czechs if the French, as they were required to do by the treaty, moved first. In view of Russian suspicions that the western democracies would be relieved to see Nazi Germany and the Soviet Union at war with one another, this Russian insistence on the terms of the treaty was eminently reasonable, nor is there any ground for doubting that the Soviet Union would have honored her commitment. It was manifestly in her interest to do so.

On September 10, as the tension between Germany and Czechoslovakia continued to mount, France inquired of Britain what aid she could expect in case of war. The British reply, intentionally chilling, was that for the first six months British military assistance would consist of two divisions not yet motorized and fifty aircraft. On the 11th the London *Times* proposed that Czechoslovakia cede the Sudetenland to Germany. Prime Minister Chamberlain now telegraphed direct to Hitler, asking if he could visit the German dictator, and on receiving

an affirmative reply he flew to Munich and journeyed on to Berchtesgaden on the morning of September 15.

Hitler told Chamberlain that the Czech crisis could be solved only if
those Czech districts that were more than 50 percent German were
transferred to the Reich without a plebiscite. This demand was accordingly presented by Britain and France to the Czech government,
not without sanctimony. "Both the French and British governments
recognize," the joint note said, "how great is the sacrifice thus required of Czechoslovakia." Although the existing alliance between
France and Czechoslovakia was to be abrogated, Britain and France
promised that they would join with Russia in a new guarantee of
Czechoslovakia's truncated borders. Two obvious difficulties, however, presented themselves. Russia had not yet been asked if she
would agree to such an arrangement. And — even more to the point
— how often can a nation be expected to put continued trust in a
forsworn ally? France was already bound to Czechoslovakia by a "sacred" pledge. That pledge broken, of how much worth was France's
word? The Czechs were given three days to make up their minds. If
they rejected the Franco-British offer, they would be left to their fate.

Faced with this betrayal on the part of an ally, the Czech government capitulated and then resigned. President Beneš had certainly
been subjected to almost intolerable pressure and in his view it would
not have been rational to have defied Germany alone. The Czech
people would have been subjected to all the horrors of a war they
could not have won, and their defeat would have been followed by the
even greater horrors of a Nazi occupation. What historian, in the
quiet of his study, will be bold enough to question Beneš's right to
make such a decision?

And yet . . . and yet . . . the Bohemian fortress line was very strong.
The thirty-four Czech divisions were finely equipped and in good
heart. The German General Staff had estimated that it would take the
German army three months to pierce the Czech defenses and overrun
the country. Much might have happened in three months. France
(though it seems unlikely) might have recovered her honor and been
shamed into keeping her word. Russia might have decided to intervene. Chamberlain's government might have fallen in the revulsion
that would surely have overtaken Britain. The German generals
might even have implemented their plot against Hitler. In any case, if
the Czechs had fought, even if they had had to fight alone, the Czech
nation would have proved itself more than the mere creature of Versailles, a matter that, as it is, must still remain in doubt.

While Beneš was capitulating, Chamberlain was on his way to Germany for the second time, to give the good news to the Führer. When

the British prime minister met Hitler in Bad Godesberg, however, Hitler told him, "I am exceedingly sorry but after the events of the last few days, this solution is no longer of any use." Hitler now raised his price, supported Polish and Hungarian demands on Czechoslovakia, demanded that all Czech forces be out of the area to be ceded by October 1, and stipulated that the area to be annexed should be given to Germany intact, with its fortifications, railways, livestock, and raw materials. All Sudetenlanders were to be released from the Czech army and all Nazi political prisoners were to be set free.

The new Czech government, headed by General Syrovy, rejected this preposterous set of demands and ordered general mobilization on September 23. Badly shaken, Chamberlain returned to London, and Britain mobilized her fleet and her antiaircraft defenses. The smell of war was in the air as it had not been since July 1914, but this time no one, even among the considerable number who would have preferred war to surrender, found it exhilarating. The British cabinet balked at trying to force the Czechs to accept Hitler's new demands, and on the 26th Britain finally informed France that she would support her if France should decide to honor her obligations to Czechoslovakia.

The German General Staff now formally pointed out to Hitler that the German army was not ready to fight a general war. Admiral Erich Raeder also warned Hitler that the navy was not prepared for hostilities. Badly frightened by the prospect of war, Mussolini now suggested a four-power conference, and Hitler agreed. On September 29 Hitler, Mussolini, Daladier, and Chamberlain met at Munich. Neither the Czechs nor the Russians were invited to attend. The talks, which began at noon, went on for fourteen hours, but when the memorandum of the meeting was signed on the early morning of September 30, Hitler had been given all that he asked for. The Czechs were granted an extra nine days to evacuate the ceded territory and the German occupation was to be in five stages instead of one. The Czech delegates were presented with the Munich agreement in the anteroom, where they had been kept waiting while the conversations had gone on, and were instructed to sign. They did so.

At Munich, Czechoslovakia lost eleven thousand square miles of territory, including all her well-fortified frontier districts in the west. The Czech economy, especially the railway system, was rendered all but unworkable. The Poles occupied Teschen and the Hungarians put forward claims to the Carpathian Ukraine. Beneš went into exile, leaving behind him a wounded nation filled with anger and despair.

Mr. Chamberlain returned to London, waving in his hand the piece of paper, bearing Hitler's signature, on which the Führer had promised to work with Britain for the peace of Europe. From the windows of 10 Downing Street the British prime minister addressed the crowd: "This is the second time there has come back from Germany to Downing Street peace with honor. I believe it is peace in our time."

Most of those who heard were anxious to believe. The London *Times*, which had so frequently supported shabby policies, declared: "No conqueror returning home from a victory on the battlefield has come home adorned with nobler laurels than Mr. Chamberlain from Munich yesterday." Very probably, a majority of the British people accepted this view at this time. Certainly the relief that there would be no war was very widespread. A few strong voices were raised in opposition. Alfred Duff Cooper resigned as First Lord of the Admiralty; Winston Churchill declared in the House of Commons that Britain had "sustained a total and unmitigated defeat." And as second thoughts began to creep in and shame tempered relief, Chamberlain's support steadily diminished.

The plea that supporters of appeasement later put forward, that British policy at Munich was designed merely to gain time while Britain built up her defenses, is, of course, mere cant. British rearmament continued after Munich at a gentle pace, while German rearmament was pressed with every effort. Britain's strength when she went to war in 1939 was relatively much weaker in comparison with German strength than it had been in 1938.

The truth is that Munich was the climax, and the symbol, of an attitude that had its roots in the First World War. That war had been unnecessary, a monumental folly, horrible beyond description. The appeasers were rightly determined that the mistake should not be made again. Where they erred was in equating the situations of 1914 and 1938. On the face of it, there were many similarities: Germany was on the one side, and Britain, France, and Russia on the other; in both instances the Germans raised the cry of encirclement; in both the sources of tension seemed to lie in the strange, ethnically diverse states of eastern Europe, about which the British people "knew very little." Yet the differences between 1914 and 1938 were enormous and fundamental. Germany, defeated and humiliated by the First World War, had given herself over to rulers who recognized no rights but their own and no means but force and fraud. To the Nazis, no engagement was binding and they knew no common cause with Europe as a whole. The only way to have faced them would have been on their own terms — steel against steel, force against force. The delusive light from the past deceived Chamberlain into believing that Britain was being given a second chance, that the mistake of 1914 could be undone, and that Germany would not have to be fought a second time.

In France a somewhat different temper prevailed. The French hatred of Germany went very deep, and there was little inclination to regard the First World War as unjust or the Peace of Versailles as vindictive. At no conscious level did the French suffer from a guilty conscience. What they suffered from was fear. The years 1914 to 1918 had left a deeper scar on France than on Britain, for it had been in France that the fighting had taken place. The public life of France had long been corrupt and embittered by faction. Some French newspapers and a considerable number of French journalists were in German pay or accepted German bribes. France, unlike Britain, had had a definite, binding commitment to Czechoslovakia, one freely entered into when it had seemed to France's advantage to do so, and one that had been repeatedly reaffirmed. That France should have failed to honor this commitment was both the measure of the French degeneration and the final betrayal that extinguished whatever remained of French morale and self-respect. Those who buy peace at such a price have no reasonable complaint if they later find themselves cheated on the deal.

During the Czech crisis Hitler had declared that his demand for the Sudetenland was "the last territorial claim I have to make in Europe." In his annual anniversary speech to the Reichstag in January 1939, he repeated his desire for peace and predicted a prosperous and calm future. By now, one would have thought, such words from Hitler would have awakened only fear and suspicion, but in fact Sir Samuel Hoare was publicly proclaiming in March that there would be a return of the "golden age." The day before Hoare made this speech, on March 8, Father Tiso, the leader of the Slovaks in Czechoslovakia, demanded a huge loan from the government in Prague, a separate Slovak army, and separate diplomatic representation, on the threat of declaring Slovakian independence. Prague reacted in the only way it could: it moved troops into Slovakia, arrested the separatist leaders, and imposed martial law.

On March 14 the German army invaded Czechoslovakia and the next day the new Czech president, Dr. Emil Hacha, was summoned to Berlin, where he was forced by threats to request that the whole of Czechoslovakia be placed under the protection of the Third Reich. German troops goose-stepped through the streets of Prague that morning, and that night Hitler slept in the ancient Czech capital. Here, as in Austria, the Gestapo at once set to work, new concentration camps were established, individual liberty was extinguished, impartial justice became a thing of the past, Jews were persecuted, and the Nazis plundered, tortured, and murdered as their fancy took them. The British government claimed that, since Czechoslovakia had disintegrated internally with the Slovak demand for independence, the British guarantee to Czechoslovakia against aggression was no longer in effect.

The Poles were obviously next in line for Hitler's attention. With the extinction of Czechoslovakia, in which Poland had greedily cooperated, Germany bordered Poland on three sides, just as she had Czechoslovakia after the Anschluss. Colonel Jozef Beck, the self-confident and irresponsible Polish foreign minister, belatedly took alarm at German suggestions that Danzig and the Corridor be returned to the Reich. But Beck, although he had far less wisdom than Czechoslovakia's Beneš, had more steel in him, and the Poles were not the Czechs. On March 26 Beck sent his answer to Hitler: he would not yield Danzig but he was prepared to negotiate. His resolution to resist Hitler's demands was certainly stiffened by the unilateral military guarantee that Chamberlain gave to Poland on March 29. France, which, of course, already had a defense treaty with Poland, agreed to associate itself with the British declaration.

Before Munich Chamberlain had refused to give any guarantee to Czechoslovakia because of the geographical position of that country. He had written, on March 20, 1938: "You have only to look at the map to see that nothing that France or we could do could possibly save Czechoslovakia from being overrun by the Germans, if they wanted to do it . . . I have, therefore, abandoned any idea of giving a guarantee to Czechoslovakia, or to the French in connection with her [sic] obligations to that country."

From the guarantee he gave to Poland almost exactly a year later, it might be supposed that this time Chamberlain had not looked at the map. The Poles were quite as inaccessible as the Czechs had been, and whereas Czechoslovakia had had a conditional promise of Soviet help, and would have welcomed it, the Poles had no such promise and would in any case have been quite unwilling to allow Russian soldiers on their soil. Czechoslovakia had possessed the Bohemian fortress line and a first-class, modern army. Nothing in Poland was defensible west of the line of the Vistula and the San, and although, on mobilization, the Poles could field an army of forty divisions, none of their formations was armored, and they lacked adequate numbers of antitank and antiaircraft guns. What was even worse was that the British guarantee to Poland was an unqualified assurance of support, with no proviso that Britain had a right to urge reason and conciliation on the Poles.

Yet it would have been a perfectly honorable course for Britain to have left the Poles to their fate, for the Polish government had sacrificed all right to sympathy by its predatory attitude toward Czechoslovakia in 1938, when Colonel Beck had acted as the accomplice of Hitler. France, it is true, had a defense treaty with Poland, but

France had already demonstrated at Munich that it was a nation that had no regard for its oath. Nor, in fact, could France do anything to protect the Poles unless the Soviet Union could be drawn in, and the Soviet Union, having been excluded from Munich, was now gravely suspicious of the west. "We nearly put our foot on a rotten plank," was the way one Russian diplomat put it. "Now we are going elsewhere."

Just as there had always been a school of thought in Germany that favored an alliance with Russia, so in Russia there were those who favored an alliance with Germany. Munich and the persistent French and British coolness to the Soviet Union strengthened the arguments of those Russians who wanted to come to terms with the Nazis. Many who would have preferred an alignment with the west now despaired. "My poor friend," a Soviet diplomat, Vladimir Potemkin, said to Robert Coulondre, the French ambassador, after Munich, "what have you done? For us I see no other way out but a fourth partition of Poland." This possibility scarcely occurred to the British, who believed that ideological differences made any rapprochement between communist Russia and Nazi Germany impossible. When, on Good Friday, April 7, Mussolini suddenly invaded Albania, Britain hastily extended guarantees to Greece and Rumania. The British government had a quite mistaken belief that by merely guaranteeing small nations it would deter possible aggressors, even when, as with Poland, Britain could not possibly intervene.

The Russians and Germans were already putting out tentative feelers to each other by April 1939. Stalin had not yet entirely given up on the west, however, and on April 16 the Soviet Union formally proposed that a new triple entente of Russia, Britain, and France be formed to resist German aggression. This offer was not acceptable to the British, who demanded that, before it was considered, Russia should give a unilateral guarantee to Poland. Consequently the talks with the Soviet Union bogged down. On the 28th Germany denounced its nonaggression pact with Poland, and Hitler repeated his demand that Danzig be returned to the Reich.

The pro-western Soviet foreign minister, Litvinov, a Jew who had married an Englishwoman, was dismissed on May 3 and replaced by the stony-faced Vyacheslav Molotov, a hard-line Communist who could be counted on to follow Stalin's lead without question or scruple. Hitler at once grasped the significance of Litvinov's dismissal. "It came to me," he said, "like a cannon shot as a sign of change in Moscow towards the western powers." The British and French, surprisingly, were less astute. They still could not bring themselves to believe that, after all Hitler's diatribes against communism, he could enter into an alliance with Stalin.

Finally, on May 27, Chamberlain agreed to send a diplomatic mission to Moscow to negotiate a mutual assistance pact. Instead of having the British mission headed by some statesman of authority — Eden had offered to go when Lord Halifax claimed he was too busy — Chamberlain selected an unknown Foreign Office official, William Strang. Not unnaturally, the Soviets took this as a calculated insult, as indeed it was. All through June the talks dragged on inconclusively, but on July 20 the British did agree to enter into military conversations with the Russians. To ensure that there was no unseemly haste over the staff talks, the British military mission, instead of flying to Moscow, was dispatched by slow cargo boat and took six days to arrive.

The French military mission was better qualified to conduct strategic conversations, but the French too were unwilling to meet the Russian demands on the vital point of aid to Poland, with or without the consent of the Polish government. The Soviet marshal, Kliment Voroshilov, who headed the Russian team, must have felt that his visitors had strayed in from Wonderland. While the talks dragged on, German armored formations massed on the Polish border, and there were still to be six weeks of excellent campaigning weather after the German harvest was in.

The Russians formed the impression that neither the British nor the French were resolute about going to war with Germany if Poland was attacked but rather that they hoped to avoid war by presenting Germany with a strong diplomatic deterrent in the form of a new triple entente. Whether such an alliance would have avoided war is problematical. What is certain is that the Soviet Union did not believe that it would. The Russians wanted a serious military convention to meet what they considered a likely eventuality, and had no desire to participate in a bluff that Hitler might very well call.

The Nazis were much more businesslike in their approach to the Russians. They had no scruples about the rights of small states and were quite prepared to promise Stalin a free hand with Finland and the Baltic nations. Stalin also realized that Hitler was becoming pressed for time. If he was to attack Poland in 1939, the invasion would have to begin early in September, so that operations could be completed before the weather broke. As long ago as April 3, in fact, Hitler had set the date for *Fall Weiss* ("Case White"), the invasion of Poland, instructing the German General Staff to be ready to begin the operation at any time after September 1. While the Russians were holding staff talks with the British and French, they were also holding secret political conversations with the Germans. On August 14 the German ambassador in Moscow, Count Friedrich von Schulenburg, told Molotov that Germany was ready to come to an agreement with

Russia on all outstanding questions, including "the Baltic sea, the Baltic states, Poland and southeastern questions."

On the evidence so far published — and it is evidence from British and French, not from Russian, sources — it seems clear that Stalin would have preferred a workable agreement with Britain and France to a pact with Hitler. Marshal Voroshilov tried time and again to get British and French agreement on basic questions, only to be met with evasions, half truths, and delays. Not until it became clear that the British at least were not negotiating seriously did the Soviet Union decide to accept the German offer. In this instance, talk about Soviet "duplicity" and "betrayal" is quite wide of the mark. The matter was one of life and death; the fate of millions hung on the outcome. But the British negotiators and their political masters appeared to have no concept of the gravity of the situation. The French at the last moment did attempt to bring pressure to bear on Colonel Beck to agree to the passage of Russian troops through Poland, but this was not done until the middle of August, and even then was not done wholeheartedly. On the 17th Marshal Voroshilov adjourned the staff talks, on the 19th Stalin told the Politburo that he would sign an agreement with Germany. The German foreign minister, Joachim von Ribbentrop, arrived in Moscow on the 23rd, and late that night the Nazi-Soviet Nonaggression Pact and its secret protocol were signed. The British government at once declared that it was still determined to fulfill its obligations to Poland.

By the Nazi-Soviet pact, Germany and Russia promised not to wage war against one another, either individually or jointly with other powers. The pact was to last for ten years and, unless renounced, was to be automatically renewed for another five years. In the secret protocol it was agreed that Poland would be partitioned between Germany and Russia, with a small rump state left to act as a buffer between them. Germany granted Russia a free hand in Latvia, Estonia, and Finland, and Russia recognized Lithuania as being in the German sphere of interest.

When Molotov and Ribbentrop put their signatures to the Nonaggression Pact, war became a certainty. The British government at once began to make emergency preparations, calling up reservists, warning merchant shipping, and manning coastal and antiaircraft defenses. In France Georges Bonnet, the foreign minister, attempted to have the government revoke its pact with Poland, but this proposal was rejected. The Maginot Line was fully manned, and without declaring general mobilization, the French army began to call up its reservists.

On August 22, assured of an agreement with Russia, Hitler advanced the date for the invasion of Poland to the 26th. The initial troop movements had already begun when suddenly, on the evening of the 25th, Hitler ordered a postponement. Britain and France had by now both declared their determination to fight, and on the afternoon of the 25th Mussolini had informed Hitler that Italy would not be ready to fight until 1942. Hitler growled that "the Italians are behaving just as they did in 1914!" but after brooding for a while he ordered a halt to the invasion of Poland. Probably he hoped for a repetition of Munich, but as it became clear that this time Britain and France could not force Poland to make concessions as they had forced Czechoslovakia to do the previous year, Hitler decided to go forward with his war. On August 31 he issued Directive No. 1 for the Conduct of the War, setting the time and date of the attack at 4:45 A.M. on September 1.

In the gray light of early morning on September 1, fifty-two German divisions in two army groups attacked Poland. The British government reluctantly declared war on Germany on September 3, and the French government, even more reluctantly, followed suit a few hours later.

Book Four

CHAPTER I

THE POLISH CAMPAIGN was the world's first example of the blitzkrieg, or "lightning war," a form of warfare that held the stage for only slightly more than two years but that, until Germany's enemies learned how to deal with it, enabled the Nazis to overrun not only Poland but also Norway, Holland, Belgium, France, Greece, Yugoslavia, and much of European Russia. The first trial of the new type of offensive took place under ideal conditions. The weather was fine, the Polish countryside relatively flat and open and therefore good tank country, the ground dry and firm. The Germans had additional aids in their considerable superiority of force and even greater technical superiority, in the configuration of the theater of operations, which greatly favored the attackers, and in the Polish dispositions, which were little short of suicidal.

The vanquished generally learn more from defeat than the victors learn from victory. Therefore it is not surprising that German soldiers should have come to understand the lessons of the First World War better than Allied soldiers did. The strategy, tactics, organization, and equipment that had been sufficient to defeat Germany in 1918 all appeared to have been justified by the outcome, for not even the waters of Lethe can wash away unpleasant memories as efficaciously as victory can. The French and British armies of 1939, and the armies of nations, like Poland, that had fallen under their influence, were, by and large, armies on the 1918 model; that is to say, they were composed basically of infantry divisions with the same kinds of weapons they had had at the end of the First World War.

Germany, on the other hand, had certain definite advantages, the more potent because they were disguised as liabilities. In the first place, the Germans, having lost, were naturally inclined to be more critical of the methods of 1918. All nations would disarm if only they could predict with certainty when the next war would occur. In this way they would not only save enormous sums otherwise spent on military equipment that rapidly becomes obsolescent, but would also be able to rearm with the most up-to-date weapons at exactly that time when they would be required for use. Obviousl·, ·he aggressor has a tremendous advantage in such a situation: he alone knows when war will come because it is he who selects the date.

Moreover, together with the physical rearmament of Germany went a spiritual rearmament that was far more impressive and frightening. Germany had emerged from the dark valley of humiliation and defeat; she was growing strong again, and the verdict of 1918 was about to be reversed. The morale of the Wehrmacht was superbly high in September 1939, and its ranks were filled with enthusiastic, confident young men in excellent physical condition.

Two main military strands can be identified in the theory of blitzkrieg, both with their roots in the First World War. When trench warfare set in on the western front, the chief problem facing both sides had been how to break the deadlock. Three methods were tried, but the two promising ones failed and the method that succeeded did so at a cost that made success almost indistinguishable from failure. The three methods were the employment of large tank forces to break the enemy front and restore a war of movement; the tactics of infiltration; and, finally, a policy of attrition by which a weaker enemy was forced to submit because he could no longer continue to trade lives even at a favorable ratio.

Tanks never achieved what had been hoped of them in the First World War, in part because they were employed prematurely, incorrectly, and on unsuitable terrain. Not until Cambrai, late in 1917, was there a fleeting glimpse of what this new weapon might accomplish, and even here the success had been short-lived. The tactics of infiltration also failed, though they came much closer to success than did the tanks. The reason for this was that the tactics of infiltration relied only on existing technology and were not dependent for success on new or undeveloped equipment.

After the war the victorious Allies largely ignored the possibilities of both the tank and of the tactics of infiltration. The French especially continued to put their faith in massive infantry armies that would hold lines or advance ponderously against them. True, some more farsighted military thinkers, especially in Britain, advocated new methods but they found little favor with the authorities. Captain Basil Henry Liddell Hart, Major General J. F. C. Fuller, and to a much lesser extent Colonel Charles De Gaulle in France argued for armored and mechanized armies, but they were little heeded or understood.

In Germany both of the failures of the First World War, the tank and the tactics of infiltration, received more attention. Blitzkrieg was the offspring of the marriage of these two concepts; infiltration would be carried out not by the infantry group moving at three miles per hour, but by the panzer division moving at thirty miles per hour. This is not to say that senior German officers welcomed without reservation the ideas of men like Heinz Guderian about the employment of armor. Had it not been for Hitler and for the whole climate of opinion brought in by the Nazi party, the Wehrmacht might have proved little more enlightened about the possibilities of armored warfare than the British and French.

The Nazis, however, as befitting men who considered themselves revolutionaries, were all for what was new, bold, and modern, and the idea of great tank forces caught their imagination. Armored and mechanized warfare had an immense attraction for them. The blitzkrieg fitted Nazi policies as a glove fits a hand. It seemed to promise exactly those results that Nazi Germany most needed if she were to resort to war — an advantage for the more highly industrialized state and for the more highly trained and technically competent army. Above all, blitzkrieg held out the prospect of a short and decisive war.

The Nazis added their own touches to the technique. They recognized no distinction between a state of peace and a state of war. Diplomacy, trade, subversion, and military operations were all instruments to be used as the occasion dictated, so once Hitler and the Nazis took up the idea of blitzkrieg they put their unmistakable stamp upon it. The military theory flourished naturally in the Nazi soil. Since the blitzkrieg was aimed at disorganizing and bewildering the enemy, open cities would be bombed, refugees would be machine-gunned from the air, fifth columns would divide and weaken the opposition, propaganda would undermine the will to resist, and terror would follow in the wake of military occupation.

The blitzkrieg had more of a psychological purpose than a physical one. This was both its greatest strength and its greatest weakness. It led to great initial success against the hidebound, the unwary, or the demoralized, but it led as well to some military imbalance. Although the new style of warfare was spectacularly successful for a time, there was always something a little gimcrack and fraudulent about it, something militarily unsound, which could succeed only by bluff and braggadocio. To use an analogy from chess, the proponents of the blitzkrieg played the man rather than the board. But though the actual errors of one's opponents may well justify otherwise unjustifiable risks and vindicate extreme boldness in execution, a military philosophy that is dependent on the errors of the adversary is potentially dangerous. It leads to overconfidence, rashness, the taking of unwarranted gambles, and, in the end, to defeat. This indeed was the future course of the blitzkrieg and of Nazi Germany. Only if it had been otherwise would it have been surprising, because an army and a military doctrine must of necessity be organic with the society from which they emerge, flesh of its flesh and bone of its bone.

At all events, in September 1939 the blitzkrieg worked even better than Hitler had hoped. The German plan took full advantage of the favorable strategic situation that had obtained since the breakup of Czechoslovakia. Western Poland was now surrounded on three sides by German-held territory — East Prussia on the north, Pomerania and Silesia on the west, and Moravia and Slovakia on the south. Poland thus presented a huge salient jutting out into German territory, like a man with his head and shoulders wedged between the jaws of some beast of prey. The simile of the head between the jaws is doubly appropriate since in this salient was situated almost all of Poland's industrial resources.

The German armies were concentrated on the two wings, north and south; much of the center was left almost empty of troops except for light covering forces. In overall command of the operation was General Brauchitsch, with two army groups under him. Army Group North, commanded by Colonel General Fedor von Bock, consisted of two armies, which between them had some twenty-one divisions, including two armored and two light divisions grouped together as a corps under General Guderian. Army Group South, commanded by Colonel General Gerd von Rundstedt, was the heavier formation, with three armies of thirty-six divisions, including four panzer and two light divisions.

The German plan called for two simultaneous encirclements. The outer one would consist of two converging arms, driving south by way of Bialystok and Brest-Litovsk and north by Lwow and the line of the Bug River to cut off all western Poland far to the east of Warsaw. The inner encirclement was intended to surround and destroy all Polish forces deployed in the Vistula Bend. Of course, the knowledge that Soviet troops would invade from the east at the appropriate moment greatly simplified the German problem.

The Poles faced this formidable array with lighthearted but ill-founded confidence. The Polish army could muster more than forty divisions, but its equipment was out of date, the Polish air force had no aircraft that could match the German, and, worst of all, the Polish high command was imbued with outmoded military doctrines and had an altogether misplaced trust in the promise of its French ally that France would — in fact and not merely in legal form — fight the war at Poland's side.

Marshal Edward Smigly-Rydz, the Polish commander-in-chief, had the word of General Maurice Gamelin that France would launch a major offensive against the Germans no later than the sixteenth day of mobilization. Along all the French frontier Germany could muster only eleven regular divisions, one division of second-line fortress troops, and thirty-six newly raised divisions, whose training and equipment were incomplete. Germany left no armored or motorized formations facing the French. On the other hand, France had 108 divisions, including an armored division, and Britain would soon have four excellent divisions in France, with the certain promise of many more to come.

After France had completed a leisurely mobilization and concentration, Gamelin pushed forward a few parties of skirmishers to the outposts of the Siegfried Line. Once there, the French commander-in-chief had said, he intended to "lean against" the German defenses to test them. If the leaning process took place, the German defenders failed to detect it, and by the end of September Gamelin had withdrawn his troops to their original positions.

Gamelin later defended himself against charges of bad faith by claiming that he made it clear to the Polish minister of war, M. Kasprzyski, that his promise to launch an offensive with "*les gros de ses forces*" ("the main body of his forces") on the sixteenth day after mobilization was not the same thing as launching an offensive with "*le gros de ses forces*" ("the main bulk of his forces"). How much honor resides in that *s*!

Smigly-Rydz had had the right to expect more, even without Gamelin's promise. He had made his own plans contingent on a French effort in the west because he had decided to defend the whole of Poland's long perimeter for as long a time as possible, making a gradual fighting withdrawal to a last bastion behind the river lines of the Niemen, the Bohr, the Narew, the Vistula, and the San. Here he would have only some 375 miles of front to defend instead of the 1125 miles of border. A general reserve was retained around Warsaw, but because of the length of the frontier this strategic reserve was weak. Polish troops were also deployed on the border with the Soviet Union.

Although the whole world knew that Poland was about to be attacked, the form and weight of the attack came as a surprise to the Poles. They had envisaged a form of warfare like that of 1914–1918, with cautious advances to contact, encounter battles, and advance guards falling back in good order on their main bodies. Instead, they were assailed by a rain of blows swifter and heavier than they had believed possible.

Two of Germany's three air fleets were deployed against Poland. Before zero hour for the ground assault they struck at Polish airfields, railway junctions, mobilization centers, and bridges. Much of the Polish air force was destroyed on the ground and that portion of it that survived was unable to do much against the overwhelmingly superior Luftwaffe. The Germans gained aerial supremacy within the first sixteen hours and were henceforth able to concentrate on helping the army forward. German paratroops were dropped to spread confusion, and the roads of western Poland became clogged with fleeing refugees. The two million Polish citizens who were Germans provided a fifth column that distracted the Poles and kept the Wehrmacht fully informed of Polish moves and dispositions.

The main reason for the Germans' success, however, was the soundness of the strategic plan and the employment of their armor. The Polish soldiers fought with their usual fanatical courage, and most German accounts give them full credit for it. The Poles died, or retreated in the hope of fighting again, or — more often than not — were simply by-passed by the speeding German tanks and motorized infantry. Within a week it was apparent that all Polish efforts to coordinate a defense had broken down. By September 7 Rundstedt's Army Group South had captured Cracow and was sweeping up to trap the Polish forces in the Vistula Bend. Meanwhile Army Group North had driven down the right bank of the Vistula and east between that river and the Warta to effect a junction of its two armies. The outskirts of Warsaw were reached the next day — a distance of 150 miles covered in just over a week and against opposition.

Although the original German plan had called for two encirclements, the Polish campaign was marked by three — or by four, if the investment of Warsaw is included. The third encirclement was brought about on the spur of the moment because of an opportunity presented by the Poles. On September 10 the Polish forces between Thorn and Lodz launched a heavy counterattack to the south, but the Germans held on the Bzura River and moved corps in from the north, south, and west. The Poles fought desperately inside the trap that had closed so quickly around them, but by the 18th all resistance had come to an end. In this Battle of the Bzura the Polish army lost the better part of nineteen infantry divisions and three cavalry brigades. The Germans captured 170,000 prisoners and much equipment.

Meanwhile, Lemberg, Lwow, Przemysl, and Brest-Litovsk had fallen, and Guderian's tanks had contact with Army Group South on the Bug River. The great strategic encirclement was now completed. On the 17th the final coup de grâce was given to whatever Polish resistance remained, for the Soviet Union, again without any declaration of war, invaded eastern Poland with twenty divisions. The Polish government fled to Rumania, and the Russians, advancing without opposition, entered Vilna on the 18th. Germany immediately began shifting divisions back to the French frontier.

As soon as Russian troops entered Poland, Hitler became desperately anxious to get the war finished as soon as possible. Rather than become involved in expensive house-to-house fighting in Warsaw, the Germans surrounded the city and subjected it to a terrible bombardment from artillery and air attack. The Polish position was hopeless, and on the 25th Warsaw surrendered.

Although Ribbentrop and Molotov had originally agreed to the existence of a small rump Poland, the German and Soviet foreign ministers met again on September 20 to revise their previous pact. This time Poland disappeared completely. The Soviet Union received a more generous reward than Germany, getting 77,000 square miles of Polish territory to Germany's 73,000 square miles. German forces withdrew from their advanced positions, followed up by the Russians.

To all intents the Polish campaign had ended on September 17 after only seventeen days of fighting. Polish casualties could not be calculated exactly, but the Germans had captured 694,000 Polish soldiers, and the number of dead and wounded must have been very high, to say nothing of heavy civilian casualties. German losses had been unexpectedly light — 10,572 killed, 5029 missing, and 30,322 wounded. The Poles were to suffer more under the joint occupation of their country than in the brief and disastrous war. Both the Nazis and the Communists began almost at once to murder those elements of the Polish population that, for ideological reasons, they considered unfit to live.

On September 28 Germany and the Soviet Union both declared that there was now no reason why the war should continue. At the end of the month the Soviet Union suddenly demanded that Latvia, Lithuania, and Estonia permit Russian military forces and bases to be established on their territories. Having no means to resist, the governments of the Baltic states agreed under protest to the Soviet ultimatum. Stalin next demanded that Finland hand over territory on the Kola peninsula, grant the Soviet Union a naval base on the Gulf of Finland, and give up land on the Karelian Isthmus north of Leningrad. When the Finns refused, nothing drastic happened for the moment.

Meanwhile, in a speech on October 6 to the Reichstag, Hitler made a definite offer of peace. The Polish question, of course, was closed. Poland would not rise again. Nevertheless, the Führer felt that he owed it to his "conscience" to make an appeal to reason. He had no demands whatsoever to make on France, and although he wanted the restoration by Britain of Germany's former colonies, this could be negotiated. He held out the prospect of general European disarmament, just as he had done after all his previous aggressions.

Since not even the Chamberlain government could accept the political obliteration of an ally, Britain rejected Hitler's offer. This did not mean that Chamberlain was considering fighting the war he had declared. For one thing, he did not believe it possible to defeat Germany. "What I hope for is not a military victory — I very much doubt the feasibility of that — but a collapse of the German home front," he wrote.

Thus the ambiguity that had marked British policy in the years of appeasement was carried over into the years of war. The British government would not make peace, but neither would it fight an outright war. Since the French were only too ready to go along with this shuffling, the result was the Phony War. The British cabinet authorized modest naval increases, decided to raise fifty-five divisions within two years (though it was soon discovered that it would be quite impossible to equip anything like that number), and added eighteen new fighter squadrons to the Royal Air Force. The British Commonwealth Air Training Plan was negotiated with Canada in December. Financial considerations were still carefully taken into account when deciding on military requirements, partly because the British government was still economy-minded and partly because the Chiefs of Staff had advised that at this stage of the war the economic sphere was the only one in which the Allies could take the offensive. This could be done, they believed, by naval blockade and by diplomatic and financial pressure. Later, when the RAF had built up its bomber strength and the problem of German retaliation had been solved, strategic bombing might be added as a weapon against the German economy.

On the outbreak of war the Royal Navy at once imposed a distant blockade on the German coast. This, of course, was far less effective than it had been in 1914, when Russia had been aligned against Germany. Still — or so British economists thought — there was the likelihood that the Nazis would eventually experience a shortage of many raw materials. Germany was especially dependent on Swedish iron ore and oil from Rumania and Poland. However, an attempt by the British secret service to set the Rumanian oil fields on fire failed, and both Sweden and Russia continued to trade with Nazi Germany.

Naval blockade was a game two could play. The Royal Navy was able to clear the seas of enemy merchant shipping, but the Germans struck back with U-boat attacks and by sowing a new type of magnetic mine in British shipping lanes. But Hitler never realized the full potentialities of the submarine and had neglected the U-boats. For the first six months of the war German sinkings of British merchantmen averaged only about 100,000 tons a month — not a light loss, but far from a crippling one. Hitler was probably influenced by his desire not to repeat the mistake of 1917; that is, to bring the United States into the war by indiscriminate U-boat attacks. If so, it was a misreading of history; the American Neutrality Acts were to do his work for him. Congress, as anxious as Hitler that the United States should not fight, forbade American ships to enter war zones and prohibited the shipment of military supplies or the extension of credit to any belligerent. At President Roosevelt's request, the embargo on the sale of arms was repealed at the end of October, but American ships were still barred from war zones and belligerents still had to pay cash for any military purchases from firms in the United States. This neutrality legislation, of course, injured the Allies, who controlled the seas, far more than it did the Nazis. The Germans could not have got American supplies in any case. During the first six months of the war, the German navy lost eighteen U-boats, about a third of its total submarine strength, and only eleven replacements joined the fleet. Nevertheless, the traditional British naval strategy of blockade, which had eventually proved effective in the First World War, was not working in the Second, and Britain, had Hitler only realized it, was in far more danger of being strangled than Germany was.

On October 14 Lieutenant Günther Prien, commanding the U-47, made his way boldly into Scapa Flow and sank the *Royal Oak* with his torpedoes, but the British evened the score on December 13, when three British cruisers, the *Ajax*, *Exeter*, and *Achilles*, engaged the *Graf Spee* off the Plate River and forced the German ship into Montevideo harbor, where she was scuttled.

The British government did not put all its faith in economic warfare; it also hoped to bring about the overthrow of the Nazi regime by psychological means. To this end, from the very first night of the war, the RAF flew regularly over Germany, carrying not bombs but propaganda leaflets. A sharp little anecdote went around service circles in Britain about the lazy RAF bombardier who was court-martialed because he had dumped his leaflets out of the aircraft without undoing the bundles. He might have hurt someone.

Daladier's government in France appeared no more capable of waging resolute war than Chamberlain's government in Britain. With self-deluding optimism both governments hoped that Italy would, at the worst, remain neutral and that Mussolini might even be persuaded to join the Allies. Casting about for some policy that would not necessitate fighting in the west, the French revived the First World War plan of sending an expeditionary force to Salonika, but the

British had enough sense to veto this suggestion. In France itself things were far from good. The French mood might perhaps be best described as one of uneasy complacency — and if that is a paradox, so was the French mood. The French army, which should have been training for war, was all too often employed as a labor force. The French fortifications, built at enormous cost in the past few years, covered the Franco-German border, but — incredibly — stopped at Montmédy. Old Marshal Pétain, when he had been minister of war, had believed that there would be no need to extend the Maginot Line to the Channel because by a few demolitions the Ardennes could be made impassable and because the northern frontier could best be defended by the French army's going into Belgium. Now, during the Phony War, French and British troops were constructing field defenses west of Montmédy, but this task was not always pushed energetically, the more so because the army knew that if the Germans invaded Belgium the field defenses would be abandoned by an Anglo-French advance.

The French army's morale should have been cause for serious concern. Ever since the signing of the Nazi-Soviet Nonaggression Pact of August 1939 the French Communist party, which had formerly been vociferously anti-Nazi, had dissociated itself from the "imperialist" war and had done its not inconsiderable best to sabotage the French war effort. In November, when Lieutenant General Sir Alan Brooke, the commander of the British II Corps, attended a ceremonial parade at General Corap's Ninth Army, he noticed to his dismay that the French soldiers were unshaven and dirty and that their uniforms and equipment were slovenly and uncared for. Worse still, most of them had sullen, "insubordinate" expressions on their faces and few of them bothered to obey the "eyes left" when they slouched past. The sedentary life in the Maginot Line, the digging of field fortifications, communist propaganda, and the lack of fighting all ate away at the spirit of the French army. By Christmas, after four months of war, total French casualties for all three services amounted to only 1433. The British Expeditionary Force did not suffer its first casualty until December 9, but for some reason British morale had not eroded.

The next outbreak of fighting, when it came, occurred not in the west but far to the north. On November 26 the Soviet Union suddenly accused the Finns of shelling a Russian village with artillery. The Finns, who were able to prove conclusively that none of their artillery could possibly have shelled the village in question, offered to submit the Russian complaint to a commission of arbitration. Stalin did not wait for the Finnish answer. Claiming that his tiny neighbor was attacking Russia "not only on the Karelian Isthmus but also elsewhere," he launched a full-scale invasion on the 29th. Russian troops first crossed the Finnish border near Petsamo in the Arctic circle, and the next day, after Helsinki and other Finnish cities were bombed, the main invasions began. Soviet forces totaling some twenty-nine divisions advanced from Leningrad up the Karelian Isthmus, in the vicinity of Lake Ladoga, and at two points across the waist of Finland by way of Salla and Suomussalmi.

The Soviet attack came as a complete surprise, in part because the Soviet Union still had a nonaggression pact with Finland. The outcome could scarcely be in doubt; the Soviet Union, a country of some 180 million people, was attacking a nation of only 3.5 million. To oppose the invaders the Finns had only nine divisions, 56 tanks to the 2000 tanks the Russians employed, and 145 aircraft to the Russian 2500. Stalin did not anticipate serious resistance. He believed that the bombing of Finnish cities would break the Finns' will to fight and that the Finnish workers would rise against their government and welcome the communist invaders.

Nothing of the sort occurred. The six Soviet divisions that attacked up the Karelian Isthmus ran into the defenses of the Mannerheim Line, which stretched across the isthmus from the Gulf of Finland to Lake Ladoga. This Soviet attack broke down in confusion, with heavy losses. The frontal attack by Lake Ladoga met the same fate. The Soviet drives farther north across the waist of Finland were at first almost unopposed. The more northerly attack advanced past Salla halfway to the Gulf of Bothnia, and the more southerly attack gained ground past Suomussalmi. Early in January, however, the Finns decided that the Russians had sufficiently lengthened their lines of communication, and launched counterattacks that virtually destroyed the invading columns.

The weather in this Winter War was appalling, with heavy snowfalls and temperatures far below zero. The Russian army had invaded with tanks and truck-borne infantry, and could not move off the roads, which were generally little more than narrow forest tracks. Finnish ski troops, almost invisible in their white uniforms, could move at will through the forests that flanked the roads. The Finns would knock out the first and the last vehicles of a Russian column, effectively immobilizing it, and would then destroy the Russian field kitchens. Often this was all that was required. The Russian soldiers, stranded on the road, then froze or starved to death by the thousands. Soviet attempts to supply isolated columns by air were rarely successful, for the Finns quickly learned the Russian recognition signals and set them out themselves, with the result that most of the air-dropped supplies fell into Finnish hands.

The world watched this unequal struggle with awe and admiration — and also with remarkable detachment. Public opinion in Britain, France, the United States, and even in Germany was strongly pro-Finnish, but none of these nations made any effective efforts to aid the Finns. The French and British governments, indeed, seriously considered sending an expeditionary force to Scandinavia, not to succor Finland, though this would have been the ostensible purpose, but to capture the Swedish iron-ore mines at Gällivare, which were supplying the German war machine with almost all its steel. This plan was so long debated that the Winter War was over before it could be implemented. This was as well, since the British and French, who were shortly to prove themselves no match for the Germans, could, even with the help of the heroic Finns, scarcely have won much success against the Germans and Russians combined.

The Finns by themselves, however, could not hope to hold out much longer. The Red Army massed fourteen fresh divisions against the Mannerheim Line, making their total force there some twenty-seven divisions. The Finns had only six understrength divisions in defense. On February 2, after a devastating artillery bombardment, the Russians launched an all-out assault along a ten-mile stretch of front around Summa. Even now the Finns continued to resist stubbornly for another ten days, but the odds were impossible. On February 13 the Russians broke through the Mannerheim Line. Simultaneously another Russian attack was launched across the ice of the Gulf of Finland against Viipuri. Here, too, the Finns fought desperately, but on March 8 their government opened negotiations with the Soviet Union and signed a harsh peace treaty four days later.

The poor Russian showing in the Winter War had a double effect. In the first place it led to some belated army reforms in the Soviet Union, and, second, it convinced Hitler that the Soviet Union would be an easy victim. Hitler would eventually have attacked Russia in any case, because this was the whole point and aim of his foreign policy. Nevertheless, if the Red Army had proved more effective in Finland, Hitler might have delayed his attack until he had first disposed of Britain, and he might have been less rashly optimistic about being able to conclude his Russian campaign in ten weeks.

At the end of September Hitler had directed OKH, the Army High Command, to prepare for the campaign in the west, but the generals managed to have the offensive postponed time after time. Meanwhile the attention of both the Germans and the Allies had turned to Scandinavia. To maintain her war effort Germany needed at least nine million tons of iron ore each year, and the neutral Swedes supplied it enthusiastically. The British cabinet believed that if Swedish iron ore could be denied to Germany, the Nazis would be faced with a major production crisis that would appreciably shorten the war. In February the British destroyer *Cossack* violated Norwegian neutrality to capture the German prison ship *Altmark* in Jössing Fjord, and released 299 British prisoners. And late in March the new French government of Paul Reynaud, who had replaced Daladier, began to press for a more vigorous prosectuion of the war. Chamberlain was much annoyed by this pressure but Churchill found strong support for his proposal to cut off the Swedish ore traffic.* The British cabinet, however, remained disinclined to make an opposed landing at Narvik, the more so since the closing of Narvik alone would do no more than embarrass the German economy. Little serious thought seems to have been given to the military problems of an invasion of Sweden although nothing short of this would really have strangled the German economy. The British government decided instead on a half measure, the laying of mines in the Inner Leads. These mines were sown on April 8, and a small British expeditionary force of eight battalions — on a reduced scale of equipment and with few supporting arms — was embarked at Rosyth and the Clyde in readiness to respond to any German reaction.

While the eight British battalions were filing aboard their ships, a German force of fifty-one battalions was also preparing to invade Norway. Hitler had issued his formal directive for *Fall Weserübung*, the invasion of Norway, on March 1, and preliminary staff studies had begun about the middle of December 1939. When the German invasion force sailed for Norway it had at its call one thousand aircraft and strong naval forces, including the cruisers *Hipper, Blücher*, and *Emden*, and the pocket battleships *Lützow,*† *Scharnhorst*, and *Gneisenau*. The German plan called for the simultaneous invasion of Denmark with two infantry divisions and some attached troops.

As the German ships sailed up the Norwegian coast under the watery light of a new moon, the British destroyer *Glowworm* sighted the *Hipper* and on the morning of April 8 rammed her. The *Glowworm* herself went down but the *Hipper* was badly damaged. In a running fight between the outgunned *Renown* and the *Scharnhorst* and *Gneisenau*, the *Gneisenau* suffered hits.

On the morning of Tuesday, April 9, the German landings began. Copenhagen was occupied almost without fighting. The Norwegians reacted differently. At Oslo the German *coup de main* met determined resistance, despite the fact that Norwegian traitors under the Norwe-

---

*Reynaud also advocated cutting off Germany's supplies of Caucasian oil, even if this meant war with the Soviet Union.

†Formerly the *Deutschland*.

gian Nazi leader Vidkun Quisling actively spread false information. Although the Norwegian government had received several warnings of the attack, the army was not mobilized. The navy and coast defenses were alerted on the night of the 8th, however, and as the *Blücher* attempted to lead the German ships into Oslo harbor the next morning she was hit twice by the ancient guns of Oskarsborg Fort and driven aground. She blew up with the loss of one thousand German lives, including the Gestapo agents who had been sent to arrest the king and his ministers. The *Lützow*, which was also hit, and the *Emden* withdrew, and landed their troops on the eastern side of Oslo Fjord. The seaborne attack had thus failed ignominiously, but after some initial difficulties the paratroops who were dropped and air-lifted into Fornebu airfield captured Oslo. Meanwhile, King Haakon and his cabinet had escaped to Hamar, seventy miles inland, where they called on Norwegians to resist.

Elsewhere the invaders had an easier time of it. Only nominal resistance was met at Kristiansand. At Sola airfield near Stavanger almost no attempt was made to resist the German paratroop landings, and the defending battalion withdrew in good order to a safer position in the hinterland. At Bergen, though the defenses had been alerted well ahead of time, only ineffectual opposition was met. Some Norwegian torpedo boats failed to press home their attack against the German invasion fleet, and the shore batteries were very late in opening fire, perhaps because of a civilized reluctance to be the first to shoot in anger. When they finally did fire, some guns, poorly maintained, jammed almost immediately. Nazi infantry landed unopposed and soon occupied the batteries. That evening a German transport struck a mine off Bergen and sank with heavy loss of life, but this was almost the only defensive success of the day north of the capital. At Trondheim the forts opened fire but hit nothing and the city was occupied without difficulty, though many young Norwegians, determined to go on fighting, escaped to the countryside. At Narvik, the Norwegian commander, Colonel Konrad Sundlo, though he had been given clear and unequivocal orders to fight, first parleyed with the enemy and then tamely surrendered the town.* Some of his troops, more spirited, refused to accept the order to surrender and escaped into the mountains.

Thus by nightfall on April 9, between first and last light of a single momentous day, every point of strategic importance had fallen into German hands. It had been a remarkable feat of arms, even if it was marred by the treachery of the attack.

*After the war Sundlo was tried for collaborating with the Nazis, cashiered, and sentenced to life imprisonment with hard labor.

The Norwegian defense had certainly been far less effective than it might, or should, have been. Treason by the followers of Quisling had not played so important a role as was at one time believed, but, then, it is a common reaction to excuse failure by the cry of betrayal. Rather it was hesitation and lack of preparation that were the main Norwegian weaknesses on April 9. The hesitation may have been caused by a shocked disbelief that the invasion was actually happening and from a natural repugnance at the prospect of shedding blood. Perhaps the Norwegians had been neutral too long to understand the world in which they and the Nazis lived. The lack of preparation may also have sprung from this same basic fault, though there was surely some serious culpability on the part of those who allowed guns to jam, battalions to retire without fighting, and torpedo boats to fail to attack. The Norwegians were to pull themselves together and under the leadership of General Otto Ruge (who, incidentally, was appointed commander-in-chief only after the invasion had occurred) were to give a good account of themselves.

Their later resistance, however, was to be in vain, for the time to have met and defeated the attack was when the invaders were at their most vulnerable, at the moment of landing or while they were still at sea. The truth was that the Norwegians had thought themselves safe. For too long they had shut the door and sat by the fire. They had deluded themselves into believing that the Nazis, because they lacked naval control of the North Sea, would not dare to invade and that the Allies would be too honorable to violate their neutrality. They neglected to defend themselves in time, and paid the penalty. All the Norwegians could hope for now was that they might be able to contain the Nazis in the south while they held out in the north until British and French troops arrived to counterattack.

Since the beginning of April, British intelligence had received numerous converging reports of the coming invasion of Norway. On the 7th a special air search discovered two of the German naval groups on their way north. The RAF bombed these forces without effect. On the evening of the 7th, the Home Fleet sailed from Scapa Flow to intercept the German ships, and the 2nd Crusier Squadron left Rosyth on the same mission.

That same evening the First Sea Lord, Admiral Sir Dudley Pound, set the tone for the British conduct of the Norwegian campaign. At Rosyth, aboard four cruisers, were the battalions earmarked for the purpose of countering a German invasion of Norway. When the First Sea Lord heard that sizable German naval forces were at sea he could think of nothing but intercepting them before they returned home. Therefore, on his own authority, Sir Dudley Pound ordered that the soldiers be cleared off his cruisers so that they could put to sea. The troops were hurriedly bundled ashore and their arms and equipment thrown after them, to lie in jumbled heaps on the quays. The plan for a combined operation in Norway had not been well thought out in the first place, but it was remarkable that the First Sea Lord, in the flush of excitement, should scrap it in this manner.

In spite of the warnings they had received, the British were surprised by Hitler's move. Nevertheless, the British war cabinet was, on the whole, optimistic, believing that the Germans had made a serious error and that they could be thrown out of Norway "in a week or two." The Supreme War Council met late on the afternoon of the 9th, with Reynaud, Daladier, and Admiral François Darlan attending for France. The French proposed that the Allies move into Belgium and occupy it, if the Belgian government could be made to agree. This was about as unlikely an eventuality as would have been possible to imagine. The Supreme War Council, although unable to agree on this suggestion, did decide that the dispatch of troops to Norway be postponed until the Royal Navy had had a chance to show what it could do. Reynaud urged that the principle objective of the Allies, when they landed in Norway, should be Narvik; its capture would cut off one Swedish ore route and it could be a staging area for an Allied advance to Gällivare. That evening the British Chiefs of Staff definitely selected Narvik as the first objective, and the cabinet agreed.

On the afternoon of the 9th the British Home Fleet, speeding for the Norwegian coast with no aircraft cover, came under German air attack. One destroyer, the *Gurkha*, was sunk, and the *Rodney* was hit. This convinced the British admiral that the Home Fleet could not operate safely in southern Norwegian waters. Projected naval attacks against Bergen and Trondheim were therefore canceled and the fleet turned north. On the 9th the Home Fleet proved unable either to bring major units of the German navy to action or to prevent the German landings in Norway. However, on the evening of the 9th the cruiser *Karlsruhe* was sunk by a British submarine; on the 10th, Fleet Air Arm Skuas sank the damaged cruiser *Königsberg* at Bergen; and on the 11th the *Lützow* was badly damaged by a British submarine. Four German troop transports were also sunk, with considerable loss of life.

The Royal Navy showed to better effect at Narvik. In the early morning hours of the 10th, in a driving snowstorm that severely limited visibility, five destroyers sailed into Ofoten Fjord to attack the ten much larger German destroyers there. The British sank two of the enemy, seriously damaged two more, and sank an ammunition ship and six merchantmen, for a British loss of two destroyers with a third seriously damaged. At a little past midday on the 13th the British

battleship *Warspite* and nine accompanying destroyers sailed into Ofoten Fjord and destroyed the remaining enemy without losing a ship.
However, about twenty-six hundred German sailors escaped ashore
to reinforce the two thousand troops who were holding the town.

Hitler was shaken by the results of the naval action at Narvik. For
days he presented a picture of "brooding gloom," which did nothing
to inspire confidence in senior German officers. At one point he declared that unless success came quickly in Norway he would call off
the campaign and immediately launch *Fall Gelb*, the invasion of
France. But before Hitler found it necessary to make so grave a decision Allied errors had retrieved the situation for him.

The First Lord of the Admiralty, Winston Churchill, was easily enthusiastic about seaborne military expeditions, as Gallipoli had demonstrated. Perhaps more than any other member of the cabinet,
Churchill was responsible for the action taken in Norway and for its
failure — which is ironic, considering the political outcome of the
fiasco. The War Office now hurriedly assembled two brigades on the
Clyde for the recapture of Narvik, but on the 11th it was decided that,
instead of risking a frontal attack from the sea, an initial landing
would be made at Harstad, a tiny port more than sixty miles north of
Narvik, and that the force would be reorganized there.

The Admiralty appointed Admiral of the Fleet the Earl of Cork and
Orrery to command the naval expedition, and the War Office selected
Major General P. J. Mackesy to command the military expedition.
These two officers had never met each other, were briefed separately,
and were given conflicting instructions. They sailed on different ships
on the 12th with different concepts of the tasks that lay before them.
When they did meet, in Norway, it soon became apparent that they
were not personally compatible, and friction soon developed. Even
old friends, however, might have been brought to the point of quar-
reling under such circumstances.

In London, meanwhile, the military coordinating committee, composed of the service ministers and Chiefs of Staff with the prime
minister in the chair, was already beginning to vacillate between Narvik and Trondheim as the objective. At about this time, too, the
Norwegian commander-in-chief, General Ruge, from his headquarters at Lillehammer began urging the British to take Trondheim. The
military coordinating committee had already agreed to make small diversionary landings at Namsos and Aalesund, 80 miles north-
northeast and 150 miles southwest of Trondheim respectively, and on
the 13th the cabinet decided to recapture both Narvik and Trondheim. On the 14th, it was decided that the 146th Brigade, then at sea,
bound for Narvik, should be diverted to Trondheim.

Before the landing the plan was changed again. Because the air staff warned against sending large ships into Trondheim Fjord without air cover, a direct attack on Trondheim was abandoned for a double pincer movement that would proceed overland from Namsos and Andalsnes, the latter being a little closer to Trondheim than Aalesund. These two attacking forces would have to move over winding secondary roads through a countryside that was still covered in deep snow. The units had no transport or supporting arms; the soldiers were not trained skiers nor did they have skis. The 146th Brigade arrived at Namsos on the 16th and 17th, but its commander and about 100 tons of its stores were taken on to Narvik in another ship. The War Office now appointed Major General A. Carton de Wiart, VC, to command at Namsos and flew him out (but without any staff) on the 15th. Three battalions of French *Chasseurs Alpins* disembarked on the 22nd.

Carton de Wiart was far too experienced a soldier to share the optimistic views held in London. Namsos was destroyed by a Luftwaffe bombing attack and was, in any case, completely inadequate as a port. On the 21st the German navy, finding the ice melted in Trondheim Fjord, landed troops on the British flank, forcing a retirement. Carton de Wiart's force was evacuated by sea between May 1 and 3, having suffered 157 casualties. The Germans now continued their advance north to relieve Narvik.

The German commander in Norway, General Nikolaus von Falkenhorst, had begun his advance north from Oslo on the 12th, moving by the main Trondheim road in the Gudbrandsdal and up the parallel valley to the east, the Osterdal. The Germans made easy progress, driving many Norwegians over the border into internment in Sweden. By the 20th in the Gudbrandsdal they had reached a point just south of Lillehammer.

The British brigade destined for Andalsnes, "Sickleforce," under Brigadier H. de R. Morgan, landed on the 18th. They had with them only a few out-of-date tourist maps of Norway, no transport, and no supporting weapons. Morgan's instructions told him both to advance north toward Trondheim and to assist the Norwegian forces to the south. On the 19th Morgan met General Ruge, who expressed great disappointment at the small size of the British contingent and demanded that the British and French place themselves under his orders as Norwegian commander-in-chief. This was a high ground to take, especially on the part of a man without previous experience in war who ten days previously had been only a colonel. Ruge claimed that his Norwegians were exhausted, all but beaten, and in desperate need of relief, but he still believed that he could check the German advance south of Lillehammer. And he insisted that Sickleforce move south to aid in this operation rather than north against Trondheim. Brigadier Morgan agreed to this, consented to split his command in two, one portion on either side of Lake Mjösa, and to place each portion under Norwegian command.

The Germans were held neither by the British and Norwegians in the Gudbrandsdal nor by the Norwegians in the Osterdal. Between April 21 and 23 the separated portions of the British brigade were overrun by German infantry supported by tanks and aircraft. Since German and Norwegian uniforms were almost identical, the British were more than once shot down by German ski troops whom they had mistaken for Norwegians. Nor did it improve British morale to discover that their only antitank weapon, the Boys rifle, had absolutely no effect on the German tanks. All that was left of the brigade, 9 officers and 300 men, attempted to escape across country through the deep snow, but most of them were eventually taken prisoner.

While one brigade was being eliminated in the Gudbrandsdal, another British brigade was recalled from France and sent to the Andalsnes area, where it disembarked on the 23rd. Two days later it met the enemy south of the town of Otta, but after a series of hopeless rearguard actions these troops were evacuated on May 1 and 2.

At Narvik — or, to speak more accurately, at Harstad — Lord Cork and General Mackesy were still at loggerheads. The navy bombarded Narvik without noticeable effect, and on the 28th a demibrigade of *Chasseurs Alpins* arrived, to be followed early in May by two more French battalions and four Polish battalions. The French, Poles, and Norwegians at last accomplished what Mackesy had been too timid to attempt. Narvik fell on the 28th but the German garrison escaped to the mountains beyond the town. This final position was about to be assaulted on June 8 when orders came for all British and French troops to get out of Norway. France was crumbling into collapse and the Norwegian campaign had ceased to have any significance. King Haakon and his ministers sailed for England on June 7. General Ruge declined to accompany them, preferring to surrender with the remnants of his army on the 9th.

The evacuation went smoothly until the ships were all at sea; then the convoy came under heavy attack. On the morning of the 8th three British ships were sunk by a German naval force, and that afternoon the *Gneisenau* and *Scharnhorst* sank the aircraft carrier *Glorious* and her two accompanying destroyers. The *Scharnhorst* was damaged in the action. On the 23rd the British submarine *Clyde* torpedoed the *Gneisenau* but did not sink her. And here the Norwegian campaign came to a close.

In Norway, from first to last, the British had deployed about one and a half divisions; the French had sent eight battalions; the Poles, four. These Allied forces, together with the Norwegians, had faced about seven divisions of German troops. German losses in the campaign were 5660; British casualties amounted to 1869; Norwegian, 1334; French and Polish, 533. The Luftwaffe lost about 200 aircraft; the British, 112. More significant were the German naval losses. At the end of the campaign the German navy consisted of only a single 8-inch cruiser, two light cruisers, and four destroyers. In a few months' time, when Hitler was contemplating the invasion of Britain, the weakness of the German navy was one of the factors that made the operation unlikely to succeed.

On the British side, the campaign had been a series of blunders, demonstrating grave inadequacies in the mechanism for the higher direction of the war. Although it had been apparent, at least from the beginning of the war, that Norway was a possible theater of operations, the British had no adequate plans ready when their own mining of the Inner Leads provoked Hitler to invade. All had to be improvised at short notice, and the British, like an impetuous Romeo, were "too rash, too unadvised, too sudden." But also too cautious, too wedded to conventional doctrines, and too hesitant. The wavering between objectives — Narvik or Trondheim — was in itself enough to cripple the campaign from the outset. This indecision was compounded by the reckless throwing in of insufficient forces when a decision was finally reached to attack both objectives. Neither objective was attacked directly; in the north the British landed at Harstad, and in central Norway at Namsos and Andalsnes. This splitting of the available force into three meant failure everywhere. In comparison with their German opponents, the British troops were ill equipped, poorly trained, and inadequately supported. Hitler's comment probably came closest to the truth. He described the British effort in Norway as "frivolous dilettantism."

Apart from the weakening of the German navy, the strategic consequences of the campaign were that Germany now had bases in Norway that would prove an embarrassment to Britain and the Soviet Union for the remainder of the war. On the other hand, the Germans had to garrison Norway, for though the population gave very little trouble, there was always the threat of another Allied landing to be guarded against. At the end of the war there were some 300,000 German troops in Norway. This number, however, should not be accepted too readily as a net loss to the German army, both because Norway was a good place to rest and refit divisions and because many of the occupation troops were not suitable for more active employment.

If anything, the political consequences of the Norwegian campaign were more important than the strategic. Many neutrals now came to believe that the German army was invincible, an opinion that came to be shared by a considerable number of French observers. This, of course, was bad for the Allies, but what was in the long run at least equally bad for the Germans was that the success in Norway helped foster Hitler's sense of his own infallibility and strengthened his ascendency over the Army High Command. The fiasco in Norway also increased the distrust that had previously not been absent between the British and French. Not least, the Norwegian campaign brought about the fall of the Chamberlain government in Britain. The debate in the House of Commons on May 7 was unusually bitter. The keynote was sounded by Leopold Amery, who addressed himself to Chamberlain in the words of Oliver Cromwell to the Long Parliament:

> You have sat here too long for any good you have been doing. Depart, I say, and let us have done with you. In the name of God, go!

The next day Chamberlain, rightly feeling that he no longer commanded sufficient support in the House or the country, decided to resign. Churchill assumed office on May 10.

In May 1940 the western Allies still entertained the most exaggerated hopes of winning the war by economic pressure against Germany rather than by heavy fighting. Nevertheless, it was recognized that Hitler might attempt an invasion of France by violating Belgian, and possibly Dutch, neutrality. Indeed, all through the winter of 1939–1940 persistent warnings of just such an attack were received by Allied intelligence. To meet an invasion of the Low Countries the French and British had two main courses open to them. They could stand on the defensive along the line of the French frontier in the field fortifications that extended the Maginot Line to the Channel, allowing Belgium and Holland to be overrun, and then launch a counterattack against the southeastern flank of the German advance in the hope of cutting off the enemy forces. Alternatively, they could advance into Belgium to meet the enemy head on and support the Belgian army. An Allied advance into Belgium appeared to offer certain definite advantages. The fighting would presumably take place on Belgian, rather than on French, territory, and the rich industrial regions of northern France would be saved for the Allies. The Germans would be denied the control of much of the Channel coast, and the Belgian field army of some twenty divisions would take its place in the Allied line.

It was decided, then, to enter Belgium as soon as the Germans invaded that country. The next question was how far into Belgium the Allied forces should go and what defensive line they should take up. Three possibilities were debated. If the British and French advanced to the main Belgian line of resistance, running from Antwerp along the Albert Canal and the Meuse, most of Belgium would be retained. Naturally, this was the solution favored by the Belgians. General Gamelin could adopt this plan only if Allied forces were invited into Belgium before an actual German invasion; otherwise it would take the Allies too long to reach the Albert Canal. And it was doubted whether the Belgians could defend the line long enough for them to come up. The Belgian government had no intention of inviting the Allies in before Belgium was invaded, so this plan was, for practical purposes, ruled out.

The next possibility considered was Plan E, which called for the Allies to advance on the left to the line of the Escaut River (the Schelde) and to push a force as far as Walcheren and South Beveland to link up with the Belgian army at Antwerp. Simultaneously, the Allies would advance along the Meuse from Groet to Namur. The disadvantage of Plan E was that it abandoned most of Belgium to the enemy.

In the autumn of 1939 a compromise was worked out. The new plan, Plan D, called for an advance as far as the Dyle River, east of Brussels, and the defense of a line from Antwerp south through Wavre to Namur. French forces would also advance along the Meuse to take up positions between Givet and Namur. In effect, Plan D called for the French and British to advance into Belgium in a great wheel, pivoting on Givet. Between the Maginot Line and the Zuider Zee there would be seven Allied armies: the French Second Army (Huntziger) covering the Ardennes; the French Ninth Army (Corap) extending up the Meuse to Namur; the French First Army (Blanchard) between Namur and Wavre; the British Expeditionary Force (Lord Gort) between Wavre and Louvain; the Belgian army (King Leopold) in the Louvain-Antwerp sector; the French Seventh Army (Giraud) advancing up the coast to South Beveland to provide a link between the Belgians and the Dutch; and (it was hoped) the Dutch army (Winkelmann) holding Fortress Holland (the central Netherlands) to the north.

Informal conversations in November between the Belgian and French General Staffs had convinced Gamelin that the Belgian mobilization would be in time to man the main line of resistance and he was assured that the Belgians would construct adequate defenses along the Dyle River. It was estimated that Plan D would shorten the Allied line by seventy or eighty kilometers and that this would enable an additional twenty divisions to be placed in strategic reserve.

The Supreme War Council approved the plan on November 17.

Beyond the right wing of Huntziger's French Second Army, where the Maginot Line proper began about Longuyon, the front would be held by four armies: from left to right the Third, the Fourth, the Fifth, and the Eighth. The French Sixth Army would be in reserve.

Plan D was certainly pedestrian in concept, for it had no strategic aim other than self-defense. No idea of delivering a great counterblow when the enemy had overextended himself was ever entertained. No thought was given to the encirclement and destruction of the German armies in the field. In Gamelin's mind the fighting would be similar to that of the First World War.

The plan also had other dangers as well as those always associated with military mediocrity. Would the Allies be able to advance to their new positions in time? Would they be able to hold those new positions even if they got there? Was the (possibly temporary) acquisition of a large area of Belgium sufficient compensation for the abandonment of the field defenses on which the Allies had been working all winter? Finally, would the enemy be obliging enough to do what was expected of him?

As a matter of fact, he very nearly was. Under pressure from Hitler to invade France at the earliest possible moment, OKH produced a plan in late October 1939. In most particulars it was what Gamelin had expected. In 1939, as in 1914, the German army was faced with the problem of how to get at France without making a frontal attack on formidable defenses. However, OKH was a good deal less imaginative than Schlieffen had been. And the problem in 1939 was more difficult than before the First World War. It was not, of course, possible to reproduce the Schlieffen Plan exactly. For one thing Schlieffen had counted heavily on the strategic surprise of a major advance west of the Meuse, and once that had been tried the surprise was lost forever. Moreover, an integral part of Schlieffen's concept had been that the French would cooperate by launching offensives of their own into Alsace and Lorraine. Now that Alsace and Lorraine were again part of France and now that the French might be presumed to have had their fill of *l'offensive à l'outrance*, it was no longer possible to anticipate such assistance from the enemy.

OKH therefore decided on a much more limited concept than Schlieffen's. Belgium and Holland would indeed be overrun, but this time the German advance would aim at nothing so grand or final as a sweep west and south of Paris and a battle of annihilation deep in the interior of France. On the contrary, the Low Countries would be invaded in an east-to-west direction, to allow the Germans to capture a stretch of coast and as much of northern France as possible and to destroy whatever Allied forces advanced to assist the Belgians and Dutch. This second aim was more a pious hope than an objective, for the German attack would be frontal, and even if it was successful, there was every likelihood that the Allies would be able to retire in good order behind the French frontier. The *Schwerpunkt* of the attack would be north of Liège, in a westerly direction toward the Belgian coast. This German plan might result in a more favorable front for the German army but it could never end the war in one swift campaign as Schlieffen's plan had been intended to do.

The new plan was greeted with a good deal less than enthusiasm by the senior German officers to whom it was confided. In particular, the commander of Army Group A, General Gerd von Rundstedt, and his brilliant chief of staff, Lieutenant General Fritz von Manstein, criticized it scathingly. Hitler himself, as early as October 25, asked, with some acumen, whether it would not be possible to shift the center of gravity to the south of Liège with the object of cutting off from the rear any French and British forces that advanced into Belgium.

Meanwhile, on January 10, two Luftwaffe officers made a forced landing near Mechelen, and the Belgians captured an operation order indicating that the German attack would come through Belgium. This incident almost certainly inclined both Hitler and OKH to seek some alternative plan. Manstein, whose criticism had annoyed OKH, was transferred to the command of a corps, but in the middle of February he was summoned by Hitler and asked to expound his views. On February 18 the Manstein Plan was formally adopted.

The Manstein Plan shifted the *Schwerpunkt* to the south of Liège, toward the lower Somme and the Channel coast about Abbeville. Rundstedt's Army Group A was now given seven of the ten panzer divisions. This armor would have to make its approach march through the wooded, hilly countryside of the Belgian Ardennes, but Guderian had assured Manstein that it could be done.

Since the French high command had long held that the Ardennes was impassable by armor, the French formations assigned to guard the exits from the Ardennes and the line of the Meuse south of Namur were of low caliber. The best French troops had been sent to the mobile left wing that would execute the wheel into Belgium and Holland. Thus the main weight of the German assault had now been directed against the weakest portion of the French defenses.

Army Group A's panzer divisions were assembled in two groups under General Paul von Kleist and General Hermann Hoth. Their task was to force crossings over the Meuse between Namur and Sedan. Four armies were allotted to Rundstedt: from north to south the

Fourth Army (Kluge), the Twelfth (List), the Sixteenth (Busch), and the Second (Weichs). In all, Rundstedt had been given forty-six divisions, and another twenty-seven divisions were held in reserve behind Army Group A's front.

Army Group B, commanded by Colonel General Fedor von Bock, was to consist of only two armies, the Eighteenth (Küchler) and the Sixth (Reichenau). The Eighteenth Army, with one panzer division and some airborne forces under command, would invade the Netherlands, while the Sixth Army, with two panzer divisions, would invade Belgium. Army Group C (Wilhelm Ritter von Leeb) had two armies, the First (Witzleben) and the Seventh (Dollmann). These two armies consisted of seventeen infantry divisions, which would contain the forty-one French divisions manning the Maginot Line and standing in reserve between the Moselle and the Swiss frontier.

Manstein saw the defeat of France as a two-phase operation. The first phase called for the overrunning of the Low Countries, the encirclement and destruction of all Allied forces in Belgium, and the establishment of a new line along the Somme to the Channel. In the second phase a new offensive to the south would defeat the remainder of the French army and take the Maginot fortifications in the rear. For Manstein's plan to work the Allies had to cooperate by moving into Belgium, just as for Schlieffen's plan to work the French had to cooperate by attacking in Alsace-Lorraine.

The Germans did their best to bait the trap. The weakening of Army Group B would mean its slower advance, which would give the British and French time to get well into Belgium. Yet Army Group B was still strong enough to overwhelm the Dutch and Belgian resistance and provide the anvil for Army Group A's hammer.

At the beginning of May 1940 the opposing forces appeared to be fairly evenly matched, and so they were in physical strength. The German army had 132 divisions: 114 infantry, 10 panzer, 6 light, 1 cavalry, and 1 airborne. This army faced a combined French, British, Dutch, and Belgian force of about 153 equivalent divisions. Each side had about 2700 tanks, but the German panzers were grouped together in panzer divisions and corps, and most of the French tanks were distributed piecemeal among infantry formations. The Germans had some 3000 first-line aircraft to oppose to an Allied total of about 1800.

The Allies, then, were not significantly weaker than their enemy. The peace-loving democracies had delayed too long in arming themselves, but the war-loving Germans attacked before their rearmament was completed. Part of Germany's advantage, of course, was that it was a single nation fighting a coalition. Far more important than this, however, was the German superiority in the military art. This was so manifest that Germany would in all probability have defeated France even if the Allies had been stronger and Germany weaker than was the case. Better strategy was only one aspect of Germany's military superiority; the German army was better organized, better led, and better trained than the armies of the Allies.

Of fundamental consequence, too, was the question of relative morale. With the exception of that of the British army, German morale was notably better than that of the Allies. The young barbarians of the Third Reich were supremely confident in themselves, their leaders, their weapons, and their cause. In contrast, the French government was riddled with jealousy and intrigue; the French high command was hidebound and inept; French junior officers complained, "We no longer dare to command and our men no longer know how to obey." Belgium and the Netherlands also had serious troubles of the spirit. The Dutch had no recent experience of war, and the Belgians, like the French, had seen too much of it. Belgium had both its communists, who thought the war an imperialist trick, and its home-grown fascists of Léon Degrelle's Rexist party. In the Netherlands there was a Dutch Nazi movement that provided traitors and fifth columnists. Both the Belgians and the Dutch, fearful of provoking a German reaction, had refused to coordinate their defensive plans with the western Allies. There had been some little unofficial liaison with the Belgians (and it had, on the whole, been misleading) but it had led to no effective exchange of ideas with the Dutch. These difficulties were compounded by the organization of the French high command. General Gamelin, the commander-in-chief, had, for no very obvious reason, interposed an extra headquarters between himself and his army group commanders by appointing General Alphonse Georges the Commander Northeast.

The Allies had ample warning that the German offensive was coming. Twice in the preceding fortnight the French military attaché in Switzerland had warned that the German attack would be launched between May 8 and 10 and that the main move would be toward Sedan. On the night of the 8th a French airman, returning from a leaflet raid over Düsseldorf, reported a German transport column, sixty miles long, driving toward the border with all the vehicles' headlights on. The next evening, the 9th, the German armies could be *heard* massing on the frontiers. A great, muted, muttering sound rose from the German start lines as scores of thousands of men and thousands of vehicles gathered for the morning's assault. Before midnight on May 9/10 the French, Dutch, and Belgian governments all received warnings of major German troop movements.

Nevertheless, the German attack achieved a sizable measure of surprise. The ground assault was preceded by air strikes against French, Dutch, and Belgian airfields. The Belgian and Dutch air forces were eliminated on May 10, and the French air force suffered considerable damage. Gamelin talked on the telephone to Georges at about 6:30 A.M. and the two agreed that Plan D would have to go into effect. Yet even this long-expected eventuality was not met with smooth staff work. The prearranged system of warning orders broke down and many French formations received only the final order to move. Yet most French units were on the road by shortly after 7:00 A.M.

At about four-thirty that morning German paratroops had dropped in the Netherlands and near the vital Meuse bridges between Roermond and Liège in Belgium. With the help of fifth columnists, two of the main bridges over the Meuse near Maastricht fell intact into Nazi hands. The Belgian fortress of Eben-Emael, at the junction of the Meuse and the Albert Canal, was taken by German glider troops, and though the defenders of the Liège forts continued to fight, they had little effect on the campaign.

While these airborne attacks were taking place, Bock's Army Group B crossed the Dutch and Belgian frontiers without any declaration of war. The Belgian army, comprising twenty-four divisions, deployed ten divisions along the Albert Canal and the line of the Meuse between Antwerp and Namur. In front of this position two divisions were stretched along the frontier as a covering force, two divisions faced Luxembourg, one division was concentrated at Brussels, and nine divisions were in strategic reserve. The French were counting on the Belgians to hold their main position on the Albert Canal for a minimum of five days, which would allow ample time for the Allies to advance and settle into their positions along the Dyle Line.

The Dutch army of ten divisions and a number of unattached units was to hold the river lines in front of Fortress Holland until Allied help arrived. The Dutch, like the Norwegians, could scarcely believe that the worst would really happen to them. Their troops were ill trained and ill equipped; their command arrangements were inadequate; and they suffered from more than their share of traitorous Nazi sympathizers. In spite of these not inconsiderable handicaps, the Dutch were able to resist for five days. It was little enough, but it was, as a matter of fact, a longer period than the German high command had counted on.

The Belgians had fought before — and heroically — in 1914 and throughout the remainder of the First World War. They were therefore better soldiers than the Dutch, and they had a larger army and a more experienced and efficient command. However, Belgium was more heavily attacked than the Netherlands and had fewer natural obstacles to assist the defense. Four German infantry corps and a panzer corps swept into Belgium between Roermond and Aachen, greatly assisted by massive air strikes. With the capture of the Meuse bridges and of Eben-Emael, the line of the Albert Canal had been turned and the panzers burst through to the west. On the evening of May 11 the Belgian army, having suffered heavy losses, began to fall back to the Dyle Line north of Louvain three days sooner than the French had calculated.

In the Netherlands the invaders were even more successful. In the north one German column drove straight toward the Zuider Zee, while the second German thrust, farther south, crossed the Meuse and the Waal, broke through the Peel line on the first day, and freed the panzer division to drive northwest toward the Moerdjik Bridge and Tilburg. The Geld valley line was broken on the 12th and what was left of the Dutch army fell back in disorder to defend Fortress Holland and cover Amsterdam and Utrecht. By now, however, Dutch resistance was almost at an end. On the 13th Queen Wilhelmina left for England and the following afternoon the Dutch capitulated. This did not save Rotterdam from being bombed by the Luftwaffe. Although this appears to have been a mistake resulting from faulty German staff work, the world not unnaturally took it as another example of Nazi brutality — which it was.

While the Dutch and Belgians were thus feeling the weight of the German fist, General Billotte's French First Army Group was swinging north and west to take up its positions. Giraud's French Seventh Army had rather more than 140 miles to go to reach Tilburg, but his reconnaissance units reached that city late on the 11th. The light French covering forces clashed on the 12th with General Erich Höpner's XVI Panzer Corps near Hammut and fought again on the 13th and the 14th, battling valiantly against odds and holding up the panzers' advance until, on the afternoon of the 14th, they were authorized to retire behind the main Seventh Army positions. On its way to Breda the main body of Giraud's army had been heavily attacked from the air and thrown into some confusion. It soon became apparent that this reckless advance into Holland would accomplish nothing, that the Dutch could not be saved, and that the commitment of an entire army so far north was a dangerous error. By the 14th Giraud was already retiring toward Antwerp. With the sudden Dutch capitulation, French troops who had gone to Walcheren were cut off and overrun; heavy French casualties were also suffered on South Beveland.

Meanwhile the British Expeditionary Force had advanced some seventy miles and the French First Army about fifty miles, to take up their positions along the Dyle Line, leaving a gap in the center between Antwerp and Louvain to be covered by the Belgian army. Because of the inability of the Belgians to hold the Albert Canal, the Allied advance had to be speeded up and the French and British formations had to scramble to get to their new positions. One strange and slightly ominous aspect of the advance was the absence of any hostile air activity. A British staff officer noted in his diary, "It almost looks as if the Germans want us where we are going," and some astute French staff officers at Vincennes worried about the same thing. At all events, by the evening of the 14th the BEF and the French First Army were more or less in their prescribed places. When they got there, however, they were disconcerted to find that the Belgians had not constructed much in the way of defenses between Wavre and Namur or along the river itself. This was contrary to what the Allies had been led to expect and it speaks volumes for French and British staff work that no attempt had been made to obtain accurate information on so vital a matter.

In the meantime, the main German thrust through the Ardennes was developing exactly according to plan. Gamelin had allotted some ninety-five miles of front to the sixteen divisions of the Ninth and Second armies. Because of the conviction that the main German effort would come north of Namur, General Corap, commander of the Ninth Army, had placed his best troops, two active divisions, on the left of his line, while his seven reserve divisions of second-class troops were strung out farther south, where the enemy attack would actually come. In both the Ninth and Second Army sectors the field defenses were incomplete and there were shortages of antitank mines and of antiaircraft and antitank artillery. Insufficient artillery ammunition had been stockpiled forward and there was not enough mechanical transport to bring up requirements. Even had these deficiencies not existed, however, there was one French shortage on this front that must in any case have proved fatal, for where courage is lacking arms are of no avail.

When the German panzers drove into Luxembourg on the morning of the 10th they met no resistance. By 8:30 A.M. they were at the Belgian border. Three German armored columns were taking this route: Guderian's XIX Corps, heading for Sedan; Reinhardt's XLI Corps, driving toward Mézières; and Hoth's group of two panzer divisions and a motorized division, heading for Dinant. Behind the tanks came the thirty-seven follow-up divisions of German infantry. Ahead of all of them came the refugees, pouring out onto the roads and moving like a flood toward the French frontier.

The two Belgian divisions in the Ardennes did not fight well; they were more intent on getting away from the Germans than on delaying them. Even the Belgian demolitions were carried out hastily, inefficiently, and without covering fire. When the Second Army reconnaissance units bumped into the German advance guards on the afternoon of the 10th, the French were roughly handled and fell back in some disorder. The French plans for the encounter battle in the Ardennes had seriously miscarried at the outset.

On the 11th the situation rapidly deteriorated still further. Attacks by Stuka dive bombers and tanks drove back the French reconnaissance units, which by nightfall had retreated nearly to the Meuse, having signally failed in their task of delaying the Germans. They had been equally unsuccessful in ascertaining enemy intentions or the strength of the attack. By last light on this, the second day of the offensive, German tanks were at Bouillon, only ten miles north of Sedan. Early the next morning Corap ordered the Ninth Army's reconnaissance units back across the Meuse. That afternoon General Huntziger, alarmed at the speed with which his covering force had been driven in, asked Georges's headquarters at La Ferté for reinforcements. Georges's chief of staff promised to send an armored division, a motorized division, and two infantry divisions. The first of these formations, however, could not begin to arrive until the 14th, and the move could not be completed before the 17th.

Early on the 12th Guderian's panzers crossed the frontier north of Sedan, and Hoth's panzer group was nearing the Meuse at Dinant. That evening Erwin Rommel's 7th Panzer Division established a bridgehead over the river near Houx. Georges now removed Huntziger's Second Army from Billotte's First Army Group and placed it under his own command. This meant that the Second and Ninth armies, at whose juncture the enemy was about to strike, were responsible to different headquarters. Although the Germans had reached the Meuse three days before they had been expected, Georges was not unduly perturbed. Not until midmorning on May 13 did the French high command realize, with a shock of horror, that the principal German blow was about to fall south of Namur. And by then it was too late.

The vital junction of the Second and Ninth armies was held by some of the worst troops in France, the 61st Infantry Division and the 102nd Fortress Division on the Ninth Army front, and the 55th and 71st Infantry divisions south of them on the Second Army front. These soldiers — Bretons, Normans, men from the Loire, and Parisians — were badly disciplined, poorly trained, and had little stomach for fighting. On May 12 General Huntziger, worried about the quality of his troops, had inserted the 71st Division into the line between the 55th and the 3rd North African divisions. This move, carried out at night, left General Grandsard's X Corps in some disarray when the German attack struck.

At three o'clock on the morning of the 13th Rommel broke out of the bridgehead at Houx and drove westward. Later in the morning a second bridgehead was established south of Houx, at Bouvignes. By midday Rommel's division had expanded the area it controlled until it was three miles wide and two miles deep. This by itself should not have been too serious for the French, for there were as yet no German tanks across the Meuse. It had been the German rifle regiments that had forced the river line — swimming, clinging to bales of straw, using rafts or assault boats when these were available — so the German foothold on the left bank was still precarious and vulnerable to counterattack. But though several French counterattacks were ordered, none was launched against the bridgehead at Houx on the 13th.

In retrospect it can be seen that May 13 was the day France lost the war. The Germans were crossing the Meuse almost as if it were no obstacle at all, but the major disaster occurred at Sedan. Here twelve squadrons of Stukas began bombing the French positions at nine o'clock in the morning, and the attack continued until four in the afternoon. The damage done was much more psychological than physical, for the Stuka was not, in fact, a good military aircraft. But on May 13 the Stukas had a devastating effect on French morale. The French artillery fell silent as the gun crews took cover and the French infantry cowered, demoralized, in their bunkers and trenches.

When the German infantry began to cross the Meuse shortly after four o'clock, they met little opposition. By last light the bridgehead at Sedan was four miles deep and four miles wide and was firmly held. The effect of this penetration on the French defenders was out of all proportion to the damage the enemy had inflicted. The troops who should have held the line and counterattacked now gave way to disgraceful panic and fled from the battlefield before they were seriously engaged. Late in the afternoon the commander of B Group Heavy Artillery in X Corps erroneously reported that he was being surrounded by German machine gunners and asked permission to retire. Entirely without foundation, the report can only have been the result of panic. However, X Corps authorized a retirement. Thereupon the artillery commander promptly ordered all ten batteries under his command to abandon their guns in Marfie Wood. This order was obeyed with alacrity.

The infantry of the 55th and 71st divisions were not long in following the artillery's example. Soon the road back to Sedan was packed with deserting French soldiers. Significantly, a large number of officers joined in the rout, as anxious to get away as their men. At 55th Divisional Headquarters, General Lafontaine, the divisional commander, was amazed to look out his window and see the road past his headquarters filled with fleeing French infantrymen, many of whom had thrown away their rifles. Lafontaine was quite unable to halt this panic-stricken exodus. Officers, when halted and questioned, claimed that they had been ordered to retire but could not tell who had given the alleged order. This type of excuse for cowardice was later to give rise to completely untrue stories of German fifth columnists dressed in French uniform. Similarly untrue was the claim made by many in this fleeing mob that German tanks were at Bulson, well to the French rear. No German armor crossed the Meuse at Sedan on the 13th. Almost all the French artillery in this sector joined in the flight, leaving their guns to fall undamaged into enemy hands. As far back as thirty miles south of Sedan, French units were swept by irrational and shameful fear. Although senior officers desperately ordered counterattacks to be launched against the small German bridgeheads, no reliable troops could be mustered to undertake them.

On the 14th a jubilant Hitler ordered all available motor divisions switched from Army Group B to Army Group A, reinforcing success. He also ordered the panzer divisions of Army Group B to move to the left flank to cooperate with Rundstedt. On this day a belated and halfhearted counterattack was launched by the French at Haut-le-Wastria near Houx, but the Germans broke it without difficulty. Although the French 1st Armored Division had also been ordered to Houx, it was not ready to attack until late on the 15th. When it did go into action, the French tanks, most of them immobilized from lack of fuel, were easy targets for Hoth's panzers, and the French 1st Armored Division was virtually destroyed without having accomplished anything useful.

On the 14th the Germans made another crossing of the Meuse at Givet. By now the 55th and 71st divisions of Huntziger's Second Army had dissolved, their soldiers and many of their officers bent only on returning home. Huntziger moved his own headquarters from Senuc back to Verdun, thirty-five miles to the rear, and ordered the French artillery to fire on surrendering French infantrymen. The panic had by now set in with equal virulence in Corap's Ninth Army. By last light on the 15th that army's XI and XLI corps had disintegrated. The 18th, 22nd, 53rd, and 61st Infantry divisions had melted away as their men joined the flight to cries of "Panzer!" and "We have been betrayed!" Perhaps in a deeper sense the second cry may have borne some relation to the truth.

By now the gaping hole in the French front could probably not have been closed by any effort, however massive, but on the 14th the French 3rd Armored Division and the 3rd Mechanized Division were ordered to counterattack at Chemy near Sedan. The divisions arrived on the scene piecemeal, so the counterattack was postponed until the next day. When it did go in, it failed ignominiously. Guderian now turned his tanks to the west and headed for the Channel coast, crossing the Bar River on intact bridges that the fleeing French had made no attempt to destroy. The panzer troops, who had had very little fighting, soon grew tired of taking French prisoners. It became the German tankmen's contemptuous practice to order groups of French soldiers to pile their weapons on the road; the German tanks would then roll over them and crush them, and the disarmed Frenchmen were dismissed, to make their own way home.

Although the German invasion was less than a week old, it was already too late to save the campaign. The enemy had still to reap the full fruits of his victory by cutting off the Allied forces in Belgium and forcing France out of the war, but the breakthrough at Sedan and the realization that a considerable portion of the French army would not fight made the Allied situation quite hopeless. On the night of the 14th Premier Reynaud appealed to Churchill for an additional ten RAF squadrons. Not unnaturally, Churchill was torn between his desire to keep France in the war and his realization that Britain could ill afford to part with any fighter squadrons that might soon be urgently needed for the defense of the British Isles. In fact, ten RAF squadrons were eventually sent to France, although the French air force was doing very little and was to have more first-line aircraft at the end of the Battle of France than at the beginning.

The French high command was incredibly slow to react to the German success on the Meuse. Even by the 15th, with his center burst asunder, the French commander-in-chief still did not order his armies to retire from Belgium. The situation there was by no means desperate, for the Germans were anxious not to force the Allies to retreat before the trap closed behind them. Attacks on the French First Army had been only partially successful and the BEF was holding firm, though the Belgian army to the north was being subjected to very heavy pressure.

On the 15th the French 2nd Armored Division began to move from its position east of Châlons to counterattack in the Sedan area. The division's tanks moved by rail, and the wheeled transport by road. As the formation approached the seething mass of disorder and desertion that lay around Sedan it got caught up in the chaos. Some of its wheeled transport headed south, out of harm's way; some of the tanks were detrained at Hirson and some at other stations. One train, driven by a panic-stricken engineer, took off on its own for the south of France. The result of all this was that the 2nd Armored Division simply fell apart and could not be reassembled for more than a week.

Thus all three of the French armored divisions that had been in existence on May 10 had been put out of action. On the 17th a 4th Armored Division, under the command of Colonel Charles De Gaulle, launched an attack to retake Montcornet. The attack seems to have been a thoroughly confused affair; the objective was not reached; and De Gaulle's force retired to the Samoussy Forest. When it attacked again on the 19th the French were very roughly handled by the 10th Panzer Division. De Gaulle requested permission to retire, which was refused, but he fell back anyway the next day.

However, from this insignificant and inauspicious little action a legend was born. De Gaulle, who in the First World War had been taken prisoner before the tank had been introduced on the battlefield, had never before seen a tank action. He may not have been a great fighting commander, but no one could deny that he had a fine way with words. His communiqués made the action at Montcornet sound like a victory, and the French were hungry for victories. Indeed, since his division had not been destroyed or scattered without fighting, there is no doubt that De Gaulle had done better than the commanders of the French 1st, 2nd, and 3rd Armored divisions. At all events, the publicity De Gaulle received was to help him on his way to the eventual leadership of the Fifth French Republic.

Wars, however, cannot be won by publicity alone, no matter how magniloquently worded, and the war was going desperately for France. Shortly after 7:00 P.M. on the 15th Reynaud had telegraphed Churchill: "We lost the battle last night. The road to Paris is open. Send us all aircraft and troops you can." That evening Gamelin warned the government to be ready to evacuate Paris, and Reynaud, looking about him for a symbol that would unite the French people, sent to Madrid to recall the French ambassador, Marshal Henri Philippe Pétain.

The next day, the 16th, Gamelin at last ordered the retirement of the French and British forces in Belgium. The Allied retreat from the Dyle Line began that night. Meanwhile, the rout from Sedan continued. On the 16th the fleeing soldiers began to reach Paris, where they promptly filled the bars and cafés, spreading fearsome stories to justify their dereliction of duty. In the Quai d'Orsay the French Foreign Office began to burn its files, and the black smoke pillared up over the capital like a symbol of defeat.

When Churchill arrived in Paris late in the afternoon he could not believe that the situation was as hopeless as the French appeared to believe. Surely, he thought, the German attack must soon run out of momentum. Then there would be the opportunity for some great counterstroke, such as the one that had saved the war in 1914 at the Marne. In his school-boy French he asked General Gamelin, "*Où est le masse de manoeuvre?*" "*Aucune,*" replied Gamelin.

On the 17th Guderian's panzer divisions were driving toward the Oise on either side of St. Quentin, and Reinhardt's XLI Panzer Corps was advancing farther north. Hoth's panzer group on the right was advancing toward Cambrai and Arras. By now, too, Höpner's XVI Panzer Corps had been transferred from Bock's command to reinforce Hoth in Army Group A. As the German armored formations were striking deep into France, Reynaud at last decided to replace Gamelin. He called back from Beirut General Maxime Weygand, the seventy-three-year-old Commander-in-Chief Middle East, who had been Marshal Foch's chief of staff in the First World War. As with his decision to recall Pétain, Reynaud hoped that Weygand's great prestige might help France to rally.

Reichenau's troops took Brussels and Louvain on the 17th, while the French First Army and the BEF continued their retreat to the Escaut. Gamelin meanwhile was forming a new Seventh Army under General Frère in a desperate attempt to establish a defensible line along the Somme and the Aisne.

When Pétain arrived in Paris on the 18th, he was appointed minister of state and vice president of the council. That same afternoon the old marshal visited Gamelin at his headquarters and was briefed on the military situation. The French position was almost hopeless, and as Pétain took his leave he shook hands with Gamelin, saying, "I pity you with all my heart." The next day Gamelin was replaced by Weygand.

On the 19th, too, Parisians were given another clear indication of how desperate their government believed the military situation to be. At a special mass at Notre Dame, cabinet ministers and high-ranking bureaucrats prayed for victory. Obviously, things were very bad indeed for so many militant agnostics to seek the help of God.

General Weygand was vigorous and energetic beyond his years. He was also a very good soldier, and it seems probable that if anyone could have saved France, he was the man. But France was past saving. For a time Weygand refused to admit this, striving manfully to bring order out of the hopeless chaos he had inherited. In spite of protests from Pétain, Weygand dismissed fifteen French generals and attempted in a way that Gamelin had never done to impose his own direct control on the battle. His plan was the obvious one of coordinated attacks northward toward the Allied forces in Belgium and southward by those encircled armies. Weygand decided that the axis of the joint attack should be along a line from Arras to Amiens.

It was already too late for such a strategy to have any chance of success. On the 19th, Gort had informed the British cabinet that he was considering retiring toward Dunkirk, but the cabinet defense committee, influenced by Churchill, resisted this plan and favored Weygand's. The cabinet sent General William Ironside to Belgium to impress their views on the British commander-in-chief. Very fortunately, however, the British Admiralty began to assemble a fleet of small vessels for a possible evacuation by sea from the Dunkirk beaches.

On the 20th Guderian's panzers, having captured Amiens, raced on to reach the Channel at Abbeville. From Abbeville they wheeled north up the coast toward Boulogne. The next day a counterattack by a British tank brigade near Arras imposed a sharp check on the German armor, but Arras and Rethel fell to the invaders despite the tank action.

Churchill flew to Paris again on the 22nd, still full of hope that a breakout might be achieved, and found Weygand attempting to form a new army group around Amiens for the northward thrust. However, on the 24th Weygand learned that the British had abandoned Arras, and he at last recognized that his plan was impracticable. Now, for the first time, he admitted that France might have to capitulate. The French cabinet on this day began to discuss the possibility of making a separate peace.

To the Germans it appeared as though *Fall Gelb* was all but over. In Boulogne the remnants of two British Guards battalions and some French marines had been evacuated by destroyers, but unfortunately the British had departed without informing the main body of French troops who were holding out in the upper town. The French, anxious to justify previous lapses of their own, were quick to claim that they had been betrayed. Under the strain of defeat the alliance was rapidly breaking up.

On the afternoon of the 24th the Belgian IV Corps had been heavily defeated by Reichenau's Sixth Army on the Lys and a gap had appeared between the Belgian army and the British Expeditionary Force. Gort and Blanchard, the new commander of the 1st Army Group, agreed to retire to the left bank of the Lys, but there seemed little hope that these beleaguered troops would not soon be forced to surrender in the open field.

Rundstedt, at least, was already turning his mind to the second phase of the operation, *Fall Rot*, the attack on French forces south of the Somme. Partly because the countryside through which the British and French were withdrawing was boggy and intersected with numerous canals and small rivers, Rundstedt did not believe it suitable for the employment of armor. Moreover, the German panzer divisions, although they had done remarkably little fighting, had covered a lot of ground and badly needed a period of maintenance and repair before being committed on the Somme. Finally, it must have seemed to Rundstedt that the British and French forces in Belgium were done for. At all events, on the 23rd he ordered his panzer divisions not to advance beyond a line running from Arras through Lens, Béthune, St. Omer, and Gravelines to the Channel. The next day, when Hitler visited Army Group A's headquarters, he confirmed this restraining order.

Notwithstanding the technical justifications for halting the German armor, it seems likely that the German high command was guilty of the error vulgarly known as counting one's chickens before they are hatched. Almost, indeed, it seemed that this might be a peculiarly German weakness — Kluck, after all, had made the same error at the Marne in 1914. Their overconfidence may also have made the Germans reluctant to press their infantry attack too vigorously, for why should they suffer needless casualties against opponents who must soon surrender in any case? Göring went so far as to declare that the air force by itself could bring about the capitulation of the British and French forces around Dunkirk. Perhaps Hitler believed this. Whatever the reason, the German panzer divisions were withdrawn to regroup in the vicinity of St. Quentin. It was the first major German error of the campaign.

By the 25th the encirclement of the British and French forces in Belgium was complete, and the Belgian army had been so weakened that it would be unable to resist much longer. As disaster deepened, so did dissension increase among the Allies. The British blamed the French for the disgraceful collapse at Sedan and were outspoken about many instances of French inefficiency and poor staff work. Weygand reproached the British for their retirement at Arras, which he claimed had spoiled his plan for a breakout. Pétain, who had disliked the British ever since the First World War, complained that Britain was fielding only one-eighth as many divisions as France.

On May 27 the British and French forgot their differences for a brief time in common anger at the Belgians, who capitulated late that afternoon. Weygand termed the Belgian surrender "an act of desertion," and it is certainly true that King Leopold made his decision to capitulate against the unanimous advice of his own cabinet. However, Churchill's representative at Belgian headquarters, Admiral Sir Roger Keyes, who was in a position to know something of the matter, claimed that Leopold had no alternative, that the Belgians had given the Allies ample notice that they might have to surrender, and that by retiring to the Channel Lord Gort had "abandoned the Belgians to their fate."

In fact, no single nation came out of this difficult situation very well. The British evacuation of Dunkirk had begun on May 26, the day before the Belgian surrender, and — chiefly because of difficulties of communication — neither the French nor the Belgians on the spot had been informed.

Initially, Operation Dynamo, the seaborne evacuation from the Dunkirk beaches, did not appear very promising. The British government estimated that no more than about 45,000 soldiers could be taken away. The order for evacuation had been issued to Gort only after Reynaud had been informed and had approved it, but the French high command did not pass this information on to either General Blanchard, the French army group commander, or Admiral Abrail, the French naval commander in the area. This led Blanchard to complain to Weygand that his forces had been imperiled because of "the precipitate retreat of the English." Blanchard was later implored to participate in the evacuation, but he obstinately refused to do so until it was too late to save much of his force. Still, it is true that Gort at first insisted that French troops be evacuated only in French ships and that there were some unpleasant scenes at the embarkation area when French soldiers were ejected from British ships.

When the Supreme War Council met in Paris on the 31st, Churchill was forced to admit that, although some 165,000 troops had already been evacuated, only about 15,000 of them had been French. Churchill promised that French troops would be given priority for evacuation wherever possible and also that the rear guard at Dunkirk would be provided by three British divisions. Between May 29 and June 4, 139,732 British and 139,097 French soldiers were embarked.

The Luftwaffe, attempting to make good Göring's rash promise, had begun to make heavy attacks on the Dunkirk area on the 27th, though RAF fighter squadrons, operating from English airfields, did their brave and not altogether unsuccessful best to keep the German bombers away. Losses, however, were heavy. Of the 861 vessels involved in Operation Dynamo, 243 were sunk. Fortunately, the weather held good and it was possible to use the seventeen miles of open beaches east of Dunkirk as well as the port itself. All this while the perimeter around Dunkirk was defended gallantly, for the most part by French troops, and the Germans made only slow progress in reducing the Allied beachhead. General de la Laurencie, the valiant commander of the French III Corps, fought his way over the Lys to

Dunkirk with the tattered remnants of his corps on the 29th, but by the next day ten German divisions were encircling the Allied lodgment, which by now had shrunk to a tiny area only forty kilometers long and some eight kilometers deep. Nevertheless, renewed German attacks on May 31 and June 1 gained little ground.

The defense could not last much longer, however, and by the early morning hours of June 4 Operation Dynamo had to be called off. The last ships pulled out at 3:30 A.M. The British rear guard under General Sir Harold Alexander was safely embarked, but some 30,000 French troops were left behind. In all, 338,000 troops had been evacuated.

While the evacuation was continuing at Dunkirk, an attempt was made to eliminate the bridgeheads the Germans had established over the Somme near Abbeville. Attacks on May 26 and 28 by two British tank brigades and two French cavalry divisions failed, with heavy losses, and on the evening of May 28, De Gaulle's 4th Armored Division, supported by the 2nd and 5th Cavalry divisions, was ordered to drive the enemy back across the river. The first French attack on the 28th made little headway. Renewing the assault early the following morning, the French succeeded in reaching the Somme at two places but were unable to eliminate the German bridgeheads. A third attack, launched late on the afternoon of the 30th, was shot to pieces by well-sited German antitank guns. When further attacks on June 2 by the French 2nd Armored Division and the 31st Infantry Division also failed, it became apparent that the Somme line was as good as lost.

The miracle of Dunkirk had been made possible partly by good fortune and the mistakes of the enemy — the calm weather, the halting of the panzer divisions, and Göring's erroneous belief that the Luftwaffe alone could prevent embarkation. But more important had been the outstanding work of the Royal Navy and of the amateur sailors who had supplied the sea lift, the air cover provided by the RAF, and the bravery and tenacity of the Allied rear guard composed largely of French soldiers. Most of the British Expeditionary Force had been saved, although it had been forced to abandon all its transport, guns, and equipment. Yet, as Churchill reminded the House of Commons, wars are not won by evacuations, however miraculous, and on June 4 Allied arms were in a desperate way. The British still had some 140,000 troops in other parts of France — most of them belonging to the four British divisions that had not moved into Belgium — and a few more British formations were dispatched to the continent after Dunkirk. This reconstituted remnant of the BEF was placed under the command of General Sir Alan Brooke.

By June 5, when *Fall Rot* was launched, the French had already lost some 370,000 soldiers, most of them prisoners. The total German losses to date — killed, wounded, and missing — were 61,418. This figure was about equal to that of the British army's losses on the first day of the Battle of the Somme in 1916. For the second phase of the Battle of France, the French army could muster only some forty-nine divisions. Of the four French armored divisions two had been destroyed and two had been very seriously damaged. The Germans had by now closed up to the Somme, the Ailette, and the Aisne, and had some 140 equivalent divisions for the coming battle.

The Royal Air Force, which had fought far more effectively than the French, had lost 196 aircraft and, except for two squadrons at Rouen, had had to withdraw to airfields in Britain.

The second phase of the Battle of France has little of the intrinsic interest of the first. As frequently seems to be the case, overwhelming superiority of force stultified the German strategic imagination. *Fall Rot* produced no such brilliant concepts as had distinguished the Manstein Plan. Instead, it was merely a matter of attacking the weak French line.

When the battle opened on June 5, the Germans at first made little progress except around Péronne, where they penetrated some twenty miles. By evening on the 6th, however, the Germans had forced the entire line of the Somme, and the French retreat had become general. The French troops were now fighting better, but it was too late, even for courage. On the 7th Rommel's panzers penetrated almost to Rouen and the next day the French Tenth Army was cut in two. On the 9th the German attack opened up on the Aisne.

The French government was divided on the question of whether to continue the war or to seek an immediate armistice. Reynaud dreamed of establishing a "redoubt" in Brittany, which was militarily impossible, and of moving the government to North Africa and fighting on from there, which was perfectly feasible. He had considerable support for the second course, though a number of ministers demanded an immediate armistice in the hope of getting the best terms they could from the Nazis. Pétain, who had never had a fiery spirit, was utterly despondent and seems to have been almost senile at times. Apart from urging surrender, he made little positive contribution to military conferences. One day his colleagues were somewhat taken aback to hear him declare: "We don't seem to be making much use of carrier pigeons. There should be a dovecote in the rear, permanently attached to supreme headquarters."

On the night of June 9/10 the French government evacuated Paris and fled to Tours. Early on the morning of the 14th the first Nazi troops entered Paris unopposed, to parade through the streets and break out huge swastika flags over the Arch of Triumph and the Eiffel Tower.

On June 10 Mussolini, feeling that it was at last safe to come to the support of his victorious ally, had declared war on France. Yet even in this last desperate hour the French were more than a match for the Italians when it came to fighting. Although only five French divisions could be spared to defend the entire length of the Italian frontier, the fascist attacks made almost no headway.

When the Supreme War Council met in Tours on the 11th, Churchill did his best to keep France in the war, but the next day Weygand informed the French government that the war was "irretrievably lost," and demanded an immediate armistice. Both Reynaud and Churchill appealed desperately to President Roosevelt for help, but even if Roosevelt had wished to respond he was powerless to bring any useful assistance to the floundering democracies of the west. By now about one quarter of the French population were homeless refugees and the armies of France were no longer capable of resistance. Reynaud asked Churchill if Britain would release France from her pledge not to make a separate peace. Although the British prime minister promised that, whatever happened, he would indulge in no recriminations, he declined to release France from her word.

The French government now fled again, this time to Bordeaux, but the end was very near. On the night of June 16 Reynaud resigned. He suggested that Marshal Pétain form the next government.

Within a few hours of taking office Pétain asked Germany for an armistice. The Germans were in no great hurry to comply and another nine days were to elapse before hostilities formally ceased. One more military event remains to be recorded. On the 18th, as a crowning irony, the French troops who were in the Maginot Line were ordered to fight their way out of the fortifications.

On June 20 General Huntziger led the French armistice delegation to the Compiègne Forest, where, in the same railway car Marshal Foch had used to dictate terms to the Germans in November 1918, the French were presented with the Nazi terms. Hitler himself had come to Compiègne to witness the last act.

When, on June 17, Pétain's new government had asked the Germans for an armistice, it had also ordered all French troops to lay down their arms, but did not see fit to communicate this information to its British allies. However, the French move was not unexpected, and on the 17th and 18th, 136,000 British and rather more than 20,000 Polish soldiers were evacuated to Britain from ports in the Cherbourg peninsula. Also on June 17, General De Gaulle fled from France in a British aircraft, and that same evening broadcast a message to the French people, urging them to rally round his person to continue resistance.

The armistice terms that France was able to obtain from her conqueror did not take into account the promise the French government had repeatedly made that the French fleet would in no circumstances be allowed to fall into German hands. Pétain's government got little in the way of concessions for this betrayal of its ally, Britain. All France, excepting only the south and southeast portions, was to be under German occupation. French prisoners of war were to remain in German captivity until the agreement had been signed, and — most shameful of all — all German political refugees in France were to be handed over to the Nazis.

On June 24 the British government publicly declared that France had broken its "solemn word" in concluding a separate armistice. Pétain and Weygand were convinced that where they had failed, the British could not hope to succeed, and Pierre Laval, the new foreign minister, actively desired Britain's quick defeat. In general, the men around Pétain began as defeatists and ended as collaborators, handing over French citizens to the torturers of the Gestapo and obeying with alacrity and subservience the vilest orders of their new masters.

Admiral Jean François Darlan became minister of the navy and forthwith canceled all plans for dispatching French warships to British or American ports. Those French vessels already in British ports had been ordered home to France on the 21st, but the British had refused to let them sail. Churchill now decided that the French fleet must immediately be seized, neutralized, or sunk.

The French warships that were in Britain were seized in a sudden surprise attack on the night of July 3. Far more important were the French naval units in North Africa. A battleship and four cruisers lay at Alexandria; the modern battle cruisers *Dunkerque* and *Strasbourg* were at Oran and Mers-el-Kebir; the unfinished battleship *Jean Bart* lay at Casablanca, and the *Richelieu* at Dakar; the rest of the French fleet was at Toulon. At Oran and Mers-el-Kebir the *Dunkerque* and two older battleships were sunk when the French refused the British terms. At Alexandria the French admiral agreed to the demilitarization of his ships. At Dakar on July 8 the *Richelieu* was seriously damaged, but not sunk, by British torpedo bombers. The result of these actions was that the Royal Navy retained its superiority over the enemy, a matter of desperate importance now that Hitler was contemplating an invasion of the British Isles. The Pétain government, now installed under German tutelage at Vichy, broke off diplomatic relations with Britain, and in retaliation for the naval actions the French air force bombed Gibraltar, but France did not declare war on Britain.

Meanwhile, Stalin had taken advantage of his agreement with the Nazis to extend the area under communist control. Between June 14 and 28, Soviet troops marched into Lithuania, Latvia, Estonia, and the Rumanian provinces of Bessarabia and northern Bukovina. In early August the Soviet government formally annexed the Baltic states.

The very completeness of the German conquest of France took Hitler by surprise. He had apparently expected no such sudden success and was now at a loss as to how to exploit it. Certainly what he hoped for was that Britain would recognize the futility of continuing the war and would make peace, thus leaving him free to turn eastward against the Soviet Union and conquer the "living space" he considered necessary for the thousand-year Reich he intended to create. But it was feckless of the German dictator to have made no contingency plans against success, for if German resources had been marshaled as they could have been, an invasion of the British Isles might have been a feasible operation early in July. As it was, there was a seven-week pause between the French capitulation and the beginning of the Battle of Britain.

In a speech to the Reichstag on July 19 Hitler appealed for a negotiated peace with Britain. What good purpose could be served in carrying on the futile struggle? Germany had no cause to quarrel with Britain and almost no demands to make on her. Germany's former colonies would have to be returned, but the British Empire as a whole would survive unscathed. In this at least Hitler was probably sincere, for he had always believed that the dissolution of the British Empire would benefit only Russia, Japan, and the United States, but not Germany. However, the British government rejected Hitler's peace offer out of hand on July 22. It was undoubtedly the right decision, though a very hard one. Who might not have been tempted by such soft and reasonable terms, especially when the alternative was so dark, so filled with pain, and so unlikely of success?

Britain's position in the summer of 1940 was little short of desperate. Even if Roosevelt was re-elected for a third term, there seemed little prospect of effective American aid. Many prominent Americans, including Joseph Kennedy, the United States ambassador to Britain, considered the British case hopeless. Nor was the opinion anything but reasonable. German arms were everywhere victorious. The Third French Republic had fallen and its Vichy successor might at any moment enter the Nazi camp against its former ally. The Soviet Union was bound to Nazi Germany by treaty, and Stalin, with the blood of Poland, Finland, the Baltic States, and Rumania on his hands, was Hitler's partner in crime. Italy had at last summoned up the courage to enter the war, and in the Far East Japan was hostile and threatening. In Britain itself there were only two battleworthy divisions fully equipped for action. The Royal Air Force was seriously outnumbered by the Luftwaffe, and although the Royal Navy was still intact, the Admiralty was not optimistic that it could prevent a landing on British shores.

Between the French surrender, on June 17, and August 13, when the Battle of Britain began, energetic preparations were made for the defense of the island. At the same time, unofficial talks were held between British and German representatives on the possibilities of achieving peace. Hitler undoubtedly hoped that men like Lord Halifax, Lloyd George, and Sir Samuel Hoare might recognize the folly of continuing the war, just as they had formerly recognized the wisdom of appeasing the Nazis; that they would oust Churchill and form a new government willing to negotiate. There was even speculation that the Duke and Duchess of Windsor, formerly King Edward VIII and his wife, might provide an acceptable substitute monarchy in such a case. Perhaps the British government actively encouraged these beliefs in order to gain time for its defensive preparations. But governments are composed of a number of men, not all of them equal to Churchill in resolution; so perhaps there may actually have been some basis for the German hope. At all events, nothing came of any of the discussions, and they may indeed have been merely camouflage.

Certainly Hitler was far from happy at the prospect of having to carry the war to Britain. The English Channel was a major obstacle before which he instinctively quailed — and not without the best of reasons. Peace was surely the Führer's best hope. But should this peace prove illusory, what alternatives were open to him?

He was determined to attack the Soviet Union at the earliest possible moment, but was reluctant to do this while an unsubdued enemy still remained in arms in the west. If Churchill was unwilling to see reason, there were three methods by which Germany might hope to change Britain's mind. First, of course, there was the possibility of direct invasion across the Narrow Seas, a hazardous and uncertain operation. Second, the German armies could turn south through Spain and Gibraltar to North Africa, capturing Egypt and Suez, isolating India, and destroying all British interests in the Middle East. However, the Spanish dictator, General Franco, was unwilling to cooperate in such an enterprise, which would in any case have entailed a vast overextension of German resources. Third, the British Isles could be interdicted by submarine and aircraft attack with the good hope that this would eventually starve the British into submission. The difficulty with this last course was that it would be slow and that the German submarine fleet would have to be greatly augmented. It was possible, also, that Hitler, who knew some history, remembered the failure of the U-boat blockade of 1917. In addition, and possibly most important, what would the Soviet Union be doing while Britain was starving to death?

Aerial supremacy over the English Channel and the landing beaches was an essential prerequisite for an invasion, and this meant that the RAF defenses would have to be destroyed before an invasion fleet could set sail. But the Luftwaffe had suffered heavy casualties in Norway, the Low Countries, and France; it had lost, in all, 2784 aircraft. Now it would not only have to replenish these losses but would also have to regroup, moving forward its airfields to within striking distance of Britain. On July 10 the Germans began attacks on British Channel convoys, but it was not until six days later that Hitler issued Führer Directive No. 16 for Operation Sea Lion. Even then all that Hitler said was that he would "prepare, and if necessary carry out, a landing operation," for which all preparations were to be completed by the middle of August.

The German admiralty had always insisted that the south coast of England was the only possible invasion area. However, the British Chiefs of Staff, not realizing the limitations that lack of shipping imposed on the Germans, considered an invasion by way of the east coast a more dangerous threat and, indeed, did not entirely discount the possibility of an invasion of the West Country by way of the Bay of Biscay ports or an invasion of Scotland from Norway. The German army hoped to land on a broad front between Dover and Lyme Bay, with 100,000 men in the first wave and 160,000 in the second. This plan called for an invasion front of thirteen divisions and was utterly beyond the capabilities of German shipping. The impossibility of providing naval and air protection on such a broad front, the limited capacities of ports of embarkation, and variable tides also made this ambitious scheme quite unrealistic. Finally, but not before the last days of August, a definite plan for Operation Sea Lion emerged.

Rundstedt, who would be in overall command, would have three armies. The Sixteenth Army would land between Hythe and Eastbourne, sailing from the ports between Rotterdam and Boulogne. The Ninth Army would land between Brighton and Worthing, sailing from the ports between Boulogne and Le Havre. In the first week an intermediate line would be established between Canterbury and Arundel, and the next objective would be a line from Gravesend to Reigate to Portsmouth. The German Sixth Army, in reserve in the Cherbourg peninsula, would either reinforce this invasion front or invade farther west, between Portsmouth and Weymouth. London was not to be directly attacked but would be by-passed and cut off.

For the first phase of the invasion, thirteen divisions would be available, though this whole force could not be carried across the Channel in one lift. The first wave was to consist of nine divisions plus airborne troops, almost double the initial assault the Allies were able to launch in Normandy in June of 1944, after years of much more intensive and farsighted preparation. The second wave was to include four panzer divisions, and by six weeks after the initial landings the German force was to have been built up to a strength of twenty-three divisions. Little help could be expected from the German navy after its heavy losses in Norway, and, of course, surprise — even tactical surprise — would be virtually impossible. All preparations would have to be made hurriedly, for after September the uncertainties of the weather would prevent invasion until late the following spring.

Invasion craft of all types began to be collected in the North German ports, and though this assembly was hampered by RAF attacks, enough remained to fulfill the requirement. Nevertheless, the invasion fleet was a sad hodgepodge: steamers, Rhine barges, motorboats, tugs, and trawlers, none designed specifically as troop transports, with differing speeds, maneuverability, and seaworthiness. Not surprisingly, at the end of July Hitler postponed Operation Sea Lion until September 15, without definitely committing himself to undertake it at all. On August 30 the navy demanded an additional postponement, and was given until September 21, with the understanding that ten days' notice would be given. On September 11 Hitler again postponed the operation, pushing up the date to September 24.

By the middle of September the British had a very good idea of where the German attack was likely to come, and had shifted their forces to meet it. Moreover, those forces had been very greatly increased, and now totaled some thirty-four equivalent divisions. Thirteen excellent divisions and three armored divisions would have met the nine German assault divisions on the beaches. In retrospect it is to be regretted that the Nazis did not make the attempt, for a very large proportion of those invading armies would undoubtedly have found a watery grave, and those who did succeed in landing, lacking reinforcement and resupply, would have been killed on English beaches.

The German army, and even some members of its high command, who should have known better, were confident that the thing could be done. The easy defeat of France had greatly swelled the hubris that always lies so close to the surface of the German national character. Yet in truth the plan for Operation Sea Lion was on a par with the Schlieffen Plan, with the plan for the Ludendorff offensives in the spring of 1918, and with the later plan for Operation Barbarossa. All were beyond German capabilities.

The German navy, with a far more acute sense of reality, viewed the entire operation with the gravest foreboding. But both the army and the navy were agreed that air supremacy would first have to be achieved. An OKW (High Command of the Armed Forces) directive, issued on August 1, outlined the priorities for the Luftwaffe in the coming struggle: first, the destruction of the RAF; second, attacks on British ports and food depots; third, attacks on warships and merchant shipping, though only when particularly favorable opportunities presented themselves; fourth, the support of German naval operations and of the invasion itself. Hitler reserved for himself the decision as to whether to permit terror attacks on the British civilian population.

Two German air fleets, the Second and Third, were deployed in France and Belgium, and Luftflotte 5 was stationed in Norway and Denmark. For the Battle of Britain, the Luftwaffe mustered 1285 bombers and dive bombers, and 1137 fighters. To meet this force, Air Chief Marshal Sir Hugh Dowding, Commander-in-Chief Fighter Command, had between 600 and 700 Hurricanes and Spitfires, but the Spitfires at least were definitely superior to the Messerschmitt 109s and 110s of the Luftwaffe.

The Battle of Britain can be divided into four distinct phases. July 10 to August 12 was a preliminary period, when the German attacks were concentrated against coastal shipping and the English south coast. Between August 13 and September 6 the Luftwaffe concentrated on RAF airfields, radar stations, and headquarters. On September 7 Göring switched the weight of his attack to London, in the dual hope of drawing RAF fighter strength into the battle and destroying it, and of breaking the British will to resist by the destruction of the capital. This phase lasted until September 19. After September 20 the threat of invasion had passed and the Luftwaffe abandoned most daylight raids, though heavy night bombing was directed against British cities throughout 1941 and 1942.

Göring designated August 13 *Adlertag,* "Eagle Day," the date of the commencement of Operation Eagle, the fight for aerial supremacy over England. However, the RAF Fighter Command husbanded its resources skillfully, and Göring was no match for Dowding. RAF Fighter Command was much aided by the network of radar stations, which gave early warning of the direction and strength of the German attacks. Although the Luftwaffe was aware that radar was helping the British, it did not attack the radar stations with sufficient strength to disable them.

On August 15 the Germans took a calculated risk by launching a 100-plane bomber force, escorted by some forty obsolescent Messerschmitt 110s, against Tyneside. Simultaneously, an 800-plane raid was launched in the south. However, Dowding had foreseen exactly this possibility and had retained seven fighter squadrons in the north, with the result that the RAF hit the Tyneside raiders hard, shooting down thirty German aircraft for the loss of only two British pilots injured. All twenty-two RAF squadrons in the south of England also fought on this day, and here again the RAF demonstrated a marked superiority, shooting down seventy-six German aircraft for a British loss of thirty-four. Another factor in Britain's favor was that any German aircraft shot down over England meant the loss of its pilot and crew, whereas British pilots were often able to parachute to safety and were frequently back in the battle in a matter of hours.

Nevertheless the period between August 24 and September 6 was a critical one. A number of British airfields were extensively damaged and some were put out of action for considerable periods of time. In these two weeks the RAF Fighter Command lost 231 pilots and 466 aircraft, nearly a quarter of its total strength, and despite there being no particular difficulty about replacing the aircraft, the supply of pilots was inadequate.

From the German naval point of view the most favorable conditions of moon and tide occurred during the period from September 8 to 10, and in Britain the code word "Cromwell" (imminent threat of invasion) was actually issued on the evening of the 7th. Yet in truth the Germans were still far from ready for the great gamble.

In the skies, the British were saved chiefly by the Germans' overestimating the extent of their own success. On the night of September 6/7 Göring switched his attacks from RAF bases and radar stations to the British capital. The next afternoon the mass daylight raids on London began. Although the civilian population of London suffered heavily, the RAF fighter squadrons were given a respite. Göring's error may be accounted for by a number of convergent reasons. On the night of August 28/29 British bombers had raided Berlin. Though they did little damage, they dealt a sharp blow to Göring's pride, the more so since he had boasted before the war that if any British bomber reached Berlin "you can call me Meyer." The Luftwaffe now argued that terror attacks on London would force RAF fighters into the air and so bring on exactly that major fighter battle that the Germans most desired. Moreover, Göring believed that the decisive phase of the Battle of Britain was already over and the RAF fighter strength effectively weakened. The way would therefore be open for the second phase of the aerial battle, which would aim at the destruction of the enemy's morale by massive attacks against his civilian population.

The German navy had had little faith in the success of Operation

Sea Lion; now the German army was becoming increasingly pessimistic. As summer faded and the elation at the defeat of France was transformed into a more sober mood, the German high command had more and more doubts. Hitler had always been a doubter, thus proving again the high quality of his military intuition. This mood found its exact counterpart across the Channel. As the Germans became uneasy, the British became confident. Churchill was later to comment dryly, "If we could have agreed equally well about other matters, there need have been no war."

Apart from the brightness of the British spirit, one other factor gave cause for hope. President Roosevelt had been seeking ways of bringing effective aid to Britain despite the constitutional restrictions that hampered him. In the first week of September a deal had been concluded whereby fifty overage United States destroyers were given to Britain in exchange for ninety-nine-year leases of British naval and air bases.

Britain was still very much in the war, and the spirit of the British people was probably never higher than at this time of extreme peril. That same British lack of realism that had for so long proved disastrous was now a positive asset, for even now few — at least among the common people — could actually envisage a British defeat.* They were proud to stand alone against the Nazi power. England was a good place to be in 1940. On September 13, RAF bombers attacked the German invasion barges at Ostend, sinking eighty of them and forcing Hitler to agree to yet a further postponement of Operation Sea Lion.

The crisis came on September 15. On this day the Luftwaffe made it supreme effort in daylight raids against London, and was beaten back at every point, with heavy losses. The RAF claimed to have shot down 174 enemy aircraft. The real figure was 58, for an RAF loss of 26, but even this was a ratio of better than two to one. And it proved sufficient. The Luftwaffe had very obviously been unsuccessful in its effort to win aerial supremacy. The year was beginning to fail, and the time of autumn fogs and equinoctial storms on the Channel approached apace. On the night of September 17, just to drive the lesson home, RAF bombers made heavy attacks on German shipping concentrated in the Channel ports between Antwerp and Boulogne, inflicting serious damage.

*The author, then a sergeant in the Canadian Army Overseas, remembers being given a lift by a middle-aged English lady, who, in the course of conversation, asked him what he thought the world would be like after the war. When he was unable to enlighten her on the point, she told him her own views: "We shall simply have to rule, that's all." And this at a time when it seemed at least problematical whether Britain would survive the winter!

Hitler postponed Sea Lion indefinitely on September 17. On October 12 the invasion was put back to the spring of 1941, never to be revived. Long before good weather came to the Channel again, the British had achieved an impregnable defensive position and Hitler had made his fatal decision to invade the Soviet Union. The German failure to eliminate Britain from the war, either by negotiation or by force of arms, was a decisive turning point in the struggle. Much of the credit must go to the fighter pilots of the Royal Air Force, for between July 10 and the end of October, German aircraft losses had totaled 1722 for an RAF loss of only 915. Churchill, whom no one has ever accused of being at a loss for a phrase, summed it up well: "Never in the field of human conflict was so much owed by so many to so few."

So FAR Britain had managed to remain in the war. But it appeared as if all the world, with the temporary exception of the western hemisphere, was now easy prey for the Nazi and communist dictators, the Japanese imperialists, and the fortunately allied Italians. During this period Winston Churchill's great qualities showed to the best advantage, for if any man was ever indomitable in the face of calamitous adversity, that man was surely the British prime minister. He was, it is true, sustained by the hope that the United States would eventually realize the hard choice that lay before her and accept belligerency rather than certain, ultimate defeat at the hands of the victorious totalitarians. Yet as 1940 drew to a close there seemed little to give substance to this hope. Congress had authorized a peacetime conscription bill, but by the incredible margin of only one vote, and though President Roosevelt was alive to the danger in which his country stood, many — perhaps most — of his countrymen did not wish to share this knowledge.

However, in March 1941 Congress passed the Lend-Lease Act, which made available to Britain, as a gift, a great flood of American armaments and supplies. Churchill later described Lend-Lease as "the most unsordid act in the history of any nation." It was scarcely that, since Britain was fighting the deadly foes of the United States while that nation enjoyed the comforts of neutrality. There is no doubt, however, that Lend-Lease was a godsend to the British, who were soon to experience a series of new disasters.

The German U-boat and aircraft campaign against British shipping was the most serious menace in 1941. Shipping losses far exceeded replacements, and in May the battleship *Bismarck* and the cruiser *Prinz Eugen* escaped into the Atlantic, where they constituted a deadly menace to Britain's North Atlantic convoys. The German ships were intercepted on the 24th in the Denmark Strait between Iceland and

Greenland, but in the first few minutes of action the British battleship *Hood* was sunk by the *Bismarck* with the loss of fifteen hundred men, and the *Prince of Wales* was so badly damaged that she had to break off the fight. For the next two days it seemed that the *Bismarck* might escape, but she was spotted by a British aircraft on the 26th some 700 miles west of Brest. After Swordfish aircraft from the carrier *Ark Royal* hit her with torpedoes and immobilized her steering gear, the *Bismarck* was sunk by gunfire from the *Rodney* and *King George V* and by the final torpedo launched from the cruiser *Dorsetshire*. The *Prinz Eugen* managed to escape to Brest.

President Roosevelt again came to Britain's aid. An American air base was established in Greenland; British warships were allowed to use repair facilities in the United States; in April Roosevelt ruled that the American "security zone," patrolled by the United States Navy, was extended eastward to west longitude 26°; and in July American troops relieved the British and Canadian garrison in Iceland. The United States Navy now escorted convoys to Reykjavik, and, without regard for the rules of neutrality, allowed British ships to accompany these convoys.

On August 9 Churchill arrived in Placentia Bay, Newfoundland, aboard the *Prince of Wales*, for a rendezvous with Roosevelt, who had sailed there on the U.S.S. *Augusta*. Like President Wilson before him, Roosevelt had a fondness for broad, idealistic statements of policy, and in the circumstances of 1941 Churchill was far readier to cooperate in such a declaration of intent than Clemenceau and Lloyd George had been in the First World War. In the Atlantic Charter the democracies renounced any territorial or other aggrandizement and declared that no territorial changes should take place except in accordance with the freely expressed wishes of the people concerned. All nations were to be able to choose their own form of government; and those that had been forcibly deprived of their sovereign rights were to have them restored. There was to be equal access for all to trade and raw materials, economic cooperation, peace, "freedom from fear and want," safety to journey on the high seas, and eventual disarmament. Wilson, perhaps, had done more to draft the Atlantic Charter than either Roosevelt or Churchill, and subsequent events indicated that the world was no more ready for such a program in the 1940s than it had been in 1918.

Admiral Raeder was forbidden to attack American ships, for Hitler intended to deal with one enemy at a time. He hoped that by late 1941 Britain and Russia would be defeated and that he would then be able to turn on the United States. Despite the order, three American vessels were sunk by U-boats in the spring and summer of 1941, and in

September the United States destroyer *Greer* was attacked by a German submarine. President Roosevelt thereupon ordered the United States Navy to shoot at sight any German or Italian warships entering the security zone. Obviously the American President had abandoned any pretense of maintaining real neutrality, but what he was unable to do was to bring the United States openly into the war, since the right to declare war belonged to Congress. Meanwhile Germany appeared to have every advantage on her side, including that of time, and it seemed that the Nazi dictator had only to exert a steady and continuing pressure, which was well within his capability, to be certain of final victory.

Between September 1940, when Hitler abandoned Operation Sea Lion, and June 1941, when he invaded the Soviet Union, the center of gravity of the war shifted to the Mediterranean theater, for the good reason that the British and Italians were both already there. The Italian forces in Africa numbered about 415,000, but General Sir Archibald Wavell, the British Commander-in-Chief Middle East, had only some 83,000 troops, most of them in Egypt and Palestine.

The logic of empire, rather than military expediency, dictated the British dispositions, as indeed it did the Italian. Their First World War experiences in Mesopotamia, Palestine, and Salonika had taught the British little of the dangers of dispersion of force, though in 1940, with the British home islands under attack as they had never been between 1914 and 1918, those dangers were greatly magnified. It could, in fact, be argued with some cogency that the entire Middle East theater was a gigantic irrelevancy, the more so since the Suez Canal was of little use and the Mediterranean all but closed to British convoys. However, Churchill, in a directive to the war cabinet issued on April 28, 1941, emphasized that "the loss of Egypt and the Middle East would be a disaster of the first magnitude to Great Britain, second only to successful invasion and final conquest [of the British Isles]." The prime minister went on to say that "the life and honor of Great Britain depend upon the successful defense of Egypt."

The British Chiefs of Staff were quick to point out that "life and honor" are not synonymous terms and that the "life" of Britain would continue "so long as we are not successfully invaded and do not lose the Battle of the Atlantic." Yet they did agree that the Army of the Nile should "fight with no thought of retreat or withdrawal." The Chief of the Imperial General Staff, General Sir John Dill, in a memorandum to the prime minister, agreed with a previous assessment of Churchill's: it was ultimately of more importance to hold Singapore, because it was "a steppingstone to Australia," than it was to hold the Middle East.

Hindsight being the legitimate prerogative of the historian, it is pertinent to point out that Singapore did in fact fall, with no very disastrous consequences except to British prestige and to an already obsolescent imperialism, and that it is therefore probable *a fortiori* that the loss of Egypt would not have been "a disaster of the first magnitude." The point is important because it is possible that the haphazard development of a theater of war in North Africa distorted the thrust of British (and later of American) strategy, leading as it did to the invasion of Sicily and Italy and to the mounting of Operation Dragoon, the belated and unnecessary invasion of southern France. Nor is it inconceivable that the decision to hold the Middle East might have been different had the British prime minister not been a man of belligerent temperament who believed that it was necessary always to engage the enemy *somewhere* and had he not been an imperialist who had himself fought at Omdurman.

In the middle of August, an overwhelmingly superior Italian force attacked British Somaliland and forced the British garrison to withdraw. By early autumn the fascist strength in Libya had been built up to nearly 300,000 men, and Mussolini was pressing his reluctant commander-in-chief, Marshal Rodolfo Graziani, to attack Egypt without delay. The ponderous Italian advance at last began on September 13, but when he reached Sidi Barrâni, Graziani, apparently believing that he had done as much as could reasonably be expected of him, settled down to defend himself in desert fortifications. The Western Desert Force, under Major General R. N. O'Connor, at once began to harass the extended Italian communications. Meanwhile, late in September, a joint Free French–British expedition under De Gaulle was defeated when it attempted to capture the Vichy port of Dakar.

On October 28 Hitler met Mussolini in Florence, to be greeted with the unwelcome news that Italy had that morning invaded Greece. The invasion, which had been backed by no adequate staff evaluation or planning, was launched from Albania as a three-pronged assault. It soon ran into difficulties everywhere. The Italian soldiers had little stomach for fighting, and the Greeks defended themselves tenaciously in the mountains before counterattacking. Within a few weeks the twenty-seven invading Italian divisions had been forced back thirty miles within Albania and were fighting, not too effectively, to contain the sixteen Greek divisions, under General Alexander Papagos, that opposed them.

On the night of November 11/12 aircraft from the *Illustrious* struck at the Italian fleet at Taranto, inflicting heavy damage. And on December 9 O'Connor's Western Desert Force attacked the inadequate Italian defenses at Sidi Barrâni and Mersa Matrûh. The distinguishing mark of the fighting was the readiness with which the Italians surrendered; one British battalion headquarters was moved to report that it was impossible to count the prisoners taken since there were so many of them, but that there were "about five acres of officers and 200 acres of other ranks."

The Italians, under the command of the Duke of Aosta, retreated headlong along the coastal road toward Benghazi, with the British in pursuit. Between December 9 and February 6, ten Italian divisions were destroyed and 130,000 prisoners captured. This remarkable feat of arms had been accomplished by a British force of little more than two divisions, and British losses had amounted to only some 500 killed and 1400 wounded. Indeed, the British might well have driven the Italians completely out of North Africa had it not been that Wavell was now ordered to supply an expeditionary force for Greece. Meanwhile, two other British forces were advancing south from the Sudan and north from Kenya to overrun Italian East Africa. Addis Ababa was taken on April 6, and five weeks later, when the Duke of Aosta surrendered at Amba Alagi, the Italian hold on Ethiopia was broken.

Hitler had been far from pleased at Mussolini's unilateral decision to invade Greece, but when he was presented with the fait accompli he made the best of it. On January 8, at a conference at Berchtesgaden, he announced his intention of sending German troops to Greece as soon as the weather permitted. At this same conference he also announced that he would occupy the rest of France, seize the French fleet at Toulon, and send German formations to assist the Italians in North Africa.

Of course, Britain was bound by her guarantee of April 1939 to help Greece. An infantry brigade had been sent to Crete, and four RAF squadrons were dispatched to Greece shortly after the Italian invasion. The Greeks, however, declined more British assistance because they feared that British intervention, while not sufficient to alter appreciably the military situation, might provoke a German attack. Churchill had high hopes of forming a "Balkan front" of Greece, Yugoslavia, and Turkey, and much diplomatic endeavor was directed to this end, though it all came to nothing. Turkey was fearful of a Russian, as well as of a German, attack, and none of these Balkan nations, prepared though they all were to defend themselves if invaded, was under any illusion about the extent of British assistance.

Late in October 1940 Hitler had occupied Rumania; and Bulgaria, bribed with promises of Greek territory, joined the Axis on March 1. The next day the German Twelfth Army began to move into Bulgaria. The British and Greeks had naturally foreseen this possibility and had at last entered into high-level talks. It was decided that the best hope of success lay in a defense of the Aliakmon River line, which ran from the Yugoslav frontier to the sea west of the Vardar River. The defense of this line, which passed through Mount Olympus, Veroia, Edhessa, and Mount Kaimakchalan, would mean the abandonment of Salonika, but Salonika could not in any case be defended unless Yugoslavia entered the war on Greece's side.

The British had wanted General Papagos to withdraw his troops from the Macedonian frontier to the Aliakmon line, but a compromise was eventually worked out whereby three Greek divisions would remain along the Macedonian border while the Aliakmon positions would be manned by British formations as they arrived and by another three Greek divisions. General Sir Henry Maitland Wilson would command on the Aliakmon position. This compromise was a thoroughly unsatisfactory one, but some sixty-two thousand British, Australian, New Zealand, and Polish troops were sent to Greece in March anyway, to take up their positions along the 100-mile stretch of front between Mount Olympus and the Yugoslav frontier.

On March 26 the Italian navy sank a British cruiser and two transports in Suda Bay, but two nights later the British sank three Italian cruisers and two destroyers off Cape Matapan.

On March 24 representatives of the Yugoslav government of the regent, Prince Paul, signed a treaty in Vienna that in effect made Yugoslavia a German satellite. The envoys had hardly returned to Belgrade, however, when patriotic elements in the Serbian population overthrew the regency and proclaimed the young king, Peter, to be the ruling monarch. A new government was formed under General Dusan Simovich, and Yugoslavia declared her neutrality. This abrupt reversal of Yugoslav policy enraged Hitler, who decided to postpone his invasion of the Soviet Union until he had taught the Yugoslavs a lesson. He ordered Göring to destroy Belgrade from the air, and Göring did his best to comply. Some seventeen thousand persons were killed in German air attacks on Belgrade during the first days of the invasion. On April 6 German forces invaded both Yugoslavia and Greece, driving down with armored columns through the Rupel Pass in the Struma valley and along the valleys of the Strumitsa and Vardar rivers. Salonika fell on April 8. The German Twelfth Army, under Field Marshal List, burst through with fifteen divisions, four of them armored. Even more dangerous was the German thrust into Yugoslavia from the east and north, which soon overwhelmed the Yugoslav defenders. The remnants of twenty-eight Yugoslav divisions surrendered at Sarajevo on April 17, eleven days after the blitzkrieg had been launched.

With this, the Greek position at once became impossible, for the

Greek divisions fighting in Albania could not be disengaged and were now being cut off by a German advance south through the Monastir gap. The German thrust also outflanked the Aliakmon line, and on the night of April 11/12 Wilson began to withdraw from that position. There was some hard fighting at Thermopylae, especially by gallant New Zealand troops, but as early as April 16 it was obvious that Greece must fall. With the concurrence of the Greek government, the British began their evacuation on the 24th. Three days before this, the main Greek army in Albania, which had fought so splendidly against great odds for so long, had been forced to surrender. The Greek armies in the north surrendered on April 23 and Athens fell on the 27th.

The British evacuation took place under extremely difficult conditions, even though it may be assumed that the British were developing some expertise for an operation they had practiced so often. By the night of April 28/29, when the evacuation came to an end, some 50,000 troops had been rescued. Many of the evacuated troops were sent to Crete, partly because there was not enough sea lift to take them back to Egypt. The British lost some 12,000 men in Greece alone; German losses in both Yugoslavia and Greece amounted to only 5650 killed, wounded, and missing.

So Greece and Yugoslavia fell under Axis domination, British arms received another stinging humiliation, and all hopes of a Balkan front came crashing down. The causes of the disaster were more political than military. The British were honor bound to assist the Greeks, and they preferred defeat in the field to allowing Greece to be overrun without honoring their guarantee. The scale of British assistance to Greece is another matter, and it is probable that honor could have been satisfied at less cost. Moreover, the decision to send a British expeditionary force to Greece had been taken on the basis of inadequate information, without any proper appreciation of the situation and without calculating how it would be possible to fight for any length of time in both Greece and the Western Desert.

The full price to be exacted for the Greek adventure had not yet been paid. Hitler decided to capture Crete by an airborne assault — a bold decision, for the odds were against the attackers both on land and sea. The British had had a garrison on Crete since the middle of November 1940, but the defense of the island had been undertaken in the most haphazard manner. Between November 19, 1940, and May 20, 1941, there had been seven British commanders, of whom Major General Sir Bernard C. Freyberg, VC, was the latest, having been appointed only on April 30. Although there were shortages of transport and artillery, and although the Germans would have aerial supremacy, the defense of Crete appeared a reasonable proposition, for after the evacuation of Greece, Freyberg had nearly forty-three thousand troops on the island, including more than ten thousand Greeks.

By the end of the first week in May British intelligence had been able to supply full details of the German invasion plan, including the date of the attack. After a preliminary aerial bombardment, paratroop and glider-borne landings would be made in three areas. One force would capture the Maleme airfield in the west; another would take Canea and Suda in the center, and a second wave here would capture Retimo airfield; the third group, in the east, would capture the airfield at Heraklion. Freyberg's plan of defense was to hold the three airfields and the area around Suda Bay.

The aerial attacks began at 5:30 on the morning of May 20 and were following at 7:15 A.M. by the first airborne landings. The first wave of attackers suffered heavy casualties, and by nightfall it seemed as though the defense was more than holding its own. Although the Germans had landed some seven thousand men, no airfield had been taken and the invaders in the central and eastern groups were in serious difficulties.

General Kurt Student, the German commander, nevertheless persisted, concentrating now against Maleme airfield in the west. By the morning of the 21st, Junker 52s were landing at Maleme, and from then on the Germans reinforced steadily. An attempt that night to bring in artillery, tanks, and two more mountain battalions by sea in Greek caïques was beaten back by the Royal Navy, with losses, and a similar fate met a second seaborne attempt on the night of the 22nd/23rd. The Germans never did manage to reinforce their assault on Crete by sea, but the Royal Navy also suffered in these engagements, losing two cruisers and four destroyers.

On the morning of the 22nd the Germans landed three more mountain battalions at Maleme. In all, the Germans brought in only some 22,000 troops; but by the 27th they had taken Canea, and on the 28th they captured Suda Bay and linked up with their forces at Retimo and Heraklion. Thus none of the German lodgments was in fact eliminated. On the night of the 28th/29th the British began to evacuate Crete, using the north coast. The next night, evacuation continued from Sphakia on the south coast and went on until the night of May 31/June 1. In all, about 16,500 troops were brought off, of whom 14,580 were British or Commonwealth soldiers. British army casualties were 15,743; the Royal Navy lost over 2000 men. The Germans suffered 6580 casualties. Whereas in Greece the Germans had had every advantage on their side, this was not so in Crete, where their single material superiority was in air power.

For the sake of the abortive Greek adventure, the British forces in North Africa had been gravely weakened, so there was a further forfeit to be paid. Wavell had had to send troops from Palestine to crush a revolt in Iraq, and when the Germans began to infiltrate Vichy-held Syria, with the complicity of the French General Dentz, Wavell was forced to dispatch a force there. Although the Vichy French resisted, Syria was occupied by the middle of June. Elsewhere things continued to go wrong for the British.

In February, General Rommel was appointed to command the newly formed Afrika Korps in Tripolitania. On April 2 Rommel took Benghazi, then proceeded to drive the British completely out of Cyrenaica, except for the Australian 9th Division, which took refuge in Tobruk and withstood all German attacks. Wavell, determined to hold on to Tobruk, reinforced its garrison with the Australian 7th Division, but two relief attempts, in May and June, both failed.

Because Churchill was determined not to be driven out of Africa, he now reinforced that theater and replaced Wavell with General Sir Claude Auchinleck. The Western Desert Force became the Eighth Army, under the command of Lieutenant General Sir Alan Cunningham. The Royal Air Force in the Western Desert was built up to a strength of some 700 aircraft and British tank strength was increased to over 700. Rommel had only 320 tanks, of which nearly half were obsolete Italian machines.

Auchinleck was clearly expected to attack to relieve Tobruk, and he did so on November 18. There was every reason to expect success since the odds were greatly in the British favor. However, the British armor, incompetently handled, was defeated in detail, and Cunningham began to consider falling back to the Egyptian border. Fortunately, Auchinleck appeared at Eighth Army headquarters, assessed the situation more realistically, and decided to stand firm. He replaced Cunningham with General Neil Ritchie on November 26. Rommel's tank strength had, in fact, been so depleted that he was forced to retire on the 27th. He abandoned his investment of Tobruk and withdrew to the borders of Tripoli. With this the 1941 campaign in North Africa drew to an inconclusive close.

By now events elsewhere had far overshadowed the fighting in the Mediterranean theater. Hitler had always intended someday to invade the Soviet Union. Even when he had been a political nonentity, dreaming wild fantasies of power, the conquest of German *Lebensraum* in the east had been his most cherished hope. He intended to annex the Ukraine, White Russia, and the Baltic states and to establish a satellite Finland that would extend to the White Sea. The enlarged Germany that would thus be created would serve as the homeland for an eventual population of 400 million Germans and would provide the firm economic base for his thousand-year Reich. It was the world's misfortune that Hitler, against all probability, had attained a position that enabled him to act out his fantasies. In September 1940 General Friedrich Paulus was given responsibility for planning Operation Barbarossa, as the invasion of the Soviet Union was code-named. Paulus completed his plan by November and it was then war-gamed.

Hitler had already greatly strengthened his position in the Balkans, for in August 1940, in Vienna, Ribbentrop had imposed a settlement by which Rumania had been forced to give part of Transylvania to Hungary, to cede the Southern Dobruja to Bulgaria, and to accept a German military mission. Although Stalin had much disliked the German influence in Rumania, for the time being he did nothing about it. On the Soviet Union's northern flank, too, Hitler had been making ominous moves, for he had sent General Eduard Dietl's mountain division from Norway across neutral Sweden to Finland. On November 21, 1940, when Molotov visited Berlin, Ribbentrop proposed that the Soviet Union join with Germany, Italy, and Japan in a four-power pact to carve up the British Empire. Stalin was quite prepared to agree but he stated as preconditions that German troops leave Finland, that a mutual assistance pact be signed between the Soviet Union and Bulgaria, that the area south of Baku to the Persian Gulf be in the Russian sphere of influence, that Japan give up her economic interests in northern Sakhalin, and that the Soviet Union control the Dardanelles. If Turkey did not agree to give up the Dardanelles, Stalin stipulated that all four powers should join in military action against her. Hitler did not reply to these Soviet demands but instead gave his approval to the Barbarossa plan on December 5.

According to Führer Directive No. 18, the aim of Operation Barbarossa was to occupy and hold a line between Archangel and Astrakhan at the mouth of the Volga on the Caspian Sea, taking in Leningrad, Moscow, the Ukraine, the Donbas, Kuban, and the Caucasus. The military objective was to destroy the Russian armies in the west and prevent their withdrawal eastward. This was to be done by powerful armored spearheads, which were to make deep penetrations and to encircle the Soviet forces. No word was said as to what would happen once the Archangel-Astrakhan line had been reached, though, as the crow flies, the length of the German front would then be somewhat in excess of 1250 miles. Presumably Hitler believed that the destruction of the Russian field armies and the occupation of almost all European Russia would remove any menace from the east. In Führer Directive No. 21, issued on December 18, Hitler ordered that all preparations for Barbarossa be completed by May 15, 1941.

On April 4 Hitler gratuitously promised the Japanese foreign minister, Yosuke Matsuoka, who was visiting Berlin, that if Japan became involved in war with the United States, Germany "would take the necessary steps at once." Meanwhile, he suggested, the best way to discourage the United States from belligerency would be for Japan to attack Singapore. Hitler said no word to the Japanese statesman of his coming attack on the Soviet Union. Nine days later Japan and the Soviet Union signed a nonaggression pact, a serious diplomatic defeat for Germany. Shortly after Operation Barbarossa had been launched, Germany suggested that Japan attack Vladivostok, but the Japanese honored their pact with Stalin — for which they were rewarded in 1945 by being attacked by the Soviet Union in violation of the nonaggression treaty.

Hitler had warned his generals that he intended a brutal, barbarous war, not one that could be conducted "in a knightly fashion." Field Marshal Wilhelm Keitel issued an order on May 13 that all captured Soviet commissars were to be executed and that any Russian civilian suspected of an offense against the invaders could be shot on the order of any officer. Most vicious of all, it was made clear that German soldiers committing crimes against Russian civilians need not be prosecuted. The aim of the war was naked exploitation and conquest. The Economic Office East was established under Göring to systematize the plunder. Commenting on its Plan Oldenburg, for the administration of conquered Soviet territory, the Economic Office East reported, "There is no doubt that many millions of people will starve to death in the Soviet Union if we take out of the country what we need." Göring, talking to Count Galeazzo Ciano, Mussolini's son-in-law and foreign minister, was more explicit. "This year," he said, "between twenty and thirty million persons will die of starvation in Russia." It is not clear whether the reason for Plan Oldenburg was the belief that Germany would require this amount of food, with the deaths of millions of Russians from starvation being merely a side effect, or whether what was desired was the depopulation of the conquered territories, with starvation being used merely as a convenient method of liquidation. Whatever the primary German motive, the outlook for those Russians unfortunate enough to fall under Nazi occupation was bleak.

Nothing was more typically Nazi than Operation Barbarossa. It was typical not only because of its wickedness but also because of the element of irresponsibility that marked the plan. Although the design was grandiose to the point of insanity, the details were poorly worked out. Estimates of enemy strength were based more on guesswork than on accurate intelligence. Hitler expected to achieve his fantastic objectives in eight weeks, and the whole plan betrays a pathological overconfidence. Hitler's calculations were breathtaking in their boldness. He expected the Soviet Union to be overthrown before the winter of 1941–1942, and it was then his intention to turn back and give Britain the coup de grâce. He did not consider that this would really be engaging in a two-front war, and had he been correct in his assessment of the time required to defeat the Soviet Union, he would have been right in this, for Britain was in no position seriously to interfere with the Nazi war plans.

The German offensive was to be launched on an enormously broad front, but the *Schwerpunkt* was to be north of the Pripet Marshes, where two great army groups, Army Group North and Army Group Center, would close a giant pincer on the Soviet armies facing them and then capture Moscow. South of the Pripet, Army Group South would drive toward Kiev from Lublin and occupy the Ukraine. Army Group North, under Field Marshal Wilhelm Ritter von Leeb, would consist of the Sixteenth Army (Busch), the Eighteenth Army (Küchler), and a force of four panzer divisions under Colonel General Höpner. Army Group Center, considerably the largest, under Field Marshal Bock, would consist of the Second Army (Kluge), the Fourth Army (Strauss), the Ninth Army (Weichs), and two armored groups totaling ten panzer divisions led by Guderian and Hoth. Army Group South, under Field Marshal Rundstedt, would consist of the First Army (Stülpnagel), the Seventeenth Army (Reichman), a German-Rumanian army (Schobert), and a force of four panzer divisions under Kleist.

Hitler had originally intended to launch his attack on the Soviet Union by the middle of May, but on April 30, as a result of the operations in Greece and Yugoslavia, he postponed the date to June 22. It has been claimed that this postponement was fatal to the German plans and that the sufferings of the Greeks and Yugoslavs therefore found their vindication in the German failure in Russia. The idea is an attractive one, but on closer examination the claim cannot be maintained. In the first place the Germans were pressed for time in Russia, not primarily because of their late start, but because of strategic errors that Hitler committed during the course of the campaign; in the second place the middle of May was really too early for the invasion of Russia. Before the middle of June, late spring rains would ruin the roads, flood the rivers, and make movement very difficult except on the few paved highways. Thus, since the initial surprise thrust had to go rapidly to yield the best results, Hitler probably gained more than he lost by the postponement.

By June 22, 1941, when Operation Barbarossa was launched, the three German army groups contained 130 divisions, of which 19 were panzer and 14 were motor divisions. Only 46 divisions were left in the rest of Europe and these included merely 1 motor division and 1 panzer brigade. Even so, the amount of force reserved from Barbarossa may have been excessive. Certainly far fewer than 46 divisions could have countered any British initiative on the continent, a possibility that was in any case unlikely. Most of the German air force was also shifted to the east; only Luftflotte 3 was left to face Britain.

Great as the German concentration in the east was, it was smaller than the Soviet concentration opposing it, for on June 22 the Russians were disposed in three very large army groups, containing, in all, 193 equivalent divisions, of which no fewer than 54 were tank or motor divisions. The disparity in actual tank strength was even greater than the overall disparity, for the Germans had only 3550 tanks to more than 12,000 Russian. The Russian tanks were at least as good as the German, though the training of the Russian tank crews and, even more notably, the abilities of the Russian tank corps commanders were markedly inferior.

To offset this numerical superiority, there were some serious Russian weaknesses. The purge of the Soviet officer corps in 1937 had inflicted great injury on the Red Army. The bulk of the Soviet forces was concentrated too close to the frontiers, which in the past two years had been extended at the expense of Poland, Latvia, Lithuania, Estonia, and Rumania. The Stalin Line, which had guarded the old, pre-1939 frontiers, had been partly dismantled, and the new, forward defense positions were incomplete. The Red Army's armored divisions had been broken up and the tanks allotted to infantry formations, and though this error had been corrected and the armored divisions reconstituted, they were still in the process of shaking down. Then, too, Stalin and the Soviet high command considered that the most likely *Schwerpunkt* of a German attack would be in the south, and the Soviet defenses were heavily weighted in that region. Colonel General Kirponos, commanding the Soviet Southwest Army Group, had 64 infantry divisions and 14 armored brigades at his disposal; Colonel General Pavlov, in the center, had only 45 infantry divisions and 15 armored brigades; and Colonel General Kuznetsov, in the north, had only 30 infantry divisions and 8 armored brigades.

Nevertheless, the Russians should have been able to put up a much stronger initial defense than they did. They were, in fact, taken by surprise, and for this there was no excuse at all. Stalin had been given repeated, detailed warnings of Hitler's intention; he was even told the correct date of Barbarossa. And these warnings had come from a variety of sources — from Soviet intelligence, from Churchill, and from the American government. German deserters had warned the Red

Army of the blow that was about to fall upon it. The reports from communist intelligence agents were the most plausible, accurate, and detailed of all, and they displayed a remarkable convergence, which should have augmented their credibility. Viktor Sokolov, the head of the Rote Kapelle cell in Brussels, Rudolph Rössler ("Lucy") in Switzerland, Leopold Trepper in Paris, and Dr. Richard Sorge in Tokyo all informed Stalin of Barbarossa. There is an instructive irony in the fact that the Soviet Union, which since 1917 had certainly spent more on clandestine intelligence than all the rest of the world together, should, in the moment of supreme crisis, have refused to believe the absolutely accurate reports of its own agents. German troop movements in Poland, Rumania, Finland, and Hungary could not be concealed, and rumors of the coming German invasion were prevalent in Moscow for weeks before the attack. Yet Stalin obstinately refused to believe the accumulated evidence.

The Soviet Union had assiduously supplied Hitler with grain and raw materials, and Soviet deliveries continued right up to the last moment. The last laden train from Russia to Germany ran through the German troop concentrations on the central front at two o'clock in the morning of June 22, much to the amusement of the German soldiers waiting to attack. There can have been few occasions in history when a ruler played into his opponent's hands as persistently as Stalin did into Hitler's.

At dawn on June 22 Count Friedrich Schulenburg, the German ambassador in Moscow, called on Molotov and read him the German declaration of war. Molotov's predecessor, Litvinov, had tried to work against Hitler in cooperation with the British and French, and had failed. Molotov had tried to work with Hitler against the western democracies, and Count Schulenburg's grave voice now informed the Russian foreign minister that his policy had failed even more disastrously than Litvinov's. When Schulenburg read out the declaration of war, Molotov exclaimed reproachfully, "Do you think we have deserved this?" It was a question that the Rumanians, the Poles, and the Finns would have had no difficulty in answering.

The German attack had already begun, at 3:15 A.M. under cover of an enormous artillery barrage. At first all went well for the invaders. Almost all the bridges along the vast front were captured intact; much of the Soviet air force was destroyed on the ground; many Soviet soldiers were on leave; some Soviet divisions were separated from their artillery; and many units were overrun and captured before they had time to deploy. Although Guderian was concerned that the panzer thrusts were not reaching deep enough, the Germans captured huge numbers of prisoners, and the Russians found no place where they could make a stand. Within four days Army Group Center had cut off and surrounded two entire Soviet armies east of Bialystok, and by July 3 all the Soviet forces in the Bialystok Bend of the Niemen River had been eliminated. Army Group Center now opened its pincers again, to close on the Soviet forces west of Minsk. The arms closed on July 10, and in this vast trap thirty-three Russian divisions were destroyed.

In the south, where Rundstedt's army group attacked in Galicia, the Russians fought magnificently and were well handled by General Kirponos. At first the German rate of advance was slow, not more than about six miles a day. Nevertheless, Rundstedt broke into the Ukraine.

In the north Leeb's armor at first made excellent time. Manstein's panzers cut through Lithuania and within four days had driven 155 miles to capture intact the bridge over the Daugava River at Daugavpils. But Manstein was halted for six days, until the infantry of the Sixteenth Army could catch up with him, and in that time the disorganized Russians were able to put their front in order and reinforce. When the German offensive resumed on July 2, it met much stiffer opposition.

These setbacks, however, were relatively minor ones. In the first three weeks of the war few people anywhere believed that the Soviet Union would not be promptly defeated. Very likely Stalin thought this himself. Certainly he was strangely invisible during the first fortnight of the war. Molotov, not the Soviet dictator, announced to the Russian people in a radio broadcast that they had been invaded, and there were persistent rumors that, when it had seemed as if his long tyranny was drawing to an end, Stalin had gone on a monumental drunk. However that may be, someone was certainly coordinating the Russian armies and trying to patch up an effective defense. Commanders who had been defeated were replaced, and sometimes executed, but except in the center, where General A. I. Yeremenko infused new life into the defense, none of these changes made any notable improvement. The Germans were apparently invincible, and their fantastic succession of larger and greater Tannenbergs depressed the Russians as much as they exalted the Nazis.

After Minsk the weather broke and for a day or two heavy rains slowed down the main German advance. But in some ways it was almost worse when the weather was fair. Except for the main Smolensk-Moscow highway, the Russian roads were poor and unpaved, and the dust was unbelievable; vehicles and weapons were clogged by it and rendered unserviceable, and it was a constant torment to the marching infantry.

In spite of these hindrances, the Germans entered Vitebsk on July

10, and on the same day Guderian's panzers got across the Dnieper. The outskirts of Smolensk were reached on the 16th. The Germans had advanced more than two thirds of the way to Moscow. So far the ambitious German timetable was being meticulously adhered to.

The Russians, however, did not collapse as the French had done. On July 15 Hoth's Panzer Group 3 by-passed Smolensk to the north and drove on to cut the Smolensk-Moscow highway. The German pincers closed around Smolensk the next day, but the trapped Russians fought on until August 7. The Germans took another 300,000 prisoners, but their own casualties had been heavy, and a pause for reorganization would be needed. The principal difference between this blitzkrieg and the one that had swept away the Third French Republic was not that the Russians fought better than the French — though they did — but rather that the distances to be traversed in Russia were so much greater than those in France, and the French road network was infinitely better than the Russian.

No sooner did the Germans pause at Smolensk than the Russians counterattacked viciously. Very heavy fighting developed in the Yelnya Bend east of Smolensk and continued throughout August. North of the Smolensk-Moscow highway the Russians also counterattacked, using for the first time their secret weapon, the multiple-rocket battery called the *katyusha*, known to the Germans as the "Stalin organ."

On August 8 General Franz Halder, the Chief of the Army General Staff, noted in his diary: "At the beginning of the war we reckoned on about 200 enemy divisions. We have already counted 360." A great deal of territory had been captured, but the principal German aim of destroying the Russian armies west of the Dnieper had not been achieved.

Part of the trouble perhaps was the extreme breadth of the front. The Germans could not have done anything about the distance that lay between Warsaw and Moscow, but had they been wise to attack the Soviet Union everywhere at once? Might not a single great drive along the Warsaw-Smolensk-Moscow axis possibly have paid better dividends? If Moscow had been taken with one irresistibly heavy blow, it would have been almost impossible for the Soviets to coordinate or reinforce their northern and southern fronts. With the center gone, everything west of the Volga would have collapsed. And could Stalin have held together a government in Asiatic Russia?

It was too late now for the Germans to entertain such second thoughts. To the south of the Pripet Marshes Rundstedt reached Zhitomir and Uman, where Kleist's panzers surrounded three Russian armies in the first week of August. Afterward the German armor swept down the south side of the Dnieper Bend to Zaporozhe, where the Russians blew up their cherished Dnieper Dam on the 24th. Meanwhile the Rumanian Fourth Army invaded the southern Ukraine and advanced to surround Odessa. In the Ukraine the Germans were initially often greeted as liberators by the local population, who had suffered much under communism, but this asset of local goodwill was thrown away by the Nazis. The brutalities of the occupying forces, particularly the SS, often turned potential allies into implacable enemies.

In the north, as well, progress was not as rapid or victory as clearcut as had been hoped for. The country was difficult and the Russians had a relatively short front to defend. Yet in spite of heavy Russian counterattacks, the Germans advanced north to take Pskov, near the south shore of Lake Peipus. The way now seemed clear for an advance toward Leningrad between Lake Peipus and Lake Ilmen, a route that would link up with the Finns, who were attacking across the Karelian Isthmus east of Lake Ladoga. However, the Germans now bumped into a strong Russian defense line between Lake Ilmen and Narva, on the Gulf of Finland, which held them up for three weeks. The advance began again on August 8 and though the fighting was very heavy, the Germans captured Novgorod, north of Lake Ilmen, on the 16th. By the end of the third week in August, Leeb's left wing was within twenty-five miles of Leningrad. Meanwhile, the Finns, under Marshal Mannerheim, had captured Viipuri.

While Leeb was advancing on Leningrad, another campaign was being fought in the Arctic. As part of Operation Barbarossa, Hitler had decided to capture Murmansk. Dietl's Mountain Corps attacked from the Petsamo area. Farther south the XXXVI Corps was to cut the Murmansk railway at Kandalaksha, and farther south still the III Finnish Corps was to cut the railway at Loukhi. None of the three attacks reached its objective. Murmansk remained firmly in Russian hands, and before 1941 was out that port was handling very large tonnages of American equipment and supplies.

In the decisive central sector Bock's army group reorganized before resuming the advance on Moscow. The German high command had no doubt that this was where the next blow should fall, and they believed with good reason that it could end the war. Moscow was the communications center of European Russia; virtually all roads and railroads led into the capital, as spokes into the hub of a wheel. If Moscow were captured the Russians would have the greatest difficulty reinforcing or supplying other portions of their front. The political effects of the capture of Moscow might also be considerable. Stalin's communist regime was hated and feared by large portions of the population, and if Moscow fell, the dictator might well fall, too. However, the one reason the German high command considered to be conclusive was that the bulk of the Red Army had been concentrated in front of Moscow for the defense of the capital. If these Russian armies could be encircled and forced to surrender, the war would be as good as over. On August 18, therefore, OKH issued an order for the capture of Moscow.

But now Hitler intervened in the direct conduct of the war. In the past, in political matters, he had frequently been right and his generals wrong, and now he had no hesitation in overruling them in a military matter. In a directive issued on August 21 Hitler declared:

> The Army's proposal of the 18th of August for the further conduct of operations on the Eastern Front does not conform to my intentions. I order the following:
>
> (1) The most important objective to be taken before the coming of winter is NOT the capture of Moscow, but the capture of the Crimea and of the industrial and coal-mining area of the Donets, and the cutting off of Russian oil supplies from the Caucasus; and to the north the investment of Leningrad and the linking up with the Finns.

Thus a clear-cut, feasible, and single military objective was set aside and for it was substituted a double-headed monstrosity. Hitler was greedy and saw too many things at once. Army Group Center was to be halted, immobile, around Smolensk, while rich new territories were to be taken in the south and Leningrad was to be eliminated in the north. Nor was it only that a double objective had been substituted for a single one. In the south Hitler wanted the Crimea, the Donbas, and the Caucasus; in the north he wanted both Leningrad and the Karelian Isthmus. Bock's armor would be sent to the Ukraine, where another giant encirclement was to be accomplished in the Dnieper Bend around Kiev, with the southern flank of Army Group Center cooperating with the northern flank of Army Group South.

On August 23 Guderian flew to Rastenburg, the Führer's headquarters in East Prussia, to plead with Hitler to abandon this plan and drive on to Moscow, but he received no support from Hitler's entourage. General Wilhelm Keitel, Field Marshal Alfred Jodl, and the other sycophants at the Führer's headquarters merely "nodded in agreement with every sentence that Hitler uttered." Hitler refused to be moved by any strategical argument. He informed Guderian, "My generals have all read Clausewitz, but they know nothing about the economic aspects of war." The orders remained unchanged.

Thus, quietly, in a headquarters far from the sound of the guns,

Germany lost the war. The Führer directive of August 21, 1941, marked a great turning point in modern history. Many horrors were still to come, and mankind has by no means moved out from the darkness of these times, but at least the world was to be spared a Nazi victory.

The new German attack in the Ukraine began on September 1 and was brilliantly successful. In fact, it was far more successful than it need have been, because it was now Stalin's turn to miscalculate. Were it not for the horror and significance of the consequences, there would be something amusing in the spectacle of the two totalitarian dictators playing out a bumbling comedy of errors against one another. Stalin, at least, had some excuse for his mistake. He was firmly convinced that the next German attack would be against Moscow along the Bryansk-Moscow axis. This opinion was shared by Marshal B. M. Shaposhnikov, the Chief of the General Staff. Quite possibly Stalin and Shaposhnikov had secret intelligence information that inclined them to this belief. At all events, the attack Stalin anticipated was exactly the one that the German high command had determined on before receiving Hitler's countermanding directive of August 21. And thus another ironic twist is added to the story: Stalin, the great spymaster, failed to believe his spies when they were right about Operation Barbarossa but believed them implicitly when they were wrong about the objective of the German September offensive.

Initially Stalin can be blamed only for crediting Hitler with more strategic ability than he possessed, but the Russian dictator soon compounded his error. Not only did he strongly reinforce the area between Bryansk and Moscow, but he persisted in believing that the attack would fall there long after there was good evidence that the Germans had turned south. In dry, sunny weather, along roads that were flanked by fields of golden stubble and tall sunflowers, Panzer Group 2 drove swiftly south to Chernigov, then east to Novgorod Severskiy, where it captured the long Desna Bridge.

Kleist's armor began to move north to meet Guderian. By now it was obvious that a gigantic German pincer movement aimed at nothing less than cutting off all the Soviet armies within the Dnieper Bend. Even old Marshal Semën Budënny, a not too bright cavalryman from the revolution, could see this. He begged Stalin to let him retreat to the Donets, but Stalin ordered Budënny to stand fast, and actually reinforced him.

In the hope that the Russians would not become aware of their danger too soon, Kleist had advanced less swiftly than he could have done, so Guderian made the better time. The two German columns met on September 14 at Lokhvistsa, 120 miles east of Kiev. Budënny's troops fought bitterly to break out of the trap, but these attempts failed, as did the frantic Russian attacks from the east, which were attempts to rescue the fifty doomed Russian divisions in the Dnieper Bend. Kiev fell on the 19th, and by the time the fighting died down on the 26th the Red Army had lost some 665,000 prisoners, the better part of five Russian armies, as well as 3500 guns and 900 tanks — undoubtedly the largest surrender of forces in the field in the history of warfare.

Hitler had the Ukraine, which he had lusted after for so long. Within the next six weeks Army Group South stood along the Kursk-Kharkov-Stalino-Taganrog line. But a price had been exacted for this success. September was gone and autumn was drawing in. The German army, and especially the panzer formations, had been gravely weakened, not least by the extra distance they had had to travel. Guderian's Panzer Group 2, which had driven so far, was operating at less than one third of its establishment, and replacements of men and machines were hard to come by.

By now Hitler had at last, and belatedly, turned his eyes back to Moscow. On September 6 he had issued Führer Directive No. 35, designating the Russian capital as the next objective, and as soon as the pincers had met at Lokhvistsa on September 14, OKH had begun to reinforce Army Group Center. Soon Bock had more than a million and a half men under his command. But even with German organization and staff work, it all took time. It was September 26 before Army Group Center could issue final orders for the attack, and it was October 2 before Operation Typhoon, as the offensive against Moscow was hopefully named, could be launched.

The Soviets also reinforced before Moscow, and General Zhukov took over command of the Western Army Group, with his headquarters at Vyazma. The advent of Zhukov was a great reinforcement by itself, for he was a relatively young, competent, and extremely ruthless commander, who more than any other single soldier among the Allies was to be responsible for the Nazi defeat. The Western Army Group was built up to a strength of six armies of forty-five infantry, six armored, and three cavalry divisions. A further five armies were held in reserve in the rear. Immediately to the south of Zhukov the Bryansk Army Group had three armies of twenty infantry, three armored, and three cavalry divisions.

The German plan for Operation Typhoon called for a two-stage battle. In the first phase, Army Group Center would make a three-pronged attack, with the Ninth Army and Panzer Group 3 advancing between Vyazma and Rzhev in the north, the Fourth Army and Panzer Group 4 advancing along the Roslavl-Moscow road in the center, and Guderian's Panzer Group 2, now called the Second

Panzer Army, attacking in the south between Bryansk and Orel toward Tula. The second phase would be the final advance on Moscow, conducted again by encircling armored thrusts from the northwest and the southeast.

Once again the fighting favored the Germans. The weather held good and the country was fairly open. In the first three weeks of October, eighty-six Russian divisions were destroyed. Army Group Center captured 663,000 prisoners and 1200 tanks, mostly in the two caldrons that were formed about Vyazma and Bryansk. The northern caldron at Vyazma was much the more successful, for here five Russian armies were trapped and eliminated by October 13. At Bryansk three more Russian armies were caught, but the ring was not so tightly held and many Russians escaped. While these caldrons were being eliminated, the advance on Moscow continued, though with reduced strength. Hitler had publicly announced on October 3 that the Soviet Union was defeated, "never to rise again."

To many observers throughout the world this seemed no more than the truth, and some despaired as they contemplated the apparent German invincibility. Most of the Soviet government evacuated Moscow, moving to Kuibyshev on the Volga, 560 miles farther east; Stalin himself, however, remained in the capital. This may have been courage, but it may equally well have been desperation. If Hitler won, there would assuredly be no place for the Soviet dictator to hide.

Hitler had already commanded that Leningrad should be utterly destroyed. Now he issued similar orders regarding Moscow. In what he thought was the moment of victory Hitler was resolved to kill as many Russians as possible. His restless and malignant mind was already turning back toward the west, and he thought of disbanding some forty German divisions so that the manpower thus released could be transferred to industry, to build aircraft and submarines for use against Britain and the United States.

But now came the first hint that all might not be well with the Nazi design. The first snow flurries occurred on the night of October 6/7. They were light and soon disappeared, but they had come exceptionally early.

As the Germans closed on the Russian capital, the Red Army's resistance appeared to be weakening. The Russians themselves were far from confident that they could save their capital, and Stalin gloomily told Harry Hopkins, Roosevelt's personal emissary, that if Moscow was lost, all Russia west of the Volga would have to be abandoned; that is, Hitler would have succeeded in establishing his final A-A Line, from Archangel to Astrakhan. On October 19 there were food riots in Moscow and anticommunist slogans began to appear on walls throughout the city. On the 20th Stalin declared martial law in

Moscow and the secret police began executing suspects. Three days later the Germans crossed the Narva and were only forty miles from the capital.

But now, providentially, the rains came to ruin the roads and bog down the German advance. For days no wheeled vehicle could move, and even the tracked panzers could struggle ahead only with painful slowness. The Russian T-34 tanks, with their wider treads, were much better in the mud. The lull in operations imposed by the weather gave the Russians a needed respite in which to bring up reinforcements. During the first two weeks of November the Russians transferred twenty-one fresh divisions from Siberia and central Asia to the Moscow front.

The Germans also badly needed reinforcements, for Army Group Center was seriously short of manpower. Germany, however, had no such reservoir to draw on as had Russia. Moreover, the German supply problems were acute. By intense efforts, railheads were established at Bryansk, Vyazma, and Rzhev, but the lines to these points were not working to full capacity. In October, too, guerrilla activity in the German rear areas began to be a serious problem, as thousands of Russian soldiers who had escaped capture took to the forests. The Russians were able to fly in leaders, arms, and supplies, and to organize these guerrilla bands into formidable forces that were to tie down an increasing number of German troops on their lines of communication.

Fortunately for the Germans, the first frost set in at the beginning of November, hardening the mud sufficiently for the transport to get moving again. The cold was uncomfortable for the troops who had no winter clothing. (None had, for the Germans had expected the campaign to be over long before winter set in.) But so far the cold was merely an inconvenience. It would be another month before German staff officers took to reading Caulaincourt's memoirs of Napoleon's retreat from Moscow.

The plan for the final attack on the Russian capital again called for a great double envelopment, with the Second Panzer Army moving north and the Ninth Army and Panzer Group 3 advancing east to the Volga Canal and then turning south. The Fourth Army and Panzer Group 4 would attack frontally by way of Istra. By and large the Germans — high command, officers, and men alike — still had no doubts of their ultimate victory. The task had been harder than they had foreseen, but they thought that it could certainly be accomplished.

Although the offensive got off to a good start on November 5, within forty-eight hours the temperature suddenly dropped. On the 7th the German army began to get its first severe cases of frostbite, and on the night of the 11th/12th the cold set in with a savage intensity and the thermometer went down to minus 20° centigrade. Even under these terrible conditions the Germans continued to struggle forward. On November 13 a momentous conference was called at Orsha. Army Group North and Army Group South both wanted to go over to the defensive, but Bock of Army Group Center believed that the enemy was nearly defeated and that one final effort would bring victory. This was also Hitler's view, and it prevailed. Haunting this conference like a ghost was the German memory of the Battle of the Marne in 1914, when a possibly winning hand had been thrown away because of timidity and lack of resolution. So does the roundabout of history bring in its ironic revenges, for though the past has indeed lessons to teach, they are lessons that are very readily misunderstood. The fateful decision was taken to continue the offensive on Moscow.

As the end of November approached, however, it was becoming apparent that the offensive would probably fail. As of November 26, German losses on the eastern front, not including the sick or the frostbitten, totaled 743,112 men, and there were almost no reinforcements. Guderian's panzers could not reach Tula; the Second Army had not taken Kursk; Panzer Group 3, which managed to capture Klin and the line of the Volga Canal on the 28th, could advance no farther; and although Panzer Group 4 took Istra and in the first week of December pushed a division out to within eighteen miles of Moscow, further progress was impossible. One small motorcycle detachment of the 2nd Panzer Division reached the suburb of Khimki, five miles from Moscow and nine miles from the Kremlin, but it stayed in this advanced post only briefly. That was the closest the German army came to the Russian capital. The German soldiers, fighting desperately in the dark evergreen forests that lay around Moscow, could see the gold spires of the Kremlin glinting in the icy air. It was a Pisgah sight, as unattainable as the Promised Land for Moses. On the night of December 4 the temperature dropped to minus 31° centigrade and the following night it went down to minus 36°.

With this halt the truth suddenly became clear. Army Group Center's great effort had failed, and the failure had left it in a most precarious position, holding some 600 miles of front against a Russian concentration of unknown strength. And for all that vast extent of front, Bock had in reserve only a single, understrength division. This was military bankruptcy, the predictable consequence of German overconfidence and of the German General Staff's willingness to gamble. Time and again in this war the dice had fallen in their favor, but now, like players who consistently double their stakes, they faced ruin. Casualties from frostbite were multiplying daily, for the army had still received no winter clothing; the panzers and the mechanical transport were freezing up and becoming immobile because of a lack of antifreeze; the horses on which the German army still so largely relied for transport were dying from the cold; and even the oil on guns and personal weapons was coagulating and rendering them unserviceable. Of the twenty-six trains a day that the logistics staff calculated were necessary to maintain Army Group Center, only eight to ten were arriving each day.

The German situation was most desperate on the central front, but neither in the north around Leningrad nor in the south was the German position secure. In September Leeb's offensive had brought the Germans to within six miles of Leningrad. On September 13 Zhukov arrived in Leningrad to take over command from Marshal Voroshilov, the first of several occasions when Stalin employed Zhukov as an emergency commander in a desperate situation. Zhukov displayed his usual energy and hardness in reorganizing Leningrad's defense, threatening to have a number of officers shot and driving his subordinates without mercy. Nevertheless, on the 16th Slutsk to the north was captured, and two days later, with the capture of Schlüsselburg on the south shore of Lake Ladoga, Leningrad was surrounded. The end seemed merely a matter of time, but OKW now ordered that Leningrad should not be taken by storm but should be starved out, and on the 17th Höpner's panzers were transferred to the Moscow front. This halting of the attack at the very moment when it seemed on the verge of success meant that in the end, of course, Leningrad did not fall at all. For one thing, the city was not surrounded in wintertime, when the ice froze on Lake Ladoga, and the Russians were able to open a winter road. For another, the Germans were never again able to regain the lost momentum that had carried them as far as Schlüsselburg. In November a German offensive to link up with the Finns east of Lake Ladoga broke down, and in December the invaders had to retreat back to the Volkhov River. All the German attempts to eliminate the large Soviet bridgehead at Oranienburg also failed.

In the south at the end of October Manstein finally stormed into the Crimea with a costly frontal assault and two weeks later he captured Kerch. The overrunning of the Crimea cost the Russians sixteen divisions and the loss of more than 100,000 prisoners, but Sebastopol still held out, reinforced now by the garrison of Odessa, which had been successfully removed by sea in October. Meanwhile, the German Sixth Army had advanced past Kharkov to occupy the Donbas, and the First Panzer Army, as Panzer Group 1 was now called, and the Seventeenth Army had captured Stalino. Rostov was captured on

November 20, and the railway bridge across the Don was seized intact, but the Russians, realizing the importance of the place, continually launched fierce counterattacks against the city across the frozen river. Although Soviet casualties were enormous, German losses were also too heavy to be endured. Rundstedt asked permission to retire from Rostov, and when Hitler refused, he resigned his command and was replaced by Reichenau from the Sixth Army. The new commander assessed the situation just as Rundstedt had done and immediately repeated his predecessor's request to be allowed to retire. This time Hitler gave way and the Germans relinquished Rostov. In some confusion, and at the cost of further heavy casualties, the invaders fell back to a winter line behind the Mius River. This was the first serious German reverse of the war and a sinister portent of things to come.

So much for the grand design, the six-week campaign envisioned in Barbarossa. A line from Archangel to the Caspian Sea had been the objective, running far to the east of Moscow and including most of European Russia. As winter set in, the reality was that the gravely weakened German armies still stood outside Leningrad, outside Moscow, and 300 miles to the west of the Caspian Sea; the Caucasus had not been penetrated; and the enemy forces in the field, in spite of huge losses, were if anything stronger and more numerous than before.

What were the reasons for this monumental failure? No single cause can be adduced for the breakdown of the German campaign, yet obviously some causes were considerably more important than others. The Russian resistance had been much fiercer than anticipated and Russian resources much larger. German arrogance had failed to make any provision against the possibility of a winter campaign. The Nazi rule in occupied territories and the barbarous treatment of subject populations had made the German task much more difficult than it need have been. Although in operations and tactics the German army had proved itself far and away superior to the Red Army, the same could not be said of German strategy. The fault was so simple and obvious that a child might have foreseen it. The German high command had attempted too many things at the same time. It had neglected the primary axiom of the single objective.

In the first place the Barbarossa plan called for an attack on an enormously broad front and for the simultaneous engagement of all three Russian army groups. Not one objective but three were set for the invading armies: Leningrad, Moscow, and the Ukraine were all to be taken, and concurrently. Quite conceivably, a single great thrust along the Warsaw-Smolensk-Moscow axis might have secured the Russian capital for the Germans by the end of August. Army Groups

North and South could have acted as flank guards for such a thrust, and once the Russian center had been demolished and the communications hub of Moscow taken, the Soviet northern and southern fronts would have been isolated from one another. Then a drive down the Volga in September might well have achieved a second victory, greater even than the Battle of Kiev. This done, Leningrad and the northern front could have been dealt with at leisure and by another overwhelming concentration of force.

The key to all this, of course, was to fight three successive battles rather than three simultaneous ones. But Hitler wanted too much, and, as a consequence, got nothing. This same fundamental error was repeated again and again. It recurs like a leitmotif in the Führer's strategic thought. When the advance against Moscow might have been successfully resumed in August, and previous mistakes rectified, Hitler turned his thrust south into the Ukraine and north against Leningrad. Again two objectives, and both of them the wrong ones. When Leningrad might have been taken in September, Hitler diverted forces back from Army Group North to Moscow, and thereby captured neither Leningrad nor Moscow. The historian, viewing the cataclysmic nature of the Russian campaign, the size of the armies, the violence of the clash, the extent of the agony, and the historic significance of victory or defeat, cannot escape a profound sense of awe that the outcome turned on so simple a miscalculation. Nor is it easy to avoid the thought that here we glimpse the workings of the hand of God.

By the first week of December, Bock had only one decimated infantry division in reserve for the whole of his overextended central front. This division was stationed, not unreasonably, behind the Fourth Army, but when the Russian blow fell, it came on the wings. On December 5 Russian counterattacks struck Panzer Group 3 on the Moscow Canal and the Ninth Army at Kalinin. The next day, the 6th, Zhukov heavily counterattacked the Second Panzer Army south of Moscow. Very heavy fighting developed, with both sides suffering grievous losses, and Guderian's force had to retreat more than fifty miles.

That first week of December 1941, and especially its final forty-eight hours, was undoubtedly the most crucial time of the war, the great climacteric, the turning point on which so much of subsequent history pivoted. For as General Ivan S. Konev and Zhukov launched their counteroffensives in the pine forests north and south of Moscow, thousands of miles away, on the other side of the world, the Japanese task force that was to blow the United States into the war neared Pearl Harbor.

At last, and only briefly, Hitler gave Bock permission to fight his battle in the center, as seemed best to him, and the German general at once ordered a fighting withdrawal to a line from Rzhev to Orel to Kursk. This was easier said than done. As the snow came down and the cold became a constant, almost unendurable pain, the Germans lost their superiority. In the winter, deep in their own country, the Russians fought better and more effectively than the Nazis. The Russians, after all, had experienced these savage winters before, and were equipped to deal with them. Warmly clad, with winterized vehicles, with a properly functioning railway net immediately behind them, they proved themselves more mobile than the invaders. Every German retirement was made difficult by the waist-deep snow that made movement anywhere but on the roads almost impossible. Much equipment had to be abandoned, and the German defense was hampered by the fact that the ground was frozen too hard for trenches to be dug. Under gloomy skies, in frequent snowstorms that limited visibility to a few feet, in freezing cold, and in a gray and white world where twilights and dawns merged almost imperceptibly into nights and days, the battered German armies fought back with a professional ferocity. Winter clothing still had not reached them in any amount, so they robbed the Russian dead of their felt boots, fur caps, and long greatcoats. It is impossible to withhold admiration from the German achievement in that terrible winter, an achievement much more significant than all the previous German victories. It is impossible to withhold admiration, but it is infinitely sad that men should have been called on to fight so well for so bad a cause.

Some senior German commanders now considered a retirement to the Berezina or even to the Niemen. They reasoned that they were still better summer soldiers than the Russians and that they should therefore fight in the summertime. A clean break to a defensible line well to the rear would give them time to reorganize, to reinforce, and to build up their shattered armies for another great drive in 1942. It was at best a counsel of despair, for how could they hope to achieve in a second year what had been denied them in the first?

Hitler, at least, saw this clearly, in one of those remarkable flashes of strategic insight that make his abilities so difficult to assess. On December 16 he issued peremptory orders against any further withdrawals, urged every German soldier to put up "fanatical resistance" where he stood, and promised to reinforce his eastern front. In retrospect it seems probable that this was the correct decision, for the Berezina and the Niemen lay far to the west and there was no certainty that the German armies could ever have reached them. If an attempt had been made to disengage in the middle of November, the thing might have been done without difficulty, but in the middle of December the option may no longer have been open. Certainly such a retreat, given the new Russian advantage in winter mobility, would have been full of terrible hazards and, had it been continued for any length of time, might well have led to the dissolution of the German army.

Hitler's order to stand fast may have been correct, but he enforced it with an inflexibility and rigidity that was self-defeating. He had seen that a full-scale retreat might lead to disaster, but this had been an emotional rather than a rational assessment. Now he demanded that no one yield a foot of ground, on pain of summary punishment. To ensure that he would be obeyed and to punish failure, Hitler began to purge the German high command. On December 1 the commander-in-chief, Brauchitsch, who was ill with heart trouble and whose condition could scarcely have been improved by the events of recent weeks, resigned. Hitler appointed himself Brauchitsch's successor and so became the Supreme Commander of the German army. At the time the Führer is reported to have said: "Anyone can issue a few tactical orders. The task of a Commander-in-Chief is to educate the army in the spirit of National Socialism. I don't know any general in the army who could do this as I want it done." The Russians had gained much by their heroic defense — a respite of time, renewed self-confidence, salvation from brutal annihilation — but not least among their gains was that the Führer had decided personally to assume the conduct of the war. Time and again in the future the German effort would be nullified and German opportunities lost because of some ridiculously wrong decision of Hitler's.

The Russian counterattacks continued throughout the winter and the Germans could do little more than hang on and attempt to survive until the weather improved. Although the major Russian attacks were launched on the wings, the Red Army also persisted, with holding attacks everywhere along the front, and as a result there was no quiet sector where the Germans had a chance to rest. Yet the Russians by no means had it all their own way. Russian infantry casualties were extremely heavy. German losses, though fewer, were also high. In the first two months of the counteroffensive they amounted to 250,000 men.

The Germans wisely made no attempt to hold a single continuous line from the Crimea to Leningrad. Instead, the invaders concentrated on holding a series of strongpoints, known as *Igels*, or "hedgehogs," the name that had been given to the defensive squares of Swiss pikemen in the Middle Ages. These strongpoints were generally synonymous with the major German supply depots, the more important ones being at Schlüsselburg, Novgorod, and Staraya Russa on the northern front, at Rzhev, Vyazma, Kaluga, Bryansk, and Orel on the central front; and at Kursk, Kharkov, and Taganrog farther south. Subsidiary strongpoints were established between these major ones. Enemy penetration between strongpoints was acceptable, since any Russian force that advanced too far between the defended localities would be in danger of being counterattacked and cut off. Yet this is an oversimplification of what actually happened, and set down so tends to impose a neatness on the situation that is deceptive, for the hedgehogs were more frequently formed by the success of Soviet operations than by the will of the Germans.

On January 15 Hitler finally agreed that Army Group Center could make a slow fighting withdrawal to a straighter and shorter line. This was done successfully, but entailed heavy losses in men and equipment. Kalinin, north of Moscow, had fallen to the Russians on December 16, and the other arm of the Soviet pincer had captured the strongpoint of Kaluga on the 26th. The Red Army next attempted a far more ambitious encircling movement, driving for Rzhev in the north and for Vyazma in the south. If these two attacks could meet, the destruction of Army Group Center would result and the war would be as good as over. The Germans held Rzhev in desperate fighting, but strong Soviet forces by-passed it to the west and advanced southwest toward Vyazma. Meanwhile, Zhukov approached Vyazma from the south.

But Army Group Center was not destined to be surrounded and destroyed in 1942. The gigantic pincers never closed. By means of vigorous counterattacks, Field Marshal Walther Model, the new commander of Ninth Army, restored the situation in the Rzhev area, and in the south the Russian advance was also stopped.

By the end of February German losses on the Russian front totaled 1,005,636 men, or some 31 percent of the original force that had launched Operation Barbarossa. The German positions in front of Moscow had been driven back between 75 and 150 miles, and at the end of February the Russians were only 50 miles east of Smolensk. The German front was nowhere secure and was everywhere being held by formations far below establishment. Nor was it possible to obtain many reinforcements now from other theaters. With the German check in Russia, guerrilla activity increased in the occupied territories. This was especially true in Yugoslavia and Greece; the occupied nations of western Europe did not at this time give their conquerors much trouble.* Army Group Center received only 9 extra divisions between December and March; in this same period the Russians threw 117 new divisions into the battle.

---

*The French, indeed, sent a contingent to fight on the Nazi side against the Russians.

In the north a Russian attempt to get behind the German Ninth Army was halted in front of Vitebsk, and an offensive along the Volkhov River resulted only in the entrapment and destruction of the Soviet Second Assault Army. On February 8 six German divisions were surrounded at Demyansk, but they fought on, supplied by air, until they were at last relieved on April 21. Kholm was surrounded on January 28, but the German defenders, again supplied by air, held out in spite of repeated attacks, heavy casualties, and an outbreak of typhus. They were relieved on May 5. These epic defensive actions may have contributed to the great German disaster the following winter at Stalingrad, for it was not possible to supply adequately by air an entire army in a pocket far from the nearest airfields. The successful experiences at Demyansk and Kholm may have led to the too-easy acceptance of Göring's assurance to the contrary.

In the south the story of the Russian counteroffensive was much the same. The Red Army captured Kerch on the Black Sea coast, and Manstein's Eleventh Army was still stuck fast outside Sebastopol. The most dangerous Russian move came around Kharkov, where the Soviets launched twin attacks in mid-January. The northern arm was halted at Belgorod, but in the south a deep wedge was driven into the German lines around Izyum. Only after prolonged and desperate fighting were the Russians finally stopped.

The Russian counteroffensives, then, everywhere failed to achieve all their aims, but they cannot be accounted a failure. They inflicted deadly injury on the German army and they demonstrated to the Russian people and to the world that the Nazis were not invincible. The Battle of Moscow was undoubtedly the decisive battle of the war — not Stalingrad or any other — for it was in the forests west of Moscow that Hitler's soldiers received their fatal check. Still dangerous and capable of inflicting much damage before it was finally killed, the German army nevertheless had lost its capability of winning the war.

CHAPTER III

THE FAR EASTERN portion of the Second World War had its remoter origins in western imperialism, but only in that peculiar, backhanded way that history so frequently appears to favor. In the nineteenth century Britain, France, Russia, Germany, and the United States had all extorted trading concessions, treaty ports, and extraterritorial privileges from a China too weak to resist. China was saved from becoming an out-and-out western colony only because her jealous exploiters imposed checks on each other's expansion.

The Japanese were determined to save themselves from a similar fate, which they did by adapting themselves, with most remarkable skill and resource, to western technology and the industrial age. By the 1890s Japan had been sufficiently educated to join with the other powers in the rape of China. After the Sino-Japanese War of 1894, and even more after the Russo-Japanese War of 1904, Japan was no longer considered an object suitable for imperialist exploitation.

But Japan had learned too well. In the trenchant phrase of Major General J. F. C. Fuller, "the disease of the West was in her bones." Like Britain an island kingdom poor in natural resources, Japan had to rely on her exports to live. Between 1894 and 1945 the Japanese perpetually sought to expand and to establish an empire that would make them economically self-sufficient. This ambition led to war with European nations on two occasions, both on Japan's initiative — in 1904 against Russia and in 1914 against Germany. (There had, it is true, been in addition a brief and unofficial, but intense, flare-up of fighting in 1939 with Soviet forces around Khalkin-Gol in Mongolia.) Nevertheless, Japan's plans for conquest, cautiously and opportunistically followed, had met no real check.

However, Japan had paid a terrible price for her successful imitation of western ways and the cult of power. The Japanese army, artificially indoctrinated with the samurai traditions of the ancient warrior class, had come to wield an altogether disproportionate influence in the state. By and large, too, the army was ignorant of the world; harsh, arrogant, and contemptuous of the materialism and supposed softness of the United States. If Nazi Germany's conceit of its own military ability was wildly exaggerated, the Japanese hubris was little short of insane. Boasting that they had never in all history lost a war, the Japanese militarists really believed themselves invincible.

Japan's entry into the Second World War was a direct result of her war with China, but it was also an indirect result of the rapacity of the industrialized West, which had led the way in the exploitation of China and the corruption of Japan. By 1939 the Japanese had conquered an enormous area of China and had brought some 170 million Chinese under their rule, but China was too large to be readily conquered. Chiang Kai-shek did little fighting, but his continued defiance was a danger and a provocation. Also in the north, Chinese communist guerrillas under Mao Tse-tung harassed the long Japanese lines of communication. Thus in 1941 nearly half of the Japanese army (twenty-one divisions out of fifty-one) was deployed in China and another thirteen divisions had to be stationed in Manchuria to watch the border with the Soviet Union.

The Far Eastern policy of the United States has never been an easy one for foreigners to understand, nor have many Americans been able to present it rationally. By long tradition isolationist as far as Europe was concerned, the United States has nonetheless frequently been willing to intervene in Asian affairs, even when these have seemed little of her concern. Over the years a China lobby developed in the United States, and in the 1930s, as Japan began to encroach on China, American affection for China was translated into hostility toward Japan.

With the outbreak of war in Europe the Japanese began to hope for greater things. The last time Europe had gone to war Japan had been able to acquire from Germany Tsingtao and Shantung in China and the Marshalls, Carolines, and Marianas in the Pacific. Surely now again a chance was being offered, a chance that, if not promptly seized, might not come again. The Japanese sincerely hated western imperialism in Asia and believed in a new era, to be heralded by the Greater East Asia Co-Prosperity Sphere. Their vision saw eastern Asia not independent, but definitely under Japanese tutelage.

To further this aim the Japanese army favored a military alliance with Germany, which would allow Japan to attack British and French possessions in the Far East. But the Japanese navy, more knowledgeable of the outside world and more respectful of American and British power, would not permit such a treaty. Moreover, Japan, which had joined the Anti-Comintern Pact in 1937, was given no advance warning of the Molotov-Ribbentrop agreement of August 1939. Japanese statesmen were confused and indignant at Hitler's apparent about-face, and concluded that it might be better to wait and see.

However, with the British defeats and the fall of France in 1940, imperialist Japanese became more restive than ever, feeling that they were witnessing "the chance of a hundred years" and that if Japan did not move quickly, the opportunity might pass. In July the American government banned the sale of aviation gasoline and high-grade scrap iron to Japan. Two months later Japan signed the Tripartite Pact with Germany and Italy, which provided that if any of the signatory powers was attacked by a nation not then at war, the other signatories would come to its aid. This was, in effect, a device to discourage American intervention in either the European war or in the Far East.

The Japanese foreign minister, Yosuke Matsuoka, who had negotiated the Tripartite Pact, was an opportunist. He did not share the opinion of most of his countrymen that the Soviet Union was predestined to be Japan's enemy. He favored inviting Stalin to join the Tripartite Pact, which would clearly have aligned all the totalitarian powers against Britain and the United States. Japan would thus turn her attention to the South rather than to the West, expanding into the British, French, Dutch, and American colonies in the Pacific. The first step along this path had already been taken, indeed, for in September 1940 the Vichy government had acquiesced in the Japanese occupation of the airfields in northern Indochina. Although the idea of a four-power pact directed against the United States came to nothing, Matsuoka nevertheless negotiated the nonaggression pact with Stalin, which was signed in April 1941.

Yet the Japanese cabinet was by no means unanimous as to what course it should follow. The Japanese prime minister, Prince Fumimaro Konoye, appointed Admiral Kichisaburo Nomura ambassador to the United States, instructing him to begin talks with Secretary of State Cordell Hull, with a view to settling Japanese-American differences. Not unnaturally, Hitler viewed these conversations with distaste, but this did not deter the Japanese.

The United States reacted in stages against Japanese aggression. In September 1940 the embargo on high-grade scrap iron was extended to all scrap metal, and late in the year the United States gave another loan to Chiang Kai-shek. At about the same time the embargo was extended again to include steel, iron ore, pig iron, and machine tools. Early in 1941, by a still further extension, the United States banned the sale to Japan of copper, brass, bronze, zinc, nickel, potash, phosphate, and uranium.

Matsuoka's desire to line up all the totalitarian states together against Britain and the United States was thoroughly argued out that spring and summer of 1941. The upshot was Matsuoka's dismissal from the cabinet in July, for by now, of course, his policy had been overtaken by events. Once again Hitler had failed to tell his Japanese friends what he intended, and by July German armies were already driving deep into the Soviet Union. When Germany pressed Japan to join her in her attack on Russia, the Japanese politely declined. Matsuoka was replaced as foreign minister by Admiral Teijiro Toyoda.

By now the United States had gained one tremendous advantage in its confrontation with Japan, an advantage that was to endure until the end. In December 1940 cryptographers had succeeded in breaking certain Japanese codes, including their highest diplomatic code, the Purple Cipher. As a result, the United States government was uniquely well informed of Japanese intentions, and in fact Roosevelt and Cordell Hull often read the decoded "Magic" messages before the Japanese ambassador received them.

In July 1941 Japanese-American relations took a sudden sharp turn for the worse when the Japanese army moved to occupy the southern portion of French Indochina. On July 26 President Roosevelt froze all Japanese assets in the United States. Britain and the Dutch government-in-exile at once followed suit. At the same time Hull broke off his conversations with Admiral Nomura.

Roosevelt's action was drastic indeed; it amounted to a declaration of economic war. At a single stroke Japan was deprived of nine tenths of her oil imports and three quarters of her foreign trade. By the end of the month Japan was forced to begin using her oil reserves, of which she had only an eighteen-month supply. Not surprisingly, therefore, when the Japanese cabinet considered the alternatives open to it, it discussed the possibility of war.

The conversations between Cordell Hull and Admiral Nomura reopened on August 6, but neither man had much to offer. Time was on the side of the United States and against Japan, for all the while the Japanese oil reserves were steadily diminishing. By the end of September they had been reduced by 25 percent.

Prime Minister Churchill did not really believe that Japan would be mad enough to attack the United States. His greatest fear, in fact, was that Japan would attack only the British and Dutch colonies in Asia and that the United States Congress would not consider this sufficient justification for a declaration of war. Roosevelt and Hull, with the help of Magic, knew better. Almost certainly the American economic sanctions would force the Japanese to go to war unless some agreement could be reached. But how could Japan get out of China and abandon the blood and toil of a decade? No Japanese government could survive such loss of face, and the first attempt to implement such a policy would undoubtedly be the signal for a military coup.

All this was well realized by the administration in Washington, but Roosevelt did not deviate from his course. The great majority of the American people, largely ignorant of the issues involved and unaware of the gravity of the crisis, still wanted peace, not war. On the other hand, the President believed that the long-term security of the United States would be jeopardized unless the Axis powers were defeated, and he dreaded the thought of a world in which totalitarianism would be triumphant. He did not, however, see the Soviet Union as a totalitarian state, and he rejected angrily any attempt to present evidence contrary to his view. He was emotionally committed to what he believed were the progressive, democratic forces in the world, and this greatly simplified his ethical problems in international affairs. In the light of the evidence, it seems probable that in the autumn of 1941 Roosevelt wanted war — against Nazi Germany if possible, but if necessary against both Germany and Japan. He maintained the economic stranglehold on Japan and refused to relax it except on terms he knew Japan would not meet.

The Japanese government twisted desperately to escape from its dilemma. Prince Konoye resigned as prime minister on October 16, to be replaced by General Hideki Tojo, who continued the negotiations in Washington. In the middle of November a special envoy, Saburo Kurusu, joined Admiral Nomura, bringing with him what the United States government knew, from its Magic intercepts, to be a final offer. It knew, too, that Japan had set a time limit on the negotiations. On November 5 the Japanese cabinet had decided that if diplomacy had not succeeded by the 25th of the month, it would ask the emperor to authorize war.

For a brief time it appeared that the United States might accept Japanese withdrawal from Indochina in return for a limited relaxation of the economic embargo for three months. Had this proposal been presented to the Japanese it seems probable that the war would not have been extended to the Pacific, for by the time the three-month period had expired it would have been obvious to the Japanese that the tide of the war had turned in the snows and forests of Russia. But, of course, that is hindsight. In November 1941 the United States government knew no more than the Japanese that the Russians would rally and save themselves. On November 26 Cordell Hull persuaded the President to take a much harder line with the Japanese. This was done the same day. Only a final settlement could be considered, the Japanese envoys were told, and this would be possible only if Japan withdrew all her forces from both China and Indochina.

The new proposal made war inevitable, and it was intended to do so. For two days after the receipt of the American reply the Japanese cabinet debated the issue, but on the 29th it reached a firm decision to go to war. Presumably it was assisted in this decision by the categorical assurance, given again by Ribbentrop on November 28, that Germany would join in war against the United States. The Japanese government was apprehensive lest Hitler demand a Japanese declaration of war against the Soviet Union in return. The Germans, however, confident that Moscow would soon fall and the Soviet Union be defeated, did not make the demand. On December 1 the Japanese decision to wage war was ratified, most reluctantly, by the emperor.

The Japanese had a plan for a war with the United States; appropriately enough, it was the brainchild of an admiral. When Admiral Isoroku Yamamoto had been promoted to commander-in-chief of the combined fleets in August 1939, he had at once begun to advocate a surprise attack similar to the one that had destroyed the Russian fleet at Port Arthur in 1904, and he boldly selected the distant naval base of Pearl Harbor, two thirds of the way across the Pacific, as his target. Detailed planning for the Pearl Harbor attack began in June 1941.

Whatever the Japanese army believed, Yamamoto knew very well that Japan could not hope to defeat the United States in war. His aim was a limited one: the establishment of a defensive perimeter in the Pacific, bending outward in a great arc from the northeast to the southwest, from the Kurile Islands to the frontier of India. Within this perimeter would lie the Philippines, the Netherlands East Indies, Malaya, Burma, and Indochina. If Japan could capture this area in the first three or four months of the war, having first destroyed the United States Pacific Fleet, it should be possible to establish a formidable defense, so strong that the United States, distracted as she would be by a war in Europe, would quail before the prospect of its reconquest.

Yamamoto and the Japanese government were, in fact, gambling on the hope that the United States would weary of war and shrink from the bloodshed that would be necessary to defeat an entrenched Japan. By a misreading of history, this calculation made some sense. The Americans were notoriously a peaceful people, however violent they might be in some aspects of their national life. Rarely, if ever, had they gone to war united. The Japanese calculation, therefore, was not unreasonable, as the later experience of America in the Vietnam War has proved. However, Yamamoto made two fundamental mistakes. The first and more serious was that the nature of the Japanese attack, with its surprise and what was branded as treachery, angered and unified the American people. The second error, of course, was an underestimation of American industrial capacity, which enabled the United States within eighteen months of Pearl Harbor to gain a decisive naval superiority in the Pacific.

At the same time as the attack on the United States Pacific Fleet, or nearly so, there would be Japanese assaults on Hong Kong, the Philippines, Malaya, Thailand, Burma, Guam, and Wake Island. All this would be done with a force of only eleven divisions. In the second phase, most of the same troops would overrun the Netherlands East Indies and Singapore and complete the conquest of Burma. Although it was ambitious, this plan was based on a just appreciation of Japanese strengths and Allied weaknesses, and it succeeded without any serious check.

Vice Admiral Chuishi Nagumo, who commanded the fleet that attacked Pearl Harbor, sailed from Japan on November 18. At five-thirty on the morning of December 7, as the task force neared its launch area, two Japanese reconnaissance planes winged their way south to Pearl Harbor and returned to report that all was quiet. This was to be expected on a Sunday morning, for Admiral Husband E. Kimmel's fleet was invariably in harbor on weekends, with many of the crews on leave. A final warning from Washington to Admiral Kimmel that war was imminent was delayed by an almost incredible series of accidents and errors. And though the Japanese submarines and bombers were both detected, the base was not alerted.

From 230 miles north of their target, the Japanese launched their first wave of aircraft shortly after seven o'clock. As they neared their target, they could see the island below them, lying bright in early morning sunlight. The first aircraft arrived over Pearl Harbor at 7:55 and the attack continued for half an hour. Only one quarter of the antiaircraft guns had crews. Many officers and sailors were on shore leave. The American warships were moored in their anchorage far too close together, neatly aligned as though the world had never been at war. At the Wheeler, Hickam, and Bellows air bases, the American aircraft were drawn up wing to wing, so that they could be more easily guarded against sabotage, and their pilots were dispersed on four hours' notice.

Within minutes the United States Pacific Fleet had ceased to exist. The *Arizona*, the *Oklahoma*, the *California*, and the *West Virginia* were in flames and sinking, as were three cruisers, three destroyers, and many smaller ships. The *Nevada*, the *Maryland*, the *Tennessee*, and the *Pennsylvania* were all very heavily damaged. At the air bases the story was, if anything, even worse. Caught on the ground, most of the American planes were never able to put up a fight. The second wave of bombers was hardly needed, but it struck at 8:40. By 11:30 the

Japanese aircraft were back on their carriers, except for the twenty-nine that had been lost. Japanese casualties were under a hundred. This compared with total American casualties of 3581 service personnel and 103 civilians.

The Pearl Harbor attack gave Japan absolute naval dominance of the Pacific, but the long-term effects were not as disastrous as at first appeared. The base installations at Pearl Harbor were in general undamaged, as were the huge oil tanks in the dockyard.

For the British the entry of the United States into the war could only be a matter for thankfulness. Much bitter fighting undoubtedly lay ahead. But now the final outcome could scarcely be in doubt. No wonder then that the news of Pearl Harbor caused the British to lift up their hearts.

For a day or two there was the threat of another danger. When President Roosevelt went before Congress on December 8 he asked only for a declaration of war against Japan. What if Hitler and Mussolini did nothing? Would the American people and their representatives, infuriated by the Japanese surprise attack, insist on turning all their strength against Japan? If this occurred, there would be two unconnected wars raging in the world. And how would Britain and the Soviet Union fare in that case? At best, American aid would be much reduced, perhaps fatally so.

In the event, Germany declared war on the United States on December 11, and Italy, willy-nilly, did the same. With this, the fears that the United States might fight an exclusively Pacific war disappeared, and Anglo-American strategy was able to follow the logical and correct course, which the British and American Chiefs of Staff had already informally agreed to, of defeating Germany first.

On December 20 Prime Minister Churchill arrived in Washington for the Arcadia Conference, which lasted until January 14, 1942. One of the achievements of the conference was the establishment of the Combined Chiefs of Staff Committee, which was the British and American Chiefs of Staff Committees meeting jointly and reporting directly to their heads of state. This machinery served the alliance well, and though the western Allies were not subsequently immune from strategic error, the debate and clash of opinion that preceded the resolution of opposing points of view did save them from making silly mistakes, such as Hitler made continually and Stalin on occasion.

The Arcadia Conference confirmed that priority should be given to the defeat of Germany, and that until this had been achieved Japan should be merely contained. It was agreed that an Anglo-American army should land in Europe in 1943, that aid should be continued to the Soviet Union, and that the strategic bombing of Germany should be increased. The British argued that in 1942 Africa should be cleared of Axis forces and occupied by British and American troops. This projected operation (code-named "Super-Gymnast") was favored by Roosevelt, who was anxious to commit American troops to action somewhere in 1942, but the American Chiefs of Staff feared — correctly, as time was to show — that the clearance of North Africa might prevent the major assault into northwest Europe in 1943. They agreed only to study the possibilities, and for the time being the matter was left there.

Four hours after the attack on Pearl Harbor, the Japanese struck at the Philippines, destroying many aircraft on the ground at Clark Field and damaging the naval base at Manila Bay. The Japanese landed on the northern coast of Luzon on December 10, and two days later another landing was effected on the southeast coast. MacArthur, foiled in his plan of defeating the invaders on the beaches, decided to abandon Manila and retreat to the Bataan peninsula. The Japanese assault on Bataan was launched on December 29, and was beaten back everywhere with heavy losses. For the next five weeks the attackers could make no headway, and the offensive was halted early in February.

Toward the end of February President Roosevelt ordered MacArthur to leave the Philippines so that he could assume command of American forces mustering in Australia. He departed reluctantly by motor torpedo boat on March 10, handing over his command to Lieutenant General Jonathan M. Wainwright and vowing, "I shall return." This abandonment of his troops by a commander, though sensible, was much criticized at the time, not least by the troops who had been abandoned.

By this time Washington had decided that there was no possibility of relieving Bataan, and the Japanese reinforced with two more divisions. A new offensive, begun on April 3, succeeded. On the 9th Major General Edward P. King, Jr., surrendered on Bataan, but the fifteen thousand troops on Corregidor, under Wainwright, continued to fight until May 6. Some outposts refused to surrender, and continued fighting until June 9.

Nowhere but in the Philippines did the Japanese advance receive any serious check. Guam fell on December 10, and Wake Island on the 23rd. The Japanese attacked Hong Kong at first light on December 8, and on the afternoon of Christmas Day the governor of the colony, Sir Mark Young, surrendered. Hong Kong had held out for only eighteen days, and it should not have been held at all.

Unlike Hong Kong, the British base of Singapore at the southern tip of the Malayan peninsula was supposed to be defensible. So long as a strong fleet was stationed at Singapore, it was believed that the Japanese would be unable to effect landings in Thailand or Malaya and so threaten the base from the landward side. Of course, in 1941 there was not a major fleet at Singapore and there was no prospect of one being sent there. Moreover, the British assumed, until the Japanese taught them otherwise, that movement off the roads in the thick Malayan jungle was impracticable. However, the Japanese landed behind the British at Kota Bahru and at Singora and Patani in Thailand. By the evening of the first day northern Malaya had been lost to the British, almost without fighting.

In the latter part of December the Japanese pushed down the east coast of the peninsula, and the British withdrew before them. On January 19 Churchill was shocked and dismayed to learn for the first time that after two and a half years of war absolutely no field defenses had been built on the landward side of the Singapore fortress. The news was almost incredible, but it was true, and it should not have been news.

In the middle of January the Japanese broke through the British line in Johore, and the British withdrew into Singapore island. After a seven-week campaign, the Japanese had cleared Malaya and were poised menacingly before the back door of the great fortress.

In spite of the losses suffered in Malaya, Lieutenant General Arthur E. Percival, the British commander, now had about seventy thousand combat soldiers and fifteen thousand service troops, but an assault on February 8 established the Japanese on the island. Fighting continued for the next eight days, but at eight-thirty on the evening of the 15th Singapore surrendered. More than eighty thousand prisoners of war fell into Japanese hands. This was by far the largest capitulation in the history of British arms, and it meant the end of the British Empire in the East.

Concurrently with their campaign against Singapore, the Japanese had invaded Burma, where the Burmese, eager for independence from Britain, often gave them considerable help. On January 16, the Japanese Fifteenth Army, under Lieutenant General S. Ilada, cut into Lower Burma from Thailand. A few days later Moulmein fell, and the defenders retreated, abandoning all Lower Burma. Rangoon was captured on March 8, after the Australian government had resolutely resisted great pressure from Churchill to divert to that city one of the two Australian divisions that were returning from the Middle East for the defense of Australia itself. This incident did nothing to improve British-Australian relations.

General Sir Harold Alexander, the British commander, retreated north to Prome, but could find no halting place. The Japanese attacked again toward the end of March, and within a month they had taken Mandalay and cut off the Burma Road. Alexander retreated northwest into northern Assam, where, in the middle of May, his depleted force finally found safety around Imphal. The rains then came and brought another disastrous campaigning season to a close. British casualties in Burma had been about three times higher than the Japanese loss of forty-five thousand men.

Meanwhile, the Japanese had landed in Borneo and the Celebes, and had taken Bougainville in the Solomons and Rabaul in New Britain, reaching out to cut off Australia from American aid. In February Sumatra fell, and in March, Java. In April the Royal Navy was forced to abandon the Indian Ocean.

Churchill now determined to seize Madagascar before the Vichy French could turn it over to the Japanese. Remembering the fate of the Dakar expedition, the British decided to do the job this time without the assistance of the Free French. The assault went in on May 5, and again the Vichy French fought their former allies, although not very enthusiastically. The port of Diego Suarez was firmly in British hands by the 7th.

The war aims of the Japanese, enunciated before Pearl Harbor, had been limited. By the end of March 1942 they had achieved all that their prewar plans had called for. It had been unexpectedly easy. But now the decision was made to extend the perimeter, to reach out for more, so that both Hawaii and Australia would be neutralized by land-based bombers. The new perimeter would include the western Aleutians, Midway, Samoa, the Fiji Islands, New Caledonia, and Port Moresby in Papua.

Thanks to their intelligence service, the Americans knew before the beginning of May that the Japanese were about to attack Port Moresby. Rear Admiral Frank J. Fletcher's naval force in the Coral Sea was now hurriedly augmented, and on May 7 the Americans sighted the Japanese invasion fleet. A bombing attack sank the Japanese light cruiser *Shoho* that day, and on the 8th the main engagement of the Battle of the Coral Sea was fought. The two fleets spotted one another almost simultaneously early in the morning and both launched air strikes. This, the first large naval battle since Jutland, was fought entirely by aircraft; the opposing ships were never within sight of one another. The fleet carrier *Shokaku* was badly damaged, as was the *Yorktown*. The *Lexington* had to be abandoned. American aircraft losses were thirty-three; Japanese, forty-three. Both fleets then left the Coral Sea, the Americans to rendezvous at Pearl Harbor, and the Japanese to return to Truk.

Admiral Yamamoto next planned to send a diversionary force to the western Aleutians to draw the United States Pacific Fleet north while the Japanese landed at Midway. When the Americans reacted to the seizure of Midway, the Japanese main fleet would be waiting for them and would destroy them in a general fleet action. It was a good plan, for the Americans would certainly have to fight for Midway just as the French had had to fight for Verdun in 1916. But the plan went wrong because the Americans, with their ability to read the Japanese codes, knew about it in good time. And in vain is the snare laid in sight of the bird. Instead of falling into Yamamoto's ambush, Admiral Chester W. Nimitz was able to lay a counterambush of his own.

Dutch Harbor was attacked by Japanese aircraft and Kiska and Attu were occupied without opposition, but there was no profit in any of this. In the Central Pacific the American fleet under the overall command of Admiral Fletcher* and the carrier group under Vice Admiral Raymond A. Spruance moved 200 miles to the northeast of Midway and awaited word of the Japanese approach. The report came in at 5:34 A.M. on June 4: Nagumo's carrier force was sailing into the area for its strike at Midway.

In the carrier engagement that followed, all four of the Japanese fleet carriers were lost and the naval balance in the Pacific was changed for good. This was the moment when Japan should have surrendered, for all that came later was anticlimactic. The war against Japan had been won in a few hours on June 4 off Midway Island.

The Battle of Midway should have forced Japan on to the defensive everywhere, but for the time being the Japanese refused to recognize the strategic consequences of their defeat and continued two offensive operations they had already begun. The Japanese army wanted to complete the conquest of New Guinea; the Japanese navy wanted to take the Solomons and the Bismarck Archipelago. So the Japanese attempted both and failed in both.

In March the Japanese had landed on the north shore of New Guinea and in July they began their second attempt to take Port Moresby. By now, however, MacArthur had adequate American and Australian forces to throw them back. A Japanese landing attempt at Milne Bay was defeated at the end of August, and by November 2 the Australians had recaptured Kokoda. After much nasty jungle fighting, the Japanese garrison at Buna was wiped out and the threat in Papua eliminated. In this campaign, Japanese casualties, almost all of them fatalities, were twelve thousand and Australian and American casualties eighty-five hundred.

The Japanese were still on the offensive in the eastern Solomons, where they had invaded Guadalcanal and begun to build an air base.

*Admiral Nimitz remained ashore in Hawaii.

When the United States 1st Marine Division and part of the 2nd Marine Division landed on the island on August 7, they encountered little opposition because most of the Japanese on Guadalcanal were service troops or laborers. However, the Japanese were unwilling to abandon their venture and they continued to reinforce Guadalcanal for the next six months. Since the Americans could not allow a Japanese air base in that area, they also reinforced. The result was the most prolonged and one of the bloodiest battles of the Pacific war. The reinforcement of Guadalcanal by both sides brought on six separate naval engagements, in which the Japanese and the Americans lost an equal number of warships, twenty-four apiece, but in which Japanese losses in transports and other craft were much the heavier.

Meanwhile the Japanese who had been landed on Guadalcanal attacked desperately but unintelligently, were shot down enthusiastically by the marines, and were made temporarily incapable of further attack. Another major Japanese reinforcement reached the island in the middle of October in spite of a naval engagement fought off Cape Esperance to prevent this from happening. The ground fighting, however, continued to favor the marines, who consistently inflicted much heavier casualties than they suffered themselves. Still the Japanese high command refused to draw the appropriate conclusions and instead stubbornly sent more troops to Guadalcanal.

By now the Americans had a two-to-one superiority on the island, and they began to push the Japanese back. Early in January even the Japanese high command was forced to realize that the situation was hopeless, and gave the order to evacuate. The evacuation was brilliantly conducted in the first week of February, when, at the cost of only one destroyer, the Japanese rescued twelve thousand soldiers from the island. The Japanese military commander, having seen the last of his men safely away, committed hara-kiri.

In the United States there was considerable criticism of the manner in which the battle had been fought and of the losses incurred. Nevertheless Guadalcanal had been a major Japanese defeat. It was not so much that Japanese casualties had totaled 25,000 men and 600 aircraft against much lower American losses. Rather it was that Guadalcanal had been a test of strength, like Indian wrestling, and the Americans had definitely proved themselves the stronger.

At the beginning of April the Japanese suffered another reverse. Admiral Yamamoto moved the aircraft carriers of his 3rd Fleet from Truk to Rabaul in order to raid Allied bases, but the effort failed when the American pilots again proved themselves superior. Not only did the Japanese lose the air battle, but Admiral Yamamoto himself, while on an inspection flight, was ambushed and killed by American naval flyers, who knew from the intercept service where he would be.

After Guadalcanal, the tempo of operations in the Pacific slowed. This coincided with, and was in part caused by, an unresolved debate between the United States Army and Navy as to who should do what in the Far Eastern theater. MacArthur urged an attack, by way of the Solomons, New Guinea, and the Bismarck Archipelago, to take the Philippines or Formosa. The navy, unwilling to trust a general with the control of its ships, wanted to relegate MacArthur to a defensive role while the main thrust was made across the Central Pacific by Admiral Nimitz' forces. MacArthur was far away and somewhat out of touch with the intrigues in Washington, but he was too powerful a figure to be treated in such a cavalier fashion. To avoid offending him, the Joint Chiefs of Staff decided to adopt *both* courses and to advance along two axes in both the South and the Central Pacific. These two offensives would converge and meet at the Philippines.

May saw the Americans land at Attu in the Aleutians and, in a hard-fought and essentially unnecessary operation, clear the island. Two months later the Japanese wisely evacuated Kiska. In August a joint American-Canadian expedition descended on the lonely island with more than thirty-four thousand troops, only to find it empty and deserted. This more than slightly ridiculous operation had no military justification, but had perhaps become a political necessity because of the fears of some Americans and Canadians living on the west coast of North America, who made many loud demands for protection against the mythical menace of Japanese invasion. Because of the agitation of these same craven groups, thousands of American and Canadian citizens of Japanese descent were forced to leave their homes and were incarcerated in inland camps for the duration of the war, an episode that in retrospect evokes nothing but shame.

In the other reasonably active Pacific theater, Burma, the Japanese were content to remain on the defensive. However, Field Marshal Archibald Wavell, with Churchill's backing, wished to reconquer some of Burma as soon as possible by an offensive into the Arakan. At first it was hoped that the Chinese might join in the attack but, as often happened when Chiang Kai-shek was involved, the plan broke down. When Wavell launched his offensive into the Arakan in December 1942, it failed. Lieutenant General William J. Slim, who was later to make his reputation in this area, was appointed to command in April 1943, but for the moment there was little Slim could do. Early in May the British were driven back and when the monsoon season broke shortly afterward, the whole endeavor fizzled out dismally.

Partly because of the failure of the Arakan offensive, Wavell was appointed viceroy of India, and a new Southeast Asia Command came

into being under Admiral Lord Louis Mountbatten with General
Joseph W. Stilwell, Chiang Kai-shek's military adviser, as his deputy.
The Fourteenth Army fell under the command of Slim. At the Sex-
tant Conference, held in Cairo in November 1943, it was decided that
the main effort against the Japanese should be in the Pacific rather
than overland from Burma and China. The reason for this decision,
of course, was the obvious success of both MacArthur's and Nimitz'
advances as compared with the situation in Burma, but it was bitter
medicine for the British to swallow.

In the summer of 1943 MacArthur moved to drive the Japanese out
of Lae in New Guinea, a task that was accomplished by September. At
the same time the Americans attacked the Japanese in the Trobriand
Islands and landed in New Georgia in the Solomons to take Munda
airfield. The long-range plan at this time was for MacArthur's forces
to work their way forward to the main Japanese base at Rabaul, but
progress was at first slow. Munda was not in American hands until
August 5. Now, however, MacArthur's undoubted military talent
came into play and he began by-passing Japanese-held islands, leaving
their garrisons to wither on the vine, rather than fighting for each island step by step. With the growing American command of the sea
and air, this policy paid excellent dividends.

In September and October 1943 the Japanese evacuated the central
Solomons and withdrew to the large island of Bougainville at the
western end of the group. This was part of a new and more realistic
policy of contracting the perimeter. In fact, the Japanese high command decided that it would be possible to give up most of New
Guinea, the Bismarck Archipelago, including Rabaul itself, the Solomons, the Gilberts, and the Marshalls. In theory the shorter perimeter should have been easier to defend, but in reality all such hopes
were vanity. The odds were lengthening every day against the
Japanese. The home islands were being cut off from their sources of
supply and Japanese industry was already short of many essentials,
including oil. Japan had always been short of merchant shipping; it
had only fifty-three million tons at the time of Pearl Harbor. Since
then American submarines and aircraft had taken a terrible toll, and
American naval superiority now increased each month.*

On November 1 the Americans struck at Bougainville. The
Japanese defenders indulged in their usual suicidal counterattacks,
losing, in March 1944, more than 8000 soldiers to American casualties
of 300, and thereby destroying their own defensive capability. Other
American landings were made in New Britain in December, and in

*By May 1943 the United States had 15 battleships to 9 Japanese in the Pacific, 3 fleet
carriers to 3, 5 carriers to 4, 11 escort carriers to 3, 134 destroyers to 87, and 104 submarines to 69.

the Admiralty Islands in February 1944. Meanwhile, in the Central Pacific, Nimitz attacked the Gilberts, landing on Makin and Tarawa on November 20. The weak garrison on Makin was overrun in four days but there was extremely bitter fighting on Tarawa. However, once again the Japanese helped their foe; their insane "banzai" charges killed so many of them that the island was cleared with relative ease. Nimitz then began to move on to his next objective, the Marshalls.

Not only in the Pacific had the middle years of the war witnessed the decisive waning of the Axis' power. In 1942 the long seesaw battle in North Africa entered its final phase. Rommel had been reinforced in Tripolitania and by the third week of January he resumed the offensive. This time it was the British who were overextended, fighting at the end of a long line of communications. Advancing on January 21, Rommel soon forced the British Eighth Army to abandon Benghazi and fall back to the Gazala line, extending southward from the coast to Bir Hacheim. Here, with the port of Tobruk immediately behind them, the British intended to make a stand. By all the rules of war their prospects of halting Rommel's offensive and inflicting heavy losses should have been excellent.

The key to the central Mediterranean was Malta, and Malta still held out, though in the winter and spring of 1942 the island was in a bad way. The Axis air offensive against it began on April 2 and was at first frighteningly successful. British convoys were unable to get through, the Grand Harbor was mined nightly by Axis aircraft, and most of the British naval forces had been withdrawn. However, with the delivery of additional Spitfires in the first half of May, the RAF slowly began to win the air battle. Much more could have been done to regain the control of the central Mediterranean had not the British air staff so strongly resisted the sending of any large force of heavy bombers to the Mediterranean theater; it feared this would curtail its cherished air offensive against Germany.

Churchill was once again at his old game of pressing his field commanders to attack before they wished to. He put very heavy pressure on General Auchinleck to launch an offensive in the Western Desert, finally giving him a direct order to do so, which he "must obey or be relieved." The political pressures on Churchill for a British offensive were, of course, strong; the Russians were demanding a second front and their sympathizers assiduously and mindlessly echoed this demand. Auchinleck agreed to Churchill's ultimatum, the more readily, perhaps, because he believed that a third course was open to him: if Rommel attacked first, the Eighth Army would be able to fight a defensive battle. This is what actually happened.

Although he had only 333 German and 228 Italian tanks to a

British tank strength of 850, Rommel began his attack on the Gazala line on the moonlit night of May 26. His main thrust came on the desert flank in the south, accompanied by a feint attack in the north. Auchinleck had anticipated exactly this and had wisely advised General Ritchie to keep his superior armored force concentrated for a counterblow. But Ritchie decided to ignore Auchinleck's advice, and the British armor was once again committed piecemeal and was again defeated.

Yet the Battle of Gazala was not going entirely as Rommel had hoped, for the good reason that the British, though incompetently led, were fighting well. By June 1 the Axis forces were down to 240 tanks to the British 420. Rommel decided to go temporarily on the defensive, concentrating his armor behind the Gazala line in a position known as "the Caldron." When Ritchie launched a badly coordinated attack on June 4, it failed disastrously, allowing Rommel to resume the offensive. In a major tank battle around Knightsbridge on the 12th and 13th Rommel decisively defeated the British armor. The next day Ritchie pulled out of the Gazala line and began to retreat to the Egyptian frontier.

Rommel took Tobruk in a storming attack on June 21, capturing thirty-three thousand prisoners. He also took a very large quantity of supplies in Tobruk, including huge stores of gasoline and thousands of serviceable motor vehicles, which should never have fallen into Axis hands. Since Tobruk harbor had been surrendered to the Germans almost undamaged, Rommel now had a major port at his back for his invasion of Egypt. It was no surprise that General Ritchie was removed from his command and Rommel was promoted to field marshal.

As Rommel turned the British smartly out of their position at Matrûh late in June, Mussolini became enthusiastic over the prospect of capturing Egypt, and flew out to Cyrenaica, complete with a white horse for his triumphal entry into Cairo. The British Mediterranean Fleet sailed from Alexandria to seek refuge in the Red Sea, and there was a good deal of panic in Egypt, though not at Auchinleck's headquarters. Auchinleck, who had now assumed command of the Eighth Army, took up his position along a line from El Alamein south to Alam Nazil, just north of the impassable Qattara Depression, with a refused flank running east at right angles along the Alam el Halfa Ridge. In the forty-mile stretch between the sea and the Qattara Depression he built four defensive localities, or "boxes," sited for all-round defense. He had good reason to feel confident, for Rommel was very overstretched, his troops were tired, his panzers short of fuel, and only fifty-five of them were fit to fight.

Nevertheless, Rommel being Rommel, he attacked on July 1 on the northern half of the front, only to find his thrust blunted by the unexpected opposition of a defended locality at Deir el Shein. The next afternoon Rommel renewed his attack but was again foiled. The Afrika Korps made another weak attack on the 3rd, which gained some ground but accomplished nothing except to increase further the disparity between the two forces. Auchinleck now ordered a counterattack, which, had it been properly executed, might have ended the North African campaign then and there. But it was slow and feeble, and for another three weeks the two hostile armies remained in their clinch, like two exhausted and punch-drunk boxers. In that time the fighting was sporadic, though often heavy — on July 21 the British lost 118 tanks to Rommel's 3 — but neither side could gain a conclusive advantage.

The First Battle of Alamein cost the British 13,500 casualties, but the Axis losses had also been high and had included over 7000 prisoners, most of them Italians. The unspectacular outcome of the battle, and the better publicity arrangements of subsequent commanders, have tended to obscure Auchinleck's success. Yet it was in July that the Germans lost the campaign in the Middle East. From now on the British were able to reinforce far more rapidly than their enemy. The 10th Submarine Flotilla had returned to Malta on July 10 and was soon wreaking havoc on Axis shipping. And by the middle of August the RAF had more than 250 aircraft on Malta. In October the Germans again mounted a sustained air offensive against Malta, but they suffered such heavy losses that the operation was canceled. Thus the outcome of the war in North Africa was never really in doubt after First Alamein.

Mussolini had perhaps realized this on July 20, when he returned to Rome without waiting any longer for a ceremonial reception in Cairo. If so, he understood the situation better than Churchill, who flew out to Cairo early in August. When he discovered that Auchinleck was not prepared to take the offensive until September he relieved him of his command, appointing him instead to the newly organized Middle East Command, which comprised only Persia and Iraq. General Sir Harold Alexander was appointed commander-in-chief of the new Near East Command, consisting of Egypt, Palestine, and Syria, and General "Strafer" Gott was appointed to command the Eighth Army. When Gott was shot down and killed on a flight to Cairo on August 7, the command of the Eighth Army went to Lieutenant General Bernard L. Montgomery. Perhaps in view of the manner in which fame was later distributed, it is not out of place to record that Lieutenant General Fritz Bayerlein, the chief of staff of the Afrika Korps, stated that in his opinion Auchinleck was the best Allied general in North Africa during the war.

The next battle began on the night of August 30, with Rommel attacking again. Like the First Battle of Alamein, the Battle of Alam el Halfa proved to be a mistake on Rommel's part. Montgomery fought the defensive battle basically as Auchinleck had laid it out for him. Attacking from the south, Rommel's panzers were stopped cold by the strong defenses of Alam el Halfa Ridge. Since his tanks were now very short of fuel, Rommel issued orders for a withdrawal, retiring almost unmolested to a position slightly in advance of his original start line. By the 7th, and by mutual consent, the battle had petered out. British casualties at Alam el Halfa were 1750, to an Axis total of 2910, of whom 1859 were German. Axis tank losses were slightly lower than the British, but Montgomery could replace tanks much more easily than Rommel, and since the British retained possession of the battlefield a number of their damaged tanks could be salvaged and repaired.

Churchill could hardly dismiss his commander-in-chief in Egypt and his commander of the Eighth Army again so soon, especially since the Battle of Alam el Halfa had been hailed as a much greater defensive victory than First Alamein. Therefore the British prime minister, much against his will, had to agree that the British offensive for which he pined would not start until October 23 — about a month later than Auchinleck had promised to attack. By the opening of the attack Montgomery outnumbered his enemy by nearly two to one in men and by more than two to one in tanks, with 1100 to 500 for the Axis. Even more serious was the general shortage of supplies, especially fuel, on the Axis side.

Montgomery's plan of attack at El Alamein called for his main thrust to be in the north between the Ruweisat Ridge and the sea, while diversionary attacks were made in the south. There would be a heavy preliminary bombardment, rather in the style of the First World War, and then the British infantry would advance to clear lanes through the German minefields. Only after this would the British armor pass through. Montgomery's first major battle was, in fact, a "set-piece" attack, meticulously prepared and launched in sufficient strength to guarantee success.

The attack, which opened at 9:40 P.M., at first went very slowly, and British casualties were high. Deep penetrations were made into the enemy's minefields but no clean hole was punched through them. Everywhere the enemy fought back viciously, and on the 25th launched strong counterattacks. At the end of the first week's fighting the Eighth Army had suffered 10,130 casualties and still had not broken through the German defenses. Montgomery now reorganized his forces for a new blow north to the sea. This attack went in on the night of the 28th, but at first it too bogged down in the German minefields.

On the German side, however, things were far worse. By now there were only about 90 German tanks left in action, whereas Montgomery still had 800. On the 30th Rommel reported that his situation was critical and that his front might break at any moment. Once again, on November 2, Montgomery shifted the direction of his thrust, but this attack, like its predecessors, was soon in difficulty. On this day British tank losses numbered nearly 200, but by now Rommel had only some 30 tanks left. Weight of numbers told: the final German counterattacks were repulsed, and by the 3rd Montgomery had finally blasted a hole through Rommel's defenses.

The previous night Rommel had decided to break off the battle and retreat to Fûka, sixty miles to the west. His troops had already begun thinning out when an order arrived from Hitler, demanding that the Alamein position be held to the last. Rommel obeyed and stopped the retreat, and his obedience might well have lost him his army. On the night of November 3 a fresh British attack broke through the German line. Through this gap poured all the British armor and the New Zealand Division to wheel north and cut off the Afrika Korps. The encirclement attempt failed, partly because it did not strike far enough to the west. The Germans managed to check the British advance long enough to pull their troops out along the coastal road, but the Afrika Korps commander, General Wilhelm Ritter von Thoma, was captured. This time Rommel retreated without paying any attention to orders from OKW (Hitler's permission arrived the next day) and he did not halt until he had fallen back fifteen hundred miles.

The pursuit was ineffectual. The British left hooks to intercept the fleeing Germans were too short; British armor halted at night while the Germans continued their retreat; commanders were often overly cautious; and traffic control was not always good. On November 6 it began to rain heavily, and though it rained on both the British and the Germans, it seemed to slow the British more. By the 7th it was obvious that Rommel had got away, despite repeated bombing attacks by the RAF.

At the Second Battle of Alamein the British captured some thirty-three thousand prisoners, about ten thousand of them Germans. Although the remnants of the Afrika Korps escaped, the British and American landings in Morocco, which began on November 8, meant that the end of the Axis' power in Africa was only a matter of time. El Alamein was the first British victory of the war, so it is perhaps natural that its magnitude and importance should have been exaggerated. Yet in military affairs, as in most matters, any distortion of reality is likely to be paid for in the long run. In this case, part of the price for the exaggeration of El Alamein was the campaign in Italy.

The decision to invade French North Africa had not been reached easily or without much dissension. In the middle of April 1942 General George C. Marshall and Harry Hopkins had gone to Britain to propose that the United States collect in the United Kingdom, by the spring of 1943, a force of forty-eight divisions and 5800 aircraft for an invasion of northwest Europe in April of 1943 (Operation Roundup). The Americans further proposed that if a German collapse occurred, or if the Soviet Union was in danger of being knocked out of the war, a smaller operation (Operation Sledgehammer) should be mounted in the autumn of 1942, to occupy Brest or Cherbourg and gain a lodgment in France. The British Chiefs of Staff and the Cabinet Defense Committee had approved both proposals by April 14, although the Chiefs of Staff expressed serious reservations about Sledgehammer. General Dwight D. Eisenhower was given command of the American forces in Britain, and the Combined Chiefs of Staff, meeting in Washington in June, agreed that nothing should be undertaken in 1942 that would delay Roundup in 1943. By midsummer detailed British staff studies had shown conclusively that Sledgehammer would not be possible in 1942, an opinion that was confirmed by the disastrous raid on Dieppe on August 19.

In this raid, carried out principally by two brigades of the Canadian 2nd Division, the folly of frontal attacks against strongly defended coastal areas was once again painfully demonstrated. It was the main lesson learned from the disaster, and after Gallipoli it should not have had to be learned at all. Although a shocking waste of excellent troops, the Dieppe raid may have helped dispel the easy optimism of American planners who believed in the possibility of seizing and holding the Cherbourg peninsula that autumn. If so, the Canadians' sacrifice was not entirely in vain.

Meanwhile, at the end of May, President Roosevelt had rashly promised Molotov that the United States would establish a second front in Europe in 1942. This promise seems to have been given without any serious staff study to ascertain whether it could be implemented. Once given, it was a constant goad to the American President, who from then on insisted that American ground forces must fight Germans *somewhere* in 1942. Sledgehammer would have been almost entirely a British operation, for the United States could have contributed a maximum of four divisions and 700 aircraft. Thus, when the British came out so decidedly against it, Sledgehammer was dead. At this juncture Churchill again suggested, as an alternative to Sledgehammer, that a joint American-British invasion of French North Africa be mounted.

The United States Joint Chiefs of Staff thought very little of this suggestion. They had all along insisted, with impeccable military logic, that, since Germany was the principal enemy, the decisive theater of the war for the western Allies could only be northwest Europe. And though the Americans agreed on the necessity of defending the United Kingdom, there was a general feeling that the United States should not be used to defend British imperial interests in faraway corners of the world. An invasion of French North Africa, in the view of the American Joint Chiefs, would be a distraction that, they accurately predicted, would make Roundup impossible for 1943. In addition Admiral Ernest J. King opposed it because it would make unacceptable demands on shipping. It was even suggested that if the British persisted, the United States should reverse its priorities and concentrate on the defeat of Japan. Roosevelt promptly vetoed this suggestion, but it took a direct order from him to bring the Joint Chiefs into line. Even then, while they reluctantly agreed to the North African invasion (Operation Torch), they reinforced the Pacific theater for the remainder of 1942 at the expense of the American buildup in the United Kingdom.

General Marshall, Admiral King, and Hopkins went to London again in July, and on the 24th the Combined Chiefs of Staff formally agreed to Operation Torch. It was General Eisenhower's opinion that this decision might mark "the blackest day in history." At all events, once the decision had been made, it was not long before Churchill's fertile mind began to toy with other strategic possibilities. As he told the British Chiefs of Staff: "The flank attack [in the Mediterranean] may become the main attack, and the main attack a holding operation in the early stages . . . We can [then] push either right-handed, left-handed or both-handed as our resources and circumstances permit."

A decision reached toward the end of July left little enough time for the detailed planning necessary before the Torch landings could be mounted in the autumn. Although he had been opposed to the operation, Eisenhower was given the overall command, which was tactful. Lieutenant General K. A. N. Anderson, a British officer, would be ground forces commander. British and American differences were by no means all resolved by Roosevelt's directive to cooperate in Torch, for the British envisaged landings in the Mediterranean as far to the east as possible so that the Straits of Tunis could be quickly dominated, but the Americans favored a landing on the Atlantic coast of Morocco, eleven hundred miles from the vital ports of Tunis and Bizerte. Landings in Morocco would conserve American shipping and give the green American troops an easier initial task, but Casablanca was surely a very long way from the decisive area. In the event,

Eisenhower proposed that the Allies should both land at Algiers, as the British wanted, and at Casablanca, as the Americans wanted. This unsatisfactory compromise was adopted, causing a larger dispersion of effort and the prolongation of the campaign.

Roosevelt believed that the Vichy French were unlikely to resist the Americans, so it was decided that the Moroccan landings should be undertaken only by American troops and that American troops should be first ashore everywhere along the coast. An American task force of 24,500 men would land north and south of Casablanca and near Port Lyautey. A second joint American-British force of 18,500 men would land near Oran in Algeria, and a third force of 20,000 would land near Algiers. A follow-up echelon of a further 44,000 troops was also provided for.

What could be done to neutralize the resistance of the Vichy French was done. But because in the murky twilight world of French politics it was by no means certain whom they could rely on, the Allies were obviously unable to give any French officer in North Africa detailed information about the proposed landings. Furthermore, in view of the security leaks that had helped to ruin the Dakar expedition and because President Roosevelt and the American State Department distrusted De Gaulle, no word of Operation Torch was confided to the Free French. Since De Gaulle could not be used, the Allies looked about for a French figurehead who might assist them in neutralizing the French garrisons in North Africa. General Henri Honoré Giraud, an honorable, rather simple man who had not been notably successful in his command of either the French Seventh or Ninth armies in 1940, had escaped from German custody and was living in unoccupied France. The State Department decided that he would do nicely and that he might even prove a useful counterpoise to De Gaulle. Giraud, under the naïve impression that he was to be the Supreme Commander of the invading Allied armies, allowed himself to be spirited out of France to Gibraltar by submarine. When the command was denied him, he was promised that he would head the French government in North Africa.

None of this elaborate plot worked out as intended. When Giraud reached Algiers no Frenchman paid much attention to him. The Americans made a deal with the Nazi collaborator Admiral Darlan, and put him, rather than Giraud, in charge of the civil government; and the long-term hope that Giraud might be a substitute for De Gaulle floundered because De Gaulle, if not honorable, was certainly not simple, and in the matter of political intrigue had nothing to learn from anyone.

The landings took place almost as scheduled on the night of

November 8. On the Atlantic coast particularly, the American landings were plagued by inexperience and confusion. Fortunately, the French did not at first resist, but they soon rallied and began to counterattack the Americans. At Casablanca a French naval force did its best to sink the American troopships but was turned back by American naval gunfire. At Algiers there was little opposition on the beaches, though two British destroyers were sunk by French shore batteries, with heavy casualties to the American Rangers they were carrying. At Oran the French fought more stubbornly and two more British warships were sunk, but by the 10th the Americans had captured the city and the French surrendered.

Admiral Darlan was persuaded to order a cease-fire. For this service, Giraud was pushed aside and Darlan was recognized as high commissioner and head of the French administration in North Africa. So blatant a pact with a Nazi collaborator caused a tremendous public outcry both in the United States and Britain, and Roosevelt and Churchill were probably much relieved when Darlan was assassinated on December 24 by a young Gaullist, who was nevertheless promptly executed for his deed.

Hitler lost little time in reacting to the Torch landings. On November 11 he invaded unoccupied France. On the 27th, just as the Germans were about to seize the French fleet by a *coup de main*, the French sailors scuttled it, sinking sixty-one of their warships in Toulon harbor. These ships would have been invaluable to the Allies for the Battle of the Atlantic and for the subsequent liberation of France, but they were at least better under the waves than in German hands.

Hitler would have been wise at this point to cut his losses and evacuate North Africa. Instead, he reinforced and was at first successful in building up a new front against the Anglo-American attacks. This initial success, however, only made the ultimate Axis defeat the more disastrous.

Meanwhile the Germans pushed boldly out from Tunis and Bizerte to seize Sousse, Sfax, and Gabès, and to secure for themselves an area large enough to be defensible. The Allies advanced slowly, their troops being inexperienced and their commanders far too cautious. By the end of the first week in December the Allies were still nearly forty miles from Tunis. A few days later the rainy season began and this further bogged down the Allied advance, but it did not stop the flow of German and Italian reinforcements. Before long, Colonel General Jürgen von Arnim, commander of the Fifth Panzer Army, had a force of four panzer divisions and ten infantry divisions. Meanwhile on the eastern flank Montgomery also approached cautiously. It was January 23 before he reached Tripoli, and there he paused to reorganize and resupply. On February 16 Rommel crossed into Tunisia with a reinforced army that now numbered seventy-eight thousand men. Since he had the advantage of interior lines and since his enemies were so cautious, Rommel was now able to turn and strike a blow at the Anglo-American army in the west. At the end of January his veteran 21st Panzer Division had swept the French garrison out of the Faïd Pass, and two weeks later, on February 14, an Axis force, spearheaded by 150 tanks, struck through this pass and overran the thinly spread U.S. 1st Armored Division, taking 3000 prisoners and creating general havoc in the Allied rear.

On February 20 the 21st Panzer Division attacked through the Kasserine Pass and then turned north, but this looked more menacing on the map than it actually was on the ground. Two days later a force of British armor and British and American infantry halted the German advance. Rommel now had no choice but to call off his offensive and turn back to face the Eighth Army. The counterblow had been a brilliant effort and the initial defeat had tended to shake American confidence more than was justified, but the attack had been too light for strategic success.

On March 6, at Medenine, Rommel suffered a serious reverse when his panzers ran into Montgomery's prepared antitank defenses. This was a trick Rommel himself had played often enough, and it cheered the British to see the tables turned. Shortly after this, Rommel, who had been ill for several months, reported sick and was replaced by Arnim. With the failure of the German attacks on both fronts, there was little the Axis forces could do but await the end.

On March 20 Montgomery attacked the German positions in the Mareth Line, which defended the entrance to Tunisia from the south. After eight days of hard fighting the British broke through. By now the entire Axis position was crumbling and the armies in Tunisia could no longer be either reinforced or withdrawn. Arnim fell back for a last-ditch stand in northeastern Tunisia and on Cape Bon. A final British-American attack on May 6 overwhelmed this position, and Tunis and Bizerte fell the next day. Arnim was captured on the 12th, and nearly 250,000 Axis soldiers followed him into captivity. This loss, which could easily have been prevented had Hitler not been determined to hold Tunisia at all costs, deprived the Axis of many excellent, veteran divisions, whose presence on the mainland of Europe would have very gravely complicated the coming Allied attack across the Mediterranean.

That attack had been decided upon at the Casablanca Conference in January 1943, when Roosevelt, Churchill, and the Combined

Chiefs of Staff met at Anfa Camp. A strategy emerged only after long and sometimes sharp debate, and what was finally agreed to did not completely satisfy anyone. Admiral King still wanted to emphasize the Pacific theater. General Marshall's thoughts kept turning longingly to the invasion of northwest Europe. The Joint Planning Staff and Lord Mountbatten wanted to invade Sardinia. But Churchill and Roosevelt, supported eventually by the Combined Chiefs of Staff, wanted to invade Sicily.

All these strategic alternatives were conditioned by the fact that the Allies now had large armies in North Africa, where they had gone for reasons that had been more political than military. There was, of course, nothing wrong with this in itself. The end of war is politics, and political considerations should often be of more weight in war than purely military ones. However, the difficulty was that the Allies had in fact no reasonable political aim in common. The broad generalities of the Atlantic Charter bore no resemblance to a plan, and — what was worse — served to conceal real divergence of views. Roosevelt and Churchill did not share the same vision of the postwar era. Roosevelt dreamed of a Wilsonian world, where war would be forever outlawed by the friendly collaboration of the victors. Churchill longed in his heart for a return to the good old days, when Britannia ruled the waves and the British Empire defied the sun to set on it. They were united in their desire utterly to defeat Nazi Germany, but in the greater realm of grand strategy, as in the lesser one of strategy, they moved forward by expedients and compromises, some of which indeed were imposed by events, but many of which resulted from national differences in their ways of looking at the war.

At Casablanca the question was what could be done with the Allied armies in North Africa once the Axis had been defeated there, which, it was calculated, would occur by the end of April. "It still would have been preferable to close immediately with the German enemy in Western Europe or even in Southern France had that been possible of achievement with the resources then available to General Eisenhower," Marshall later wrote. But an invasion of western Europe in 1943 was no longer possible. Neither time nor the available shipping would permit it. The bulk of the Allied forces in North Africa could have been transported back to the United Kingdom, but then they would have had to wait there — training but not fighting — until 1944. Many of them could certainly have done with the training, but while the Soviet Union was still engaged in bitter combat on the eastern front, such a policy was considered politically unacceptable. Whether in fact it was so is another matter, for by now, with Stalingrad invested and the German drive to the Caucasus turned back, it was obvious that Russia was not going to be defeated. Also it is very difficult to see how the Soviet Union, now that the tide had turned, could have made a separate peace with Hitler, even had the Nazi dictator been willing to entertain such a possibility.

The chief decisions taken at Casablanca were that the Mediterranean should be opened as soon as possible so as to economize on shipping, that the bomber offensive against Nazi-controlled Europe should be continued and enlarged, and that Italy should be driven out of the war. To achieve these ends it was decided to invade Sicily during the full-moon period of June, or possibly of July. General Eisenhower was appointed Supreme Commander Mediterranean, with General Alexander as his deputy. Admiral Sir Andrew Cunningham was to be naval commander-in-chief, and Air Chief Marshal Sir Arthur Tedder air commander. This was all definite enough so far as it went, but as yet no decision was taken as to what should happen after Sicily had been captured.

At Casablanca Roosevelt and Churchill announced that they would demand "unconditional surrender" from the Axis powers. This war aim does not seem to have been given any serious consideration before it was promulgated, and it is rarely wise to make major decisions casually over lunch. The announcement of unconditional surrender, though it marched admirably with the mood of the time, could only complicate the Allies' military task, for it stiffened their enemy's will to resist and undermined those in Germany and Italy who plotted an overthrow of the Nazi and fascist regimes. Such an announcement was not necessary to keep Russia in the war, for by January 1943 the Russians also scented victory and had much reason to seek revenge. Unconditional surrender can now be seen as an emotional rather than a rational aim. Even if it was felt that Germany's sins deserved so harsh a retribution — and this was certainly a very reasonable point of view — what benefit could come from trumpeting the fact abroad before victory had been achieved? Time enough to refuse the enemy terms when the enemy is beaten.

In May another conference, Trident, was held in Washington, and by now the British Chiefs of Staff were pressing for an invasion of Italy. The fascist regime was in imminent danger of collapse, and an invasion of Calabria would almost certainly bring it down. At the very least, the British said, Germany would be forced to divert troops to Italy or the Balkans. If the Germans tried to hold both, they would not have sufficient resources to do so. The Balkans could then be occupied by the Allies and — again the delusive hope! — Turkey could be induced to join the war. It was also argued, rather more speciously, that an Italian campaign would be the best possible preparation for an invasion of northwest Europe in 1944, since it would draw off large numbers of German defenders. What this last argument overlooked was the fact that Italy was almost ideal defensive country and that even in more open terrain the defense can usually be maintained with between half and one third the troops that the offensive requires.

Reluctantly Marshall and the Americans finally agreed to this reasoning, though they insisted that the cross-Channel invasion should be given clear priority and that operations in the Mediterranean should be definitely subsidiary to Roundup, which was now renamed Overlord to emphasize this order of priority. The Americans also insisted that a firm date be set for Overlord and that large forces, including seven divisions from the Mediterranean theater, should be specifically earmarked for it. To all this the British Chiefs of Staff agreed, and May 1, 1944, was set as D-Day for northwest Europe.

Yet even when the joint Anglo-American invasion forces for Operation Husky landed in Sicily on July 10, it had still not been decided whether to invade Italy as the next step. Churchill, however, was determined on an Italian campaign. He wrote to General Jan Smuts on July 15 that if the Americans would not cooperate in that venture the British would do it themselves. The Mediterranean was the one theater where the British could cooperate as equal partners of the Americans without being dominated by the superior strength of their great ally. Perhaps, too, Churchill really believed his own unfortunate phrase to Stalin about "the soft underbelly" of Europe.

The plan for the invasion of Sicily called for the landing of two armies, the British Eighth Army under Montgomery and the United States Seventh Army under General George S. Patton, Jr., both under the operational control of General Alexander, the commander of the Anglo-American Fifteenth Army Group. The British would land at five spots along a forty-mile stretch of beach on the southeast, south, and southwest tip of the island between Syracuse and Pozzalo. The Americans would land at three places some thirty miles to the British left on the west-coast beaches of the Gulf of Gela between Cape Scaramia and Licata. No port was to be directly attacked in the first assault — a lesson that had been thoroughly learned at Dieppe eleven months before — and initial maintenance would be over only the open beaches. In the summer of 1943 this was a radical decision, but the planners rightly assumed that usable ports would soon be in Allied hands. An airborne assault by portions of the British 1st Airborne Division and the American 82nd Airborne Division would precede the main seaborne attacks, the British dropping west of Syracuse and the Americans near the Ponte Olivo airfield four miles inland from Gela.

The naval plan for Operation Husky called for 1375 merchant

ships to be assembled off the Sicilian coast, after sailing from Britain, the United States, Egypt, Algeria, Malta, and northern and southern Tunisia. This great converging armada lost only six ships from submarine attack, and assembled promptly at the rendezvous just after midnight on July 10. When the landings began a few hours later, at four-thirty in the morning, while it was still dark, they went much more smoothly than the Torch landings in North Africa had done. Surprise was complete, in part because a storm and high seas on the 9th had convinced those in charge of the Italian coastal formations that no invasion was possible for the next twenty-four hours. The 4300 Allied aircraft, in 113 British and 146 American squadrons, that supported Operation Husky gave the invaders aerial supremacy over Sicily and its adjacent waters.

The Allied plan specified that after the seaborne and airborne assaults had taken Syracuse, Licata, and the airfields in the south a firm base would be established behind a line from Catania to Licata, to be followed by the capture of Augusta, Catania, and the airfields around Gerbini. Then the rest of the island would be overrun. It was a sound plan but a cautious one. There was no maximizing of results here, but the Allies had had enough bitter experience to justify caution, or at least to excuse it.

Field Marshal Albert Kesselring, who had been appointed Commander-in-Chief South in December 1941, was in operational control of all German ground and air forces in Italy and the western and central Mediterranean area. These were few enough for the work they had to do. The debacle in Tunisia had left the European mainland opposite the African shores almost denuded of reliable troops. Had the Allies launched their invasion more promptly, they would have had a much easier time of it. By July 10 something had been done to improve the Germans' situation. Although, contrary to British expectations, Hitler decided to hold both Italy and the Balkans, he was still able to find troops to defend Sicily. By the time of the Allied invasion there were two German armored divisions in Sicily. In addition, there were four Italian divisions and six Italian coastal divisions, though none had much fighting value. In all, at the time of invasion, there were about 40,000 German troops in Sicily and some 230,000 Italians.

The Allies landed eight divisions simultaneously in Sicily, putting 150,000 men ashore on the first day — a larger effort than was to be made on the Normandy beaches the following year. The landings were almost unopposed, since the two German panzer divisions were being held in reserve inland for counterattack. All the initial objectives were captured with ease, and the Italians surrendered in droves.

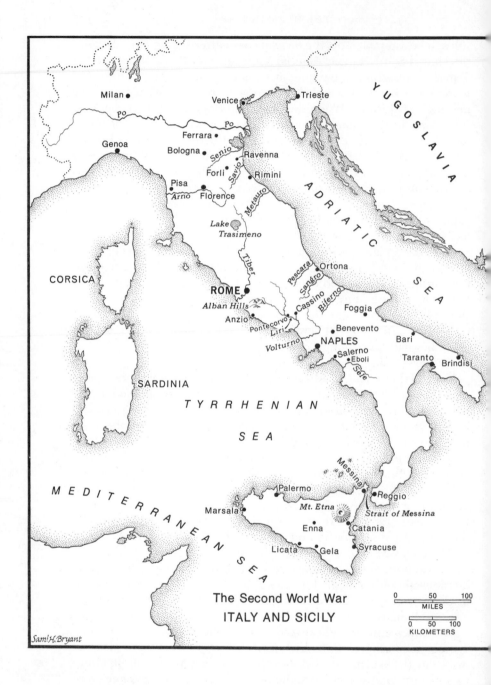

The Second World War
ITALY AND SICILY

Sam!H.Bryant

Syracuse fell to the British that same evening, its port facilities undamaged, and Licata with its port and airfield fell to the Americans. The airborne landings, however, had been disastrous. Errors of navigation had led to a great dispersal of the drops. Many British gliders fell into the sea, and the American paratroops were scattered over a fifty-mile area. Nevertheless, by the morning of the 11th both the Seventh and Eighth armies had established sizable bridgeheads and were driving inland.

Counterattacks were beaten off on the 11th and 12th, and by the 13th the Allies had established a firm base and controlled the port of Augusta. The Eighth Army advanced toward Catania on the east coast and toward the communications hub of Enna in the center of Sicily, while the Seventh Army advanced up the southwest coast and also drove inland toward Enna. However, on July 15 enemy resistance suddenly stiffened on the British front as the German formations were encountered in front of Catania. Consequently the Eighth Army's right was held up south of Catania, while the Seventh Army, having mainly Italians to deal with, soon overran all western Sicily. This was the opposite of what had been planned, for it had been intended to hold on the left and advance on the right.

When the Americans captured Campofelice on the north coast on the 22nd, Sicily was cut in two. The hardest struggle, however, was in the east, where the Germans skillfully defended Mount Etna, which dominated the coastal road from Catania to Messina. Both sides reinforced. By the end of July the Germans had seventy thousand troops on the island, in four divisions; the Allies had twelve divisions. The Sicilian countryside was eminently suited for defense, being mountainous, almost roadless in the interior, and with ancient stone towns and villages perched on high crags to dominate the valleys. As usual, the Germans used ground to the maximum advantage, but even so, with the Italian collapse in the west, they could do no more than defend for a while the northeastern corner of the island around Messina so as to gain time for the better defense of the mainland.

A dramatic development on July 25 made time all the more vital for the Germans. Late that evening Radio Rome interrupted its programing to announce that King Victor Emmanuel had accepted the resignation of Mussolini. The Italian people had never been enthusiastic about the war, and — as Lenin had said of the tsar's soldiers in 1917 — the Italian army had "voted for peace with its legs." Mussolini, of course, had never dreamed that events would turn out as they had. In the summer of 1940 he had thought that the German "New Order" was secure in Europe, and, as he had callously said at the time, "I need a few thousand dead so as to be able to attend the peace conference as a belligerent." Now, with Italy's African empire lost and Sicily all but overrun, even the Fascist party turned against its leader. Aware of the danger in which he stood, Mussolini had gone to Feltre on July 19 to meet Hitler, with the intention of telling him that Italy would have to make a separate peace, but when the moment came Il Duce's nerve had failed and he had said nothing. The first air raid on Rome, which occurred while Mussolini was at his rendezvous with Hitler, helped convince the Fascist Grand Council that the dictator would have to go. The king called on Marshal Pietro Badoglio to head the new government.

None of this was unexpected by Hitler, who was not for a moment deceived by Badoglio's announcement that Italy would continue in the war. The Germans had a contingency plan ready against the day of Italy's defection, and on the 30th they implemented it. German formations seized the passes into Italy and began to pour into the country. By the end of the first week of August the Germans had fifteen divisions in Italy, including the four fighting in Sicily.

For the defenders of Sicily it was high time to go, for the American Seventh Army had linked up with the British Eighth Army in front of Messina. The evacuation began on the night of August 10 across the Straits of Messina. In spite of the almost total Allied naval and air supremacy, the Germans got clean away, suffering almost no losses in the withdrawal. By the morning of the 17th, when the Americans entered Messina, the Germans had gone and were even then in Italy, reorganizing to fight again. Among the German troops evacuated were 13,500 wounded, many of whom would also fight again. German losses in Sicily were 6663 captured, 13,500 wounded, and about 5000 killed. Italian casualties amounted to about 2000 killed, 5000 wounded, and 137,000 taken prisoner. The Allied losses in killed and wounded were 19,245.

In spite of the favorable casualty ratio, however, the Sicilian campaign had been unimpressive. For thirty-eight days four German divisions had outfought and outmaneuvered an Allied force of more than twelve divisions. It is true that the ground had favored the defense, but it had, after all, been the Allies who had chosen the ground — and the points of invasion. To some at least it appeared as if the job had been done the hard way after leisurely preparation had wasted time that the enemy put to good use. By landing at the southernmost tip of Sicily, where fighter cover was guaranteed, the British and Americans had condemned themselves to fighting up the entire length of the island to Messina. No attempt had been made to exploit Allied sea power by subsequent amphibious landings at the enemy's rear.

Still, it was a victory of sorts. Italy was on the point of being driven from the war and the Allied aim of drawing German divisions away from the eastern front was being fulfilled. On July 20 the American Joint Chiefs of Staff formally sanctioned the invasion of the Italian mainland.

On August 15 Marshal Badoglio secretly opened negotiations with the Allies for a separate peace, and Badoglio's representative had instructions to go even further and say "that when the Allies landed in Italy, the Italian Government was prepared to join them against Germany." Thus did Italy, in the most remarkable manner, repeat her performance of the First World War by changing sides. However, the declaration of war on Germany was not made by the new Italian government until October 13. On August 16, at a commanders-in-chief's conference in Carthage, the Allies decided to invade southern Calabria (Operation Baytown) with the Eighth Army and to launch a second, and main, invasion in the Bay of Salerno (Operation Avalanche) with General Mark Clark's Fifth Army, which would have under command the U.S. VI Corps and the British X Corps.

At the beginning of September the Germans had a total of sixteen divisions on the Italian mainland: six south of Rome in the new Tenth Army commanded by Colonel General Heinrich von Vietinghoff, two around Rome itself to keep the Italians in order, and eight north of the Apennines in Rommel's Army Group B.

In faint moonlight on the night of September 23, in a perfectly calm sea, the Eighth Army's two assault divisions were set ashore on the beaches north of Reggio Calabria under cover of a barrage fired from Sicily and from warships offshore. Because of navigational errors most of the assault troops were put down on the wrong beaches, but on this occasion it was a matter of no consequence; there was no opposition. Those Italian soldiers who were encountered readily volunteered to help unload the Allied landing craft and were of considerable assistance in this task. The Allied soldiers pushed rapidly inland, and within a week, despite vile roads and German demolitions, had penetrated seventy-five miles up the peninsula.

With the announcement of Italy's capitulation, the Germans at once disarmed the Italian army and air force, a simple task ironically called Operation Axis. The Italian minister of the navy, Admiral Count de Courten, had visited Field Marshal Kesselring's headquarters on the 7th and, with tears in his eyes, had informed him that the Italian fleet would put to sea the next day to attack the British Mediterranean Fleet. The Italian navy, he said, was resolved to "conquer or perish." The Italian fleet did sail on the 8th, but its mission was not death or glory; it was surrender. The Germans managed to sink the Italian flagship *Roma* with a radio-controlled glide bomb, but the rest of the Italian navy achieved its aim of submitting to the Allies.

At three-thirty on the morning of September 9 the main Allied invasion force began to go ashore in the Bay of Salerno. The British landed on the northern beaches with two divisions; on the British right the U.S. 36th Division landed on the southern beaches. It had been an open secret that the Allies would land at Salerno — even the Italians had guessed it — and General Vietinghoff had alerted his troops the previous day and had disarmed the Italian 222nd Coastal Division and taken over its positions. Against all probability, the Fifth Army commander, General Clark, counted on achieving tactical surprise and would therefore not permit any naval bombardment. In the British sector this order was wisely not obeyed, and the coastal batteries were silenced. In the sector of the U.S. 36th Division, however, Clark was obeyed, with the result that the assault troops suffered severe losses from heavy and unanswered fire.

The Germans immediately struck hard at the invaders. In the British sector none of the first day's objectives was taken, though the troops did manage to get almost two miles inland. In spite of its losses on the run-in, the green U.S. 36th Division managed to drive its left flank forward nearly five miles after landing, but its right made little progress and did not succeed in linking up with the British to the north. For the first two days the Germans concentrated mainly against the British sector in the north, this being the direct route to Naples. During this period the Allies made steady but unspectacular progress, especially on the right, where the Americans extended their beachhead to a depth of ten miles. On the 10th the British captured Salerno, but the two Allied bridgeheads were still separated and in very grave danger as German reinforcements came up.

German counterattacks secured the heights around the northern rim of the beachhead, over which passed the roads to Naples, and pinned the British X Corps to the coastal strip. This achieved, the Germans next turned to the task of driving the British and Americans farther apart as a preliminary to eliminating them one at a time. On the 12th the British were driven back, with heavy losses, and the next day the Germans hurled the Americans back more than five miles, and at one point came to within 800 yards of the beach.

The Germans had a more spectacular success when, on September 12, a force of 100 glider-borne SS troops, under the command of SS Hauptsturmführer Otto Skorzeny, landed at the hotel on Gran Sasso mountain in the Abruzzi where Mussolini was being held prisoner and spirited the former dictator away. Hitler then established his confederate as the nominal head of a republican fascist regime in northern Italy. But though this rescue had good propaganda value, it did nothing much to help win the war.

Despite General Alexander's urging Montgomery to drive his

Eighth Army northward faster, it was still 200 miles away and advancing with extreme caution. By the night of the 13th the fate of the Salerno landings hung in the balance. In the sector of VI Corps, all unloading from ships was halted, and General Clark, apparently losing his nerve, asked the naval task force commander, the American Vice Admiral H. Kent Hewitt, to prepare either to evacuate the VI Corps and move it to the X Corps sector or vice versa. This was a naval impossibility and would undoubtedly have led to a military disaster. Fortunately it was not attempted. Instead, Alexander and Eisenhower, shaken by Clark's suggestion, rushed in reinforcements. All the resources of air power were turned against the Germans counterattacking the Allied perimeter. On the 14th more than two thousand sorties were flown by Allied aircraft. The navy also pounded enemy positions with heavy and accurate fire. On the night of the 13th/14th, thirty-eight hundred paratroopers of the U.S. 82nd Airborne Division dropped into the VI Corps sector, and on the 14th the British 7th Armored Division began coming ashore. And, at long last, on the 15th, the advance guard of Montgomery's Eighth Army appeared at Sapri, only forty miles south of Salerno. By the next day the Allies had seven divisions ashore, with some 200 tanks, whereas the Germans, who had sent in the last of their available reinforcements, could muster only four equivalent divisions, with fewer than 100 tanks. The Germans counterattacked for the last time that morning but made little headway. That evening, just as patrols of the Eighth and Fifth armies were meeting on the right of the VI Corps, Vietinghoff decided that the chance of eliminating the Salerno beachhead had vanished and ordered a retreat to the next defensible position, the line of the Volturno River, twenty miles north of Naples.

The next stage of the Italian campaign was marked by slow Allied advances up both coasts, the Eighth Army on the Adriatic side and the Fifth Army on the west. And now the full difficulties of fighting step by step up the peninsula became apparent. The central mountain spine of the Apennines divided the country in two; only the coastal roads were suitable for maintaining a major thrust; and the rivers, strong, swift, and flowing down each side of the Apennines to the sea, were major obstacles to northward movement. All in all, it would have been difficult to find terrain easier to defend. The Fifth Army, which had suffered some twelve thousand casualties at Salerno, did not take Naples, thirty-five miles away, until October 1. The Allied planners had hoped Naples would fall by September 12. This rate of advance was to prove typical of the entire campaign, and was indeed to be reduced rather than accelerated as time went by.

In the last week of September the British landed at Bari and took the undefended Foggia airfields, but German resistance now hardened. It was only after hard fighting that the British pushed on to the Biferno River. Then the autumn rains set in, slowing the offensive still more. Not until November 3 did the Eighth Army get through the German defenses and then all that happened was that the enemy withdrew to another river line, that of the Sangro, seventeen miles to the north.

On the west coast progress had been equally painful, and for similar reasons. The Fifth Army was unable to attack the Volturno line before October 12, and the defenders held there until the 16th, when they withdrew in good order some fifteen miles to the Garigliano, the Rapido, and the Liri rivers, where they had prepared a new line. Behind this Kesselring was busily fortifying his Winter Line, although he did not think the Allies would continue their offensive into central and northern Italy, since there seemed little point to it. By now there were eighteen German divisions in Italy, but the decision to hold south of Rome meant that some panzer divisions, concentrated in the Po valley, could be released for the eastern front. Beyond all this, and appealing to both the Allies and to Hitler, was the magic of the name of Rome.

The next German defense line ran across the Italian peninsula at its narrowest part, just eighty-five miles from sea to sea. In the east the Sangro River formed a barrier that could be crossed only at a great cost in blood; in the center the Abruzzi mountains were all but impassable; and in the west the Garigliano River lay athwart the road to Rome, while the valleys of the Liri and the Sacco, running north, were accessible only through narrow defiles. Kesselring exerted every effort to make this naturally strong position impregnable. In November a new Fourteenth Army was created under Colonel General Eberhard von Mackensen, and this, together with the Tenth Army, came under Kesselring's command on the 21st.

On November 8 Eisenhower ordered that Rome be taken as soon as possible, and the same day Alexander ordered a three-phase offensive. The Eighth Army on the Adriatic side would attack toward the Rome-Pescara highway, to threaten the rear of the Germans opposite the Fifth Army and apply leverage to force them out of their positions. The Fifth Army would then attack frontally up the Liri and Sacco valleys. This combined effort, it was hoped, would bring the Allies to within fifty miles of Rome, and then a third amphibious attack would be launched in the vicinity of Anzio.

Montgomery's offensive on the Sangro began on November 20 in terrible weather. After a week's desperate fighting, a bridgehead was gained across that river. Beyond the Sangro, however, lay ridge after defensible ridge and mountain torrent after mountain torrent. A further major effort on the 28th carried the Eighth Army past the first ridge. The enemy thereupon retired to the Moro on December 10. The fortified ruins of the town of Ortona, two miles farther north, held up the Allied advance until the Canadian 1st Division, in some of the bitterest fighting of the war, successfully stormed the place on the 28th. Beyond Ortona lay the Riccio River and beyond that again the Pescara. In what was left of 1943 the Eighth Army reached the banks of the Riccio before the offensive bogged down hopelessly for the winter, ten miles short of the Pescara. At the turn of the year both Eisenhower and Montgomery left the Mediterranean theater, where the bright hopes of the summer now seemed so dim, to return to Britain for the preparation of Operation Overlord. General Maitland Wilson became Supreme Commander Mediterranean, and General Sir Oliver Leese took over command of the Eighth Army. In his farewell message to the troops General Montgomery said, "We have been successful in everything we have undertaken." And looked at narrowly, from a certain point of view, it was almost true.

On the western side of the peninsula General Mark Clark fared no better. The Fifth Army had attacked on December 2, making some progress; but ahead lay the Rapido River and behind that again the main defenses of the Gustav Line. And the Fifth Army, which had not been competently handled, had suffered nearly forty thousand casualties since it landed on the Salerno beaches on September 9. In November and December the army's strength had been further reduced by fifty thousand sick and by the transfer of the British 7th Armored Division and the U.S. 82nd Airborne Division back to England for Overlord. Clark renewed his offensive on December 7, but it had not even reached the Rapido before it was abandoned early in January 1944. Rome was still more than eighty miles away.

In Russia, meanwhile, the vast tragedy of the war continued to run its course. Hitler had decided on another great summer offensive to knock the Soviet Union out of the war. There was, in sober truth, little hope of this after the events of the winter, but the German army was still very strong and, division for division, in summer fighting still immensely superior to the Red Army. The German high command had considered the possibility of remaining on the defensive, and some senior officers had held that after the losses of the winter this would be the wiser course. Against this was the counterargument that time was on Russia's side, that American and British supplies would replace the Red Army's losses of material, and that the Russians could afford an adverse casualty ratio of at least three to one and still remain in the war. In fact, Hitler had led the Third Reich into a desperate situation from which there was probably no escape. At the time, however, this was not entirely obvious either to the Germans or to their enemies. The outcome of the war seemed to hang still in the balance, though the Stavka had good cause for hope and the German high command had good reason for dread.

Most senior German commanders favored another attack on Moscow. But Hitler had reverted to his previous plan of holding in the center and attacking on both flanks, of capturing both Leningrad and the Caucasian oil fields. The Leningrad portion of the plan was held in temporary abeyance, for even Hitler could see that he had to be less ambitious now than he had been the previous year. Nevertheless he was incapable of restraining himself for long; he was already being lured by another grandiose dream, that of joining the Caucasian offensive with Rommel's capture of Egypt and of an advance to Persia.

In Führer Directive No. 41, issued on April 5, Hitler laid down his intentions for the summer offensive. The Russian infiltrations into German rear areas were to be eliminated, the surrounded German garrisons at Demyansk and Kholm were to be relieved, and the Russian pocket at Volkhov wiped out. The sixty-mile Soviet salient at Izyum would also be pinched out. Next, the Kerch Peninsula would be cleared and Sebastopol captured. When all this had been accomplished, the main German offensive would be launched toward Voronezh on the Don. The line of the Don south from Voronezh would be cleared in conjunction with a second thrust from Rostov, which would encircle any Soviet formations remaining in the Don Bend. "As the Don front becomes increasingly longer in the course of this operation," Hitler wrote, "it will be manned primarily by formations of our Allies." The Hungarians would hold the northern portion, the Italians the center, and the Rumanians the southeastern sector. Once the Don Bend had been cleared, German armies would move east to cut the Volga at Stalingrad and would only then thrust down between the Donets and the Don into the Caucasus toward the Terek River, Tiflis, and Baku. The Second Army and the Fourth Panzer Army were assigned the task of taking Voronezh, and the Sixth Army and the Fourth Panzer Army would then clean up the Don Bend.

As we have seen, the first part of this plan was accomplished in April and May, with the relief of Demyansk and Kholm and the elimination of the Volkhov pocket. On May 8, Manstein's Eleventh Army launched its attack in the Crimea, where three Russian armies were holding the Kerch Peninsula. Manstein struck at the southernmost portion of the Soviet line, punched a hole, and drove to the rear of two of the Soviet armies. The Russians broke and fled, trying

The Second World War · THE RUSSIAN FRONT

Sam! H. Bryant

to escape back to Kerch, where they might make their way across the strait to the mainland. Manstein forestalled this by capturing Kerch on the 16th. The better part of two armies were trapped and the Germans took 170,000 prisoners.

Four hundred miles farther north Bock was to attack on May 18, to pinch out the Izyum salient. However, Marshal S. K. Timoshenko had massed five armies and strong armored formations in the Izyum Bend and north of it, around Volchansk, for an offensive of his own. The Russian plan called for simultaneous attacks north from the Izyum salient and south from Volchansk, to encircle the main German base at Kharkov.

Fortunately for the Germans, Timoshenko got his blow in first, on the 12th. Initially both attacks made rapid progress. The thrust from the north was halted twelve miles from Kharkov, but the southern attack drove as far west as Krasnograd. Indeed, it stretched too far, and Bock took the opportunity for dealing a deadly counterstroke. On May 17 a heavy attack struck the Russian western flank south of Izyum. One force thrust up to the Donets and into Izyum, while farther west the Germans fought their way north to Bairak on the northern Donets Bend. Largely because Stalin himself intervened and refused to allow any withdrawal, two of Timoshenko's armies were encircled. The trapped Russians made desperate attempts to break out, but they were cut down in swaths and the German lines held. Both Soviet army commanders and their staffs were killed, and the Russians lost 239,000 prisoners, 1250 tanks, and 2026 guns.

After twenty-seven days of vicious fighting Sebastopol fell to the Germans on July 3. The Russians had lost their great Black Sea naval base, and Manstein was rewarded by being promoted to field marshal.

On the morning of June 28, the main German offensive opened with a drive toward Voronezh on a wide front between Kursk and Belgorod. The attack of the Fourth Panzer Army went well, carrying the Germans halfway to Voronezh in the first two days. On the 30th Paulus' Sixth Army launched its converging attack northeast toward Voronezh. However, the Russians, warned in time, evacuated the Don Bend, falling back across the river in good order. Although the Germans secured a bridgehead over the Don at Voronezh on the evening of July 4, the Russians defended the town itself bitterly, and it was the 13th before most of the place was in German hands. There had really been no need to take it at all, as Hitler with one of his flashes of insight had realized. But the German army's sense of timing, which had been so exquisite before, often seemed to be slightly off in the summer of 1942. Even before Voronezh fell, however, panzer formations had already been turned south, to drive down the corridor between the

Donets and the Don. The Hungarian Second Army took over the defense of the northern Don line and the Sixth Army began to advance down the right bank of the river.

The Russian withdrawal behind the Don, combined with the German victories at Kharkov, Kerch, and Sebastopol, readily convinced Hitler that the Russians were "finished." On July 13, therefore, he changed the original plan and diverted the Fourth Panzer Army straight south instead of allowing it to proceed to Stalingrad. This meant, in effect, that the planned attack on Stalingrad had been halted, since the Sixth Army by itself would not be strong enough for the task. What the Führer had in mind was the encirclement of the Russian forces around Rostov, to be followed by the simultaneous capture of both Stalingrad and the Caucasus. Now, instead of the German objectives being taken in succession — Voronezh, Stalingrad, Rostov, and the Caucasus — Hitler would try to take his two major objectives, Stalingrad and the Caucasus, at the same time by simply dividing his forces.

Hitler therefore split Army Group South in two. Field Marshal Sigmund von List's Army Group A, consisting of Rouff's Seventeenth Army, Kleist's First Panzer Army, Manstein's Eleventh Army, and later for a time the Fourth Panzer Army, would cross the lower Don and operate south toward the Caucasus. Army Group B, consisting of the Sixth Army, the Hungarian Second Army, the Italian Eighth Army, and the Rumanian Third Army, would hold the Don line, capture Stalingrad, and cut the Volga waterway. Field Marshal Bock, who objected to his battle being thus "chopped in two," was dismissed, and Weichs was given command of Army Group B.

By Führer Directive No. 45, issued on July 23, the Seventeenth Army and the Rumanian Third Army were to advance down the Black Sea coast to Batum; the First and Fourth Panzer armies were to capture the oil fields at Maykop and Grozny, by driving down the Rostov-Tiflis highway, and were also to send a force farther east along the Caspian shore to Baku. The Sixth Army was to take Stalingrad alone and then exploit southeast along the Volga to Astrakhan. The German front in south Russia, now about 750 miles long, would by these operations be stretched to a length of some twenty-five hundred miles. The only link, and a tenuous one, between Army Group A in the Caucasus and Army Group B on the Don and at Stalingrad would be a single motor division stationed at Elista. And by now the Führer was so convinced that the conquest of Russia would be merely a mopping-up operation that in August he sent five divisions of Manstein's Eleventh Army from the Crimea to Leningrad for a renewed attempt to capture that city, and he sent the SS Panzer Grenadier Division Leibstandarte and the Motor Division Grossdeutschland to France.

The Germans had no success on the Leningrad front. The heroic city still withstood all efforts to capture it. Since its prewar population of three million had been reduced by some 600,000 deaths from famine in the winter of 1941–1942, and nearly a million more had been evacuated by November 1942, enough supplies could now be brought in over Lake Ladoga to keep Leningrad alive. The divisions from the Crimea were thrown into bitter battles along the Volkhov to halt Soviet attacks and had all they could do to stabilize the front.

Meanwhile the focus of the fighting had been shifting steadily southward. Kleist's First Panzer Army had driven east between the Donets and the Don, but few Red Army troops were caught in the corridor. By July 20 the Germans stood on the lower Don above Rostov. In Rostov itself, NKVD units held out until July 25.

In the next three weeks Army Group A advanced on a broad front south of the Don, moving across the Kalmyk steppe toward the heights of the Caucasus, 300 miles away. On the right the Rumanian Third Army marched down the coast of the Sea of Azov; next to it Rouff's Seventeenth Army reached Krasnodar on August 10. On the 9th Kleist's First Panzer Army took Maykop and seized the oil fields, but they found all fuel stocks and equipment destroyed. On the left Hoth's Fourth Panzer Army drove south to the Manych River and stormed across it to take Voroshilovsk. All this advance was relatively easy and rapid. German morale in Army Group A was very high.

Then, suddenly, in the middle of August, the swift progress slowed. Gasoline ran short, and resupply was slow. And once the mountains were reached, the Russian defense stiffened. Movement anywhere but on roads became difficult, and artificial obstacles harder to by-pass or outflank. The Russians laid ambushes in the sunflower fields, but only rarely were large bodies of their troops brought to action.

The Seventeenth Army captured Novorossisk on September 10. Its next objective, Tuapse on the Black Sea coast, lay just ahead. But Rouff's soldiers were never to reach Tuapse. The Russians halted the German advance at Mozdok, sixty-five miles from Grozny, and contained the small German bridgehead over the Terek River.

Hitler blamed everyone but himself for the breakdown of the Caucasian offensive. He insisted on immersing himself in details, poring over his huge map sheets until the small hours every morning, and sleeping late the next day. His health deteriorated and his judgment became increasingly impaired. But this withdrawn, desperate psychopath was still in supreme command of Germany's armed forces. When his immature, amateurish plans went wrong, he simply changed his commanders in the field. Field Marshal List was dismissed from the command of Army Group A and replaced by Kleist; Colonel General Franz Halder, the Army Chief of Staff, was replaced by General Kurt Zeitzler. Hitler was as determined as ever to capture Baku, but the new offensive he ordered had no chance of success. Strong Russian counterattacks, blizzards in the mountains, supply difficulties, and the exhaustion of the troops brought all German offensive operations in the Caucasus to an end by mid-November.

Disappointing as the results of the Caucasian offensive had been, a far worse disaster was about to be visited on the other southern group of armies, Army Group B. On July 12 Stalin had ordered that Stalingrad and the line of the Volga were to be defended to the last, and the Stavka decided to fight west of the Don. The previous signs of poor Russian morale had now disappeared and the Red Army was fighting heroically. The Russian supply position was also much improved by the summer of 1942. Most of this improvement was due to Russian production and to the miracles of organization that had been performed in transferring factories from European Russia to east of the Urals. American Lend-Lease and British aid had also been of some help, particularly American motor vehicles and canned goods.

To assist in taking Stalingrad, General Hoth's Fourth Panzer Army was ordered on July 30 to cooperate with the Sixth Army. Even so, it was not until August 8 that panzer forces managed to encircle the nine Soviet divisions and seven armored brigades west of Kalach, and it was another two weeks before the trapped Russians were eliminated. This victory was the last successful German encirclement of the war. Not until August 21 were the Germans able to establish bridgeheads across the Don.

The main German offensive against Stalingrad began in the early morning of August 23, with panzer formations driving across the forty miles of steppe. The advance went perfectly, for these rolling plains were ideal tank country, and the disorganized defenders were easily by-passed. That same evening the west bank of the Volga was reached on a five-mile front at Rynok, some thirty miles north of Stalingrad.

The defense of Stalingrad was entrusted to General Vassily I. Chuikov, who commanded the Sixty-second Army within the city, while part of General M. S. Shumilov's Sixty-fourth Army was holding the Germans back from the Volga to the south. General A. I. Yeremenko was in overall command of the Stalingrad Army Group, with Nikita Khrushchev as his political commissar. During the last week of August and the first two weeks of September the German attacks made some progress, though the attackers had to pay a price in blood for every foot they advanced. On September 10 the Germans finally reached the Volga south of Stalingrad. The city was now besieged on three sides, the defenders had the two-mile-wide Volga at their backs, and the Russian Sixty-second Army had been separated from the Sixty-fourth. On September 21 and 22 two German infantry divisions and a panzer division broke through to the center of the city and reached the Volga, thus cutting the Sixty-second Army in two. However, the Russians still held a ferry crossing in the northern portion of Stalingrad and a bridgehead on the west bank of the Volga, six miles south of the city. Much farther to the northwest, at Serafimovich, they held another bridgehead over the Don. The Germans were soon to learn how dangerous it was to permit their enemy to retain such footholds.

The fighting in Stalingrad was unlike anything the Germans had experienced in this war. Every ruined building was converted into a strongpoint, and gains were measured in yards, just as they had been at Verdun and the Somme in the First World War. There was no room here for maneuver or encirclement. All attacks had to be frontal, and under these conditions the stolid Russians gave at least as good as they got. By October 3 the Russians had reinforced Chuikov with six fresh infantry divisions. The Russian artillery, moreover, was in relative safety on the east bank of the Volga, and a very large number of guns and *katyusha* rocket batteries were massed there.

Hitler was as resolved as ever to take both Stalingrad and the Caucasus, though by now it was obvious that he might get one or the other but could not possibly gain both. Possibly, too, he allowed himself to be influenced subconsciously by the spell of names. At least it is interesting that he should have set such store by the capture of Stalingrad and Leningrad, the cities of Stalin and Lenin. It was almost as though, like some primitive necromancer, he attached a mystical significance to the proper nouns. He sent the Rumanian Third and Fourth armies to the north and south of Stalingrad respectively, to strengthen the Sixth Army's flanks, but even so those flanks were dangerously weak. On the left for 350 miles the line of the Don was held by Italian and Rumanian formations and to the right the Ergini Hills were held by the Rumanians.

As October came and went the German attacks continued against the Dzerzhinsky tractor factory, the Barrikady artillery factory, and the Red October steelworks. The tractor factory and a portion of the Red October works were taken, but by the end of the month the Russian defenders could sense that a good deal of the force had gone from the German offensive.

All this while the Russians had been assembling two powerful army groups north and south of Stalingrad, under the overall direction of

General Zhukov and his chief of staff, General Vassilevsky. The Stalingrad Army Group to the south was under the command of Yeremenko; the Don Army Group to the north was under General C. Rokossovsky; and farther west along the Don the Southwestern Army Group was under General Vatutin. The Germans were aware of this ominous buildup of forces on the flanks, but Hitler would not relinquish his hold on Stalingrad — of which he now controlled nine tenths — nor could he reinforce the threatened sectors.

First of all the Russians prepared a holding attack on the central front between Velikye Luki and Rzhev to pin down German reserves and prevent their dispatch to the south. The main blow fell on November 19, beautifully timed to strike the Germans at their moment of greatest weakness. Nevertheless the Russians could not reasonably have hoped to achieve the success they did. Every canon of military common sense dictated that Paulus would retire when he found himself threatened by encirclement. This, in turn, would uncover Army Group A in the Caucasus and force it to retreat. Only if, by great good fortune, the Russians could break through to Rostov before Army Group A could pass through that bottleneck would more be gained than the liberation of a large area of Russia and the ruin of the German summer offensive. But the vain imaginings of Hitler, back in faraway Rastenburg, were more potent aids for the Soviet cause than all that Zhukov or the Red Army could do.

In a dense fog Rokossovsky's Fifth Tank Army attacked at dawn from the Russian bridgehead over the Don at Serafimovich, and his Twenty-first Army farther south attacked from Kletskaya. Between them, these two armies had a combined strength of three armored corps, two cavalry corps, and twelve infantry divisions. They drove forward in the direction of Kalach to cut the railway to Stalino. The Rumanian Third Army, holding the bend in the Don between Serafimovich and Kremenskaya, disintegrated in the face of this attack. Having broken through, Rokossovsky's forces turned southeast toward Kalach. Farther west Vatutin's troops broke through the Rumanians and cut the Stalino railway, to establish a block against possible German counterattacks.

On the 20th Yeremenko's Stalingrad Army Group launched its offensive against the Rumanian Fourth Army south of Stalingrad. Again the Rumanians broke, abandoning their artillery. The objectives of this offensive were to drive through the Ergini Hills, cut the railway to Novorossisk on the Black Sea, and then wheel northwest to meet Rokossovsky's armies at Kalach. The Russian pincers closed on November 23, and the German Sixth Army of about twenty divisions, or 250,000 men, was encircled by approximately sixty Soviet divisions. As yet, however, although the German position was certainly critical, it was by no means desperate, for the embracing Russian arms were still thin. Major General Arthur Schmidt, Paulus' chief of staff, favored a breakout to the southwest, and as soon as possible, before the Russians tightened their grip. A preliminary to a breakout, however, would have to be an airlift to bring in gasoline for the Sixth Army's tanks and gun tractors. This should not have presented any insuperable problem since the Germans still possessed a good airfield at Pitomnik within the perimeter. Schmidt estimated that the Sixth Army could commence its breakout on November 27.

Weichs at Army Group B agreed that a breakout should be made, but Hitler set his face against any retreat, and on the evening of the 21st issued orders that Stalingrad be held at all costs. Both Göring and the Luftwaffe chief of staff, General Hans Jeschonnek, told Hitler that the Sixth Army could be supplied by air, provided the nearby airfields remained in German hands and the weather remained good. In the second half of November 1942 there was little probability of either of these conditions being met. The necessary number of transport aircraft simply were not available; the weather in winter, not surprisingly, was often bad; and when the Germans lost their airfields at Morovskaya and Tatsinskaya, the number of daily aircraft flights into Stalingrad had to be reduced by two-thirds. For this effort, the Luftwaffe lost 488 aircraft and over a thousand air crewmen. However, some 42,000 wounded, as well as a number of specialists, were flown out of the pocket.

On November 27 Manstein was appointed to command the newly formed Army Group Don, consisting of two army-sized combat groups under General Hollidt and General Hoth, which would attempt to relieve Stalingrad. Manstein commanded as well the Sixth Army and the remnants of the Rumanian Third Army. He planned a strong counteroffensive south of the Don, along the Kotelnikovski-Stalingrad axis, by Hoth's army, in conjunction with an attack along the Chir inside the Don Bend by Hollidt's army. Hoth's thrust would be the main one since his forces were only sixty miles from Stalingrad, did not have to force a crossing of the Don, and initially were opposed by only five Russian divisions. Hollidt's attack on the Chir would provide flank protection for Hoth.

Hoth's attack went in on the morning of December 12 but ran into difficulties as the Russians reinforced. Hoth's panzers took a week to advance thirty miles to the far side of the Aksay River, but by the 20th the Germans stood on the banks of the Mishkova, only about twenty-five miles away from the Sixth Army. Hoth's men could see the glow of Stalingrad in the sky, and the time had come, in Manstein's opinion, for the Sixth Army to launch an attack to link up with Hoth's forces. Hitler, however, was still forbidding any retreat from Stalingrad. On the Chir, too, the Russians were preventing any German advance toward the Sixth Army. Manstein therefore compromised by ordering Paulus to maintain his positions at the same time as he attacked southwest toward Hoth on the Mishkova.

All this became academic on December 21, when three Russian armies under General Vatutin and General Golikov attacked in a blinding snowstorm across the frozen middle Don west of Serafimovich. This offensive broke right through the Italian Eighth Army on a sixty-mile front and flooded into the Don Bend from the north, threatening to overwhelm Hollidt's army on the Chir and to capture the German airfield at Morovskaya. Manstein was forced to take Hoth's best panzer division, the 6th, away from him and send it hurrying north in an attempt to stem the Russian advance. When the Russians attacked Hoth on the 24th, the German relieving force was driven back beyond the Aksay. All this time, too, Rokossovsky tightened the ring around the Sixth Army and drove it closer in to Stalingrad.

This breakthrough on the middle Don sealed Stalingrad's fate, but, even worse, these new Russian attacks posed a much more serious threat. If Vatutin's formations captured Rostov, the whole of the German southern front would be encircled, Army Group Don and all Army Group A in the Caucasus would be cut off, and the war would be over at one stroke. If the Rostov Gate fell, the Germans stood to lose not an army of 230,000 men, but two army groups of over 1.5 million. This indeed was the Russian plan, known as Operation Saturn, which had been adopted by the Stavka on December 3. That this ambitious plan failed was, in no small measure, the result of the continued resistance of the Sixth Army within Stalingrad.

The last hope for the defenders died on Christmas Day, with the retreat of Hoth's relieving columns. The bread ration was reduced to fifty grams per day, and all rations were withheld from the wounded. The cavalry and transport horses were slaughtered and eaten, and the defenders made a thin, watery soup from the bones of dead horses dug out of the snow. But still the Sixth Army held on. After Paulus rejected a demand for surrender on January 8, the Russians launched heavy attacks to split up the starving, exhausted garrison. On the 30th Hitler promoted Paulus to field marshal as an inducement for him to fight to the last, but the next day he surrendered. General Strecker, with what was left of the XI Corps, held out for two more days in the northern sector, defending the Barrikady gun factory and the Dzerzhinsky tractor factory, but he too surrendered on February 2, and a stillness fell on Stalingrad. Inside the pocket the Russians captured ninety-one thousand German prisoners, including Field Marshal Paulus and twenty-four generals. The remainder of the Sixth Army was dead. Of the German prisoners taken that day only about six thousand survived to return to Germany at the end of the war.

On January 12, in bitter subzero weather, two Russian armies launched converging attacks from the east and west to break the encirclement of Leningrad. Within six days the two drives met on the Baltic shore near Schlüsselburg. A land corridor had been cleared through the German ring around Leningrad, though the city remained under artillery fire.

On the central front, the Russians had captured Velikye Luki in December and the Germans could hope to do no more than hold a defensive line here in 1943. To make this easier they withdrew to a straighter, shorter line in front of Smolensk. This German withdrawal was marked by much brutal treatment of the local population, with mass shootings and hangings, the deportation of young men to slave labor camps in Germany, and the murder and starvation of Russian prisoners of war. As the Red Army advanced into these territories to liberate them, what the soldiers saw made them grimmer than ever.

On December 29 Hitler had at last, and grudgingly, authorized a withdrawal of Army Group A in the Caucasus. These German formations were in relatively good condition, although the "Caucasus round trip" had not improved the troops' morale. It was far from certain that the First Panzer Army and the Seventeenth Army would escape in time, for the Russian pressure to capture Rostov was very great. The Fourth Panzer Army was being driven back toward it, and an even more serious threat developed on January 12, when General Golikov's Voronezh Army Group smashed through the Hungarian Second Army on the Don west of Voronezh, inflicting about 100,000 casualties and destroying the Hungarians as a fighting force. Voronezh fell on the 26th, and the Russians pressed south down both banks of the Don toward Rostov. Late in January, Russian advance guards were within fifty miles of the place and the situation of the German troops retreating from the Caucasus appeared critical. However, Rostov was not taken until the middle of February, and by that time the First Panzer Army had been able to slip through the bottleneck. Because it had not been possible to evacuate both armies in the Caucasus over the available road network, the Seventeenth Army had been directed west to the Taman peninsula, where it could be supplied across the Kerch Strait. Thus 300,000 excellent troops rested, inactive, in the Taman peninsula throughout all the desperate fighting of that summer in the eastern Ukraine.

By February 2 the Russians, sweeping forward on a very broad front, had seized a bridgehead over the Donets southwest of Millerovo. On the 7th they took Kursk and on the 9th Belgorod, and two Soviet armies captured the great German supply base of Kharkov on the 16th. Naturally, the Russians were exultant at their success, and Stalin promoted himself to a marshal of the Soviet Union.

However, Manstein, who had by now been placed in command of the reconstituted Army Group South, which included all German formations in south Russia, was able, if only temporarily, to retrieve the situation. When he counterattacked on February 21 he caught the Russians off balance and drove them back as rapidly as they had recently advanced. By early March Izyum on the Donets was again in German hands; on the 14th Manstein recaptured Kharkov. By the 19th, when Belgorod fell, most of the area between the Dnieper and the Donets was again under German control. Except for the Seventeenth Army in the Taman peninsula, the Germans were in much the same geographical position in south Russia as they had been at the beginning of 1942.

But it was not the same Army Group South as in 1942. The Sixth Army had been destroyed and all four of Germany's satellite armies had been written off. The force that remained had been grievously weakened by casualties and there was no possibility that these losses could be replaced. One sinister result of the manpower shortage was that the Germans now began large-scale deportations of young Ukrainians to Germany as slave laborers.

When the April thaw came, Manstein knew that all hope of a German victory had gone. He still hoped, however, to achieve a stalemate, to institute an elastic defense that would inflict such casualties on the Russians that they would agree to a compromise peace. Almost certainly there was never any basis for such a hope, but Manstein, though brilliant, had more than his share of the German overconfidence. Even if he had not been so frequently thwarted by his political master, Adolf Hitler, Manstein could not have achieved a draw after the winter of 1943. The odds were too great and the Russians had suffered too much at the hands of the invaders to allow them to escape so easily. And, of course, there *was* always Hitler — interfering, frustrating his commanders, and making absurd decisions. But, then, it was really unfair of Manstein and the German generals to complain of this. They had long ago willingly delivered themselves into his hands, sworn their oath of fealty to him, and loyally supported him so long as Germany seemed to be winning the war.

As the front congealed in April a huge salient jutted out from the Russian lines around Kursk. This salient, which extended from just south of Orel to Belgorod, was 100 miles long and 80 miles deep from east to west. In the spring of 1943 the German high command was seized with the not very original idea of pinching off this salient and destroying the Russian forces within it. The forces available were fewer than before, but they were still very strong. In all, some twenty panzer or motor divisions, ten infantry divisions, and over a thousand aircraft were assembled for Operation Citadel. Kluge, commanding Army Group Center, would attack from the north with the Ninth Army, and Manstein's Army Group South would attack from the south with the Fourth Panzer Army and the army-sized Army Detachment Kempf.

Assembling this force took time, and then Hitler interfered again, to postpone D-Day until the middle of June. For one reason or another, there was a second postponement until the beginning of July. This delay was put to good use by the Russians, who had no doubt where the German blow was going to fall. Stalin once again sent Zhukov to the threatened area, and the Russians worked frantically to strengthen their defenses. More than 400,000 mines were laid; more than 6000 antitank guns were dug in; the area was honeycombed with field entrenchments; reinforcements were shipped in; and a new reserve army, under Colonel General I. S. Konev, was formed to give depth to the defense.

Zhukov, remembering the disaster that had befallen Timoshenko's offensive at Kharkov the previous May and the effectiveness of the Russian counteroffensive at Stalingrad, recommended that the Red Army await the German blow at Kursk, inflict what damage it could on the attackers, and then counterattack. However, in early May General Vatutin, the commander of the Voronezh Army Group, and his political commissar, Khrushchev, suggested a pre-emptive attack between Belgorod and Kharkov. Stalin was impressed and it was all that Zhukov and Vassilevsky could do to persuade him to let the German attack go in first. At last Stalin agreed to wait and appointed Zhukov to coordinate the Central, Bryansk, and Western army groups.

Operation Citadel opened at three o'clock in the afternoon of July 4, but in spite of heavy artillery and air support, the Germans found it hard going. The new Panther tanks proved a disappointment, and panzer losses were enormous. The Ninth Army's attack from the north got partway into the Russian defenses, then bogged down after only twelve miles. The Fourth Panzer Army managed to advance thirty miles and actually got clear of the Russian defensive zone by July 11, but it emerged from that zone so weakened that it could go no farther. Manstein wanted to continue the battle, but Hitler closed down the offensive on the 13th. The battered German formations fell back to their start lines.

One day before this, Zhukov had launched the Russian counteroffensive. As was often the case with Russian attacks, this one was staggered in time and space, beginning with the Western and Bryansk army groups in the north and moving progressively south. On August 5 the Russians captured Orel and Belgorod, and on the 23rd Kharkov was retaken. Army Group South fell back to the Dnieper along a 500-mile front, with no guarantee that it would be able to hold this so-called Winter Line. Stalin ordered the first of the victory salutes to be fired in Moscow, and Russians everywhere now knew for certain that the war was won. The Battle of Kursk was convincing confirmation of Stalingrad.

In late September and early October the Red Army crossed the Dnieper on a broad front at many points; the Crimea was cut off; and in November Kiev fell. By the end of October on the central front the Germans had been driven out of Smolensk.

At Teheran in November the three political leaders of the major Allied powers all met together for the first time. Yet despite the victorious balance of the year, there was a shadow over this conference, or at least over British relations with the Soviet Union. In April 1943 the Germans had announced that they had discovered a number of mass graves in the Katyn Forest, near Smolensk, containing the bodies of thousands of Polish officers and NCOs who had been Russian prisoners of war and whom the Russians had murdered. At first there was little inclination to believe them. The Germans had certainly murdered enough people to make any such claim suspect. True, some fifteen thousand Polish officers and NCOs had been taken prisoner by the Russians when the Soviet Union invaded Poland in 1939, and no word had since been heard of them. Russian officials were all suspiciously vague in reply to the persistent inquiries of the Polish government-in-exile. Some of these missing Poles had now undoubtedly turned up as corpses in the Katyn Forest, and though the Russians, of course, claimed that they had been shot by the Germans, the strong weight of the evidence began to make it appear that for once Dr. Goebbels was telling the truth when he accused the NKVD of the crime. When the Polish government requested an international inquiry by the Red Cross, Stalin refused, and suspended diplomatic relations. He then set up his own rival Polish government in the Soviet Union, staffed by communists.

This was an unhappy taste of things to come. The British had no desire to see a communist totalitarianism replace the Nazi brand in much of Europe, but Roosevelt and those about him refused to be alarmed. At Teheran, in fact, the Americans sided with the Russians against the British, primarily because Roosevelt still believed he could work with "Uncle Joe." As a consequence, Stalin certainly received the not inaccurate impression that he could do what he liked with Poland after the war. (The fate of the new Soviet republics of Estonia, Latvia, and Lithuania was not even discussed.) Stalin agreed that the strategy of the Allies should be coordinated in 1944, and for this he received a firm promise that Britain and the United States would open a second front in France not later than May of 1944.

And so, before the victory over Nazism was won, much of its benefit was already being thrown away.

Before this chronicle of the middle years of the Second World War is closed, it is necessary to look briefly at two other campaigns fought in 1942 and 1943, one an inconclusive Allied victory and the other an equally inconclusive Allied defeat.

Between the end of June 1940, when France collapsed, and the end of June 1941, when Hitler invaded the Soviet Union, the Second World War was a classic contest between an overwhelmingly superior land power and a superior sea power. During this period Britain never had the same dominance of the oceans of the world as Germany had of the European land mass, but she was able to more than hold her own. The German navy had been assured by Hitler that no war was probable before 1946, and the German naval building program had been leisurely and not very rational. On September 1, 1939, Admiral Karl Dönitz, in command of the German U-boat fleet, had only seventy-four U-boats built or in the building, and of these only fifty-seven were ready for operations. Not until the summer of 1939 had Dönitz been able to convince the admiralty to concentrate on building the medium-sized, ocean-going Type-VII submarine that he considered most suitable for attacks on convoys.

Nevertheless the U-boats had considerable success in 1940 and 1941, especially after a wing of Focke-Wulf Condor aircraft was allotted to Dönitz in January 1941. The early spotting of British convoys enabled the German submarines to coordinate their attacks and converge on their targets in time. In 1940 and 1941, too, the threat of German surface raiders was very real, stretching British naval resources. The British were able to survive the Battle of the Atlantic in the first two years of the war because their enemy was unprepared, because they had American help, and because their own countermeasures were astute and timely. But the margin of survival was sometimes desperately small. Dönitz had always calculated that he would need to sink 600,000 tons of British shipping each month to win the U-boat war, and for this he needed 300 operational, ocean-going U-boats. He never even approximated that figure, in spite of its being a goal well within German capabilities. At the end of December 1941 Dönitz had ninety-one U-boats in service, though not much more than one-third could be on duty at one time. Worse still, thirty of them, at Hitler's insistence, were relegated to the Mediterranean or to Norwegian waters, where targets were fewer.

When Germany declared war on the United States — something that Dönitz in his blindness had long advocated — the German U-boat commander hoped to begin his submarine campaign with "a roll of drums." It was a good Nazi phrase, but it was not to be acted out. Dönitz had rightly sensed that the American democracy would be slow to adjust to wartime conditions and that if he could concentrate his U-boats off the American coast he would reap a rich harvest. In fact, he was unable to get any of his submarines to American waters until early in February, and then only in small numbers. Even at that date those that did reach the American seaboard did very well indeed. Dönitz had been right in his understanding of American psychology. The United States Navy at first obstinately refused to institute a convoy system, despite — or perhaps partly because of — the urgings of the Royal Navy; American merchant ships and shore radio stations paid no attention to communications security; the cities on the United States Atlantic coast remained ablaze with lights; and American beacons and navigational aids continued to function just as though the world were not at war. Not until April 1942 did the United States begin to organize convoys. It was July before the convoy system was extended to the Caribbean, and it was not instituted everywhere until August. For these very good reasons Dönitz sent all his available U-boats to the American coast, to operate off Cape Hatteras and in the Caribbean, and after April in the Florida Strait. Because oil tankers frequently fell victim to the U-boats, the United States had to introduce gasoline rationing.

However, once the United States Navy organized convoys, the rate of sinkings dropped dramatically. Accordingly, on May 23 Dönitz withdrew his submarine packs from American coastal waters, to concentrate on the Caribbean and other areas. On July 19 he switched his attack back to the North Atlantic, to the Great Circle route between the North Channel and Newfoundland.

This opened another phase of the Battle of the Atlantic, the one that was to see the climax of the ocean war, and was to last from August 1942 until May 1943. For most of the period the Germans appeared to be winning. The number of U-boats in operation steadily increased and so did the amount of Allied tonnage sunk. By the use of U-tankers, which first came into service in March 1942, the U-boats' time at sea and range was greatly extended. A U-boat pack could now follow an Allied convoy right across the Atlantic to North America; then it could lie in wait off the coast in the hope of picking up an eastbound convoy that could be attacked all the way back until the pack once again found its safe refuge in French harbors.

By October 1942 Dönitz had 40 U-boats operating in the North Atlantic, a far cry from the 300 he considered necessary, but enough to do great damage. In 1942 the western Allies lost 7,699,000 tons of merchant shipping, and though they built seven million tons, the balance was still strongly against them. Nor did tonnage figures tell the whole story. Merchant crews could not be replaced as easily as could lost ships, and the rate of sinkings, if it continued, could hardly help being bad for merchant seamen's morale. All Allied strategy depended on control of the seas: the campaign in North Africa, the projected campaigns in Sicily and Italy, the war in the Pacific, and the ultimate hope of launching Overlord against the coast of France.

Yet the RAF Bomber Command and its commander, Air Chief Marshal Sir Arthur Harris, strongly resisted all suggestions that aircraft be diverted from the bomber offensive to assist in winning the Battle of the Atlantic. Harris was ever ready with arguments to support his case; he was backed by the Chief of Air Staff, Sir Charles Portal; and he had — at this time — the ear of the prime minister, who in turn was under the influence of his court wizard, the scientist Lord Cherwell. Yet the long-range and very-long-range aircraft of Bomber Command would certainly have been better employed in Coastal Command. The "Black Pit" in the middle of the Atlantic, where Allied convoys were out of reach of air cover, was the area where most sinkings occurred, and when in fact air patrols were extended and the Black Pit eliminated, sinkings dropped sharply. The bombing of U-boat pens was undertaken, but not in 1941 or 1942, while they were being built. Only when the steel-reinforced concrete had hardened did Bomber Command begin to fly sorties against the U-boat bases at Brest, Lorient, St. Nazaire, La Pallice, and Bordeaux. Between the middle of January and the end of February 1943, some two thousand sorties were flown against Lorient alone, but no U-boat was even slightly damaged by this enormous, belated effort. In general, Harris cooperated in the anti-U-boat war only reluctantly and gave as little aid as he could.

In 1942 and early 1943 it seemed possible that the U-boats would delay or prevent all the Allied plans. The German admiralty was often able to decode convoy route signals, which enabled Dönitz to concentrate a wolf pack across a convoy's path. Naturally, the Torch landings in North Africa in November 1942 drew the U-boats there and for a time the rate of sinkings off the Moroccan coast was high. However, the German naval staff insisted that the U-boats remain too long in the Mediterranean area, even after it was obvious that escort forces for North Atlantic convoys had been dangerously reduced because of Operation Torch. Even so, in November 119 Allied ships amounting to 729,160 gross tons were sunk.

Dönitz got his U-boats back to the North Atlantic as soon as he could, and in December a pack of twenty-two attacked Convoy HX217, though without much success, chiefly because Allied aircraft forced the U-boats to submerge, and prevented their pressing home the attack. At the end of December an attack on Convoy ONS154 was more successful, and by now Dönitz had more submarines at his disposal. During 1942 the German U-boat strength grew from 91 to 212. With the January storms, shipping losses declined, but they soared again in February. Late in January a U-boat pack attacked Convoy SC118 and in a running, five-day fight sank thirteen ships for a loss of three submarines. In February Convoy ON166 lost fourteen ships. In all, sixty-three Allied ships totaling 359,328 tons were lost in this month. By early March Dönitz was able to attack all fast HX convoys and most slow SC convoys. Between March 16 and 20 a pack of forty-four U-boats attacked Convoys HX229 and SC122. In this engagement only one U-boat was lost, but thirty-two ships were sunk and nine badly damaged. During the month as a whole, 108 Allied ships of 627,377 tons went down, and what was most appalling was that 85 of them had been sunk in convoy. U-boat losses in March were only thirteen.

After this calamitous month President Roosevelt ordered an investigation, which resulted in a number of very-long-range Liberators being taken away from the bomber offensive and assigned to reconnaissance duties in the North Atlantic. More important in defeating the submarines was the formation of "support groups" of destroyers, often built around an escort carrier. These hunter-killer groups had no responsibility for the protection of convoys but were able to hunt U-boats to the death. The support groups operated in the vicinity of convoys — that was where the U-boats were to be found — but once the battle was joined they could concentrate solely on the kill. By March 1943 six support groups were operating in the North Atlantic. They were assisted by a number of technical devices: airborne radar, High Frequency Direction Finder ("Huff-Duff"), Hedgehog antisubmarine mine salvos, Torpex depth charges, and rocket-firing aircraft. The very-long-range Liberators were able to cover the Black Pit and bring the whole of the North Atlantic under aerial surveillance. Oil- or grain-carrying ships were fitted out with a flight deck, given three or four Swordfish aircraft, and attached to convoys as "merchant aircraft carriers." In the summer of 1943, when the Murmansk route was temporarily closed because of the prohibitive loss suffered during the endless Arctic days, the British were able to release two more destroyer flotillas for support group work.

All this proved too much for the U-boats. In the last week of April two U-boat packs attacked Convoy ONS4, but were promptly counterattacked by the 5th Support Group, under Captain Abel Smith, RN, in the carrier *Biter*, and lost two submarines without damaging any ship in the convoy. May was a disastrous month for Dönitz. On the 4th a pack of forty-one U-boats closed on Convoy ONS5, but again the fight went against the submarines, of which six were sunk. The last two weeks of May proved even worse. In the middle of the month Convoy SC130 was attacked by thirteen U-boats, but the convoy sailed right through the submarine patrol line without loss, and three U-boats were sunk and two damaged. In the whole of May forty-one U-boats were sunk, as compared with fourteen in February, thirteen in March, and twelve in April. Dönitz could not afford these losses, so he withdrew his submarines from the North Atlantic for the time being. The U-boat war continued, but German submarines were never again the deadly menace they had once been. In September the Germans introduced the acoustic torpedo, but Allied scientists soon discovered a countermeasure. That autumn Dönitz shifted his submarines to the area around Gibraltar and to the southern routes, but here again they were defeated.

Success had been achieved by six support groups, some forty or fifty Liberator aircraft, and twelve ocean escort groups, but as the German naval historian Jürgen Rohwer has pointed out, it is interesting that in the records of successful attacks, either by U-boats or by support groups, the names of a few commanders and ships recur again and again. Thus it would seem that the training, flair, and determination of a relatively small number of men were ultimately of more importance than the number of ships involved.

The other inconclusive battle of these years was the Combined Bomber Offensive, known as Operation Pointblank. But whereas the struggle against the U-boats gradually brought a defensive success, the bombing of targets in Germany in 1942 and 1943 was an almost complete failure. The reasons for this failure went a long way back — probably, in the case of the Royal Air Force, as far back as April 1, 1918, when it was first established as an independent, separate service. The only justification for a separate air service was that it could perform a separate task, that it was inherently more than a supporting arm for the army and navy. The only truly separate task that an independent air service could perform was that of "strategic" bombing, and after 1918 the new Royal Air Force proclaimed, as an article of faith for which there could in the nature of things be no supporting evidence, that strategic bombing by itself would be sufficient to win wars. Without such a claim, there could have been no reason for the air force's remaining independent.

However, since no bomber force was technically capable of anything approaching accuracy, bombing would have to be area bombing. This meant indiscriminate attacks against an enemy's civilian population. So out of the desire for service independence, rather than on the basis of any wartime, empirical evidence, was created the theory that the terror bombing of civilian populations would win wars. This theory made it unnecessary to try very hard to improve bombing accuracy. In fact, as late as midsummer of 1941, as the Butt Report, issued in August of that year, clearly demonstrated, the *majority* of Bomber Command crews never approached nearer to their target than five miles. The strategic bombing theory was dominant in the RAF long before the war, and in spite of mounting evidence during the war years that the theory was false, it remained dominant until nearly the end.

Part of the reason for this, of course, was that after the British Expeditionary Force had been driven off the continent in 1940 there was no other way of waging offensive war against Germany. A man of Churchill's temperament found it fatally easy to listen to the siren voices of those air force officers and scientists who assured him that the war *could* be won, and won without the necessity of fighting major land campaigns. Although the British prime minister was too astute really to believe that air power by itself could defeat Nazi Germany, he was, as he said, prepared to try, "providing we do not neglect other methods."

The United States Army Air Force, not being a separate service, was spared the same necessity for self-justification as the Royal Air Force. As a consequence, American airmen held more sensible and balanced views on the role of air power in war. No reputable American airman in the Second World War claimed that air power could win a war by itself. (This fallacy came later, it is true, but only after the United States had followed the British example and created a third independent service.) When the United States Eighth Army Air Force under General Ira Eaker arrived in the United Kingdom in August 1942, it was supposed to bomb truly strategic targets in Germany — war industries, dockyards, oil refineries, and communications — not set fire to the homes of German workers so that they would be discouraged from working in the factories that Allied bombers could not hit. But the Eighth USAAF was no more capable than the RAF of precision bombing.

The views of the RAF Bomber Command on terror bombing did not go unchallenged even at the time. Sir Henry Tizard, an eminent defense scientist and no friend of Lord Cherwell's, produced evidence to prove that Cherwell's advocacy of area bombing was based on erroneous arithmetic. Some felt that there was much to be said for bombing Germany's oil supplies rather than the built-up areas of her cities. The Royal Navy desperately wanted to have Bomber Command help kill U-boats. Some even thought that the RAF might do more to support the army fighting in the Western Desert or in Italy. Only a very few considered the moral aspect of the problem, although ethics can no more be safely neglected in war than in peace. The political end of war is concerned with the kind of world desired once the war is over, and it is a truism, so obvious that even politicians should understand it, that bad means invariably corrupt good ends. Thus the barbarization of war is a self-destructive formula, except for barbarians, because the postwar world will always reflect the lowered standards of the war. This, indeed, is part of what happened in the two world wars of this century, and those who advocated and approved terror bombing have much to answer for.

In 1939, Bomber Command had discovered that it could not bomb by day without suffering unacceptable losses, and since it could not bomb by either day or night with anything approaching precision — and did not have the desire, the training, or the aircraft to support the army and the navy — it turned to the area bombing of Germany by night. For a considerable time its effort was very limited. Between September 1939 and January 1942 the average number of monthly night sorties of the Bomber Command was only 1625, but when Sir Arthur Harris became the commander-in-chief of the Bomber Command on February 23, 1942, greater things were in store. Lübeck was burned on March 28; Rostock was destroyed in April; and on May 30 the first thousand-bomber raid wiped out most of the residential district of Cologne. This was followed by other thousand-bomber raids: on Essen on June 1 and on Bremen on the 25th. At this time, though Britain was in the process of losing the Battle of the Atlantic, the Chief of Air Staff fought hard against diverting any of his bombers to help the navy, and General Wavell was complaining:

> When after trying with less than 20 light bombers to meet an attack which has cost us three important warships and several others damaged and nearly 100,000 tons of merchant shipping, we see that over 200 heavy bombers attacked one town in Germany.

But to "Bomber" Harris these pleas from the navy and army were merely irritants; he had his eyes fixed intently on the fiery hearts of burning cities.

In 1942, Bomber Command continued to increase in size and efficiency. By April, four squadrons of Lancasters were in service; on May 30, "streaming" was adopted for the raid on Cologne, saturating the defenses and reducing the time over target. In the course of the year the navigational aids Gee and Oboe were introduced, to be followed in January 1943 by H_2S. Pathfinder squadrons of small, fast Mosquito aircraft also came into service in 1942. Interestingly enough, Harris at first opposed the Pathfinders because he feared that increased precision would bring demands for an end to area bombing; he was more than happy to keep his cudgel. The B17s and B24s of the Eighth USAAF conducted only twenty-seven operations between August and December 1942, but on the whole the Americans were satisfied with the results. Not until 1943 were they to learn, at heavy cost, how mistaken was their belief that the unescorted bomber could defend itself on daylight raids over Germany.

After the futile raids on the U-boat pens in January and February, the 1943 Bomber Command offensive began with a raid on Essen on March 5. For the next five months Harris struck again and again at the Ruhr. The most spectacular raid was that made against the Ruhr dams on May 16, when the Möhne and Eder dams were damaged, for the loss of eleven aircraft out of nineteen attackers. However, both dams were repaired within two months and the damage done to German industry was slight. All told, in the Ruhr raids Harris lost more than 800 of his Halifaxes, Sterlings, and Lancasters. Although millions of Germans were made homeless, German industrial production increased dramatically during the year. In particular, the fighter strength of the Luftwaffe grew until by the middle of 1943 fighter production had tripled. Four great incendiary raids on Hamburg at the end of July and the beginning of August burned out 70 percent of the city and killed perhaps eighty thousand persons in the resulting fire storm. Only 59 bombers were lost, a rate of under 3 percent. In the middle of November, Bomber Command turned on Berlin. In eight raids between November 18 and December 30 much of the German capital was gutted, for a loss of 183 aircraft, or under 4 percent. Meanwhile the Eighth USAAF had been finding daylight raids over Germany prohibitively expensive. On the 10th a raid on Münster resulted in a loss rate of 11 percent, and, even more disastrously, when 291 bombers attacked Schweinfurt on October 14, 65 American planes were lost and another 138 damaged. The German fighter force had won a decisive victory, for between October 8 and 14 the Americans lost 148 bombers. General Arnold decided to stop temporarily all deep-penetration raids. Against such losses could be set Air Chief Marshal Portal's claim at the Teheran Conference in December 1943 that six million Germans had been rendered homeless, but the Chief of Air Staff also had to admit that the Combined Bomber Offensive had not achieved its aims for 1943 and was in fact three months behind schedule.

CHAPTER IV

DURING 1944 and the first four months of 1945, Nazi Germany senselessly played out an end game it could not hope to win. The same was true of Japan. The Allied doctrine of unconditional surrender may have been partly responsible for this, but by far the greater share of responsibility rests with the nature of the German and Japanese regimes themselves. The Nazis especially, because of their crimes against humanity, had not the slightest reason to hope for a merciful peace. If they obtained justice, they would be utterly destroyed. Hitler himself lived in a world of fantasy, hoping against all reason that some miracle would save him. Perhaps the Soviet Union would fall out with the western Allies. Perhaps the new weapons that Germany was developing — the V-1 and V-2, the Snorkel submarine, the jet aircraft — would turn the tide. So he deluded himself.

And so the war went on. The Russians recaptured Zhitomir on the last day of 1943, and Kirovograd on January 8. Despite the spring thaw, the Soviet offensive continued. The Russians had been taught by stern masters — war, the enemy, terrible defeats — but by now the Red Army was notably better than it had been in the past, particularly in its command and staff structure. By 1944 the Soviet Union was undoubtedly capable of defeating Nazi Germany single-handedly.

The next Soviet drive to liberate the Ukraine began on March 4. This prolonged and violent battle resulted in the encirclement of some twenty-one German divisions near Chernovtsy. However, the relieving attacks of Army Group South were partially successful. On April 4 the Russian ring was breached and the survivors of First Panzer Army escaped, though they lost all their artillery.

The Germans, now driven back to the foothills of the Carpathians, were isolated from their comrades to the north and had to rely on a line of communications that ran through Rumania. Meanwhile, Sebastopol was recaptured on May 9, and by the 12th the whole of the Crimea had been liberated. In the south General Ferdinand

Schörner's Army Group Southern Ukraine (previously Army Group A) held a shaky line between the Black Sea and the Carpathians, and Field Marshal Walther Model's Army Group Northern Ukraine (previously Army Group South) extended north of the Carpathians to the Pripet Marshes.*

The Stavka had decided that its next major blow would be launched in Byelorussia against the flanks of the huge salient being held by Field Marshal Ernst Busch's Army Group Center. Between Polotsk in the north and the Pripet Marshes in the south, a distance of more than 450 miles, the front of Army Group Center curved out to the east, enclosing Vitebsk, Orsha, Mogilev, Bykhov, and Bobruisk. This front was held by three seriously depleted German armies, from north to south General Reinhardt's Third Panzer Army, General Tippelskirch's Fourth Army, and General Jordan's Ninth Army. Most of Army Group Center's thirty-two divisions held frontages some fifteen miles in length, though on Hitler's orders a division was allotted to each of the strongpoints of Orsha, Mogilev, and Bobruisk, and three divisions to Vitebsk.

Hitler, OKH, and Model all believed that the next Russian offensive would fall in Galicia, against Army Group Northern Ukraine. As a consequence, Model got what reserves were available, leaving Army Group Center with only two divisions in reserve for the whole of its front. Yet Hitler rejected all suggestions that Army Group Center should be allowed to withdraw to the Berezina, even though such a retirement would have shortened the front by some 150 miles and would have deprived the Russians of the leverage they could get from converging flank attacks.

For Operation Bagration, as the offensive was code-named, the Russians concentrated the majority of their forces on the flanks, for from the beginning the Stavka envisioned a deep penetration and encirclement west of Minsk. What was aimed at was nothing less than the destruction of Army Group Center. Frontal attacks in the center were designed to prevent a clean German withdrawal and, as it turned out, were almost unnecessary.

The preparations for this enormous offensive could not be concealed. From June 10 on, Army Group Center was aware that huge concentrations were building up opposite it. Thus Field Marshal Busch, his army commanders, and their staffs had to await the storm, knowing that it would come, but were forbidden to take the appropriate measures to lessen its severity.

The Soviet offensive opened on June 23, one day after the third

---

*Kleist and Manstein had been relieved of their commands by Hitler, and Model, on transfer to Army Group Northern Ukraine, had been replaced as commander of Army Group North by General Fritz Lindemann.

anniversary of Operation Barbarossa. It went excellently from the beginning. Vassilevsky's First Baltic and Third Byelorussian army groups achieved a quick breakthrough against Third Panzer Army on both sides of Vitebsk. Zakharov's Second Byelorussian Army Group, driving toward Mogilev, reached the Dnieper on the first day, and on the 24th, Rokossovsky's First Byelorussian Army Group advanced toward Parichi.

Possibly there was still time for Army Group Center to have extricated itself without suffering too severely, but Hitler refused to abandon Vitebsk. As a result, before nightfall on the 24th the German LIII Corps was all but surrounded and its flanking corps to the north and south had been thrust away centrifugally, leaving a twenty-five-mile gap in the German line. Farther south the Fourth Army withdrew its left to keep in touch with the retiring right wing of the Third Panzer Army. In the south, in the Ninth Army's sector, the First Byelorussian Army Group burst through south of the Berezina and advanced rapidly toward the Bobruisk railway.

On the 25th, on the Ninth Army's front, Rokossovsky's troops continued to advance northwest, threatening to cut off Bobruisk. In the center, on the Fourth Army's front, the Russians cleared the area between the Dvina and the Dnieper and closed in on Mogilev and Orsha. To the north around Vitebsk a breakout attempt by the surrounded LIII Corps was smashed, with heavy losses. The next day, the 26th, the net began to close as Rokossovsky's First Byelorussian Army Group began to get behind the Ninth Army west of Bobruisk and, on the northern flank, Vitebsk fell. By June 27 two German corps, XXXV and XLI Panzer, some forty thousand troops, were surrounded east of the Berezina. Orsha fell on this day and the remnants of the LIII Corps surrendered in the north.

With these successes, the Russian Supreme Command issued new orders for the next phase of the operation. The First Baltic Army Group was to take Polotsk and press on toward Glubokoye. In the center the Third and Second Byelorussian army groups were to advance on Minsk, and in the south the First Byelorussian Army Group was to drive on Baranovichi by way of Slutsk. The aim of these orders was nothing less than the encirclement of the entire Army Group Center, but as Zhukov was later to remark, "The strength and disposition of our troops fully corresponded to the object of the operation." Late on the 28th, Field Marshal Busch was relieved of his command and was replaced by Field Marshal Model, who for the moment also continued to command Army Group Northern Ukraine. Model had his Führer's confidence and henceforth Hitler was to agree to all Army Group Center's suggestions, but by now it was far too late. On the 29th Slutsk fell, the Fourth Army continued its all-too-slow withdrawal in the center, and Soviet armor appeared south and west of Polotsk, to cut the railway to Molodechno.

By the evening of July 3 the Russians had taken Minsk and were flowing past it to the north, completing the encirclement of three German corps and two panzer corps, more than 100,000 men. A week later the 57,000 survivors surrendered. In a fortnight's fighting Byelorussia had been liberated and Army Group Center's three armies destroyed. Twenty-eight German divisions were wiped out in Byelorussia, with a loss of 350,000 men, almost twice as many as at Stalingrad.

The Russians continued their drive to the west toward Daugavpils, Vilna, Bialystok, and Brest-Litovsk. The pace of the Russian advance would now be decided more by logistical considerations than by fighting.

By July 18, eight German divisions had been surrounded at Brody and the Russians were advancing on a broad front toward the Vistula and the frontiers of Germany. On the 27th Lublin and Bialystok were captured, and the Russians established bridgeheads over the Vistula. Brest-Litovsk was liberated on the 28th, and to the south the Second and Third Ukrainian army groups entered Moldavia, which induced the Rumanian and Hungarian governments to surrender. The Russian advance continued into Walachia, until, by late August, Marshal Timoshenko's soldiers stood along the Danube from south of Bucharest to the Black Sea. On September 5 the Soviet Union declared war on Bulgaria, but with the overthrow of the Bulgarian government on September 9 the Red Army halted its advance.

No such easy liberation was granted to Poland. When the requests of the Polish government-in-exile for an investigation of the Katyn Forest massacre had become embarrassing, Stalin appointed a "Committee of Liberation," composed of his own creatures, and installed it in Lublin, where it operated under Soviet direction as the "government" of those Polish territories that had been recaptured from the Nazis. This device enabled Stalin to dismiss as mere "quarrels between two rival groups of Poles" any differences that arose between the Polish government-in-exile and the Soviet Union.

As the Red Army approached Warsaw at the end of July 1944, Soviet radio broadcasts appealed to General Tadeusz Bor-Komorowski's Home Army of Polish resistance fighters inside Warsaw, and to the Polish population, to rise against the Nazis. Since the Red Army was now only nine miles from Warsaw, Bor-Komorowski gave the order for Operation Tempest, the rising of the Polish underground in Warsaw, to begin at five o'clock on the afternoon of August 1.

At first the Poles were successful. The Germans, taken by surprise, quickly lost about half the city, and the Poles secured several bridges across the Vistula. But the Red Army now halted in its tracks and went over to the defensive, leaving the Polish resistance to continue the unequal fight alone. There was no military reason for this Russian action, and those few western historians who have attempted to excuse the treachery by the plea of military necessity seem to have been influenced less by the evidence than by their "progressive" sympathies.

As the Germans reinforced their garrison in Warsaw to some eight divisions, including three SS divisions, they began a ruthless house-by-house extermination of resistance. Stalin meanwhile refused repeated requests from the British and Americans that he come to the assistance of Bor-Komorowski, and flatly rejected a British proposal that Royal Air Force aircraft should drop supplies to the Polish insurgents and then be allowed to land in Soviet-held territory for refueling before the return flight. Nevertheless, the RAF did begin to fly to Warsaw from Italian airfields on August 10, but losses were heavy and few supplies got through.

On August 20, on Churchill's initiative, the British and American governments made a strong joint representation to the Soviet government, but once again Stalin categorically refused to move a man. Conditions within Warsaw were now horrible beyond description, as the SS murdered tens of thousands of Poles and sent tens of thousands more to concentration camps. The population was starving and epidemics of disease raged unchecked. The Lublin Committee now announced that General Bor-Komorowski was a criminal and a traitor and that he and his staff would be court-martialed once the Red Army captured Warsaw.

As yet, however, the Red Army was making no attempt to capture Warsaw. Instead, Stalin was allowing the Nazis to exterminate those Poles who might have resisted the postwar communization of their country. The Russians, nine miles away, passively watched the martyrdom of Warsaw for six weeks. By then the Nazis had done the communists' work for them and it was time for the Soviet Union to establish an alibi. Accordingly, on September 13 Red Army troops at long last crossed the Vistula to seize the suburb of Praga, and Soviet guns, which had all along been within range, began to shell German positions. On the 18th, American Flying Fortresses began to airdrop supplies and were allowed to land for refueling in Russian-held territory. But it was all too late — and the Russians had intended that it be too late. The few survivors of Bor-Komorowski's Home Army surrendered late on October 2, after having waged a heroic battle against hopeless odds for sixty-one days. In August and September 1944 more than 200,000 Poles died in Warsaw, many of them women and children. Nazi casualties were 26,000, of whom 17,000 were killed.

Meanwhile, in the west, the Allies had continued their slow advance up the Italian peninsula. Plans had been made for an amphibious landing by the U.S. Fifth Army at Anzio, thirty-five miles south of Rome, combined with a strong attack against the German defenses in the center around Monte Cassino. The second operation began on January 17, and on the 22nd an American-British force, under the command of the U.S. VI Corps, made a landing from the sea at Anzio. Field Marshal Kesselring reinforced the threatened areas with commendable promptness.

To the south the Americans suffered very heavy casualties while crossing the Rapido River, and the British bogged down after advancing about four miles. Although the Free French in the high mountains did better, the Allies had clearly failed in their attempt to break into the Liri valley. What was even worse, the Allied troops at Anzio spent time consolidating their beachhead instead of driving vigorously inland to the Alban Hills, only some fifteen miles distant. The result was that the Germans successfully contained the beachhead and began launching strong counterattacks to drive the Allies into the sea. Mackensen, commander of the German Fourteenth Army and in overall command at Anzio, soon had five divisions reinforcing the hodgepodge of units with which he had first contained the landing. Obviously, instead of the Anzio landings providing the crowbar that would pry the enemy out of the Gustav Line, the troops isolated in the bridgehead would have to be rescued by the overland advance from the south.

Plans for a renewed assault on the Gustav Line were made at Alexander's headquarters at Caserta on February 28. The Allies transferred the bulk of their strength west of the Apennines, assigning a smaller sector — from the Liri River to the Tyrrhenian Sea — to the U.S. Fifth Army, and moving most of the British Eighth Army to the Cassino front. Meanwhile, Kesselring, prodded on by Hitler, launched three major counterattacks against the Anzio beachhead without eliminating it. The final attack, at the end of February, was beaten back with very heavy losses by the U.S. 3rd Division, and thereafter the Germans went over to the defensive. During this time, however, successive Allied attempts to capture the dominating feature of Monte Cassino all broke down.

The Allied blow fell in the Liri valley just before midnight on May 11, when thirteen divisions of the U.S. Fifth and British Eighth armies advanced between Cassino and the sea. Four days later the six divisions now under the U.S. VI Corps would attack from the Anzio beachhead to link up with the forces inland. Opposition was fierce and casualties heavy, but the Allied attacks were pressed home persistently over the broken ground and through the vineyards and coppices of scrub oak until by the 14th most of the Gustav Line was in Allied hands.

Moving much more rapidly, the African troops of the French Expeditionary Corps crossed the Aurunci Mountains and the U.S. II Corps advanced steadily along the coast. On May 16 the Germans began to withdraw to the Hitler Line. Two days later the Poles at last occupied Monte Cassino, which had so long defied all Allied attacks. To the west, French African units swept on to within a few miles of Pontecorvo. However, the attack from the Anzio beachhead had to be postponed until it could be launched simultaneously with a set-piece assault on the Hitler Line.

The Canadian I Corps broke through the Hitler Line on May 23 after very bitter fighting, and the British XIII Corps kept pace on the right. On the same day the U.S. VI Corps broke out of the Anzio beachhead, while the U.S. II Corps made good progress up the coast. On the 24th, Canadian units reached the Melfa River, and the next day the U.S. VI Corps linked up with the U.S. II Corps near the coast. The Anzio beachhead, which had caused the Allies so much anxiety, had been successfully merged with the rest of the Allied front more than four months after it had first been formed.

General Alexander had ordered the U.S. Fifth Army to drive to Valmontone, which would have cut Highway 6 and isolated all German forces south of Rome. However, Mark Clark, a publicity-conscious commander, whom many of his troops suspected of harboring high political ambitions, wanted the prestige of being the first to enter Rome. Instead of fighting his way on to Valmontone, Clark switched four divisions north toward Rome and continued toward Valmontone with only the 3rd Division and the Special Service Force. Kesselring was thus able to get the Hermann Göring Division to Valmontone in time to hold open the German escape route. A great opportunity was missed here, and though Clark was given a tumultuous welcome in Rome, it was all for nothing — he never became President.

Kesselring was in no hurry to fall back to the Caesar Line, which stretched across the peninsula from the Tyrrhenian Sea near Velletri to the Adriatic northwest of Pescara. He intended to take full advantage of the numerous river obstacles, defiles, and ravines that ran athwart the Allied axis of advance. Alexander ordered the Fifth Army to capture Rome while the Eighth Army broke through the Caesar Line and advanced east and north of the Italian capital. Thus, at the end of May, the Fifth Army was fighting desperately to clear the Alban Hills (which might well have fallen without much opposition to a determined advance on January 17) while three corps of the Eighth Army continued to claw their way north and west over some of the best defensive territory in the world.

On June 1, the U.S. II Corps at last cut Highway 6 at Valmontone, then turned left to advance on Rome. The next day the U.S. VI Corps on the right moved forward against weakening opposition to the Via Appia, the straight and ancient road that led north to Rome. On June 3 the two Allied armies established contact. By now the German Fourteenth Army was withdrawing from the Caesar Line and the German Tenth Army was swinging back its right flank to a new position some twelve miles north of Highway 6. Because of these moves, the two German armies lost contact with one another just as the two Allied armies gained contact, and the enemy exposed himself to a stroke that never fell. Mackensen's Fourteenth Army in particular, situated west of the Tiber in relatively open country, might possibly have been destroyed by a more rapid Allied pursuit, but Alexander's plan called for only a step-by-step advance. The western world, however, could rejoice when American units entered Rome on June 4, to be greeted with great enthusiasm by the populace.

The spring offensive had cost the Allies more than forty thousand casualties to the German thirty thousand. Substantial German forces had been held in Italy when they might otherwise have reinforced the defenses in France, but rather more Allied troops had also been retained in the Mediterranean theater when they might otherwise have participated in the invasion of northwest Europe. Operation Anvil was now revived — and renamed Dragoon, since it was obviously going to be launched too late to serve as any sort of anvil — and, against strong British objections, was scheduled for August 15. General Alexander was ordered to give up for Dragoon three American and four Free French divisions. The British commander had argued forcefully, but perhaps rather speciously, that if he could retain these troops he could not only force the Pisa-Rimini line but could break out of Italy altogether through the Ljubljana gap and overrun Austria. Alexander was supported by the British Chief of the Imperial General Staff, Field Marshal Lord Alanbrooke, but the Americans were adamantly opposed to the scheme. In this they were almost certainly right, although the alternative they espoused, Anvil-Dragoon, could exert little influence on the campaign in France. The truth probably is that Allied strategy had taken a wrong turn with the invasion of the Italian mainland, and that the results of that error could never later be rectified. Two days after the fall of Rome the

Italian campaign was upstaged by the Allied invasion of northwest Europe.

Operation Overlord was one of the few really decisive battles of world history. Had the venture failed, Nazi Germany would still have lost the war, but such an outcome would have meant the overthrow of all the West, beyond hope of early rally or return. These facts will be disputed in some quarters even now, and they were certainly not self-evident at the time. In the spring of 1944 it seemed that what was at stake was the outcome of the war.

The cross-Channel invasion was an immensely hazardous and difficult operation, for the enemy had had four years in which to strengthen his Atlantic defenses with artillery, minefields, wire, concrete emplacements, and beach and underwater obstacles. The reasons for his not doing a better job were the competing requirements of the Russian and Italian theaters, and the insistence by Hitler, who was replacing strategy with intuition, on the heavy reinforcement of such nonessential areas as Norway and the Channel Islands.

The cross-Channel invasion was a gigantic set-piece operation, and the time available for preparation meant that little was left to chance. Heavy fire support was to be provided by aerial bombing, naval gunfire, and guns and rockets fired from the assault craft. Specialized landing craft were developed for tanks and infantry. Amphibious tanks were built, as were special assault vehicles for clearing beach defenses, armored bulldozers, flail tanks for blasting lanes through minefields, and mounted flame throwers for use against pillboxes. The experience at Dieppe had convinced the planners of the futility of attempting to capture a major port in the initial assault, so the logistical support of the invading force would have to come in across open beaches. Elaborate beach organizations were therefore devised, and artificial harbors, known as "Mulberries," were constructed, to be towed across the Channel and placed in position off the coast. Rhino ferries, built on pontoons, were to move material and equipment to shore from larger ships. Plans were made for gasoline pipelines to be laid across the Channel. The Allies were very good at all of this.

The operational plan for Overlord was begun in May 1943 by Lieutenant General Sir F. E. Morgan, a British officer. Morgan, who was given a target date of May 1, 1944, was forced, because of shortages of landing craft, to limit his plan to an assault on a three-divisional front. He had little choice as to the landing area. The overriding consideration was the capacity of the beaches to maintain a large invasion force, and only two areas within fighter cover met this requirement: the beaches in the Pas de Calais and those in Normandy between Caen and the Cotentin Peninsula. The Pas de Calais had the advantage of the shorter sea route, but offsetting this was the fact that the enemy considered it the most likely area for an invasion and had therefore made his defenses very strong. The German defenses in Normandy were weaker, though Rommel, now in command of Army Group B, was working frantically to strengthen them. The Normandy beaches were excellent for the Allied purpose; good airfields could be constructed inland; and the major port of Cherbourg was near at hand. Therefore the decision was made to land in Normandy.

At the Quadrant Conference in Quebec in August 1943 the COSSAC (Chief of Staff to the Supreme Allied Commander) plan, calling for the invasion of Normandy, was approved in principle. Since American forces would constitute a substantial majority of the armies invading the continent, the Supreme Allied Commander would have to be an American. The British had to accept this, but they did successfully resist a proposal that the Supreme Commander also be responsible for the Mediterranean theater. Late in 1943 President Roosevelt appointed General Dwight D. Eisenhower Supreme Commander, and Eisenhower brought with him as his chief of staff another American, General Walter Bedell Smith. The Deputy Supreme Commander was Air Chief Marshal Sir Arthur Tedder; the naval commander, Admiral Sir Bertram Ramsay; the air force commander, Air Marshal Sir Trafford Leigh-Mallory. By a somewhat unusual arrangement, a British ground commander was appointed for the assault phase. General Montgomery, commander of the 21st Army Group, would command in France until the Allies had three army groups in action, at which time Eisenhower would set up his headquarters on the continent and assume control of operations. Possibly the appointment of Montgomery as ground commander for the critical assault phase was tacit recognition of Montgomery's experience in operational command and of Eisenhower's comparative lack of such experience.

At all events, both Montgomery and Eisenhower at once demanded that the invasion frontage be extended. The revised plan called for an assault on a five-divisional front by two armies. The U.S. First Army (Lieutenant General Omar N. Bradley) could attack on the right with two divisions, and on the left the British Second Army (Lieutenant General M. C. Dempsey) would attack with one Canadian and two British divisions. Three airborne divisions, two American and one British, would be dropped on the flanks of the invasion area on the night before D-Day.

At Eisenhower's insistence all Allied air forces in Britain except the RAF Coastal Command were placed under him before the invasion.

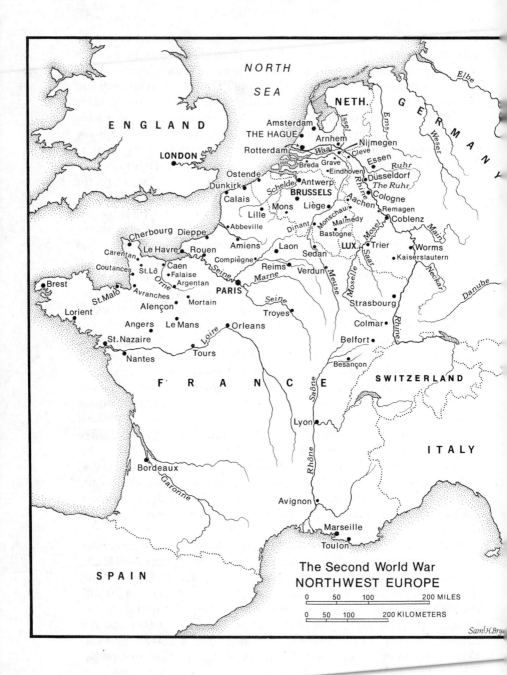

The Second World War
NORTHWEST EUROPE

0   50   100   200 MILES

0   50   100   200 KILOMETERS

Sam⋅H⋅Bry

However, the reluctance of airmen wedded to the concept of strategic bombing to cooperate even in the greatest battle of the war delayed the necessary centralization of control. The U.S. Ninth Air Force was not taken off Operation Pointblank and given to Eisenhower until March 10, 1944; the RAF Bomber Command and the U.S. Eighth Air Force continued on their unregenerate way until April 14. Operation Pointblank had, however, seriously depleted German fighter strength. Once the bombers were under Eisenhower they were directed against the transportation system of northwestern France, attacking railroads, bridges, rolling stock, and marshaling yards, as well as airfields, coastal batteries, and radar sites. Since these attacks could not be too concentrated lest they reveal the intended invasion area, as many bombs were dropped on the Pas de Calais as on targets in Normandy. Nevertheless, by D-Day all the Seine bridges below Paris had been destroyed, as well as most of the Loire bridges. This had an enormous influence on the battle in the beachhead since the Germans had great difficulty in bringing up reinforcements.

The timing of the assault depended on the weather, the tides, and the moon. Weather acceptable for a landing could not be counted on before the beginning of May; the landings had to be made near low tide so that beach obstacles would be visible; and a moon was needed for the airborne drops. Originally it was hoped that Overlord could be launched early in May, but the extension of the invasion area required extra shipping, which took time to assemble. Also the Allied air forces, having begun late, wanted more time to complete their interdiction program. Accordingly, Overlord was postponed until the next favorable date, which would come between June 5 and 7. This delay, though unavoidable, was dangerous, both because the Allies needed as long a summer campaigning season as possible and because they knew that the enemy was preparing some sort of secret weapon for launching against the British Isles from sites along the Channel coast.

Long-range plans called for a buildup of forces in the Normandy-Brittany area, followed by a breakout. The U.S. First Army was to take Cherbourg and drive south to St. Lô; the British Second Army was to attack inland to the south and southeast of Caen. After the breakout two army groups would pursue the enemy to the German border, while the third army group, invading France from the south, would drive up the Rhone valley and take its place on the right of the Allied line. In the subsequent advance the army group on the extreme left would be given priority because the northern pathway into Germany presented the fewest natural obstacles and because such a thrust would most directly threaten the industrial area of the Ruhr. The

Rhine, however, would be closed along its length; there would be a further period of buildup, followed by a double envelopment of the Ruhr and the overrunning of the rest of Germany. This plan was, in fact, adhered to rigidly even when the complete collapse of German forces in France seemed to provide a great opportunity for more rapid exploitation.

Bad weather on June 5 forced a twenty-four-hour postponement and it seemed that the operation might have to be delayed at least two weeks. However, when the Allied meteorologists forecast good weather for a thirty-six-hour period beginning early on the 6th, Eisenhower ordered the invasion to go ahead.

On the German side sixty-seven-year-old Field Marshal Gerd von Rundstedt's two army groups contained fifty-eight divisions, though most of them were seriously understrength. Rommel's Army Group B consisted of the Fifteenth Army of eighteen divisions in the Pas de Calais area, the Seventh Army of eleven divisions in Normandy, and of a corps of three divisions in the Netherlands. Army Group G, commanded by Colonel General Johannes Blaskowitz, consisted of thirteen divisions of the First Army in the Bay of Biscay region and the Nineteenth Army on the Mediterranean coast of France. Of the ten panzer or panzer grenadier divisions in Rundstedt's command, three were in Rommel's Army Group B, three in Blaskowitz' Army Group G, and four in OKW reserve, from which they could not be moved except by Hitler's personal order.

Rundstedt and Rommel disagreed about the best method of defeating an Allied invasion. Rundstedt, knowing the lack of depth of the German defenses, did not believe the Allies could be pinned down on the beaches; he wanted to concentrate his panzer forces well to the rear so as to be able to launch a powerful, coordinated counterattack. He envisaged the main battle as being fought well inland a week or more after the landing. Rommel, drawing on his experience in North Africa, did not believe that the panzer forces could move except slowly, and by night, in the face of Allied air attacks; he wanted to concentrate well forward and to fight his main battle on the beaches as soon as possible. Both theories were based on an admission of German inferiority, and the event was to prove that both Rundstedt and Rommel were right in their apprehensions. The result of their disagreement was a compromise that met the requirements of neither commander. The question as to whether Rundstedt's or Rommel's concept was the better is probably academic, for it seems probable that neither could have succeeded.

The Allied attacks, launched from east to west by the British 3rd Division on Sword beach, the Canadian 3rd Division on Juno beach, the British 50th Division on Gold beach, and the U.S. 1st and 4th divisions on Omaha and Utah beaches, struck the German 352nd and 716th divisions as well as part of the 709th Division. Of the German armor only the 21st Panzer Division was in the actual invasion area around Caen, but the 12th SS Panzer Division, the Hitlerjugend, was nearby, and the Panzer Lehr Division was stationed only seventy miles away.

All day Monday, June 5, Allied ships set out for France. More than seven thousand ships, divided into two great task forces, were involved in the operation. Minesweepers cleared ten channels through the German minefields, but the Germans did not detect the approach of the assaulting forces. That night heavy bombers attacked German coastal batteries, though not very effectively. As H-Hour neared, other bombers attacked the beach defenses, but most of the bombs fell too far inland because of the crews' fears of hitting the approaching landing craft. More than 170 squadrons of fighters and fighter bombers escorted the assault armadas, and patrolled the skies above the beaches to such good effect that it was three o'clock on the afternoon of D-Day before a single German aircraft appeared over the invasion area.

At fifteen minutes after midnight on June 6, the United States 101st Airborne Division began landing north of Carentan behind Utah beach, and the United States 82nd Airborne Division came down on the extreme right. A few minutes later the British 6th Airborne Division dropped on the left flank. The American paratroops were dropped inaccurately, suffered very heavy casualties, and failed to achieve as much as had been hoped. The British paratroops landed much more tightly and were able to capture all their objectives.

The infantry assault craft had to contend with four-foot waves as they made the run-in to the beaches, a trip that varied in length from seven to eleven miles. Some of the amphibious tanks could not be launched because of the high seas. Fortunately, the naval bombardment was much more accurate than the aerial bombing had been. The first German submarines to reach the invasion area arrived on June 9, far too late to be effective. As the infantry swarmed ashore they suffered casualties but not nearly as many as Allied planners had anticipated.

Not until the first Allied paratroopers landed were German formations put on the alert. Rommel had been in Germany on June 6 and did not get back to his headquarters until that evening. He at once demanded reinforcements — the infantry division that was cooling its heels on the Channel Islands, the five infantry divisions in reserve in the Pas de Calais, a portion of an infantry division from Brittany, and the four panzer divisions in OKW reserve. OKW rejected all these demands, though they were exactly the right ones. By June 10 Rommel had received as reinforcements only the 12th SS Panzer Division, the Panzer Lehr Division, and one infantry division.

The Allies were also unable to reinforce as quickly as they had hoped. On three of the five invasion beaches the attacks had been entirely satisfactory, even though Caen and many other objectives had not been taken. The British and Canadians had linked up Juno and Gold, and the Americans on Utah had overcome the difficulties of their terrain in a highly efficient manner. On the British Sword beach a counterattack by part of the 21st Panzer Division had driven to the sea before it was halted and thrown back; although the situation was satisfactorily stabilized here, Sword was not linked to the Canadians on its right. The real trouble on D-Day occurred on Omaha beach, where the U.S. 1st Division suffered extremely heavy casualties at the hands of the German 352nd Division. The Americans here had declined the proffered help of British flail tanks and armored assault vehicles, and the troops paid the price. When darkness fell, the Omaha beachhead was only slightly more than a mile deep at its deepest point, and only a hundred tons of supplies had been landed.

The mood in higher Allied headquarters was one of tempered optimism. Casualties had been far lower than had been feared — only some 9000. And though only 87,000 men had been put ashore instead of the planned 107,000, only half the intended 14,000 vehicles, and less than one quarter of the intended supplies, the enemy reaction had been less fierce than it might have been. The events of the next few days amply confirmed the Allied optimism, for the buildup continued steadily, German counterattacks were delayed and disrupted by Allied air power, and the enemy reinforcements were held in the Pas de Calais because of the fear of a second Allied landing there. Within a week the Allies were firmly established in France, past all possibility of being dislodged, airfields had been built, and the odds were steadily shifting in the Allies' favor.

Montgomery's plan was to draw the major portion of the enemy strength to his left flank against the British and Canadians so that the Americans could more easily overrun the Cotentin Peninsula, capture Cherbourg, and then break out to the Seine. There were, of course, disappointments and setbacks. Although the plan had called for its capture on D-Day, Caen did not fall until the second week of July, by which time there were a million Allied soldiers in France. The important road junction of Villers-Bocage, southwest of Caen, held out even longer. Although the U.S. VII Corps cut across the Cotentin Peninsula between June 14 and 18, Cherbourg did not fall until the 26th, when it was discovered that its port facilities were so thoroughly demolished as to be unusable. A freakish Channel storm between June

19 and 23 sank much Allied shipping and destroyed the Mulberry off Omaha beach. A strong British attack to take Caen failed late in June, after Rommel had committed all his available armor.

By the end of the month both Rommel and Rundstedt had decided that they could not hope to hold back the Allies much longer. As early as June 17 they had met the Führer at Soissons and had vainly attempted to make him understand the situation. Rommel told him bluntly that Germany should make peace, but when Hitler met his generals again at Berchtesgaden on the 29th all he did was rant about how his V-1s and V-2s would win the war by destroying London. The first flying bomb attack had been launched against London on the night of June 12/13, yet now Hitler rejected out of hand his generals' suggestion that the flying bombs would be better employed against the Allied bridgehead and the invasion ports. A few days later, on July 2, Rundstedt was dismissed from his command and replaced by Field Marshal Günther von Kluge. Rommel was seriously wounded on July 17, when his staff car was attacked by a British fighter bomber,* and Kluge had to take over the direct command of Army Group B.

Meanwhile, on the front around Caen seven of the eight German panzer divisions had been drawn away from the American sector where the Allied breakout was planned. After hard fighting Caen was taken on the 9th, and the U.S. First Army advanced slowly and painfully through the broken country on the right flank. Between July 15 and 18 a five-corps attack south of Caen by the British Second Army made good initial gains before it was halted by deeply sited antitank guns. Kluge reported to Hitler that his front might break at any moment.

On July 18 the U.S. First Army captured St. Lô, and General Patton's U.S. Third Army and General H. D. G. Crerar's Canadian First Army became operational. The major breakout attempt could now be made in the west. Once again the western attack would be assisted by a British-Canadian offensive in the east. Bad weather delayed the launching of the American offensive, Operation Cobra, until July 25, and on the same day an attack by the Canadian II Corps resulted in exceptionally fierce fighting, in which little ground changed hands, but that kept the enemy's attention firmly fixed on his eastern flank. Kluge was slow to appreciate the danger developing in the American sector and did not reinforce his left until the 27th. By then it was too late, for by the 30th the Americans had captured Coutances and Av-

---

*Rommel had been involved in the July 20 bomb plot against Hitler, and when the plot failed his complicity was discovered. Because of his popularity with the German people he was given the choice of committing suicide rather than standing trial. For the sake of his family he killed himself by taking poison on October 14, 1944.

ranches and the enemy was in full retreat. On August 1, the U.S. 12th Army Group became operational under Bradley; it consisted of Patton's Third Army on the right and General Courtney Hodges' First Army on the left. Patton directed the major portion of his force south and east against negligible opposition, urging his tank columns forward with a real sense of urgency.

However, once again the Allied tendency to adhere to prearranged plans prevented full exploitation. Instead of directing every available formation toward the Loire, the U.S. First Army was swung west, to cut off the Breton peninsula. The diversion into Brittany brought little profit. The ports were strongly garrisoned, and though Brest was taken on September 19, its capture had no real significance. The ports of St. Malo, Lorient, and St. Nazaire, on the other hand, were quite properly allowed to hold out for the rest of the war. Once again, in the high councils of the western Allies, methodical, preplanned, step-by-step strategy was preferred to dash, improvisation, initiative, and an instinct for the enemy's jugular.

Fortunately, Hitler again came to the Allies' assistance; he ordered an abortive counterattack with five panzer and two infantry divisions on August 7. On the large-scale maps at OKW the scheme must have looked attractive, for the thrust along the Mortain-Avranches axis would, if successful, have cut off the advance elements of Patton's Third Army. The trouble was that the counterattack never had any hope of success. When it was launched on the night of August 6/7, Mortain was captured but the American formations on the ground slowed the German advance, and on the 7th the fighter bombers of the U.S. Ninth Air Force and of the British 2nd Tactical Air Force brought the enemy offensive to a standstill. Patton pressed on to capture Le Mans on the 9th.

The enemy was still holding successfully south of Caen but an enormous hole had been torn in his left wing, through which American armor was pouring. At this time the only sensible course for the Germans would have been to fall back with all speed behind the Seine and attempt to form a new defensive line there, at least until a defensive line could be established on the Rhine. By the first week of August, of course, there was no guarantee that such a strategy would have been successful, and indeed it probably should not have been. The Germans had already lingered far too long in Normandy. Hitler's counterattack at Mortain had thrust his forces so far into a potential trap that there seemed to be no way of extricating them.

For once the Allies adapted their plans to the changed situation, abandoning for the time being their previous intention of casting a wide net around the German Seventh Army and Panzer Group West by blocking the escape route between Paris on the Seine and Orléans on the Loire. Now, thanks to the abortive Mortain counteroffensive, a shorter encirclement became feasible. If the Canadian First Army could drive south past Falaise and the U.S. Third Army could drive north from Argentan, the Germans would suffer a military defeat from which they would be unlikely to recover. In the second week of August there was a real chance of an almost immediate end to the war. The credit for this new concept must go to General Bradley, who outlined the idea to Eisenhower and Montgomery on August 8.

The Canadian First Army was already attacking south toward Falaise in an operation (Totalize) that had begun well on the night of August 7/8. The withdrawal of German panzer forces from the Caen front had left only one infantry division holding the line against the Canadian attack, with the greatly understrength 12th SS Panzer Division in reserve. However, although the Canadians advanced nine miles, there was no breakthrough and Falaise was not taken.

Meanwhile Patton's Third Army was making much better progress. The Americans crossed the Sarthe River near Le Mans on the 9th, drove on to reach Alençon some twenty-five miles to the north on the 11th, and continued in the direction of Argentan. The gap was closing fast, and with every mile that Patton advanced north, the possibility increased that the bulk of the German forces in France could be destroyed. Unfortunately, the boundary drawn arbitrarily on the map between the U.S. 12th Army Group and the British 21st Army Group proved a more effective obstacle than the German defenses. This boundary had been fixed some eight miles south of Argentan, and though the Americans reached it late on the 12th and drove across it to within two or three miles of Argentan, they were halted the next afternoon. The U.S. XV Corps had to stop at Argentan because Bradley and Eisenhower feared "a head-on meeting" between the advancing Americans and Canadians, which might have resulted in "a calamitous battle between friends." Such a decision is almost impossible to understand, and it is even more difficult to understand how it can have been made by Bradley, one of the best of the American commanders and the man who had first conceived the idea of the shorter encirclement.

The responsibility, of course, was Eisenhower's, and here again the Supreme Commander demonstrated that he had little real grip on operations. Had the Americans pushed on to close the gap, there might well have been accidents between them and the Canadians, though it is most unlikely that these would have been on any sizable scale. And almost certainly if the gap had been closed at any time up until August 17, the war would have been over early that autumn. Patton was quite rightly furious at the check imposed on him, but the fatal order stood, and for three precious days the Americans stayed idly on the defensive around Argentan while Patton sent two divisions east to the Seine. It was not until August 16 that Montgomery intervened as ground forces commander and ordered Crerar's Canadian First Army and Bradley's Americans to converge on Trun, ignoring the army group boundary.

Almost simultaneously with this renewed Allied effort to close the gap, Kluge ordered his forces to attempt their escape. He was relieved of his command the next evening and was replaced by Model. On the airplane that was taking him back to Germany, Kluge committed suicide by taking poison, leaving a letter for Hitler in which he urged the dictator to "end the hopeless struggle." Model ordered the II SS Panzer Corps, of four divisions, to hold the northern flank of the escape route against the Anglo-Canadian forces, and the XLVII Panzer Corps, of two divisions, to hold the southern flank against the Americans. The German Seventh Army and the remnants of what had been Panzer Group West were to escape eastward as quickly as possible. By early morning on the 18th the bulk of the German forces were east of the Orne and German troops were escaping from the pocket in a steady stream.

On the 17th the Canadian First Army had at last taken Falaise, in the face of fanatical German resistance. Regrouping of the American forces at Argentan delayed the advance to Trun until the morning of August 18, when the U.S. V Corps at last moved north. Chambois was entered almost simultaneously on the early evening of the 19th by the Americans and the Poles, and the gap was at last closed.

During the 17th and the 18th the desperate Germans were pounded mercilessly by the Allied air forces. In perfect flying weather the British and American pilots were presented with wonderful targets. On the 18th, 3057 sorties were flown, and on the 19th, 2535. Since every available road and track was crowded with German transport moving eastward two abreast, it was almost impossible to miss. Allied artillery also took a terrible toll. The entire area of the gap was soon littered with German dead and with destroyed or abandoned tanks, guns, and vehicles.

But the enemy, even in these frightful circumstances, fought well. The German Seventh Army was placed under the command of the Fifth Panzer Army on the 19th, when the Seventh Army's commander, General Paul Hausser, was seriously wounded. On the 20th the Germans launched coordinated attacks to extricate the encircled Seventh Army. The Seventh Army attacked northeast and north while the II SS Panzer Corps attacked from outside the caldron.

These attacks were successful. A hole was bored in the encircling Allied line between St. Lambert-sur-Dives and Trun, through which between 40 and 50 percent of the surrounded forces managed to escape. The fierce battle continued along the line of the little Dives River all through August 21. When it died down late that night the battle of the gap was over, and with it the Normandy phase of the northwest Europe campaign. German casualties in Normandy exceeded 400,000, of whom about half were prisoners. Allied casualties between D-Day and the end of August totaled 206,703; of that total, United States forces had suffered 124,394 casualties.

Once the Battle of the Falaise Gap was over, the Allied armies advanced to the Seine to attempt the second, wider encirclement that Montgomery had long planned. There was, however, to be no second encirclement. Colonel General Sepp Dietrich's Sixth SS Panzer Army fought a skillful rearguard action to hold the crossings of the lower Seine while the disorganized remnants of the Seventh Army got across. In spite of bad flying weather between August 20 and 23, Allied air power inflicted severe damage on the German forces waiting to get across the river. Well over four thousand German vehicles, guns, and tanks were destroyed at the Seine crossings — a figure that seems most impressive until it is remembered that Dietrich nevertheless managed to ferry some twenty-five thousand of his vehicles to safety on the far bank. The enemy's rearguard actions to defend his twenty-four crossing places were, many of them, classics of their kind, illustrating what well-trained troops, skillfully deployed, can achieve even in the face of greatly superior forces.

While the Allies were fighting hard to get across the lower Seine, the U.S. V Corps and the French 2nd Armored Division thrust on to Paris, which was liberated on August 25, amid scenes of wild rejoicing. It was the second major capital in the west to fall that summer, and its liberation was a portent — if one was needed — that final victory was not far off.

At the time, indeed, it appeared as though the war was as good as over. This belief in itself may have had some influence on subsequent events. Although the Allies had accomplished much of what they set out to do, their efforts fell considerably short of what might have been achieved. Success was great, but was not maximized. The amphibious operation on D-Day, the largest of its kind ever attempted, had been meticulously and intelligently planned and, on the whole, competently executed. Fortune, of course, had played its part in the success of the landings, but fortune, like the rain, probably falls on both sides almost equally. German errors undoubtedly contributed greatly to the Allied achievement. Hitler's belief that a second major landing would be made in the Pas de Calais had been assiduously nourished by Allied deception. The patent weaknesses in the German command structure, and in particular Hitler's interference in operations, was built into the German system of government.

Weaknesses in training and tactical ability were more evident on the Allied side than on the enemy's. This leads to the regrettable but inescapable conclusion that German formations were on the whole more effective than their British, Canadian, or American equivalents. Perhaps the western democracies, by the very nature of their society, produced less competent armies than did the abominable Nazi regime. What the West did produce, and what was undoubtedly the principal source of its success, was an abundance of equipment and material resources and an aerial superiority that overwhelmed the enemy.

In the strategic sphere the secondary Allied landing in the south of France, coming as it did on August 15, made little sense. The port of Marseilles was certainly open for heavy traffic within a month, but Marseilles was a long, long way from the Rhine. The American insistence on Operation Dragoon was symptomatic of a certain inflexibility that distinguished the American high command in its conduct of the war. Many members of the high command, including the Supreme Commander, considered that decisions taken after long reflection and debate in the weeks and months that preceded their implementation were inherently sounder than decisions taken under the heavy pressure of events, when the emotions of the moment might warp judgment and lead to error. This philosophy paid good dividends in set-piece operations like the D-Day landings, where most of the factors were known and could be carefully weighed ahead of time. Unfortunately, war is not merely a matter of set-piece operations, and the source of the major Allied failures in Normandy — and later in the war — was an inability to improvise, to capitalize adequately on success.

Model soon realized that he could not hold the line of the Somme and Oise rivers. As a first priority the Germans had to save what was left of their Fifteenth Army, strung out along the coast between the Seine and the East Schelde. These formations began withdrawing on August 28, but it seemed very doubtful whether they could be got out in time. By August 31, the British Second Army was at Amiens. The U.S. First Army was driving toward Maubeuge in Belgium and the U.S. Third Army was advancing northeast toward Reims. The Canadian First Army had been directed along the coast to overrun the Havre peninsula and capture Le Havre, Dieppe, and the Channel ports as far north as Bruges.

As the distance from the Normandy beaches lengthened, the Allies began to experience difficulties in maintaining their armies. The destruction of bridges in France slowed the opening of railway lines, so virtually everything had to be moved by truck. In Normandy, ammunition supply had been the main administrative problem, but with the breakout gasoline became the critical item. By the time Brussels and Antwerp fell, on September 3 and 4, the Allied lines of communication were nearly 300 miles long. Some formations had to be grounded so that their transport could be pooled and used to keep the spearheads moving. By now Patton's Third Army had reached the Meuse at Verdun and had sent out advance guards to the Moselle near Metz, but it could go no farther because of the shortage of gasoline. So rapid had been the Allied advance and so completely off balance were the Germans that when the British 11th Armored Division, after a drive of sixty miles since first light, captured Antwerp on September 3, it found the dock facilities of that great port almost intact. If Antwerp could be opened, all of the Allies' supply problems would be solved with one stroke. However, Antwerp is an inland port, some fifty miles from the sea, and before it could be used the approaches to it along the Schelde would have to be in Allied hands. This should have presented no particular difficulty, for on September 3 the three corps of the German Fifteenth Army were still to the west of Antwerp and south of the Schelde. Had the British Second Army at once advanced north from Antwerp to Breda, the Fifteenth Army would have been surrounded and the island of Walcheren and the South Beveland peninsula could soon have been occupied.

Most wars are wars of missed opportunities, but during August and September 1944, the western Allies achieved a truly spectacular record in this regard. The fact that they also achieved even more spectacular successes has tended to obscure this. At all events, Montgomery, who had been promoted to field marshal on September 1, perhaps as compensation for his direct subordination to Eisenhower on that date, gave no orders for rapid northward exploitation from Antwerp, and the German Fifteenth Army got away. Between September 4 and 23, when the German evacuation of the area south of the Schelde was completed, the grateful enemy managed to save 86,000 men, 616 guns, and 6200 vehicles.

Perhaps Montgomery was distracted by other matters at the time. Certainly he was engaged in a considerable controversy with the Supreme Commander as to the future conduct of the campaign. On September 1, as had long ago been decided, the Supreme Commander took over direct operational control of Montgomery's 21st Army Group and Bradley's 12th Army Group; Montgomery ceased to be ground forces commander, becoming equal with Bradley in subordination to Eisenhower.* Eisenhower intended to stick to the plan devised by SHAEF (Supreme Headquarters, Allied Expeditionary Force) the previous May. In May of 1944 it had seemed probable that when the Allies got beyond the Seine they would still be fighting against well-organized German armies, but by the beginning of September the actual situation was very different. German Army Group B, now commanded by Model since Rundstedt had been again recalled on September 4 to serve as Commander-in-Chief West, had about twelve divisions with which to cover some 250 miles of front; its armor had been reduced to fewer than eighty tanks with which to oppose some 1700 Allied tanks; and the Allies had almost complete command of the air. When the British Second Army got to Antwerp on September 3, it was only ninety miles from the Rhine.

On August 23 Montgomery had proposed to Eisenhower that the old, pre-D-Day plan be abandoned and that the Allies stake everything on a single thrust north of the Ruhr by "a solid mass of some forty divisions." Such a thrust, he claimed, would not only capture the Ruhr but would also open up the Channel ports, give the Allies valuable air bases in Belgium, and clear the rocket sites from which England was being bombarded. Montgomery also proposed that the command structure that provided for a single ground forces commander be continued — and after the stunning German defeat in Normandy there did seem to be some validity in this suggestion. His proposal for a single thrust, Montgomery argued, would also make the best use of the limited resources available. It would be better for at least some Allied formations to be given adequate maintenance so that they could exploit a fleeting opportunity than to hamstring all Allied formations by providing inadequate maintenance thinly but evenly over the entire front.

There was a very great deal to be said in favor of Montgomery's concept. And in purely military terms there was not much to be said in favor of the American alternative. Even if Allied resources had not been sufficient to maintain a force of forty divisions — Montgomery himself was soon talking in terms of a thrust by twenty divisions — a single Allied offensive would almost certainly have been sufficiently powerful to reach the Rhine and well beyond. General Siegfried Westphal, Rundstedt's chief of staff, later made the intelligent comment that *any* single concentrated thrust in September would have sufficed to bring about the collapse of the German forces in the west.

*General Jacob Devers' 6th Army Group, consisting of the French First and U.S. Seventh armies, became operational and passed under Eisenhower's command on September 15.

And General Günther Blumentritt, Westphal's predecessor, remarked, almost reproachfully, that a single thrust north of the Ruhr would certainly have enabled the western Allies to occupy Berlin and Prague ahead of the Russians.

Eisenhower, of course, was well aware that Montgomery's plan would require most of Bradley's 12th Army Group and all of General Jacob Devers' 6th Army Group to be halted so that the northern offensive could receive absolute priority in administrative support. He also believed, as he told Montgomery, that American public opinion "would not stand for it." And he knew, if he accepted Montgomery's proposal, what reaction could be expected from Bradley, Hodges, and Patton. These, however, are exactly the kinds of pressures a Supreme Commander is paid to withstand. During the campaign in northwest Europe, the Allies suffered some 750,000 casualties — and about 500,000 of these were suffered after the pause in September.

On August 24 Eisenhower agreed that the immediate "principal offensive mission" of the 12th Army Group would be to act as right-flank guard to Montgomery's advance and that Montgomery could coordinate the action of his army group with that of Bradley's left wing. A divergent attack eastward toward Metz would be delayed but not canceled. On September 4 Eisenhower formally ordered the 21st Army Group and the portion of the 12th Army Group northwest of the Ardennes to secure Antwerp and take the Ruhr, and the rest of the 12th Army Group to occupy the Siegfried Line opposite the Saar and to capture Frankfurt. Just as Hitler saw too many tempting prizes in Russia, Eisenhower saw too many in Germany. "An attack without *Schwerpunkt*," Hindenburg had long ago said, "is like a man without character." In any case, the Allies were now committed to an advance to the Rhine on a broad front and to offensives against both the Ruhr and the Saar.

For his part, Montgomery was too concerned with his northern attack to pay much attention to the opening of Antwerp. At a meeting on September 10, Eisenhower stressed the vital importance of getting Antwerp working for the Allies at an early date, but agreed that the 21st Army Group could first attempt to seize the crossings of the lower Rhine and the Maas. This was another compromise. It was far from being the advance of "a solid mass of some forty divisions" that Montgomery had advocated, but it *was* an advance in the vital northern sector. If it succeeded, the right flank of the Siegfried Line would be turned and the bulk of the German Fifteenth Army might be cut off. Absolute priority of supply was given to the 21st Army Group for this operation, which was code-named "Market Garden," but this decision was not taken by Eisenhower until September 12, and then only because Montgomery told him that otherwise a postponement would be inevitable.

Operation Market Garden called for the U.S. 101st Airborne Division to capture the canal crossings north of Eindhoven, the U.S. 82nd Airborne Division to take the bridges across the Maas at Grave and the Waal at Nijmegen, and the British 1st Airborne Division to drop farther north around Arnhem, where it would seize the bridges across the lower Rhine. This airborne, or Market, phase of the operation would be followed by an overland advance by the British XXX Corps (Lieutenant General Sir Brian Horrocks) to link up with each of the airborne divisions between Eindhoven and Arnhem. The British Second Army would then drive on to Zwolle preparatory to an advance along the eastern face of the Ruhr. The attack on the Ruhr was to be carried out in conjunction with an offensive by the U.S. First Army from a bridgehead across the Rhine between Bonn and Cologne. The plan was really no substitute for the heavily weighted advance Montgomery had desired. This attempt to drive seventy miles to Arnhem in two days actually was "a pencil-like thrust," and its success depended on winning a series of simultaneous battles, failure in any one of which would mean failure of the whole.

The first paratroops dropped early in the afternoon of September 17, taking the enemy by surprise. Dropping-accuracy was excellent in all three areas. The two more southerly drops were successful. The U.S. 101st Airborne Division took Eindhoven on the 18th and the U.S. 82nd Airborne Division captured the bridge at Heumen and the major bridge at Grave the same day. The bridges across the Waal at Nijmegen were not taken until the 20th, but they, too, were captured before the enemy could destroy them. The Guards Armored Division, moving by road from the bridgehead over the Meuse-Escaut Canal, linked up with both divisions on the 18th and pushed on to Nijmegen, where it was halted by stiffening German resistance. Two thirds of the operation was thus a brilliant success, but it had to succeed completely to justify itself.

At Arnhem the British 1st Airborne Division, with the Polish Parachute Brigade under command, suffered a series of misfortunes. In the first place, the British plan called for the paratroops to drop not on the objective, but some seven or eight miles to the west. The division did not all drop at once; half was to go in the first day, a quarter on the second lift, and the last quarter on the third lift. And just as the air lift was inadequate, so was fighter bomber support.

The II SS Panzer Corps had recently been withdrawn from the line and sent to Arnhem for resting and refitting, and was thus at hand to attack the British dropping zones. General Student, the commander of the German First Parachute Army, and Model, commander of Army Group B, were both immediately at hand to take charge, and they were highly competent, experienced officers. Once on the ground the British troops found that their wireless sets would not work. And — most serious of all — the British XXX Corps was unable to force its way north to link up with beleaguered paratroops. The weather also turned bad, so the scale of air supply and air support had to be sharply reduced. As a consequence, the remnants of the British 1st Airborne Division were withdrawn on the night of the 25th/26th.

With the failure of Market Garden, Europe was doomed to another winter of war. There was now no option for the Allies but to regroup, clear the Schelde Estuary, and prepare for a final offensive in the spring. Even now, Montgomery was slow to realize the importance of Antwerp. Le Havre had been taken on September 12, but demolitions had been so thorough that the port could not be used for nearly a month. On September 22 the Canadians fought their way into Boulogne, but again enemy demolitions delayed the use of the port until October 12. Calais was taken on October 1 but could not be used until November. In any case the capacity of all these ports together was insufficient to sustain a major offensive in the north, though the problem of gasoline supply was solved with the opening, late in October, of an underwater pipeline from Dungeness to Boulogne. The port of Dunkirk was invested but not attacked, and the German garrison held out until the end of the war.

In the middle of September, the Canadian First Army began the task of clearing the enemy from the Antwerp approaches. After two weeks of hard fighting the Allied lines had been advanced a few miles east of the city and both the Albert and the Antwerp-Turnhout canals had been crossed, but there were still Germans in the northern suburbs of Antwerp itself, and the enemy held Walcheren Island, the South Beveland peninsula, and the "Breskens Pocket" on the mainland south of the West Schelde.

While the clearance of the Antwerp approaches was going on, Allied operations elsewhere suffered from lack of adequate supplies. The British Second Army advanced slowly east and south toward Krefeld. The U.S. First Army, with Cologne as its objective, bogged down in close and bitter fighting around Aachen, which did not fall until October 21. And though Lieutenant General William H. Simpson's U.S. Ninth Army came into the line on Bradley's left flank on October 22, the strategic situation was not much improved. The Germans, forced back on their own lines of communications and taking every advantage of excellent defensive country, gave ground very stubbornly indeed. Patton's U.S. Third Army took Metz in November, but halted in front of the Siegfried Line and the Saar River. All the bright hopes of the summer had now narrowed down to the opening of Antwerp and the improvement of the administrative situation.

Only Eisenhower's insistence on the importance of Antwerp forced Montgomery to give "absolute priority," on October 16, to the clearance of the Schelde approaches. By the end of October, South Beveland and the eastern flank around Antwerp were secured, and by November 2 the Breskens Pocket was eliminated, after vicious fighting among the dikes, flooded fields, and polders. By November 8, Walcheren Island was taken. The first Allied convoy entered Antwerp on November 28, marking the end of the supply famine.

On October 18 it had been decided that the capture of the Ruhr should be left to Bradley's 12th Army Group. The U.S. Ninth Army would assist the British Second Army in clearing the west bank of the Rhine opposite the Ruhr. The U.S. First Army would seize a bridgehead over the Rhine south of Cologne, and to the south the U.S. Third Army would keep pace with the First. The Ruhr itself would be taken by a converging offensive by the U.S. Ninth, First, and Third armies. Farther south still General Devers' 6th Army Group would advance to the Rhine.

In spite of setbacks and delays, there were no deviations from this plan. In the wet November weather the British advanced to secure the line of the Maas. The U.S. Ninth Army then captured Gelsenkirchen and plodded forward to the Roer, which was reached on December 3. Seventeen American divisions were committed to this offensive, but on the right U.S. First Army had to fight bitterly to clear the Hürtgen Forest. The Roer could not be crossed because the Germans held the Schmidt dams, which could have flooded the area. When aerial bombing failed to destroy these dams, they had to be taken by laborious infantry assault, which began on December 13. All along this northern portion of the long battlefront, winter rains swelled the rivers, flooded the fields, and made movement off the roads almost impossible. In the south Devers' army group had launched an attack in the Vosges on November 14. The U.S. Seventh Army made slow going of it until the French burst through the Belfort Gap and advanced to the Rhine, thus turning the enemy's flank. Sarrebourg was taken on November 21, and Strasbourg fell the next day, but the French failed to clear the west bank of the Rhine and the Germans continued to hold out there around Colmar.

Eisenhower's broad-front strategy had meant that the Allies had to hold a front of almost 500 miles. Of course the enemy had to defend himself over the same distance, but the Siegfried Line and the Rhineland defenses enabled him to economize on troops. General Hasso von Manteuffel, commander of the Fifth Panzer Army, drew what was surely the right conclusion when he commented after the war, "Minor attacks planned and launched in a great variety of different ways [by the Allies] were unsuccessful everywhere and completely failed to create the preliminary conditions for a bigger offensive." Allied strategy had degenerated into a series of relatively weak, disconnected advances. This dispersion of effort forced Eisenhower to economize where he could, and he felt it safest to do so in the broken, hilly countryside of the Ardennes. Bradley's 12th Army Group had strong concentrations both north and south of the Ardennes, but between Trier and Monschau, in the same general area where the Germans had made their spectacular breakthrough in 1940, seventy-five miles of front were held by only the four divisions of Major General T. H. Middleton's U.S. VIII Corps. The risk was recognized and it was rightly calculated that an enemy counterattack in this area could be contained. The strength of the German blow, however, came as a serious surprise.

The Ardennes counteroffensive was the brain child of Hitler, who selected the area around Eifel and chose Antwerp as his objective. The idea was impossibly ambitious and displayed that interesting combination of lack of realism and a shrewd instinct for an enemy's weakness that often characterized the concepts of the Führer. Had the actual situation of his own forces corresponded to what he believed it to be, the concept would have been brilliant. As it was, the German plan was based largely on fantasy. The drawing in of autumn weather seriously curtailed Allied aerial reconnaissance, enabling the Germans to build up an extraordinary concentration of armor, undetected by Allied intelligence. Hitler managed to collect two panzer armies, the Sixth SS (Dietrich) and the Fifth (Manteuffel), and he reinforced his Seventh Army (Brandenburger).

Hitler issued the general plan of the battle on November 3. After infantry attacks had broken the American front between Monschau and Echternach, the armor would drive through, by-passing resistance and ignoring open flanks. The Meuse would be crossed between Liège and Namur, and the offensive would continue to Antwerp. If successful, this would cut the lines of communication of the U.S. First Army and the 21st Army Group, would result in the capture of vast Allied supply dumps, and would probably destroy twenty-five to thirty Allied divisions.

The *Schwerpunkt* of the attack was to be in the north, where the German lines were closest to the crossing of the Meuse. Here Dietrich's Sixth SS Panzer Army, of nine divisions including four panzer divisions, was to cross the Meuse on both sides of Liège and drive on to cross the Albert Canal between Maastricht and Antwerp. To the south, Manteuffel's Fifth Panzer Army, of seven divisions including four panzer divisions, was to cross the Meuse from a point west of Liège to Namur, advancing to act as flank guard for the SS troops. Farther south still Brandenburger's Seventh Army, of seven divisions, was to advance to the Meuse as a flank guard for the Fifth Panzer Army. Between six and seven additional divisions were to be in reserve.

Most of the German higher commanders involved felt that Antwerp was too far away for the panzers to reach and they deprecated the width of the frontage of attack, some 125 miles. They were sure that they could break the overextended front of the U.S. VIII Corps but did not believe they could reach the Meuse in the first two days, as the plan demanded. Also they very rightly worried about Allied counterattacks from both flanks at the base of the penetration. Hitler refused to modify the plan, and from his point of view he was right. Even large-scale local tactical successes were of no use to him. Nothing short of a miracle could now save the Third Reich, so he played for a miracle. Thus, in a sense, the German pattern in the west in late 1944 was a repetition of the one adopted in the spring of 1918, though Hitler's Ardennes counteroffensive never had the chance of success that Ludendorff's March offensive had had.

The German attack began on the morning of December 16 and gained its greatest initial success in the center, where the Fifth Panzer Army broke clean through the front of the U.S. 106th and 28th divisions. The Sixth SS Panzer Army achieved mixed results. Stavelot was reached the first day and panzer forces advanced toward the headquarters of the U.S. First Army at Spa. A green American division, the 99th, retreated in considerable disorder, but the veteran U.S. 2nd Division fought splendidly and frustrated the enemy's plan of quickly reaching the Meuse.

The American high command reacted reasonably quickly. The U.S. 7th Armored Division was sent down from the north on December 17 to support the left wing of the U.S. VIII Corps. It reached St. Vith, south of Monschau, and held out at this important road junction for the next three days, assisted by some rallied units of the 106th and 28th divisions. This stand threw the Germans off schedule, and though renewed attacks by the German LXVI Corps finally forced the Americans to withdraw, on the night of December 21, the delay had enabled Hodges to bring up the U.S. 1st and 9th divisions to hold the northern shoulder around Monschau.

Bastogne, in the south, was an even more vital communications center than St. Vith, in the north; but here, too, an American armored division, the 10th, intervened promptly in the battle. On December 19 the Panzer Lehr Division reached Bastogne, some thirty miles from its starting line, but even though it was reinforced by the 26th Volks Grenadier Division, it was unable to capture the town, where elements of Middleton's VIII Corps and the U.S. 101st Airborne Division were resolutely holding out. The Fifth Panzer Army now ordered the XLVII Panzer Corps to by-pass the Americans surrounded at Bastogne and drive on westward.

That day at Verdun, at a conference attended by Eisenhower, Bradley, Patton, and Devers, Patton suggested that the enemy should be allowed to advance in the center so that he could subsequently be cut off and annihilated. (His actual words, as quoted by Eisenhower, were: "Hell, let's have the guts to let the sons of bitches go all the way to Paris. Then we'll really cut 'em off and chew 'em up.") There was much to be said for the idea. Of all that group gathered at Verdun, Patton had the most highly developed killer instinct, but Eisenhower replied that the Germans were not to be allowed to cross the Meuse.* The plan decided on was to hold in the north around Monschau and to launch a strong counterattack from the south. Patton was ordered to concentrate three divisions around Arlon and to launch his counterattack along the Bastogne-Houffalize axis not later than December 23.

The next day, the 20th, Eisenhower placed all the Allied forces north of the German penetration under Montgomery's command. These consisted of the Canadian First and British Second armies, the U.S. Ninth Army, and part of the U.S. First Army. Bradley remained in command of the American forces south of the penetration. Montgomery at once imposed a coherent plan on the battle, moving the British XXX Corps to guard the crossings of the Meuse around Namur and deciding not to counterattack until he had stabilized the situation and could strike a coordinated blow. His conduct of operations was excellent and contributed substantially to the Allied success. Unfortunately, he held a press conference on January 7 in which, according to the reports, he implied that he had been called in only in the nick of time to save his American allies from defeat. The press accounts, adroitly misrepresented by German propaganda, did nothing to foster inter-Allied goodwill.

The Fifth Panzer Army continued to make some progress and could almost certainly have made more had it not had to provide much of its own left-flank protection because of the slowness of the

---

*General Horrocks, commanding the British XXX Corps, had much the same idea. He wanted to let the Germans cross the Meuse between Louvain and Namur in order to destroy them more completely. Montgomery gave Horrocks the same reply that Eisenhower gave Patton: none of the enemy was to be allowed to cross the Meuse.

German Seventh Army's advance. Also Hitler was unwilling to shift the *Schwerpunkt* of the offensive from the area of the Sixth SS Panzer Army to that of the Fifth Panzer Army, partly at least because he favored the ideologically sound SS over the army. He eventually sent the 2nd SS and 12th SS Panzer divisions to support the Fifth Panzer Army, but this move came too late.

By the 24th, leading elements of the Fifth Panzer Army had driven to within three miles of Dinant, but this was as far as the enemy offensive reached. In the north the Sixth SS Panzer Army could make no progress, and in the south the Seventh Army had fallen far behind. Bastogne still held out, with the aid of airdropped supplies, and the weather now began to clear, allowing the Allied air forces to attack German communications with great effect. The German offensive now ground to a complete standstill. The defensive perimeter of Bastogne had been reduced to only sixteen miles, but the Americans continued to resist ferociously. When a heavy attack on Christmas Day was beaten back, the Fifth Panzer Army went over to the defensive. In the late afternoon of December 26 a spearhead of the U.S. 4th Armored Division from Patton's Third Army fought its way into Bastogne.

This was the signal for a renewed series of strong German attacks. They continued on Hitler's orders until January 3, engaging a maximum of nine German divisions. The American defenders, in one of the epic fights of the war, repelled all the assaults until, on January 3, counterattacks by the U.S. VII Corps in the north and the Third Army from the south, both directed toward Houffalize, finally forced the Germans to stop trying to capture Bastogne and turn their attention to extricating themselves from the salient they had created. The enemy did have one success of a kind when, on New Year's Day, the Luftwaffe launched an attack on American and British airfields, destroying 260 aircraft for a German loss of 200. The Allies, however, could much better afford such a loss than could the Luftwaffe, so here, too, the Germans received the worse of the exchange.

The German withdrawal began on January 10, but the two Allied attacks did not meet at Houffalize until the 16th. By the time the pincers closed, the enemy had escaped again, though he had had to abandon large numbers of vehicles and much equipment. By the end of January the Germans, having lost much irreplaceable equipment, were back at their starting line, much reduced in numbers and — for the first time — convinced that they had lost the war. The task of conducting a successful defense on the western borders of the Reich had now become patently impossible. The Americans suffered some seventy-six thousand casualties in the Ardennes fighting and the German toll was probably higher.

Possibly the single most important factor in the Allies' eventual success was their command of the air; after December 26 panzer units were allowed to move only by night, and when the weather cleared the Allied aerial superiority was decisive. Hitler's last throw had probably prolonged the war by six weeks. More significant in the long run was the fact that it had been made in the west, for the Soviet offensive that began on January 12 was to carry the Red Army far into areas that would otherwise have been conquered by the western Allies.

The last phase of the Second World War in northwest Europe has only a slight and somewhat morbid interest for the student of military affairs, for the German forces were so outnumbered, so bankrupt of strategy, and so overwhelmed by material superiority that they were unable to put up any effective defense. This was not the case in Italy. In the fighting south of Rome, Kesselring had had to commit eighteen of his twenty-three divisions, and most of these had suffered very heavy losses. Early in June, however, OKW had sent some eight divisions to Italy to slow the retreat of the Fourteenth Army and to form a reserve in Lombardy. Consequently, Kesselring was able to reunite his Tenth and Fourteenth armies and to slow the Allied pursuit. He managed to find six divisions to use as a reserve and for work on the fortification of the Gothic Line in the northern Apennines while he held the front with nineteen divisions. By August 4 the Germans were behind the Arno and, on the Adriatic side, the Metauro, in relative security.

Although the Gothic Line was 200 miles long, its defenses were formidable, and only the last 50 or so miles on the Adriatic coast ran through reasonably flat terrain. On paper, at least, the enemy also enjoyed numerical superiority; he had twenty infantry and six panzer or panzer grenadier divisions plus six Italian divisions to the Allies' seventeen infantry and four armored divisions. All the German formations, however, were so far below strength that a comparison on a divisional basis is misleading.

Alexander's plan of attack called for an assault by the Eighth Army toward Rimini on the Adriatic, followed by a secondary offensive with five divisions through the central mountains toward Bologna. The attack on the Gothic Line began at midnight on August 25/26, taking the enemy by surprise. A bridgehead across the Metauro was seized without difficulty, but the advance to the Foglia River entailed some hard fighting, and three days passed before the Eighth Army found itself up against the Gothic Line proper. By September 2, however, the British V Corps and Canadian I Corps were well inside the main Gothic defenses on a twenty-mile front.

Hopes were high in the Allied armies during those sunny September days. The dust was atrocious but the Adriatic was unbelievably blue, like the robe of Our Lady of Victories. Traffic signs along the roads leading to the front read, "Drive carefully if you want to see Vienna." However, Kesselring threw in his last reserve and successfully halted the Allied advance. Heavy rain began to fall on September 6 — unusually early — and for eighteen bitter days, when air support was minimal and the countryside beside the roads turned into swamp, the Allies could only inch forward. Rimini fell on September 21, but an offensive toward Bologna by the Fifth Army, begun on October 2, had to be abandoned after twenty-five days of slow progress. By this time the Eighth Army's advance had also stopped, seven river lines and fifty miles short of the Po.

One more outburst of sharp fighting was to occur in the last month of the disappointing year. On November 28, Alexander ordered both the Eighth and Fifth armies to make one more attempt to take Bologna. The operation would begin by a crossing of the Santerno River by the Eighth Army on December 7, followed by an advance up Highway 9. The Fifth Army would drive up Highway 65.

Kesselring had been hospitalized as the result of a motor accident, and Vietinghoff had assumed command of Army Group C. General Leese had been sent to Burma as Commander-in-Chief Allied Land Forces Southeast Asia, and command of the Eighth Army passed to General Sir Richard L. McCreery. Maitland Wilson was sent to Washington early in December, when Sir John Dill, the head of the British Joint Staff Mission, died. Wilson's place as Supreme Allied Commander Mediterranean was taken by Alexander, who was promoted to field marshal on December 5. General Mark Clark assumed command of the Allied armies in Italy as commander of the 15th Army Group. The Fifth Army was taken over by Lieutenant General Lucian K. Truscott, Jr., who had distinguished himself as the commander of the U.S. VI Corps at Anzio.

The Allies, short of ammunition,* with limited air support because of bad weather, without adequate reinforcement, and fighting in extremely difficult country, were unable to take Bologna in 1944. Indeed, in view of these factors the wisdom of ordering the offensive at all may be questioned. On December 4 the Canadians took Ravenna, and the Eighth Army struggled on across the Lamone River to the Senio, which was reached by the middle of the month. Clark now warned his army commanders that there would be one final "all-out attack" to take Bologna and cross the Senio, but when a German coun-

---

*As far back as the middle of August, Wilson had warned that the curtailment of production of certain types of gun ammunition would result in a worldwide shortage. Production was resumed too late, and by the middle of November the Allies in Italy were seriously short of ammunition.

terattack on December 26 had a limited success against the U.S. 92nd Division, Alexander ordered his forces to go over to the defensive and "to concentrate on making a real success of our spring offensive."

During January the Eighth Army lost three divisions, which were sent to Greece to help prevent the takeover of that country by the communist organization ELAS, or People's National Army of Liberation. This diversion of force was necessary but it tied down some eighty thousand Allied troops until near the end of the war. Moreover, the Canadian I Corps was withdrawn from Italy during February and March, to come under the command of the Canadian First Army. When the Combined Chiefs of Staff met in Malta on January 30, on their way to the Yalta Conference, they decided that the Italian theater had served its purpose, and directed Alexander to do no more than conduct "limited offensive actions . . . to contain the Germans."

The Allied armies in Italy still consisted of 536,000 men in the spring of 1945, as well as some 70,000 Italians organized in four combat groups. Ammunition and equipment shortages had been rectified, and the Luftwaffe could deploy almost nothing against the 258 squadrons, totaling more than 4000 aircraft, at Alexander's disposal. Some 60,000 Italian partisans were operating in the German rear, forcing Vietinghoff* to use troops he could ill afford as a guard for his lines of communication.

General Clark's plan was to launch converging attacks to trap the German forces between the Apennines and the Po. The Fifth Army would thrust along the Bologna-Verona-Lake Garda axis, while the Eighth Army drove northwest toward Ferrara and then northeast toward Venice and Trieste. So that full air support could be given to each army, the Eighth Army would attack three days before the Fifth Army.

At seven o'clock on the evening of April 9, the main offensive began with an assault-crossing of the Senio by the British V Corps and the Polish II Corps. Because of the close and broken nature of the countryside, each Allied advance, of even a few miles, had to be planned virtually as a set-piece operation. Truscott's Fifth Army attacked on the 14th, with the U.S. IV Corps driving up the left bank of the Reno. Under cover of massive air support, the U.S. II Corps attacked up the east bank of the river on the 15th, but it was not until the 20th that the last German defenders in the Apennines were overrun and the Americans broke through to cut Highway 9 west of Bologna.

The German front now began to collapse, forcing Vietinghoff to

*Vietinghoff took over command of Army Group C on March 11, when Kesselring succeeded Rundstedt as Commander-in-Chief West.

order a retirement to the Po. The Allies closed the trap on the 23rd, when the Fifth and Eighth armies linked up west of Ferrara. By the 25th organized resistance south of the Po came to an end. Some of the enemy got away by swimming the river, but more than fifty thousand German soldiers were captured.

The campaign in Italy was now as good as over. Gone were the painful advances measured in yards, with each yard being paid for in blood. As the Allied armies fanned out into the plain of the Po, there was no longer anything to stop them. The partisans in northern Italy redoubled their activities in these days, and on the 28th they shot Mussolini and his mistress, Clara Petacci, near Lake Como, and hung the bodies by their heels in a public square in Milan. Barbarous though the episode was, the world recognized its rough justice. Venice was entered on the 29th.

Long before this — as early, indeed, as February — some senior German commanders in Italy had been seeking a way to surrender, but negotiations had dragged out until after the Allies had launched their offensive. On April 29 the instrument of surrender was signed at Caserta, but Kesselring, who the day before had been made Supreme Commander of both the northwest Europe and Italian theaters, refused to sanction it. However, the news of Hitler's suicide satisfied his misguided sense of honor, and on May 1 Kesselring consented to the capitulation. When the cease-fire came into effect at noon on the 2nd, the remaining 207,000 Germans in Italy surrendered.

On the eastern front, meanwhile, a Soviet offensive, begun on June 9, had driven Finland out of the war by September 19. Five days before this, the three Baltic army groups and the Leningrad Army Group launched an offensive against Army Group North, attacking toward Riga. The Germans fell back nearly 200 miles to avoid encirclement, and the First Baltic Army Group, strongly reinforced, then drove west to the Baltic, which it reached on both sides of Memel on October 10. Army Group North retreated into Courland, where it was cut off.

Belgrade was occupied on October 20, 1944, by the Third Ukrainian Army Group and Yugoslav partisans. The Second and Third Ukrainian army groups then advanced up the Danube valley toward Budapest. As the Russians penetrated into the Hungarian plain, German resistance stiffened, for troops from Army Group E in Greece and Albania and from Army Group F on the Adriatic and Aegean reinforced the defense of the German Sixth and Eighth armies. The Russians reached the outskirts of Budapest in the first week of November but were unable to capture the city immediately. A bridgehead was seized over the Danube south of Budapest on

November 29, and the Russians then struck north to Lake Balaton. A fresh offensive encircled Budapest on December 29. On that day a provisional Hungarian government declared war on Germany. Budapest did not fall at this time, however, and for the next six weeks was the scene of bloody fighting.

On the 600 miles of front that ran along the Narew and the Vistula to the Carpathians, the Germans had only some seventy-five under-strength divisions. Hitler still refused to withdraw Army Group North and shorten the Vistula line. Instead, he decided to save the 150,000 Germans surrounded in Budapest. He moved the IV SS Panzer Corps from Warsaw to Budapest at the end of December, and in the middle of February, when the Ardennes counteroffensive had failed, he moved the Sixth SS Panzer Army to Hungary. In January the Germans made considerable progress, coming to within twenty miles of Budapest, but on the 27th Marshal Fyodor Tolbukhin counterattacked and the relieving forces were thrown back. Budapest fell on February 13, with the loss of 110,000 German prisoners.

The final Russian offensive of the war had begun on the morning of January 12 and, predictably, struck the attenuated German line along the Vistula. Marshal Ivan S. Konev's First Ukrainian Army Group broke out from the Baranovichi bridgehead between Cracow and Sandomir with seventy divisions. The enormously outnumbered Germans could put up no effective defense. Zhukov's First Byelorussian Army Group attacked two days later from bridgeheads south of Warsaw. Konev took Kielce on the 15th and drove on to cross the middle Oder at several places. Zhukov captured Warsaw on the 17th, took Lodz, and by-passed Poznan on the 22nd. His troops had reached the Oder on a broad front by February 3. Berlin lay only thirty-five miles farther on. Meanwhile Rokossovsky's Second Byelorussian Army Group and Marshal Ivan Chernyakhovsky's Third Byelorussian Army Group drove northwest into East Prussia, reaching the Baltic east of Danzig by the 26th and cutting off the twenty-five German divisions in East Prussia. A hole 200 miles wide had been torn in the Vistula line and through this the Soviet forces poured at will.

But by the end of the first week of February, when the Germans were standing on the Oder-Neisse line, their front had shrunk from 600 miles to a mere 200. Hitler rushed reinforcements to the east and for a brief time, while the Red Army drew its breath, it appeared as though the front had stabilized. Farther south in Hungary, the Second and Third Ukrainian army groups counterattacked on March 16 and achieved a clean breakthrough on both sides of Lake Balaton. Two weeks later the Red Army crossed into Austria.

With the thousand-year Reich crumbling, the leaders of the Allied powers held yet another conference, this time at Yalta in the Crimea. The Yalta Conference opened on February 4, with Stalin in a strong bargaining position. President Roosevelt took the chair, at the Russian dictator's tactful request, and it soon became apparent that the President was dominated by two principal ideas: he was determined, at almost all costs, to obtain Russian cooperation in the war with Japan and in the postwar world, and he saw, in the same noble vision that had inspired Wilson a generation earlier, international affairs being run by a parliament of nations that would have no further need of alliances, spheres of influence, or balances of power. Men's views of history, like their ethics, are ultimately shaped by their metaphysics, and Roosevelt's only metaphysic was a liberalism whose premise was the perfectability of man.

At the Moscow and Teheran conferences, no firm decisions had been taken as to the future of Germany, so at Yalta this and other unresolved war aims had to be settled quickly; otherwise victory would take the Allies unawares. Churchill, who had undoubtedly been Britain's greatest wartime leader since Pitt, was nevertheless a man of his class and generation. His vision of the world was perhaps too much in conformity with the past: he foresaw the continued existence of the British Empire, of European pre-eminence, and of social and political values that the two great wars with Germany had already destroyed. Thus Roosevelt looked starry-eyed toward a future impossible of realization and Churchill clung to a past that could not be revived.

Stalin was a realist. The rootless grandson of a Russian serf, he had no past to look to, and as a convinced Marxist his vision of the future was limited by the dogmas of power. He agreed to join Roosevelt's United Nations and to join the United States in its war against Japan within two or three months after the defeat of Germany. He agreed also to Churchill's request that France should have a zone of occupation in Germany after the war. For these modest concessions he sought and was granted advantages that enabled him, within a few years, to fix his grip on all of eastern Europe. In the Far East he was promised the Kurile Islands, Southern Sakhalin, the port of Dairen, Port Arthur, an interest in the Manchurian railways, and a sphere of influence in Outer Mongolia. At his insistence the eastern border of Poland would be the Curzon Line and the temporary western border of Poland would be the line of the Oder-Neisse rivers. The Lublin Committee, now recognized by the Soviet Union as the provisional government of Poland, would be broadened by the inclusion of some Polish exiles, and although Poland was promised "free" elections, Stalin successfully resisted all suggestions that those elections be supervised by an impartial international body. Britain was the junior partner of the United States at Yalta, and Churchill could do little to make his views prevail. The Soviet Union was in a very strong position, with her armies already occupying most of the territory that Stalin coveted.

So Yalta fixed the pattern for the postwar world — or so it seemed for a decade or two. New factors, unforeseen in 1945, have now cast a somewhat different light on Stalin's diplomatic victory at Yalta. Perhaps the realist did not get the best of the bargain after all. The rise of communist China and her quarrel with the Soviet Union, provoked in part by the concessions Stalin received at China's expense at Yalta, have raised the question as to whether the east European satellites of the Soviet Union are an asset or a liability.

But this was for the future. Meanwhile, in the west, Eisenhower's ponderous plan was to clear the west bank of the Rhine from Nijmegen to Coblenz while the U.S. Seventh Army eliminated the Germans holding out in the area bounded by the Moselle, the Saar, and the Rhine rivers. The Ruhr would then be taken by a double envelopment from north and south. When all this had been done, the Allies would advance deeper into Germany.

The Canadian-British attack between the Maas and the Rhine went in on February 8 under the cover of one of the heaviest barrages of the war in the west. Much of the ground was flooded and the attacking infantry had to be carried into battle in amphibious "Buffaloes." The main defenses of the Siegfried Line were penetrated on the second day, but it was February 23 before the U.S. Ninth Army could attack north toward Düsseldorf. By then nine German divisions had been sent to oppose the Canadians and the British XXX Corps. Nevertheless, Cleve was captured on February 11 and the Reichswald was cleared by the 13th; by the 20th the Canadian First Army had forced its way ahead between fifteen and twenty miles. However, much hard fighting still lay ahead in the Hochwald and at Xanten.

The American attack on the 23rd, launched by six divisions of the U.S. Ninth and First armies, initially met considerable resistance, but the German defenses had been thinned to reinforce the Canadian front and by March 2 the Americans had captured München-Gladbach and linked up with the Canadians west of Venlo. The U.S. First Army captured Cologne and the U.S. Third Army reached the Rhine and cut off the enemy forces in the Eifel. By the 11th, the 21st Army Group held the line of the Rhine between Düsseldorf and Nijmegen, and the U.S. 9th Armored Division of the Third Army had captured the undestroyed Ludendorff railway bridge across the river at Remagen. Five American divisions were soon dug in on the east bank, where they held out despite repeated German attempts to eject them. On the 9th, the U.S. Third Army reached the Rhine at Andernach and soon established contact with the First Army.

On March 15, Lieutenant General Alexander Patch's U.S. Seventh

Army attacked the Siegfried defenses on the southern face of the triangle bounded by the Moselle, the Saar, and the Rhine; the Third Army attacked the apex north of Saarbrücken; and Major General Manton Eddy's XII Corps struck south toward Mainz and Worms. By the 21st the west bank had been cleared from Coblenz to Mannheim, and four days later all organized resistance west of the river had ceased. Some 293,000 Germans were taken prisoner during the clearing of the Rhineland; total German casualties were about 360,000.

In the "Thunderclap" attack on Dresden by RAF Bomber Command on the night of February 13/14 and by the Americans the following day, this city of 600,000, which was then crowded with refugees, was almost obliterated. Total casualties are a matter of speculation, but they were enormous — and totally unnecessary, since this slaughter of civilians did nothing to win the war.

Montgomery's plan to cross the Rhine with the 21st Army Group was perhaps overly deliberate, considering the state of the German defenses. The crossing was made by two British and two American divisions between Wesel and Rees on the evening of March 23. Only light resistance was encountered and the attackers pressed rapidly inland. The next morning the U.S. XVIII Airborne Corps, consisting of the British 6th and U.S. 17th Airborne divisions, landed close behind the front. By the 28th the Allies had established a large bridgehead over the lower Rhine.

Now the Canadian First Army was directed into Holland, and the British Second and U.S. Ninth armies toward the Elbe. The right wing of the Ninth Army and the U.S. First Army would encircle the Ruhr. On March 25 the First Army attacked eastward to link up three days later with the U.S. Third Army near Gressen. On April 1 contact was established between the First and Ninth armies at Lippstadt, and the Ruhr was isolated. In this ruined waste Model's Army Group B, which still had some 325,000 soldiers, was trapped. By the 19th all resistance had collapsed. Model committed suicide; he was neither the first nor the last of Hitler's marshals to seek this way out of his difficulties.

Germany was now at its last gasp. Isolated units sometimes still fought hard but there was nothing that could be called a coordinated defense. Kassel was stubbornly defended and the U.S. First Army had to fight for a week to subdue resistance in the Harz Mountains. Elsewhere the Allies advanced at will, sometimes discovering caches of Nazi treasure and sometimes liberating the prisoners in horrible Nazi concentration camps. The Allied armies poured into the Reich through a 200-mile-wide gap.

On the northern flank the British Second Army crossed the Weser and raced toward Bremen and the Elbe. Lübeck was captured on May 2, thus saving Denmark from being liberated by the Russians. The Canadian First Army liberated Holland and drove into Germany toward Emden and Wilhelmshaven. The Ninth Army had reached the Elbe near Magdeburg on April 11, and the following day American columns crossed the river only seventy-five miles from Berlin. The U.S. First Army closed up to the Mulde, a tributary of the Elbe, after capturing Leipzig on the 18th. Patton's Third Army crossed into Czechoslovakia and was within striking distance of Prague when Eisenhower ordered it to halt along the Carlsbad-Pilsen-Budejovice line.

In the south Devers' 6th Army Group drove to the Swiss border and linked up with Alexander's troops advancing in northern Italy. The U.S. Seventh Army captured Nuremberg on April 20, on the 22nd the French captured Stuttgart. Munich was entered on the 30th and Salzburg and Berchtesgaden were taken on May 4. There was no "National Redoubt" in Bavaria and no fanatical Nazi resistance there.

On the afternoon of April 12, President Roosevelt had died at his home in Warm Springs and was succeeded in office by Vice President Harry Truman. The British prime minister, Winston Churchill, was to be dismissed from office in July by the British electorate, a strange reward for his years of service during the darkest times of the war. Thus the two great partners of the western Allies both had new leaders to implement the peace. It made far less difference to the future that the German dictator committed suicide in his bunker beneath the Reichschancellery in Berlin on April 30 when Russian forces were almost upon him.

Marshal Zhukov had broken through the Oder-Neisse defenses on the 16th and had reached the suburbs of Berlin within five days. Meanwhile Konev had driven down to the ruins of Dresden.

Eisenhower ordered his troops to halt on the Elbe on April 21, the same time as he ordered the halt in Czechoslovakia. On that day the Russians and Americans met at Torgau on the Elbe, and Germany was cut in two. On May 4 the representatives of Admiral Dönitz, whom Hitler had designated as his successor, surrendered all the German forces in northwest Germany, Denmark, and Holland to Montgomery in a brief ceremony on Lüneburg Heath. Army Group C made a similar surrender in the south the next day. After the signing of a general surrender at Reims on the 7th, the Second World War in Europe officially came to an end at midnight on May 8.

In the Far East the war against Japan had been as much as won by the end of 1943, though bitter fighting remained to be done. In the Southwest Pacific MacArthur, with eight American and seven Australian divisions, strongly supported by naval and air forces, moved along the northern New Guinea coast in a series of leapfrogs that brought him ever nearer his obsessional goal, the Philippines. Between May and September the Americans captured Wakde, Biak, Noemfoor, and Morotai islands, while the First Australian Army was conducting an expensive, and probably unnecessary, mopping-up campaign in eastern New Guinea and the Solomons. The conquest of Rabaul, which would certainly have been a bloody affair, was not now considered necessary.

Meanwhile, Nimitz was making good progress in the Northern Pacific area. In February Kwajalein and Eniwetok were captured, and Truk in the Carolines was hit hard by a carrier strike. On June 15 some twenty thousand Americans landed on Saipan in the Mariana Islands, but the thirty-two thousand Japanese defenders resisted so desperately that the American forces had to be heavily reinforced. On the 19th, when a carrier force under Vice Admiral Jisaburo Ozawa attacked Vice Admiral Marc A. Mitscher's Task Force 58 in the Philippine Sea, the Americans shot down 227 Japanese aircraft for a loss of only 26 of their own planes. This "Great Marianas Turkey Shoot" destroyed the Japanese carrier capability for the rest of the war.

On Saipan heavy fighting continued until July 9, costing the Americans over three thousand dead and ten thousand wounded. Virtually all the Japanese defenders were killed. Tinian was taken at the end of July, and after Guam fell on August 11, B29 Superfortresses began bombing Japan.

On July 18 General Tojo was replaced by General Kuniaki Koiso, who was resolved to persevere in the war. By now Japan was seriously short of oil, largely as the result of tanker sinkings by American submarines based in Australia and Pearl Harbor. Indeed, the Japanese supply system was so mortally damaged that it is doubtful that the capture of the Philippines was necessary to complete the strangulation process. However, American public opinion and MacArthur's desire to fulfill his promise to return made it very difficult to adopt the strategy suggested by Admiral King and other naval officers, which was to by-pass the Philippines and strike next at Taiwan or Okinawa as a prelude to the invasion of Japan proper.

On the morning of October 20, four divisions of General Walter Krueger's Sixth Army landed on Leyte in the central Philippines. Between October 23 and the 26th this invading force was in acute danger because of a sudden threat to its transports and supply ships in Leyte Gulf. Admiral William F. Halsey's 3rd Fleet was lured north by Ozawa's fleet carriers, leaving the San Bernardino Strait un-

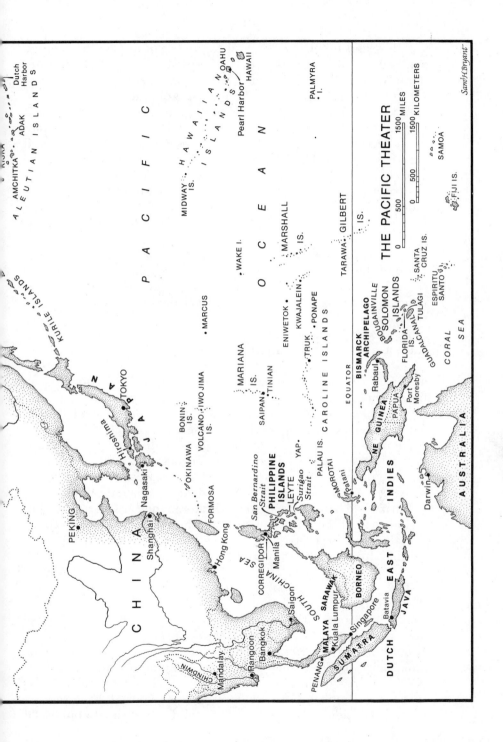

THE PACIFIC THEATER

Sam H. Bryant

ALEUTIAN ISLANDS
Dutch Harbor
ADAK
AMCHITKA
KISKA

KURILE ISLANDS

PACIFIC OCEAN

HAWAIIAN ISLANDS
MIDWAY IS.
OAHU
Pearl Harbor
HAWAII
PALMYRA I.

WAKE I.
MARCUS

MARIANA IS.
SAIPAN
TINIAN

VOLCANO-IWO JIMA IS.
BONIN IS.

OKINAWA

JAPAN
TOKYO
Hitoshima
Nagasaki

FORMOSA

PEKING
CHINA
Shanghai
Hong Kong

San Bernardino Strait
PHILIPPINE ISLANDS
LEYTE
Surigao Strait
YAP
PALAU IS.
MOROTAI
Patani

CORREGIDOR
Manila

SOUTH CHINA SEA
Saigon
Bangkok
Rangoon
Mandalay
CHINDWIN
PENANG
MALAYA
SARAWAK
Kuala Lumpur
Singapore
Batavia
BORNEO
JAVA
SUMATRA
DUTCH EAST INDIES

MARSHALL IS.
ENIWETOK
KWAJALEIN
TRUK
PONAPE
CAROLINE ISLANDS

TARAWA
GILBERT IS.

EQUATOR

BISMARCK ARCHIPELAGO
Rabaul
NE GUINEA
PAPUA
Port Moresby
BOUGAINVILLE
SOLOMON ISLANDS
FLORIDA IS.
GUADALCANAL
TULAGI
SANTA CRUZ IS.
ESPIRITU SANTO

CORAL SEA

Darwin

AUSTRALIA

SANTA CRUZ IS.

FIJI IS.
SAMOA

0   500   1500 MILES
0   500   1500 KILOMETERS

guarded, and two Japanese naval forces began to pass through the San Bernardino and Surigao straits respectively. Although Vice Admiral Thomas C. Kinkaid's 7th Fleet severely defeated the Japanese forces emerging from Surigao Strait, Vice Admiral Takeo Kurita's 1st Attack Force passed unchallenged through the San Bernardino Strait into Leyte Gulf. Halsey turned back much too late, but Kurita, suddenly deciding that his line of retreat was being cut off, timidly retired before he did much damage. This Battle of Leyte Gulf cost the Japanese four fleet carriers, three battleships, nine cruisers, and eight destroyers. Although many American ships were badly damaged, only one light carrier, two escort carriers, and three destroyers had been sunk. After Leyte Gulf, Japan was no longer a naval force to be reckoned with.

On land the Japanese belatedly decided to offer their main resistance on Leyte rather than on Luzon. By December Yamashita had some sixty thousand soldiers on Leyte, but by then Krueger had three times as many. For the Japanese, who had neither naval nor aerial superiority, the reinforcement of Leyte was a difficult and enormously expensive task. Shipload after shipload of troops drowned en route as a result of aerial attacks, and of the 1600 aircraft the Japanese tried to fly into the island only some 400 arrived. By New Year's Day all organized resistance on Leyte had been crushed. American casualties, including wounded, were under sixteen thousand; Japanese casualties were about seventy thousand, almost all of them killed.

On December 15 the weak Japanese garrison on Mindoro, just south of Luzon, was overcome. Krueger's Sixth Army now launched the main assault against Luzon. The Japanese had only a handful of aircraft available for defense, but their kamikaze attacks were to sink seventeen American ships and seriously damage another twenty.

Burma had become a secondary theater in the Far Eastern war, just as Italy had in the European one, and the front in China was comatose. Early in 1944, however, Stilwell began to advance into Burma, up the Hukawng valley, and in the Arakan a British corps moved southward toward Akyab.

The Japanese also took the offensive in March, attacking into Assam in an attempt to capture Imphal and Kohima. General Sir Geoffrey Scoones's IV Corps of three divisions held out in Imphal and was supplied by air, while a small British force under Colonel Hugh Richards held Kohima. The Japanese offensive, persisted in too long, failed in June, when Lieutenant General Montagu Stopford's XXXIII Corps, moving down from the north, linked up with a strong sortie from Imphal. Japanese losses in this campaign were very severe; more soldiers died of starvation and disease than of wounds. Of the eighty-five thousand troops the Japanese deployed, some sixty-five thousand died. British casualties amounted to about seventeen thousand. Stopford now captured Ukhrul and mopped up the surrounding area while the IV Corps advanced south into the Imphal plain, pursuing the retreating Japanese to the Chindwin River, which was reached in July.

In China a Japanese spring offensive forced the United States Fourteenth Air Force to evacuate a number of its forward airfields, but Stilwell's advance on the northern front in Burma (with five Chinese divisions, the British 36th Division, and the "Mars Brigade," which included an American regiment) resulted in the capture of Myitkyina on August 3. With the fall of Myitkyina the Japanese lost their main base in the north, and suffered some ten thousand casualties in the fighting. Stilwell's aim now was to cross the Irrawaddy and link up to the east with Chiang Kai-shek's Yunnan armies, which were advancing from the Salween River toward Namhkan. Stilwell himself was recalled in October because of persistent disagreements between himself and Chiang. He was replaced by Major General Albert C. Wedemeyer as adviser to the Chinese Nationalists and by Lieutenant General Daniel Sultan as field force commander on the northern front. The advance against the Japanese Thirty-third Army was delayed when Chiang recalled two of his best Chinese divisions to help check a Japanese advance on Kunming in China, but Bhamo and Indaw both fell in December. On the 16th of that month Sultan's troops made contact with General William J. Slim's Fourteenth Army. By the end of January 1945, Sultan was at Namhkan and had linked up with the Yunnan armies. The land route to China was now reopened.

In the Arakan, Slim launched an offensive, on December 12, to seize the airfields south of Akyab, which fell without resistance on January 2. Mountbatten's plans to clear central Burma and capture Rangoon had to go forward even though it was known that the monsoon came early in May and would end the campaigning season. In March 1945 the British 19th Division advanced from its bridgehead over the Irrawaddy to capture Mandalay on the 9th. The 7th and 20th divisions drove south to reach Prome on May 2. At the same time the 5th and 17th divisions entered Pegu just north of Rangoon. The previous day British paratroops had dropped on Elephant Point, Rangoon, and on the 2nd amphibious assault troops found the city abandoned by the Japanese. That afternoon the monsoon broke.

After the Battle of Leyte Gulf and the liberation of the Philippines the war against Japan entered its final phase. The American plan was to capture Iwo Jima in the Bonin Islands and Okinawa in the Ryukyu

Archipelago as preliminaries to a landing on the westernmost Japanese home island of Kyushu in November of 1945. After Kyushu had fallen, the main island of Honshu would be invaded. No one was in any doubt that this program would entail bitter fighting and heavy losses, for Japan would be defended desperately and the Japanese army still numbered well over five million men.

At dawn on February 19, 1945, Admiral Spruance's forces landed on the tiny island of Iwo Jima, which was dominated to the south by the extinct volcano, Mount Suribachi. Iwo Jima was only 750 miles from Tokyo, and its possession by the Americans would enable fighter escort to be provided the B-29s attacking Japan from the Marianas and would provide an emergency landing field for returning bombers. By now the air offensive against Japan had brought much of the country's industrial life to a standstill. Yokohama, Tokyo, and Nagoya, the center of the Japanese aircraft industry, had been almost destroyed, but though it was obvious that Japan had lost the war, the ruling military clique refused to contemplate surrender.

The fighting on Iwo Jima was intense, but by the end of the third day the marines controlled one third of the island. On February 23 a patrol of the 28th Marine Regiment hoisted the Stars and Stripes on the summit of Mount Suribachi, and were caught in the act by a photographer, who thus obtained one of the world's most famous photographs. By March 15 Iwo Jima had been subdued. American casualties totaled 20,196, of whom 4189 were killed. The 23,000 Japanese defenders were almost all killed; only 200 prisoners were taken.

Two weeks later, on Easter Sunday, April 1, six American divisions landed on the southwest coast of Okinawa. The Americans had little difficulty on the beaches; it was not until they advanced southward that they met the main Japanese resistance.

In a desperate but pathetic attempt to relieve Okinawa, what was left of the Japanese navy set sail on April 6. The huge battleship *Yamato*, accompanied by cruisers and destroyers, was engaged by some 400 aircraft of Task Force 58 when it was spotted in the East China Sea fifty miles southwest of Kyushu. At a little after noon on the 7th the *Yamato* went down. Most of the other Japanese vessels were also sunk. In any case, none had fuel for the return journey.

A major American offensive to clear the southern portion of Okinawa was launched on April 9, and thereafter the fighting was perhaps the hardest in the war. Sugar Loaf Hill was captured and recaptured before the marines finally secured it on May 21. The 96th Division had an equally hard task in capturing Conical Hill. Shuri was taken on May 30. The last organized Japanese resistance was crushed on June 22. It had been an incredible fight. The Americans had lost 12,520 killed and another 36,631 wounded. The Japanese dead totaled 109,629. Only 7871 prisoners were taken.

With Okinawa in American hands, the next step was the invasion of Japan proper. The task was an intimidating one, for the best estimates of the American Chiefs of Staff indicated that United States forces could expect a minimum of half a million fatalities before the war ended. Fortunately, this desperate venture proved unnecessary.

As early as August 2, 1939, Dr. Albert Einstein had written to President Roosevelt, advising him that there was a possibility of making an atomic bomb of frightful power. Roosevelt, without informing Congress, authorized the Manhattan Engineer District Project to produce this new weapon. Before the first successful test some $2.5 billion had been spent on research, development, and manufacture. Dr. Vannevar Bush, the Chief of the Office of Scientific Research and Development, headed the research teams of British, American, and Canadian scientists, and Major General Leslie R. Groves headed the Manhattan Project itself. Two large plants were built, at Oak Ridge, Tennessee, and at Richland, Washington, and a laboratory operated at Los Alamos, New Mexico. The Germans were also interested in developing an atomic bomb but they had no success. However, this was not known by the Allies until very late in the war, so the Manhattan Project was a race against time.

As it was, a test in the desert of New Mexico on July 16, 1945, was outstandingly successful. The single bomb, exploded on top of a steel tower, had a force equivalent to the detonation of 20,000 tons of TNT. President Truman and Prime Minister Churchill, at the Potsdam Conference, were informed of the results of the test on the 17th. The cryptic message read: "Babies satisfactorily born." On July 24 Truman told Stalin in guarded terms that the United States had a new bomb of tremendous power, but the Soviet dictator did not grasp the import of the information.

By this time Japan was already seeking for terms. Early in July a message from the Japanese emperor to Stalin had intimated that Japan would make peace, though not on the basis of unconditional surrender. Stalin, incidentally, had been very tardy in relaying this information to his allies. Truman, Churchill, and their senior civil and military advisers were almost of one mind that the atom bomb should be used. It was indeed a horrifying weapon, but so are almost all weapons. If the war could be brought to a speedy end, many lives — both Allied and Japanese — would be saved, including the lives of the half-million American soldiers who would probably otherwise be killed in the conquest of Japan. On July 26 an ultimatum by the

United States, Britain, and China, calling on Japan to surrender unconditionally, was rejected. The next day eleven Japanese cities were
warned by leaflet that they would be heavily bombed. Six of these
cities were attacked by Superfortresses the next day. Twelve more
cities were warned on July 31, and four of them were bombed on August 1. A final warning was given on the 5th, and when the Japanese
government still made no move, the *Enola Gay*, a B-29 piloted by Colonel Paul W. Tibbetts, took off from the island of Tinian in the
Marianas on August 6 with an atomic bomb aboard. The *Enola Gay*'s
destination was Hiroshima.

At a quarter past nine that Monday morning, August 6, the *Enola
Gay* released her bomb, which descended five miles by parachute and
exploded before it hit the ground. In a single blinding flash 60 percent of Hiroshima was wiped out. Destruction was total over an area
of four and one-tenth square miles. Of Hiroshima's population of
340,000, some 88,000 were killed outright and another 37,000 were
injured.

Incredible as it seems, even this did not at once convince the government of Japan to surrender. Therefore, on August 9, a second
bomb was dropped over the city of Nagasaki in Kyushu with similar
results. The Russians had been convinced more readily than the
Japanese. On August 8 the Soviet Union hastened to issue a declaration of war against Japan, to become effective the next day. On August 14 the Japanese government finally accepted the Allies' terms
(which had been modified to provide that the emperor could be retained as head of state, but without political power).

And so the Second World War ended. On Sunday, September 2,
the Japanese surrender was formally signed aboard the U.S.S. *Mis-
souri* in Tokyo Bay in the presence of General MacArthur, General
Wainwright, and General Percival. By evening there were thirty-three
thousand Allied troops ashore in Japan, the advance guard of the occupation force. For the first time in six years most of the world was at
peace.

CONCLUSION

THE IMMEDIATE RESULTS of the wars were plain enough to see after 1945. The map of Europe was redrawn; Germany was divided; Poland was shifted bodily to the westward; Lithuania, Latvia, and Estonia became provinces of the Soviet Union; Bulgaria, Hungary, Rumania, Poland, Czechoslovakia, and East Germany became satellites. This process was accompanied by forced mass movements of population and by the exodus of refugees. Europe was cut in two by the Iron Curtain, and the Cold War became the predominant fact in the international situation.

In the defeated nations some of the guilty were brought to trial, as were some collaborators in liberated countries. Between November 1945 and the beginning of October 1946 a handful of Nazi war criminals stood in the dock at Nuremberg. The top echelon of the Nazi hierarchy had already escaped from human justice by suicide. Hitler and Goebbels killed themselves in Berlin; Himmler crushed a cyanide capsule between his teeth while being interrogated on the Lüneburg Heath in the British zone; Ley committed suicide before he came to trial; Göring managed to kill himself in prison in Nuremberg. Of the others, Ribbentrop, Kaltenbrunner, Rosenberg, Frank, Streicher, Frick, Sauckel, Seyss-Inquart, Keitel, and Jodl were hanged. Hess, Funk, Raeder, Neurath, Dönitz, Schirach, and Speer were imprisoned. The tribunal that tried these men was often criticized for containing Soviet representatives, for the Soviet guilt in waging aggressive war was as patent as the German. Nevertheless, the criticism was a technical one and offered no real reason why the Nazis should not be punished. The evidence of Nazi crimes adduced at Nuremberg was nauseating in its horror and irrefutability. The war-crimes trials were also criticized for working on the basis of post facto law, for punishing men for crimes that had not been defined as crimes before they were committed. This type of shallow legalism, had it been listened to, would not have strengthened the rule of law but would have undermined the whole moral basis of law. To have spared mass murderers who had sent millions of innocent victims to the gas chambers because no legal body had previously ruled that such mass murder was illegal would have been a criminal abrogation of responsibility.

In each of the occupied zones of Germany, trials of lesser war criminals were held and some twenty-four defendants were sentenced to death. Hundreds of German men and women who were equally guilty either escaped justice or received lighter sentences. Liberated France condemned old Marshal Pétain to death for treason, a sentence later commuted to life imprisonment. Pierre Laval was shot, and then after a year or two France sensibly attempted the impossible task of forgetting all about her recent history. Vidkun Quisling was shot in Norway. In eastern Europe communist vengeance fell alike upon collaborators and ideological opponents. Cardinal Mindszenty was imprisoned in Hungary and Archbishop Stephanich in Yugoslavia after "trials" that were travesties of justice. Kings were replaced by dictators in Rumania, Bulgaria, and Yugoslavia and in Italy by an unstable republic.

In Japan, too, there were trials of war criminals. General Tojo and six others were hanged. General Honjo and Prince Konoye committed suicide. Other military and political leaders were sentenced to terms of imprisonment. Then, to all appearances, Japan embraced democracy with enthusiasm.

The Cold War probably began with the Bolshevik seizure of power in Petrograd on October 25, 1917, but the West as a whole did not begin to recognize this until sometime late in 1946. In spite of the concessions made at Yalta and the generally cordial atmosphere at Potsdam, the Soviet Union and the western Allies were unable to agree on the kind of peace they sought. The foreign ministers of the United States, Britain, France, and the Soviet Union met in London and Moscow in the second half of 1945, and in Paris, New York, Moscow, and London in 1946 and 1947, but could not frame a peace treaty with Germany. Treaties were signed with Italy, Rumania, Bulgaria, Finland, and Hungary in February 1947, and one with Austria in May of 1955. Faced with similar difficulties in the case of Japan, the United States unilaterally signed a peace treaty with that country in April of 1952.

The Second World War spelled the end of the European colonial empires overseas, although the largest empire of all, the Russian, actually increased its territory and its subject population. The British, under the leadership of Clement Attlee's Labour government, voluntarily liquidated their empire, partly out of the sincere conviction that the imperial day was dead and partly from the realization that Britain no longer had the power to defend all those places on the map that had formerly been painted red. The French showed less wisdom. In Madagascar, Indochina, and Algeria they tried to suppress their colonial rebels, and although they were successful for a time, in the end they failed ignominiously.

The military coups and the civil and foreign wars that have plagued so many of the emerging nations may indicate the failure of the imperial powers to prepare their colonies for self-government or may indicate the beginning of a much wider trend, which has become visible where resistance to it was softest. In any case, few responsible persons in the former imperial powers regret the loss of empire, for the realization has gradually come home to them that though oppression is bad for the oppressed, it is in the long run worse for the oppressors. The last surviving empire in the world, the Russian, has so far maintained itself because the Soviet authorities have been ready to suppress dissidence with naked force and because the subject nationalities are on the same land mass and have contiguous borders with the old Russia.

Another result of the world wars, even more complete and dramatic than the end of empire, was the revolution in warfare itself that came about with the introduction of nuclear weapons. The conflict that began in 1914 and ended in 1945 was certainly the last of its kind. That particular fire has blown itself out. Either there will be no major war between the powers in the future, or universal death will descend upon the planet. The odds on one or the other are probably no better than fifty-fifty, although as nuclear capabilities proliferate among the nations these odds obviously shorten in favor of death. The United States and Britain held a brief monopoly on nuclear power, but the Soviet Union soon exploded its own bomb, aided by treason in the West. Since then France, China, and India have demonstrated nuclear capability, and it is probably too late to prevent further proliferation. It is even possible, indeed, that nuclear weapons may become available to private criminals, instead of (as up to now) merely public ones.

At all events, any increase in potential force is almost invariably accompanied by a decrease in real liberty. Gunpowder made all men alike short; nuclear power leads to superpowers. There can be no democracy, and little equity, on the international scene when two or three powers possess the ability of destroying all life on earth. The great conflict of the twentieth century, of course, has resulted in additional state power in all political systems; it has curtailed freedom in the democracies as well as in the dictatorships. Moreover, the net result of the wars in the world as a whole has been that totalitarian systems have expanded and democratic systems have contracted. Between 1914 and the present, liberty has all but bled to death. And now, beyond the state, there looms the shadow of the superstate, where the oppressions of government can be exercised at a higher level.

Between 1914 and 1945 war became total war. Just as Trotsky saw the revolution in Russia becoming "permanent revolution," so have we seen the German Wars become permanent war. There has been no peace since 1945, nor could there be, for war became an end in itself, self-perpetuating and incapable of conclusion. This is evident not only in the Cold War, but in the alternatives to all-out war that have naturally had so much attraction in the post-Hiroshima era. The coup d'état, subversion, and guerrilla war have experienced unprecedented revivals, and with obvious causes. There would seem to be every reason to expect this trend to continue. In most ways this is a regrettable development, for these alternatives to war have all the drawbacks of war but lack war's better qualities. They merely substitute slyness for courage, treason for comradeship, massacre for combat, and subversion for loyalty. The Trojan horse may be an intelligent substitute for the phalanx, but it is also far meaner and less noble.

Yet, at least in the older democracies of the West, another, and opposite, danger has become apparent. Here the peril is not so much that men and nations are seeking alternative forms of violence as that they have overreacted to the slaughter of the world wars and are abandoning all military virtue and military values. The progressively more unrestricted violence that overwhelmed the world between 1914 and 1945, that led to the mass murders in the Nazi concentration camps and to area bombing, was self-defeating as well as wicked, but the repugnance that these events aroused has taken a wholly irrational turn. The reaction has manifested itself against all the former philosophical structure of the Western world.

In the "liberal" societies of the West the eunuchs are inheriting the earth. This can be seen in a new and excessive tenderness toward criminals, in the abolition of capital punishment, in the rejection of all forms of discipline, and in a softness that denounces the validity of all objective standards and the renunciation of all sanctions. The process is a reciprocating one: the questioning of values leads to the abandonment of sanctions, and the weakening of sanctions leads to the rejection of values. Nor is it surprising that the softness that has crept over the West since 1945 has been accompanied by cowardice and cruelty, the hallmarks of the soft. It is no accident that the same states that refuse to put a murderer to death have generally been ready to encourage the murder of unborn innocents. Morality has been stood on its head in the name of compassion, but now, as formerly, society can readily be divided into the hardhearted kind and the softhearted cruel.

Civil society, just like military society, needs discipline if it is to function properly. Discipline is the acceptance of reasonable standards and the enforcement of those standards. To function properly, all organized forms of society — the family, the city, the nation-state — need to be organized in conformity with some set of values, and depend to some degree on coercion for the maintenance of those values. As Max Weber long ago said (although he stated the case too restrictively), "All political formations are formations of violence." Only discipline preserves freedom — a paradox, perhaps, but one that will become more and more painfully easy to understand as society becomes more and more libertarian, chaotic, and violent. For violence, too, is the end result of the lack of discipline, but it becomes the mindless violence of the mugger, the motorcycle gang, or the rampaging mob. Man's fallen nature being what it is, violence we must have. The problem is to harness it to the service of order and justice, to moderate and temper it so that it is minimal in relation to the ends it serves. Thus force should neither be renounced nor made the justification of policy, a point of view that the disciplined soldier understands very well.

Of the remoter consequences of the German Wars it is still too soon to speak with confidence. The results are still unfolding, often bringing surprises in the process. For instance, the satellite states of eastern Europe, seized by Stalin and placed in subjugation by him, seemed far more a source of Soviet strength a decade ago than they do today. The United States, which in the 1950s appeared so strong to friend and foe alike, was humiliated in the 1960s and early 1970s and forced to withdraw from a confrontation with the North Vietnamese — a result that, however gratifying to Americans who were opposed to the conflict, gives little confidence to other allies of the United States throughout the world. Moreover, as Soviet communism and western democracy confronted one another, each tended to adopt the more unpleasant aspects of its opponent's system. Ever since the Bolsheviks seized control of Russia in 1917, communism had been a fraud, its proclaimed ideals of internationalism, peace, and economic justice no more than the manipulative tools of power. As communist cynicism and bad faith appeared to succeed, the West did not scruple to adopt similar methods. The transition from Bastogne to My Lai marks a falling off that is steeper and far more tragic than the decline between Marathon and Chaeronea.

Probably what the world is witnessing in this century is the death of a civilization, and of a civilization, moreover, that was more universal than any of its predecessors. The wars were not entirely responsible for this, though without them life could probably have been maintained. What was begun by murder is now being completed by suicide. Major military confrontation between communism and democracy has been rendered less probable by the threat of nuclear annihilation, and, as the West continues to decline, conflict becomes less necessary for a decision. The heirs of Christendom have become more materialistic than the dialectical materialists, and are therefore less vital and less able to sustain life. The East can afford to sit by our sickbed for a time, secure in the knowledge that softness and corruption are the harbingers of death.

In all this dark scene the only comfort lies in the hope of change, a change that must in some sense be a returning as well as a new venturing forth. There are at the moment few signs of either, but one reflection at least gives some reason for a lifting up of the heart. There is still in the West a remembrance of higher values and some determination to return to them. If that determination can crystallize and manifest itself in time, the outlook will by no means be black, for whatever else the soft society may be able to do, it will be completely unable to defend itself.

Notes

Index

NOTES

Book One — Chapter I (pages 3–21)

page
6 "... reconciled as to ... Waterloo ...": Bismarck to Baron Courcel, French ambassador, Nov. 1884, quoted in Erich Eyck, *Bismarck and the German Empire* (London, 1958), 273.

"Endeavour always to be one of three ...": R. W. Seton-Watson, *Britain in Europe 1789–1941 A Survey of Foreign Policy* (New York, 1937), 502.

"... satiated power ...": William L. Langer, *European Alliances and Alignments 1871–1890* (New York, 1950), 451.

7 "... oysters and champagne ...": Count von Hatzfeldt-Wildenburg in 1901, Freiherr Hermann von Eckardstein, *Lebenserinnerungen and politische Denkwürdigkeiten*, 3 v. (Leipzig, 1919–21), II, 188, quoted in Michael Balfour, *The Kaiser and His Times* (Boston, 1964), 204.

"... nightmare of coalitions." Eyck, 185.

7 "... my map of Europe": Bismarck to E. Wolf, Dec. 1889, quoted in L. Albertini, *The Origins of the War of 1914* (Oxford, 1952), 3 v., I, 34.

8 "... no easy task ...": A. J. P. Taylor, *Bismarck: The Man and the Statesman* (New York, 1969), 137.

11 "... Pomeranian musketeer": ibid., 167.

14 "... honest broker": ibid., 170.

14n. Lord Salisbury: R. J. Sontag, *Germany and England: Background of Conflict 1848–94* (New York, 1969), 218.

15 "... European coalition against Russia": Albertini, I, 34.

17 "... large appetite but very poor teeth": Taylor, op. cit., 212.

18 "... the way to Berlin led through Vienna": A. F. Pribram, *The Secret Treaties of Austria-Hungary*, 2 v. (Cambridge, Mass., 1921), II, 8.

18 General Skobelev: Albertini, I, 42.

20 "... a moderating influence in Vienna": *Die Grosse Politik den europeäischen Kabinette (1871–1914) Sammlung der diplomatischen Akten des Auswärtigen Amtes* 39 v. (Berlin 1922–27), V, 1022. (Hereafter referred to as GP).

20 "We remember they are waiting for us in Alsace-Lorraine": ibid., VI, 133.

Book One — Chapter II (pages 22–47)

page

22 ". . . juggling five balls": Hermann Hofmann, *Fürst Bismarck* (Stuttgart, 1922), I, 183.

23 ". . . crossing the bar": Lady G. Cecil, *Life of Robert, Marquis of Salisbury*, 4v. (London, 1931–32), IV, 96.

23 *"Wehe meinen Enkeln"*: Friederich von Holstein, *Private Papers*, 4 v. (Cambridge, 1955–63), II, 422.

". . . like a balloon": A. Ponsonby, *Henry Ponsonby, Queen Victoria's Private Secretary: His Life from His Letters* (London, 1942), 363.

"I'll let the old man snuffle on": quoted in Taylor, 235.

24 newer and more sophisticated industries: E. J. Hobsbawm, *Industry and Empire: An Economic History of Britain since 1750* (London, 1968), 144–63.

25 ". . . fig leaf of absolutism": Balfour, 23.

". . . ingeniously continued chaos": *War Diary of Crown Prince Frederick*, quoted in Balfour, 69.

Thirteen thousand bottles of wine: E. Ludwig, *Bismarck*, 485, 595.

25 Telegram to Hinzpeter: W. Schröder (ed.), *Das persönaliche Regiment: Reden und sonstige öffentliche Aeusserungen Wilhelm II*, 92.

26 ". . . peaceful, clear and loyal policy": Balfour, 136.

31 ". . . secret military supplement [did not have] to be revealed to French [legislature]": P. Renouvin, *Revue d'Histoire de la Guerre Mondiale*, October 1934, 298.

32 Boisdeffre on mobilization: *Ministere des Affaires étrangères — L'alliance franco-russe. Origine de l'alliance 1890–1893. Convention militaire 1892–1899, et convention navale 1912*, (Paris, 1918), 42 annex. (Henceforth referred to as A.F.R.).

33 France training 30,000 more recruits a year than Germany: G. Ritter, *The Schlieffen Plan: Critique of a Myth* (London, 1958), 143.

34 army strengths 1914: Albertini, I, 550–51, 576.

German army increase: Balfour, 176.

34 ". . . he approached all questions with an open mouth": ibid., 145.

Flying Dutchman: ibid., 140. Balfour regards this story as possibly apocryphal.

41–2 Kruger telegram: ibid., 194.

43 The British government came under sharp criticism: Albertini, I, 98.

43 unite the naval power of Britain with the military power of Germany: Sir Edward Grey, *Twenty-five Years: 1892–1916*, 2 v. (London, 1925), I, 43.

44 ". . . it would not be impossible for her to reach an understanding with Russia or France": GP, XIV, 3793.

45 ". . . as long as the injustice of 1871 has not been righted": Albertini, I, 108.

Book One — Chapter III (pages 48–91)

page

48 ". . . the equilibrium of European forces": A.F.R., 94.

48 ". . . a conservative defensive pact": Albertini, I, 84.

49 the kaiser a direct descendant: J. Hohlfeld, *Dokumente der deutschen Politik und Geschichte: Das Zeitalter Wilhelm II*, quoted in Balfour, 217.

50 ". . . our future lies on the water": Balfour, 206.

50 German industries more efficient than British: Hobsbawm, 155, 161–62.

51 ". . . hammer or anvil": Albertini, I, 112–113.

51n "Copenhagen 'em:" Admiral Sir John Fisher, *Memories and Records*, 2 v. (London, 1919), I, 22.

52n no plan of campaign, John Ehrman, *Cabinet Government and War: 1890–1940* (Cambridge, 1958), 15–16.

53 *"arbiter mundi"*: GP, XIV, 3867.

52–53 kaiser sends British a plan for winning South African War: Balfour, 223.

53 Franco-Italian treaty, 30 June 1902: A.F.R., II Series, 1901–11 (Paris, 1929–40), 329.

55 Baron Hayashi: *British Documents on the Origins of the War 1898–1914*. G. P. Gooch and Harold Temperley, eds. (London, 1926–38), II, 103. (Henceforth referred to as BD).

55 terms of Anglo-Japanese treaty: ibid, II, 125.

56–59 Belgrade coup 1903: for a fuller account see D. J. Goodspeed, *The Conspirators: A Study of the Coup d'Etat* (New York, 1962), 1–32.

61 The tsar reluctantly took the French advice: Albertini, I, 152.

61–62 terms of Entente Cordiale: BD, II, 417.

62n ". . . except a clause or two of no importance" Grey, I, 49.

63 ". . . if we let our toes be stepped on": GP, XX, 207–209.

64 kaiser's speech in Tangiers: A.F.R., VI, 222.

64 Royal Navy unable to run on wheels: BD, III, 122; A.F.R., VI, 491; GP, XX, 344.

65n ". . . the greatest mischief-maker": GP, XIX, 6220.

65 "What is signed is signed": GP, XIX, 6248.

66n Lord Lansdowne denies *Le Matin* report: BD, III, 97–98.

66 ". . . *vous avez débauche l'Italie*": Albertini, I, 164.

67 "all preparations were ready": BD, III, 210, 219.

68 Grey's memorandum to cabinet 20 Feb. 1906: ibid., 299.

70 Crowe memorandum: ibid., III, 397–420.

71 Comparison British and German university students: Hobsbawm, 152–53.

73 terms of Anglo-Russian agreement: BD, IV, 618–20.

74 Stolypin refuses to listen to Izvolsky: S. B. Fay, *The Origins of the World War*, 2 v. (London, 1928), I, 372.

76–77 Vesnich-Izvolsky meeting: ibid., I, 380.

77 the kaiser was furious: GP, XXVI, 8939.

78n Aerenthal's account of Buchlau: *"Osterreich-Ungarns Aussenpolitik von der Bosnischen Krise 1908 bis zum Kriegsausbruch 1914"*, 8 v. (Vienna, 1930), I, 79 quoted in Albertini, I, 206–07. (Henceforth referred to as Oe-U.)

78n Sir Francis Bertie and Sir Arthur Nicolson told Grey: BD, V, 293.

78 French assurance to Franz Josef: Oe-U, I, 365.

79 reactions of Slavs not all the Serbs could have wished: Freiherr Alexander von Musulin, *Das Haus am Ballplatz* (Munich, 1924), 171.

79n population of Bosnia-Herzegovina: Fay, II, 93.

80 "Not a single pig, not a single plum tree": Conrad von Hötzendorf, *Aus meines Dienstzeit 1906–1918*, 5 v. (Vienna, 1922–25), III, 127.

81 Bülow's telegram to Pourtalès: GP, XXVI, 9437.

81 Grey had also proposed mediation: ibid., XXVI, 701; Fay, I, 392.

82n ". . . how well-intentioned, friendly, courteous and successful": Prince Bernard von Bülow, *Memoirs: 1905–09*, 4 v. (London, 1931), II, 388–89.

82n "shining armour": Balfour, 295.

83 terms of circular note: BD, V, 782.

83 *"C'est ma guerre"*: *The Diary of Lord Bertie of Thame, 1914–1918*, 2 v. (London, 1–24), I, 66.

84n Poincaré-Izvolsky slush fund: Fay, I, 270, 339, 458.

84–85 Prince George murders valet: V. Dedijer, *The Road to Sarajevo* (New York, 1966), 382.

"The day of your joy will come": Fay, I, 384–85.

85–86 kaiser's interview with Colonel Berkeley: GP, XXIV, 8249–74.

86 McKenna tells House of Commons: BD, VI, 155; GP, XXVIII, 10266, 10264, 10274.

88 terms of Racconigi agreement: Albertini, I, 307–09.

88 "We shall come out some day": F. Stieve, *Izvolsky and World War* (London, 1926), 68.

89 tsar to Georges Louis: quoted in Fay, I, 292.

90 Mansion House speech: BD, VII, 412.

90 Grey to Bechendorff: "In the event of war between Germany and France . . .": Fay, I, 290–91.

90 ". . . with the aid of the English army on its left wing": *Un Livre Noir; Diplomatie d'avantguerre d'apres les documents des archives ~~~~~, 1910–1917*, 3 v. (Paris, 1926), II, 421 (Henceforth referred to as *Un Livre Noir*); Fay, I, 292.

91 ". . . had no reason for existence other than . . .": A. Charpentier, *Les responsibilités de M Poincaré*, (*Evolution*, Paris, 1926), 2.

Book One — Chapter IV (pages 92–113)

page

92 Albert Ballin warns kaiser: B. Huldermann, *Albert Ballin* (Berlin, 1922), 216 ff., quoted in Albertini, I, 334.

93 Grey's draft formula: BD, VI, 537.

93 Poincaré telegram to Paul Cambon: A.F.R., 3rd, II, 269.

94 "Freedom will be sensibly impaired:" W. S. Churchill, *The World Crisis 1911–1918*, 4 v. (London, 1949) I, 112.

95 "There is no more conspicuous example:" D. Lloyd George, *War Memoirs*, 6 v. (London, 1933–36), I, 49.

95–96 "From time to time in recent years": BD, X, 416.

96 Poincaré to Izvolsky: "The only difference consists. . ." *Un Livre Noir*, I, 362–68.

97 Conrad urges attack on Italy: Conrad, II, 15.

97 Berchtold "loved racehorses and women": J. Jovanovich to L. Albertini, 6 Mar. 1938, quoted in Albertini, I, 384.

98 eager instruments of his will: I. E. Gueshoff, *The Balkan League* (London, 1915), 112–17; Albertini, I, 364–65.

99 Charikov's proposal to Izvolsky: GP, XXVII, 159 ff., 170 ff.

100 Geshov meets Milanovich: Albertini, I, 365.

100–101 terms of Serbo-Bulgarian Treaty: Gueshoff, op. cit., 117–27.

101 Serbian foreign minister warns French ambassador in Sophia: A.F.R. 3rd, III, 48.

101 terms of Greek-Bulgar, Bulgar-Montenegrin treaties: Gueshoff, 127–33.

102 *"Mais c'est là une convention de guerre"*: A.F.R., 3rd, III, 264.

102 "Britain would join with France in the attack on Germany": *Un Livre Noir*, II, 338–45.

102 Millerand's staff appreciation: A.F.R., 3rd, III, 359.

103–104 Panafieu protested: ibid., IV, 39.

104 Sazanov attempts to stop war: Albertini, I, 376.

104 Franco-Russian program for Balkan wars: ibid., 376, 387.

104 Russo-Austrian Joint Note: Fay, I, 438.

104 Paul Cambon questions whether Sazonov in control: A.F.R., 3rd, IV, 107.

105 Conrad urges separation of Serbia and Montenegro: J. Szilassy, *Der Untergang der Donaumonarchie: Diplomatische Erinnerungen* (Berlin, 1921), 222 ff.

105 Conrad recalled as Chief of General Staff: Albertini, I, 384.

105 "If Russia goes to war, France goes to war": *Un Livre Noir*, I, 345–46.

105 Izvolsky's report on French attitude: ibid., i, 368–72.

106 "The French Government urgently begs us": ibid., II, 18–22.

106 "France wanted one of those outright diplomatic triumphs": ibid., II, 303–06.

107 General Wilson's report to Nicolson: BD, IX, 656.

108 formation of Union or Death: E. A. Popovic, "Organizacja Ujidinjenje ili Smrt," *Novo Europa*, 11 June 1927, 396, quoted in Albertini, II, 26–28.

108–109 Black Hand assassination attempts: S. Stanojevich, *Die Ermordung des Erzherzogs Franz Ferdinand* (Frankfurt, 1923), 51, quoted in Albertini, II, 30.

109n attempted murder of Prince George: Dedijer, 383.

109–110 Liman von Sanders crisis: Albertini, I, 543–45.

110 Blondel told the Rumanian government: Oe-U, VIII, 9902; Albertini, III, 570.

110 Rumania was under no obligation: *Un Livre Noir*, II, 377–84.

110 Rumania would try to join the stronger side: ibid.

111–113 assassination of archduke: R. W. Seton-Watson, *Sarajevo* (London, 1926); Albertini, II, 1–119.

113 Harrach's account: T. So,nosky, *Franz Ferdinand der Erzherzog-Thronfolger, Ein Lebensbild* (Munich, 1929), 220, quoted in Albertini, II, 37–38.

Book One — Chapter V (pages 114–158)

page

115 Princip, Ilich, and Grabez members of the Black Hand: Albertini, II, 42, 55.

115 Tankosich instructs murderers: A. Mousset, *Un Drame historique: l'attentat de Sarajevo* (Paris, 1930), 162–63.

115–116 L. Jovanovich on Serbian government's foreknowledge: *Krv Slovenatva*, reproduced *Journal of British Institute of International Affairs*, March 1925; L. Magrini, *Il dramma di Sarajevo. Origini e responsabilita della guerra europa* (Milan, 1929), 106–08, 115, quoted in Albertini, II, 100–101.

116 Milovich's report to Pasich: Dedijer, 388.

117 Ciganovich spying on Black Hand for Pasich: Albertini, II, 97–98.

117 Disagreement between Black Hand and Old Radicals: ibid., II, 69–70.

118 Artamanov's pledge of Russian support: Col. Bozin Simich as quoted by Victor Serge, *Clarté* (Paris, May 1925); Albertini, II, 82–86.

119 Léon Descos's letter to Viviani: A.F.R., 3rd, X, 469.

119–120 Tisza opposes strong action: Albertini, III, 175–76.

120 ". . . stained itself by an assassination": *Die Deutschen Dokumente zum Kriegsaugbrach — Vollständige Sammlung der von Karl Kautsky zusammenge- stellten amtlichen Aktenstucke mit eigigen Ergänzungen, Neue durchgesehene und vermehrte Ausgabe, 4 v.* (Berlin, 1927), I, XIX (Henceforth referred to as DD).

121 Grey suggests direct Russo-Austrian conversations: BD, XI, 79.

121 "conversations *à deux* would be very dangerous": ibid., XI, 76.

121 Professor Fay: Fay, II, 366–67.

122 "shadow of impending calamity": S. Sazonov, *Fateful Years 1909–1916* (London, *1928*), 151.

122 "no intention of playing the role of mediator": A.F.R., 3rd, X, 539.

122 Austria counting on Russia not to intervene: *Die internazionalen Bezrehungen im Zeitalter des Imperialismus. Dokumente aus den Archiven der Zarischen und des Provisorischen Regierung*, 5 v. (Berlin, 1931–34), i, IV, 247 (Henceforth INT. BEZ).

122 military measures prior to mobilization: BD, XI, 60.

123 Jaurès demands withholding of Poincaré's visa: Albertini, II, 188.

124 Paléologue's account of banquet: M. Paléologue, *An Ambassador's Memoirs* (London, 1923), 3 v., I, 22–23.

124 Szápáry on Poincaré's attitude: Oe-U, VIII, 10461.

125 Serbian government refuses to investigate murder: BE, XI, 27; DD, I, 12.

125 Hartwig's death: Oe-U, VIII, 10170, 10193; A.F.F., X, 499; Freicherr von Giesl, *Zwei Jahrzente im Nahem Orient* (Berlin, 1927), 259–61; Albertini, II, 276–79.

125n Pasich's foreknowledge of 1903 coup: J. Jovanovich to L. Albertini, 2 Jan. 1938, quoted in Albertini, II, 108.

125–126 terms of Austrian ultimatum: Oe-U, VIII, 10395.

126 Paléologue does not report Russian mobilization: A.F.R., 3rd, XI, 216, 259; Albertini, II, 582–89.

126–127 "Russia cannot allow Austria to crush Serbia . . .": BD, XI, 125.

127 Berchtold promises not to annex Serbian territory: Albertini, II, 683–85.

127 Serbia's appeal to Russia: ibid., 346–64.

127 Sazonov's advice to Serbian government: ibid., 354.

127–128 Serbian reply to Austrian ultimatum: Oe-U, VIII, 10648, 10860.

129 British suggest four-power mediation: Albertini, II, 431.

129 "If [Austria] could make war on Serbia . . .": BD, XI, 188.

129 "We shall try all we can to keep out of this . . .": DD, II, 374.

130 ". . . the absurd and obsolete attitude . . .": BD, XI, 192.

130 Wilhelm II to Jagow: DD, II, 293.

130 Bethmann's appeals to Vienna: DD, II, 384.

131 Bethmann appeals for British neutrality: DD, II, 373; BD, XI, 362.

131 Grey's comments on Bethmann's offer: Albertini, II, 507.

132 "I felt impatient at the suggestion . . .": Grey, I, 330–31.

132–133 "England shows her hand . . .": DD, II, 368.

133 ". . . complete readiness to fulfill our obligations . . .": Baron Schilling, *How the War Began in 1914: Being the Diary of the Russian F.O. from the 3rd to the 20th of July 1914* (London, 1925), 43.

133 "accelerate our armaments . . .": INT. BEZ, i, V, 221.

134 "Kindly impress on M. Sazonov . . .": DD, II, 342.

134 "We cannot escape our destiny . . .": S. K. Dobrorolski, "La mobilisation de l'Armée russe en 1914," *Revue d'Histoire de la Guerre Mondiale* (Paris, April–July, 1923).

134 "Of course, military measures . . .": DD, II, 359.

134–135 Paléologue conceals Russian general mobilization: A.F.R., 3rd, XI, 359; Albertini, II, 582–89.

135 [Russia] " should not immediately proceed . . .": ibid., XI, 305; BD, XI, 294.

135 "Sazonov must be firm . . .": Paléologue, op. cit., I, 19.

136 "In doing so we have no other reason . . .": BD, XI, 319.

137 Moltke to Conrad: "Stand firm . . .": Conrad, IV, 152.

138 French government decides to go to war: Albertini, III, 78n.

138 German ultimatums to Russia and France: DD, III, 490–91.

139 "Germany expects . . .": ibid., 492.

139 San Guiliano outlines Italy's position: ibid., 419, 534.

139 "Your uncle would have given me a different answer": Helmuth von Moltke, *Erinnerungen, Briefe, Dokumente 1877–1916* (Stuttgart, 1922), 19–21.

139n Moltke's objections overridden: DD, III, 575, 578.

139–140 Lichnowsky-Grey conversation: ibid., 562; Grey, II, 312; Fürst von Lichnowsky, *Heading for the Abyss* (London, 1928), 75–76.

140–141 "Lord Lansdowne and I . . .": Albertini, III, 399.

141 "Have you ever thought . . .": Lord Morley, *Memorandum on Resignation, August 1914* (London, 1928), 19.

141 "I heaved a sigh of relief . . .": R. Recouly, *Les heures tragiques d'avant-querre*, (Paris, 1922), 55.

142 Treaty of London 1876: Grey, II, 3–6.

142 "The Cabinet consider . . .": J. A. Spender, *Life of Herbert Henry Asquith, Lord Oxford and Asquith*, 2 v. (London, 1932), II, 81.

142 "Belgium has always been faithful . . .": DD, IV, 779; *First Belgian Grey Book* (Paris, 1914), 22.

143 ". . . a brief outburst of profanity . . .": Baron de Bassompierie *"La nuit de 2 au 3 août 1914 aux Ministère des Affaires Étrangères en Belgique,"* Revue des Deux Mondes, 15 Feb. 1915.

143 "Italy, with that clarity of insight . . .": A.F.R.: *Livre Jaune Français*, No. 159.

143 Albertini, III, 86.

145 ". . . the interior of [their] enormous empire . . .": Gerhard Ritter, *The Schlieffen Plan: Critique of a Myth* (London, 1958), 25.

147 ". . . securely billeted in the fortress . . .": ibid., 162.

148 ". . . too scrupulous, too reflective . . .": Prince von Bülow, *Memoirs*, 4 v. (Boston, 1931), II, 201.

148 ". . . a hostile Holland at our back . . .": Ritter, 166.

149 "However awkward it may be . . .": ibid.

150 "Only one . . ." Major General Sir Charles E. Callwell, *Field Marshal Sir Henry Wilson: His Life and Diaries* (New York, 1972), I, 78.

151 "There was a strange temper in the air . . .": Churchill, *World Crisis*, I, 188.

151 "The light had grown more livid . . .": Theodor Wolff, *The Eve of 1914* (New York, 1936), 443.

Book Two — Chapter I (pages 161–183)

page

163 "The wrong — I speak only . . .": R. A. Lutz, *Fall of the German Empire: Documents 1914–1918*, 2 v. (Stamford, 1932), I, 13.

164 ". . . brushing the Channel with his sleeve . . .": H. Rosinski, *The German Army* (London, 1939), 137.

166 "The enemy will be attacked wherever encountered": Cyril Falls, *The Great War* (New York, 1959), 46.

168 ". . . in conformity with the movements of the French army": Sir George Arthur, *Life of Lord Kitchener*, 3 v. (London, 1920), III, 55–56.

174 The British Regular Army had . . . lost 86,237 men. Brig. Gen. Sir James E. Edmonds, *A Short History of World War I* (New York, 1968), 75.

175–181 Eastern Front 1914: Major General Max Hoffmann, *War Diaries and Other Papers* (London, 1929); Erich Ludendorff, *My War Memories 1914–1918*, 2 v. (London, 1919); Major General Sir Alfred Knox, *With the Russian Army*, 2 v. (London, 1921); W. S. Churchill, *The Unknown War* (New York, 1931; N. N. Golovine, *The Russian Army in the World War* (New York, 1932).

Book Two — Chapter II (pages 184–202)

page

186n "We have to wage war as we can, not as we would like to": Dardanelles Committee, 20 Aug. 1915, quoted in P. Guinn, *British Strategy and Politics 1914 to 1918*, (Oxford, 1965), 171.

190 "I suppose we must now recognize . . .": Arthur, III, 85–86.

190 "A great Power does not wage war by halves": R. Recouly, op. cit., 55.

190n ". . . like a lighthouse . . .": Lloyd George, *Memoirs*, II, 751.

192 ". . . in conjunction with the Serbians, the Rumanians and the Greeks": Guinn, 52.

192 ". . . knocking the props from under her": Lloyd George, I, 219–26.

192–196 Gallipoli campaign: A. Moorehead, *Gallipoli* (London, 1956); B.O.H., C. F. Aspinall-Oglander, *Gallipoli*, 2 v. (London: HMSO, 1929–32).

192 ". . . invisible portcullis . . .": General H. Kannengiesser, *The Campaign in Gallipoli* (London, 1928), 26.

193–194 Carden replied, as was expected of him: Churchill, *World Crisis*, II, 533.

197 "... one bright spot on the military horizon ...": Guinn, 105.

197n "... a wonderful poster": Lloyd George, II, 750.

200 "... the British were not pulling their weight": J. Terraine, *The Western Front 1914–1918* (London, 1964), 138; *Douglas Haig, the Educated Soldier* (London, 1963), 154.

201 "... [we must] act with all our energy ...": Robert Blake, ed., *The Private Papers of Douglas Haig, 1914–1919* (London, 1952), 102.

201 "Your attack will find particularly favorable ground between Loos and La Bassée": H. B. Liddell Hart, *The Real War 1914–1918* (London, 1930), 188.

202 "Stop the attacks of the Tenth Army ...": Edmonds, 139.

202 "... of 19,500 square miles of German-occupied France ...": Churchill, II, 803.

Book Two — Chapter III (pages 203–224)

page

204–205 "France has arrived almost at the end of her military effort": Reicharchiv, *Der Weltkrieg 1914–1918* (Berlin, 1925–1944), X, 2–9.

206 "... *un terrain à catastrophe* ...": A. Horne, *What Price Glory: Verdun 1916* (London, 1962), 51.

209 "We have the formula!": ibid., 235.

209 "They will not be able to make us do it again ...": Lieutenant Jubert, quoted in A. Horne, *Death of a Generation* (London, 1970), 116.

211 "England's difficulty was Ireland's opportunity": D. J. Goodspeed, *The Conspirators*, 45.

211–214 Battle of Jutland: H. H. Frost, *The Battle of Jutland* (Annapolis, 1936); D. Macintyre, *Jutland* (London, 1958); A. J. Marder, *From the Dreadnought to Scapa Flow*, 5 v. (Oxford, 1961), IV.

215 "the French army will cease to exist ...": *Private Papers of Douglas Haig*, 144–45.

215 "... looked on at this outburst of excitement": ibid., 144–45.

219 "And so the great secret was sold": Lloyd George, II, 646.

220 "No one who has not visited the front ...": Liddell Hart, *The Real War* (London, 1970), 247.

223 "The fight must be to a finish ...": *Times*, 29 Sept. 1916, quoted in Guinn, 171.

223 "... the door that should be kept open ...": Lloyd George, 509–12.

Book Two — Chapter IV (pages 225–244)

page

226 "With Falkenhayn we lose the war militarily ...": D. J. Goodspeed, *Ludendorff: Genius of World War I* (Boston, 1966), 201.

232 "*L'heure est venue!*": Brig. Gen. E. L. Spears, *Prelude to Victory* (London, 1930), 130–31.

232 "Our friends are being murdered!": John Williams, *Mutiny 1917* (London, 1962), 36.

233 "The Commune awaits you.": ibid., 1962.

234 "For the last two years most of us soldiers . . .": *Private Papers of Douglas Haig*, 234.

236 ". . . a duck's march . . .": Callwell, *Wilson*, I, 359.

237 ". . . success seems reasonable certain . . .": Haig's outline plan quoted in Lloyd George, IV, 2152–56.

237–238 "If we fail to beat the enemy . . .": Viscount Reginald Esher, *Journals and Letters*, 4 v. (London, 1934–38), IV, 137.

238 "*L'offensive des Flanders doit être assurée* . . .": Pétain to Haig, 30 June 1917. Quoted in D. J. Goodspeed, *The Road Past Vimy* (Toronto, 1970), 122.

240 ". . . this secluded little community . . .": Lloyd George, IV, 2224.

243 ". . . to restore British prestige . . .": Brig. Gen. John Charteris, *At GHQ* (London, 1931), 268.

244 "I will not attempt to deal with the question of Russian territories . . .": Speech 5 Jan. 1918, *War Cabinet Report for the Year 1917* (Cd 9005, 1918, Cmd. 325, 1919), Appx. III.

244 "You ask what is my policy?": Lewis Douglas, "Clemenceau," *The History Makers* (London, 1973), 19.

Book Two — Chapter V (pages 245–263)

page
250 Pétain "had a terrible look": *Private Papers of Douglas Haig*, 298.

250 "We must fight in front of Amiens": Falls, 335.

252 "*La bataille d'Hazebrouck est finie*" Brig. Gen. Sir James E. Edmonds, *History of the Great War, Military Operations France and Belgium 1918* (London: HMSO, 1925), III, 24.

256 "What am I risking after all?": Marshal Ferdinand Foch, *The Memoirs of Marshal Foch* (London, 1931), 427.

257 "the black day of the German Army . . .": General E. Ludendorff, *My War Memories 1914–1918*, 2 v. (London, 1919), II, 679.

257–258 "We must draw only one conclusion": General H. von Kuhl, *Der Weltkrieg 1914–1918*, 2 v. (Berlin, 1930), II, 409.

259 "Those Americans will lose us our chance . . .": Liddell Hart, op. cit., 467.

260 ". . . ten, eight or even four days . . .": Max von Baden, *Erinnerungen und Dokumente* (Stuttgart, 1927), 346.

Book Three — Chapter I (pages 267–289)

page
268 ". . . the pips squeak . . . ": Harold Nicolson, *Peacemaking 1914* (Boston, 1933), 18.

268 ". . . the only disinterested men at the peace conference": Charles Seymour, *The Intimate Papers of Colonel House*, 4 v. (Boston, 1928), IV, 280–83.

270–271 "A hundred years is a very long time": D. Lloyd George, *The Truth About the Treaties*, 2 v. (London, 1938), I, 141–42.

273 "I feel that we are bound in honor": Seymour, IV, 343n.

279 "They hired the money, didn't they?" Frank P. Chambers, *This Age of Conflict: The Western World — 1914 to the Present* (New York, 1962), 203.

279 "... an almost microscopic shortage ..." ibid., 143.

Book Three — Chapter II (pages 290–326)
page

299 "Rearmament is too serious a business ...": John Wheeler-Bennett, *The Nemesis of Power: The German Army in Politics 1918–1945* (London, 1964), 310.

304 The British Mediterranean fleet ... unable to control the Mediterranean: A. J. P. Taylor, *The Origins of the Second World War* (London, 1961), 92–93.

306 "... their own back garden": quoted in W. Shirer, *The Rise and Fall of the Third Reich* (New York, 1960), 293.

318 "Both the French and British governments recognize how great is the sacrifice ...": ibid., 389.

319–320 "... peace for our time": J. W. Wheeler-Bennett, *Munich: Prologue to Tragedy* (London, 1966), 181.

320 "... a total and unmitigated defeat": *House of Commons Debates*, 5 Oct. 1938, Col. 366–68.

322 "You have only to look at the map ..." Keith Feiling, *The Life of Neville Chamberlain* (London, 1946), 347–48.

323 "We nearly put our foot on a rotten plank ...": A. J. P. Taylor, op. cit., 192.

323 "My poor friend, what have you done?" Potemkin to Coulondre, 4 Oct. 1938, Robert Coulondre, *De Staline à Hitler: Souvenirs des deux ambassades 1936–1939* (Paris, 1950), 165.

323 "It came to me like a cannon shot ...": "Notes on Hitler's Conference with his Commanders-in-Chief, 22 August 1939," *Documents on International Affairs* 1939–46, I, 446.

325 "... including the Baltic sea, the Baltic states, Poland and southeastern questions": *Documents on German Foreign Policy*, VII, 62–64.

326 "The Italians are behaving just as they did in 1914": Paul Schmidt, *Hitler's Interpreter* (New York, 1951), quoted in Shirer, 556.

Book Four — Chapter I (pages 329–378)
page

333 "... lean against" the Siegfried Line: General Maurice Gamelin, *Servir*, III, (1947), 47–50, quoted in J. R. M. Butler, *Grand Strategy, II, September 1939–June 1941* (London: HMSO, 1957), 60.

333 "... *les gros de ses forces* ...": Alistair Horne, *To Lose a Battle: France 1940* (Boston, 1969), 96.

336 "What I hope for is not a military victory ...": Feiling, 418.

338 French soldiers unshaven and dirty: A. Bryant, *The Turn of the Tide: A Study based on the diaries and autobiographical notes of Field Marshal the Viscount Alanbrooke KG, OM* (London, 1957), 71.

338–340 Russo-Finnish War: C. L. Lundin, *Finland in the Second World War* (Bloomington, 1957); W. Erfurth, *Der Finnische Krieg* (Wiesbaden, 1950); V. Tanner, *The Winter War* (New York, 1955).

341–347 Norwegian campaign: J. L. Moulton, *The Norwegian Campaign of 1940* (London, 1968); B. O. H., T. K. Derry, *The Campaign in Norway* (London; HMSO 1952); B.O.H., S. W. Roskell, *The War at Sea*, I (London; HMSO 1954); C. de Wiart, *Happy Odyssey* (London, 1950).

349 "You have sat here too long . . .": W. S. Churchill, *The Second World War: The Gathering Storm* (London, 1948), 659.

349–370 Campaign in France and the Low Countries: B.O.H., Major L. F. Ellis, *The War in France and Flanders 1939–1950* (London, 1953); A. Goutard, *The Battle of France 1940* (London, 1958); A. Horne, *To Lose a Battle: France 1940* (Boston, 1969); J. Williams, *The Ides of May: the Defeat of France, May–June 1940* (London, 1968).

362 "We lost the battle last night . . .": P. Reynaud, *Memoires* (Paris, 1960), I, 321.

363 "*Où est le masse de manoeuvre?*": Churchill, *Their Finest Hour*, 46.

363 "I pity you with all my heart": John Williams, *The Ides of May: the Defeat of France, May–June 1940* (London, 1968), 211.

368 carrier pigeons: Reynaud, op. cit., I, 458.

371–377 Operation Sea Lion: R. Wheatley, *Operation Sea Lion* (London, 1958); W. Ansel, *Hitler Confronts England* (Durham, N.C., 1960); P. Fleming, *Operation Sea Lion* (New York, 1957).

375–378 Battle of Britain: D. Middleton, *The Sky Suspended: The Battle of Britain* (New York, 1960); A. Galland, *The First and the Last: The Rise and Fall of the German Fighter Forces 1938–1945* (New York, 1954); B. Collier, B.O.H., *The Defence of the United Kingdom* (London, 1957), *The Battle of Britain* (London, 1962); P. Wykeham, *Fighter Command* (London, 1960).

377 "If we could have agreed equally well about other matters . . .": Churchill, *Their Finest Hour*, 316.

378 "Never in the field of human conflict . . .": ibid., 340.

Book Four — Chapter II (pages 379–408)

page
379 ". . . the most unsordid act . . .": ibid., 569.

381–383, 387 Desert War: R. J. Collins, *Lord Wavell* (London, 1947); R. Woolcombe, *The Campaigns of Lord Wavell 1939–1943* (London, 1959); C. Barnett, *The Desert Generals* (London, 1960).

381 ". . . The loss of Egypt and the Middle East . . .": Butler, *Grand Strategy*, 506.

381 ". . . the life [of Britain would continue] as long as . . .": ibid.

385–386 Crete: D. M. Dawson, *Crete* (Wellington, 1953); G. Long, *Greece, Crete and Syria* (Canberra, 1953); I. S. O. Playfair, *The Mediterranean and the Middle East* (London, 1960).

388–408 Russian campaign 1941–42: W. Anders, *Hitler's Defeat in Russia* (Chicago, 1943); B. H. Liddell Hart, *History of the Second World War* (London, 1970); J.F.C. Fuller, *The Second World War 1939–1945* (London, 1948); P. Carell, *Hitler Moves East 1914–1943* (Boston, 1964); W. Goerlitz, *History of the German General Staff 1657–1945* (New York, 1953); H. Guderian, *Panzer Leader* (New York, 1952); F. Halder, *Hitler als Feldherr* (Munich, 1949); G. E. Blau, *The German Campaign in Russia: Planning and*

Operations 1940–42 (Washington, 1955); Cyril Falls, *The Second World War* (London, 1948); *The Memoirs of Marshal Zhukov* (London, 1971).

389 [Germany] "would take the necessary steps at once . . .": H. Feis, *The Road to Pearl Harbor: The Coming of the War Between the United States and Japan* (Princeton, 1950), 184.

389 . . . was not to be conducted "in a knightly fashion": General Halder's evidence, 22 Nov. 1945, *Nuremberg Documents, Nazi Conspiracy and Agression*, VIII, 645.

389 "There is no doubt that many millions of people . . .": ibid., V, 378.

389 "This year between twenty and thirty million persons . . .": *Ciano's Diplomatic Papers* (London, 1948), 464–65.

392 "Do you think we have deserved this? ": Churchill, *The Grand Alliance*, 367.

396 "My generals have all read Clausewitz . . ." P. Carell, *Hitler Moves East: 1914–1943* (Boston, 1964), 102.

406 "Anyone can issue a few tactical orders . . .": Walter Warlimont, *Inside Hitler's Headquarters 1939–45* (New York, 1964), 214.

Book Four — Chapter III (pages 409–467)

page

409–424 Far Eastern Theater 1941–1943: H. Feis, *The Road to Pearl Harbor* (Princeton, 1950); *Hearings before the Joint Committee on the Pearl Harbor Attack*, 39 v. (Washington, 1946); S. E. Morison, *History of United States Naval Operations in World War II*, 15 v. (Boston, 1947–1962); L. Morton, *The Fall of the Philippines: U. S. Army in World War II* (Washington, 1953); W. Slim, *Defeat into Victory* (London, 1957); E. J. King, *United States Navy at War* (Washington, 1945); S. W. Kirby, *The War Against Japan*, 5 v., (London, 1957–58); H. G. Bennet, *Why Singapore Fell* (Sydney, 1944); L. Wigmore, *The Japanese Thrust* (Canberra, 1957).

409 "The disease of the West . . .": Major General J. F. C. Fuller, *The Second World War: 1939–1945* (London, 1948), 128.

424–433 Desert War: C. Barnett, *The Desert Generals* (London, 1960); F. De Guingand, *Operation Victory* (New York, 1947); A. Moorehead, *Montgomery* (New York, 1946); B. H. Liddell Hart, ed., *The Rommel Papers* (New York, 1953).

424 ". . . obey or be relieved": B.O.H., Major General I. S. O. Playfair, *The Mediterranean and Middle East* (London: HMSO, 1960), III, 204.

430 ". . . the blackest day in history": Harry S. Butcher, *My Three Years With Eisenhower* (London, 1946), 29.

430 "The flank attack may become the main attack . . ." J. M. Dwyer and J. R. M. Butler, *Grand Strategy*, III, 637–38.

434 "it would still have been preferable to close immediately . . .". *The War Reports of General George C. Marshall, General H. H. Arnold, Admiral Ernest J. King* (New York, 1947), "Biennial Report of the Chief of Staff of the United States Army, July 1, 1943 to June 30, 1945," 156.

435–445 Italian campaign: Montgomery of Alamein, *El Alamein to the River Sangro* (London, 1948); I.S.O. Playfair, B.O.H., *The Mediterranean and the*

Middle East, 6 v. (London, 1960); G. W. L. Nicholson, *The Canadians in Italy* (Ottawa, 1957); B. H. Liddell Hart, *History of the Second World War* (London, 1970); M. Clark, *Calculated Risk* (New York, 1950); F. D. Guingand, *Operation Victory* (London, 1947); P. Badoglio, *Italy in the Second World War* (London, 1948); *The Memoirs of Field Marshal Kesselring* (London, 1953); E. Linklater, *The Campaign in Italy* (London, 1951).

436 "...soft underbelly...": Michael Howard, *The Mediterranean Strategy in the Second World War* (New York, 1968), 34.

439–440 "I need a few thousand dead...": Marshal Pietro Badoglio, *Italy in the Second World War* (London, 1948), 15.

441 ...tears in his eyes...B. H. Liddell Hart, *The Other Side of the Hill* (London, 1951), 359.

445 "We have been successful in everything we have undertaken": Col. G. W. L. Nicholson, *The Canadians in Italy* (QP, Ottawa, 1957), 339.

460–464 Battle of the Atlantic: S. E. Morison, *The Battle of the Atlantic* (Boston, 1946), *The Atlantic Battle Won* (Boston, 1956); S. W. Roskill, *The War at Sea*, B.O.H., 3 v. (London, 1956–61); H. Busch, *U-boats at War* (London, 1955); D. Macintyre, *U-boat Killer* (London, 1956).

461 "a roll of drums": Dr. Jürgen Rohwer, "The U-Boat War Against the Allied Supply Lines," *Decisive Battles of World War II: The German View*, H. A. Jacobsen and J. Rohwer, eds. (New York, 1965), 269.

464–467 Bomber offensive: C. Webster and N. Frankland, *The Strategic Air Offensive against Germany*, B.O.H., 4 v. (London, 1961); A. Harris, *Bomber Offensive* (London, 1947); R. Saundby, *Air Bombardment* (London, 1961); G. Dickens, *Bombing and Strategy* (New York, 1949).

466 "When after trying with less than 20 light bombers...": Butler, *Grand Strategy*, III, Pt. II, 510.

Book Four — Chapter IV (pages 468–514)

page
470 "The strength and disposition of our troops...": *The Memoirs of Marshal Zhukov* (London, 1971), 533.

476–499 North West Europe campaign: Montgomery of Alamein, *Normandy to the Baltic* (London, 1947); D. Eisenhower, *Crusade in Europe* (London, 1958); L. F. Ellis, B.O.H., *Victory in the West* (London, 1962); R. E. Merriam, *Battle of the Ardennes* (London, 1959); R. E. Urquhart and W. Greatorex, *Arnhem* (London, 1958); C. P. Stacey, *The Victory Campaign* (Ottawa, 1960); M. Schulman, *Defeat in the West* (London, 1947); H. Speidel, *We Defended Normandy* (London, 1951).

485 "...a head-on meeting...": Dwight D. Eisenhower, *Crusade in Europe* (New York, 1948), 278–79.

486 "...end the hopeless struggle...": Col. C. P. Stacey, *The Victory Campaign: The Operations in North West Europe 1944–1945* (Ottawa: QP, 1960), 255.

491 American public opinion "would not stand for it": Chester Wilmot, *The Struggle for Europe* (London, 1952), 468.

497 "Hell, let's have the guts...": Eisenhower, op. cit., 350.

INDEX